CHOICE AND CHANGE

The Psychology of Personal Growth and Interpersonal Relationships

Sixth Edition

APRIL O'CONNELL

VINCENT O'CONNELL

NOVA Southeastern University
Santa Fe Community College
Gestalt Institute

Prentice
Hall

Upper Saddle River, New Jersey 07458

Library of Congress Cataloging-in-Publication Data

O'Connell, April
    Choice and change : psychological theory applied to personal growth, interpersonal relationships, and living and working with others / April O'Connell, Vincent O'Connell.—6th ed.
      p. cm.
    Includes bibliographical references and index.
    ISBN 0-13-088413-8
    1. Personality. 2. Maturation (Psychology) 3. Adjustment (Psychology) I. O'Connell, Vincent, II. Title.

BF698.027 2001
155.2'5—dc21

                       00–038533
                       CIP

VP, Editorial director: Laura Pearson
Associate editor: Jennifer Blackwell
Managing editor: Mary Rottino
Production liaison: Fran Russello
Editorial/production supervision: Bruce Hobart
   (Pine Tree Composition)
Prepress and manufacturing buyer: Tricia Kenny
Cover art director: Jayne Conte
Cover designer: Maureen Eide
Marketing manager: Sharon Cosgrove

Once again,
to all of you
who are now or will be
working along with us in the vineyard.

This book was set in 10/12 Times Roman by Pine Tree Composition, Inc., and was printed and bound by R.R. Donnelley & Sons Company. The cover was printed by Phoenix Color Corp.

 © 2001, 1997, 1992, 1989, 1985, 1980, 1974 by Prentice-Hall, Inc.
A Division of Pearson Education
Upper Saddle River, New Jersey 07458

Printed in the United States of America

10 9 8 7 6 5 4 3 2 1

ISBN 0-13-088413-8

Prentice-Hall International (UK) Limited, *London*
Prentice-Hall of Australia Pty. Limited, *Sydney*
Prentice-Hall Canada Inc., *Toronto*
Prentice-Hall Hispanoamericana, S.A., *Mexico*
Prentice-Hall of India Private Limited, *New Delhi*
Prentice-Hall of Japan, Inc., *Tokyo*
Pearson Education Asia Pte. Ltd., *Singapore*
Editora Prentice-Hall do Brasil, Ltda., *Rio de Janeiro*

CONTENTS

7   THE PSYCHOLOGY OF HEALTH: The Holistic Approach to MindBodySpirit Well-Being   144

8   THE PSYCHOTHERAPIES: Many Types, Many Applications   171

9 ABNORMAL PSYCHOLOGY: Trying to Function in Dysfunctional Ways   198

10   INTERPERSONAL COMMUNICATION: Creating Harmonious and Enduring Relationships at Home, at Work, and at Leisure   227

11   MARRIAGE AND FAMILIES: Learning to Live with Other People   257

PREFACE

To Our Student Readers: Welcome to *Choice and Change*. We have written all the editions of our text with you in mind so that you would have a textbook that you would actually enjoy reading. Textbooks don't have to be dull—especially not in psychology which is all about you, your family, and your friends. So we have made sure to include many examples of the text material.

Meet Culturally Diverse Students Much Like Yourselves and the People You Know. In addition, you will encounter some students (very much like yourselves or like people you know) in the very first box (page 1 of Chapter 1) as they struggle for self-understanding and self-actualizing. Their concerns and problems reflect their wide diversity in age, racial and ethnic background, and educational/vocational goals.

> Meet Eduardo Sanangelo, the youngest child of an Hispanic-American family, anxious to start his studies even though English is his second language.
>
> Meet Shannon McCrory, beautiful but struggling with shyness and poor self-esteem as she believes herself to be physically handicapped and socially backward.
>
> Meet Jonnimae Jones, African-American and single mother of teenagers determined to make something of herself.
>
> Meet Martha Vining, Italian-American and dealing with having married a man outside her Italian culture.
>
> Meet Dan Westwind, Native-American, going to the "white man's college" after many years and having to confront his hostility to the white society.
>
> Meet Alec Riordan, Caucasian-American, working out his anger at his family for their prejudicial world view.
>
> Meet Natasha Petrovicc, who (along with her family) is a refugee from a previous Soviet bloc country and experiencing some culture shock in the New World.

Follow these students in chapter after chapter as they dialog with their professor and with each other about the topics covered in the text.

Read also the Written Verbatim Comments of Actual Students. Over the course of years, we have collected many written responses from students much like yourselves and reproduced many of them throughout the text. So watch for boxes that say *Students Verbatim* that are actual real-life comments by students.

Become a Psychonaut by Responding to the Boxes Which Invite You to Do Reflective Writing. Many of the boxes invite you to explore your own experiences and reactions. You might want to keep a journal so that at the end of the course you will have a written record of your own self-exploration. Keep this journal. It will even be more interesting to you in years to come for you will have a written record of what you were thinking and feeling and figuring out during this course—a time capsule of this one segment of your life.m

Correspond with us (your authors) if you like. We would like to hear from you. Tell us what you liked about the book or didn't like. Share with us your experiences that are similar or different from the scenario students in the boxes. Ask us questions or tell us about yourselves. We may not be able to respond instantly but respond we will. You can reach us at april.o'connell@santafe.cc.fl.us.

Acknowledgments

We would like to thank the following people for their critical reviews: Thomas J. Mullane, Point Park College, Pittsburgh, PA; Pamela West, Blackhawk Technical College, Janesville, WI; Sharna Olfman, Point Park College, Pittsburgh, PA; and Jonathan Segal, Trinity College, Washington, DC. Thanks also to our associate editor Jennifer Blackwell who coordinated the efforts of all.

The authors wish especially to thank the following persons who have contributed so generously to this edition: Lois-Ann Kuntz, a co-instructor of a team-taught course for several years; Rick Dery, who edited the manuscript so accurately and perceptively; Josephine Lescarbeau, who kept our computer going; Sheila Lescarbeau and Sharon Watson, who worked on painstaking details; Steve Hopkins, the copy editor, whose sensitivity to language and ideas is greatly appreciated; and the staff at Pine Tree Composition who were so wonderful to work with: the production editor, Bruce Hobart, who maintained his sense of humor throughout the project; Theresa Lowe, who has a voice worthy of a career in radio; and the operator, Tyla Giroux for her skill in putting the pages together.

Finally we wish to acknowledge the spirit and energy of some extraordinary college administrators—their hard work, their compassion for others, and their dedication to the educative process have been awesome and inspiring: Larry Tyree, President of Santa Fe Community College; Pat Grunder, Vice-President for Educational Resources; Michael Reiner, Chair of Social Sciences/History; and Joanna Clark and Betty Odum, instructors in Arts and Sciences.

Finally, we need to thank the library staff, particularly June Littler and Mary McCarty, without whose help this edition would never have been finished on time.

April O'Connell   Vincent F. O'Connell

1 THE PSYCHOLOGY OF SELF
Self-Concept, Self-Esteem, and Self-Actualizing

Box 1.1

SCENARIO
One Identical Letter, Five Very Different Reactions

On a bright, sunny day in May, six people each received the following formal letter from the Admissions Office of the college to which they had all applied.

Dear Prospective Student,

With regard to your application to be admitted as a freshman to State College, we are sorry to inform you that we cannot process your application officially at this time. You passed the math examination, but your scores on the reading and composition portions are below the cutoff level for immediate acceptance.

We can, however, admit you to our pre-college program. The pre-college program is designed to bring students up to passing levels in these courses. You have already passed your math, so you need register only for the reading and composition classes. Since your scores were just below the established cutoff scores, we are confident that you will have little trouble in passing the two exams within one term. Since you only have to take two pre-college classes, you can also take an actual college course. We suggest a psychology course which will help you make some decisions about your educational/vocational objectives and your life-career in general.

Please call us for an interview with one of our academic counselors at your earliest opportunity, so we can register you and plan for your further education.

Very sincerely yours,

I. L. Andrews
Dean of Admissions and Records.

Eduardo Sanangelo (22 years, Hispanic-American) was elated! He threw his cap into the air, caught it, and rushed into the house shouting, "I'm in! I'm in! Well, sort of in. I can't register as a freshman right away but I have been admitted on the pre-college level. They have these courses you can take to bring you up to level and then you get in! I knew my English wasn't good enough. But I passed the math so all I have to do is take two English courses, and I'm in!"

Jonnimae Jones (30 years, African-American, single working mother of two teenagers) read the letter, and then clutched the letter to her heart. Her eyes were misty but she was smiling as she whispered to herself, "I can do it. I know I can. I've come this far. It won't be easy, but I'm going to make it."

Shannon McCrory (17 years, Caucasian, and just graduated from high school) leaned her head on her father's shoulders and wailed, "Oh, Pa, does this mean I got to go to college? They'll laugh at me. I don't have nice clothes and I sound like the hillbillies on TV." Shannon didn't give voice to her most troubling anxiety, but her father knew what it was. He put his arm around her. "Girl, there ain't nothing you need be ashamed of. Folks know you're the prettiest and smartest girl hereabouts. But, honey, you ain't gotta do nothin' you don't want."

Dan Westwind (38 years, Navajo Native American) had been working on an old truck until he saw the Chief walk toward him with a letter in his hand. The old man handed Dan the letter. After reading the letter, Dan turned to the Chief and said, "For me to go an extra term will cost more money." The old man shrugged. Dan understood the shrug: He was to go no matter what the cost. Dan nodded, folded the letter, and put it in his pocket. Neither man said anything more. Dan waited respectfully until the old chief left and then resumed working on the truck.

Box 1.1

SCENARIO (continued)
One Identical Letter, Five Very Different Reactions

Natasha Petrovicc (24 years, Caucasian and a newly arrived refugee from the Balkans) put her hand to her mouth in astonishment. She had only applied to the college at her husband's urging. And now she was accepted. This was not the way things happened in the old country. There you had to be one of the rich elite. Or know somebody in the Politburo. It was all too new, too wonderful . . . and too scary all at the same time. Waves of dizziness overcame her and her legs gave way from

under her. She found herself sitting on the ground quite faint and frightened.

Nat Bernstein (19 years, Caucasian, Jewish, son of Dr. Ellen Bernstein and Dr. Harry Bernstein) walked into his parents' bedroom, took a gun from the bottom drawer of his father's bureau, and put a bullet through his head. He was pronounced dead-on-arrival (DOA) at the hospital.

How We Cope with Life Events Depends on Our Personality Style

The introductory scenario describes an identical event in the lives of six people. How each of those six people reacted to this identical event was dramatically different. Given the encouragement of the Dean's letter, what could account for Nat Bernstein's suicide? What accounts for the exuberant response of Eduardo Sanangelo and the unemotional response of Dan Westwind? Given the burdens that Jonnimae Jones is carrying—member of a depressed minority, single working mother of two teenagers—what gives her the self-confidence that she can "make it"? What are the factors behind Shannon's lack of confidence and Natasha's dizziness? The answers to these questions, of course, involve what we call "personality" or personality style.

Personality Includes Every Dimension of Human Experience

The general public tends to think of personality as our "public image"— what we show to others when we put our "best foot forward." But the psychological definition of personality involves much more than our public image (see Tip 1.2). Our personality involves our physical characteristics and general health. (When we are feeling sick, we may become irritable and pessimistic when we are ordinarily cheerful and optimistic.) Personality also involves our **cognition** or mental abilities. (If a brilliant individual suddenly develops a brain tumor, not only is his intellectual ability severely hampered, his personality will undergo a dramatic change as he struggles with his impairment.) Our personality also includes our **worldview,** which is how

---

Tip 1.1 Why Did These Six People React As They Did? At the end of this chapter, we look into some of the possible reasons why each of these peoples reacted as they did. (If you would like to know immediately, turn to pp. **16–21**.)

Tip 1.2 Defining Personality: Unique, Dynamic, Consistent. Most professional definitions of personality include three characteristics: uniqueness, dynamic organization, and consistency. *Uniqueness* means that no two personalities are exactly alike (not even those of identical twins). *Dynamic* means that our personalities are not static but fluid and changeable in mood and intensity from moment-to-moment. Yet despite these moment-by-moment changes, most of us develop a fairly *consistent* personality patterning which is recognizable to others.

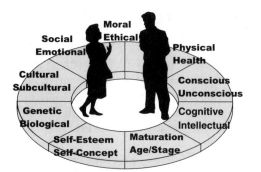

Figure 1.1 Personality consists of every dimension of human existence.

we perceive the possibilities for living and which also partly determines our moral/ethical and spiritual values. (A person who believes the "world is a maggot hill" will interact with others quite differently from a person who believes, as Will Rogers did, that "a stranger is a friend I haven't met yet.") In a later chapter we shall see how our personalities are also influenced by the **culture** (for example, Hispanic, African-American, Mid-Eastern, etc.) we were born into, as well as by all the **subcultures** of our profession, place of work, religious affiliation, and clubs and recreations. In short, personality includes just about everything we know about ourselves (see Figure 1.1).

In addition to what we know about ourselves, personality also includes many things we don't know about ourselves, called the **unconscious** parts of personality (Freud, 1900). Even though we may be unaware of the unconscious aspects of our personality, they influence our personality style throughout our lifetime.

Two Core Dimensions of Personality: Self-concept and Self-Esteem

Two core dimensions of personality involve our *self-concept* and our *self-esteem*. Self-concept and self-esteem are sometimes used interchangeably as if they mean the same thing; but while these two terms are closely related, their meanings are somewhat different.

Self-Concept: How We *Think* of Ourselves

Our **self-concept** has largely to do with factual information—how we *think a*bout ourselves in terms of our gender, sibling rank, race, nationality, religion, etc. When we are young, our self-concept is a matter of destiny—we are born into it. As a child, we may say, "There are four of us children—I'm the oldest." As we get older, we may identify ourselves in terms of our family's religion. We say, "In our house, we're Baptist/Catholic/Jewish/Muslim." Still later, our self-concept enlarges to include the region of the world we come from. A man smiles as he says, "Ma'am, ah'm from TEXAS" and that tells us that his self-concept includes a very strong identification as a Texan. Very often, our self-concept is the way we introduce ourselves to others: "I'm Doris Davidson, your neighbor three doors down from you, and I'm organizing a crime-watch organization in our neighborhood." Or the way others introduce us: "This is Jim Delericio. He's your son's Little League coach."

Self-Esteem: How We *Feel* About Ourselves

If our self-concept is how we *think* about ourselves, our **self-esteem** is how we *feel* about ourselves. Other terms that mean almost the same thing are self-respect, self-liking, self-confidence, self-worth, self-regard. There have been hundreds, perhaps thousands, of studies done on self-esteem. The findings have been remarkably consistent; namely, that our self-esteem affects every area of our life—for good or for ill (Rogne, 1991). Some of these findings are summarized below.

The Consequences of Positive Self-Esteem. When we have positive self-esteem, we feel joyous, exuberant, happy. We will enter into new situations with optimism. We will make constructive goals for our life-careers and we will be proud of ourselves when we accomplish those goals! We will accept our negative feelings as well as our positive feelings without being ashamed of them or denying them. We will not be overly dismayed by those moments of confusion and worry that visit us all. We will understand that everyone—no matter how successful—has periods of despair as well as joy, heartache as well as happiness. We will look forward to learning new skills and knowledge or to taking on new job responsibilities. We will be more open about the problems in our lives, and we will seek counsel and advice from others. If we run into frustrating situations, we will not give up after one or two attempts. We will maintain the attitude that most problems can be solved—if not by us, then by someone else whom we can consult. We will accept the responsibility for our lives and make decisions with confidence. If our decisions result in negative situations, we won't tell ourselves that "nothing we do comes out right!" Instead, we'll simply "go back to the drawing board."

The Consequences of Poor (or Negative) Self-Esteem. When we have negative self-esteem, we feel alternately depressed, helpless, unable to cope, and inferior to others in our personal, social, and vocational arenas. We will have an exaggeratedly low estimate of our abilities and believe we are of little worth to anyone. Even when people compliment us on our special skills and talents, we will tend to minimize them and describe them as "really nothing." We will tend to hang back from entering new situations and think "I can't do this . . ." or "I could never learn to do that . . ." When we feel unable to cope with a situation, we will reject the help of others (parents, siblings, close friends, co-workers) because we are ashamed to let others know how inadequate we feel. In fact, we may act "tough" to cover up our sense of inferiority. We may be very defensive (hurt, upset, angry) if someone offers friendly suggestions or constructive criticism. People who have extremely low self-esteem tend to blame other persons for what is going wrong in their lives because that is the only way they know how to manage their overwhelming feelings of inadequacy and failure (Baumeister, 1991).

Sometimes Our Self-Concept and Our Self-Esteem Can Be Diametrically Opposed

Although our self-concept and our self-esteem are usually positively correlated, in some people they may be diametrically opposed to each other. An example will illustrate. A colleague of ours has earned a national reputation as a medical researcher. We were surprised, therefore, when she came to our office one day, fell into a chair, and blurted out:

I'm a sham. I've been playing a game all my life. People come up to me and compliment me on my research and all I want to say at that point is, "Oh, shut up! I don't want your compliments." But of course I don't. I just smile and say "thank you." But inside I feel so angry. I really want to say to them, "I'm not as great as you think I am. I may be good at research, but that's because I spend so much time at it. If the truth be known, I'm just a lonely person with no one to love and no one to love me. I spend a lot of time at my research lab because I have no other place to spend it. I have no friends, only colleagues. I haven't had a romantic involvement in years. In fact, I think I signal men to stay away. It's easier to reject them than to suffer the fear that eventually they'll reject me.

This woman had a positive self-concept as a competent medical researcher but her self-esteem was negative. Deep within this woman was a hurt and bewildered child that she kept hidden from others, which some writers call the *child within*. Frequently, the very people who seem the most "successful" on the outside are the very people who are the most shy of revealing how lost and hurt is the child that still resides in their emotional memory (Capacchione, 1991). (For other examples of battered self-esteem, see Box 1.2.)

Most of Us Are Combinations of Positive and Negative Self-Esteem. Generally speaking, most of us are combinations of both positive and negative self-esteem. If we have been strong and athletic all our lives, we will have positive self-esteem in regard to sports. On the other hand, if we were so good at sports that we neglected our studies in high school, we may now have low self-esteem regarding our academic skills. College professors frequently hear students say, "I do well in English, but I'm terrible in math. I just can't do it." Or "I'm really dumb in English. I like science and math, but writing comes hard to me, and I always get poor marks in composition." Even celebrities who seem "to have it all" have areas in which they feel limited or insecure or inferior to others! No one feels adequate every day in every way in every area of their lives (Sanders, 1991).

Box 1.2

STUDENTS VERBATIM
How My Self-Esteem Got Battered

Female: When I was in grade school, no one knew I had a hearing problem. They thought I was mentally retarded and I was put into a class for special education.

Female: In the fifth grade, I had buck teeth and I was fat. No one knows how awful it is to be called "fatty" and "rabbit." My teeth got fixed and I lost my baby fat. I think I look nice now, but I have to watch my weight all the time.

Male: I didn't have a lot of friends when I was in second and third grade so I became a bully. Boy! Was that dumb! That just made everybody hate me even more. I didn't get friends until I won some athletic awards in high school. Then I became a better person.

Male: My dad was a drunk. I hated to bring anyone home because I never knew how he would be. When he was drinking, he would call my girlfriends awful names, and then he and I would get into fights.

Male: My mother was always dating jerks who would treat her extremely bad, but I wasn't old enough to do anything about it for years. This made me feel really low.

Male: In eleventh grade, I didn't make the first string on the football team. I had to sit out almost every game sitting on the benches watching our team. It was humiliating.

Female: In my senior year, my boyfriend (we were intimate for many months) suddenly dropped me for my best friend. I felt betrayed. It was hard to face my friends because I felt so small. I cried for weeks.

Male: When I was in the fourth grade, I was held back by my parents—they held me back, not the school. So there I was left back and all my friends went on to the next grade. Boy, did I feel dumb.

Female: In high school once, I was not dressed for cheerleading because I didn't know we were going to cheer. I just happened to have my cheerleading outfit in my car. So I went there to change into it, and suddenly a policeman was looking in at me. I almost got arrested for indecent exposure.

Female: I'll never forget this. In kindergarten, a boy pushed me down and knocked out one of my front teeth. I didn't realize then that another tooth would grow in. I didn't smile for weeks, I was so embarrassed by my looks.

Male: Here's one for the books: In high school, my dad let me have a car which I wrecked. I had to take my date to the Senior Prom so he let me rent a car. I had an accident with that one too.

Reflective Writing: Now describe how your self-esteem has gotten battered in the last year.

Rituals and Rites of Passage Enhance Our Self-Concept

Now it so happens that our self-concept is enhanced naturally as we go through our life-careers. That is because as we get older and as we traverse from one part of our lives to another, our self-concept is enhanced by what are called *rites of passage* (VanGennep, 1908). To encourage you to become a good swimmer, swimming classes marked your progress in titles from "minnow" status to advanced "porpoise" status. And so it goes throughout our society. When you obtain your educational degrees, these advances in your educational status will be publicly acknowledged by graduation rites. When you become a parent, you may celebrate your new status through a baptism rite (if you are Protestant or Catholic) or the rite of circumcision (if you are Jewish or Muslim). When a person dies, the friends and relatives of the person mourn the person's passing through funeral rites. **Rites of passage** are all those formal ceremonies by which society acknowledges and celebrates changes in our status, and these rites are composed of repeated rituals. Rites not only enable the person to recognize his or her new status, they enable the person's community to recognize them as well. As a child, you went through many rites of passage. Every time you were told you were promoted to the next grade, you couldn't wait to bring home your report card that had the new grade written in black-and-white. You may have gone through a first communion or confirmation (if Protestant or Catholic) or a bar mitzvah (or bas mitzvah) if you are Jewish. If you were in the Cub Scouts or the Brownies, you may have gone through the rites of "flying up" into the Boy Scouts or the Girl Scouts. In Boy Scouts and Girl Scouts, you promised "to do my duty to God and my country and to live up to my Girl/Boy Scout laws." (For more examples of present-day rites and rituals around the world, see Box 1.3).

Example: The Societal Significance of Marriage Rites. Consider, for example, the marriage rites of a young couple. Not only does the marriage rite help family and friends to acknowledge that the man and woman have changed their status from *single* to *married,* this change of status is also most significant to a host of societal agencies. For example, the Internal Revenue Service allows the married couple to figure their taxes in a different way, generally quite advantageously. Health insurers will allow one of the two persons to add the other to his or her health benefits. Future employers look favorably on married men as more stable and reliable employees. Real estate agents are much happier to rent or sell to a married couple than to a single person. Married status even affects how we conduct trials. Courts of law insist that all witnesses "tell the truth, the whole truth, and nothing but the truth." If they do not, they can be cited for any number of violations of the law: contempt of court, obstruction of justice, perjury. The sole exception is the married partner of the defendant. The law says that we do not have to testify against a spouse. Such are the powers that come with the change of status from single to married.

The Sacred Rites of Ordination. Highly significant to every culture are the sacred rites they have evolved. These rites serve to acknowledge a person's progression into sacred orders. The person is now acknowledged as a prophet, minister, priest, nun, vestal virgin, oracle, medicine man, witch doctor, shaman, rabbi, lama, elder, deacon—just to name a few examples. Sacred rites signal to the community that the individual has undergone a transformation of status from worldly life (also called secular or profane life) to the sacred life. By whatever name they are called, these individuals have chosen (or have been chosen) to give up certain worldly pleasures that the rest of us enjoy (wealth, sex, marriage, parenthood, etc.) so that they may be of service to their communities.

Box 1.3 — Present Day Rites of Passage: Some Beautiful, Some Healing, Some Not-So-Nice

Nobel Prize Award Ceremony. There may be no more dignified rite than the ceremony that accompanies the awarding of the Nobel prizes for literature, economics, science, and peace (including service to humanity). Held in midwinter in both Oslo and Stockholm, it is a formal, candle-lit affair attended by dignitaries from all over the world.

Hollywood's Oscar Awards. The huge annual celebration produced by the Hollywood film industry in which movie people are awarded "Oscars" for a multitude of specialties, including of course, acting. It is probably the most famous of modern rituals. It is an annual rite which millions of people around the world tune in to watch on TV.

A Medical Ritual. The present medical pre-operation procedure of washing hands for six minutes may be far longer than is necessary for obtaining septic operating hands. The kinds of anti-bacterial soaps used today do not need six minutes for achieving septic conditions. Furthermore, after the six-minute hand-washing, the hands of the physician are encased in truly sterile rubber gloves. Nevertheless, the ritualistic hand-washing is a powerful bodymindspirit cleansing and preparation for what is to come (Akir & Gluck, 1998).

Shamanic Healing. Shamanistic healing, such as practiced by our Native American population, is a ritual performed by a medicine man with the use of many symbols, while the person's family and friends are gathered around the sick person in a communion of prayer and chanting.

Reading of Minutes. A humorous example is the reading of minutes at the beginning of every meeting. With the exception of a few persons who have a particular motive for paying attention, most people confess their minds wander during the reading. So what does this ritual accomplish? It provides a way for people (who have not been together for some time) to reunite as a group (McEarchern, 1998).

Female Genital Mutilation. One of the saddest of rituals is that performed on females in the Middle East and Africa, in which the clitoris is surgically removed by a physician or even a nonmedical member of the community, generally when the female is pubertal or prepubertal. Not only does it impair the woman's ability to partake in a loving sexual act, it is often so dangerous as to be fatal. This centuries-old practice is supposed to ensure the woman's fidelity to her spouse since sexual passion is thereby diminished or made non-existent. Genital mutilation has been condemned by the United Nations, as outlined in the *Convention of the Elimination of All Forms of Discrimination Against Women* (Gray, 1998; Leonard, 1996).

Initiation into Barrio Street Gangs. Acceptance into these street gangs depends on a physically violent rite of passage. In order to be accepted into a barrio gang, the prospective initiate must undergo a physical ordeal in which he voluntarily allows several members of the gang to attack him. He is expected to fight back but cannot show any signs of weakness or fear. This ritual serves as a way of eliminating weaker fighters. It also serves as a ritual of gang bonding and confirmation of the male gender role (Vigil, 1996).

We Have Adapted Many of These Sacred Rites to Our Secular World. So meaningful are the sacred rites to us today that we have incorporated many of them into our secular society. For example, physicians recite the Hippocratic Oath in which they promise to carry out many principles of life-giving service to others. In fact, all professions have developed mission statements and codes of ethics that are intended to convey a highly developed social conscience and moral behavior. Our elected leaders at all levels take an oath to uphold the laws of our country to the best of their ability.

In fact, social scientists are now actively advocating the use of traditional rituals and rites of passage, or the invention of new ones, in order to enable people to accept traumatic events, to heal physically and psychologically, and to build a sense of community with others. For example, some sociologists and therapists who study family life recommend the building of specific family rituals to build the child's self-concept and self-esteem. Examples of such rituals include giving thanks before meals, kissing a child before going to school, family shopping for clothes before school begins in the fall, and family celebrations at religious and nonreligious holidays (Parker, 1999). Even going together to an annual community parade is a ritual that rebonds the family (Rothenbuhler, 1999).

Unlike Our Self-Concept, Our Self-Esteem Gets Battered Throughout Our Lives. Rites of passage enhance our self-concept. But while rites of passage enhance our self-concept, our self-esteem is not so easily enhanced. In fact, if anything, our self-esteem is battered almost every day of our lives. From our earliest years onward, our society has been constantly calling attention to our errors. If we didn't get a good mark in school, our parents may have berated us for our "failure" to live up to their expectations. Our playmates often said mean things to us. When we wrote a composition in high school, the paper may have come back with a passing grade but that didn't seem to compensate for all those red markings all over it. Society has developed many ways to communicate its displeasure with us. By contrast, we don't get as many positive "strokes."

Does it get any better when we become adults? Not on your life! As adults we may be yelled at by the boss and that doesn't enhance anyone's self-esteem one whit. We get into a fierce quarrel with friends and family, and we get assaulted with name-calling and accusations of misbehavior. We're driving along a sunny highway and suddenly we become aware of a siren shrieking and a blue light that tells us a policeman wants us to pull over. There we are with a ticket for speeding, which deflates both our pockets and our self-esteem. It is no different for celebrities. If a movie star begins to lose "box office" ratings, they find themselves no longer esteemed by the public or movie producers. And what do you think a political figure feels when the election results suggest that he or she has lost the public confidence? The continual battering at our self-esteem is simply part of "the human condition."

The Time of Lowest Self-Esteem: High School. Most adults report that their self-esteem was at its lowest ebb during high school, more than at any other time of their lives. Furthermore, the low self-esteem we probably all experienced in high school was not something we could easily talk about—if at all. If we tried to tell our parents how "unpopular" we believed ourselves to be, they generally tried to "buck us up" with remarks like, "Oh, that's silly, you've nothing to be ashamed of," or they didn't listen to us at all. We couldn't share our feelings of misery with our friends because it would have been generally too embarrassing. Ironically, at no time in our lives do we long to be accepted by our peers as we do in high school. Ironically, that is the time that acceptance by our peers is the hardest to achieve. Adolescent groups demand strict conformity to group standards of behavior and mete out harsh punishment to those who don't comply with their rigid codes of dress, language, dating, etc. The slightest deviation from the "in-group" standards results in jeers, sarcasm, and eventual outright rejection. If the reader doubts these studies, we have only to point to the figures on absenteeism, truancy, and dropouts from high school. If the high school years were not so unhappy, there would not be as much delinquency and teenage violence (including the carrying of knives and guns to school) at ever younger ages. Nor would there be as much suicide and attempted suicide in the adolescent years (Woods, 1990).

But the Good News Is . . . There Is No Better Time to Enhance Self-Esteem Than in Your College Years! If the high school years are the years of lowest self-esteem for most people, the good news is that the adult years are the time when we can consciously develop more positive self-esteem. You can begin to discover your areas of interest and what you are "good at." You can find others who share the same interests as you, whether these interests are sports, journalism, art, auto mechanics, computers, electronics, drama, politics, or the human service professions. Sharing common interests becomes the basis of friendship rather than what people look like or what they wear. The college experience enables students to discover and acknowledge their skills and competencies and enhance their self-esteem.

Locus of Control: Internal and External

Is it really possible to raise our self esteem? Yes . . . IF we are willing to believe we can, and IF we are willing to consider alternate choices, and IF we are willing to make changes. Unfortunately, many people believe they are doomed to live the life they are leading. Like the people of ancient times, they feel they are the pawns of demons and gods that rule the universe. The ancients believed they had little control over their lives. For example, no matter how earnestly Oedipus tried to avoid the terrible fate that had been predicted for him, he was doomed to commit the terrible acts of regicide (killing of the head of state), patricide (murdering his own father), and incest (marrying and cohabitating with his own mother). It is the kind of thinking which assigns the control of one's life to external (and usually demonic) forces. The language of this worldview includes such terms as *fate, kismet, karma, predestination, the will of the gods,* and *"It is written on the wind."* Psychologists today call it **external locus of control.** People who hold this worldview see little possibility of changing their lives (Rotter, 1990).

But developing new behavior patterns is not easy because change does not come easily to the human personality. Call it habit or conditioning or "fear of the unknown," we tend to cling to our present circumstances, no matter how difficult they are. Listen to people describe their difficult life situations: abusive relationships, jobs that they hate, families that are dysfunctional and in which everyone is driving everyone else crazy. They believe they are at the mercy of circumstances beyond their control. Like primitive peoples of ancient times, they believe they cannot change themselves or the circumstances of their lives. When you suggest to them that they might do something about their situation, their responses often sound something like this:

> *I know my husband/boyfriend is abusive, but I couldn't survive economically without him.*
> *I have no choice in this matter. My hands are tied.*
> *I can't do anything. It's just hopeless.*
> *I hate my job but everyone says I'd be a fool to leave, so I guess I've got to stay where I am.*

This inability to recognize the choices available to us or to make constructive changes in our lives has been termed **learned helplessness** (Seligman, 1990). These unhappy people are convinced they have no other choice than to live or work in situations that are making them miserable. They remain where they are, leading lives of "quiet desperation." Like ancient primitive peoples, they believe themselves to be the helpless pawns of fate, the worldview of ancient peoples (Rotter, 1990). For example, people who suffer from ongoing depression believe, like Oedipus, that there is nothing they can do to lead a more joyful life. They live without hope.

People who have an **internal locus of control** believe that they are able to direct their lives and can change their circumstances. The fact that you are reading this text means that you believe education will improve your life. What has been discovered through research is that people who set goals and accomplish them have an internal locus of control. An internal locus of control is one of the outstanding personality traits of highly evolved and integrated persons,

---

Box 1.4

SELF-EXPLORATION
Have You an Internal or External Locus of Control?

Respond to the following items. Then add up the internal and external responses below and reflect.

1. Do you consult your astrology to see if it's going to be a good day?
Yes = External No = Internal
2. Do you believe that students get good grades by studying?
Yes = Internal No = External
3. Do you believe "it's who you know rather than what you know"?
Yes = External No = Internal
4. Do you believe in "lucky" and "unlucky" days?
Yes = External No = Internal
5. Do you believe that hard work is generally rewarded by employers?
Yes = Internal No = External
6. Do you believe that "somebody up there likes/hates" you?
Yes = External No = Internal

7. Are most of the problems in your life caused by other people?
Yes = External No = Internal
8. Do you have the know-how to take care of most of life's stresses?
Yes = Internal No = External
9. Have you had success in most of your undertakings?
Yes = Internal No = External
10. Are you generally anxious about the future?
Yes = External No = Internal

Totals: Internal _____ External _____
Do you have an internal or external locus of control?

Reflective Writing: Give an example of your behavior which reflected an external locus of control and then an example which reflected an internal locus of control.

---

persons whom Abraham Maslow called "highly self-actualizing." (Check your own locus of control in Box 1.4.)

The Scientific Study of Highly Integrated, Creative, and Self-Actualizing Persons

Prior to World War II, most studies of human personality came from three sources: (1) the "Average" person (particularly the college sophomore taking psychology courses), (2) people suffering from serious personality disorders, and (3) experimental animal research. One text (we won't say which) was dedicated "To the white rat without which this book would never have been written." We really knew very little about the healthy and creative person. When Sigmund Freud was asked this question: "You have told us a lot about the unhealthy person. What is the healthy person like?" He could only answer in a now famous phrase, *Arbeiten und Lieben* ("To Work and To Love"). He could not say any more.

For many years, American psychology was dominated by what we now call the **mechanistic** or **reductionist** theory of human personality. According to this model, human beings are nothing but the sum total of their genetics, their early experiences, their conditioning, and the sociocultural determinants involved in their society. Sigmund Freud, along with other reductionists, believed that the achievements of human civilization are simply serendipitous events (accidental by-products) of our need for food, sex, and other biological needs (Freud, 1962). For example, to satisfy our need for shelter, we learned to build huts, and then we invented architecture. To satisfy our need for food, we learned to cook, and then we invented haute cuisine. To protect ourselves from the cold, we invented fur clothes, and then we invented fashion. A noted ethnologist, Desmond Morris (1967, 1970), asserts that we humans have aggrandized ourselves by thinking that we are a unique species. In his model of personality, we are nothing more than

Figure 1.2 Are we simply "naked apes" who live in a "human zoo?"

"naked apes" who live in "human zoos" (see Figure 1.2). The two formulators of conditioning, Ivan Pavlov and B. F. Skinner, both came to believe that the laws of conditioning account for all our human personality. All in all, the assumptions that underlie the reductionist and mechanistic theories involve a worldview that human personality is predetermined, inescapable, and prescribed.

Then, after World War II, psychologists sailed into a new direction. They began to publish studies of successful executives, productive scientists, and creative writers, poets, and artists of all types. To be sure, there had been hints and clues for over half a century. Gordon Allport, a president of the American Psychological Association, suggested we consider ourselves as **human becomings;** a species always in process of development and evolution (Allport, 1955).

But it was Abraham Maslow (1954) who described how we "human becomings" reach high levels of *self-actualizing* in a model of human evolution he called a **hierarchy of needs** (see Table 1.1). What he was saying was this: As we grow in age and maturity, our needs and motivations change. That should not be surprising since we all know that the wishes and joys of childhood no longer satisfy us when we become adults (*"When I was a child, I thought as a child . . ."*). But Maslow also pointed out that until our basic *deficiency needs* are satisfied (hunger, thirst, warmth, shelter), we cannot reach the higher human *meta-needs* involving love and belongingness, esteem, cognition, aesthetic, and self-actualizing needs. Maslow's hierarchy of needs model involves seven levels (see Figure 1.3).

Maslow's Hierarchy of Needs

In deriving his hierarchy of needs, Maslow studied what he called highly self-actualizing persons, whom he described as the "shining lights" of any society. Early on, he said, they set goals for themselves and achieve what they have wanted to achieve in their lifetimes (Maslow, 1954). Moreover, their achievements are not for themselves alone but for the betterment of humankind. They may be writers struggling to alert us to the ills of our society. They may be scientists looking for a cure for some dread disease. They may be artists and musicians who break through to new illuminations of color and sound. They may be humanitarians spending their life in service for others. Maslow used the **case study method** (see Box 1.5) with subjects that included living persons (Albert Einstein and Eleanor Roosevelt) and historical figures (Abraham Lincoln). Albert Einstein, Eleanor Roosevelt, and Abraham Lincoln all achieved their personal dreams and their dreams for their societies.

Self-actualizing persons, said Maslow, have a strong belief that they have some control over their lives. Despite the setbacks and tragedies they endure, they recover and they continue with their life-career. They do not blame others for their limitations. They do not fob off their inadequacies on "an unhappy childhood" or "second-class citizenship." They know that while the blaming game may comfort us, it isn't very productive. They know we will all be visited occasionally with heart-breaking life situations but they keep going, unwilling to be overcome by

Table 1.1   Maslow's Seven-Level Hierarchy of Needs

Physiological Needs.   Physiological needs are the basic needs to survive, such as air, food, water, and clothing for warmth. People deprived of these needs will seek to satisfy them by any possible means including working for "slave wages," begging, prostitution, and stealing. A sound mind needs a sound body for functioning fully at every level. Globally, we are becoming aware of the need for good nutrition, pure water, and a nontoxic environment.

Safety and Stability Needs.   Our many homeless people wandering the streets and running from the police have no protective shelter and, in times of freezing temperatures, are sometimes found frozen to death on the streets. But simple shelter is not enough. Our home should be a place of sanctuary. If our domicile is a place of constant turmoil, physical violence, alcoholism, etc., we are living in a kind of hell. If we are having trouble with a roommate, we may hate to return to our apartment. Be it ever so humble, all of us need our home to be a stable sanctuary of safe retreat.

Love and Belonging Needs.   When we are children, our needs for love and belonging are fulfilled by a close and caring family. As we transit into adolescence, we long for acceptance by other teenagers. As adults, these needs are met in our own family grouping. But what if we did not have such an ideal growing up? Some men and women, whose home life was marked by divorce or death, may search for a life-partner to fulfill their longing for the absent father or absent mother. Or suppose our life-partner turns out to be alcoholic or drug addicted. In that case, our love and belonging needs will not be fulfilled very often—unless we enjoy the caretaking role of co-dependency. Belonging needs are also met by affiliating with a club, a profession, a church, a political party—or simply a group of friends.

Esteem Needs.   In addition to being loved and cared for by others, human becomings have a need to give as well as to receive. We need to make a contribution to our society. For some, this will come through great political, scientific, or artistic achievement. But we do not have to become public figures to achieve our esteem needs. We can contribute also by working with charitable organizations. Or we can take a leadership role in one of the many civic groups in any city, town, or village. One of the most significant avenues for achieving our esteem needs is through a work of our liking, one we believe to be valuable and of service to others. We study hard for a profession we can pour our hearts into, whether it be in teaching, in auto electronics, in law enforcement, or in the many human service areas.

Cognitive Needs.   Our need for knowledge may lead us to become research scientists. Or we may have a "nose for news" and become investigative reporters. Formal education, of course, is the most direct route to satisfy our cognitive needs, but we keep learning in other ways as well. We read the morning newspapers and listen to the nightly newscasts to keep up with "what's been going on" or with the latest athletic standings. We patronize the local library because we are "history buffs" or find biographies to be of more interest than fiction. We take adult education classes to enlarge our leisure recreations or technical skills. In fact, the more technological our society becomes, the more driving becomes our need to know more about our world. We are a curious species with an unquenchable thirst for knowledge.

Aesthetic Needs.   The aesthetic needs involve a quest for creating beauty in our lives. This need is so intense in some people that they devote their entire lives to creating works of art and music. Others will satisfy their aesthetic needs by designing clothes, automobiles, planes, or household goods. Profit-oriented corporations know that "a thing of beauty" is "good business." Community planners are careful to preserve the natural beauty of the earth along with planning new traffic routes. All of us express our aesthetic needs in some way or other, whether it be arranging the furniture in our homes or offices, tending our gardens, or sending our children off to school as neatly and attractively as possible.

Self-Actualizing Needs.   Maslow described self-actualizing as the need to express the highest potential that we are capable of reaching. People who have become self-actualizing live according "to their own lights," pursuing their goals and dreams throughout their lives.

Figure 1.3 Abraham Maslow's Hierarchy of Needs

obstacles or tragedy. Self-actualizing personalities strive always toward the "farthest reaches of personality," and by their insights and achievements enable their societies to evolve as well. They know too that the older we get, the more times we will have to mourn the death of those we dearly love. That is part of "the human condition" (Arendt, 1970). (They know that the only way to avoid these experiences is to die young.) But they are determined to live as courageously and authentically as possible. They know also that the responsibility for our lives is squarely on our own shoulders and ours alone. In fact, the only person any of us can change is first person singular—the person we refer to as "I."

But What About Our Responsibility to Raise Moral and Ethical Children? You may feel some concern about your children—present and future. Aren't we responsible for them? Yes, of course, we are! Especially when they are young. The socialization process of the child (teaching the child to live according to the standards of society) is one of the primary functions of the family. We do our best to raise our children to be morally responsible adults. But as they get older, we must be careful that in our sincere desire to raise morally responsible children we do not become domineering and over-demanding and insisting on absolute conformity to our ideas of how they should be. Our children, like ourselves, are also *human*

Box 1.5

RESEARCH METHODOLOGY
The Case Study

The case study applied to a physically ill person. The case study method, which had its origins thousands of years ago in the physician/patient relationship, is a summary record of many observations of one subject—the patient. When we are ill, the physician makes the following kinds of observations:

> Observation 1: Interviews us and listens to our symptoms.
> Observation 2: Does a cursory clinical exam with stethoscope; looks in our mouth and has us say "Ah-h-h."
> Observation 3: Secures analysis of our bodily fluids, such as blood and urine.
> Observation 4: Sends us to a laboratory for other exams, such as a chest X-ray and EKG.

One subject: Many observations. The physician then makes a diagnosis and prescribes treatment.

The case study applied to an educationally disadvantaged child. A psychologist gets a referral from a teacher about a child who is failing in his subjects. She will then compile as much data on this child from the following kinds of observations:

> Observation 1: Perusal of the child's cumulative folder.
> Observations 2, 3, and 4: Observe the child in class, in the lunchroom, and on the playground.
> Observation 5: Interview the parents of the child.
> Observation 6: Interview the child through a battery of tests, such as IQ and achievement tests.

One subject: Many observations. The psychologist summarizes the data into a report for the school and inaugurates a plan of action to help the child.

The case study applied to an event. The case study approach can be applied to events as well as to persons. When there has been a major accident, various kinds of research teams study every available bit of data to learn the nature and cause(s) of the accident. In the famous case of the crash of the Boeing 747 over Lockabie, Scotland, thousands of persons collected the bits and pieces of the airplane over many miles of ground. The "black box" recordings were analyzed by specialists in that area. The CIA and the European Interpol network examined passenger lists, freight lists, passports, etc. Intelligence agencies of every nation pooled their findings to discover who and what had blown up the airplane.

One subject: Many observations. The investigators make a judgment about the cause of the crash.

PRO: Advantages of the Case Study Method. A case study is a comprehensive picture of one subject and very necessary in order to diagnose the person's problem and to develop a treatment or action plan. No other method analyzes a single person or event so profoundly. In the healing arts particularly, the case study is an essential method to uncover the underlying etiology of a problem. By healing arts, we mean not only medicine, but also psychotherapy, special education, physical therapy, speech and hearing therapy, etc.

CON: Limitations of the Case Study Method. On the other hand, we have to be cautious about applying the case study findings about a single person to other people. Discoveries from one subject cannot be generalized to a population without corroboration. Scientists feel much more secure when they study larger samples of (say) one hundred, or a thousand persons, or even several thousand persons. Another problem of case study work is that it is very, very expensive in terms of time, professional staff, and financial resources. Nevertheless, problems of expense are disregarded when what is being studied is an epidemic, a plane or auto accident, or a homicide investigation.

becomings (Allport, 1955) and they also need some life-space to evolve according to "their lights" as well.

Toward Your Own Self-Actualizing: An Always New and Never-Ending Process

While many self-actualizing people become our great leaders, scientists, writers, and political figures, others are never publicly known. They live quietly but very creatively, knowing that the quest toward self-actualizing does not have to involve external fame or financial wealth. It can be an inward spiritual journey, illustrated by a Japanese koan which goes as follows:

> *Two brothers sought knowledge.*
> *The younger brother took a trip around the world;*
> *The older brother took a walk around his garden.*
> *They both learned much.*

Nor is it as important to self-actualizing persons to achieve their life goals, said Maslow, as it is to have life goals to achieve. They are fulfilled simply by following their star, or for working at something that has meaning, or living compassionately for the benefit of others in society.

Strengths and Limitations of the Humanistic Model. We said earlier that no model of human personality can be perfect. In our finite understanding of the world, any model must be thought of as the best we have now, until something better comes along. Let us consider both the strengths and the limitations of the growth model.

The first strength of the humanistic model is that human personality is not reduced to the status of conditioned laboratory rats or mindless robots. We do not fold, bend, adjust or otherwise mutilate the person in order to accomplish institutional goals. We do not squeeze the person into a job. Instead, we attempt to help the person find a job for which he or she has the ability— a job which would also be fulfilling. We don't force the person into a personality mode of "normality" since what is considered "normal" is different in different cultures. Instead, we encourage the person to discover and express his or her innate individuality provided it does not injure or prevent the growth of others. The basic assumption of the growth model is that "human becomings" are thinking creatures, capable of conscious choice and change. The growth model affirms the ability of the individual to transcend the limitations of limiting, injurious, or poverty-stricken circumstances and to unfold, harmonize, and expand the Self within.

But since no theory is ever perfect, let's consider the limitations of the humanistic model. Obviously, the humanistic model is a model of hope and challenge, but critics of this approach say (and rightly so!) that taken to its extreme, this emphasis on the individual can lead to unbridled hedonism: "Me first and always!" As well, many terms in the growth model are hard to nail down. What is meant exactly by the terms "self-actualizing" or "self-esteem"? And when it really comes right down to it, do we have a Self at all? Is the Self simply another word for "Soul"? If so, then the Self has no place in psychology; it belongs to the realm of theology, say some critics.

There is another problem to consider. The growth model had its inception during the most positive period of world growth and reflects a Keynesian model of continuous economic expansion. Today we are confronting the consequences of that economic philosophy. We are running out of fossils fuels. Our world ecology is under toxic siege. In our search for ever higher standards of living, we ignored global ecology. Now we are confronting the depletion of our rain forests and the pollution of our earth, sea, and sky. Our nation, along with many others, is now confronting monumental debt which must be paid sometime, if not by our generation, then by the generations that come after us. Eventually, the humanistic model must either expand to focus on the survival of the human species or be replaced by another theory that incorporates a more global worldview. It may well be that the primacy of the whole human race and the need to save our planet from global destruction must eventually take precedence over the primacy of the individual.

Studying Human Personality Via the Case Study Method

Knowing what we know now about the case study method as a means of investigation, with its strengths and limitations, we will now use it to reconsider the six people described in the opening scenario, Box 1.1. All six people received the same identical letter, but each reacted quite differently. By providing more information about their personality style and their life experiences, we will be better able to understand their dramatically different responses. Let it be clearly

understood, however, that in the case study approach, we can only draw some hypothetical conclusions. Nevertheless, the case study approach is used in many research studies so it is a good place to begin our understanding of research methodology.

Case Study: Eduardo Sanangelo. Eduardo was the fourth and youngest child of the Sanangelo family. More important, he was the first son. Eduardo's parents had despaired they would ever have a male child to carry on the family name, so Eduardo seemed an answer to their earnest prayers. Little Eduardo was welcomed into the world with much celebration in his large extended family in rural New Mexico.

Little Eduardo became the center of family life, the joy of his parents. For his four older sisters, it was like having a wonderful baby doll that could walk and talk and play with them. When it came time for Eduardo to begin school, his parents lectured him repeatedly about the importance of working hard at school and "doing everything the teacher tells you to do!" His sisters were given the job of making sure he did his homework correctly. All the importance placed on "learning" and being personally tutored at home by one or the other of his sisters proved to be of lasting value. Eduardo proved himself not only on the playing fields but also in the classroom. His grades were excellent, and it was the family's high expectation to send him to the big university in Albuquerque. His high school math and science grades gave him the confidence to go for an engineering degree. He would be the first in his family to go to college!

He was also a little nervous about his English language competency exam, since English was his second language. Nevertheless, he applied to the local college and took the entrance exams. Does his exuberant response to the letter surprise anyone?

Case Study: Jonnimae Jones. Jonnimae was born into a large migrant family in which poverty and hunger were the rule. When Jonnimae's father could not find employment, he took his drunken despair (and loss of manly self-esteem) out on his wife and children. Jonnimae learned to stay very still and not call attention to herself so she escaped most of the brutality, but her mother's bruised face and the screaming of her brothers and sisters would remain forever

in her memory. Schooling was always a hit-and-miss affair, but somehow Jonnimae managed to learn to read (fairly well) and write (with many misspellings) and to do elementary sums. In fact, when her illiterate parents discovered her ability to add numbers, they made her the money manager of the family so as to stave off the creditors. Eventually, the other illiterate migrants began asking for her help in interpreting letters or official documents. "Miss Jonnimae," they would say holding up a piece of paper, "Can you tell me what this says?" It made Jonnimae feel good.

As is the case with so many below-poverty-level adolescents, Jonnimae was pregnant and married by the time she was 16. When they were first married, her husband was proud of being "the man Jonnimae married," but his pride turned to resentment (about the hours she spent helping other people) and jealousy (of their respect and awe of her). Within a few months, her husband began to exhibit the same abusive pattern as her father: bouts of drunken despair and rage, which he took out on Jonnimae, followed by abject guilt and sorrow and promises to her that he would "be better" to her in the future. By the time Jonnimae was 20, she was the mother of a girl and boy. Still, the physical and verbal abuse became more and more frequent and more and more intense. After one particularly violent beating, Jonnimae ended up in the hospital with a shattered face and several broken bones. With a social worker's help, Jonnimae initiated both a court restraining order and divorce proceedings. But Jonnimae knew that neither a court restraint nor a divorce decree would prevent her husband from "claiming his rights" as husband and father. Quietly (and telling only her parents where she was going), she took herself and her children off to the city where she found a room for rent and a job as a dishwasher.

She was a hard worker—and honest. When the manager discovered her ability to do sums and make accurate change, he made her permanent cashier. The additional pay enabled her to get a tiny three-room apartment for herself and the children. For a few years, Jonnimae was happier than she had ever been. But something kept nagging at her. She could hear her mother's voice urging her to get an education: "You're good with people, Jonnimae. You can make something of yourself." It seemed such an impossible dream. Nevertheless, one day, with a lump in her throat and a queasy stomach, Jonnimae walked into the college's administration offices. She waited quietly in the corner until her turn came. The fact that the counselor turned out to be an African-American like herself made the words easier to say: "I want to be a nurse." The counselor was startled. She had seldom heard such a clear statement of vocational aspiration.

"Well, do have a seat," replied the counselor, "and let's see what we have to do to get you there." That had been the beginning. Now this letter! Nothing could stop her now, nothing!

Case Study: Shannon McCrory. Even as a baby, passersby would stop to gasp at the beautiful toddler with silver-blonde hair and sky-blue eyes. So what could be so anxiety-provoking for Shannon that she was scared to go to college? Just this! Shannon had been born with a club foot. Shannon's mother stated later, "She was not a 'blessed event' at all." In the hospital, she refused to have anything to do with the baby. The attending physician diagnosed her mother as having a "postpartum depression." Shannon's young father turned to his mother for help. Although now in her forties, Shannon's grandmother was glad to take care of the child since her own three children had all "left the nest." The arrangement was to be temporary—only until Shannon's mother came back "to her senses" again. But, as Fate would have it, Shannon's mother became pregnant again, and a prenatal exam revealed she was carrying twins. Everyone now agreed that it would be best to keep Shannon with her grandmother—for just a little longer. Weeks turned into months and months into years. Eventually, there was not even any more talk about Shannon going back to the family.

Although Shannon had looked forward eagerly to "making friends" with children of her own age, the reality was otherwise. Her club foot and ungainly walk produced aversion in the other children. And although only one or two of her classmates made fun of her openly, the other children tended to avoid her. For the first time in her life, Shannon began to see herself as an "ugly cripple." By the time other children got used to her club foot and tried to approach her, she kept them at a distance. She loved the learning activities, but by the end of the day she waited eagerly for the bus to take her back to the warm safety of her grandmother's house.

On the way to the college to take her admissions exam, Shannon became sick to her stomach. Her father had to stop the car so she could "upchuck" on the side of the road. She managed to get through the exams, but her head ached all day and when she turned her paper in she knew she had not done well. The test results that came were no surprise to her. Shannon was relieved. Now maybe she didn't have to go to college. She could stay home and take care of her grandmother (who was quite old now). Furthermore, now that she could be of help in the house, even her mother seemed more accepting of her in a distant way. When her mother was having "one of her spells," it was Shannon who cooked the evening meal for her father and "the boys." If she was scared to go out into the world, she knew that at least she could be useful to her family and that made her feel valued.

Case Study: Dan Westwind. Dan knew the extra money needed to go to college was not the issue. The basic issue was that the tribe needed him to be their representative to the Bureau of Indian Affairs. Dan had been given a grave responsibility and he would undertake whatever was necessary on behalf of his people. But he did not look forward to going through years of schooling to get the neccesary degree. Still, in the ways of his people, Dan stoically accepted whatever came his way and did not question the designated path that was chosen for him. ¡Que sera, sera!

Like some other traditional societies, Dan's life-career had been chosen by the tribal elders. When the tribal elders had decided to send one of their own people to the white man's college to become a lawyer, Dan had been the obvious first choice. Of all their people, Daniel had spent more time than anyone else in the white man's world, even graduating from their high school. He also had a trade, having worked as a car mechanic in Albuquerque for several years.

But there were several problems connected with Dan as a choice. He was already near 30 years of age. He would be close to 40 before he could call himself a lawyer. Furthermore, they knew he hated the white man's world because of what had happened to him in the city. What the Elders knew went like this: While having coffee one day at a diner, Dan had discovered that his waitress was half Native American. They found themselves "simpatico" and were married. Soon they had two sons. Although he didn't like the city and often looked longingly toward the mountains of his home, Daniel seemed to be making the transition from mountains and desert to life in the city. In actuality, Daniel hated living in the city. He hated listening to the white men "joking around" with their "squaw waitress," asking her whether she thought there would be another Indian uprising. He resented the way the white car owners spoke to him as though he was just a "dumb Indian." Still, he kept his peace. Then disaster hit. While crossing the street one day, his wife was killed by a white hit-and-run driver. Shocked and grief-stricken, he brought his sons back to his mother's house. He then went on an alcoholic binge that lasted for three months. He woke one morning to find himself in City Hospital full of tubes leading to hanging bags of intravenous fluids. He had been in the hospital for one week. His mother and the Navajo governor were sitting across from him.

Through the pain he could hear the nurse speaking to him, "If you tried to kill yourself with alcohol, you were almost successful." Daniel knew it was true.

The Governor waited until the nurse had left the room before he spoke: "Mourning time is over. It is time to live. If you don't want to live for yourself, then you can live for your people. There is much work for you to do."

His mother said simply, "The boys need you. They need their father. Come home."

So Dan went home. That was three years ago. He picked up the pieces of his life and went to work as a mechanic for a service station in the village, and in his spare time served as a maintenance person for the Navajo community. If there was a chance for personal happiness (a concept he only dimly understood), Dan knew it could only be where he could see his beloved mountains. Nevertheless, when the elders told Dan of their decision, Dan would do what he had to do. But the only relief he could envision to the bleak future of the next few years of his life were the times he could allow himself to journey back to the Navajo reservation.

Case Study: Natasha Petrovicc. Natasha Petrovicc is not just an immigrant to the United States. She and her husband, Gregori, and their two children are actually refugees from a former communist bloc country. Gregori had no English at all when they came to the United States, so he is working as a custodian in the local elementary school. It was he who persuaded Natasha to go back to school so she could get a good job which would help them all.

"You speak good English," Gregori said to her one day. "You are the one to get an American education so you can get a good job. Me, what can I do? I am no good at speaking English. No one understands me. I cannot read the English. As janitor, I know what I must do and Mister Evans, the principal, he likes that I am nice to the children so I get on. But I can't get a better job until I know more how to speak English. So you must be the one to go to the college and become educated."

"But what about the children? Who will take care of them? Who will cook the food? Who will clean the house?" cried Natasha.

Gregori said, "I will take care of everything here. We will put Nikki and Reza in the nursery school near my school. I will take them there. I will bring them home. I will cook the meals. I will keep the house clean. You must not concern yourself with these things. You must concern yourself with your classes at the college. You must make good marks. You must find something good to work at. You must do these things for all of us. You can teach all of us to speak good English. You can help the children with their homework to get good grades. We have not come to this country to live like peasants forever. We have come to make a good life for ourselves."

So Natasha applied to the college. She had not expected to be accepted. It was all happening so fast. While she was happy to be far from the violence that seems never to end in the "old country," she was having difficulty getting used to the newness of everything in the "new world." At times, she would experience dizzy spells. Sometimes, she even felt wistful for the "old country"—horrors at the thought! She sometimes felt depressed—all this while being grateful to be in a country free of brutal political violence, free of state police, free of prying neighbors ready to report your every word or action.

Case Study: Nat Bernstein. Receiving the Dean's letter was only the trigger-point for what happened. Nat's whole life seems to have been a disaster. Nathan was born to a Jewish family in which education and academic achievement were valued and fostered. Both parents were college professors. Nat's older brother, Aaron, graduated from Princeton with a Ph.D. in physics. By 36 years of age, Aaron was well on his way to a successful academic career.

If Aaron was the "model son," Nathan was the "problem child." By 10, he was smoking cigarettes and then grass with the gang. He stole his father's liquor and money enough to buy drugs. He dropped out of school at 16, watching TV during the day and skipping out at night with his friends, doing "God-knows-what," said his parents in despair. Eventually, petty crimes followed, and from then on, he was in and out of juvenile detention centers. Nothing seemed to help Nat. Not counseling sessions or halfway houses for his drug abuse. He always ascribed his difficulties with the law on the "lousy police" or "the system." He screamed four-letter words at his parents.

To begin with, Nathan was two months premature. Furthermore, it was a complicated "breech birth," and the baby had to be isolated with a life-support system for several weeks before his parents were allowed to take him home. Even the pregnancy had been difficult, according to Nathan's mother. At various times during her pregnancy, she had experienced nausea, anoxia, swelling of the ankles, and high blood pressure. Nathan's problems continued throughout infancy. He was colicky. Strange faces would start him crying. He would scream for fifteen or more minutes when he was left at the nursery school, according to the caretakers. He did not initiate play with other children. In grade school, he showed extremes of behavior. When he wanted to, said his teachers, he could do better than anyone else in the class. But he was "moody." He would sometimes sit staring. Or he might suddenly hit one of his classmates "for no reason."

Eventually, the school counselor recommended that he be given a complete psychological and physical evaluation. Diagnosis: epilepsy of the "petit mal" type. Petit mal epilepsy does not result in "fits" or "convulsions." The epileptic episodes last only for a few seconds, not even long enough to fall down. Nathan's particular type of petit mal epilepsy was preceded by noises (sometimes even bits of speech), called an epileptic aura. The bits of speech he would hear were similar to what he had heard at home. "Why aren't you more like your brother, Aaron!" "You'll be the death of me." Not realizing these comments were coming from his own brain memories, he thought his classmates were ridiculing him. With angry "knee-jerk" responses, he would turn around and hit them.

When he was 18, Nat took off. For eighteen months, no one knew where he was until he showed up at his parents' home again, looking somewhat better than he had for some time.

He had a young woman with him whom Nat introduced as Amber, his "soul mate." Amber seems to have been a good influence on him, so his parents allowed them to share a room in their house, although an intimate relationship without marriage was painful for them. At mealtimes, the two young people would introduce the family to "New Age" concepts. Things seemed to be working out better for Nat. With Amber's encouragement, he finished high school at night. He even contemplated enrolling in the local college and took the necessary entrance exams. Little by little, however, Nat's previous behaviors returned: drug addiction, petty theft, drunken sprees, and obscenities toward his parents and even Amber.

One night, Amber left quietly without even writing a note. Nat got drunk, cried a lot, and called her obscene names. That night he had a bad trip on drugs. The Dean's letter came in the morning mail. He dropped the letter, went into the house, and shot himself.

Box 1.6

APPLICATION
Applying the Case Study Method

After you have read all the previous brief case studies, respond to the items below:

Eduardo Sanangelo:
1. Name three factors in his background that could account for Eduardo's cheerful and optimistic nature?
2. What do you think his chances are for doing well in college? Support your answer.

Jonnimae Jones:
1. Identify three factors in her childhood and adulthood that contributed to her positive self-esteem in regard to her ability to "make something" of herself.
2. List three character traits that make her a good prospect for becoming a nurse.

Shannon McRory:
Suggest three possible motivations for Shannon's lack of self-esteem and reluctance to go to college despite her brilliance as a student?

Dan Westwind:
1. What are Dan Westwind's chances for success in terms of coping skills and purpose?
2. Describe his self-concept and personality style.

Natasha Petrovicc:
1. Although she is happy to be away from the violence of the old country, why does she sometimes yearn to go back?
2. What might be happening that results in her occasional dizziness?

Nathan Bernstein:
1. How do you evaluate Nat's self-esteem?
2. Name four factors that could be involved in his self-destructive behavior.
3. What evidence is there that Nat does not understand his problems?

Box 1.7

SCENARIO REVISITED
How Do We Go About Becoming More
Highly Self-Actualizing?

Professor Weitzman has just finished calling the class role. Eduardo has his hand raised.

Eduardo: You know, Professor, when I came to college, I had pretty good self-esteem. Now I'm not so sure of myself. After our last class discussion about how all of us can have areas of low self-esteem, maybe I have low self esteem and just don't know it! (*class laughter*)

Professor Weitzman: Eduardo, with your generally optimistic attitude, I don't know how you could have too many areas of low self-esteem. (*more laughter*)

Martha: Seriously, Professor Weitzman, how do you get to be self-actualizing?

Professor Weitzman: Well, you've already started that just by reading your text and thinking about yourself and others and perhaps what you want to do with your life. Very soon, we will be forming small groups of five to eight students. In these groups, we will provide you with further opportunities for self-analysis and for trying out new interactions with your group members.

Eduardo: Isn't there anything we can do now? Today?

Professor Weitzman: Well all right, we can take just a few minutes to do something that might get you started at a personal level. Turn to Maslow's hierarchy of needs in the textbook. Let's see how many of these levels we can identify in our own lives. We'll start with the lowest level—the level of physiological needs. Can anybody identify with that level? (*There is an uncomfortable silence.*)

Dan: I can. . . . Three years ago, I was drinking heavily. I didn't care about anything, not even my life. Every cent I got I spent on liquor. I wasn't eating much. I panhandled. I was a bum. I ended up in the hospital.

Professor Weitzman: Thank you, Dan. That couldn't have been easy to say.

Dan: Talking about it is part of my treatment plan.

Professor: Now the level of safety and security? (*Again a silence and then a timid hand goes up.*)

Natasha: I think I can. My husband, my children and me—we are refugees. In my country, there was so much bombing, and killing, and raping. We were always in fear for our lives. Even now when we hear sirens, our hearts . . . how do you say . . . pound?

Eduardo: That fits for sure, doesn't it, Professor?

Professor Weitzman: I would say so, indeed! The level of love and belonging anyone?

Shannon: That's been me most of my life. My mother never wanted me around so I had to stay with my grandmother and she was kind. I've got a great dad too but because of my . . . deformity . . . the kids in school didn't like me. I just didn't belong. I've made a few friends at college, but I still don't feel at home here yet.

Dan: Well, I don't either.

Natasha: Not me either.

Professor Weitzman: As we go through this course, we may discover that our need to belong somewhere manifests throughout our life spans, although it takes many forms.

Alec: I'll try the next one—the cognitive needs. First I've got to explain to you all that I come from a very prejudiced family. I didn't know that when I was growing up, but when I got to high school, I began to realize it. So I pulled away from my entire family. Now I've got questions and I'm looking for answers. I want to know what makes people prejudiced. In a country where we are supposed to respect others different from ourselves, why do some people hate others? It baffles me. Why? Why? Why? I want to find answers.

Jonnimae: Aesthetic drive! The other people in the class will probably think I'm crazy but it's true for me. It's mathematics. When I look at a row of figures in my accounting courses and they all come out the way they should—all pretty and balanced—it just seems very aesthetically satisfying. I feel that way about chemistry too. I like making models for my chemistry class. Am I crazy or what?

Professor Weitzman: I confess that's a new one for me but I don't call that crazy. I call that creative. Now I'll take the next one. Who do I think is making strides toward the level of self-actualizing?

Eduardo: You, Professor?

Professor: Yes. And you. And you! And all of you in this class. Call that a little idealistic but that's my philosophy and I'm sticking to it. (*class laughter*)

Alec: But that doesn't answer my question. Why do prejudice and hatred exist in a free society. It's really tearing me up.

Box 1.7   SCENARIO REVISITED (continued)

Professor Weitzman: There are no simple answers, Alec. Human behavior is the result of many factors: Our genetic predisposition, our conditioning and life experiences, how we are brought up, and the culture and subculture we were born into.

Alec: Are you saying that we are predetermined by our biology and upbringing? That we can't escape? That sounds like that old Calvinistic predetermination!

Professor Weitzman: There are some who say that—and we'll be discussing the reasons for their positions.

Alec: We can't escape what we've been born into? I'm getting away from my prejudiced family.

Professor Weitzman: Whoa, Alec! I hold firmly to the humanistic school of psychology; namely, that we do have *free will* and we *can* go beyond the givens of our birth. But it is a basic tenet of scientific inquiry that we consider all perspectives even if they disagree with our own. So let's give all points-of-view a fair hearing.

IMPORTANT TERMS AND CONCEPTS TO KNOW

becomings	hierarchy of needs	negative	self-actualizing
blaming	high school	personality	self-concept
case study	internal	physiological	self-esteem
cognitive	locus of control	rites of passage	unconscious
conscious	learned helplessness	safety and security	

MAKE YOUR OWN CHAPTER SUMMARY BY FILLING IN THE BLANKS BELOW

Use the "Important Terms and Concepts to Know" to fill in the blanks below.

Personality. How we cope with life events depends on our _____ style. It includes every dimension of the human experience, such as _____ factors (what we know about ourselves) and _____ factors (what we don't know about ourselves).

Two key dimensions of personality. These include _____ , which is how we think about ourselves and _____ , which is how we feel about ourselves. The self-concept is generally enhanced as the result of achievements which society acknowledges through _____ . Sometimes we can have a very positive self-concept but a _____ self-esteem. Most of us are a combination of both positive and _____ self-esteem. The era of lowest self-esteem for most persons are the _____ years.

Locus of Control. People who have high self-esteem have an _____ locus of control; for example, they believe they can effect positive changes in their lives. People who have an external _____ indulge in the _____ game. They believe they do not have the ability or opportunity to change their lives, which Martin Seligman calls _____ .

Growth of Personality. Unlike other species, we can grow, mature, and evolve throughout our lifetime. Gordon Allport urged us to think of ourselves not so much human *beings* as human _____ . The ability to grow, change, and evolve was one of the characteristics of Maslow's _____ subjects.

Abraham Maslow. This psychologist constructed a seven-level _____ . The two lowest level needs are composed of the _____ needs and safety-and-security needs. The next five levels are composed of the love and belonging needs, the esteem needs, the _____ needs, the aesthetic needs, and the self-actualizing needs. Maslow warned us that we must not consider these levels as permanent achievements; for example, a person who is homeless can be said to be at the _____ level of needs.

The Farthest Reaches of Personality. Most personality theorists agree that the highest levels of human development must include the physical, the emotional, the _____ or intellectual, and finally the moral/ethical/spiritual dimension.

The research methodology. The reader is introduced to the _____ method of research in this chapter.

2 SOCIAL PSYCHOLOGY AND THE FRONTIERS OF TRANSPERSONAL, POSITIVE, AND PEACE PSYCHOLOGIES

Reading from bottom middle and to the left, upwards counter clockwise: Nelson Mandela, Martin Luther King, Jr., Mahatma Gandhi, Emile Zola, Abraham Lincoln, Mother Theresa, Rachel Carson, Dian Fossey, Andre Sakharov. Social psychology has largely focused on "man's inhumanity to man," what causes some individuals and groups to behave with heartless cruelty. But over and beyond such inhumane behavior, there have always been those persons who have reached beyond the limitations and narrow structures of their society. They have been described as highly integrated, creative, self-actualizing, fully functioning, self realized, and individuated. Such individuals not only transcended their cultural time-and-place, they also enabled humanity to achieve a more compassionate worldview.

Box 2.1

SCENARIO
The Powerful Social Forces That Influence Human Behavior

Professor Wietzman: We have been discussing the various factors of personality such as self-concept and self-esteem. But we can never really understand human behavior until we include the cultural context in which the person exists. That's a fancy way of saying that many of our attitudes and behaviors are the result of societal influences—the person's racial, ethnic, religious affiliations, and other groups to which he or she belongs. Prejudice, hate-crimes, and genocide can all be viewed from the perspective of the person's group membership.

Alec: I'm glad we're getting into this, Professor. Why is there so much hate crime? I have a personal reason for asking this. I come from a really prejudiced family. It was only in the last two years of high school that I learned how prejudiced they are. I moved out as soon as I could.

Professor Wietzman: First of all, Alec, I have to tell you that there isn't anyone entirely free of prejudice. We are all of us prejudiced to some degree.

Eduardo: Hey, I resent that, Professor! I don't think I'm prejudiced. I accept everybody as being equal to me.

Professor Wietzman: Eduardo, what vocational area are you aiming for?

Eduardo: I'm going to be an engineer.

Professor Wietzman: Would you employ a woman as an engineer?

Eduardo: A woman! Why would a woman want to be an engineer when she'd be so much better at being a . . . a teacher or social worker maybe.

Martha: Talk about prejudice!

Professor Wietzman: To be specific, that's called *gender bias.*

Eduardo: (*now a little rattled*) I thought prejudice meant thinking that a certain ethnic group has . . . bad traits.

Professor Wietzman: Prejudice simply means *pre-judgment*, making assumptions about someone without knowing them. One example is called *stereotyping*, assuming that somebody has certain characteristics because they are members of a certain group.

Alec: But just what makes us stereotype people?

Professor Wietzman: To answer that, we need to understand the terms, *cognitions* or *cognitive schemas*, which are thoughts, ideas, or perceptions about the

---

Box 2.1   SCENARIO (continued)
                  The Powerful Social Forces That Influence Human Behavior

---

way things are or should be. We have cognitive schemas for just about everything in our social world and these cognitive schemas guide our actions.

Martha: Eduardo has a cognitive schema that women shouldn't try to be engineers.

Alec: So racial and ethnic prejudice has to do with rejecting anyone who doesn't fit our cognitions about what it is to be a good person or a good American?

Professor Wietzman: Very good, Alec. That's part of it. Cognitive schemas are the result of many factors—past experiences, our defense mechanisms, our age—just about everything. Anything that threatens to disrupt our cognitive schemas makes us uncomfortable, and we have an innate tendency to reject it. Cognitive schemas are the way we make judgments.

Shannon: Would cognitive schemas account for popularity? Is that why there always seem to be *in-groups* and *out-groups*?

Professor Wietzman: Certainly, that would be a factor.

Martha: How about parents who object to their son's choice of a wife because "she isn't our kind"? That's what my in-laws said when they met me. I'm Italian and they didn't think I was good enough for Rodney. I guess I didn't fit into their cognitive schema about what kind of wife would be right for Rod. Fortunately, Rod didn't feel the same way.

Professor Wietzman: You've all given good examples of cognitive schemas.

Alec: We keep talking about cognitive schemas. Isn't that just another name for *prejudice* and *attitude*?

Shannon: And *stereotypes*? And *either/or thinking*?

Professor Wietzman: Yes, yes, yes, and yes.

Li Ho: I'm beginning to get it. *Cognitive schema* is a larger, more general term and includes all the other terms.

Professor Wietzman: That's getting closer but the term also has less judgmentalness about it than the other terms. Not all our cognitive schemas are as negative as the examples you have provided.

Jonnimae: I listened to Alec describing his prejudiced family and how he got outside of the . . . prejudicial cognitive schema of his family. I think that's amazing. I've heard that it is very difficult to get beyond prejudice.

Professor Wietzman: It is difficult because many of the prejudices and attitudes we have were learned so early in our lives that they seem built into the very fabric of our personality structure. Nevertheless, by learning how groups influence our behavior, we can begin to develop wider cognitive schemas and enlarge our worldviews.

The Discipline of Social Psychology: Society, Group Membership, and the Individual

Social psychologists focus on the very questions we ask ourselves when we learn about tragic events via the public media:

> *What makes people participate in the atrocities of war and genocide?*
> *Why do some people not help another in an emergency, whereas others are "good Samaritans"?*
> *Why do people choose to become gangsters and live outside the law?*
> *Why do people give up their liberties and even their lives to follow a cult leader?*

While social psychologists have not discovered all the answers to these questions, they have discovered a few of them.

Our Cultural Groups Shape Our Attitudes

If we have grown up in an affluent family that held that the making and spending of money was the ultimate value in life, then we may very likely grow up to think of money as the basis of "the good life." If we have grown up in a home where the adults express fear or hatred and prejudice and other such attitudes toward other ethnic groups, then we may very likely become fearful or hateful toward those groups.

Our attitudes are *also* shaped by the groups we admire and would like to belong to. If we have grown up watching the respect paid by gangsters to their gang leader and if we yearn for that kind of respect ourselves, we may try to become more violent and brutal than the other gang members. In fact, throughout our lifetime, we are learning to conform to the behavioral expectations of our professions, our political affiliations, our civic and church associations. Group membership makes us feel stronger and more secure. We feel we belong somewhere and it seems to fulfill Maslow's third hierarchical level of love and belongingness. That's the bright side of the coin; the other side of the coin is darker. By definition, *in-groups* make for *out-groups*. Once we become an in-group member, those who are not part of this group are, by definition, members of the out-group.

Research in social psychology had its beginnings at the end of the nineteenth century when a French scientist, by the name of Émile Durkheim (1884), studied the social factors involved in suicide. While his research parameters are somewhat primitive (when compared to research today), many of Durkheim's basic findings are still valid today. What he discovered was that many people who committed or attempted to commit suicide were isolated from their **primary groups** (the families they were born into) and their **secondary groups** (their friends and close associates). At the time of their suicide, they had left their homes in other parts of France and were living in Paris, had not yet established new relationships or friends, nor a way to make a secure living for themselves. Far from home, lost, bewildered, and running out of funds, they fell into despair. Feelings of failure and having no one to turn to for help prompted them to end their miserable existences.

Adorno's Study of the Authoritarian Personality

After Durkheim, there followed some sporadic investigations, but the great impetus came with the rise of Nazi Germany and the atrocities of that era. One of the earliest of these studies was that conducted by Theodor Adorno and his associates (1973), and it is still noteworthy because it defined the "authoritarian" personality type. The authoritarian personality is considered so valid a personality type that it has been incorporated into (literally) thousands of research studies ever since.

Adorno was himself German-born. Witnessing the takeover by the Nazi regime, he emigrated to the United States in 1934. After World War II, Adorno organized a research team at Berkeley, California, to investigate whether Americans could become as fanatic and Fascistic as the Germans and Italians under the regimes of Hitler and Mussolini. The specific questions posed by Adorno and his research team were as follows:

How could the German people have been induced to follow such despotic leaders?
What is the personality style of people who blindly obey terrible orders such as happened in theHolocaust?
How could the nation that produced some of the greatest musicians, philosophers, scientists, and humanitarians the world has ever known also produce the atrocities of the Nazi regime?

And most compelling of all their questions:

> *Could the atrocities that happened in a Fascist state also happen in a democracy?*
> *Could Americans, who have been brought up in a democracy, be as easily regimented*
> *as the Germans?*

Their research findings were shocking even to the investigators. What they discovered was that even in a prevailing democratic climate, a large percentage of people can be described as "highly authoritarian." Highly authoritarian subjects were defined as follows:

- They blindly follow authority without question (as did the Germans during the Hitler regime).
- They have a lack of positive self-esteem. In fact, they tend to feel vulnerable and defenseless. Belonging to an authoritarian organization provides them with some measure of security and self-esteem.
- While they are dominant and authoritarian and expect unquestioning obedience from their children and employees, they are nevertheless very submissive to those who are their superiors in authority. In other words, said the researchers, they could have made "good Nazi soldiers."
- They have a strong tendency to agree emphatically with statements such as "Obedience and respect for authority are the most important virtues children should learn," and "Most of our social problems would be solved if we could somehow get rid of immoral, crooked, and feebleminded people," and "People can be divided into two distinct classes: the weak and the strong."
- They are harshly judgmental about others, particularly minority groups. They tend to view racial, ethnic, religious, and other minorities as "enemies of democracy." By contrast, low-authoritarian subjects (defined as more open-minded and democratic) were more egalitarian and were willing to accept all ethnic groups as equal to the WASP (White Anglo-Saxon Protestant) dominant population group of that time (the late 1940s and early 1950s).
- Their cognitive schemas are *dogmatic, stereotypic,* and exemplify *rigid either/or thinking.*

Authoritarian Personalities: Dogmatic, Stereotypic, Rigid Either/Or Thinking.
Dogma refers to a set of beliefs held to be true and absolute without evidence or proof. *Dogmatic* individuals not only subscribe to a prescribed set of beliefs, they often behave in an "arrogant" fashion toward those who believe otherwise. In our personal lives, we all know dogmatic people who are absolutely convinced that what they believe is right and that other people are wrong. They do not like to listen to others who have a different opinion, particularly if that opinion comes from a minority group they dislike or from a person younger than themselves. You may know such a person who says, "Until you're my age, keep your opinions to yourself."

Not only were Adorno's authoritarian subjects dogmatic, they also fell prey to stereotypic thinking and all-or-nothing thinking. **Stereotypes** are the cultural assumptions that people who belong to a certain group all share the same personality characteristics. Stereotyping people is a normal cognitive process. It is sometimes called a **cognitive shortcut**—how we clump events together in chunks to make sense of our world. If we had to cogitate (think deeply) about the thousands of objects and people we encounter over the course of the day, we would hardly be able to function at all. Cognitive shortcuts make life simpler and easier to manage when it comes to objects and events, but when these shortcuts are applied to people, they can be the basis of much of our prejudicial thinking. **Gender stereotyping** seems to be the most common, but all segments of our population get their fair share of stereotyping.

Women are emotional, illogical, and passive.
Men are macho, logical, and aggressive.
Jews are clever in business affairs.
Blacks have rhythm.
Italians are passionate.
Germans are methodical.
The British are reserved.
Accountants are conformists.

Lawyers are manipulative.
Artists are uninhibited.
Old people are unhealthy and dull-witted.
The Scots are tight with money.
Blondes are airheads.
Computer programmers are nerds.

Now there may be some truth to the perception that accountants are more conforming than (say) artists and entertainers—after all, accountants have to understand thousands of IRS rules and conform to them. But there are always exceptions to any stereotype, and we miss the real person when we view him through stereotypic glasses: *I may be a woman and a blonde, BUT I AM NOT AN AIRHEAD!*

Either/or thinking is the tendency to think in terms of black and white. When adults indulge in either/or thinking, they tend to see a few people as "good guys" but almost everyone else as "bums" or "SOBs." They view people like the heros and bad guys of Hollywood Westerns—as wearing white hats and black hats. The democratic personality tends to view almost all people as having some good in them.

How Can We Know Whether We Are Holding a Dogmatic Position on an Issue? Ends versus Means. One way to know is to examine ourselves: Do we justify the *means* in pursuit of the *ends*? Many terrible deeds have been committed by **dogmatic** people out of their conviction that since they know what is right, others are not only wrong—they must be purged of their misbeliefs or simply wiped out. The Inquisition came into being to root out not only the Devil but also to discover anyone suspected of "heretical thinking." The purpose of the Inquisitors was to save the heretic's soul through any means, including torture—even if the body died in the process. Two centuries later, the very Puritans who sailed to the New World for reasons of religious freedom became, in turn, equally dogmatic—resulting eventually in the witch trials and witch burnings in Salem, Massachusetts.

In a democracy, the *ends* may never justify the *means*. We are involved with the "due process of law" as much as we are involved with "law-and-order." That is why our Supreme Court defends our liberties of free speech and free assembly even to those who are political adversaries of democracy. Sometimes we may become horrified that permission to march has been granted to white supremacist groups. But, unless these groups are conspiring to overthrow our constitutional government or commit a crime, the Supreme Court has declared that they have as much right to assemble and to speak as does anyone else (see Tip 2.1).

Tip 2.1   The Devil's Advocate. Even during the times of the Inquisition, the medieval Catholic Church allowed for a defense of the accused person by appointing a cleric to defend them. For, said the Church, even the Devil deserves to be heard, and the defense counsel-cleric became known as the "Devil's Advocate."

There seems to be a positive correlation between authoritarianism and education. One social scientist identified the authoritarian cognitive style (dogmatic, stereotypic, and rigid either/or thinking) as more prevalent among those who come from lower educational levels. We become more open-minded and democratic in our thinking as we become more and more educated (Leung, Lau, & Lam, 1998).

Solomon Asch's Studies of Conformity

Another burning question for social psychologists of the post–World War II decade went something like this: *Just how were the German people made to conform to the racist philosophy and brutal tactics of the Nazi war machine?* Much research has been undertaken to answer this question and social psychologists have come up with a few insights for us. One line of investigation, under the direction of Solomon Asch (1951), demonstrated just how easily people can be made to conform even when conforming went contrary to their beliefs or perceptions.

A typical experiment would be set up as follows. Asch would invite about eight college students to a classroom to judge the comparative length of similar lines (see Figure 2.1). Now it's important to understand that of all the students in each experimental session, only one student was a real subject. All the others were "stooges" or confederates of the experimenter—but of course the real subject (let's call him Student S) did not know that. As far as Student S was concerned, they were all real subjects like himself.

In the beginning of the experiment, all is rather hum-drum. All the students agree that Line X is most similar to Line B. But after a few rounds, something seems to go wrong. The first five students state that Line X is most similar to Line A or Line C (see Figure 2.1). Movies of this experiment clearly show that Student S is obviously puzzled. He looks at the lines again. He squints at them. Sometimes he even wriggles nervously in his seat. What will he do because of his difference of opinion? Will he go along with the crowd? Or will he candidly express his opinion in the face of overwhelming public opinion? About 35 percent of the time, Student S conformed to public opinion and agreed with the other (stooge) students. But that was only the beginning.

Asch then concerned himself with the 65 percent who were able to diverge from public opinion? He wondered what would happen if he increased the public pressure on them. Would they be able to maintain an independent stance? This is how Asch increased the social pressure: He instructed the stooges that if Student S turned out to be an independent type, they were to laugh at him and make derisive remarks about his intelligence, etc. The public pressure was effective. Now 75 percent caved in under this increased public pressure.

When all the real subjects were asked later why they gave in to public opinion, they offered two major responses. The first was that in the light of what everyone was saying, they began to doubt themselves and their own senses. They thought that maybe there was something wrong with their eyes or the lights in the room. The second common response was that they knew their own perceptions were right but they "didn't want to make waves."

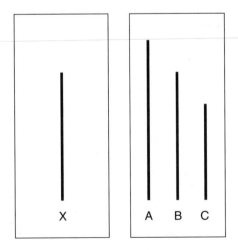

Figure 2.1 Asch's Study of Conformity

So what Asch did was to change the experimental conditions. Student S continued to listen to the other students but was allowed to give his own answer in private. Without the public condemnation, Student S did not change his own belief that he was mistaken.

Asch was dismayed by the results of his studies, not just because people will give in to public pressure but for the fact that his particular subjects were college students!—presumably, the nation's most intelligent young people. Subjected to enough social pressure, the majority could not resist the pressure of social conformity. They kept still. *Is that what happened to the Germans who said nothing while their friends and relatives were dragged off to concentration camps? They just kept still?*

But there are also some brighter results in these generally dismal findings. No matter how much pressure was applied, 25 percent of the subjects did not conform, not when they were questioned privately, nor when they were ridiculed publicly. They were able to remain a "minority of one." Another finding: If Student S had at least one confederate, he was much more able to stand up against the social pressure. In fact, he was unlikely to conform. It reminds us of the saying: *A good friend is a strong defense.*

Milgram's Experiments in Obedience

Stanley Milgram, a former student of Asch, was so concerned by the massacre of villages of men, women, and children during the Vietnam War that he undertook a project to determine just how far Americans would obey orders, no matter what might result. His research in this area is now known as the "obedience experiments" (Milgram, 1974).

What Milgram did was to post an advertisement in the local newspaper for volunteers to take part in a university experiment. The volunteer would receive $4.50 an hour (a good hourly rate at that time). When the subject appeared at the office, he was introduced to another person who apparently had also answered the advertisement. The Experimenter appeared and told the two men that the experiment was to discover the effects of punishment on learning and that one of the subjects would be the Teacher and the other would be the Learner. These roles were drawn from slips of paper in a hat in a seemingly random manner. Both the Teacher and the Learner were conducted to a booth where the Learner was strapped into a chair. The straps, explained the Experimenter, were merely to prevent excessive movement, but then an electrode was placed on the Learner's wrist and some electrode paste was applied in order "to avoid blisters and burns." If the Learner asked if the shocks would be painful, the Experimenter replied that while the shocks may be painful, they would not do any permanent damage.

The Teacher was then conducted to a second booth from which he could not see the Learner and where he was shown an apparatus that registered the voltage of electric shock in units from 15 to 450 volts. The Teacher was then given a booklet full of questions. He was told to ask the Learner a question through an intercom. If the Learner answered correctly, the Teacher was to go on to the next question. If the Learner answered incorrectly, however, he was to be punished with a shock, starting at 15 volts and going up to the highest volt level, 450 volts.

As you may have already guessed, the Learner was really a stooge. (Both slips in the hat read "Teacher.") All the Teacher knows is that as the shocks increase in intensity, the Learner begins to cry out that he is in pain and pleads to be let out of the experiment—at least in the beginning. The Learner's protests get louder and louder. Then he yells out, "I can't stand the pain," and he begins to scream in agony. At a certain point, he screams out that he has a heart condition. At 300 volts the Learner begins to pound on the wall. Still the testing goes on. The reader should not get the idea that the Teacher is impervious to the cries of the Learner. Movies of this experiment clearly show that the Teacher is perspiring and visibly shaken. He turns frequently to the Experimenter (who is dressed in a pristine white lab coat) and questions the Experimenter anxiously about the Learner's welfare. Perhaps they should stop? But in a cool and unemotional tone of voice, the Experimenter merely replies that "the experiment must continue." The Teacher continues asking questions and administering shocks (he thinks).

Eventually there is no more screaming—just silence. No matter how many times the Teacher tries to get a response from the Learner, there is only this ominous silence. As far as the Teacher knows, the Learner could be dead. Yet approximately 66 percent of the Teachers obeyed "the Authority" right up to the 450 volt level. Whatever this happened, the Teachers often behaved in strange ways. One man giggled every time he heard a scream. A few of the people who truly believed that the Learner was dead were asked how they felt. They replied in a variety of ways. One man replied, "So he's dead. I did my job." A few even placed the blame for the Learner's death on the Learner himself. *It was his own fault for being so dumb.* When Milgram's experiment was **replicated** (repeated) in Australia, South Africa, and in several European countries, the results were similar or even more dramatic. In one German study, 85 percent of the subjects were found to be obedient to the end.

Disturbed that Americans, born and bred in the very country which has been so concerned with "human rights," would obey authority to this extent, Milgram wondered if college students would show more resistance to such inhumane orders. But a replication of the study with Yale undergraduates yielded similar results. *What about women who are supposed to be the "gentler sex"?* But women Teachers also administered heavy shocks to the Learners. Perhaps the subjects were influenced by the impressive environment of Yale University where the experiment was taking place. So the experiment was tried in a dingy store in a nearby town—and still the same results.

Milgram came to some dismal conclusions:

- Independent thinking and moral/ethical judgment are not built-in attributes of a free society. Evidently, some people will do things because some more powerful authority tells them to.
- When faced with the painful dilemma of hurting someone and obeying some authority, most people will obey "the authority." Comparisons were drawn to the Nazi concentration camp officers who complied with orders to murder millions of people.
- An implication from this comparison was that the Nazi murderers were merely average bureaucrats following orders and trying to do their jobs as well as they could.

Zimbardo's Prison Experiment

Another classic experiment was carried out by Philip Zimbardo (1976) of Stanford University, who provided more information about group membership and how it defines our roles and how we behave. But the most astonishing finding of this experiment is how swiftly our social roles change our behavior. The experiment was supposed to run for two weeks. But what happened in the first few days was so shocking that Zimbardo called off the experiment after six days.

Zimbardo's purpose for running the experiment was "to understand just what it means psychologically to be a prisoner or a prison guard" (Zimbardo, 1976, p. 277). The pay was advertised as $15.00 per day—quite a decent rate for college students at that time. Of more than 70 students who answered the ad, they ended up with "about two dozen" young men who were *"mature, emotionally stable, normal, intelligent college students from middle-class families."*

We have taken pains to describe the subjects because of what ensued. As far as Zimbardo and his team were concerned, their subjects were the *"cream of the crop of this generation"* and none had any criminal record or had been in any serious difficulties growing up.

The next step was to select the college students who would be the prisoners and those who would be the prison guards. This selection was made by a genuine flip of a coin. The prisoners were picked up unexpectedly at their homes by an actual city policeman in his squad car, handcuffed, taken to the city jail where they were fingerprinted, stripped, searched, deloused, given a prison number, and put into a prison cell.

In the meantime, the "prison guards" were made aware of the dangers of guarding prisoners (as is done in actual prisons) and were told they could make up their own rules to maintain law and order with one exception—they could not physically hurt the prisoners. The events that happened next horrified the research team. The behavior of the guards became increasingly "cruel and inhumane." Some guards treated the prisoners like "despicable animals," who took pleasure in making the prisoners perform senseless and demeaning actions. The research team watched with amazement as the prisoners became not just docile but servile. Although the prisoners were free to leave at any time, none asked to leave. In fact, Zimbardo had to forcibly insist that three prisoners leave because of the severe emotional symptoms they were exhibiting, such as hysterical crying, confusion in thinking, and severe depression. Eventually, Zimbardo had to stop the experiment and release all the prisoners after only six days.

What Makes Decent Human Beings Make Morally Wrong Choices? Some Theories and Explanations

When we discussed the findings of Adorno's investigation into the *authoritarian* personality, it was shown that those people who are the most likely candidates for joining antidemocratic hate groups are from less-educated groups, even prison groups. But in the experiments by Asch, Milgram, and Zimbardo, the subjects were often college students, professional people, and perfectly decent citizens judged to be morally upstanding and mentally healthy. The question then arises: What are the dynamics that underlie the willingness of people to behave in such reprehensible ways, without regard for human existence? Overall, these studies point to the following factors:

- Power as a corrupting force of human personality;
- The dehumanizing effect of a demeaning environment;
- The human tendency to conform to membership in a group;
- The inability to resist overwhelming public group pressure;
- The powerful influence of social roles, such as the roles of *authority, prison guard,* and *prisoner.*

Even when we enter the workplace, the pressure to conform continues. The pressure may come from the corporations we work for, the professions we go into, and the political parties we belong to. Simply put, like other gregarious species, we follow the herd. In the political arena, it is called "getting on the band wagon." Milgram's experiments in obedience suggest that our societal structure has such a built-in awe, fear, or reverence for those in authority that we will obey orders even when they endanger human life. Zimbardo's prison experiment has helped us understand the power of our social roles. The simple act of donning a uniform may cause human beings to take on, with extraordinary swiftness, the psychological attributes that the uniform represents. In the Zimbardo experiment, the prison guards became authoritarian, punitive, harsh, abusive, and inhumane. The prisoners became passive, submissive, and psychologically demeaned. Indeed, we are reminded that *"power corrupts and absolute power corrupts absolutely"* (see Tip 2.2).

Carl Jung: Deindividuation

Another theory thought to hold considerable validity is the phenomenon of *deindividuation.* Carl Jung was, at one time a student and then a colleague of Sigmund Freud. It was he who formulated the concepts of *individuation* and *deindividuation* (Jung, 1955). *Deindividuation* is what happens when people are taken over by what is sometimes called "mob psychology." It is what makes perfectly decent people do terrible things in the frenzy of a crowd that they would not do alone and "in their right mind"—such as yelling "Jump! Jump!" to a potential suicide victim fourteen flights up. Fraternities have hazed a pledge to death. Posses have lynched a person without trial. At such times, these people are not acting as individuals. **Deindividuation** is what happens when people lose their individual identities and behave in accordance with the actions of a mob. Deindividuation is augmented under conditions of anonymity, when wearing uniforms, and in the dead of night. Under just such conditions the Ku Klux Klan would meet and carry out its dark and dreadful deeds. **Individuated persons** have the courage and the ability to stand up and be counted. It takes a person firmly rooted from his or her "center" to resist the pressure of conforming to public opinion. (We describe individuated persons later in this chapter.)

Some political leaders have been expert in techniques of deindividuation. Significant in Hitler's rise to power were the techniques by which the Nazis transformed huge assemblies of people into a mass of deindividuated and mindless robots. Movies taken at the huge coliseum at Nuremberg record the dramatic rites and rituals used to orchestrate human emotions and human behavior. Against the darkness of increasing night and against a backdrop of flaming torches, there would begin a hypnotic beat of drums. Then someone would begin the chanting of the two words "Heil Hitler" over and over again. The drum beats and the chanting were kept up for some minutes until the assembled Germans had become mesmerized—now a mass of deindividuated and mindless beings ready to follow their leaders without question. Deindividuated behaviors have been described as "emotional, impulsive, irrational, regressive, or atypical for the person in a given situation" (Forsyth, 1983, p. 322).

When Will People Help? The Bystander Effect

On March 13, 1964, around 3:00 A.M., something so shocking took place on the streets of New York City that it spawned a line of investigations ultimately called the *bystander effect.* The event was the murder of a young woman. But it wasn't simply the murder itself that shocked the nation but the circumstances of her death.

Tip 2.2   On the corrupting power of power. This theme has been repeated by many persons down through the ages. The phrase we have used comes from a letter written by Lord Acton to Bishop Mandell Creighton (1887). Tacitus, the Roman philosopher born in A.D. 55 wrote that "the lust for power, for dominating others, inflames the heart more than any other passion." William Pitt in a speech to the House of Lords in 1770 said "Unlimited power is apt to corrupt the minds of those who possess it." Edmund Burke repeated this a few years later when he wrote in his essay on "A Vindication of Natural Society" the following words: "Power gradually extirpates from the mind every humane and gentle virtue."

Box 2.2   Ethics in Psychological Research

Asch, Milgram, and Zimbardo all received many honors and awards for their work, but they also received strong criticism for putting their subjects through such stressful situations. These experiments and others resulted in additions to the code of ethics of the American Psychological Association. The additions prohibit social scientists from performing such psychologically painful experiments. Even though the Teachers in Zimbardo's experiments were later debriefed by explaining the nature of the experiment and by actually seeing that the "dead Learner" was really alive and unharmed, the APA said that debriefing the subjects later does not justify the agony they initially went through. *Even for the sake of discovering more knowledge, the ends do not justify the means.* The APA guidelines are extensive and cover many professional topics. We present below some of the guidelines that pertain to ethics in research methodology. The APA code of ethics is phrased in professional language, so we have paraphrased them in simpler terms for the sake of clarity.

1. *Concern and care for all experimental subjects must be maintained in the design of the research and in the carrying out of the research design.* The researchers must take steps to ensure the physical safety and health of both human and animal subjects. For human subjects, care includes "due concern" for the person's dignity along with his or her physical welfare. In other words, the subjects must not be put into situations that demean them in any way.
2. *The research must be carried out with approval from the host institution.* No psychological research can be conducted in any institution without prior approval. A description of the research must contain clear disclosure. In other words, the host institution may not be deceived.
3. *The people who are to be used as subjects must give their informed consent.* Informed consent

means that the researchers provide a general description of the study in clear and simple language. There is to be no deception of any kind, although in order to prevent bias on the part of the subjects, certain details can be left out until after the research is over.

4. *All subjects are free to participate or not.* The researcher will provide the subjects with the clear message that they have a right to refuse to participate. If they do participate, they may withdraw at any time.
5. *Informed consent also involves the use of filming or recording of any kind.* All citizens are protected by what the U.S. Supreme Court has called "expectation of privacy," which means that we do not record activities in places that are supposed to be private, such as our homes, public bathrooms, and store dressing rooms. In environments where there is no "expectation of privacy," that is, in naturalistic observation, the researcher is free to record such behaviors, for example, as observing how people go through customs or line up at a ticket counter, etc.
6. *Information about the nature of the research should be made available to the subjects as soon as the opportunity permits.* If for reasons of mitigating bias, the subjects are not told about the precise nature of the research but have given their informed consent, the researcher has a responsibility to disclose this information to them at the earliest possible time. This information includes the purpose of the research, the results, and conclusions.
7. *The subjects' anonymity and privacy must remain intact.* Under no circumstances is any information to be made public that would disclose the identification of the subject, the purpose of the subject's inclusion in the research, or any personal information about the subject.

Detectives investigating Genovese's murder discovered that at least 38 of her neighbors had heard her screams for help over the course of 30 minutes and some had witnessed at least one of the attacks on her. Except for one man who had shouted "Leave that girl alone," no one had come to her aid, not even by calling the police. The police who investigated the murder were shocked by the apparent indifference of the apartment dwellers who were her neighbors. These decent New Yorkers turned off their lights and some went back to sleep after the first attack. They were awakened again by the second and third assaults. When questioned as to why they didn't intervene in this nightmarish and brutal event, they replied that "We didn't want to get involved." The murderer himself said he knew no one would do anything (Dorman, 1999). The term *Genovese Syndrome* was coined to describe this do-nothing-to-help attitude and behavior.

The Genovese murder gave rise to many questions: *Are New Yorkers simply too selfish and self-absorbed to help another human being in dire trouble? Are big city dwellers really so alienated from their neighbors that they avoid getting involved when someone needs help? Are there special circumstances that determine whether or not we will help our neighbor?*

Diffusion of Responsibility

Two of the people who were shocked by the murder were two young psychologists working in the New York area at the time. They decided to investigate the Genovese Syndrome. The first of these research investigations (Darley & Latané, 1986) revealed that one variable in whether someone will help or not help another individual is the number of people in the vicinity. In effect, the more people in the vicinity, the less likely one will stop to help. When there are many persons in the vicinity, passersby assume that there are enough people to help already. In fact, in staged experiments, subjects who thought there was no one else around to help were much more responsive and willing to help (75 percent on average) than those who were aware of other people in the vicinity (53 percent on average). The staged experiments involved many different apparent emergencies, such as fire, asthma attacks, flat tires, faintings, etc. Another reason for diffusion of responsibility is that people tend to hang back if they are not sure how to help and assume that other people in the vicinity know more what to do (Latané & Nida, 1981).

Cultural differences. Cultures which are small, rural, and traditional (such as those found in Latin America and the Pacific Rim) are more likely to go to the aid of someone in trouble than highly technological cultures (such as the United States, Great Britain, and Germany). Traditional societies, including countries such as Thailand, Peru, Malaysia, and Guatemala tend to value group membership, group achievement, and group productivity. Loyalty and concern for each other are valued more than individual achievement. These traditional cultures were also more willing to help other people. Even in the United States, people in small towns are more likely to help than in large cities (Amato, 1981). This difference may be accounted for by the fact that people in a smaller town have a better chance of knowing each other. In a large city, a person can walk for miles without meeting anyone they know. In a world of strangers, we are less likely to be a "good Samaritan."

Social Loafing: Another Variation of Diffusion of Responsibility. The phenomenon we discuss now is no doubt familiar to all of you reading this book. In either your high school or college classes, or in your job, or anywhere you have to work with others to achieve a goal, have you ever noticed that some of the people seem to do very little of the work? In fact, they sometimes seem to be expert in doing virtually nothing and (as if that isn't disagreeable enough) seem happy to share the credit for work done by others. This phenomenon is called **social loafing** and is defined as reduction in effort by individuals when they work in groups as compared to when they work alone. In fact, the more people in a group, the less productive it is (Kravitz & Martin, 1986). And why? Because with more people, there is more duplication of services, or group members may work at cross purposes. This contributes to a *diffusion of responsibility*. If the reader has heard people bemoaning the inefficiency of large bureaucratic organizations, the cause may be, in large measure, attributed to diffusion of responsibility and social loafing (Latané, Williams, & Harkins, 1979).

Attribution Bias Theory

One of the distinguishing characteristics of the human species is our need to discover reasons for things. In psychology, the answers we derive are called *attributions*. Attributions consist of judgments we make about what has caused a situation. There are two types of attributions: internal and external. When we believe the cause of an event is due to a person or a group of people, it is called *internal attribution* or **character attribution.** When we believe the cause of an event to be something in the environment, it is called *external attribution* or **situational attribution** (Jones, 1990). Example: Suppose we give a friend a very important letter to mail and the letter doesn't arrive at its destination on time. Naturally, we will try to determine what happened. We may decide that our friend never mailed the letter (because he was lazy or forgetful), which would be a *character* attribution. Or we may decide that the letter got lost in the mail which would be a *situational* attribution. So far, so good.

But the problem is that we tend to indulge in self-serving **attribution bias.** If we experience good fortune (such as a raise in salary or being selected as "salesperson of the year," we will attribute our good fortune to our character (we worked hard, we had the best sales record, etc.). But what if someone else in the company gets the raise or is selected "sales person of the year"? We are apt to attribute that person's selection as the result of the situation—he or she was in the "right place at the right time" or that the person was "buddy-buddy" with the guys in the front office—not because he or she did a good job.

Attribution bias may also account for why we tend to assign negative qualities to groups different from ourselves. Thus racial and ethnic groups will attribute negative qualities to each other: black versus white; Jews versus Arabs; Turks versus Greeks, and so on. Attribution bias also works along a geographical veriable. Northern Americans will tend to judge Southern Americans more harshly than themselves. Northerners are apt to label Southerners as "rednecks" and Southerners still talk (only somewhat kiddingly) of the "damyankees" (Little, Sterling & Tingstrom, 1996). (See Tip 2.3.)

Festinger's Dissonance Theory

Deep within the human psyche is a driving force for harmony of body, mind, and spirit. In other words, human beings feel the need to be consistent in their thoughts, feelings, and behaviors—a natural and constructive motivation. If we are acting contrary to our cognitive schemas in some way, we become uncomfortable and anxious. We are then in a state Leon Festinger (1957) called **cognitive dissonance.** When we become acutely aware of our discomfort, we seek to adjust whatever it is that is out of harmony with our deepest concerns and beliefs.

A good example has to do with smoking. There may not be an American alive who is not aware of the dangers of smoking. If a person is still smoking, he is in a state of **cognitive dissonance.** To harmonize his cognitive schema with his behavior, he has either to stop smoking or to change his understanding of its danger. If the desire to smoke is uppermost, he can rationalize his smoking by pointing out that his father smoked heavily and died at the ripe old age of 93. In this case, the person has changed his attitude about smoking to harmonize with his smoking

---

Tip 2.3 A popular present-day comedian, Jeff Foxworthy, makes good-natured fun at his own "redneck" in-group and the enthusiastic rseponse he gets from both Northerners and Southerners indicates that his attribution jokes surely reflect this geographical bias.

Box 2.3

SCENARIO REVISITED
The Farther Reaches of Human Nature

Eduardo: Caramba! Professor, this chapter is sure getting me down.

Alec: Seems like all we learn comes down to the equation I've heard my prejudiced father say a hundred times—that "people are no damn good"! (*General murmuring and agreement from other class members.*)

Shannon: Aren't there any studies that show the good side of people?

Professor Wietzman: One of the unfortunate aspects of studying human personality is the fact that it is a lot easier to discover the negative aspects of human nature than the positive aspects.

Martha: Why is that?

Professor Wietzman: Let's take an analogy. What happens when you go to your primary care physician for an annual checkup? What does he examine you for?

Martha: Why, to see if there is anything wrong with us that should be taken care of, of course.

Professor Wietzman: And what has he told you?

Martha: Well, at my last checkup, he told me I need to watch my cholesterol. It's getting a little high . . . Oh! He asked me if there was any arthritis in my family. I told him my mother suffers from it. So he told me to get on an exercise regimen since I may be at "high risk" for arthritis. That was sure a downer.

Professor Wietzman: Did he tell you what was right with you?

Martha: Right with me? What do you mean?

Professor Wietzman: Is your heart in good condition?

Martha: My heart? I guess so. He didn't say there was anything wrong with it.

Professor Wietzman: Exactly. It is much easier for physicians to discuss what's wrong with you than to discuss what's right with you. Well, similarly, it's a lot easier for social scientists to concentrate on the psychopathologies of personality than it is to focus on what is nonpathological, even *transcending* in personality, by which is meant the noble and illuminating in human nature.

Alec: Yeah! Pick up any newspaper and what do the headlines read! All the terrible things going on in the world! Good news doesn't sell newspapers or raise TV ratings.

Professor Wietzman: Sad but true. The abnormal and the pathological have been the traditional areas of research in both physical and mental health. But the situation is beginning to change. As we shall discover in the chapter on health, a fairly new initiative in medicine is to focus not so much on disease but on health. Similarly, there are some recent initiatives in psychology that focus not so much on what is wrong but on what is right—even uplifting—in human nature.

Alec: I would have thought psychologists would have been enthusiastic to study healthy people for a change.

Professor Wietzman: Psychological researchers have spent many decades investigating the abnormal personality, the so-called "average" personality, and laboratory animals. In fact, I remember one textbook that was dedicated to the white rat "without whom this book would never have been written." (*Class laughter.*) It takes a long time to change a cognitive schema—even in the sciences. It will be interesting to watch the directions of these new initiatives. They are variously called *transpersonal psychology*, *peace psychology*, and *positive psychology*.

---

behavior. But if the facts of lung cancer, emphysema, and a shortened life span are brought to the smoker's shocked attention (such as through the death of a loved one from a respiratory disease), that realization may finally motivate the person to quit. The reader may even know someone who has said something like this: *I smoked heavily until I saw my dad die of lung cancer.*

A Shifting Focus: Transpersonal, Positive, and Peace Psychologies

Across all cultures and down through history, there have always been individuals who were able to **transcend** (go beyond) the limits of their in-group membership. They have been the great scientists ruthless in their determination to dispel superstition. They have been the great saints and reformers the world over seeking peaceful ways to interact with each other. They have been the dogged scholars who have sought to uncover the truth hidden by propaganda and lies. As social critics, they were willing to risk reputation and ridicule to point out the "wrongs" in their society. The public media have sometimes called them *icons,* which suggests they have charismatic and larger-than-life qualities. But they were not just charismatic icons. They were (and are) real people who struggled as do we all. But despite their own pain and heartache, they carried on and ultimately enabled their society to reach a more profound understanding of what it means to be a member of the family of humankind. Let us then study these *transcending personalities.*

An APA Headline: Psychologists Leading Movement to Shift Scholars' Attention Away from Societal Ills and Toward Studying What Is Good, Healthy, and Uplifting (Ruark, 1999). What's right with human personality is a lot harder topic to investigate than what is wrong with human personality. Nevertheless, under the direction of Martin Seligman, the 1998 president of the American Psychological Association, a group of psychologists are spearheading a movement to change the emphasis from a *disease* model to a *health* model of personality. They are calling their movement positive psychology and they want to change the focus from what is wrong with people to what is right—even inspiring—in human interaction. They are asking the following questions:

What exactly is the "good life"? Can it be defined?
What kinds of experiences are joyous, fulfilling, and long-lasting?
What qualities enable people to flourish and find "happiness"?
What kinds of institutions and other environments foster these experiences and qualities?
How can we foster peace in our time, not just find ways to make peace, but also to eradicate the causes of war, such as poverty, oppression, world hunger, etc.?

Positive psychologists are rejecting the reductionist theory of human motivation that states that our behaviors, which are seemingly kind, caring, and generous, can be reduced to methods for avoiding pain, guilt, shame, and other negative emotional states. Positive psychologists do not believe that humankind is motivated solely by self-serving reasons. They believe that much of what people do is not for selfish gain but comes out of genuine moral and ethical concerns and the old-fashioned qualities of virtue. These positive psychologists are calling for "co-conspirators" from across many disciplines and fields to join them in this quest. Eager responses have come from many different disciplines and the membership now includes humanistic scholars, philosophers, theologians, business executives, evangelists, and social commentators (Ruark, 1999). Moreover, the peace psychology movement is open to all of us regardless of our academic degrees or socioeconomic status—a quite surprising modification of APA rules and regulations!

So let us take a closer look at people Maslow (1954) called **transcending personalities**—those persons who have gone beyond the limitations of the worldviews of their culture and who have moved their society to another level of psycho-socio-philosophic humanism. What can the research tell us about them? We want to discover the personality traits by which they were (and are) able to live so valiantly and to gain such stature. Perhaps then we too can live valiantly and creatively. We may not become known for what we do. But we can take heart that while we are only one of the "workers in the vineyard," we have nevertheless joined the ranks of the great reformers, saints, and scholars of all ages and times.

Box 2.4

STUDENTS VERBATIM
Student Choices for Transcending Personalities

The frontispiece of this chapter (p. 25) depicts persons chosen by students as transcending personalities because they challenged the worldview of their time and era and broke through to larger cognitive structures of what it means to be a man, or a woman, or a citizen of the world.

Abraham Lincoln (1809–1865) rose from log-cabin poverty to become the sixteenth president of the United States. He is known not only as the president who fought to save the Union, but also as the writer of the *Emancipation Proclamation*, which freed the slaves.

Emile Zola (1840–1902), a famous scholar and novelist, was already internationally famous before taking on the entire French government (including the French army) in the so-called "Dreyfus affair." Alfred Dreyfus, a Jewish officer, had been falsely accused as a traitor, convicted of treason, and sent to the infamous prison of Devil's Island. Zola sacrificed his health and his safety through his outspoken document *J'accuse* (I accuse), written to clear Dreyfus. He had to flee to Great Britain for his life, dying only a year after Dreyfus' release.

Mahatma Gandhi (1869–1948) challenged the entire British empire by breaking Britain's hold on India. He did this by organizing India's peoples of color to resist the oppressive colonial regime through nonviolent and peaceful means. Ultimately, he won his country's freedom. He was assassinated by an Indian who differed from him politically.

Eleanor Roosevelt (1882–1945), an extremely shy person as a child, broke through the traditional mold of the silent First Lady of the White House and became one of the greatest humanitarians of her day. When opera star Marian Anderson was refused permission to sing by the DAR (Daughters of the American Revolution) because of her color, the First Lady brought the issue of discrimination to national attention by resigning from the DAR and inviting Marian Anderson to sing on the steps of the Lincoln Memorial. A crowd of 75,000 white and black persons gathered on Easter Sunday, April 9, 1939, an event which made international news. Later, as a representative to the United Nations, she became an international spokesperson for women, children, and all oppressed peoples.

Martin Luther King, Jr. (1929–1968), a minister who had modeled his passive (and peaceful) resistance movement on the principles outlined by Mahatma Ghandi, organized the year-long black boycott of the local bus company in Montgomery, Alabama. He won significant civil rights for African-Americans—and, like his role model, he too was assassinated. He is famous for his "I Have a Dream" speech given before 200,000 demonstrators in Washington, DC.

Nelson Mandela (1918–) became a lawyer through a correspondence school. He spent most of his life working and fighting for the cause of the opressed peoples of color of South Africa. He was condemned to prison for many years. In the face of world criticism, the government of South Africa offered Mandela the opportunity of release if he would cease his political agitation. He refused and spent more years in prison. Finally released in 1990 and an old man, he still maintained his stance in favor of a government for *all* peoples. He was awarded the Nobel Prize for his humanitarianism in 1991 and elected as president of South Africa from 1994 until 1999.

Andrei Sakharov (1921–1989) was a Russian physicist who opposed the building of atomic weapons. He supported East-West cooperation and human rights. Along with his wife, Yelena Bonner, he became a leading dissident of the oppressive Soviet regime in power. In 1975, he was awarded the Nobel Peace Prize, but he exiled to Gorky five years later, where he lived under terrible conditions. He was restored to favor in 1986, and elected to a high official position in1989.

Albert Einstein (1879–1955) was awarded the Nobel Prize for physics in 1921. He was removed from his teaching post by the Nazis because of his antiwar politics and his Jewish background. He emigrated to the United States when he was offered a teaching post at Princeton University. His theories helped develop the atomic bomb. Nevertheless, he continued to speak out against war and the use of atomic weapons for the rest of his life, and everywhere he supported world peace.

Mother Theresa (1910–1997), born in Macedonia, became an Irish nun and then worked as a missionary in India. Seeing the poverty and degradation of people dying on the streets, she organized an Indian order of sisters to shelter and administer to the sick and dying. She received the Nobel Prize for humanitarianism in 1979.

Dian Fossey (1932–1966), supported by the National Geographic Society, studied the mountain gorillas of Rwanda, Africa, and became an activist to save the

Box 2.4

last 250 surviving animals from extinction. Because she openly confronted those who were killing the gorillas for money, she was murdered in her sleep. Her book *Gorillas in the Mist* became a best seller, and was then made into a movie. Today there is an institute and fund to carry on her work for the survival of the mountain gorillas.

Florence Nightingale (1820–1910), born to an aristocratic family, gave up thoughts of a comfortable life by becoming a nurse and organizing the first army nurse corps ever. With 38 women, she sailed for the Crimea, and there she and her nurses cared for the wounded and dying soldiers in terribly primitive and filthy conditions. She returned to England with only a handful of surviving nurse volunteers and suffered physically for the rest of her life. Nevertheless, she continued actively supporting the improvement of hospitals, nurse's training, and the care of the ill.

Harriet Tubman (1829–1913) was born a slave, but escaped and became an abolitionist. She returned to the South time and time again, each time at risk to her own life, to help African-Americans travel to the North via the Underground Railway. She is sometimes called the "Moses of her People."

Rachel Carson (1907–1964), a naturalist who worked as marine biologist for the U.S. Fish and Wildlife Service, wrote the classic book *Silent Spring* to alert the world to the ecological dangers of agricultural pesticides. She worked intensely all her life toward protecting the ecology of the earth. She pioneered the conservation movement of the 1960s just before her death.

Reflective Writing: From your studies or your own personal reading, whom would you nominate as a transcending person? State your reasons. When you have described the qualities you would like to emulate, see Tip 2.4.

Ten Characteristics of Transcending Personalities

In describing the characteristics of these highly evolved persons, we are using a **metastudy** approach (a method of analyzing many research studies and drawing conclusions from the overlapping data). Such an undertaking, however, involves inherent research difficulties which students should be aware of (see Box 2.5). Nonetheless, we have pulled together some of the findings of the many studies of outstanding personalities described previously. As we compare and contrast their findings with the "average" population, we shall be looking for what we can apply to our own living. On the way to this understanding, we may discover some of the factors that go into what has been called variously self-actualizing, self-realized, individuated, creative, fully-functioning, and transcending personalities.

1. Affectively, they are characterized by an emotional "richness." Some people close themselves off to anything that borders on sadness, pain, or suffering. But when they close themselves off to negative emotions, they are also closing themselves off from a significant part of their personalities (Jung, 1955). It's as if they are saying, *I don't want to experience any more pain. If that means I have to live without the happier emotions and remain in some kind of neutral and gray limbo, so be it.* People who choose to narrow their emotional range like this are existing as half-people.

Tip 2.4   On the qualities you admire about your role-model. We emulate what we admire. Whatever qualities you stated you admired in Box 2.4 are the qualities you are developing within yourself. You may add those qualities to your self-esteem.

Box 2.5

RESEARCH METHODOLOGY
The Metastudy Approach

For almost one hundred years now, there have been literally thousands of studies in the area of personality. Some hundreds of these studies have been done on the same topic. For example, by 1985, there were well over 3,000 studies done on "job satisfaction". Meta-analysis is a specific analytic technique for averaging the results of many studies or drawing out commonalities.

PRO

1. *Summarizes many research studies and draws out commonalities and differences.* A metastudy elicits data from a multitude of studies and draws some overall conclusions. A person can review one single metastudy instead of the hundreds that have been done.
2. *Provides a jumping-off place for other studies.* Other investigators can then use the metastudy data and conclusions as a starting place, rather than having to go back and review all the studies for the last 90 years.
3. *A metastudy is valuable for pointing out needed research areas.* If well done, a metastudy can make needed recommendations for future investigations by pointing out the limitations of previous studies, as well as by noting promising lines of investigation.

CON

1. *The terms and definitions may sound similar, but they may actually cover somewhat different areas.* The result may be nothing more than comparing oranges and apples.
2. *The target populations may not be synonymous.* If the samples and populations of the research studies are not carefully defined, the conclusions drawn may not be warranted. Commonalities may appear where there are none. Or there may seem to be no commonalities because the dissimilar samples and populations have canceled out their respective research findings.
3. *Earlier research findings may be outmoded.* In this era of great social and technological change, studies done a few years apart may reflect changes in the attitudes and the cognitive schemas of the sample subjects.

By contrast, Maslow's study of highly self-actualizing people revealed that they accept both sides of themselves, "the light" and "the dark." Whereas other people might use many defensive mechanisms to avoid looking too deeply into themselves, studies of creative artists corroborate that they are more open to the "dark side" of their personalities (Sumerlin & Bundrick, 1996). They are not frightened to explore the dark sides of their personalities. They do not run away from occasional morbid thoughts or intense dreams. In fact, highly creative scientists were eager to explore the meaning of their dreams and to express other aspects of themselves that other persons might keep hidden (see Figure 2.2). Their ability to accept the light and the dark of their personality structure makes them capable of transforming their pain and suffering into works of art or scholarly and scientific pursuits (Feist, 1998). They are "psychonauts" of their inner space.

2. Perceptually, they make more accurate assessments of what we call "reality." Because they are less defensive about "the light and the dark" in themselves, they are more able to interpret reality accurately. Maslow found that his highly self-actualizing subjects were not fooled by artifice. On the contrary, they were wonderfully apt in perceiving artificiality and phoniness. Because they were less fooled by external appearances, they are more able to judge the character of a person. They were not impressed by status or degrees or appearance. While others may think that "clothes make the man," Maslow said, his self-actualizing subjects knew that character cannot always be judged by how a person appears on the outside. (Some of our most successful white-collar criminals are dressed immaculately and speak articulately and come from the "best schools.")

Figure 2.2 They are characterized by emotional richness and able to accept the "light" and "dark" aspects of themselves. They know that all experiences are grist for self-knowledge and growth.

3. Intellectually, they are life-long learners. And they are truly *human becomings*, as Allport described the human species. They become more knowledgeable year by year. They become more skilled in the social graces. As they get older, they become more able to cope with things that would have devastated them earlier. They develop their gifts and talents, and continue to learn new skills.

Almost every study done on creative artists and scientists confirm that they search for new areas to explore. They are happy in their work and derive joy from it when they are engaged in designing or doing something new. They want challenge. Time and again, studies seem to show that what creative people want—whether they are artists or composers or scientists—is the challenge of discovery and of learning something new (Csikszentmihalyi, 1997). And they become wiser over the years. They understand that personality integration is a life-long process. Abraham Maslow made this very telling observation: *We may be born intelligent but wisdom is something that happens as the result of many years of living on this earth.*

4. Socially, they are less conforming, highly individuated, and more willing to be themselves. Being more individuated, they have less need of a mask or "persona" (Jung, 1955) but which we tend to call a "public image" (see Figure 2.3). Enmeshed in our conditioned habits, it is very difficult to break with ingrained ideas. Yet Maslow discovered his highly self-actualizing persons could embrace new ideas. All the great thinkers of the world—philosophers, scientists, writers, economists, etc.—had to break with what they have been taught was true. This ability involves shaking themselves loose from outmoded traditions and "conventional wisdom" (Galbraith, 1985) and breaking through to new ideas. As difficult as it may be, the ability to go against the tide of public opinion has been the distinctive quality of every great reformer. By definition, that is the reformer's purpose. Sometimes, they have had to suffer the consequences of their courage by being publicly ostracized, or imprisoned, or put to death. Regardless of the consequences, however, they are people willing to "stand up and be counted." They live authentically.

5. Behaviorally, they exhibit an internal locus of control. In study after study of the highly integrated and self-actualizing person, one theme is particularly dominant—that of self-determination. Highly self-actualizing persons, said Maslow, take responsibility for their lives, for their actions, and for their own destinies. They have an internal locus of control (Rotter, 1990). They are determined to carry on despite crises, setbacks, tragedy. Highly self-actualizing persons are just as vulnerable as the rest of us to the trials and tribulations of living. None of us is completely in control of our environment or our destiny. We are born into a society not of our choosing, and we shall assuredly die whether we are ready for it or not. There are powers and events over which we have little or no influence: death of the people we love, natural catastrophes, accidents, and all the chance events of the natural world. No matter how hard we work to achieve position, esteem, security, and prestige, and to deal honorably with the world, there is always the possibility that our dreams and

Figure 2.3 Authenticity Highly individual persons are more willing to be themselves and so have less of a mask.

plans may go awry. There is, then, a reality to the Greek description of the Fates.

The Fates notwithstanding, however, highly integrated persons do not give up in the face of hardship or tragedy. They too have moments of loss of confidence and discouragement. But they refuse to wallow in their negative emotions. They make mistakes as do the rest of us, but they acknowledge them and learn from them. Despite moments of anxiety, guilt, shame, sorrow, and grief, Maslow's subjects did not allow themselves to get entrapped in self-pity and self-blame. William Ernest Henley, the crippled poet, exemplified this attitude when he wrote that he was determined to be "the master of my fate . . . the captain of my soul."

6. Cognitively, they are able to live in the here-and-now. They do not stay bitter or resentful about the lacks in their lives, either in the past or the present. One of the most notable characteristics of these personalities is how they transcend the difficulties that beset their lives. They "recycle" their painful experiences and use the raw material of their suffering as grist for their creativity. When asked what makes a good writer, Ernest Hemingway replied, "An unhappy childhood." Studies of illustrious persons reveal that they, too, can come from a home situation that was not perfect. As a matter-of-fact, many seem not to have been close to their parents. This lack of closeness may have pushed them toward early independence, self-support, and achievement. Since they had little adult support, they apparently learned how to rely on themselves. Abraham Lincoln's mother died when he was eight, and his father was a rather indifferent parent and provider. In fact, after his wife died, Lincoln's father seems to have left Abe and his sister, both less than 10 years of age, to fend for themselves for several weeks in their wilderness home, while he went off to seek another wife. Charles Dickens' childhood of poverty, debtors' prison, and workhouse abuse was the basis of most of his remarkable novels that we so revere today.

7. Physically, they transcend their limitations and suffering. History is replete with courageous examples of people transcending their physical limitations. Michelangelo spent years on his back, which he had broken in a fall, in order to paint the Sistine Chapel above him. Beethoven wrote his last five symphonies while growing more and more deaf. When the Curies, Marie and Pierre, were working on developing radium, both became afflicted with radium poisoning. Pierre died of it and although Marie's fingers were horribly burned because of it, she continued to distill the metal until she had enough to distribute to other scientists. The painter, Henri Matisse, became crippled with arthritis in his older years so that he had to have paint brushes tied to his fingers to go on working. We can only feel inspired by William Ernest Henley's poetic cry: "I thank whatever gods may be for my unconquerable soul."

8. Philosophically, they have a multicultural worldview. In a nutshell: they are democratic (Sumerlin & Bundrick, 1996). Because they are less narrowly dogmatic, they are more accepting of other traditions and other ways of life. While they respect multicultural differences, they tend to see the underlying universals of other faiths, other religions, other philosophies, and other political persuasions. They view these diverse cultural traditions as expressing a fundamental human quest, the quest to understand the meaning of life, and to live according to the highest possible principles and values. What does make us feel spiritually fulfilled is living life so that the meaning of it outlasts us. No one can choose that meaning for us. Choosing that meaning is our responsibility and only ours.

9. Politically, they often become activists for human rights. Transcending personalities are not content with understanding others, they become activists in their striving for human rights for all persons, regardless of their religion, race, age, ethnic affiliation, or socioeconomic status. Even in free and democratic societies, there have been occasions when people give up their political, economic, and social freedoms to a cult and a cult leader. But transcending persons have refused to give away their freedom to think and to act. The German religious leader Martin Luther nailed his ninety-nine theses on the doors of a corrupt church and spoke the words that still ring across the centuries. "Here stand I—I can do no other. God help me! Amen." His namesake, Martin Luther King, Jr., was able to stand up for his people and be counted. In South Africa, Nelson Mandela was offered release from prison if he would cease agitating for freedom for all South Africans—and he refused.

10. Spirituality, they live their life for meaning. Agreeing with Jung, Viktor Frankl (1962) urged humankind to live their lives with meaning or they shall surely suffer from **noogenic neurosis,** by which he meant a state of apathy, aimlessness, and boredom. At the age of 37 years, Viktor Frankl was a practicing physician and psychiatrist who was sent to the Nazi concentration camps because he was a Jew. He survived and when released wrote of his experiences and the meaning he had derived from it. Said Frankl: *A life lived solely for pleasure is not true happiness. The pursuit of pleasure and living solely for ourselves eventually leaves us feeling empty and unsatisfied—or with the taste of bitter ashes—and so we fill it up with more pleasure, a cycle that never ends.* Maslow noted that his subjects had a deep and abiding feeling of identification with all of humankind and a general desire to help others however they could. More recent statistical studies have confirmed Maslow's observation that highly self-actualizing people want to live a life of meaning and purpose (Sumerlin & Bundrick, 1996).

Transcending personalities have a steady love of humankind (even when they disappoint us), which in Latin is called *caritas*. In Greek, it is called *agape*. Today, we may call it *compassion* or *lovingkindness* or *good will toward all*. Whatever it is called, this quality is the dominant personality characteristic of the great saints and reformers of the world. In other times, said Maslow, they might have been men and women "of the cloth," that is, priests, ministers, rabbis, monks, nuns, etc. Today, they can be found in every segment of our secular world as well. Instead of becoming a minister or priest, the spiritually oriented person may be a diplomat who wearily boards yet another jetliner to fly to yet another far-off place to forestall yet another intertribal war. Or it may be a judge in a courtroom doing her best to mete out justice and mercy within the parameters of obsolete laws. Or it may take the form of our next door neighbor knocking on our door for the sake of some charitable organization.

In essence, transcending personalities find joy in working for transpersonal goals. Alfie Kohn (1998), who is a *positive* psychologist, summarizes some research on "happiness." He describes a fairly common worldview in our culture that having a lot of money will make us happier than we are now. Those individuals who subscribe to this point-of-view entirely will spend a lifetime making money. They will bet on the stock market and watch the ups-and-downs on their

Box 2.6

SCENARIO REVISITED
The Eternal Quest

Eduardo: Professor! These . . . self-actualizing people . . . they sound too good to be true.

Li Ho: How can anybody live up to that? I always think of my family, as multicultural as they are, as very caring for each other but they have their faults. The way the text discusses these people, they sound like angels come down to earth.

Professor Wietzman: Good comments. Those criticisms have been leveled at Maslow's descriptions. His answer was that they also had qualities that could be called faults. He said they were not perfect. In fact, Maslow said that if highly self-actualizing persons have a fault, it is in their anger and hostility to people who are phoney or pretend to be something that they are not. Many of his subjects admitted they had difficulty controlling their irritation when confronted by lying and other kinds of dishonesty.

Martha: Is that all? They can't be faulted for that!

Professor Wietzman: Maslow also said that voicing their true thoughts and feelings resulted in sometimes seeming rude and somewhat insensitive. Barron who studied creative artists found the same thing. Sometimes, this seeming rudeness was simply part of their honesty. If we are not used to such honesty at first, we later come to appreciate it because we have learned we can trust what they say to us. If they seem to lack diplomacy, at least they do not engage in duplicity; that is, they do not say one thing to us and something totally different to someone else. In other words, they are trustworthy.

Shannon: But, Professor, how do we get to be a transcending person?

Professor Wietzman: It's a life-long quest. There is no single way. As a wise man is reputed to have said, "There are many paths to the mountain top." And we will be discovering some of those directions throughout these chapters and how we can apply them to our own lives.

Shannon: Does it take a long time?

Professor Wietzman: All our lives.

Dan: That let's me out! I'm halfway through my life.

Martha: Me too—almost.

Jonnimae: Me too.

Professor Wietzman: Whoa! That's not what I meant. It's what the philosophers have called the "Eternal Quest." There is no set beginning or end to this quest. It's similar in analogy to the way Gordon Allport described us, not as human beings but as human becomings— always "in process" and always evolving.

Eduardo: Professor, some of us in this class are just college students starting out in life. How can we work for peace or transpersonal values? Most of us don't have the time or the money to do much more than survive.

Professor Wietzman: That's an understandable comment. You can't afford much by way of energy, or time, or money while you are so busy with your college education and personal lives. But what about this as a suggestion? We have so many global problems at the present time. Choose some cause that is dear to your heart. Then find a reputable organization that is working for that cause. Support it by contributing a few dollars. Some not-for-profit organizations actually have a minimal student rate.

Dan: I am concerned about the way we are polluting our environment. What would a few dollars do?

Professor Wietzman: Not much financially, but your membership is valuable in many ways. For example, your membership would indicate your support and that adds political clout. Furthermore, you may get newsletters or magazines that update what is being done and what you can do on a personal basis. As an informed citizen, you can educate others in your circle of friends and family.

computer screens. They may work at two or three jobs "to get ahead," and get ahead they do, buying a better car, a better house, and getting an even better job. But studies of their happiness indicate that these progressions in their life may make them happier at the time of acquisition but their happiness level soon reverts to their normal levels of dissatisfaction. Research indicates that, once the poverty level has been passed and people have reached a modicum of financial security, an obsession for more and more money stems from an underlying void somewhere else in their lives. The void may be a lack of positive self-esteem, a lack of love in their lives, or a feeling they have nothing of value to offer others except money. But, says Kohn, the compulsion to acquire more and more money to fill the void in their lives is futile. The research suggests that the more people are driven by a desire to be wealthy, the poorer is their psychological health (Kasser & Ryan, 1996). Furthermore, many, many studies have confirmed this survey result: when workers are asked what they want from their work, money ranks far behind such variables as a pleasant place to work with good people to work with and a lot of challenge. One sociologist has made a memorable statement: *The idea that everybody wants money is propagated by wealthy addicts to make themselves feel better about their addiction to money* (Slater, 1980, p. 25). Certainly, Frankl would have agreed to that. *Happiness,* said Frankl, *is not achieved by pursuing it*; *happiness is a by-product of giving ourselves to transcending purpose* (Frankl, 1962).

IMPORTANT TERMS AND CONCEPTS TO KNOW

authority	deindividuation	metastudy	smaller
authoritarian	dissonance	more	social loafing
bias	dogmatic	obedience	social roles
bystander	geographical	positive	stereotype
character	group	self-actualizing	traditional
conformity	meaning	situational	worldview

MAKE YOUR OWN CHAPTER SUMMARY BY FILLING IN THE BLANKS BELOW

Use the "Important Terms and Concepts to Know" to fill in the blanks below.

Social psychology focuses on the dynamics of _____ membership.

T. W. Adorno studied the _____ personality and discovered that being born and raised in a democracy is no guarantee against the prejudice and intolerance. His authoritarian subjects exhibited a high degree of _____ thinking, a tendency to adhere to a set of beliefs and to obey leaders without question. They also demand strict obedience from their subordinates and tend to _____ people, which means assigning them personality attributes based on their racial, ethnic, religious, or other group membership.

Solomon Asch studied _____ , the tendency to "follow the herd" and discovered that it is difficult for people to resist peer pressure.

Stanley Milgram discovered that most people will obey impersonal _____ even if, in doing so, it may endanger another human being.

Phil Zimbardo reported on his prison experiment and discovered that our _____ have a powerful effect on our thinking and behavior.

Attribution bias is a phenomenon that has been studied in several ways. When we assign the cause of an event to a person, we are making an internal or _____ attribution. When we assign the cause of an event to the environment, we are making an external or _____ attribution. Unfortunately, we tend to indulge in attribution _____ with those who are different from ourselves in race, religion, ethnicity, and even _____ area.

Leon Festinger coined the term cognitive _____ to indicate that a person is experiencing disharmony in his/her set of beliefs or behaviors.

Group dynamics are affected by size. Kitty Genovese's murder shocked the nation and instigated a series of studies investigating the _____ effect. It was found that the _____ people at the scene of an emergency, the _____ the motivation to help. But cultural differences have an effect on this phenomenon. Smaller, more _____ societies will provide more help than large urban technocracies. In the working situation, the larger the group, the more _____ occurs.

Carl Jung explained the dynamics of mob psychology as the result of _____ .

New directions have been initiated that have to do with establishing more peaceful ways of relating to each other, both on a person-to-person basis and worldwide. Abraham Maslow initiated the study of the healthy and creative person, whom he termed as highly _____ . Among other characteristics, he described his subjects as able to transcend the _____ of their time and culture. A past president president of APA, Martin Seligman, initiated a thrust he calls _____ psychology (now an APA division) and is calling for "co-conspirators" from every discipline.

Victor Frankl urged us to live our lives with _____ .

3 PERSONALITY THEORY
Emotional/Social Influences Throughout the Life Span

He was not always right. Some of his theories have fallen by the wayside, but he changed our understanding of the nature of humankind. His genius is shown by the sheer number of concepts we still use today of which the following are only a few:

anxiety	Freudian slips	reaction formation
castration complex	id	reality principle
catharsis	introjection	regression
conversion hysteria	obsessive-compulsive	repression
defense mechanism	Oedipal complex	sibling rivalry
displacement	pleasure-pain principle	sublimation
dream interpretation	preconscious	superego
ego	projection	suppression
Elektra complex	psychotherapy	unconscious
free association	rationalization	

For his theories of personality development, Freud drew on biblical history, all the great mythologies, literature, and folklore of the Western world.

Box 3.1
SCENARIO
My Daughter Is So Bad! What Can I Do with Her?

Jonnimae and her sister, Sarakate, are in Jonnimae's apartment, catching up on the events of the last two years while keeping an eye on Sarakate's two children. Four-year-old Janie is busily devouring her cookies, and the baby is holding on tightly to his bottle. The two women continue talking until the baby begins to whimper. His bottle is now in the hands of four-year old Janie.

Sarakate: Janie, did you take the baby's bottle?

Janie: No! He dropped it! I was just picking it up.

Sarakate: No, he didn't! You took it from him! (*Sarakate grabs the bottle from the little girl, slaps her hand, and gives the bottle back to the baby.*) That's for hitting him! (*She slaps the little girl again.*) And that's for lying to me! (*Howling, Janie crawls away from the group, lies down on the floor, and begins to suck her thumb.*) She's why I've come, Jonnimae! I don't know what's gotten into her, I swear I don't. She has temper tantrums. She's sucking her thumb again. She steals the baby's bottle and actually drinks from it. Four years of age and still drinking from a bottle! It just shames me. I've spanked her till her back side is red. (*A scream* from the baby interrupts the conversation. There is an angry-looking red spot on the baby's arm. Sarakate picks up the little girl and shakes her.*) Jonnimae, what am I gonna do with her? She's so mean to the baby! She's got a mean streak in her, I swear she does! And she used to be so good. What's the matter with her?

Jonnimae: In my psychology class, I learned it's a natural thing to be jealous of a baby brother. It's called sibling rivalry.

Sarakate: Oh, I know children can be jealous of each other. I was jealous of you, Jonnimae, because you were so smart and everybody admired you. But I wasn't mean like Janie.

Jonnimae: Oh, yes! You pulled some lies on me, telling Mama that I hit you! Then I'd get whipped.

Sarakate: I'm sorry! I don't remember that, but I know you wouldn't lie to me. Only isn't there anything I can do to stop Janie from being so mean to the baby?

Jonnimae: There must be, for sure. But first we have to understand what's going on inside Janie. Then maybe we can figure out what we can do about her.

Sigmund Freud: Revealing the "Darker Side of Human Nature"

Prior to Freud's appearance on the social scene, people tended to explain differences in human nature in ways that do not have much meaning for social scientists today. The Medieval Church spoke in terms of "saints" and "sinners." Calvinistic sects explained human behavior as the result of predetermination: Only a few souls were predestined to be worthy of entrance into heaven. The vast majority of humanity, according to the Calvinistic worldview, was doomed to lead a sinful life which leads to hell.

The secular world, too, developed an idea that had to do with heredity. Some people were presumed to come from good stock, whereas others had "bad blood." Since royal blood was deemed to be superior, royal families were careful not to marry their children to a "commoner." Eventually, the idea of inherited superiority was extended also to the wealthy who had made achievements in the secular world. By the end of the nineteenth century, statisticians in England were coming to the conclusion that "giftedness" was a matter of heredity. On the other side of the English Channel, French social scientists were devising an intelligence test that would identify "slow learners," who, it was presumed, were dullards because of their genetic inheritance.

Also running rampant was a political philosophy called **social Darwinism,** which provided a pseudo-explanation for social stratification: Why some people are destined to be rich and others poor. Simple!—cream rises to the top. In other words, people who are on the top got there (or their forebears got there) by virtue of some kind of inherited superiority. Conversely, those on the bottom (or their forebears) were there because of some kind of inherited inferiority. Get the picture?

Now into all this smug self-satisfaction of the wealthy ruling classes, a book appeared on the publishing scene entitled, *The Interpretation of Dreams.* The author was, of course, Sigmund Freud (1900). It was Freud who provided us with the first inkling that it is not just our inheritance that accounts for our personalities. Environmental experiences also play a large part. It was a revolutionary idea and it shook the educated elite out of their complacency. In the hundred years since the publication of that book, Sigmund Freud has been idolized, vilified, lionized, and demonized. He was called a lunatic, a sex fiend—even the Anti-Christ by the Church. What he was, in actuality, was simply a scientist attempting to explain human nature as the result of how we are brought up. It came as a shock for that complacent *fin-de-siecle* (circa 1890–1910) European society to be told that how they were raising their children was producing illness. In fact, Freud came to the conclusion that adult personality is fully formed by age six. (In his later life, he revised this figure to age three.)

It is difficult for young people growing up today (with our more open attitudes toward human sexuality) to imagine the sexual repression of one hundred years ago, the society in which Sigmund Freud lived and worked. It was a society that gave legitimacy to the **double standard** of sexuality—what was considered appropriate behavior for men was not considered appropriate for women. For one thing, it gave tacit permission for aristocratic men to lead double lives. Overtly, these men assumed the posture of respectable husbands and fathers. Covertly, their evenings were often spent in brothels in the company of prostitutes or with their paid mistresses who came from the *demimonde* of Europe (see Tip 3.1). In England, it was the end of the Victorian period, which may have been the most sexually repressive era in all of English history. Aristocratic men married "good" women in order to have children and carry on the family line, but they often turned elsewhere to "have fun" with sexually permissive women. In Europe, it was not unusual for these men to introduce their pubescent sons to their first sexual experience by escorting them personally to the brothels or to an obliging maid servant (with a payment of money for their services).

No such equivalent behavior was permitted of "good women." Women were expected to remain virginal until introduced to the sexual act by their husbands. Many aristocratic women were so ignorant of sex and repulsed by the process of birth that they remained frigid all their lives. It was not unusual for mothers to teach their daughters that sex was something women had to endure "in order to have children." Women wore clothing that hid every part of their bodies except their face and hands. We say words now that once would have caused a woman to "swoon" in public. So careful were the Victorians to refrain from using the words "breast" and "thigh," they began to refer to these parts of the chicken as "light meat" and "dark meat," terms we still use today (Mencken, 1963).

Freud's Metaphor of the Iceberg. Freud likened the human personality to an iceberg (see Figure 3.1). Only 10 percent of an iceberg is visible above water. The other 90 percent is hidden beneath the surface. In like manner, said Freud, only 10 percent of our personality is conscious. Most of our motivation is hidden—even from ourselves—in what he called the **unconscious** part of the personality. This unconscious aspect is composed of the **id** (our biological urges and drives) and the **superego** (what society has taught us we must and must not do). The id and the superego wage war throughout our lifetime. Out of this eternal warfare, said Freud, the third part of the personality emerges—the *ego* which is the only part of the personality which is conscious. It is the task of the **ego** to keep a balance between the pleasure-seeking *id* and the prohibitions of the *superego*. It is not easy for the beleaguered ego to keep the unruly id in check and, at the same time, to prevent the superego from becoming overly punitive. Instead of the metaphor of an iceberg, Freud might better have used the metaphor of an active volcano, because the unconscious aspects of personality, like molten magma, are in constant (*dynamic*) turmoil. Furthermore, every so often, bits and pieces of these unconscious urges and anxieties erupt into our everyday living as slips of the tongue-and-pen, dreams, fantasies, defense mechanisms, and physical symptoms. How these three parts of our personality (id, superego, and ego) develop, said Freud, comes about through five stages of growth, which he called the *psychosexual development* of the person.

Freud's Theory of Psychosexual Development: Five Stages of the Libidinal Drive

From his studies of human nature, Freud arrived at this conclusion: Human sexual development does not suddenly manifest at puberty. He believed that we are all born with a strong sexual drive which he called the **libido.** If that sounds shocking, it is because we need to understand how Freud conceived of the libidinal drive. In its narrowest sense, the **libidinal drive** is the drive toward sex and procreation, but in its widest sense, it is the drive toward pleasure and caring and all those emotional satisfactions that make life worth living. Without this libidinal

---

Tip 3.1 The *Demimonde* of Europe. *Demimonde* is a French word having the connotation of what we might call "not quite respectable people," particularly women who were actresses, ballet dancers, and cabaret singers. Readers who have had humanities or art courses may be familiar with paintings that depict the turn-of-the-century *demimonde*. Toulouse-Lautrec made posters of the famous can-can girls. Degas painted ballet girls in their tutus. Whistler and other artists painted Lily Langtry, a society beauty who became Prince Edward's mistress and later an actress.

Only 10% of the personality is conscious.

Like an iceberg, 90% of our motivation is beneath our awareness, and inaccessible to us.

This part of our personality does become accessible at certain times—in our dreams and nightmares; in our fantasies; in our slips of the tongue or pen; and in our defense mechanisms.

The ego is the "compromiser" that mediates between the urges and "I want" of the id and the "you must not!" of the superego. The ego, then, is the "battleground" on which the id and the superego play out their eternal conflict.

The superego is composed of all the "voices of society."

Freud equated the superego with what we call "conscience."

The baby is born "all id," and is a complex of all the primitive and biological drives of the self. It is dominated by the pleasure-pain principle.

EGO

SUPEREGO

ID

Eventually, as the superego develops, the pleasure-pain principle is gradually overlaid and dominated by the reality principle. But the id is never completely held in check. Every so often, the id manages to break through the prohibitions of the superego.

Figure 3.1 Freud's Topology of personality.

drive for pleasure, there would be no desire to live—a state of being we sadly observe in suicidally depressed people. According to Freud, the libidinal drive normally develops in five stages from birth to puberty. Each of these stages has a psychological aspect as well as a sexual aspect, which is why Freud called it the *psycho*sexual theory of development of the individual (Freud, 1900).

1. The Oral Stage and the Biological Urges of the Id. Freud explained that in this first stage of psychosexual development, the libidinal drive is centered around the mouth. We only have to observe a baby happily sucking on bottle, breast, thumb, or pacifier to witness the intensity of the libidinal drive. Just try taking the nipple away from a baby and the result may be a "force twelve" howling. Today we are not shocked by this concept because we know that if the baby doesn't find pleasure in sucking and swallowing, or if these reflexes are poorly developed, the baby may "fail to thrive." But in Freud's day, the idea that a baby could have a libidinal drive was anathema! But Freud further observed that even as adults, we find pleasure in many kinds of oral activities. We love to eat. We nibble when we are bored or anxious. In the absence of something to eat, we may chew on a pencil, on our fingernails, on a stick of gum, or even (like an author of your text) on our eyeglasses. Finally, expressions of love, tenderness, and caring often begin with kissing the child or adult we love. (We might mention also that Freud was sometimes teased by his colleagues for his own oral habit—the cigar he was almost never without—and which eventually killed him.) This baby id is dominated by what Freud called the **pleasure/pain principle**, which means simply that the baby seeks only pleasure and avoids pain. Now most of us try to avoid pain and pursue pleasure, but we have learned that in our pursuit of our pleasure we must avoid causing pain to others. Since the baby is not aware of other people, his pursuit of pleasure may cause pain to others (see Box 3.2)

2. The Anal Stage and the Development of the Superego. According to Freud, the baby is the center of family life. In a healthy family, the baby is loved and cared for in a paradise where all his needs and wants are fulfilled. But he will not be permitted to exist forever in this Garden of Eden. Eventually, his teeth will break through his gums and nursing will become too painful for Mother to continue. Moreover, Mommie (or whoever is the chief caregiver) will get tired of constantly changing his diapers and will decide that it is time for toilet training. He is expelled from his Garden of Eden by being weaned away from the breast and seated on the "potty." The **socialization** process (of weaning and toilet-training) is the impetus for the next stage of psychosexual development. But there is more going on at this stage than just weaning and toilet-training. The baby is learning that he cannot do *whatever* he wants *whenever* he wants and *wherever* he wants. He cannot have the breast or bottle any more; he must learn to drink from a cup. He cannot hurt other people—even innocently. If he pulls Mommie's hair, she will get annoyed. Nor can he hurt his baby sister or brother. The pleasure/pain principle is giving way to the **reality principle**; i.e., the baby is learning that if he continues to do these things, some dire consequence will follow.

Box 3.2

HELEN KELLER:
The Unbridled Id (Before the Child Is Socialized)

We can get some insight into a child's primitive psychology (before the child is socialized) from Helen Keller's autobiography. Helen was blind and deaf from about six months of age. Her family loved her but did nothing to socialize her. She lived in a sightless, soundless chaos and was allowed to do whatever she wanted, even grabbing food off everyone's plate. Eventually she was socialized and taught sign language. She even went on to graduate from college. She was obviously a brilliant person, and when she was eighteen, she wrote her autobiography, describing her lack of conscience and fierce sibling rivalry with her baby sister.

. . . I think I knew I was naughty, for I knew it hurt Ella, my nurse, to kick her, and when my fit of temper was over, I had a feeling akin to regret. But I cannot remember any instance in which this feeling prevented me from repeating the naughtiness when I failed to get what I wanted. . . . After my teacher, Miss Sullivan, came, I sought an early opportunity to lock her in her room. I went upstairs with something which my mother made me understand I was to give to Miss Sullivan, but no sooner had I given it to her than I slammed the door to, locked it, and hid the key under the wardrobe in the hall. I could not be induced to tell where the key was. My father was

obliged to get a ladder and take Miss Sullivan out through the window—much to my delight. Months after I produced the key . . .

. . . For a long time I regarded my little sister as an intruder. I knew that I had ceased to be my mother's only darling, and the thought filled me with jealousy. She sat in my mother's lap constantly, where I used to sit, and seemed to take up all her care and time. . . . One day I discovered my little sister sleeping peacefully in [my doll's cradle] . . . I rushed upon the cradle and overturned it, and the baby might have been killed had my mother not caught her as she fell."

Source: Helen Keller, *The Story of My Life* (New York: Globe Books, 1962) pp. 24–29.

Although the baby railed against toilet training in the beginning, the toilet-training process eventually becomes quite pleasurable. There are rewards for "doing his duty." People praise him and caress him and kiss him! He also discovers certain pleasurable feelings result by controlling his bladder and bowel. His libido is becoming focused on the anus and the child comes to associate being loved with being clean; i.e., making "doodoo in the potty." ("Doodoo" in his diapers means he is not a good boy and is not loved.) Feces or any kind of dirt comes to be associated with "being bad." He has entered the ***anal*** stage of psychosexual development.

Keep in mind, also, that while the child is being weaned and toilet-trained, he is also being taught all the rules and commandments of five thousand years of civilization—the *do's* and *don'ts* of his society: *Thou shalt do this! Thou shalt not do that! Thou must do this! Thou must not do that! Thou should do this! Thou should not do that!* It is a lot to learn, but if the socialization process is successful, learn it he does. All these do's and don'ts become introjected (absorbed) into the baby's unconscious as the superego. We should not break things. We should say "please" and "thank you." We shouldn't say "bad things." The **superego** (which means "over I" in Latin) contains all the "voices" of the child's society and makes up the second part of the unconscious aspect of personality. In fact, *Freud equated the superego with the conscience.*

3. The Phallic Stage and the Development of the Ego. At about the age of three or four, the male child discovers that if he manipulates his penis in a certain way, he experiences paroxysms of pleasure. The libidinal drive now becomes focused on the penis, and the psychosexual development of the child enters the third or **phallic stage** (*phallus* is Latin for penis). In Freud's day, the little boy was given dire threats that if he continued "to play with himself" his penis may get diseased or even wither and break off! To validate these threats, he discovers to his horror that little girls have lost their penises! Freud thought these threats led to the **castration complex** in little boys—the fear of losing the penis or having it destroyed in some manner or other. More modern research indicates that the castration complex may exist in little boys even in homes where the parents are permissive and understand that masturbation is a "normal" developmental phase of children (Conn & Kanner, 1947). Freud also thought that girls must have a penis envy because they do not have such a pleasurable organ. (Ah, well, we'll forgive Freud for his lack of understanding of female psychology.)

The Oedipus Complex and the Elektra Complex. During the phallic stage, the child begins to develop a special attachment to the parent of the opposite sex. Freud called the special mother-son attachment the **Oedipal complex.** Oedipus was the Greek hero who (all unwittingly) killed his own father and married his own mother. Little boys frequently resent their fathers, who take so much of their mothers' time, and boys may, in fact, wish their fathers dead. Of course, "dead" to a little boy does not have the same connotation as it does to an adult. The little boy simply wants to get rid of this male giant who grabs his mother's attention. He wants her all to himself. Little girls and their fathers often develop a strong father-daughter attachment, which Freud called the **Elektra complex** after another Greek myth. In fact, Freud came to believe that ancient mythologies represent the primitive worldview of ancient humanity and also the primitive psychology of the young child today.

Sibling Rivalry. Not only are small children resentful of the parent of the same sex, they are also resentful of anyone who takes their parents' time and attention. A three- or four-year-old child who has been the "baby" of the family may become quite jealous of a new baby in the house. Even if the older child has been looking forward to a brother or sister "to play with," the actual event is a big let-down. Instead of a brother or sister to play with, the new baby turns out to be a rival, stealing the attention he or she used to get. Listen in on the quarrels older children engage in. "You're Mama's favorite, you always have been!" and the retort: "Well, Daddy always gives in to you!" (see Box 3.3). Parents are always hopeful that sisters and brothers will develop loving relationships with each other, but Freud pointed out that, in fact, history has not proved that hope to be borne out very often. Cain killed his brother Abel out of jealousy, and the Biblical Joseph was sold into slavery by his ten older jealous brothers. History is replete with examples of bitter rivalries of brothers such as the famous King John who was willing to let his brother, Richard the Lionhearted, languish in a prison rather than raise the money to ransom him out and regain his throne. In a conscious or unconscious attempt to regain some of the attention he used to have, the older child may start having "accidents" again, begin thumb-sucking again, and even ask for a bottle. Freud called this behavior **regression,** which is reverting to a more primitive behavior pattern—as in the opening Box 3.1 Scenario.

4. The Latency Stage: The Libidinal Drive Becomes Dormant. At the age of six or seven, the child's psychosexual development enters the fourth stage. At this time, the strong libidinal drive seems to lose some of its power and becomes quiescent, which is why Freud called it the **latency stage**. Freud observed another phenomenon associated with this stage. Children begin to pair off with members of their own gender. Up until now, children have been happy to have anyone to play with: young, old, male, or female. Now, the boys develop a gender bias; in fact, they regard girls as "the enemy." On their part, girls begin to show disgust for the boys they used to play with and wholeheartedly agree that "snips and snails and puppy dog tails, that's what little boys are made of!"

5. The Genital Stage: The Beginning of Adult Heterosexuality. The latency stage comes to an end at puberty. Not only does the libidinal drive come to the fore again, it does so with even greater intensity and strength than ever before. The "enemy gender" now becomes the object of the young man's sexual interest. In order for normal heterosexual development to be achieved, the young man must withdraw some of the emotional attachment from his mother and redirect it to a younger person of the opposite gender. Similarly, the young girl must also withdraw some of her emotional attachment from her father and direct it toward younger males. This process is, according to Freud, the resolution of the Oedipus and Elektra complexes.

But What Happens When Normal Psychosexual Development Goes Awry? Fixations and Neuroses

Until this point, we have been describing what Freud considered as normal development. However, society places so many taboos and prohibitions on sexual expression that the course of psychosexual development hardly ever runs smoothly. But if the socialization process has gone awry, the person develops fixations of behavior which are primitive expressions of emotional development. Freud called these fixated behaviors by the term **neurosis** (see Tip 3.2).

Tip 3.2 Neurosis as a Professional Term Is No Longer Used. Mental health professionals have agreed to eliminate the term "neurosis" from professional use because of its lack of definitional preciseness. However, this term has been in use for almost one hundred years, so it behooves the readers to be familiar with it.

Box 3.3

STUDENTS VERBATIM
On Sibling Rivalry

Read the paragraphs below and then respond to the question at the bottom of this box.

Female: I was the older child, but a lot of times I would be punished for upsetting my little sister, even when it was she who had been the aggressor. I remember many times when she would beat on me and then cry and pretend I hit her. I would promptly be either spanked or severely reprimanded and it wasn't even me.

Male: I love my kid brother now, but I remember the day my parents brought him home. There they were at the doorway, my mother holding the baby. I remember how furious and jealous I was. (I was three years old at the time.) When my mother held the baby down for me to kiss, I bit him instead. I don't remember what happened after that, but it couldn't have been pleasant.

Female: I was the youngest of three girls, each two years apart. I would always meddle with my sisters' toys or tear them up as soon as they would get them. They would have to take care of me when both my parents worked. I was the dominator of the house, and my sisters didn't like me. I don't blame them. I knew I was getting away with murder. My parents always blamed them instead of me.

Male: My three brothers and I get along OK now, but when we were growing up I can't remember anything good that we did together. We didn't just quarrel—we physically fought all the time. The funny thing is I think my Dad actually encouraged our fighting with each other, but I don't know exactly how he did that. The only time we got along was when somebody outside the family tried to pick a fight with one of us or bully us. Then we all hopped on him.

Reflective Writing: Now reflect on your own experience with your siblings.

---

1. Fixation at the Oral Stage: The Passive-Dependent Personality. If the socialization procedure was not successful, the person becomes fixated at the *oral stage* of psychosexual development, and for that reason, the person is sometimes said to have an **oral personality.** Either the caregiver didn't insist on the child becoming toilet-trained and picking up his toys and clothes, or the child's refusal to do so was too strong for the caregiver. Freud explained that these personality types may appear to be grown up, but underneath their adult clothing they are still emotional infants who expect others to take care of them. Their fixation at the oral level may include overeating to the point of obesity, drinking to the point of being alcoholic (they are still on the bottle), and the seeming inability to do anything by themselves including making decisions. They sometimes expect others to "pick up" after them and/or wash their dishes. Passive-dependent personalities frequently marry a "Mommie" or "Daddy" type to take care of them, and are amazingly successful in manipulating other people "to do" for them. Students sometimes identify such a person as their roommate. "What can we do?" they often ask us, to which we can only answer (somewhat sadly), "You alone probably can't do anything except find yourself a more grown-up roommate."

2. Fixation at the Anal Stage: The Obsessive-Compulsive Personality. This person's socialization was overdone, or at least that's what Freud believed (see Tip 3.3), and the person is fixated at the anal stage of development. He may have been made so anxious about making a "mess" in his pants that he became obsessively fearful of anything resembling feces, dirt, germs, or even just untidiness. The reader may recognize this person as the "eternal house-

---

Tip 3.3 On the Obsessive-Compulsive Personality. While Freud accurately described this personality type, we no longer attribute this disorder solely to an overly strict toilet-training. While an overly demanding socialization process may be involved, the genetic evidence is strong that it "runs in families."

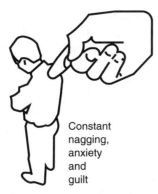

Constant
nagging,
anxiety
and
guilt

Figure 3.2 The Superego.
If the superego is over-
dominant, the person will
be vulnerable to continual
anxiety and guilt no matter
how hard he or she tries to
be "good" (clean, neat
perfect).

keeper" who is constantly washing, dusting, sweeping, and cleaning everything in sight. Even if this person has just finished cleaning, she can see specks of dirt everywhere she looks. Up she must go and clean again. To visit this person may be a very uncomfortable event, since no sooner do we finish drinking from a cup or glass than she has whisked it away, cleaned it, and returned it to the cupboard. Sometimes this anxiety about dirt gets transformed into an obsession about money. The person exhibits miserliness and the tendency to focus on unimportant details. At the office, he may make a good bookkeeper because he will know just where every cent (the smallest of details) has gone. But because he is so preoccupied with the pennies, he loses sight of the dollars (the big picture) and so does not make a very good accountant. An over-active superego, said Freud, is not a person with a good conscience but a person who is so laden with guilt that he is tormented all his life with feelings that his best is never good enough.

3. Fixation Before the Genital Stage: The Oedipal Complex Is Not Resolved. Freud explained that the resolution of the Oedipal complex occurs after puberty when the adolescent male withdraws his emotional attachment from his mother and redirects his libidinal drive toward other females. This resolution must be achieved if the young boy is not to remain under his mother's domination the rest of his life. The reader may, in fact, know of a man who is still so attached to his mother that he puts her wishes and her desires and her needs before those of his wife and children. They also may marry someone who takes the place of "Mother" and who will play the dominant role in the house. In like manner, a young woman who has not resolved her Elektra complex may remain "Daddy's little girl" the rest of her life. Or she may marry someone "just like Daddy."

Freud also thought that **homosexuality** was another result of the unresolved Oedipal complex. Since the mother has such a dominant hold on the young boy, he is unable to disengage from her emotionally. Freud theorized that in order to stay "loyal" to his mother, the young lad does not form attachments to women, but forms attachments to men instead. In that way, he does not betray his mother by loving other women. Freud's explanation of homosexuality does not hold up today. More and more evidence has been gathered concerning the biological underpinnings of homosexuality. Freud's explanation might possibly account for a percentage of homosexuality, but it would seem to be a small percentage.

The Repetitive Nature of "Neurosis." How serious does a behavior have to be to qualify as a "fixation" or "neurosis?" All of us have left-over behaviors of the oral stage or anal stage. We chew gum or smoke a pipe, for example, but does that make us an "oral personality? We may enjoy a clean house, but does that make us an obsessive-compulsive personality? If we clean our house or car and then relax and enjoy ourselves, we are not displaying obsessive-compulsive behavior. If, on the other hand, we have to get up several times in the night to check that all the doors and windows are locked, then we may have an obsessive-compulsive reaction to our anxieties. Mental hospitals frequently have patients who have scrubbed their hands with a harsh abrasive hundreds of times a day until they have patches of raw skin up to their elbows. These patients are extreme cases of obsessive-compulsive disorder.

Freud's "Long Shadow" on the Twentieth Century. Almost overnight, Freudian theory changed our understanding about the nature of human personality. We know now not "to beat the devil" out of a child. Nor do we shame a little boy when he masturbates. Freud brought to light the significance of dreams and instituted the whole area of psychotherapy as we know it today. He created a lexicon of psychological terms, most of which we still use today (see the frontispiece to this chapter, p. 49).

If the scientific and medical communities were put off by Freud's strong views on human sexuality, there was one group, at least, that responded very positively to his theories; namely, the creative artists and writers of both Europe and America. Almost overnight, authors such as Eugene O'Neill, Henry Miller, and E. M. Forster were writing erotic books revealing the libidinal behaviors and fantasies of modern men and women. The Irish novelist James Joyce created an extraordinary novel, *Finnegan's Wake,* in which the narration is almost solely the protagonist's stream of conscious and unconscious thoughts. Salvador Dali painted dream-like landscapes where clocks ooze over tables and fences. Marc Chagall actually painted his dreams and his child-like memories of growing up in Russia. T. S. Eliot's poem "The Love Song of J. Alfred Prufrock" is a complex flow of free associations of an aging man who acknowledges the urges of his libidinal drive and is repulsed by them.

Another spin-off from Freud's theory of personality is the technique frequently used in movies and TV in which psychological motivation is revealed through flashbacks. In the midst of the story-line, the action of the hero or villain is suddenly interrupted, and we see instead some event in the life of a little boy or girl. All of us recognize what is going on. We are being let in on some incident of the person's past, some conscious or unconscious memory. But the most literate person of the nineteenth century, if he or she were to watch the movie with us, would be utterly baffled by these interruptions and flashbacks. Such has been the influence of Sigmund Freud on artistic and literary expression. He was not always right, and we can find many errors and limitations in his theories of human psychology (see Box 3.4). And on this side of the Atlantic, we oversubscribed to some of his theories. Nevertheless, he was a giant, and we midgets who stand on his shoulders and criticize him are not taller than he.

The Neo-Freudians: Modifying and Adding to Freudian Theory. Despite public condemnation, Freud's theories about the "dark side of human nature" began to attract men and women from various professions. Many of the people who came to study with him were already well-known psychologists, psychiatrists, physicians, philosophers, or merely very educated lay persons. Eventually, they formalized their association into what ultimately became known as the International Psychoanalytic Congress of Vienna. The president was (of course) Sigmund Freud, and its expressed purpose was to continue to investigate human personality using Freud's new methods of free association, psychoanalysis, dream interpretation, and so on. For a while, the group members worked amicably together, but eventually conflicts began to splinter the group. Eventually, some of the members of the group were forced to form their own "schools of analysis" in order to pursue their particular insights. Together, they are called the neoFreudians and include many names the reader will encounter from time to time if he or she pursues further study in psychology, counseling, education, social work, and other mental health professions. The neo-Freudians were not opposed to Freud's theory of a powerful libidinal drive as a motivator of human behavior—not at all. However, the neo-Freudians believed that there are also other factors to account for what we do and why, such as the desire for *self-esteem, competency, power*, and *innate (*inherited*)* individual differences of personality. The neo-Freudians we discuss in this chapter are Alfred Adler, Carl Jung, and Erik Erikson (who is sometimes called a "second generation neo-Freudian").

Alfred Adler: The Individuality of Our Life Styles and the Striving for Competence and Power

In English, we use the term *life style* to mean financial status or the leisure and recreational activities we prefer and can afford. But Alfred Adler, who originated the term, meant something quite different. Adler defined his concept of **life style** as the unique underlying theme (or themes) that motivates each individual throughout the life span (Adler, 1954). He likened

each human life to a river that bubbles up from its source, twisting and turning as it travels—sometimes with calm passages and sometimes through rapids—before it reaches its final destination. To catch hold of the person's theme, we must consider everything about that person: the person's values, attitudes, goals, aspirations, as well as the person's seemingly strange choices at times. In some people, this theme is easy to identify. A career politician wants to reach a level of power so as to effect change in government. An artist wants to produce works of beauty and may even be willing to live a life of poverty to do so. A scientist is searching for some kind of truth. These are easy life styles to understand.

Figure 3.3 Alfred Adler. He added the drive for competence and power to our understanding of personality.

Living a Life Lie. Other persons, however, seem to lead such confused, chaotic, even self-destructive life styles, they appear to have no unifying theme. To continue Adler's metaphor, the flow of their lives seems not like rivers that have a direction but like churning whirlpools going nowhere or dark pools of stagnant water. That is, however, where we are mistaken, said Adler. Each person is seeking to express his or her underlying life theme, no matter how bewildering and contradictory their life styles may seem to us. The reason for their unhappy or destructive life styles is that they are living a life lie. A woman may be working successfully but really wants to live a more traditional wife-and-mother life as a homemaker. A man may want to enter the arts, but instead he is working in the family business (for which he has no liking). The therapist's job is to help the person discover his and her unique life theme and enable them to develop a life style that is more harmonious with that theme (see Box 3.5).

Two Sources of Our Uniquely Individual Life Styles. How is it that human beings have such different life themes leading to such different life styles? Adler's answer: A person's life style develops from two principal sources: first, from the person's sense of inferiority and the need for power; and second, from what he called *gemeinschaftsgefühl* (Adler, 1954).

The Inferiority-Superiority Complex

Small children live in a world of tall and powerful giants who control their lives and tell them what to do. These giants are superior to them in every way—in strength, in everyday skills, in language—and particularly, in power. This superiority of their parents and older siblings is

Box 3.4

EVALUATING FREUD
How Well Do His Theories Stand Up Today?

It is more than a hundred years since Freud's first major writings appeared on the publishing scene. Since then, he has been both praised and vilified. He was called a "sex maniac" and the "Anti-Christ." He was neither, of course. He was a proper Austrian gentleman, physician, and neurologist. He was often astonished at what he had unearthed in the repressed memories of his patients and even in himself. From our perspective today, we can more objectively assess Freud's theories and concepts. Under the scrutiny of modern scientific research, some of his theories still stand up and some have fallen by the wayside. We list below only a few of the positive and negative criticisms.

On the Minus Side

1. **Limitations of the case study method.** Freud's major method of investigation was through the (retroactive) case study. It is particularly apt for diagnosing disease, but when we apply this method to psychological disorders, we are on dangerous ground. We can read anything we want into a person's past history and assign erroneous reasons for a person's problems.
2. **Lack of empirical evidence for his theories.** Freud's division of the personality into the id, the superego, and the ego has probably met with the most severe criticism since empirical proof of these concepts is impossible. Science demands that empirical proof should be more concrete than "inner" material such as dreams and fantasies.
3. **Overlooked the influence of genetics and culture.** Freud was almost completely in the environmental camp of the nature/nurture debate. Convinced as he was that adult personality is formed by a child's experiences in the first six years of life, he ignored

the area of genetics, neurobiological pathology, and cultural and subcultural differences. We know now that human nature is multidetermined and multivariate.
4. **Little understanding of female psychology.** As an example, we only have to mention his concept of "penis envy."

On the Plus Side

1. **Positive influence on child rearing.** He changed our assumptions in the area of child rearing, parenting, and education. Example: We no longer advocate punishing children for masturbating or "beat the devil" out of them.
2. **Women given back their right to full sexuality.** Instead, frigidity became the twentieth century "neurosis."
3. **Formulation of the psychotherapeutic approach.** His greatest achievement may be the beginning of psychotherapy as we know it. He demonstrated that physical symptoms could be eliminated through the "talking cure."
4. **Use of dream interpretation.** He helped us to understand that dreams are another expression of the person and meaningful indeed (discussed in Chapter 14).
5. **Formulation of anxiety and defense mechanisms.** He formulated many of the defensive behaviors that we still consider valid today.
6. **Concept of unconscious forces on personality.** The concept of the unconscious had been discussed for a hundred years prior to Freud, but it was he who gave it sum and substance through the evidence of dreams, repressed memories, slips-of-the tongue, etc.

overwhelming and intimidating for the child, leading to intense feelings of *inferiority*. The more inferior (incompetent) the child feels, the more he strives for *superiority* (so as to have some kind of power and control in life). This desire to overcome our inferiority and become competent and powerful leads to what Adler called the **inferiority-superiority complex.** We make up for our weaknesses and limitations by achieving superiority in other areas of our personality, which Adler called **compensation.** All of us compensate, said Adler, which means that we try to overcome our limitations by developing other areas of our personality. In that respect compensation is a healthy defense mechanism. In fact, Adler believed that if we didn't feel inferior to some degree, we would not strive to achieve anything at all. Adler attributed his own personality to his childhood frailty (and subsequent feelings of inferiority) and his academic brilliance to his striving for superiority.

Box 3.5

STUDENTS VERBATIM
Living a Life Lie

Students often feel confused because they are not sure what they want to do with their lives or what vocation they should enter. If they are living a life lie, their anxiety and confusion is often phrased as the following: Who am I really? If I could understand who I really am, I would not feel so confused and anxious all the time. Why do I feel so different from the other members of my family? Why do I feel like a phoney? What kind of work do I want to do? Why did I do such a stupid and crazy thing? Fortunately, college is the "golden opportunity" to discover more authentic ways to live.

Female (22 years): My mother has always told me to study to become a nurse. My mother is a single parent who has had a tough time raising the two of us. So she wanted us to have the security of a good job "to fall back on." I got accepted at the nursing school, but after two terms I know I have made the wrong choice. I just don't want to be a nurse. I'm living a life lie. Shall I just quit? What do I say to my mother—after all she's the one who paid for all this? Yet I know I don't want to do this.

Male (21 years): I thought to get on at college, I had to do everything my roommates and their friends did.

I went out drinking and smoking grass and doing really dumb stuff. My grades began to suffer but I didn't care. I thought I was being real cool. When I got put on academic probation, I had to look at what I was doing. I had to stay with my roommates until the lease was up and then I moved out. I have some serious roommates now and I'm doing better in school.

Female (18 years): I didn't realize what a life lie I was living when I was in high school. I wanted to be accepted by the "popular" group so I did everything like them, using a lot of make-up and very sexy clothing. I dropped my previous friends and hung around the popular crowd. I let myself become intimate with the popular boys because that was part of the game—even boys I didn't like. Then I came to college and realized that I didn't want to be like them anymore. I wanted to be myself. I'm really glad I came to that realization. I feel so much freer now and able to live the way I should live.

Reflective Writing: Reflect upon some time you were living a life lie and what enabled you to live more authentically.

Compensation versus Overcompensation. Some persons, however, *overcompensate* for their low self-esteem. The reader may have noticed that tall, strong men often seem very gentle in their dealings with others. They move and talk quietly. Since they know they are superior in height and strength, they don't have to "throw their weight around." By way of contrast, Adler described the *Napoleonic complex:* How very short men need constantly to prove themselves superior in one way or another. Napoleon Bonaparte was very short, and Adler suggested that his drive to conquer all of Europe was his unconscious attempt to overcompensate for his short stature. We cannot know, of course, if this was actually the case, but it is interesting to note that another world conqueror, Alexander the Great, was also small in stature in comparison to the Greeks of his time. A second example: A little girl who feels unloved because her sister was her father's "favorite" may spend a lifetime proving herself attractive to men. She spends exorbitant amounts of time, energy, and money on clothes, makeup, and hair styling. She engages in flirtations or love affairs and may even become a breaker of men's hearts—the French *femme fatale*. To love her is to suffer heartbreak. Another example: The little boy who feels outstripped by his siblings may pursue a vocation in business in which he seeks to outstrip others through aggressive—even ruthless—competitive methods. Sometimes the drive for superiority can be hidden under a camouflage of virtue. For example, the person may strive to become superior in "goodness" in a way others may not appreciate. The person may not be so much "good" as either a "martyr" trying to make others feel guilty or "holier than thou," indicating that the rest of us are "sinners."

Gemeinschaftsgefühl: The Development of Character

If human nature were nothing but this striving for power and superiority, we would exist only in a dog-eat-dog world in which everyone is seeking to overcome others. Fortunately, that is only half the story. There is, said Adler, another very powerful drive within the human heart—not one that seeks to overcome others—but one which seeks to affiliate with others, to unite with others, to cooperate and bring out the best in others. Ideal mother love is an example of this drive. He called this drive to be of service to others ***gemeinschaftsgefühl.*** Our German-speaking colleagues tell us that this word is impossible to translate precisely into English but that it has overtones of *love, caring, lovingkindness,* or perhaps simply as *compassion.* Persons who have a highly developed *gemeinschaftsgefühl* have a compassionate love of all humankind despite our human foibles and follies and apparent madnesses at times. So taken was Abraham Maslow by this quality in what he called self-actualizing persons that he included *gemeinschaftsgefühl* as one of their personality characteristics (Chapter 1, pp. 11–13).

Persons with a highly developed *gemeinschaftsgefühl* manifest a goodness that we instantly recognize, but not of the "holier than thou" kind that makes us feel inferior. They arouse in us a sense of happiness and joy. We are glad to be in their company. To use a present-day adage, they perform "random acts of kindness" and "senseless acts of beauty." Across cultures and down through the ages, there have always been those whom biographers have described as "saint-like" or "enlightened" or as representing a highly evolved moral/ethical orientation. They continue to manifest joy and spirituality despite the setbacks, obstacles, and tragedies in their lives. The person with a highly developed *gemeinschaftsgefühl* may be described as growing always in wisdom and in grace.

Birth Order

It is not just the giant-sized adults that make a child feel inferior or superior. It also happens through rank and gender of birth order. Much has been researched on birth order and many books have been written on the subject in the last fifty years, but it was Alfred Adler who first called our attention to the child's place in the family constellation (Adler, 1929, 1959). Adler hypothesized many effects of birth order. More recent research has added to and modified his original observations, but most of his insights into the effects of birth order have been somewhat validated by empirical research (Sulloway, 1998). Consider the following hard data.

Firstborn children go on to college and graduate school and become university professors more often than their younger siblings. They also make up the majority of doctors, lawyers, accountants—in fact—they more frequently go into all the professions. They are also "overrepresented" in corporate leadership, political office, and even in the field of aerodynamics—almost all the famous astronauts were first born. Does this mean that firstborn children have more intelligent genes? Of course not. But it does mean their parents were more motivated to help them succeed. Whether it is writing a school report, or playing in Little League, or taking private lessons in music or dance, parents of firstborn children were willing to chauffeur them, pay for what they needed, and encourage their skills and talents. By the time the younger siblings come along, parents begin to run out of energy, time, and money, with the result that later-born children are not so closely supervised. Oldest siblings often accuse their parents of letting their younger sibling "get away" with things the oldest child could not. "Boy! I wasn't allowed to do the things he's allowed to do!"

Being closer to their parents, firstborn children *introject* (observe and imitate) more of their values and behaviors. Consequently, when firstborns become adults, they fit more comfortably into adult society and, consequently, are more at ease in the corporate structure. Furthermore, their parents have often given them the job of taking care of their younger brothers and sisters and so first-borns develop more responsibility toward "the family good" and later "the corporate good." But a sense of responsibility also results in guilt when they do not live up to what they think they should do or should be. Consequently, first-borns tend to be more guilt-ridden and more anxious generally with a tendency to worry more than later-born children.

Younger children often accuse their oldest sibling of being "bossy" and abusive. Since younger siblings do not have the physical or verbal power of the older siblings, they develop crafty strategies to get even. As younger children, we may have screamed to make our parents think we were being hurt by our older sibling. We may have become expert in blackmail and extortion, "I won't tell Mom what you said if you won't tattle on me about the cake." Being born later, we were not pushed to make good grades so we probably put more emphasis on having fun than on our studies. We grew up to be much more spontaneous and popular with our friends, more interested in physical sports, or expressing ourselves in the arts. We are not nearly so responsible as our firstborn siblings; nor are we as burdened with guilt as they are (Sutton-Smith & Rosenberg, 1970).

Only children are much like first-born children with these exceptions: Not having had to vie for parental attention or having experienced sibling rivalry in the nursery, only children tend to have more open, trusting, and optimistic attitudes toward life. While some only children become the traditional "spoiled rotten" stereotype, most only children are generous in dealing with other children because they have not had to fight for time, attention, or material things. Unfortunately their lack of experience of sibling rivalry results in a certain naiveté. Not having witnessed the hair-pulling, tattling, jealousy, lying, and betrayal that goes on in the nursery, they tend to be surprised, even astonished, by what they observe in others. They are continually asking others, "Why are they doing that? Why did she say that? Do all people do that? Do others feel that way?" Unfortunately, because they are quite naive about the ways of the world, they are also more likely to be "taken in" by schemers and scoundrels (Sulloway, 1997).

Adler's Creative Self versus Freud's Conflicted Self. While both Adler and Freud placed heavy emphasis on early environment as a major factor of personality, there were several major differences. While Freud attempted to describe personality in terms of the libidinal drive, Adler added the need for competence and power. Another difference is that Freud's model of the personality is a conflict model (the id versus the superego) while Adler's model involves a *creative self* that guides the person along and through the shoals and rapids of life. This creative self uses the raw material of both his heredity and his experiences in life to interpret and give meaning to his life. Adler likened the person's creative self to an artist who conceptualizes a portrait of himself and then works to live up to this self-portrait. In short, this creative self drives us to do what we do. In most of us, the self-portrait we have imaged for ourselves is healthy, but some people create an unhealthy one which accounts for what seems to be destructive behaviors. Today we would perhaps call these self-portraits by terms introduced in Chapter 1: *self concept* and *self esteem*.

Carl Jung's Four-Stage Transpersonal Model of Human Existence

Carl Jung was another personality theorist who had to break with the Freudians. He did not believe (as Freud did) that the human personality was fully formed by age six. Jung's model of personality described four great chapters or eras covering the whole life span, each of which has

Box 3.6

GEMEINSCHAFTSGEFÜHL
The Outer Expression of Which Is Cheerfulness & Joy

The following is excerpted from Adler's own writings (1959). Although Adler confessed to being the pampered child, others have described Adler as having exemplified the qualties of gemeinschaftsgefühl.

. . . we can easily measure anyone's *gemeinschaftsgefühl* by learning to what degree he is prepared to serve, to help, and to give pleasure to others. The talent for bringing pleasure to others makes a man more interesting. Happy people approach us more easily and we judge them emotionally as being more sympathetic . . . There are people who appear cheerful, who do not go about forever oppressed and solicitous, who do not unload their worries upon every stranger. They are quite capable, when in the company of others, to radiate this cheerfulness and make life more beautiful and meaningful. One can sense they are good human beings, not only in their actions, but in the manner in which . . . they speak, in which they pay attention to our interests, as well as in their entire external aspect, their clothes, their gestures, their happy emotional state, and their laughter . . . [By contrast]. . . . There are some people who are absolutely unable to laugh because they stand so far from the innate bond that connects human beings that their ability to give pleasure or to appear happy is absent . . .

. . . There is [also] another little group of people who are utterly incapable of giving anyone else joy since they are concerned only in embittering life in every situation which they may enter. They walk around as though they wished to extinguish every light. They do not laugh at all, or only when forced to do so, or when they wish to give the semblance of a joy-giver.

Self-Reflection: Describe someone you believe to have a highly developed *gemeinschaftsgefühl.*

unique characteristics, needs, and motivations (Jung 1955). The four eras include *childhood, youth, maturity,* and *old age* (see Figure 3.4). He was also responsible for originating and describing a concept that we have taken much to heart—the *midlife crisis.* The midlife crisis became a focal point of Jung's theories about human existence since he considered this juncture in our lives a time when we can become truly, authentically ourselves—a process he called **individuation** (Jung, 1955).

1. Childhood (from birth to about 20/25 years). Many of the readers may be surprised to discover that Jung would regard them as still in the stage of childhood. According to Jung, childhood is roughly that stage from birth to the late teens and early twenties. It is the "dawn of life" in which the person is emerging out of the "Universal Unconscious" into an individual self-identity distinct from the other family members. But until a person is financially self-supporting, Jung regarded the person as being protected and harbored within the safety of the family unit.

2. Youth (about 20/25 years to 37/38 years). Jung described the second stage of youth as "the morning of life" in which the young adult is setting out on his independent life-career. The tasks of youth are twofold. The first is the development of an *ego complex,* by which Jung meant a level of consciousness characterized by a "high degree of self-identity and continuity of personality." We seem to know who we are and what we want from life. The second task is *acquisition:* the acquisition of whatever we think to be essential to our happiness and well-being. From our early twenties to just before age 40, we go about the job of acquiring job and career, spouse and children, house and furnishings, and, of course, always a bigger and better automobile—all those material objects we believe will bring us satisfaction and happiness. It

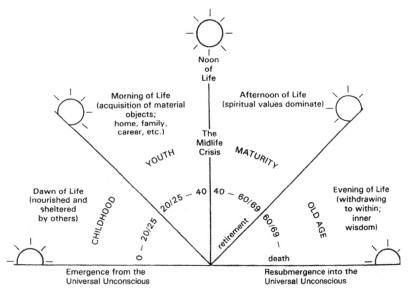

Figure 3.4 Jung's Four Stages of the Life Span. Where Freud beleived adult personality to be fully formed by age six, Jung posited four age/stages, each of which has needs and values different from the others and which influences our personality and character.

is at this time that we define our life goals in terms of family, money, position, and success in our life-career. It is a time of competition, struggle, hard-work, and task-directed behavior.

Figure 3.5 Carl Jung. The psychologist who reintroduced the terms *soul* and *spiritual* into psychology.

The Midlife Crisis (from 37/38 years to about 42/43 years). In contrast to Freud's "neurotic" patients who were so emotionally disabled they were unable to work or live harmoniously with others, Jung's patients were often the great and near-great of Europe. When they came to Jung, they were unable to put into words just what was troubling them. In fact, they sometimes described themselves as having "everything that life has to offer." Yet, as they approached their fortieth year, they had become aware of "an emptiness" or "void" or some "lack" in their lives. Somehow, life had ceased to have any meaning. Jung described their problem as **spiritual bankruptcy.** In their pursuit of worldly "success," they had neglected the spiritual dimension. By **spiritual dimension,** Jung was referring to all those non-materialistic values we all need in our lives: tenderness and caring within the family grouping; intimate friendship and challenging companions; moments of deep conversation and quiet intimacy; and the appreciation of nature, whether awesome or beautiful. What had been neglected were the needs of the Soul. In fact, Jung entitled one of his books

---

Box 3.7
SELF-EXPLORATION
Is This True of Your Sibling Experience?

This self-exploration can be answered in either of two ways: as if applied to yourself or a sibling. But remember to use your judgment about the sibling rank. Example, a third child born seven or eight years later than the second born may very well be like another firstborn child. A middle child, but the first son in a family, may be treated like a firstborn.

Firstborn Children: Are these statements true or false of your own experience?

1. Tends to be more conforming to parental values and societal staus quo.	T	F	?
2. More supervised in educational and extracurricular activities by parents.	T	F	?
3. More motivated to go on to college and/or professional school.	T	F	?
4. More willing to assume responsibility.	T	F	?
5. More emotionally identified with parents.	T	F	?
6. More communicative and verbal than later born.	T	F	?
7. More apt to seek help from parent, friend or physician when hurt or puzzled.	T	F	?
8. More apt to be bossy and verbally assertive or aggressive.	T	F	?
9. More willing to be concerned and caring about other members of the family.	T	F	?
10. More tendency toward introverted, quiet leisure activities (reading, gardening, running).	T	F	?
Totals			

Middle-Born Children: Are these statements true or false of your own experience?

1. More distant from parents, hostile and suspicious of authority and rebellious of rules.	T	F	?
2. Less inclined to study and make good grades.	T	F	?
3. Tends to be more popular in school and have more friends.	T	F	?
4. More willing to take time to have spontaneous fun.	T	F	?
5. More engaged in sports and action-oriented activities.	T	F	?
6. More aggressive and acting-out behavior (temper tantrums, crying, fighting).	T	F	?
7. More apt to go into positions that allow independent action (dentist, forester, truck-driver, artist, writer).	T	F	?
8. More apt to keep problems to self rather than confide in parents or other adults.	T	F	?
9. More democratic in group decision-making process.	T	F	?
10. Gets into more trouble than other members of the family.	T	F	?
Totals			

Modern Man in Search of a Soul. The therapy, of course, was to enable them to get in touch with their **transpersonal** *needs:* more time with their family and friends, more time for the contemplation of nature, and ways they could be of service to those now living or to those who come after us.

3. Maturity (about 42/43 years to retirement). If men understand what is happening to them and if they process the midlife crisis successfully, they now devote themselves to these suprapersonal values as they confront the "second half" of their lives. They make friends with their children, who are becoming young adults. With their adult children "leaving the nest," husbands may seek ways to share activities with wives, something they have not done in many years. Now they have time to take the vacations they have longed for and to visit with relatives and friends they haven't seen in many years. They may start building their "dream house,"

Box 3.7
SELF-EXPLORATION (continued)
Is This True of Your Sibling Experience

Youngest Children: Are these statements true or false of your own experience?

		T	F	?
1.	More willing to play the comic and make people laugh.	T	F	?
2.	More eager to make a name for yourself and show up your older siblings.	T	F	?
3.	More able to negotiate with people in a friendly way.	T	F	?
4.	More willing to consult others when in trouble or confused.	T	F	?
5.	Enjoy other people so long as they treat you as an equal.	T	F	?
6.	More willing to get help when hurt physically.	T	F	?
7.	More willing to let others "have their way."	T	F	?
8.	Learned crafty ways to get back at your older siblings.	T	F	?
9.	Tend to watch others to discover what mood they are in.	T	F	?
10.	Still feel you are not taken seriously enough at times.	T	F	?

Totals

Only Children: Are these statements true or false of your own experience?

		T	F	?
1.	Apt to be very verbal.	T	F	?
2.	Feel close to adults.	T	F	?
3.	Apt to be bewildered by fighting and jealousy of other children.	T	F	?
4.	Tend to be fairly self-confident about self and abilities.	T	F	?
5.	Tend to be easy going in temperament and trusting of other persons.	T	F	?
6.	Tend to be more oriented towards professional school and graduate degrees.	T	F	?
7.	Tend to be trusting of others and bewildered when others betray that trust.	T	F	?
8.	Not so able to deal with direct confrontation, over-sensitive and hurt when bawled out.	T	F	?
9.	Generally have an optimistic attitude towards life.	T	F	?
10.	More able to draw on "inner resources" so as to develop the imagination and talents (art, writing, etc.).	T	F	?

Totals

Reflective Writing: If any of these sibling categories accurately reflects your experience, state how. If your responses do not reflect your experience, explain how.

which they can now afford. They value leisure time over the need "to make money" and begin to "throttle back" at work. If a man is a physician, he may now take Wednesdays off to join some friends on the golf greens. Or he may decide he needs to make a major midlife vocational change. He may leave his "fast track," super-competitive job and buy that small bookstore he has always wanted. He looks for ways to give of his time, energy, and money to charitable organizations. Unlike the "do-gooder," he does so because he finds joy in the giving.

Successful processing of the midlife crisis leads to what Jung called **individuation.** The man after 40 truly has a chance of becoming "his own person." He is unshackled from the compulsion to live up to someone else's standards of behavior. He need not be who *they* think he should be or do what *they* think he should do with his life. Unlike adolescents (who are living through the most unindividuated time of their lives), people in their maturity are now free to be who they are and to pursue their own needs and the values *they themselves* want to express (Jung & Aniela 1964).

On the other hand, if he misconstrues the changes he needs to make to resolve his midlife crisis, he may destroy everything he has built up for the last two decades. He may suddenly divorce his wife, abandon his children, buy a sports car, and take up with a woman half his age. His adult children may tell their friends, "Dad's gone completely crazy." Jung would say that he really isn't going crazy. He is misconstruing his midlife crisis. The changes he needs to make are not so much external as *internal*. Instead of making a transition to the next level of conscious maturity, he is reliving his youthful stage, what people call "chasing his youth."

4. Old Age (from retirement to death). If we have processed the midlife crisis successfully and evolved to a more transpersonal life style during the stage of maturity, we will be able to live out the "evening of life" in dignity and peace. Our spiritual values now allow us to confront the last part of our lives with acceptance and grace. We do not regret the ending of existence, because we know that we have lived our lives as well as we could. We know our lives have been worthwhile and that we have touched the bodies, minds, and hearts of others when we could. The older person is preparing to reemerge into the Universal Unconscious again. Time now to focus on the inner world and "things of the spirit." But, not just yet! There is one more task left to do. If the task of youth was acquiring an ego complex and the task of maturity was individuation, the task of old age is to inspire in the younger generation the understanding that renunciation of worldly goods leads to luminous wisdom. Then: *Consumatum est.*

Daniel Levinson and the *Seasons of Our Lives:* Validating Jung

Jungian psychology has always had a respectful place in European psychology, but psychologists on this side of the Atlantic generally were skeptical about Jung's theories. They always seemed more mystical than scientific (see Box 3.8). But some of his concepts have received validation from psychologist, Daniel Levinson. Levinson described himself as the prototype of the academic professor living a quiet, intellectual career and content to spend his life more-or-less in the way he started out in his twenties. No one was more surprised than he when around the age of 40, he found himself divorced, remarried, and undergoing other major changes in his life. Until then, he had only a vague familiarity with Jung and had never really given his theories much credence. But after the events of his age-40 transition, he decided to investigate the phenomenon of the midlife crisis (if there was such a beast) and its parameters. Some of the questions he and his staff investigated were as follows: *Had Levinson himself truly gone through a midlife crisis? Who else is affected by midlife crises? Only the highly educated elite like himself? Or is it a more universal experience in our technological society?*

The Universality of the Midlife Crisis

Over the next decade Levinson and his research staff followed the lives of four groups of ten men and their families, forty in all. The four groups were chosen from four different walks of life: physicists (representing the scientific profession), business executives (representing men motivated by money, power, and position), novelists (representing the world of artists), and plumbers (representing blue-collar workers). Levinson's research has been criticized as being composed of a very small sample. True, but until then, no forty functioning (healthy) persons had ever been so thoroughly investigated with a longitudinal case study approach (Levinson, Darrow, Klein, Levinson, & McKee, 1978).

Box 3.8

EVALUATING JUNG
Psychologist or Mystic?

The Minus Side. If Freudian psychology was attacked as being nonverifiable in the laboratory, Jungian psychology has been even more heavily criticized in this direction. Freud himself thought that Jung's emphasis on the transpersonal and spiritual dimension of human existence was delving into nonscientific areas. As we investigate more of Jung's theoretical concepts, we may find ourselves agreeing with his critics. Furthermore, his writing is sometimes so obscure that it is difficult for psychologists to agree just what he means by certain terms. What did he mean, for example, by the *Universal Unconscious?* It is difficult sometimes to know whether he is talking psychology or theology (he came from a long line of ministers.)

The Plus Side. Despite these harsh criticisms, we cannot lightly dismiss Jung—too many of his concepts have touched a genuine chord in the general population. While Jung's transpersonal view is one of the reasons that experimental psychology has tended to avoid Jung's theories of personality, developmental and social psychologists have found validity in many of Jung's theoretical formulations, particularly concerning the midlife crisis and the process of individuation. In fact, the midlife crisis has become one of the most popular underlying themes for movies, TV dramatizations, and books. In classes, students readily volunteer real-life examples of the midlife crisis from their own families. As a term, it has even passed into popular usage in the media and in everyday conversation. Furthermore, as the reader will soon note, Jung's four age/stage model became the basis of two other models that have received wide acceptance in psychological circles: Daniel Levinson's model of personality development and Erik Erikson's eight-stage model of the life span.

But As Well, There Are Major Transitions at the End of Every Decade

Levinson and his associates substantially validated Jung's midlife crisis theory. Yes, the midlife crisis does exist. Somewhere around 40, men undergo a sweeping transformation of interests, values, and needs. They *do* become more oriented toward transpersonal (spiritual) values. Furthermore (and this finding was astonishing to the researchers), the midlife crisis seems to be universal. It is not confined to the intellectual elite but crosses social, educational, and economic lines. Blue-collar workers as well as college professors underwent a profound self-examination and reorientation at this time in their lives. In fact, the midlife crisis is related to one variable and one variable only, that of age—simply the number of years the man has lived on this earth. Levinson and his team discovered that while the age-40 transition may be the major one of our lives, other crises occur (even if of lesser intensity) at age 20, age 30, and age 50. As a major postulate, Levinson emphasized that *no life structure can ever be perfect or permanent. Whether they know it or not, men are constantly structuring and destructuring and restructuring their lives.* (See Table 3.1.)

    The Age-20 Transition. The first transition occurs between the ages of 18 and 22 years, during which the young person leaves home to try out many new types of life structures. This trying out of life styles involves many changes, many hopes, and many disappointments. If he doesn't go on to college, he may try out one job after another by quitting or getting fired. Or he may run off to join the circus, take to the open road, or join the armed services. He may fall in and out of love several times. If he goes on to college, he may change his major several times, and even change his college. These flip-flops and changes are not to be considered as failures but as gaining more experience of life. In adolescence, teenagers develop a life dream. This life dream is usually unrealistic because adolescents do not have enough life experience to form

Table 3.1   Levinson's Eras and Cross-Eras of the Life Span

Stage	Age	Movement or Life Structure
Childhood	0–17/18	Childhood
Major Transition	18–22	Passage from adolescence to novice adulthood
Novice Adulthood	22–29	First independent life structure as a novice adult
Minor Transition	28–33	Age-30 transition
Early Adulthood	32–38	Second life structure; now speaks with a "voice of authority"
Major Transition	37–43	The great "midlife" transition
Middle Adulthood	42–60/65	Third life structure: Leadership, mentoring, transpersonal values
Major Transition	60–65	Transition to retirement
Late Adulthood	65–	Fourth life structure: May simply "kick back" or begin a new life-career

more realistic life goals. For example, an adolescent may have had a life-dream of becoming a physician. He has not yet realized that he lacks the money or the academic credentials for medical school. When he comes to recognize these obstacles, he may either abandon his life dream entirely or modify it to something he can achieve, such as becoming an x-ray technologist or emergency medical technician. He may even begin to consider himself a failure, but by the time he is 22 or 23 years of age, in all probability he has found a genuine direction for himself. In his twenties, he has found himself, so to speak, and knows what he wants to do. He may go on to graduate school or he may get himself a job and build his life-career more solidly. He is building his first independent life structure of home, family, and life-career. He is a "novice adult."

The Age-30 Transition. His life progresses fairly satisfactorily throughout his twenties. Then, toward his thirtieth birthday, he begins to experience dissatisfaction with the life structure he has built up. He tries to correct the "flaws" he perceives in his life-career. If there have been severe difficulties in the marriage, he may find himself thinking about divorce or separation. Or he may "have a fling," after which he may make a recommitment to his home and family. If he has been working for others, he may decide now is the time to start working for himself. It may only be a small business, but he will be "his own boss." Or he may decide to go back to school and get a degree so he can move up in his line of work or even go into a different line of work. Although it is not easy to carry a full-time job, be a spouse and parent, and attend school part time, he usually makes better grades than he ever did before. Having successfully come through the destructuring and restructuring of the age-30 transition, he will build a second life structure, no longer a "novice adult," but a person who speaks with a "voice of authority."

The Age-40 and Age-50 (and so on) Transitions. In addition to validating Jung's midlife crisis, Levinson added some other observations. The age-40 transition may be precipitated by "marker events" such as a heart attack or the loss of one or both parents. The death of his parents causes him to acknowledge his own mortality. If his father dies, he may realize that he must become "his own father." There is no one else left to blame for his own failure to live as he wants to live. Now, it is not "success" that he wants to pursue but "quality of life" for his remaining years on earth. He may try for his "big dream" before "it is too late." For example, he may quit his job as one of many editors of a publishing company to work full-time at being a novelist. Or he may decide to get off the "fast track" and move from city to country life. If the man has successfully "processed" his age-40 midlife crisis, he comes out on the other side with a more stable psychology and with a new appreciation for the transpersonal joys of life. If he does not process the midlife crisis successfully, it will only recur with more severity at the age-50 transition.

What Does Levinson Have to Say About Women? *The Seasons of a Woman's Life.* After Levinson completed his research into the lives of men, he decided to investigate the same kinds of questions in a population of women. What he has to say about women probably could have been predicted by every woman reader of this text past the age of 40. Levinson remarks frequently that the most overwhelming impression for him is the discovery of **gender splitting.** Levinson explains this term as meaning that frequently women give up their adolescent dreams of becoming "somebody" at the end of high school. Instead of pursuing their life dream, they give it up in favor of marriage, home, and family. This was true for 85 percent of women. In their thirties, these women experience something akin to having forfeited something by being "a good girl" and devoting their lives to husband and children. Convinced that they are no longer needed in the house to care for the children (who are leaving the nest), many go back to work. A few decide to go back to college to pursue their earlier dream of a career in the health professions, education, guidance and counseling, law enforcement, and so on. In our own classes, these women often demonstrate an eager motivation to learn and to achieve what they missed earlier by getting the top grades in class.

What about the other women who *did* pursue careers? Of the 15 percent who did pursue their life dreams, Levinson found them to be a somewhat happier group of women, although they too felt there was something missing from their lives. If they went wholeheartedly for a career and did not have children, they regretted not having children and tried to fill in that loss by developing personal relationships with nieces, nephews, stepchildren, and the like. If they did have one child before their biological clock ran out (one was about all they could manage with a career), they regretted not having given their child a brother or sister "to play with." If they "tried to have it all" by doing a part-time career and combining it with more family life, they admitted that by-and-large they neglected their families at certain times for the demands of their career. When these career women were asked if they would have given up their careers in order to have the families they dreamed of, most of them answered in the negative. They valued their careers even if they missed the traditional home-and-children role. Levinson's "bottom line" conclusion: No woman has a "perfectly happy life" any more than a man. Life is not perfect. Life is a matter of making choices. (Levinson, Levinson, & Johnson, 1994).

Erik Erikson's Eight-Stage Psychosocial Theory of Personality

In the years between World War I and World War II, literally thousands of studies were done on various aspects of human development. These piecemeal studies seemed a jumble of chaotic, confusing, and seemingly contradictory investigations. Then, midway through the century, a psychologist by the name of Erik Erikson pulled many of these theories and research studies together in an eight-stage model he called a psycho*social* theory of human development (1950). As he outlined his model, each stage has a specific **life crisis** which must be confronted and successfully resolved in order to achieve the **life task** of that age/stage. Successful achievement results in a positive personality trait, an achievement of character. Failure to achieve it results in a negative personality trait (see Table 3.2). Psychologists have found Erikson's model so useful in describing the life span experience that it is included in almost every text book dealing with any aspect of psychology.

Table 3.2   Erikson's Psychosocial Model of Development

	Age/Stage		Life Task	vs	Failure	Character Outcomes
I	(0–1 yrs.)	Infancy	Basic trust		Mistrust	Hope and drive
II	(1–3 yrs.)	Toddler years	Autonomy		Shame	Self-concept and willpower
III	(4–5 yrs.)	Play years	Initiative		Guilt	Direction and purpose
IV	(6–12yrs)	School years	Industry		Inferiority	Method and competence
V	(10–22?)	Adolescence	Identity		Role confusion	Devotion and fidelity
VI	(to 40?)	Early adulthood	Intimacy		Isolation	Affiliation and love
VII	(40–65?)	Middle adulthood	Generativity		Stagnation	Production and love
VIII	(65–?)	Old age	Ego integrity		Despair	Renunciation and wisdom

Stage I. Basic Trust versus Mistrust (Infancy). Noting that the human infant comes into the world a helpless entity, Erikson said that the child needs to develop **basic trust** in people to love him and to care for him physically and emotionally. This special kind of "mothering" provides the child with the emotional security that he is wanted and loved. Being wanted and loved leads to the positive character traits of *drive* and *hope*. He now has the *drive to grow* and the *hope that good things will continue to happen to him*. If the infant is neglected, abused, or rejected by the caretakers, he or she will become sickly or retarded physically, intellectually, and emotionally—if the child survives at all. We know that children left in orphanages and hospitals for too long can become emotionally withdrawn (Bowlby, 1969; Provence & Lipton, 1963). They may even "fail to thrive." Or they may develop a severe personality disorder that lasts all their lives.

Stage II. Autonomy versus Doubt and Shame (Toddler Years). Somewhere between seven months and two years, infants are accomplishing the life task of autonomy. **Autonomy** is the desire for self-control and the willpower to accomplish it. They are beginning to feed themselves, to crawl, and eventually to walk by themselves. In fact, they struggle for independence; wiggling out of their parents' arms to go where they want to go. They are gaining control of the bodily functions of bladder and bowel. They are learning to use language that gets them what they want ("Cookie!" will get them something good to eat). Now, too, children are learning they can say "No!" to the world, sometimes with such fury (as in a temper tantrum) that the world is forced to listen. But, says Erikson, it is equally important that children learn that the world can say NO to them too! No, they are not to hit their mommies. No, they may not throw food on the floor. If children do not learn to abide by the rules and regulations of society, they may remain aggressive and rebellious, always side-stepping the law and always a little bit "shady."

Figure 3.6 Erik Erikson. Constructed an 8-stage model of the life span.

On the other hand, if children learn to be "too obedient," they may allow and even encourage other people to control their lives.

Stage III. Initiative versus Guilt (Play Years). At about three years of age, children are acquiring initiative. **Initiative** means children are being able to organize the chaos of every-day events into meaningful organization. In contrast to the toddlers of Stage II who live in an eternal *here-and-now*, children in this stage are beginning to understand the concepts of morn-ing, noon, and night. They are getting a sense of their immediate geography and can play out-doors unsupervised (but "only on this side of the street—and don't cross the road!"). They can walk down to their friend's house, knock on the door, and say, "Can you play?" In fact, play-ing is the process by which they are developing, growing, and maturing through this stage. They are acquiring imagination and can invent games to play by themselves. They are also learning to play cooperatively with others. Part of this cooperative play is learning to share toys. They can even slide off Daddy's lap if little brother insists on being picked up. All of these learnings are leading to the lasting outcomes of (self-) direction and (his own) purpose of life. Erikson believes this is the beginning of becoming a *moral* person. If the child does not learn to be cooperative, he will remain forever at odds with his peers, trying to win out over them com-petitively and always aggressively "on the make." This is the person who wants always "to be in control" of personal relationships.

Stage IV. Industry versus Inferiority (School Years). Until children go to school, they are involved in the serious task of playing. Then around age six, they are sent to school. Their life task from six to adolescence, said Erikson, is **industry** (learning to work) to prepare them for adulthood. To achieve adult competency in Alaska, children must learn to build igloos. On the African veldt, they must learn to track the spoor of an animal. In the South Pacific, they must learn to fish. In our technological society, children must become literate. They must learn to read and write and do arithmetic so that as adults they can become employable and manage their personal affairs. Failure to achieve this life task of industry results in inferiority, which of course means not only a very negative self-esteem but a severe handicap throughout their adult life. If that sounds harsh, consider the plight of illiterate adults. They are unable to fill out a job application. They cannot read directions on a label or instructions on the simplest gadget. They cannot read a map. They cannot order meals from a restaurant menu. They may be very, very intelligent people, but they are functioning at the level of mental retardation.

Stage V. Identity versus Role Confusion (Adolescent Years). Erikson characterized adolescence as "the big crisis" in complex technological societies. One reason is that while young men and women may be biologically ready for sexual cohabitation, the rules of our society say they must not "give in" to this drive, and so they live in suspended psychobiolog-ical tension, sometimes for many years. A second reason is that while adolescents have the power and drives of an adult, they often still have the emotions of a child. In fact, many parents have said that when their children became teenagers they suddenly lost all their previous "sense and sensibility." The sweeping psychobiological changes that come about at puberty result in alternating bouts of giddy elation to crashing loss of self-confidence. The self-esteem of most high schoolers is so fragile that anything can seem a major catastrophe. Teenagers deem them-selves to be "fat" or "stupid" or "unattractive" or "unathletic" or "unpopular" (or whatever), the slightest negative comment or rejection will confirm that sense of unworthiness (Erikson, 1950).

The big task of adolescence is **identity.** In the hunt for their own identity, adolescents often reject their families and their families' values. But their newly developing adolescent self-identity is not yet very secure. They cannot stand alone. They cling to each other, copying each other's clothes, slang, musical preferences, hair styles, and so on. In the struggle to find their identity, they may try on many roles, adopting other people's mannerisms until they find a life style that fits their unique temperament. With the accomplishment of the task of identity, the lasting outcomes are devotion (to a sociopolitical movement or religious institution) and fidelity (toward their further education and life-career).

Stage VI. Intimacy versus Isolation (Young Adulthood). Adolescents think in terms of "I" and "me." The task for young people entering adulthood is learning to think in terms of "we," "ours," and "us," pronouns that have to do with spouses, children, and all our "significant others." Erikson called the life task of this stage **intimacy.** Intimacy involves sexual intimacy, of course, but it also involves psychological intimacy. We learn to share our hearts and minds and souls with other human beings. Intimacy involves not only sharing our joys and aspirations, but also our fears and anxieties. Intimacy makes possible genuine partnership in interpersonal relationships: friendships, life-partners, and warm relationships with co-workers. The lasting character traits are those of altruistic love and affiliation with others.

If adults retreat from intimacy, they are subject to an alienating sense of isolation and the inability to relate to others. They may develop protective devices to keep others at a distance. They may be described by others as snobbish, cold, rude, or even arrogant. They feel alienated from others and do not take part in community affairs, church, or social gatherings. They may even become reclusive, hiding in their houses away from society. They are also vulnerable to developing such sociological evils as prejudice and discrimination and to committing criminal acts, stemming from feelings of dissatisfaction and hatred.

Stage VII. Generativity versus Stagnation (After the Midlife Passage). After the midlife passage, the adult experiences the need to give something back to the community and to be of service to others. Erikson called this need **generativity,** helping younger persons become productive and creative. For some, it may be the simple task of enabling their adult children to buy a home and get started on their life-careers. It may take the form of fostering the creativity of younger persons at work and mentoring their leadership skills. It may take the form of leadership in state or local politics. Generativity prevents the stagnation of personality. The identification being accomplished in this life task is that of being a **transpersonal** human being, one who is aware of the universal themes of life and death, birth and rebirth, joy and suffering, and compassion for others. At this time, we become concerned not only for our own heirs, but for all the inheritors of our planet. This transpersonal identity results in the two characteristics of *production* and *care*. We are fostering others to be productive citizens and leaders who will be caretakers of the next generation.

Stage VIII. Ego Integrity versus Despair (Aging Years). The identification to be acquired in this last stage of the life span is that of being a spiritually integrated human being. We all know people who, as they got older, became wizened not only in body but also in mind and spirit. We are not talking here about the ravages of Alzheimer's disease. We are talking about those persons who became mean-spirited, grasping, bitter. Charles Dickens depicted such a person in his well-loved *A Christmas Carol* in the personage of Scrooge. It is not a small achievement to live out our lives with ego integrity; i.e., maintaining a sense of joy and peace despite the ending of life. Erikson calls the successful outcomes of this awareness *renunciation* and *wisdom*. When we meet older people who have achieved this understanding, we are awed by the way they are living out their lives. They have let go of the anxieties and strivings that mark the rest of the human life span (Kubler-Ross, 1975). They have gone beyond the plane of our common human foibles.

Are there any such older persons? Some of the readers may know such a person in their own lives and can affirm that such ego integrity is possible. Students often tell us that this person has been a guiding light for their own development. To those readers who do not know such a person, we point to some of the extraordinary historical figures of civilization who achieved this transpersonal level of awareness even in their final years: Socrates, Diogenes, Plato, Einstein, Albertus Magnus, Blaise Pascal, Benjamin Franklin, Carl Jung, Albert Schweitzer, Jean Piaget, all of whom worked joyfully into their eighties and nineties. We can also point to Mother Teresa of India; the American artists Grandma Moses and Georgia O'Keefe; Margaret Kuhn, who founded the Gray Panthers in her sixties and worked for the organization until well into her nineties; the Delaney sisters, two African-American women, an attorney and a physician, who wrote their joint autobiography around their one hundredth birthday; as well as two remarkable women who worked internationally from their sixties on, Eleanor Roosevelt and Margaret Albright.

Age-Locking versus Breaking Out of the Old Age Stereotype. All societies have divided the life span into distinctly different time zones, with distinctly different rights and responsibilities. The mere fact of age seems to mold social roles—and our society is no exception. And so it has been down the centuries and across cultures. From the time we enter school, we are divided into age zones, and certain tasks and behaviors are expected of us. Seating ourselves in a restaurant we may scan the people around us and think: *This place is full of old people. I don't think I'll come here again!* Or an older person may decide not to move into a certain apartment complex because there are too many college students there. From our adolescent or grown-up children, we may hear, "Mom, you aren't really going to wear that dress, it's too young for you. You'd look ludicrous!" or "Dad, you aren't really going back to school at your age!" We have tended to be stereotyped by our birthdays into an age-locking. Old age has traditionally been considered a "major touchstone by which individuals organize and interpret their own lives" (Neugarten, & Neugarten, 1987).

But that was in the early 1980s. Fortunately, we are beginning to break through such restraints. Because we are so much longer lived than previous generations, people in their middle age no longer believe they are on a fast trajectory toward old age and death. Menopausal depression is not a psychological necessity of a woman's midlife. In the forties and fifties, most men and women experience themselves as being at the height of their powers. With children "leaving the nest," parents are freer to be themselves and to revel in their increased leisure. The traditional role of grandparents has altered in many ways from the days when Grandma spent her time in the kitchen baking cookies and Grandpa puttered around the house. Grandparents, these days, are having more fun, traveling more places, engaging in more activities than ever before. They may take a trip out west in a recreational vehicle or a cruise in a Caribbean "love ship" or go to Disneyworld with the grandchildren. Old age (as we have known it in the past) doesn't look like it used to. When their adult children chide them with, "For heaven's sake, act your age," they respond, "We are." However, to live healthily and happily in our older age, we must prepare now in terms of living a healthful life style, build a firm financial retirement, maintain an emotional/social network of friends and family and create an interesting post-retirement career.

Box 3.9

SCENARIO REVISITED
What Can Sarakate Do With Janie?

Since that first visit by Sarakate to see Jonnimae (see the opening scenario, Box 3.1), Sarakate has come often to visit and discuss children. The two sisters are presently in the park watching Janie and the baby.

Jonnimae: Janie is certainly being a loving older sister now. She looks so cute wheeling her baby brother in his carriage.

Sarakate: She is *now* but she still sometimes gets whiney and sulks or pulls a tantrum if I pick up the baby and don't have time for her.

Jonnimae: But only sometimes?

Sarakate: Yes . . . and only when she's tired. I have to admit that there's been a big change in her since I started paying more attention to her.

Jonnimae: Whatever you've been doing has certainly made a big change in her.

Sarakate: Well, after what you told me about how jealousy is normal in kids, I stopped thinking that Janie is just being a bad girl. You told me she was just trying to get some of the attention she lost when the baby was born. So I figured out ways to pay her attention when the baby was sleeping or on his bottle. Don't laugh at this, Jonnimae—I even bought her a bottle of her own. And she drinks from it too.

Jonnimae: Laugh! I think that's wonderful.

Sarakate: Do you think that will keep her babyish all her life? I wouldn't want to do that.

Jonnimae: I asked my psychology teacher about that too and he said not to worry about that. She'll give it up when she's ready.

Sarakate: You know, Jonnimae, I feel so guilty about having whipped Janie. Only that's the way we were raised and I didn't know any different.

Jonnimae: I feel the same way. I'm learning so much about children in my class. I only wish I had known all this stuff earlier when my kids were younger. I spanked them too.

Sarakate: Do you think I've ruined Katie's personality? You know, like Freud said, that our personalities are formed by the time we're six years old? Do you think my whipping has ruined her for good?

Jonnimae: I asked my psychology teacher that too. He said adults make many mistakes with children but as long as we have loved them and not abused them, they'll forgive us our mistakes. (*Smiling*) And it seems to me right now that Janie is looking like a happy child. You couldn't have done too many things wrong. She's even sharing her cookie with her brother. You can't ask much more than that at her age.

IMPORTANT TERMS AND CONCEPTS TO KNOW

age-locking	id	midlife	pleasure-pain
anal	identity	neurosis	psychosexual
biases	individuation	obsessive-compulsive	psychosocial
competence	inferiority-superiority	Oedipus/Oedipal	restraints
ego	intimacy	oral	sibling rivalry
Elektra	latency	passive-dependent	stereotypes
four	libido	perfect	superego
gemeinschaftsgefühl	libidinal	permanent	transpersonal
generativity	life crisis	phallic	trust
genital	life task		

MAKE YOUR OWN CHAPTER SUMMARY BY FILLING IN THE BLANKS BELOW

Use the "Important Terms and Concepts to Know" to fill in the blanks below.

Sigmund Freud developed a _____ theory of development which consists of five stages. In the _____ stage, the baby is an unconscious being which Freud called the _____ , and which is ruled by the _____ principle. He also posited a strong _____ drive which is socialized in the second or _____ stage with the beginning of toilet-training and weaning. In this stage, the child is introjecting the rules and regulations of society, which coalesce as the _____ (which Freud equated with the conscience). Throughout the individual's life, the id (with its constant striving to express biological urges) and the superego (the warnings and inhibitions of society) wage eternal warfare. It is the job of the _____ (the only conscious aspect of the personality) to hold them in check and to maintain a satisfactory balance between them. In the _____ stage, the child develops a strong attachment to the parent of the opposite sex, called the _____ complex in male children and the _____ complex in female children. The last two stages are called the _____ stage (when the libidinal drive is more quiescent) and the _____ stage (when the individual is capable of fully adult sexuality). Freud helped us to understand that if children suffer childhood trauma, they will not develop normally but be emotionally fixated at an early stage of emotional development, which he called a _____ .

The neo-Freudians were those physicians, psychiatrists, and psychologists who, while agreeing with Freud's libidinal theory, believed that other factors also influence human personality.

Alfred Adler stressed the need for _____ , and described the _____ complex, which is the way many people overcompensate for their feelings of inadequacy. He also believed that human beings have a counterthrust to their personality, which seeks to affiliate with others in loving and kind ways, which he called _____ .

Carl Jung posited _____ great stages. He helped us understand the "second half of life," ushered in by the _____ crisis at around age 40. At this point in his life, the man suffers from what Jung called spiritual bankruptcy and his task in life is to develop _____ values. If a person resolves the age-40 transition successfully, he begins to live according to his needs and values and less according to other people's values, a process called _____ .

Daniel Levinson validated Jung's midlife crisis, but added that we seem to undergo transitions at the end of every decade. No life structure, he said, can ever be _____ or _____ . Throughout our lives, we are in a constant process of structuring, destructuring, and restructuring.

Erik Erikson developed an eight-stage model of the life span, which he called a _____ theory of development, each stage having its special _____ to resolve and _____ to achieve. The first life task is that of basic _____ , which needs loving "mothering." The big crisis in American society, said Erikson, comes at stage V, when the adolescent boy and girl are learning the task of _____ . The task of young adulthood is _____ , when we learn to say "we" instead of the adolescent "I." After the midlife crisis, the person's task is _____ , the willingness to become mentors to the next generation and to work for other suprapersonal values. We are living longer and healthier but to live _____ , we must prepare now for that future.

Age Zones are the expressed cultural _____ we have toward persons who differ from us in age. Fortunately, we are breaking out of this _____ and living not just longer but more youthful lives.

4 COGNITIVE AND MORAL DEVELOPMENT
How We Become Thinking Adults and Moral/Ethical People

(1896–1990)

Using the research technique of naturalistic observation, Piaget pioneered the study of the cognitive and moral/ethical development of children.

Box 4.1
WHERE IS OUR MIND?
What Is it We Call Thinking? How Does Morality Develop?

Professor Weitzman writes the three questions above on the blackboard and then turns to the class.

Professor Weitzman: Who wants to try to answer these questions?

Eduardo: That's easy. The mind is in the brain of course. We think in our brains.

Professor Weitzman: Suppose we were deaf and blind and could not smell or taste or feel. Could we still think?

Eduardo: No. The brain needs information from our senses. If we didn't have senses, we couldn't think.

Professor Weitzman: So you're saying that our minds are also in our eyes, ears, tongue, nose and skin?

Eduardo: What? Oh, I . . . I don't know. Maybe. Yeah, I guess so.

Professor Weitzman: That's what John Locke, the British philosopher/psychologist, concluded 250 years ago. He said we are born a *tabula rasa* or "blank slate." Slates were what school boys took to school to do their lessons on with chalk. When we are born, we have nothing in our "minds." Then over time, the infant's mind absorbs sensory data from our vision and our hearing and all our other senses that coalesce in our minds as "ideas." When we are little, we

have only a few ideas. As we get older, we get more and more ideas in our "minds" until we are adult thinkers. Is that your model, Eduardo?

Eduardo: Well, more or less, yes.

Professor Weitzman: Actually Eduardo's model goes back almost 2,500 years. Locke had taken his model from Aristotle except that Aristotle had used the analogy of a wax tablet because that is what they used for writing in Greek times—a tablet that was made from bee's wax. People wrote on the wax tablet and when they were finished they could simply smooth it over and use it again like Etch-a-Sketch. (*class laughter*)

Eduardo: It seems like everything always goes back to the Greeks somehow.

Professor Weitzman: Actually, Aristotle differed from other Greek philosophers who thought that the mind was located in the heart. Consider their reasoning. When we are excited about something, our hearts pound. To this day, we emphasize a vow or a declaration to the flag by touching our heart. Furthermore, the heart is magnificently red and warm and pulsating. The heart seems a lot more alive than the brain, which just seemed to be motionless like a dull gray mushroom. So it was a radical idea for Aristotle to

| **Box 4.1** | **WHERE IS OUR MIND? (Continued)**
What Is it We Call Thinking? How Does Morality Develop? |

suggest thinking takes place in the brain. Anyway, John Locke built on Aristotle's thesis and for almost 300 years philosophic science accepted this model for how we develop our thinking ability. This model is called the quantitative model. It seemed logical and self-evident and most people, like Eduardo here, accepted it. Then early in the twentieth century, along came a Swiss psychologist who said, "No, that's not quite right." And the name of the psychologist . . . anybody know it?

Alec Riordan: We just studied him in my algebra class. Jean Piaget! He's sure hard to understand.

Professor Weitzman: That's because he proposed a very radical new theory that was hard even for social scientists to understand. We call this newer model the *qualitative* theory of cognitive development. In the upcoming chapter you will study this theory and another of his theories; namely, how a child develops his moral/ethical character. It was such a radical theory that it took some decades before American psychologists could take it seriously. Furthermore, Piaget did not write in English, and it took a few years before we got good translations of his work. But that

wasn't the only factor that impeded our acceptance of Piaget. We are a large country. We have a large population. When we do a study, we try to get as large a sample as possible. Piaget drew his conclusions from small samples through simply observing children's reactions. We call this research method by the term **naturalistic observation.** But the most serious criticism probably was that some of his observations were of his own children. Why do you suppose that made us so nervous?

Li Ho: Bias! That is a grave criticism. We are taught in my science courses to be very careful how we go about selecting our population and samples.

Professor Weitzman: And that's absolutely right. But what we did not appreciate was how keen an observer Piaget was. You see, he had been a naturalist long before he became a psychologist and he was very used to observing nature—even as a child. He was such a good observer that he had his first scientific paper published when he was only 11 years old—on a rare species of insect. Genius frequently shows its promise very early on.

Jean Piaget: The Pioneer of Cognitive Development

The beginning of any new field of science seems to need an intellectual giant to pioneer a foothold. Astronomy had its Galileo. Physics had its Isaac Newton. Emotional development had its Sigmund Freud. In the area of **cognition** (the professional term for *thinking*) that giant turned out to be Jean Piaget. Now no textbook in psychology, education, mathematics, science, philosophy, or moral/ethical development can ignore his contributions. Moreover, said Piaget, if we want our children to grow up to be *moral* adults, we need to understand how they become *thinking* adults. Why? *Because,* said Piaget, *cognitive development and moral development go hand-in-hand* (Piaget, 1973).

Piaget's Qualitative Four-Stage Model of Cognitive (Thinking) Development

What Piaget was saying is as follows: Children do *not* have the same cognitive processes (thinking) as adults. They may use the same words we use but they do not *think* like we do. They do not have the same perceptions as we do. They do not reason as we do. In point of fact, their entire worldview is alien to ours. According to Piaget, adult cognition develops in four stages, which he called **organizations of mind**—four evolutionary leaps of consciousness that may even reflect the development of the human race (see Table 4.1).

Table 4.1   Piaget's Age/Stage Model of Cognitive and Moral Development

Cognitive Age/Stage	Cognitive Limitations	Cognitive Achievements	Moral Age/Stage	Morality
Stage 1.	No mediation.	Object permanence.	Amoral.	No conscious awareness of any sort.
Sensory-Motor (Birth to 2 years)	Only reflexive schemas (Example: see-reach-grab-put-in-mouth)	Constancies of size, shape, color. Symbolic function is beginning. Beginning of time: past (memory) and future (imagination).		
Stage 2. Pre-operations (2 to 7/8 yrs.)	Cognitions are concrete, functional, egocentric, animistic. Cannot decentrate. Worldview is magical. Metaphors are not understood.	Can mediate one idea but one idea only. Can make choices. Symbolic function makes language possible. "A puddle is to jump in."	**Stage 1. Moral realism or moral restraint**	No real morality. If child is good has learned obedience. Does not understand why rules exist. Justice without mercy. Centrated on effect.
Stage 3. Concrete Operations (7/8 to 10/12) yrs.	Thinking is concrete and many abstract concepts (terms such as freedom, democracy, allegiance) will not be understood.	Can mediate two ideas, making possible mathematical operations. Child can decentrate. Worldview is less magical, more realistic.		
Stage 4. Formal Operations (11/12 yrs. to adulthood)	Most creative in areas of expertise; less creative in other areas.	Is able to perform hypothetical reasoning which makes possible true creativity and scientific thinking. Comprehension of abstractions (human rights, due process, compassion)	**Moral relativity or moral cooperation**	Ushered in by rule-making. Children are learning that people make rules for good of all. Centrated on rule-making. Centrated on "fair" and "not fair." Morality is becoming internalized. Can now temper justice with mercy.

1. The Sensory-Motor Stage (birth to 2 years). Like Freud, Piaget regarded the new-born baby as a rather unorganized complex of primitive but very strong reflexes, as seen in the activities of *reaching for objects* and *grabbing them,* etc. During this stage, the baby has no **mediation;** i. e., the baby does not have any perceptions or ideas or thoughts or in his head. Well, if the baby does not have any mediation, what does it have? It has a sensory-motor organization of "mind," which means that it *must* respond *motorically* (physically) to whatever stimulus breaks through to its sensory awareness. Sensory stimuli can be internal (coldness, wetness, hunger, pain) or external (light, sound, or a caretaker's face moving across its visual field). An example should help clarify the term *sensory-motor.*

Let us suppose that we are dangling a string in front of a four-month-old kitten so as to catch its (sensory) visual attention. Can that kitten just watch that string? No, that kitten must respond (motorically) by trying to catch it with its paws. It is a natural animal instinct or reflex—call it what you like. Similarly, if we dangle a set of keys in front of a four-month-old baby so as to catch her (sensory) visual awareness, the baby must respond (motorically) by reaching-grabbing-and-putting-them-in-her-mouth (if she can). Neither the kitten nor the baby has any choice in the matter—no choice but to respond. However, during the sensory-motor stage, the baby will be developing many sensory/perceptual abilities which will make mediation possible by two years of age. These abilities include the development of the *constancies, object permanence,* the ability to make *symbolic connections,* and finally the beginning of *memory.*

Box 4.2

**RESEARCH METHODOLOGY
Naturalistic Observation**

Piaget's observations of the schoolboys at play (p. 91) during recess is a good example of the research method called naturalistic observation. *The value of naturalistic observation is that the subjects are being observed not in the artificial laboratory situation but in their natural habitat: real people, real children, real animals—all behaving in natural ways.*

On the Plus Side. Naturalistic observations frequently reveal behaviors that are not observed in the laboratory. A prime example is that of Jane Goodall's observations of chimpanzees in the wild. Until her naturalistic study, no one had observed chimps devising tools with which to scoop up ants and termites. Chimps had never done that in the zoos or university laboratories. People (and that includes children) act quite differently in the artificiality of the laboratory. Moreover, when people know they are being observed their behavior changes. So researchers devise many ways to observe subjects without their knowing, such as using two-way mirrors, tape recorders, and movie cameras. We need to mention also that all research in the sciences must begin with naturalistic observation.

On the Minus Side. The biggest disadvantage of naturalistic observation is the lack of scientific control. There are so many variables interacting with each other in "real life" that the significant variables may be overlooked or misinterpreted. There is no way to be sure of what is cause and what is effect. For example: Millions of dollars are being spent in naturalistic observation of courtrooms to discover what factors influence jury members to make their judgments of innocent or guilty. But in the end, no one can say for sure what leads to the jury's decision. Is it the demeanor of the defendant? The sincerity (or lack of it) of the witnesses? The testimony of "experts"? The eloquence of the attorneys in their final summation? The demographic variables of the jury members? The judge's instructions to the jury? Are the jury members being influenced by the general atmosphere in the court? Has the defendant already been tried by the media? Many factors are involved and simple naturalistic observation cannot determine the cause-and-effect relationships.

The Development of the Constancies, Object Permanence and Stranger Anxiety.   In their first few weeks of life, objects enter and leave a baby's visual field without any meaning. As the weeks and months go by, certain face-objects (bottle-object and Mommie-face-object) will come to have meaning (*MMMMMmmmm . . . milk*), but many visual objects still simply come into the baby's visual field and out again without much connectedness. Then, little by little, the objects begin to have meaning. Sights and sounds become connected. Objects, colors, shapes, size take on meaning. These are called the constancies. Then, Piaget observed that somewhere between the sixth and eighth month, the baby develops a dim awareness that objects exist even if they cannot be seen, a cognitive skill which Piaget called **object permanence.** Piaget had observed that by eight months, most babies will engage in searching behavior for an object they cannot see any more. If you take away the keys with which they have been playing, they continue to look for them—at least for a few seconds. (More recent investigations have shown that object permanence comes earlier than Piaget could determine—not because Piaget was inaccurate, but because we have more sophisticated technology with which to measure a baby's visual focus. An interesting consequence of object permanence is the development of **stranger anxiety.** Since infants can now recognize the familiar face-objects of their immediate family, they are also able to recognize unfamiliar face-objects. Furthermore, if these unfamiliar face-objects come too close, small babies may get frightened and begin to cry. It is a good idea to introduce new people slowly now to help the baby get used to the new face-objects (see Tip 4.1.)

The Beginning of Memory.   Object permanence is demonstrated by the baby's *searching behavior.* But this same searching behavior for a hidden object, said Piaget, also demonstrates the development of *past memory*—if only for a few seconds duration. By eleven months of age, Piaget noted, infants are also developing a sense of *future* time. By way of illustration, Piaget provided this real-life observation: One day, his youngest child, Lucienne, was watching her mother put on her hat. Suddenly Lucienne began to cry. Lucienne was now capable of recognizing that *Mommy is here now but she will soon be gone*—a demonstration of her ability to construct a future time. This ability to think in future tense may be the single most important distinction between human beings and other life forms. Why so? Because this cognitive skill leads to the cognitive abilities we call imagination, planning, logic, creativity, inductive reasoning, and hypothesis-making (Piaget, 1970).

The Development of the Symbolic (Semiotic) Ability.   Lucienne's crying behavior also indicates another development; that is, the beginning of the *symbolic (semiotic) function:* "Mother-putting-on-her-hat" had become the symbol for "Mommy-is-leaving." The development of the symbolic function is another achievement of *homo sapiens* and will ultimately lead to the "miracle of language."

Tip 4.1 The Constancies Are Not Necessarily a Permanent Achievement: They Can Be Lost! Just because we achieve the constancies of size, shape, color, etc. in infancy, does not mean they are permanent achievements. People who are in the midst of an acute schizophrenic episode can lose these constancies. People and objects can become distorted, magnified, or seem shrunken. People who suffer from diseases of the nervous system, as in Alzheimer's disease, can also suffer loss of their constancies and lose their perceptions of time and space. Furthermore, in times of great distress, any of us can have visual hallucinations in which objects and people become distorted and unreal.

The infant is acquiring many symbolic sight-and-sound connections over the next two years, like "Mommy" and "Daddy" and "All gone" and "Cookie." In fact, the average two-year-old will have developed up to a hundred symbolic connections for speech and be able to comprehend several hundred more (Clark, 1991). By two years of age, so many of these symbolic connections will have occurred that the infant will undergo an evolutionary leap to the second organization of mind—the *stage of **preoperations***. Why did Piaget believe this transition to be an evolution in the child's consciousness? Because, said Piaget, it is at this second stage that the human species is capable of mediation (thinking).

2. The stage of preoperations: The ability to mediate one idea in mind (2 years to 7/8 years). By two years of age, the child is capable of **mediation** which is to say that the child can now hold one idea in mind. This new ability allows children to finally have some choices in their lives, at least to the extent of agreeing or disagreeing with what is going on. (*Do you want a cookie? Yes! Do you want to take a nap? NO!*). Before this stage, the child could only cry if unhappy; now the child can agree or refuse to do something. The two-year-old can now say NO!— or express it in a temper tantrum. This ability to make a choice is not insignificant. *Piaget equates choice with intelligence.* According to Piaget, the more choices a life-form has, the more intelligent it is (see Tip 4.2). *But the preoperative child can hold one idea in mind and one idea only.* Don't try to give a three-year old two commands at the same time (*Sally, go get your other shoe and pick out a pair of socks to wear*). By the time Sally has found her other shoe under the bed, she may run and give it to you. Picking out a pair of socks has faded from mind.

By four years of age, the child may have as many as several thousand words in his speaking vocabulary. Because he has become such a grand conversationalist, adults may think he is capable of adult reasoning. Such is not the case, said Piaget. Although the four-year-old has an astonishingly good grasp of language, he has a very different **phenomenology** (thought processes and worldview) from adults. Among other properties, the child's thinking is concrete, functional, egocentric, and animistic (Piaget, 1970). Let's consider these properties one at a time.

Concrete Thinking. A child's concrete thinking means that children have a very literal phenomenology. For example, suppose you take your eight-year-old little boy and your four-year-old preoperative little girl to the supermarket with you. If you are like many parents, you may say, "If you are good in the store and don't whine and fuss, you may each have a quarter to spend." Unthinkingly, you give your only quarter to your four-year-old little girl and two dimes and a nickel to your eight-year-old little boy. You explain to your preoperative four-year-old that her quarter is worth the same as her brother's two dimes and a nickel. Does she understand that concept? No, she very probably does not! Very soon, tears may be streaming down her face. After all, her brother got three monies and she got only one!

The preoperative child's concrete thinking also means they will not "catch on" to jokes or understand metaphors. "Oh, dear," said a lady to her husband, "The sewing machine has developed a birdie. We'll have to take it to the repair shop." Of course, what the lady meant

---

Tip 4.2 Piaget: Intelligence as Availability of Choices. Piaget believes that the more choices we can make, the more "intelligent" we are. A baby can only cry if it is in pain. A two-year-old who gets hurt can either cry *or* run to someone for help. A ten-year-old can cry *or* run to someone for help *or* apply a band-aid. An adult can cry *or* go to someone for help *or* apply medicine *or* go to the emergency room. Creative intelligence for Piaget is simply the number of other possibilities and alternatives we are capable of pursuing.

was that the sewing machine had developed a loud, shrill whining noise. A few minutes later, she discovered her five-year-old son staring sadly at the sewing machine. Realizing that her son had taken her words at their literal meaning, she quickly explained that there wasn't really a bird in the sewing machine, that "a birdie" was simply another way of saying "noise like a bird." (For other examples of a child's thinking, see Box 4.3.)

Functional Thinking. Functional thinking means that children understand the objects in their world in ways that make sense to them. The function of a bed is to sleep on it. The function of a glass is to drink from it. The function of a spoon is to eat with it. All well and good. But now ask a little boy what a mud puddle is for, and he answers, "To splash in." And what are rocks for? To throw of course. Ask a little girl what sand is for and she answers, "To make sand castles." At this age, children are making sense in the best way they can. They are seeking to discover what philosophic scientists call "the nature of things."

Egocentric Thinking. Be careful of Piaget's use of the term, **egocentric.** He does not mean it as we generally use it; that is, someone who is so self-centered that he thinks only of himself and rarely of other people. What Piaget means by *egocentrism* is the special worldview of the child which Piaget phrased as follows: A child is only able to understand his own perspective and not the perspective of other people. The common Piagetian example goes like this: Suppose you place a four-year-old child in front of a table with several objects on it, objects such as a ball, a book, and a toy car. Ask him to hold the teddy bear while you arrange the objects so that the ball is nearest to him and the toy car is nearest to you. If you ask the child which object is nearest to him and his teddy bear, he will correctly say "the ball." So far, so good. But let's take this example a bit further. Ask him to let you hold the teddy bear. When he gives you the teddy bear, you ask the child what is nearest to his teddy bear *now.* He will still say "the ball." Unlike adults, he cannot perceive the world from any perspective but his own (see Figure 4.1). Here is a real-life example you may have had. A four-year old runs in excitedly with a picture she has drawn and holds it up for you to see. But she is holding the blank side toward you and the picture side toward herself. So you say, "Hold the picture so we can see it." What does she do now? She doesn't turn it around; she simply holds it higher, the blank side still facing you (see Tip 4.3).

Figure 4.1 The Preoperative Child's Egocentric Worldview. When asked what is closest to the teddy bear the adult is holding, the child will point to the ball. He can only see the world from his perspective.

Animistic Thinking. Primitive peoples of the past (and some traditional societies even today) held an *animistic* view of life. **Animism** is defined as the belief that *natural phenomena have supernatural causation.* Rivers, mountains, and clouds have special gods or demons that cause floods or landslides or thunderstorms. Cause-and-effect is magical and inanimate objects have animate life. For example, in the nineteenth century, when the Easter Islanders were asked how their 40-ton long-eared statues got to the seashore (so many miles from the quarry), the Easter Islanders replied, "They walked there of their own accord." Children demonstrate this same animistic thinking: *Q: How did the cookies get into your room?*

Box 4.3

STUDENTS VERBATIM
The Concrete (Literal) Thinking of Preoperational Children

Male (17 years): I'll never forget this because I got spanked for it. Once I called my father a "smart Alec." I thought I was saying something nice, like he was really very smart.

Female (20 years): When I was young, I was really confused by the term "turning over a new leaf." I knew it meant something good so whenever I was outside with my mother, I kept turning over leaves. She thought I was looking for bugs.

Male (24 years): I had no idea what people meant when they said they had a "frog in their throat." I really used to imagine a frog and I hoped it wouldn't happen to me.

Male (24 years): When I was in kindergarten, I didn't understand the difference between "on accident" and "on purpose" which really got me into trouble. One day, I knocked a kid down while we were at recess. When the teacher asked me if I did it *on accident* or *on purpose*, I said "on purpose." I got sent to the corner for the rest of the day.

Female (42 years): When I was between four and seven, they still used radios a lot. I believed that radios actually had people in them talking and singing. It was always a mystery how all those people could fit into such a small box.

Male (22 years): I misunderstood the word *divorce* when I was about five. That was when my parents got a divorce. I must have asked why Daddy was leaving, because I remember my mother saying, "Because of the divorce." I thought it was some type of monster that was driving my daddy away from me.

Male (19 years): When my little brother went out to play and come back in, my mother would ask him, "And where have you been, pray tell?" But one day, he got really angry when she asked him and shouted, "Nowhere! And stop calling me *Praytell!* My name is *Joey.*"

A: I dunno. I guess they just got there. It is a world where the witches and ghosts of Halloween make a lot of sense and where things "go bump in the night." Or consider this example of animistic thinking: A little girl gets her hand caught between the door and the jamb. After the screaming and tears are over, what does she do? She goes over to the door and kicks it! *There, you bad door, take that and that and that!*

3. Concrete operations (from 7/8 years to about 11/12 years). In this third stage of cognition, children are losing their magical view of the world and their understanding of *cause-and-effect* is becoming more realistic. They are acquiring a *few* adult cognitive abilities, but *only a few.* If we don't recognize the cognitive limitations of this stage, we may misconstrue the child's behaviors. Even worse, we may make cognitive demands of which the child is not yet capable—with disastrous results. On the other hand, a child at this stage will be able to enjoy jokes (primitive ones at least) that depend on the double images of puns. *Q: Why is Goofy standing on the corner with bread in his hand? A: He's waiting for a traffic jam.* (The child can now hold in mind both the image of the *jam* we eat and the image of a traffic jam at the same time.)

Tip 4.3 Why Children Seem to Say Cruel Things to Each Other. Remember that cognitive development and moral development go hand-in-hand. Here is an everyday example most readers will be familiar with. We have already described the preoperative child's egocentric thinking, the inability to view the world from any other perspective but his or her own. This self-centered perspective is one of the reasons children sometimes say "cruel" things to each other. The preoperative child may say to a little girl with crossed eyes, "Boy, are you funny looking!" To a younger brother or sister who can't do something, "You're sure dumb! I'm not going to play with a dummy any more." Children of this age cannot yet comprehend how they would feel if someone said the same thing to them. In other words, children have not yet developed the capacity to understand another's feelings.

The Achievement of the Conservations. The ability to hold two concrete ideas or images in mind results in the achievement of conservations. In order to grasp fundamental mathematical processes, to comprehend number sets and simple algebraic equations, and to grasp scientific principles, the elementary school child needs to have developed what Piaget called the *conservations*. Conservation is the recognition that although *something may change in form, its essence remains the same;* that is to say, that the certain properties are retained (conserved). For example, even though water, ice, and steam appear to be different, they are different only in form, not in the essential aspect of H_2O.

Let's apply conservation to the psychology of a four-year-old preoperative little girl and her eight-year-old brother who is now firmly in the stage of concrete operations. Suppose you have two beakers of orange juice that are identical and you want to divide them equally into a tall, thin glass and into a short, fat glass (see Figure 4.2). Right in front of your two children, you pour the two equal beakers into the tall thin glass and the short fat glass right up to the brim of both glasses. You had better give the tall, thin glass to your four-year-old and not the short fat glass. Why? Because your eight-year-old will understand that both glasses (the tall thin one and the short fat one) have an equal amount of orange juice, but your four-year-old will not. If you give her the short, fat glass, she will think you have given her brother more orange juice because his is the taller glass. Preoperative children, said Piaget, are **centrated** on the two properties of height and length. Your eight-year-old has now achieved the ability to **decentrate** and to remember the previous image of the two beakers containing equal volumes of orange juice, but your four-year-old cannot understand this. She has not yet achieved *conservation of liquid amount.* **Centration** is the term Piaget used for concentrating (centering or focusing) on one property to the exclusion of others.

Here's another example. Let us suppose you have two clay balls of equal mass. You give one clay ball to your little preoperative girl and you keep one clay ball. Now ask your little girl: *Whose clay ball is bigger? Yours or mine? Or are they both the same?* Your four-year-old will probably answer quite correctly: *Both the same.* So far so good. But now you take your clay ball and roll it out into a long, thin snake and ask the same questions. What does she answer? You've got it! She answers that *your* clay is larger because it is longer. She has not yet achieved *conservation of substance.* There are many conservations to be achieved in the stage of concrete operations. But eventually the child will achieve them, laying the groundwork for the next and final stage, the stage of formal operations.

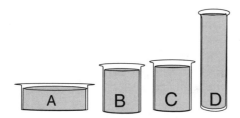

Figure 4.2   Conservation of Liquid Amount. The preoperative child is centrated on height and length. If we show a four-year-old that beakers marked B and C have the same amount of liquid in it, she will understand that. But if we pour beakers B and C into beakers A and D to the brim right in front of her and ask which has more, the child will answer D. D is taller and that seems to the child to have more than the short, fat beaker A. The child in the stage of preoperations cannot remember the previous image of two beakers (B and C) as having had an equal volume of liquid.

Achievement of the Conservations and the Ability to do Arithmetic. There are many types of conservations to be learned during this stage, including the conservations of number, length, area, weight, volume. They do not all arrive at the same time. They are achieved one-by-one at different ages between 7 and 11 to 12 years of age. The importance of understanding the development of these conservations is this: Until the child achieves these conservations, she will not be able to understand even the simplest mathematical processes or grasp elementary laws of physics. If we insist on having her learn a mathematical process before she achieves the necessary conservation, she will simply get discouraged at her failure to understand. Furthermore, her discouragement will *generalize* (spread) to everything having to do with mathematics. Text books on education are now urging teachers-in-training to make sure the child has the necessary conservations before demanding that he understand, for example, the logic of number sets and beginning algebraic equations. If we do attempt to teach these processes, we will be setting the child up to hate math (see Tip 4.4).

The Ability to Perform Multiple Classifications: A Larger Worldview.   The school age child is now developing a larger worldview. If we were to give a box full of objects to our preoperational four-year-old and ask her to pick out everything that has to do with eating, she will pick out the toy objects that represent vegetables, fruits, and candy, etc. Around 7 or 8 years, she will also be able to pick out plates and cups and silverware. In another year or two, she will pick out farm animals and fruit trees. As she approaches eleven years of age, she will understand that grocery stores and bakeries and ice cream shops can also be included. Her extended multiple classification system will enable her to understand number sets, the reversibility of simple algebra, biological phyla and species, etc. She will also be developing an understanding of abstract nouns as compared to concrete nouns.

Limitations of the Concrete Operational Stage.   The child in this stage is also much less egocentric. She is more able to understand another point of view besides her own. But, while the child is giving evidence of more adult logic, there are still certain limitations to her thinking. For example, children in this stage are still not able to engage in inductive logic. They cannot derive a new hypothesis from observed events. If we insist that they do so, we will make them "hate science," because they couldn't carry out the assignment. They can appreciate ecological world problems (and in fact are quite worried about them, these days) but we should avoid asking them to dream up new solutions—that is just simply beyond them. They can pick out the best possible answer in a multiple choice question, but most children of this age will lose heart if we require abstract essay answers from them. Educational psychologists advise against enrolling children in academically rigorous schools which demand sophisticated skills before their cognitive processes have reached the needed level of maturity (Elkind, 1989).

4. The Stage of Formal Operations.   The big leap to adult consciousness is the ability to think abstractedly, a powerful property of the stage of **formal operations.** With this ability, adolescents will be able to make deductive and inductive hypotheses from observations they have made. They will be able to make repairs on their bikes or cars that they have never come up against before. They will be able to think up new ideas and demonstrate true creativity. In fact, they are becoming problem-solvers. Piaget described this new ability as being able to derive new operations from previous ones. With their developing abstract abilities, adolescents can

---

Tip 4.4 Who Hates Math? As a case in point, have the teacher ask members of the class to raise their hands if they "hate math." We bet the majority of the class will raise their hands. And why? Piaget would say we insisted on teaching certain mathematical concepts before these students had achieved the necessary conservation. Piaget would ask: *Why must we hurry the child by pushing him to learn when he is just not ready?* In three, four, or five months time, the child will have achieved the conservation necessary and solve the arithmetic problem with ease and liking.

appreciate the similes and metaphors of literature (especially those of love poetry when they develop a crush on a school mate). Adolescents are also developing the ability to see themselves more objectively in terms of society. They can identify themselves according to their gender, their ethnic roots, and their religious orientation, quite apart from the orientation of their family. (*My family is racist but I think that's wrong!*) They are beginning to make independent judgments in terms of their own identity and independent choices in terms of their own life (*My dad wants me to go into business, but I think I'd rather teach*).

Piaget's Theory of Moral/Ethical Development: A Two-Stage Theory

After his monumental work on cognitive development, Piaget could have spent the rest of his scientific career continuing to fine-tune his cognitive model. But Piaget was concerned about something we are all concerned about now: How children develop their moral/ethical character; which is to say, how they develop their ideas of "right" and "wrong." Freud had attributed our "character" to our emotional development. Piaget approached the area of moral/ethical development from another perspective altogether. One of the notations we made earlier in this chapter was that Piaget became firmly convinced that cognitive development and moral development go hand-in-hand. In other words, *children cannot reach a certain level of moral/ethical development until they have attained a certain level of intellectual functioning.* For example, we can't expect a child of five to have the same kind of compassion as we adults do for people who are economically or physically disabled. In fact, a person with a disfigurement of some sort may even frighten them. As a result of his research, Piaget proposed a two-stage theory of moral/ethical development.

1. The Stage of Moral Realism (also called the Stage of Restraint). Before the age of ten, said Piaget, the child has no real morality. Children as young as three years of age can learn the rules of the house. But children obey these rules simply because they must, not because they understand the reasons for the rules. Why should he not go out into the street? Because he might be hit by a car? Well, he doesn't really believe that can happen to him. If he obeys the injunction not to play in the street, it is because Mama said so! Besides, he might get caught—and that means trouble! Before the age of ten, said Piaget, children have not developed any real internalized code of ethical principles. If children are "good," it is because they have developed **obedience.**

Centrated on Effect, Not Cause. An interesting difference between adults and children is this: While adults focus on **causation,** young children are centrated on **effect.** What that means is that adults want to know *why* a person did something while young children look only at *how much damage was done.* For example, consider the following dialogue between an adult and a five-year-old.

Q: A poor boy and a rich boy both stole bread. What should happen to them?
A: They should go to jail.
Q: But the rich boy had money and the poor boy didn't.
A: Then he should ask his mommy for it.

Consideration of motivation and extenuating circumstances are cognitive skills that children have not yet developed.

Justice, Not Mercy. A child's moral/ethical judgments are based on justice without mercy, and the young child's sense of justice is harsh, grim, and uncompromising. If punishment is meted out, it is meted out to all and to all alike—no exceptions for extenuating circumstances. If the eight-year old boy is going to be punished for stealing a toy from the toy store, so should his two-year-old sister who also picked up a toy. He does not understand yet that she was not "stealing," but simply copying his behavior. If we tell him that his baby sister "didn't know any better" and was only following his example, he will think we are "favoring" her. If we punish him and not his baby sister, he will be angry and think he is not being treated "fairly." Nor should we, as teachers or coaches, turn a miscreant's fate over to his classmates. Their justice will be more like the Old Testament's "an eye for an eye and a tooth for a tooth"—and worse. The young child's worldview understands only black-and-white morality, the morality of folklore, fairy tales, and fables. When Hansel and Gretel are rescued from the cannibalistic witch, do they show any mercy? Not on her life! They push her into her own oven to burn to death.

2. The Stage of Moral Relativity (also called the Stage of Cooperation). It took humankind a millennia to evolve from the just God of Genesis to the compassionate God of Amos, to the merciful God of Micah, and to the loving God of the New Testament. Today, if a person has committed a crime out of extreme provocation, the law no longer demands "an eye for an eye and a tooth for a tooth." Today, the law considers *mercy* as well as *justice.* After years of physical brutality, a woman takes a shotgun one night and murders her husband. A brother and sister kill their father because he has sexually molested them for years. Justice versus mercy has become a dominant theme not only in the courts of law, but also in theology, religion, psychology, education, and literature. One of the most beautiful speeches in all Shakespeare has to do with the difference between justice and mercy. In *The Merchant of Venice,* the lovely and intelligent protagonist, Portia, describes justice as "an attribute of Kings," but mercy is an "attribute of God himself" (see Box 4.4). Piaget says that children transit from justice to mercy in the second stage of moral/ethical development, the stage he called *moral relativity.* Moral relativity has to do with consideration of individual situations and extenuating circumstances. Even then it will be many years before most of us can truly appreciate the profound maxim of Native Americans: *Never judge a person until you have walked a mile in their moccasins.*

Centrated on Rules. The stage of relativity is ushered in with an intense preoccupation with rules—to the point of obsession. Using the investigative technique called naturalistic observation (see Box 4.2), Piaget concluded that children will spend as much time arguing

---

Box 4.4   **PORTIA'S SPEECH ON THE QUALITY OF MERCY**

The quality of mercy is not strain'd,
It droppeth as the gentle rain from heaven
Upon the place beneath: it is twice bless'd;
It blesseth him that gives and him that takes:
'Tis mightiest in the mightiest; it becomes
The throned monarch better than his crown;
His scepter shows the force of temporal power,
The attribute to awe and majesty,
Wherein doth sit the dread and fear of kings;
But mercy is above this sceptered sway,

It is enthroned in the hearts of kings,
It is an attribute to God himself,
And earthly power doth then show likest God's
When mercy season's justice. . . .
Though justice be thy plea, consider this,
That in the course of justice none of us
Should see salvation: we do pray for mercy,
And that same prayer doth teach us all to render
The deeds of mercy.
—*The Merchant of Venice,* IV, i,184

about rules of a game as playing it. Piaget gives the following wonderful illustration. A group of boys were let out for recess in his native Switzerland. It was winter, and the boys were delighted at the snow that had fallen over night and made preparations for a snowball fight. But before they started making the snowballs, they got into a heated discussion over the "rules of the game." They decided, for example, how the two teams would be chosen and how they would elect the captain of each team. Then they argued over what would be "fair" and "not fair," and what the forfeit would be if someone broke a rule. (Snowballs made with stones and rocks would not "be fair.") This discussion lasted so long that the boys hardly had a chance to play before they were called in from recess. But that was of little importance, according to Piaget, their play was making "the rules."

Fair Play for All. Piaget explained that the centration on rule-making is not just play. The social fabric of our society is composed of house rules, school rules, club regulations, community ordinances, federal laws, and of course our religious commandments. All of these injunctions are the gears by which the whole machinery of our society is kept together so that people can live together in fairly peaceable ways. What children are really learning at this ten-to-twelve-year-old stage is how to be *rule-abiding* so that later they can be *law-abiding.* In the earlier stage, children do not consider the reasons for rules, only that you have to obey them. Rules exist because God or Mama or Daddy made them. Now children are learning that *people* make rules, people like themselves, in order for everyone to get "fair play." Fair play becomes the rallying cry of children as they enter the second stage of morality. In fact, our civil law is just such a matter of deciding what is "fair." While most judges and juries decide on this question for individual cases, it is the purpose of our higher courts to decide what is "fair" for groups of people. The only real difference is the terms being used: The higher courts use more sophisticated terms, terms like *human rights, equal rights,* and *civil rights,* but both the courts and children are considering issues of fair play.

Hartshorne and May: Morality Is a Developmental Process . . . and Situational

One of the first scientific explorations of children's morality was carried out in the 1920s in the New York City public schools, from grade 1 through grade 8 (Hartshorne & May, 1930). The psychologists defined morality by such terms as honesty, trustworthiness, and self-control. What they observed was that all the children in grade 1 cheated (looked at answers on the teacher's desk) and stole (took cookies from another desk) when they had an opportunity and if they thought they would not get caught. Little by little, as the children progressed from grade 1 through grade 8, fewer and fewer children engaged in stealing or cheating when the opportunity arose. The researchers concluded that, more often than not, children develop honesty and self-control by getting caught, or by observing others getting caught, or by admonitions of what can happen if they do get caught. *Morality,* the researchers concluded, *is a process that develops over time, bit-by-bit.*

The researchers also discovered that this developmental process is situational. A child might do something "wrong" at home that he wouldn't dream of doing in school. Somehow it's okay to take money from Mom's purse, but he would never take money from the teacher's purse. Another example: The 12-year-old child might think it wrong to steal something from "old Mr. Swenson" who owns the neighborhood convenience store "because he's nice and he doesn't have a lot of money." But somehow it's okay to steal from a large department store "because they're rich, and anyway, they have insurance." Even as adults, we may be scrupulous in our personal dealings with other individuals, but we may feel it's okay to pad our expense account or evade a few tax rules on our IRS return. Honesty and trustworthiness turn out to be situational even among the adult population.

Lawrence Kohlberg's Model of Moral/Ethical Development: Three Levels, Six Stages

While psychologists on this side of the Atlantic were still puzzling over Piaget's terms and concepts, a young American became fascinated by Piaget's model of moral development. His name was Lawrence Kohlberg (Kohlberg, 1981, 1984). While still in graduate school, he decided to devote his life to investigating Piaget's theories. Was Piaget's qualitative approach valid? Could it be applied to elementary school children in the United States as well as in Switzerland? Or were there cultural differences? Piaget had concentrated on grade school children; was it possible to investigate children above and below this age range? How can we foster the development of moral character in children? This last question, of course, will be of much interest to any of the readers who are or will be parents, teachers, coaches, Sunday school teachers, scout leaders, 4-H leaders, and so on.

What Kohlberg did was to devise a series of ethical problems and to ask a child to make a moral judgment concerning them. Then, after the child decided what was "right" or "wrong," Kohlberg pursued the child's reasoning with a series of follow-up questions. Why did the child make this judgment over that judgment? The following ethical problem is a fairly typical example: Two boys have accidents. The first boy breaks six plates while getting a plate for the table at his mother's request. The second boy breaks only one dish, but he breaks it because he was sneaking cookies. Who did worse: The first boy or the second boy?

Level One: Preconventional Morality (3–10 years). Agreeing essentially with Piaget, Kohlberg (1984) said that young children (before the age of ten) have no real morality. They are at the preconventional level of moral development. Kohlberg validated Piaget's observation that a young child's judgment is based on the tendency to centrate on *effect* (six plates versus one plate) while adults tend to focus on *causation*. In the above example of the broken plates, most adults will say the second boy did worse because he did something he wasn't supposed to do. Adults look at motivation; the reason behind the accident. But a young child will say that the first boy was "naughtier" because he broke six plates and the other boy broke only one. Consideration of causation will not emerge, generally, until the child reaches the conventional level of morality.

Stage 1: The Stage of Obedience/Disobedience (3–7 years). At the first stage of the preconventional level, the child's morality is based on obedience (just as Piaget had said). He refrains from doing wrong to avoid getting punished.

Q: Why should children not do bad things?
A: So they won't get in trouble. Or so they won't get spanked.

Stage 2: Hedonistic Self-Interest. The morality of the second stage of the preconventional level (from around seven to ten years) is based on hedonistic self-interest. Although the child may seem to be a little more considerate of other children, he is motivated mainly out of self-interest. If he is generous toward others, it is because he may reap rewards later.

Q: Why should you let Johnnie play with your toys?
A: If I let him play with my toys now, he'll let me play with his toys.

Kohlberg noted that this preconventional level can be applied to the general population as well as to young children. Ask any career criminal in prison what he did wrong, and more frequently than not, the answer will be "I got caught." Other adults who are at the preconventional level are those who sell you a used car that has hidden serious defects, the "carny" who looks at all the visitors as "marks" to get money out of, and (sadly) the "con man" we trusted with our hard-earned money.

Level Two: The Conventional Level (10–13 years). At around ten years of age, children begin to exhibit a morality based on the standards of society. It is also the morality of most Americans, said Kohlberg. It is a conventional morality in which there is a right/wrong dichotomy. Certain things are right and everything else is wrong—black and white, no shades of gray.

Stage 3: Good Girl/Good Guy Reputation. In stage 3 (about ten years of age), the child's moral reasoning is based on what others will think of him or her. He wants his parents to be proud of him. He wants others to like him. He acts in ways that will earn their trust and liking.

Q: Why should you be good?
A: So Mommie and Daddy will be proud of me.
Q: Why should you not tattle?
A: So the other kids will like me.

Stage 4: Respect for Law, Duty, and Authority. At about twelve or thirteen, the child enters the fourth stage of morality, a stage that is characterized by a respect for society at large. The child comes to respect impersonal authority, understands the need for law and order, and is developing the concept of "doing one's duty." They are beginning to understand the concepts behind the solemn oaths we take, such as the Scout's Oath and the Pledge of Allegiance. All of us formally accept this level of self-governance when we say the "Pledge to the Flag."

Q: Why should we obey laws?
A: (12-year-old) If we didn't have laws, some people would get more and that wouldn't be fair.
Q: Why do we have laws?
A: (16-year-old) If we didn't have laws, there would be anarchy, and that would be awful.

Level Three: Postconventional Morality (Age 13 and up). Well, is there anything beyond conventional morality? Yes, said Kohlberg, there is another level. Some people develop a personal conscience that is so strong that they are willing to follow their own higher ethical standards rather than the standards of conventional morality. It is not an easy task to follow one's conscience rather than societal standards. It requires "taking thought." It requires recognizing that societal rules and laws sometimes lag behind the moral issues of the day. It requires a recognition that if we always "go by the book," we may be committing a *legal* right but a *moral* wrong. Their inner direction leads them to see beyond the "letter of the law" to the "spirit of the law."

Stage 5: Contractual/Legalistic. This stage involves being committed to upholding rules whenever possible but being willing to bend them a bit when needed in individual cases. For example, health care procedures in hospitals frequently require a multitude of official procedures and paper work that are very time-consuming, sometimes involving delays for days. In certain life-and-death situations, health-care workers develop "shortcuts" so as to save the patient's life. They do the procedures first, and fill out the required paper work after the fact.

Q: Have you ever "broken" the law?
A: Not really, although sometimes I have had to be very liberal in my interpretation.

Stage 6: Individual Conscience. People who have reached this sixth stage of post-conventional morality are willing to disobey "unjust laws." They are following their individual conscience. An example of this, of course, are those civil rights workers who broke the unjust laws of desegregation before the Civil Rights Act of 1954. The idea of disobeying unjust laws brought down condemnation upon Kohlberg from many critics. They accused Kohlberg of encouraging delinquency, perhaps even anarchy. His answer to these critics came by way of quoting Socrates, Ralph Waldo Emerson, Chief Justice Louis Brandeis, and Martin Luther King, Jr.

Mark Twain. Mark Twain provides a literary example in *Huckleberry Finn.* In the early part of the story, Huck runs into Jim, who is an escaped slave on-the-run. Huck has been taught by the "good people" of Hannibal, Missouri, that slaves are the property of their masters. To help a slave run away is just the same as stealing the master's property. A person can go to Hell for stealing! But Huck regards Jim as a friend. He thinks about the beatings Jim will get if Huck returns Jim, a heart-wrenching thought for Huck. At this point, Huck engages in a monologue just as soul-searching as Hamlet's "To Be or Not To Be" (a speech in which Hamlet ponders the issue of suicide). Huck makes his choice based on his own individual conscience rather than on the societal standards of Hannibal, Missouri. Although he imagines the gates of Hell are opening wide in front of him, and he knows he will never be able to return to Hannibal, he chooses to befriend Jim. He shrugs and guesses he will "just have to go to Hell." Huck and Jim sail to freedom on that famous raft down the Mississippi.

Who Reaches the Highest Levels of Moral/Ethical Development? College Students Like You! Kohlberg concluded from his research that only 10 percent of the American population ever reach this sixth stage of moral development. Who are these persons? Kohlberg described them as middle class, college-educated people. It is the middle class, college-educated young people of any country who not only develop the highest levels of morality and ethics, but who are willing "to stand up and be counted." They have the ideals and physical energy to move their society to new levels of justice, mercy, and "fair play." In other words, they may very well be each of you, the readers of this book. We also believe that many more of you will reach those levels than did Kohlberg's subjects. Your generation is a much more sophisticated and "savvy" generation than the generations of Kohlberg's research studies. You are a post-Watergate, post-Vietnam, post-Kennedy/Martin luther King Jr. assasination, post-Berlin war, post-Chernobyl, post-Soviet Union generation. You pay more attention to news broadcasts. You are more attentive to newspaper editorials. You tune in to presidential debates on TV. You are more apt to make your voices heard. You keep an eye on your governmental officials. You know and understand the need for freedom of the press and all media. As such, all of you are potential Stage 6 candidates.

Box 4.5

SCENARIO REVISITED
Evaluating Piaget and Kohlberg

Professor Weitzman: Let's take stock a minute here. There is no doubt about the contributions of Piaget and Kohlberg. They have given us some valuable insights into how people develop along the moral/ethical dimension. Does this accord with your own experience? (*Some hands are raised.*) All right, let's start off with . . . let's see . . . Eduardo?

Eduardo: You've made Piaget much easier to understand. But there's something bothering me, but I'm not sure how to say it.

Professor Weitzman: Give it a try.

Eduardo: In my family, even in my whole village, we think going along with the group is a good thing. We do things together. We look out for each other. Kohlberg makes it sound like if you go along with the crowd, you're not being very mature.

Alec: Yeah, but Eduardo, you told us yourself you're the first person in your village to go to college. That must make you stand out.

Eduardo: It is true I'm the first man from my village to go to college. And that makes me different. But when I get my first job, my wife will understand I have to help my mother and my two sisters with money and help around their place. So it isn't just for me that I'm going to college. It's for my whole family. And I'll have to help whoever else I can in the village.

Professor Weitzman: Eduardo's comments are cogent. Critics have pointed out that Kohlberg's perspective leans very heavily toward the Western industrial/technological direction and it does not allow for variations of culture. There has been much research in many areas to suggest that there are several cultural dimensions that should be taken into account in terms of morality.

Li Ho: I'm from Hawaii and I have a lot of different ethnic blood in my veins—Hawaiian, Japanese, Chinese, Anglo—like most Hawaiians. And I have to say that the only set of relatives I have that don't group together are my Anglo relatives. Is that because the others are all Asian?

Professor Weitzman: No, we feel sure that this dimension has more to do with *size* and *technology.* I've been to Israel and the Israelis lean more in the direction of collectivism, which is to say that they are very group-oriented. Collectivism is more inherent where people can see each other on a fairly frequent basis—daily or weekly or even monthly. The point is that they recognize each other when they pass each other and they greet each other in some fashion. So size has much to do with it, such as a tribe, a clan, or a village where everyone knows each other to some degree. Even in Israel, people are more willing to help in the kibbutz than in the city of Jerusalem. Size makes a difference.

Dan: I'd have to say that is true for my tribe. I'm not a good example but we are expected to help each other.

Shannon: It's kind of like what I feel when my father and I drive in to Albuquerque. I feel so out of place and unsure of myself. I even feel lost and out of place here—I don't know anyone.

Jonnimae: I'd like to add two objections. (*Professor Weitzman nods*) First, you kept on saying he . . . he . . . he . . . were their subjects all boys? Weren't there any girls at all? Also, when my children were just little things, they once in a while showed caring and concern for each other. I don't mean they were perfect. They fought like sisters and brothers do. But if one was hurt, the other tried to help in some way. They would come running for me to help. And once Angie took off her band-aid to give to her little brother when he scratched himself. Isn't that a kind of morality?

Professor Weitzman: Good comment. You're touching on some criticism leveled at the Piaget-Kohlberg theory. In fact, the chapter now discusses some of your objections.

Post-Piaget and Kohlberg: More Research Developments (and Controversies) about Moral/Ethical Development

Kohlberg's principles of moral development are already taking their place in institutions of educational and religious instruction. Churches sponsor discussion groups of moral/ethical issues for adolescents and young adults. Sunday school teachers are leaning away from lecturing on morals and toward listening to children discuss their concerns. Colleges of education are urging all those who will be working with children to raise ethical issues for children to consider that are within their scope of understanding and ability to make judgments. But since the time of Piaget and Kohlberg, research studies have pioneered some additions, deletions, and amendments to their work. This is not to devalue their efforts at all, for we are, at the present time, only building on and fine-tuning their seminal work.

Can Young Children Empathize? It Looks Like They Can

One of the limitations of the work done by Piaget and Kohlberg was their dependence on the child's language ability. Until the children are three years of age, their verbal ability is quite primitive. In order to take advantage of good language skills, Piaget began with six-year-olds. Kohlberg reached down to the three-year-old level, which is the age that most children have enough linguistic ability to engage in a question-and-answer dialog if it is kept simple. But if we discover that very young children seem to be able to demonstrate empathy completely without words of any sort, would that indicate that very young children demonstrate an *empathetic morality?* That is what developmental psychologists asked and tried to find out.

Observational studies have confirmed that very young children do indeed demonstrate a well-developed sense of empathy—particularly, if it is someone they know and identify with. For example, children who were present when their parents are hurt either physically (father having a bad headache) or emotionally (mother having received bad news and crying) react with discernible empathy and comfort. They wanted to help the parent or to "fix" the problem. For example, after one mother had an argument with her husband and broke down crying, her not-quite-two-year-old daughter climbed on her lap and became physically affectionate (Zahn-Waxler and Radke-Yarrow, 1986).

But the ability to be empathetic may begin even earlier than two years. Some years ago, Martin Hoffler began observing infants and babies right from birth. Several researchers have traced evidence of empathy to early infancy (Dunn, 1988; Hoffler, 1991). What they say goes something like this: Empathy evolves along with the concept of a Self in babies. Newborn babies do not have a sense of Self; they cannot distinguish between themselves and other people. For example, when neonates hear other infants cry, they themselves begin to cry—and they cry more fiercely than when they hear any other loud noise. Sometime later in their first year (the studies do not agree on just when), infants begin to get a sense of themselves as distinct from other persons. Now when they hear other babies crying, they may not themselves cry. Instead, they may turn in the direction of the crying. Or if they are toddlers, they may run to their mothers and climb on her lap, very unhappy until the crying ceases. Sometime during their second year, they may even try to help the crying child by offering their teddy bear or comforting them. As they get older, their repertory of helpful, comforting behaviors increases.

In addition to cognitive growth, researchers have also discovered other variables that have a bearing on the development of empathy, including genetics (hovering around 50 percent), parent-child warmth or distance, parent-child verbal interaction, and gender. Girls tend to exhibit more empathy and at an older age. Is that because girls are innately caring and maternal? Or is it that parents teach their girl-children to be more caring? We really don't know yet. We do know that boys identify more with other boys and men identify with other men more than they do with women. The reverse is also true: Women identify and empathize more with women. Our ability to identify with and feel empathy for others more like ourselves generalizes to people of the same ethnic roots, the same social status and the same circumstances as ourselves.

Carol Gilligan's Care Orientation: Gender Differences in Moral Development

Piaget and Kohlberg did all their work (or most of it anyway) with young boys and adolescent males, a strong criticism from a society that is promoting gender equality. Carol Gilligan, a psychologist at Harvard, decided to take up the challenge of whether or not their research findings were applicable to women. Or do women have a different structure to their moral character? After years of research, Gilligan published her findings on the moral structure of adolescent girls and boys (Gilligan, 1982). Since the publication of her book *In a Different Voice: Psychological Theory and Women's Development* (1982) many other researchers, worldwide, are investigating her findings in the light of their particular culture, vocation, and educational mission.

Universal Principles of Abstract Justice versus Care and Concern for Others

Well, what were her findings? Namely this: Women do differ from men in their moral structure. Given moral dilemmas (that have no easily judged right or wrong) men are more concerned about abstract principles of equality and fairness (*We hold these truths to be self-evident: that all men are created equal . . .*). Given the same moral dilemmas, women respond in terms that have to do with concern about the person over a principle and relieving the burdens and sufferings of others. Men solve problems by looking to rules, fairness, and reciprocity. Women solve dilemmas by wanting to help solve the hardships of others even if there is some sacrifice to themselves. Men were found to be more narrowly and self-first focused (Box 4.6). There is even some evidence that men consider themselves first and women consider others first (Perry & Mcintire, 1994; Skoe, 1998). Does that mean that these two modes are innate and biologically significant? Perhaps in part but we really need more research in this interesting distinction between the two genders.

Culture-Based Orientations. What most of the research studies have found is that some cultures are more justice-oriented and some cultures are more care-oriented. An investigation of 95 Native American college students discovered that the care response was more representative of their worldviews (Arvizu, 1995). Studies done in Hawaii, Taiwan, and Israel also reflect a slightly higher care orientation over justice orientation (Change, 1996; Cherry, 1994; Yeh & Creamer, 1995). What social scientists and educators are now pondering is how to incorporate more care orientation into our children. While a justice orientation can have noble results,

---

| Box 4.6 | Men and Women's Preferred Mode of Responding to Moral/Ethical Dilemmas |

Men were more apt to respond in this manner.	*Women were more apt to respond in this manner.*
We ought to worry about our own country first and let the rest of the world take care of itself. I find it hard to be sympathetic toward starving people in foreign lands when there is trouble in our own country. It's not really my problem if others are in trouble and need help.	I would agree to a good plan to make a better life for the poor, even if it cost me more money. Americans should change their eating habits to provide more food for the hungry in other parts of the world. I get very upset when I see people treated unfairly.

---

it can also swing the other way—toward slogans and pseudo-principles that are really rationalizations for selfish disregard of human needs and human suffering.

Social or Observational Learning: What We Witness We Imitate

We have always known that children learn simply by being around others, watching and imitating them. This is how children learn to speak their native language. It is how we are all **enculturated** to the mores and folkways of our ethnic background. Children of each culture pick up these behaviors more through observation of adults than through being told to behave in certain ways. But psychologists had very little empirical evidence for social learning until Albert Bandura (1986) demonstrated it through his classic experiment with the Bobo doll.

In 1965, Albert Bandura set up the following experiment. Nursery school children watched three films with Bobo, a balloon clown that rights itself every time it is pushed. In all three films, an adult aggresses against Bobo. In the first film, the aggressive adult is rewarded with candy, soft drinks, and praise for the aggressive behavior. In the second film, the aggressor was criticized and spanked for the aggressive behavior. In the third film, there were no consequences at all for the behavior. Bandura's intention was to study the outcome of these three aggressive behaviors on the nursery school children. Immediately after the film, each child was left alone in a room filled with toys, including the Bobo doll. The child's behavior was observed through a one-way mirror. Children who watched the film where the aggressive adult was reinforced with candy, soft drinks, and praise imitated the behavior more than the children who saw the adult being punished. What about the children who watched the film where neither positive or negative consequences occurred? *They also behaved more aggressively toward Bobo,* which was startling to Bandura. What does this experiment suggest about the maxim parents sometimes say to their children: *Do as I say, not as I do?*

As an example, let's consider a hypothetical student by the name of Eddie, age 14. Eddie has been in and out of juvenile correctional institutions for most of his young life. He comes out of a family characterized by alcoholism, physical abuse, and poverty. He has never been friends with anyone but those who live in the same inner-city circumstances as he does. He and his friends have been shoplifting beer, cigarettes, and clothes ever since they were in the lower grades. Sometimes they get caught by the police and go through the legal system, many times ending up for weeks in a juvenile institution. His father, his uncle, and his friends have all "done time." They brag when they outwit the cops and curse their "luck" when they land in jail. Eddie may hate his alcoholic father, but he probably admires his father's ability to steal radios, TVs, and other items. Eddie has been modeling his behavior according to what he has seen and what he admires.

One day he happens to join a basketball game at the local YMCA. He gets on well with the game and the guys and particularly the coach. In fact, he begins to want to be like the coach and so the coach becomes a role model. The coach, on his part, takes a personal interest in him and encourages him to keep his grades up and to let go of the friends with whom he had been shoplifting. The coach introduces him to some other young people of his age. Now Eddie has the possibility to make other choices and changes in his personal life. Whether he does so or not depends on the effectiveness of the role-modeling process.

What Can We Do Now to Foster Care-Orientation in Our Children?

Many social scientists are investigating this question, both nationally and worldwide. Of course, it takes many years to discern whether or not certain parenting and school practices in early childhood through to high school result in the successful attainment of the care mode of personality in both genders. We await the results of these longitudinal studies with a great deal of anticipation. But in the meantime, we can provide the reader with some recommendations presented by the American Psychological Association to offset the external influences of violence, such as daily violence on TV, a generally hostile neighborhood, and a culture that exalts "heroes" who are violent and even criminal.

- Treat children with the same kind of respect and dignity you would like them to show others: *Thank you for getting the newspaper this morning, when I was so sick, and bringing it to me.*
- Let them know how highly you regard their kind behaviors: *I saw you help that little girl up on the playground. That was so kind of you. It makes me very proud of you.*
- Let them know how strongly you feel about their unkind acts: *When you punched your sister, it made her cry. We don't like behavior like that. Treat your sister more kindly. If you are upset with her, talk to her first; and if that doesn't work, talk to me.*
- Provide them with books that promote compassionate behavior, but not the kind that have "goody two-shoes" characters. Look instead for books which show ordinary people who perform acts of caring and concern.
- Find out about movies your children want to see. If they are excessively violent or if they glamorize criminals, do not sit down to watch these movies with your children. As they get older and can watch these kinds of movies themselves, have discussions with your children that deal with other ways the characters could have acted. A little discussion goes a long way in having teenagers reflect on the movie. Reflective critiquing will partially negate an accepting attitude to everything they view.
- Educate your children about famous altruists. Local museums and your public library will be very helpful in finding books and other materials that foster appreciation of outstanding historical or living persons. Ask them who they admire and why.

IMPORTANT TERMS AND CONCEPTS TO KNOW

Bobo	effect	model	realism
care	egocentric	moral/ethical	relativity
concrete	formal operations	obedience	rule-making
concrete operations	functional	observational	sensory-motor
conservations	hypothetical	permanence	situational
constancies	justice	postconventional	social
conventional	justice-orientation	preconventional	stranger
decentrate	mediate	preoperations	three
developmental	mediation		

MAKE YOUR OWN CHAPTER SUMMARY BY FILLING IN THE BLANKS BELOW

Use the "Important Terms and Concepts to Know" to fill in the blanks.

Jean Piaget's theory of cognitive development posits four age/stages of "mind" from birth to adulthood. The _____ stage begins at birth. The baby has no _____ (thoughts or ideas). During the first two years, the baby's sensory modalities become connected and the baby develops the _____ of size, shape, and color. In addition, the baby develops object _____ (the understanding that things exist even if they are not seen) and exhibits _____ anxiety. The _____ stage begins at about two years of age and continues to between seven and eight years. The child can now _____ one idea but only one idea. The child's cognitive processes are _____ or literal; that is, he will not be able to understand abstract ideas, sophisticated jokes, metaphors, allegories, and so on. In addition, the child's thinking is _____ , which means that every object has a use which pertains to the child. The child's

perspective is also _____ , which means that children cannot view the world from any perspective but their own. The stage of _____ develops between 7 and 11 to 12 years of age and is marked by the ability to mediate two or more ideas at the same time, which means the child has the ability to _____ from the properties of height and length. The child develops the _____ of mass, volume, weight, etc., making it easier for the child to understand basic arithmetical facts, simple algebra, and number sets, etc. The stage of _____ is the adult stage of cognition. After 12 years, the child will develop the ability to analyze, be logical, and engage in _____ reasoning.

Piaget's theory of moral/ethical development is based on this central assumption: Cognitive and _____ development go hand-in-hand. His model of moral/ethical development is a two-stage theory. In the first stage, the child has no innate moral/ethical system. If he is good, it is because he has learned _____ . An adult looks to motivation or cause, but a young child is centrated on _____ . The child's sense of morality is grim and based on _____ , which does not allow for underlying motivation or extenuating circumstances. The concept of mercy does not develop until much later on during the second stage. This second stage is ushered in by centrating on _____ , and what is "fair" and "not fair."

Lawrence Kohlberg fine-tuned Piaget's stage theory of _____ development to a three-level, six-stage model. Young children, career criminals, and "con men" are all at the level of _____ morality, which is based on self-interest. The majority of Americans are at the _____ level, which is based on law-and-order and respect for abstract authority. The final level of morality, called _____ morality, is reached by a small percentage of Americans, generally middle class, college-educated youth—people like those of you reading this text.

Hartshorne and May's studies revealed that honesty is _____ . All children in the first grade will cheat and steal if they think they won't be caught. Little by little, as they progress up to the eighth grade,

fewer and fewer of them will cheat or steal. Morality is also _____ ; that is, they may steal from a big department store but not from the neighborhood convenience store where they know the "nice owner."

Carol Gilligan has proposed two modes of moral-ethical development. Males tend to use a _____ while females tend to use a _____ orientation. These two orientations have also been found to be culture-related.

Albert Bandura had investigated _____ learning or _____ learning. One particularly striking illustration of this type of learning was demonstrated by the famous _____ experiment in which children witnessed an adult abusing or being kind to an inflated clown doll.

Teaching children to be law-abiding and ethical depends on the stage they are in. At the _____ level, they need to be constantly reminded of the rules (since it is so easy to forget them). At the _____ level, conformity to peers is important. The _____ level depends on individual conscience and requires the kind of experience provided in homes and classes where children are listened to as well as heard and where there can be frank exchange of opinions and discussion.

5 CONDITIONING AND LEARNING
How We Have Been Conditioned and How We Can Use Conditioning to Build Constructive Habits

Top to bottom: A dentist prepares a frightened patient by putting him through deep relaxation. A dog has been trained to detect narcotics. A man with migraine is learning to control headache through biofeedback. Soldiers are given treatment for post-traumatic disorder. A woman has given birth after Lamaze training. A child is learning appropriate classroom behaviors.

Box 5.1
SCENARIO
What Would You Like to Improve on?

The graduate student from the university, Jill Smith, is sitting with a small group of eight students. She waits patiently as each student thinks about the question she has just written on the board, which reads

WHAT IMPROVEMENT WOULD YOU LIKE TO MAKE TO YOURSELF?

As each of the students volunteer a habit, Jill writes it on the board.

Jill Smith: I never ask anyone to volunteer until I go first. So what I would like to work on is getting more exercise. I used to get a lot of exercise but my life has become so sedentary, I'm beginning to feel like an old lady with aches and pains.

Eduardo: Quit smoking! Before I came to college, I was working with a bunch of men, all older than me, and I wanted their respect. I thought smoking would make me look like a man. But it is not good for me.

Annamaria: Lose some weight. Not eat so much. I'm Italian, and Italians just love to cook and eat what they cook. Everybody kept telling me I had to eat for two when I was pregnant. Three pregnancies,

I ate for six people. I"m so fat, I feel like a baby elephant.

Alec: I'll add my name to learning how to study better. I'd rather be anywhere than sitting at a desk and studying.

Jonnimae: You can add my name and write "better study habits." I fall asleep the minute I lean back on my bed at night and open a book. I go right to sleep. I just can't stay awake.

Dan: Yeah! I go along with Alec and Jonnimae. I need better study habits.

Martha: And I'd like to stop yelling at my son. I do it all the time.

Jill Smith: Is there anything you'd like to work on, Shannon?

Shannon: (*almost whispering*) I'd like to get over being so shy.

Jill Smith: Shannon, that's a tough one. The others have selected specific behaviors. You have a deep-seated personality trait and that is not so easy to change. But that doesn't mean we shouldn't list it as a goal for you and see what kind of specific goal we can develop, a small step toward helping you be not so shy. (*Jill turns*

Box 5.1

SCENARIO (continued)
What Would You Like to Improve on?

to a dark-haired girl who hasn't said anything since the beginning of the class.) Natasha, we haven't heard from you since the beginning of the term. Would you like to work on something?

Natasha: I . . . not speak English . . . good. . . . not know . . . always . . . what people . . . always say . . . English is so fast.

Jill Smith: I understand that. How about we make a goal improvement for you . . . that you practice English more.

Natasha: No . . . too much . . . mistakes . . . I make.

Shannon: Is it OK if I help Natasha practice speaking? We have the same lunch hour and another class together. We could talk together if that's all right with Natasha. . . . (turns to Natasha) . . . I don't have anyone to eat with. Maybe we could eat together and study for our classes together . . . if you would like.

Natasha: (brightening up) Would like that . . . thank you many times.

The blackboard list looks as follows

Eduardo:	Stop smoking
Martha:	Lose weight
Annamaria:	Stop yelling at son
Dan:	Better study habits
Jonnimae:	Better study habits
Alec:	Better study habits
Shannon:	Less shy, more assertive
Natasha:	Practice speaking English
Jill:	Get more exercise

Jill Smith: The first thing we need is knowledge about how conditioning comes about. Once we have some knowledge about how we've been conditioned to be how we are, perhaps we can discover some ways to decondition those old behaviors in ourselves and then condition some new habits we do want. We can make conditioning work for us instead of against us.

Classical Conditioning and the Science of Learning

Learned behaviors come about as the result of our life experiences and are (relatively) permanent. Some learning takes place in the formal atmosphere of school and college, but most of our attitudes and communication style are acquired in more informal ways as we grow up and as we interact with our family, friends, peer groups, and so on. We begin our discussion of how we learn with exploring how we are conditioned to be who we are. Conditioning can be a difficult subject to absorb in the beginning, but if the readers can stay with it, they will learn how to use conditioning toward making constructive changes in their lives (see Tip 5.1).

Ivan Pavlov: A Dog Is Conditioned to Salivate to a Bell

We made the point in earlier chapters that any new area of investigation seems to need an intellectual giant to make a foothold in an unknown scientific area. The intellectual giant who got us started on the scientific investigation of how we learn was a Russian physiologist by the

Tip 5.1 Maturational versus Learned. From time to time in this or other textbooks, you will come across other terms that mean the same thing as *maturation* and *learning*. It's a good idea to make note of these other terms as follows: *Maturational:* Inherited, genetic, biological, inborn, innate, and even reflexive (a term fallen out of favor). *Learned:* Environmental, experience, conditioned, upbringing, sociocultural variables, situational influences.

name of Ivan Pavlov. He was a superb scientist and so dedicated to science that he was willing to work in unheated laboratories in the freezing winters of Russia, protected from the cold only by wearing his overcoat, fur-lined Russian hat, and gloves. Before his monumental work in conditioning, he had already received the Nobel Prize in 1904 for his work on the physiology of dogs. Today we revere him as one of the great pioneers of psychology. Yet, ironically, until his dying day, Pavlov insisted he wasn't a psychologist—he was a physiologist. He said he didn't even *like* the discipline of psychology because of its lack of scientific rigor (Fancher, 1979). Nevertheless, Pavlov contributed to psychology its first rigorous scientific methodology, which he called *conditioning.*

What Pavlov discovered came about in this way. His original research objective was to study the amount of salivation produced by a dog within a given period of time on the presentation of meat powder. To do this, he harnessed a dog so it could not move very far. Pavlov had invented a device very similar to the dentist's implement for removing saliva from your mouth. But instead of having the saliva washed away, the saliva was collected in a beaker so it could be measured. But a major problem began to arise. The problem involved a curious time factor. In the beginning, the dog began to salivate immediately upon the bowl of meat powder being placed in front of him. But in very short order, the dog began to salivate at the mere sight of the bowl, and then to the sight of the lab assistant carrying in the bowl. A few more days, and the dog began to salivate at the sound of the door opening and even earlier than that—to the sound of the footsteps coming down the hall. The lab researchers just could not keep the timing at a fixed point. Now another lesser intellect might have given up on the experiment as impossible to carry out. But Pavlov realized that they had stumbled on a very significant phenomenon. What they had stumbled on was conditioning (Pavlov, 1927)

"Unconditioned" Means "Un-Learned."   In a typical experiment, Pavlov would place some meat powder in front of the dog. The dog would, of course, salivate to it. Because the dog does not need to learn to salivate to meat powder, Pavlov called the meat powder an **unconditioned stimulus (UCS).** The dog's behavioral *response* of salivating to the **UCS** is now called an **unconditioned response (UCR)** because the dog didn't have to learn to salivate *(Memory Jog: for unconditioned, think unlearned.)* The next step was to establish the fact that the dog did not salivate to a bell. When we ring a bell in the hearing of a dog who has never heard a bell before, does the dog salivate? No, of course not. At the sound of a bell, a dog might cock his ears or orient his head toward the sound, might cock his head or even paw it but the dog will not salivate. For that reason, Pavlov called the bell a *neutral stimulus* (NS) for salivation.

"Conditioned" Means "Learned."   The third step in Pavlov's procedure was to *pair* the meat powder (the UCS) with the bell (the neutral stimulus) several times; that is, every time the meat powder was presented to the dog, the bell was sounded. After several *pairings* of bell (NS) and meat powder (UCS), what happened when the bell was sounded by itself? If you say that the dog now salivated, you are right. Pavlov called this salivating behavior a conditioned response (CR). Very simply, a **conditioned response (CR)** is a *learned* response. The fact that the dog is now salivating to the bell means that the bell is no longer a *neutral* stimulus for salivation. The bell has become a **conditioned stimulus (CS)** for salivation. Pavlov further discovered that a conditioned stimulus **generalizes** (transfers) to other stimuli within the same *sensory modality*. He called this transfer **stimulus generalization**. The dog would also salivate

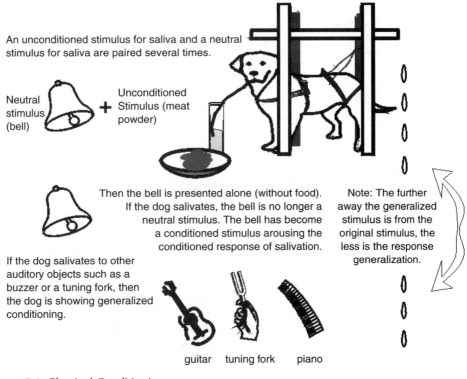

An unconditioned stimulus for saliva and a neutral stimulus for saliva are paired several times.

Neutral stimulus (bell) + Unconditioned Stimulus (meat powder)

Then the bell is presented alone (without food). If the dog salivates, the bell is no longer a neutral stimulus. The bell has become a conditioned stimulus arousing the conditioned response of salivation.

Note: The further away the generalized stimulus is from the original stimulus, the less is the response generalization.

If the dog salivates to other auditory objects such as a buzzer or a tuning fork, then the dog is showing generalized conditioning.

guitar   tuning fork   piano

Figure 5.1 Classical Conditioning

to other *auditory* stimuli, such as bells with a higher or lower pitch or even to buzzers, which Pavlov called **generalized stimuli** (see Tip 5.2).

"Experimental Extinction" Means "Forgotten/Deconditioned." What will happen to the conditioned response of salivation if we keep ringing the bell over and over *without the presentation of meat powder*? If you reply that the dog will stop salivating, you are again quite right. But Pavlov used a more *empirical* term: He said that **experimental extinction** had been achieved, which simply means that the dog no longer salivated to the bell. So the bell was put away for a while and the researchers turned their attention to other projects. Then one day someone rang the bell accidentally and, to the astonishment of everyone in the laboratory, the dog was salivating again. This sudden reappearance of the conditioned response of salivation

---

Tip 5.2 You May Have Conditioned Your Pet! If you have ever had a pet, you may have observed this example of conditioning in your own home. Just pick up the leash and your dog instantly becomes excited. The leash is now a **conditioned stimulus** for the **conditioned response** of anticipating a walk. Or perhaps you have a cat that you feed with a can of cat food. The moment you use the electric can opener to open the can, your cat comes running, tail up, at the sound of the buzzing. The buzzing of the electric can opener was originally a neutral stimulus but after a few pairings of buzzing and the smell of food, the buzzing became a **conditioned stimulus** (CS) for the **conditioned response** (CR) of running-to-the-kitchen. The cat may also come running at the buzzing of the alarm clock, which would be **generalized responding.**

had occurred *by the simple passage of time.* Pavlov called this sudden reappearance of the salivating behavior **spontaneous recovery.**

Higher Order Conditioning. After Pavlov had conditioned the dog to salivate to a bell, he discovered he could use the bell in place of the unconditioned stimulus (meat powder). In other words, Pavlov could use the conditioned stimulus of the bell to condition the dog to salivate to an electric light or to the whirring of a fan, etc. In fact, Pavlov managed to achieve four levels of higher order conditioning in this way (see Table 5.1). It was because of the phenomenon of higher-order conditioning, that Pavlov concluded that conditioning is the basis for all human learning and human personality.

John Watson Applies Conditioning to a Human Baby

Pavlov worked only with dogs. It was an American psychologist, John Watson, who first applied conditioning to a human being. Watson had been an engineering student before studying psychology. When he got into psychology, he became disgusted with the lack of scientific rigor in the young science of psychology. Upon hearing of Pavlov's work on the conditioning of dogs, Watson was seized with excitement: Here at last was an empirical method worthy of being called scientific. He decided to apply it to a baby, known to us only as "Baby Albert." Watson and his assistant, Lucille Raynor, performed the following experiment (Watson & Raynor, 1920).

They selected a nine-month old baby in a foundling home who seemed to exude good physical health and a happy, cheerful nature. They put into Baby Albert's crib several white, furry objects, such as a white Santa Claus beard, a white muff, a real white rabbit, and a real little white

Table 5.1   Higher-Order Conditioning

Pavlov suggested that higher-order conditioning is how simple conditioning leads to the complexities of human cognition.	*Unconditioned Stimulus*		*Neutral Stimulus*		*Becomes a Conditioned Stimulus*		*Conditioned Response of Salivation*
STEP ONE The meat powder is paired with a bell until the bell elicits the conditioned response of salivation.	⌣	+	🔔	=	🔔	→	💧💧💧💧
STEP TWO The bell is now used in place of the unconditioned stimulus and paired with the sound of a buzzer, which elicits salivation (although not as much as the original conditioned salivation).	🔔	+	◉	=	◉	→	💧💧💧
STEP THREE The buzzer is now paired with an electric light until salivation. The response is quite weak now.	◉	+	💡	=	💡	→	💧💧
STEP FOUR The electric light is paired with the whirring of a fan, and a very weak conditioned response is elicited.	💡	+	🌀	=	🌀	→	💧

Pavlov suggested that higher-order conditioning is how simple conditioning leads to the complexities of human cognition.

Every higher stage of conditioning elicits weaker and weaker response of salivation as symbolized by the lessening of salivary drops. Pavlov was unable to go beyond fourth-order conditioning in dogs.

Figure 5.2 Baby Albert. The baby that was the first human being upon whom conditioning was experimentally demonstrated.

laboratory rat. Albert showed no signs of fear to any of these objects, including the little white rat. In fact, he tried to grasp all the white, furry objects, including the little white rat, and—as babies are wont to do—to put them in his mouth.

Having established the fact that Albert did not fear any of these white furry objects, the next part of the experiment was carried out three months later (Watson didn't tell us why he waited three months) when Albert was twelve months old. Watson and Raynor put the white rat into the baby's cage . . . er, crib, but this time they made a loud noise every time Baby Albert tried to reach for the little white rat. Now all babies have a natural reaction (a reflex or unconditioned response) to loud noises. They cry, or fall over on their faces, and show other signs of distress. That's exactly what Baby Albert did. The experimenters now stopped making loud noises, but continued to put the white rat into Albert's crib to see what Albert would do. If the readers have already guessed that Albert cried and showed other signs of distress, they are right. Clearly, Albert had been conditioned to fear the little white rat via Pavlov's **classical conditioning.** Furthermore, Albert's *conditioned* fear of the little white rat *generalized* to anything that was white and furry such as the Santa Claus beard, the white rabbit, and the white muff. Upon putting these other objects into the crib, Baby Albert cried, fell over on this face and showed other types of distress.

What Happened to Baby Albert? Students generally ask what happened to little Albert? Did he remain scared of white furry objects? We simply don't know since Watson never published anything further. Was there any attempt to help Albert get over his fear of white furry objects? Alas!—no, so far as we know. This experiment could not be performed on a human subject today because of the establishment of *ethical procedures* by psychology and other professions. As for Baby Albert, his name has gone down as one of the "famous children" of psychology, along with others the reader has encountered in previous chapters: Helen Keller and Piaget's three children. What we have been describing is called **aversive conditioning,** which means conditioning resulting from painful stimuli.

The Russians and Ferdinand Lamaze Adapt Classical Conditioning for More Natural and Gentle Birthing

Another application of classical conditioning comes from Russian medicine. Philosophically, the Communist regime was committed (at least in theory) to a policy of equality and education for all peoples. (This didn't work out in practice considering their treatment of their minorities.) This official position of equality included equal opportunities for all women. Consequently, many Russian women became physicians and for many years now most Russian physicians are women (Haavio-Mannila, 1995). The preponderance of women in the medical profession doubtless led to a deep concern for women having a difficult labor. After intensive study, the Soviet physicians decided that a significant reason for women having so much pain during labor is that they have been *conditioned* to fear the birth process. They reasoned as follows: Young women often had to listen to terrible tales about women having difficult labor (like Aunt Olga) or even dying in childbirth (like Cousin Tatiana). These stories so scared the young woman having her first baby that she worked against the birth process by being "uptight" and by clenching her hands and bracing her entire body, instead of relaxing her body and "letting go."

The Soviet physicians decided to **decondition** the negative emotional mind set of the pregnant women and to **condition** a new mind set about the birth process, not as an illness but as a phenomenon of health. First, they taught the young women about the physiology of their bodies and the process of birth, in order to enable them to understand what goes on during birth. Then they taught the pregnant women how to breathe during labor, how to press down in rhythm to the contractions, and so on. This training was so successful anesthesia was no longer used in 90 percent of the births. The Russians called their natural birthing the *psychoprophylactic method (PPM)*. So why do we call it the Lamaze method? When the French physician Ferdinand Lamaze heard about the astounding results the Russians were reporting, he went to the Soviet Union to learn their techniques and brought them back to the West. Besides, it was the era of the "cold war" and we were not about to admit that anything good could come out of the U.S.S.R. Today, the Lamaze method of birthing or modifications of it are used all over the world (Lamaze, 1956).

B. F. Skinner's Operant Conditioning: We Also Learn Through Our Own Exploratory Behaviors

For many years, it was assumed that classical conditioning accounted for all human learning. Then a young man from Harvard, B. F. Skinner, introduced the psychological world to another approach to conditioning, an approach he called **operant conditioning** (Skinner, 1938). Skinner agreed that classical conditioning was scientifically sound, but he pointed out that it is a very unnatural way to learn. Under normal circumstances, bells and food do not occur simultaneously very often. Classical conditioning, he pointed out, *depends on someone artificially putting two dissimilar stimuli together*. The bell and the meat powder were put together in a scientific laboratory. And, many times, we do the same thing. We teach dogs to bark by offering the dog a treat (uncondition stimulus) and urging them to "Speak!" (neutral stimulus). We sometimes teach children to be polite by putting a cookie in front of them and prompting them with the word "please."

But, said Skinner, in everyday life, people learn (are conditioned) through their own voluntary behavior, and they discover for themselves positive or negative consequences (reinforced, nonreinforced, or punished). For example, when a two-year-old toddler accidentally puts his hand on a hot stove, chances are that he will not put his hand on that stove again. No one paired the *unconditioned stimulus* (pain) with the *neutral stimulus* (hot stove) together. The child was exploring his environment and discovered, on his own, that if he puts his hand on a hot stove it hurts! Skinner would call that *one-trial conditioning*. He will not do *that* again. No one had to teach him that. He learned it on his own. Skinner boldly asserted that most of our learning happens through just this kind of operant conditioning. Learning as the result of avoiding pain is called *aversive learning*.

A Typical Operant Conditioning Experiment

Analyzing a typical **operant conditioning** process will illustrate Skinner's basic approach. A rat is put into a so-called "Skinner box." A typical *Skinner box* is simply a cage and a container filled with food pellets. The container of food pellets is attached electrically to a very delicately balanced lever inside the cage so that when the lever is touched, even slightly, it releases a pellet of food (see Figure 5.3). Now when a rat is put into a Skinner box for the first time, it will run around all over the box sniffing and crawling in the corners and trying to climb the wall (presumably looking for a way out). As the result of this exploratory behavior, the rat will hit (accidentally) the delicately balanced lever with its nose or its tail or its haunches or whatever, and out comes a pellet of food.

Of course the rat will eat the pellet of food and search for more pellets and again it will hit the lever (accidentally) and down will come another pellet of food. When this spontaneous *emitted behavior* becomes *purposeful* behavior is hard to say, but very quickly (in a matter of minutes) the rat is hitting the lever and eating the food, perhaps up to 20 times a minute until it is satiated. Notice! Nobody paired the food and the lever. In the course of the rat's exploratory behavior, one of the behaviors (pressing the lever) was reinforced (food pellets) and that behavior increased in frequency.

The World as a Giant Skinner Box. The point of all the foregoing is that Skinner believed that the world is a giant "Skinner box" in which we human beings are being rein-

---

Box 5.2

**SCENARIO REVISITED
How Have You Been Conditioned?**

Jill Smith: How many of you can identify how you have been conditioned?

Annamaria: I can right off! I''ve been conditioned to associate food with love and prosperity and good times and all the good things of life. "Antonio's engaged! Let's celebrate" which means "let's eat!" "Let's celebrate if Antonio gets unengaged." As long as there is food on the table why should we worry? And what's more!—Don't try to refuse food. That's how Mama shows her love. If we refuse to eat second helpings of pasta, we're rejecting Mama's love.

Martha: Besides, Italian food is so-o-o good!

Annamaria: So I eat to cheer myself up. I eat when I get lonely. I eat when I'm nervous. It's so comforting to eat because that represents good times and love. So what do I do?

Jill Smith: We replace eating with something else that makes us feel good.

Shannon: I guess I've been conditioned to being scared people will make fun of me because . . . of my . . . club foot.

Jill Smith: I'm sure it wasn't easy for you in high school, Shannon.

Martha: I guess I've been conditioned to yelling and nagging. That's what my parents and grandparents were always doing. Yelling and screaming! And now I do that with my son. How do you stop it?

Jill Smith: We call that social learning. But, yes, that is how you were taught to raise your children. Your par-

ents and grandparents were your role models. Now you need to develop a better role model for your son, so he can be a better model to his children.

Alec: This is hard to talk about but everyone else is sharing, so I will too. I've been conditioned to be prejudiced. I live near my grandparents and they grew up in the 1930s and I guess lots of people were prejudiced then. I know it's wrong, and I'm working on unconditioning all the prejudices they inculcated in all us grandchildren. Some of us are almost free of it but my older brother—he is still so prejudiced, we can hardly have a friendly conversation.

Jill Smith: Alec, your attitude is fine. But to relieve your mind, we are all prejudiced to some degree. Some people are prejudiced about gay people. Other people can't abide people who are fat. In high school, it is fashionable for the athletes to be prejudiced about the ones that get A's in class and call them "nerds." A famous French writer by the name of Voltaire said, "We really do not think at all; we merely rearrange our prejudices." Life is not perfect and people are not perfect.

Alec: So what can we do about all this prejudice?

Jill Smith: Keep working to understand our prejudices—just as you did. We can educate our children to understand what it means that "all men (and now women) are created equal." If some of you become teachers, you can help your students to understand that also. In other work places, you can make sure that you exemplify a democratic attitude toward all.

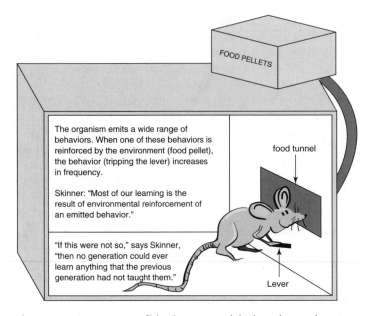

Figure 5.3 Operant Conditioning: A model of a "Skinner box."

The organism emits a wide range of behaviors. When one of these behaviors is reinforced by the environment (food pellet), the behavior (tripping the lever) increases in frequency.

Skinner: "Most of our learning is the result of environmental reinforcement of an emitted behavior."

"If this were not so," says Skinner, "then no generation could ever learn anything that the previous generation had not taught them."

forced or nonreinforced continuously. One of Skinner's basic assumptions concerning human nature is that we have no such thing as free will. Concepts such as *freedom* and *free will* are simply illusions. Why we do what we do (our learned behaviors) is because they have been reinforced by somebody or a group of somebodies in our society. Skinner categorized reinforcers into two kinds: primary reinforcers and secondary reinforcers. Animals respond mainly to **primary reinforcers**, such as water and food and escape from pain. Humans respond to these kinds of primary reinforcers, too, but we respond also to **secondary reinforcers** such as smiles, money, prizes, honors, applause, and phrases such as "Thank you" or "How thoughtful your present was." Parents, teachers, scout leaders, our peer groups, athletic coaches, our employers—all of these people are constantly reinforcing or extinguishing our behaviors in one way or another all the time (see Figure 5.4).

What We Think of as "Punishment" May Actually Be Positively Reinforcing. Skinner made the point that the most effective way to extinguish a child's behavior is through **nonreinforcement** (ignoring the behavior). Why? Because if we punish a child for an undesirable behavior, what we may really be doing is reinforcing it—*simply by giving attention to it.* Let's analyze an example from real-life.

Can you remember back in your grade school of some child who was the class clown or class cutup? He was usually a child who was not doing very well in his school work and he took out his frustrations by acting up in class or challenging the teacher with "sassy" remarks. Of course, the child was yelled at constantly by the teacher or sent to the office. You may recall how the other pupils giggled and egged the boy on to talk back and misbehave. (They didn't dare get in trouble by acting up, but they got much vicarious enjoyment out of his misbehavior.) The class clown was getting a lot of positive reinforcement from his classmates. Realizing this, the teacher usually instructed the other students not to giggle when he misbehaved. But of course her admonitions did no good, and they continued to giggle.

What the teacher may *not* have realized was that her own behavior of yelling and scolding him was also positively reinforcing to the child and actually *increasing* his misbehavior. As Skinner pointed out, any attention, even punishing attention, can be reinforcing. So how

Tip 5.3 For Test-Taking. Notice that Skinner never uses the word *stimulus*. He said that he did not know what the stimulus is. Is it the food? Or the rat's own hunger pangs? Or the delicately balanced lever? Skinner would simply not theorize about it. Skinner only uses the word *reinforcer*. Therefore if you come across a test item that has the word stimulus in it, the item must be referring to Pavlov's *classical conditioning*.

Figure 5.4 Skinner's World Skinner believed that the world is a giant Skinner box, which is continually shaping our behavior with reinforcements we value. Can you identify these reinforcers?

do we tell if we are extinguishing the behavior or positively reinforcing the behavior? Skinner said: Simply look at the consequences. If the undesirable behavior decreases or extinguishes, your actions have been **nonreinforcing.** If the undesirable behavior increases, then your actions (no matter how negative or punishing you thought them to be) were actually **positively reinforcing**.

Behavior Modification: Reinforcing the Desirable Behaviors through Environmental Engineering

Fortunately, most of a child's undesirable behaviors (such as thumb-sucking) will decrease in frequency and eventually drop out *(be extinguished)* simply by being ignored. Unfortunately, we can't always ignore a child's behavior. If the child is screaming insults in a classroom with 30 other children, a teacher is unwise to ignore it since the other children may follow suit! So what can the teacher do instead? For such situations, Skinner suggests that we devise a behavior modification program with techniques he called **environmental engineering**, such as *immediate feedback, time out* and *shaping of behavior*.

Immediate Feedback. A very important aspect of environmental engineering is **feedback** to the child about how the behavior is being perceived, whether the response is correct or incorrect, appropriate or inappropriate. *To be effective, the feedback must be immediate and clear.* The faster and clearer the feedback to animal, child, or adult, the faster the learning.

For example, let's take a child who is not doing well in arithmetic. The teacher is too busy to help her. She sits there helplessly while all the other children are doing their "independent seat work." What this child needs is a tutor to sit right down beside her, one-on-one, and to provide her with immediate feedback about what she is doing right and where she has gotten off the track. The tutor should correct any errors—then and there! One-on-one tutoring is the best instruction anyone can have—not just the little girl who is failing her arithmetic, but any and all of us—whether it is baseball, football, basketball, or soccer.

Time Out. Now to get back to that poor teacher with the child screaming insults at her in the class! For this situation, Skinner devised the technique of *time out*. **Time out** means putting the child in an environment that is nonreinforcing. If he is sent to sit in an office where other problem children are sitting, they will soon be giggling at each other, making faces, and if they are creative (as most children are), they will soon be inventing a sign language to communicate silently. The company of other children in the office turns out to be *positively* reinforcing. So what kind of an environment is nonreinforcing? How about a room that has nothing in it but a desk and chair! We are talking boredom here. There's not much that is reinforcing about boredom.

The child must be told that he can go back to the classroom whenever he demonstrates appropriate classroom behavior. Don't tell him what that behavior is—let him tell you. Most children know how they are supposed to behave. If he says he doesn't know, you reply (in the kindest and most reinforcing way imaginable) that you know how smart he is and you feel sure he can figure it out on his own. He may pout some now because this particular gambit isn't working as it has in the past. But eventually he will get so-o-o-o bored that he will tell you how he should behave. "Wonderful," you respond, "Do you think you can do that in the classroom?" He growls a grudging "Yeah," and you tell him that when he goes back, he must repeat his answer to the teacher. You feel sure she will let him return to his seat. No yelling here! No screaming! No lecturing! Just positive reinforcement when he makes the correct response. Boring time-out when he doesn't!

The Many Applications of Behavior Modification

Behavior modification has proved to be a highly reliable way to change behavior and the spin-offs have been many and varied. For example, cigarette smoking is a very difficult habit to stop and it amounts to a virtual addiction. Smokers want to quit the habit but have a very hard time doing so. In fact, in a survey conducted by the American Lung Association (Gemignani, 1998), seven smokers in ten said they hoped to quit and had tried repeatedly to give up tobacco. The most frequently used method to stop was "cold turkey," which turns out to be the least effective way, amounting to a mere 5 percent success rate. Pharmacological aids, nicotine replacement products, and anti-smoking medications (patches and gum) have been loudly touted by TV advertisement and have a higher success rate. Even antidepressants and tranquilizers have only a modicum of success. However, when these treatments are combined with a behavior modification program which has been devised by the smokers and therapists, the success rate is much higher.

Behavior modification is the basis of training animals, such as the porpoise shows at Marine Land. It is often used to help parents deal with defiant and unruly children or to build

---

Box 5.3   Evaluating Environmental Engineering as an Educational Method

Environmental engineering has had a lot of critiquing, not only by other psychologists, but by educators, philosophers, and commentators on the social scene.

On the Plus Side
1. **Effective in teaching specific new behaviors or eliminating undesirable ones.** There is no doubt that conditioning is a rapid-fire way to teach something new or to modify undesirable behavior.
2. **Many applications for psychology, education, health, and other areas.** Many techniques of environmental engineering are already in use in a number of institutional settings, such as the classroom, drug and alcohol rehabilitation half-way houses, juvenile detention centers, etc.
3. **Can be applied to our own personal lives.** We can all of us apply environmental engineering in our professional, social, and personal arenas.

On the Minus Side
1. **Does not teach creative thinking.** While environmental engineering is an effective way to induce desirable change, it is not a panacea. For one thing, it is not a creative act in that it does not foster original thinking.
2. **Can lead to some undemocratic usage.** Environmental engineering amounts to control of the person's behavior. We are manipulating the person just as we manipulate robots or animals we want to train. In that respect, it is contrary to our democratic belief in the worth and dignity of our constitutionally given freedoms.
3. **Has been used punitively.** At its worst, conditioning can be used for brainwashing, thought control, and political oppression—as it has been done in totalitarian and communist countries (Farber, 1957).

Box 5.4

Female (24 years): Whenever the phone rings in my apartment, I have an urge to say "Financial Aid" because I worked in that department for three years.

Male (26 years): Once when I ate 11 hotdogs in a row (just to win a bet), I got sick and upchucked for hours. Now I can't touch a hotdog.

Male (18 years): When I was a kid and my mother called me by my first and middle names, I knew I was in trouble.

Female (26 years): My father used to beat me with a belt with brass studs on it. To this day, the sound of someone clicking open their notebook makes me nervous.

Female (19 years): Maybe I shouldn't say this, but when my boyfriend lights a candle, I know we are going to have sex.

Male (32 years): I think all guys are conditioned like this. I check my zipper three or four times when I leave a men's room. I was once embarrassed when some kids in grade school made fun of me because I had forgotten to zip it.

Female (19 years): When I was in grade school, I had to come in from playing at five in the afternoon because that was when we kids had to eat without fail. Now I get hungry when it's five o'clock even if I've just eaten.

Female (23 years): Has anyone noticed that just walking into a movie theater makes you yearn for popcorn? It gets to me every time, even after just eating.

Male (41 years): When I was young, I used to visit my grandfather at the farm. He used to have me come in the barn and he'd help me learn how to whittle or make things or just help him. That's how I got to be so handy. But the barn was filled with wood chips and sawdust. It was a wonderful place. Now whenever I smell wood or sawdust, I get a very pleasant sensation.

Reflective writing: Reflect on some feeling or behavior that has been conditioned in you or someone else.

the self-esteem of educationally disadvantaged children. It is being employed with patients with Alzheimer's disease, with children who have eneuresis and with adolescents who have eating disorders. (See Box 5.3 and also the frontispiece to this chapter on p. 102 for more examples of how behavior modification is being applied).

Using the Facts of Learning and Conditioning to Develop Better Study Habits

One of the most practical applications of behavior modification is in developing efficient study habits. When we discuss *efficient* study habits, we are discussing being able to study *less* with *more* results. But before we can discuss these techniques, we need to learn about memory; that is, what helps us to remember and what is involved in forgetting. The prevailing theory today is that we have at least three kinds of memory: *sensory* (or *trace*) *memory*; *short-term* (or *working) memory*; and *long-term memory*. The purpose of discussing these three kinds of memory is to understand that we need methods by which to move information from our sensory memory through to our short-term memory and finally into our long-term memory (see Figure 5.5).

Three Types of Memory: Sensory, Short-Term, Long-Term. Our **sensory** or *trace memory* lasts for a very brief period—milliseconds, in fact. It is composed of all the thousands of stimuli that impinge on us from moment to moment: auditory sounds, stray thoughts, colors and forms, momentary bodily feelings, the dynamic whirlwind of passing emotions, unconnected bits of memory, smells, tastes, changes of temperature, etc. We are hardly aware of most of them, so quickly do they pass through our millisecond trace memory. A minute percentage, a very minute percentage, lasts long enough to pass on to our short-term memory.

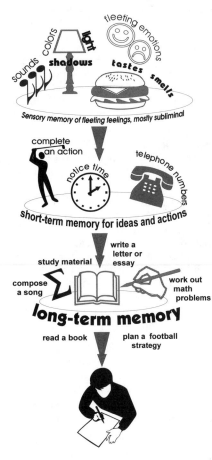

Figure 5.5 Three Types of Memory.

Our **short-term** or *working memory* is very busy. It functions for many everyday purposes, such as looking up and dialing a telephone number. We remember the number just long enough to dial it, and then we forget it. Another example of our short-term memory is when we scan newspapers for an item that might interest us. Unless we have a photographic memory, we probably couldn't tell you what most of the articles were about since our lack of interest lets them fade right out of our short-term memory. It really is very convenient to have a short-term memory. If we had to remember everything that ever happened in our lives, the clutter in our minds would interfere with our everyday functioning. The Russian psychologist, Alexander Luria, studied a person with a remarkable photographic memory. He could scan a newspaper quickly and remember every article and every word he had read. What Luria discovered was that this kind of photographic memory is not a blessing at all, but a curse. When asked to summarize an article, the man was unable to do so. Every word he read would release a flood of visual images and associations, which actually incapacitated his ability to isolate the essential points of the article (Luria, 1982).

Storing Material Into Our Long-Term Memory: How to Study Less and Remember More. A famous early German psychologist discovered that once something gets into our **long-term memory**, it has a good chance of lasting forever (Ebbinghaus, 1913). What makes something proceed to our long-term memory? Meaningfulness, clarity, and how compelling it is in terms of size, color, sound, etc. If it attracts our attention with much compelling force (like a car accident), we will likely store it somewhere in our memory to be recalled many times (see Figure 5.5). There are a variety of techniques for getting material into our long-term memories and the reader may already have developed many of them. But some of them will be new to the reader. Furthermore, most of these techniques are based on validated research studies so they are not just good ideas, but based on the scientific facts about how we learn, forget, and remember.

1. Become a proactive learner. The most basic element to improving your memory as you study is to realize that learning (putting something into our long-term memory) is not a passive process of simple absorption, as if our memory was a sponge. Most of us have had a similar experience to this first grader. The teacher called on him to read orally, which he did in very fine fashion. "Very good," said the teacher, "Now can you put what you read in your own words?" The little boy shook his head. "No, ma'am, I can't" Surprised, the teacher said, "But you read the material so well," "Yes, ma'am," replied the little boy, "only I wasn't listening." Sometimes, when we think we are reading, we realize after a couple of paragraphs that we haven't been paying attention (all those words we scanned dropped right out of our short-term memory). Getting something through to our long-term memory is an act of will, a very active process involving a mind-set to remember and determination to do so.

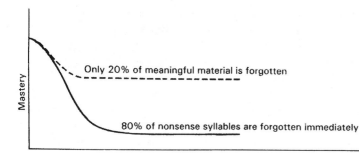

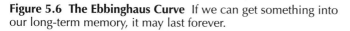

Only 20% of meaningful material is forgotten

80% of nonsense syllables are forgotten immediately

Figure 5.6 The Ebbinghaus Curve If we can get something into our long-term memory, it may last forever.

2. Make the material meaningful: avoid rote memory. Don't fall into the trap of learning facts or memorizing names without knowing what they mean. That is called rote memory. Yes, you can memorize a formula or a series of names but they fade very quickly from memory. In fact, what you learned may not even last until you take the exam. Every time you commit something to memory, understand what it means. Lock the new material into something you already know.

3. If you do have to memorize, concentrate on the nonsalient features. If you do have to memorize a list like the twelve cranial nerves, you need to be aware of the **serial position effect**. In a list, the two salient aspects are the beginning and the end of the list. The terms in the middle of the list do not stand out (are not salient) and will fade fast. Advice: Over-memorize the middle part of the list.

4. Use mnemonic devices that are meaningful. Everyone uses mnemonic devices, and they are very useful. But make sure the mnemonic device relates to what you are trying to remember. Many graduate students in medicine and psychology are asked to learn the twelve cranial nerves, that start with the *ophthalmic* nerve, the *occulo-motor* nerve, the *optic* nerve, and then go on to the last nerve, the *hypo-glysseal* nerve. There is a traditional sentence that students sometime use to remember the order that goes like this: *On old Olympic's towering tops, a Finn and German vaulted a hedge.* Each of the beginning letters is the same as the beginning letter of a cranial nerve. There are two problems with this mnemonic device. The first is the sentence we are memorizing has little to do with neurology. The second problem is that if we accidentally skip one of the words, we've lost all the rest of the nerves that come after. Two much better mnemonic devices are the ones we had to learn in the early grades to help us with our reading and spelling. They are both related to the material we are trying to remember, and they both employ rhythm and rhyme which makes it much easier to store in our long-term memory.

To distinguish when we use *ei* or *ie*:	To remember how to pronounce the words *boat, read, raid, etc.*
I before e *Except after c* *Or when sounded like A* *As in neighbor or weigh.*	*When two vowels go walking,* *The first does the talking.* (In each of the words above, the first vowel is spoken while second vowel is silent.)

5. Using distributed and massed practice appropriately. Some students insist they do their best studying under pressure, meaning that they wait until the last minute to crash-study for exams. That is an example of **massed practice.** (We generally agree with them since that is usually the only time they really study.) **Distributed practice** means to study or practice some each day (usually for a much briefer period of time). Which do you think is better? Well, if you are practicing the piano, or studying for a psychology exam, or learning Spanish, or working out on the football field or in the gym, then definitely distributed practice is the most efficient. Seven hours of practice on Sunday is not nearly as good as one hour of practice each day of the week. There are situations, however, when massed practice is better: when the material you are working on demands much thinking or organization, such as a physics problem or a term paper or anything that requires a large time frame. That doesn't mean you should wait until the night before to write the term paper. Actually, you should write the paper sometime before the due date and then redraft in the week or so before its due!

6. Use motor learning: It is highly resistant to extinction. One of the best-known facts of learning and forgetting is this: Any activity that has been learned with some kind of muscular involvement (motor learning) is highly resistant to extinction. Those of you who have done a lot of swimming and diving know that even if you haven't been in the water for several years, you do not forget your diving or swimming techniques. You may have lost some of your stamina or polish, but you won't have forgotten how to stroke or dive. The same is true of music. Ask a musician if he remembers how to play a certain song, and he may screw up his face as he tries to remember the melody. In short order, however, his fingers will be reaching for all those old familiar chords even though he may not have played the piece in several years. So how can you use motor learning to become a better student? The answer: Take notes. When you write, you use your muscles. As a matter of fact, if you're the type who likes to write lists, you may have already discovered that once you have written your list, you may not even have to refer to it. Writing the items helps you remember. So take notes. Take notes in class. Take notes when the teacher is lecturing. Take notes as you read the text.

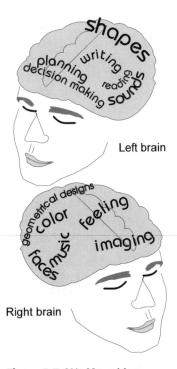

Figure 5.7 We Have Many Kinds of Memory By using a multisensory approach and both our left and right brain, we establish more neural connections between different parts of our brain.

7. Use a multisensory approach. If using motor learning is an effective way to remember what you are studying, think how much more effective it is when you use more than just your muscle memory. We have many kinds of memory that involve our senses. We have several kinds of visual memory: a memory for faces, a memory for geometric designs, a memory for color, etc. We have many kinds of auditory memory: a memory for names, a memory for music, a memory for speech. We also have memory for scent, for feeling and touch, and for taste, etc. (see Figure 5.7). How do we know we have different kinds of memories? From the area of neurological pathology. A lesion to one part of the brain may result in loss of the memory for faces. A lesion to another part of the brain may result in the loss of memory for color, etc. The more of these sensory memories we use in our learning, the more connections we make in our brain—and the more opportunity to get the material into our long-term memory. Use both sides of your brain when studying: Combine music, art, muscular movement with language and math concepts.

8. Provide yourself with immediate feedback. If you can make flash cards with questions and answers on possible exam items (as has been done commercially with language vocabulary cards), you are providing yourself with *immediate feedback*.

9. Make yourself specific study objectives. If you just go home and say to yourself, "I will study for two hours," your study objective is a matter of clock-watching. You will pay more attention to the clock than to what you are studying. *Gosh! Only forty-five minutes. I've still got an hour and fifteen minutes to go. (Sigh.)* Make your study objective the material you are learning. *OK., I'll take notes on Chapter 6 of my history and do the first part of my art assignment.* Then when you are finished with your two objectives, you have a feeling of satisfaction for having accomplished your study objectives. Now *reinforce* your studying behavior by whatever is good for you: Call a friend, turn on TV, go to the movies, whatever.

10. Set the material by reviewing, reviewing, reviewing. You've heard this many times before so we won't elaborate except to say that reviewing solidifies your learning in your long-term memory.

Box 5.5

SCENARIO REVISITED
My Son Sucks His Whole Hand? It's Driving Me Crazy!

Martha: My ten-year-old son sucks his whole hand. It's driving me crazy! (*Class laughter*). Well, at least four fingers. He puts all four fingers in his mouth. There I am vacuuming, and he begins his hand-sucking and he's driving me crazy with it. I yell at him every time he does it, and what Skinner says is that my yelling at him is reinforcing that behavior? (*Jill Smith nods.*)

Martha: But I don't want him to suck his fingers in school.

Eduardo: I'll give you odds he's not sucking his fingers in school.

Martha: How do you know that?

Eduardo: Cause the other guys would make fun of him.

Jill Smith: Does your son know he gets a rise out of you every time he does it?

Martha: He knows I can't stand it!

Jonnimae: He's jerking your collar, baby! My brother used to do that to my mother. She couldn't stand anyone sniffling. Whenever she got on his case about something, he'd start sniffling. She'd say, "Stop that sniffling. I can't stand it. Go blow your nose." He got out of a lot of bad situations like that.

Jill Smith: It probably entertains him to see you fly off the handle. Children are very smart, a lot cannier and

foxier than their parents. I'm not saying they are wiser than we are. Wisdom comes with years of living on this earth and learning from many life experiences. But children in this age group like to see if they can outfox their parents.

Martha: So I shouldn't say anything at all? Can I at least turn away so I don't have to watch it?

Jill Smith: That's a good idea. Your back is not very reinforcing. Just calmly turn your attention to something else so he doesn't know he's "jerked your collar" again.

Martha: (*A few weeks later.*):"It's working! I wasn't sure I could hold my temper because I still seethe inside. I don't show it though. He's not sucking his hand as much any more. I know it will take more time, but I'm wise to it now." (*The class reinforces her new behavior and success with a lot of hand-clapping and expressions of congratulations.*)

Reflective Writing: Reflect on some behavior on your part by which you unwittingly reinforced undesirable behavior in someone else. Record your insight. Then devise a strategy by which you no longer reinforce that behavior.

Box 5.6

RESEARCH METHODOLOGY
Experimental Conditioning

On the Plus Side

1. Experimental conditioning turned the study of psychology into a genuine science. With the discovery of both classical and operant conditioning, psychology "came of age" as a science in its own right. Psychology finally had developed a rigorous scientific methodology for measuring the psychological variable we call learning.

2. Experimental conditioning can be done under rigorous laboratory conditions. As a method of research, conditioning is the example par excellence for how we learn, and its conclusions are unassailable for the laboratory situation. In contrast to naturalistic observation, survey, case study, etc., laboratory conditioning can control all the relevant variables. By controlling all the variables we can finally make a statement about cause-and-effect. Only experimental research under laboratory conditions can isolate the determining factor or factors. With all other methods, we can make a statement about "probable cause," but this probable cause is always based on inference—which means we think we know what is going on. But until the "probable cause" is supported by experimental research, the hypothesis must always remain tentative.

3. The experimental observations are empirical. *Classical* and *operant conditioning* have both derived terms that do not depend on inference. Terms such as *unconditioned response* and *extinction* and *spontaneous recovery* do not infer what's going on inside the "mind" of the rat, or the dog, or the person. Two independent observers can agree that the subject in question is demonstrating this behavior. The behavior can be turned into numerical data and graphed.

4. Animal subjects can be used. Since many laboratory experiments cannot be done on human beings, animals are used in this type of experimental research.

On the Minus Side

1. The artificiality of the laboratory situation. The laboratory situation is least like real life. The very fact that the conditioning takes place in a laboratory makes the environment artificial. Under real life circumstances, there may be not just one or even two variables influencing the behavior of the person. Most human behaviors are multidetermined.

2. Generalizing research on animals to humans. The big problem is applying the results of laboratory conditions to human beings who are much more complex in nature and subject to many more environmental influences of real life.

IMPORTANT TERMS AND CONCEPTS TO KNOW

aversive	free will	models	operant
baby	freedom	modification	reinforced
classical	genetic	motor learning	role models
conditioning	generalized	multisensory	spontaneous recovery
extinguished	Lamaze	nonreinforced	time out
extinction	learned	neutral	unconditioned
feedback	learning	observational	

Box 5.7

SCENARIO REVISITED
Eduardo Reports on His Behavior Modification to Stop Smoking

Eduardo: I've made a discovery, a very important discovery! I know why it is so hard to stop smoking! Smoking is not one habit. It's a hundred habits.

Martha: Oh, come on, you're going to tell us that's why you can't quit—because it's a hundred habits?

Eduardo: Oh, I'm quitting all right. I've made my mind up to that! But I'm quitting them one at a time.

Jill Smith: Tell us about it.

Eduardo: Well, you know how you told us to keep a journal of the target behavior for a week or two? Well, I did that. Here's what I discovered. I smoke when I drink coffee. I smoke when I have a beer. I smoke when I begin to play the guitar. I light up when I start the car. I smoke after every meal. I light up when I open my books to study. See what I mean?

Jill Smith: So how are you quitting?

Eduardo: Well, you said to avoid places I smoke. So I don't go to the bar and have a beer any more. Good for me anyway, not to drink beer. I was getting a beer belly.

Jill Smith: Any other habits broken yet?

Eduardo: Yeah, I used to smoke first thing getting up in the morning. Isn't that terrible—to put all that poison in your system first thing! Whew! Now I say to myself I will not smoke until after breakfast. Pretty soon, I stop that habit too. I'm just doing one at a time. But I've broken two more habits.

Jill Smith: They are?

Eduardo: Well, I stopped smoking in the car completely. That's one. And I stopped using a cigarette to start my guitar playing. I love playing my guitar. I don't need a "starter." I think my hardest ones to break will be not smoking after a meal. That's my most enjoyable

Eduardo's List: Smoking Is a Hundred Habits

1. Waking up
2. After breakfast
3. With coffee
4. Starting car
5. With beer
6. With coffee
7. Playing guitar
8. Begin studying
9. In-between classes
10. After last class
11. With Roger (a friend)
12. Watching TV
13. After lunch
14. After dinner
15. On the telephone
16. As a study break
17. Decision-making
18. Offer one to girls

time to smoke. But I know I'll succeed. I'm determined.

Jill Smith: Eduardo is mentioning something essential to self-modification procedures, the determination to change. Eduardo, what do you use for reinforcers?

Eduardo: After I break a habit, I let myself go to the movies. If I find myself lighting up a cigarette with coffee, I make myself run around the building three times. I'm out of breath then and I don't feel much like smoking. It's a good way to keep myself in shape too.

MAKE YOUR CHAPTER SUMMARY BY FILLING IN THE BLANKS BELOW

Use the "Important Terms and Concepts to Know" on facing pace 118 to fill in the blanks below.

Etiology of Behavior. Generally speaking, there are two types of behavior, called maturation and _____ . Maturation is the result of our _____ encoding.

Ivan Pavlov. A Russian physiologist, Ivan Pavlov, introduced the world to the process of _____ . What Pavlov discovered was that any _____ stimulus (such as a bell) can be made to be a conditioned stimulus by pairing it with an _____ stimulus (such a meat powder). Furthermore, once the conditioning to the

---

Box 5.8

Jill Smith: Now lets bring all these facts of conditioning and learning to a practical every day level. Jonnimae, do you remember how you described your studying problem when we first began our unit on conditioning?

Jonnimae: Sure, I said I get sleepy the minute I start to study in my bedroom.

Jill Smith: But where in your bedroom? (*Jonnimae looks puzzled. Then a look of understanding spreads over her face.*)

Jonnimae: Oh my gosh! I see what you mean! I study on my bed!

Jill Smith: Good! You've discovered something. Can you put it in Pavlov's empirical language?

Jonnimae: I'm conditioned to sleep on my bed. So when I try to study on my bed, I get sleepy instead.

Annamaria: *Mama mia!* I use the kitchen table to study and nibble and nibble and nibble.

Jonnimae: Does that mean I can't study in my bedroom? I don't have much privacy.

Jill Smith: Well, at least not on your bed. What you need to do is to make a place that you don't do anything else but study. It can be a desk or simply a chair in the corner of the room, even your bedroom. What you will be doing is conditioning yourself to study there. The minute you sit down in that chair or at that desk, it will arouse the conditioned response to study.

Jonnimae: Well, I'm going to get myself a desk and chair. No more studying on the bed.

Annamaria: And no studying on the table for me! That's where I eat and eat!

Jonnimae: I think I've got a good memory for figures, but how do you use color memory or music memory for studying?

Shannon: I think I know how a little. I call them my "study tricks." For example, I make diagrams and charts and I color them. I love to make models of molecules for chemistry. All it takes is a few cotton balls for the atoms and some toothpicks to hold them together to make molecules. I guess you could use clay or plastic styrofoam, too.

Eduardo: I sometimes put names and dates and facts to music. I got that idea from my humanities course. The teacher gave us this one to help us remember who wrote it: (Sings the opening bars of Schubert's "8th Symphony.")

This is the symphony that Schubert wrote and never finished.

This is the theme in G. . . .

I make up words to songs that help me remember things. English is a hard language to learn how to spell. In Spanish, everything is spelled the way it looks. But not English. So I put hard English words to music. Here's one to La Cucaracha. *Ought* is a hard word. It has all those silent letters: *u* and *g* and *h*. So I hum in my head (*sings to La Cucaracha*)

O-U-G-H-T   O-U-G-H-T

That's the way to spell the word.

(*Laughter from the other students.*)

Martha: Is there any truth to the idea we have a left-brain and a right-brain and they do different things?

Jill Smith: The jury is still out on that but there seem to be definite differences. Even daydreaming seems to function more on the right. But of course both brains are involved in everything we do and the more we use both parts of the brain, as many areas of the brain as we can, the more fixed becomes the concept in our memory banks. Got some ideas you can use now, Jonnimae?

Jonniemae: I think so. Kind of makes studying less of a chore and more fun.

---

bell had occurred, the salivation response _____ to other auditory stimuli.

When the bell was presented many times without the meat powder, the conditioned response of salivation eventually stopped again; in other words, the behavior _____ . Surprisingly, after a period of time when the bell was rung, the dog began salivating again. Pavlov called this reoccurrence of salivation by the term _____ .

Applications of classical conditioning. The Russians used the facts of conditioning in their educative practices and in their birthing procedures, now called the _____ method.

John Watson. Pavlov worked only with dogs. It was the American psychologist John Watson who applied conditioning to a human _____ , called Albert. Watson conditioned Albert to fear a little white laboratory rat. Painful conditioning is also called _____ conditioning.

B. F. Skinner. Skinner formulated _____ conditioning. Skinner did not believe in such concepts as _____ and _____ . He believed the world to be a giant Skinner Box in which we are constantly being positively _____ with smiles, money, honors, applause, etc. In addition to the shaping of desired behavior, Skinner proposed two other techniques of environmental engineering: putting the child in a nonreinforcing area, which he called _____ , to correct bad behavior, and stressing the effectiveness of immediate _____ for learning. Behavior _____ is a way for us to change behaviors in ourselves or in our children. One of the important elements of learning new ways of behaving is to provide children and adolescents with positive _____ they can imitate.

Guidelines for effective studying. One of the most important of these guidelines is to use _____ learning because it is highly resistant to _____ (forgetting). Another helpful studying technique is to use a _____ technique, which utilizes many sensory modalities.

6 ANXIETY AND DEFENSE MECHANISMS
Causes, Complications, and Coping Strategies

When physical pain overwhelms us, we lose consciousness; when psychological pain threatens to overwhelm us, we escape via our defense mechanisms.

Box 6.1

SCENARIO
What Is Causing Your Anxiety?

Jill Smith, the graduate student from the state university, is leading a small group discussion.

Jill Smith: The assignment today is to share an anxiety and how you handle it. I never ask a group to do anything I wouldn't do. So I'll share mine first. I imagine all kinds of things that could go wrong with what I've planned . . . so I devise two or three alternate lesson plans—just in case. I have only had to change plans once, but it sure is comforting to have them at hand. Dan?

Dan: I have a rage inside me when I'm around "whites." Sometimes I'm not sure I can control it. I'd like to hit some of these cowboys right in the jaw when they start kidding around with me.

Eduardo: I'm surprised that you get that kind of kidding, Dan. Indians . . . I guess I should say "Native Americans" . . . have become our folk heroes these days.

Dan: Yeah, we've become folk heroes all right, only we're still getting the short end of the stick. That's why I'm here in college. To do something—not just for my tribe, but for all Native American nations . . . About the kidding. . . later, after it's all over, I know what they say is in good fun, only I don't see it that way at the time. I don't feel in control.

Jill Smith: Let's see what we can do about your trigger response of anger, Dan. Shannon, I know your shyness is causing you anxiety.

Shannon: Is it ever! I'm so shy, it's hard for me to say "no" even when I don't want to do something.

Eduardo: This is embarrassing for me to admit, but when I don't get a good grade on a test, I make up all kinds of excuses why I didn't study more, like . . . I was sick or I had to help a friend. And I know deep in my heart I just didn't study enough.

Martha: I do something I really would like to get over. If I've had a hard day at work or school and one of my kids gets a little playful, I snap at them. Of course, I feel bad immediately and try to make up for it. But I'd like to get over snapping at them.

Alec: I'm going to pass for the time being.

Jonnimae: I'll tell you when I get anxious! When I walk into an exam. Even when I have studied for it and I think I really know the material, I freeze! I can't remember anything. I just blank out!

Jill Smith: As we have just shown, we all have our own anxieties. Anxiety is a part of life. There is no such thing as a life without anxiety. What we can do is learn to cope with our anxieties in better and better ways.

Symptoms of Anxiety: Their Many Shapes and Forms

It was Freud who first defined our present understanding of anxiety. He differentiated *anxiety* from *fear.* We generally know what we are afraid of, be it another person or a test we don't think we'll pass or not having enough money to pay our bills. Anxiety, on the other hand, is a more diffuse emotion, which cannot always be easily identified. Anxiety can be felt psychologically as "nervousness," without knowing why, or expressed as "knots in the stomach" or "weak in the knees." The symptoms and complications of anxiety are legion! (See Table 6.1.)

To truly understand the phenomenon of anxiety, we must comprehend this basic fact: *Anxiety is painful.* The pain of anxiety may come from a sense of guilt, from a secret shame, from the memory of an abusive past, from fear of the future, from negative self-esteem, and so on. But wherever it comes from or however it is experienced, anxiety is painful. When we experience overwhelming physical pain, our body defends itself by losing consciousness. We faint. We pass out. In like manner, when the pain of anxiety becomes overwhelming, we defend against that pain by losing conscious awareness of it. We may lose the conscious awareness of the pain but the anxiety manifests in other behaviors. Freud called these behaviors **defense mechanisms.**

Defense Mechanisms Protect Us from the Pain of Anxiety . . . But Are Also Barriers to Our Further Growth

Here is a scenario you may all be familiar with. You're in an argument with someone and the other person is telling you something about yourself "for your own good." When you protest, the other person accuses you of being "defensive." Don't let anyone ever play that game with you! We all have defenses. We need our defense mechanisms to survive. Just as we need our physical immune system to protect us against infection, so too do we need our emotional defense system to protect us against overwhelming anxiety.

Unfortunately, our defense mechanisms can also be barriers to our further growth and evolution. As children, we may have learned that a temper tantrum not only helped us cope with our feelings of frustration, it also got us our parents' attention. If we continue to use that defense as an adult by stamping our feet or shouting, other adults will consider us as childishly immature. That kind of reputation will block our chances for jobs that require "maturity"—a cool head to handle the problems that come up. Furthermore, our defense mechanisms distort reality. Instead of seeing what is really going on "out there," our vision and our hearing is being filtered through a haze of anxiety, anger, panic, worry, etc. In the words of two famous psychologists, our defense mechanisms make us "deaf, dumb, and blind" (Dollard & Miller, 1966).

Table 6.1 Common Symptoms of Anxiety: Their Number is Legion!

Alcoholism	Grinding teeth	Minor acne	Picking off lint
Allergies	Headaches	Mouth clucking	Procrastinating
Anger (excessive)	Heart palpitations	Muscle cramps	Puckering lips
Clammy hands	Heartburn	Muscle spasms	Rocking
Crying (excessive)	Hyperactivity	Nightmares	Rubbing hands
Drug addiction	Insomnia	Night terrors	Sighing (constant)
Facial tics	Junk food eating	Oversleeping	Stuttering
Fainting	Lip biting	Perspiring	Sweating (profuse)
Fatigue (constant)	"Lump" in throat	Phobias	Tongue clicking

Figure 6.1 Defense mechanisms. They can be barriers to our further growth.

Defense Mechanisms Can Be Injurious to Others! Unfortunately, our defense mechanisms may also be detrimental to the growth and well-being of others. In fact, they may be very harmful to those we love the most. For example, an alcoholic parent may take out the frustration of losing his job by abusing his wife and children. It behooves all of us, then, to study ourselves diligently so that we can become more productive persons, more loving family members, and more self-actualizing individuals.

The Etiology of Anxiety: Genetics and Environment

Anxiety is present from the very beginning of our life on earth. In fact, children experience anxiety even more intensely than adults because children do not know how to express their anxiety. We can observe anxiety even in infants, as Watson did with Baby Albert. Moreover, infants can become terrified by events we think nothing of—the sudden disappearance of Mother or the sudden appearance of a stranger's face (stranger anxiety) in their field of vision. But, in fact, the etiology of human anxiety may begin long before then. It may begin at birth, or even before. Difficulties in the uterine environment or a difficult birth process may make us more vulnerable to human anxiety. Furthermore, anxiety and our ability (or inability) to cope may be genetic in part.

The Genetics of Personality

The nature/nurture question is one of the enduring philosophic/scientific quests of psychology. *How much of our personality is due to our genetic inheritance (nature) and how much to our environmental experiences (nurture)?* The strongest evidence for the genetic component of personality comes from several sources:

- Twin studies: identical twins who were separated at birth and raised in different environments.
- Studies of genetic defects among relatives: parents, siblings, cousins, children.
- Comparisons of adopted children with their biological versus adoptive families.
- Molecular biology: the study of DNA material and personality traits.

The research data so far suggest quite strongly that certain types of anxiety and emotional disorders definitely "run in families." The only issue now to be argued over is: *How much of our personality is due to nature (genetics) and how much is due to nurture (environment)?*

The concept that some people are genetically disposed toward anxiety may seem strange at first, but it coincides with other personality traits that seem to have a genetic component. Alcoholism, the trait we call "shyness," and many serious mental disorders have all been identified as heavily genetic in origin. Is it any more unusual for the trait we call "anxiety" to also have a strong genetic component?

The Twin Studies. In the first half of the 20th century, twin studies clearly established the genetic aspect of intelligence. Identical twins raised apart are much more similar in intelligence to each other than they are to their adoptive family members—no matter how differently they are raised. IQ has a concordance factor of about 75 percent. Other personality factors, however, also have an astounding mean (average) concordance factor, which hovers around 50 percent. To summarize the research briefly, studies of twins separated at birth and raised in different environments are strikingly more similar to each other in personality traits, in attitudes, in what they like to do for work and leisure, preferences for clothes, jewelry, hairstyle, etc., than to their foster or adoptive families (see Box 6.2).

Ethnically and Racially Distinct Characteristics. When a population remains stable over a period of centuries (does not move around and does not interbreed with other populations), there is a tendency for certain genes to increase in frequency in that gene pool—for good and for ill! Africans have a deficient gene in their genetic pool which makes them susceptible to sickle-cell anemia. Northern Europeans are susceptible to cystic fibrosis, a lung disease that ultimately proves fatal. Scandinavians are susceptible to phenylketonuria (PKU) which, if not treated, can result in mental and physical retardation. Mediterranean peoples, such as Italians, Greeks, and North African Arabs, are susceptible to thalassemia anemia. East European Jews are susceptible to Tay-Sach's disease. Both Jews and Africans have higher-than-average allergic reactions to milk products. The genetic differences of these populations do not mean they are inferior. Despite the pride that the royal families of Europe take in their "royal blood," their inbreeding has produced a high frequency of hemophilia. So much for the superiority of royal blood!

On the other hand, stable genetic pools can produce other characteristics that are neither favorable nor unfavorable. The Scandinavians and Highland Scots of Europe, the Masai of Africa, and the Sioux Nation of America are genetically tall. Does that mean that they are superior? No, only that they are taller. We are finally getting over our nervousness about racial or ethnic differences and are able to celebrate our multicultural diversity. In addition to physical characteristics, research has even revealed that "emotionality" differs significantly in different racial and ethnic groups (Freedman, 1974).

Environmental Influences Before and During Birth

The fact that some identical twins do not fall victim to the same problems also suggests there may be a penetrance factor. By **penetrance factor,** geneticists mean that the difference in the twins could also be related to something that happens in the womb. Contrary to what was once believed, the placenta does not protect the baby against infection. We have long known that certain diseases are very toxic to the developing baby, among which are rubella (German measles), diphtheria, and scarlet fever. Now we know that many other elements can penetrate the placenta and violate the baby's uterine development. In terms of identical twins developing in the womb, one of the babies could be affected and not the other. The popular media have publicized the tragedy of the "cocaine babies" who are born with what amounts to an addiction to cocaine. They lag physically, mentally, and emotionally for months, even years, after birth. Women who drink alcohol increase the chance of their babies being born with birth defects, particularly with fetal alcohol syndrome, characterized by physical deformities and intellectual retardation (Rosenthal, 1995).

Box 6.2　RESEARCH METHODOLOGY
The Twin Studies (Genetics Are Constant and Environment Varies)

For almost 40 years, the University of Minnesota has been the site of an investigation on the characteristics of identical twins. Some of these twins, who were separated at birth and brought together for the first time, showed such extraordinary similarities that the researchers were actually "spooked" by their similarities, despite the enormous differences of their adoptive family environments. Some of the outstanding examples will illuminate.

The Jim Twins. The research study began with the study of identical twins who, by some strange token, were both named "Jim." They were both adopted into working-class Ohio families, but never knew each other before the study. Both were good in math but poor in spelling. Both had worked as part-time deputy sheriffs. Both vacationed in Florida. Both preferred Chevrolets. Both liked the same brands of liquor and cigarettes. And as if that were not enough, when they got anxious, they both chewed their fingernails to the nub.

The Ring Twins. Bridget and Dorothy were 39 years old when they met for the first time. Both twins had extraordinary fondness for beautiful hands. Not only did they both have manicured nails, they both wore seven rings on their hands and three bracelets.

Roger and Tony Twins. Roger was raised in Florida by highly educated Jewish parents and Tony in an Italian family in Philadelphia. They were found to have identical IQ scores and similar jobs. They liked the same toothpaste, aftershave lotion, and cigarettes, and the same type of women . . . , and (get this!) they had similar gift-giving preferences. After they met, they gave each other a surprise gift: identical shirt-and-tie sets.

The German/Jewish Twins. But perhaps the most extraordinary example is that of two boys, one raised by a German Nazi mother, the other by his Jewish Hispanic father in the Caribbean. Besides looking very much alike, both wore pin-striped suits, a small mustache, and rimless glasses. Considering the extreme differences of their growing up, the investigators were amazed at their similarities.

The strong personality genetics of twin studies have been confirmed by a massive Swedish study involving five hundred pairs of Swedish twins, both identical and fraternal. So far, the personality factors listed below have been established as having a strong genetic component and the list keeps growing!

Mental Factors	Anxiety/Emotional Factors	Worldview	Work and Leisure
Intelligence (IQ)	Alcohol & drug addiction	Optimism	Television viewing
Mental speed	Self-esteem & shyness	Alienation	Leadership
	Crime & violence	Religiosity	Job satisfaction
	Depression & "neuroticism"	Authoritarianism	Thrill-seeking
	Extraversion & dominance	Traditionalism	

Sources: Bouchard, Lykken, McGue, Segal, Tellegen, 1990.

Criticism of Genetic Theory of Personality

1. **Concordance Rate is Only 50–75 percent.** If genetics were the sole causative factor of personality traits, the concordance rate would be 100 percent or very close.
2. **Environment Plays Equal Part.** Critics have warned us not to fall into the nature camp too wholeheartedly. If the heritability traits hover around 50 percent, it still leaves 50 percent to the environment.
3. **Blaming the Victim.** By focusing on the genetic aspect of personality, we are ignoring the real causes of violence and crime; namely, poverty, racism, illiteracy, and unemployment. Biology may contribute to violence but environment tips the balance.

Otto Rank: The Birth Trauma

Otto Rank (1884–1939) was among the first professionals to join Sigmund Freud in Vienna. Rank was particularly impressed by what he called birth trauma, by which he meant the pain and suffering the baby must experience as a result of hours of labor and the contractions that ultimately eject him from the uterus. Rank pointed out that birthing can be so brutal (even to the point of strangulation by the umbilical cord) that the human psyche is forever marked by this experience. Rank believed that although the adult cannot consciously remember this experience, every time the man or woman sustains a threat in adult life, it must trip an unconscious memory of those early awful hours of the birth contractions (Rank, 1941). Rank's birth trauma theory was not taken very seriously in the United States, but some European health professionals took it very seriously indeed.

Ronald Laing: Rebirthing Therapy

Ronald Laing, a British psychiatrist, laid much of the blame for a patient's dysfunctional behavior on the confused communication and interaction that goes on between a dysfunctional parent and young child. In these parent/child communications, the child is always wrong, no matter what the child says or does (Laing, 1970). As a consequence, the child develops double-bind thinking (see Box 6.3). As an adult he manifests such "crazy knots" in thinking and emotional judgment that sane thinking is impossible. Laing evolved a therapy in which the patient symbolically "died" to his present confused existence, and was then "reborn" in a symbolic birth process. Part of the therapeutic treatment actually involved the patient in a facsimile of the birth procedure, attended by his therapeutic family and other friends who welcomed the reborn person into a world where people do not lie or say one thing and mean another. Clear communication—without lies, without pretense, without phoniness, without false compliments—is what the reborn patient is taught. "Don't lie just because the truth may hurt" is the dictum by which the newborn adult now lives. We can cope with hurt feelings. Lies (even kindly lies) distort reality and make for "craziness." Laing insisted on truth (even if it hurts), so that we can think clearly and sanely.

William James' "Twice Born" and the "Born Again" Experience

Before the reader rejects Laing's rebirthing theory, remember that many Christian sects call their members "born again Christians." They have had an experience so extraordinary that they describe it as "being reborn." Psychologists do not as yet have much understanding of this phenomenon, but the whole attitude of "born-agains" toward living and being-in-the-world has undergone a profound transformation. The pioneering American psychologist William James also referred to a rebirth experience. He described two kinds of persons: those who go about their lives in unquestioning optimism and those—like himself—who, at some time in their lives, go through a severe, even suicidal, depression. In order to survive the crisis of depression, the person must go through a psychological rebirth, and James even called them the "twice-born" and counted himself among them (James, 1890).

Box 6.3

RONALD LAING
The Knots of Double-Binding Thinking

Ronald Laing has provided many examples of double-bind ideas, which he calls "crazy knots" of thinking that result in no-win situations for the person.

Child-Parent Double-Bind. When my mother loves me, I feel good. She loves me now so I must be a good person now. When she does not love me, I feel bad. When she does not love me, I must be a bad person.

Child-Parent Double-Bind. I hate my father when he beats me. But if I hate my father I am a bad person. I do not want to be a bad person. I will not hate my father when he beats me. I will love my father when he beats

me. Besides my father says when he beats me, it is because he loves me.

Parent-Child Double-Bind. A child should respect parents. When she does not respect us, we beat her. She learns to respect us when we beat her.

Female Double-Bind. I am not worthy of respect. Therefore I cannot respect anyone who respects me. When you respect me, I suspect you are not worthy of my love. When someone rejects me, I respect that person. The only way I can love you is if you reject me.

Frederick Leboyer's Gentle Birth

On this side of the Atlantic, we are acknowledging the birth trauma theory via the gentle birth methods of Frederick Leboyer. Leboyer, a French physician, took a step beyond the natural childbirth methods such as the Lamaze method. While Dr. Lamaze had focused primarily on the mother's birthing experience, Leboyer focused on the baby's birth experience. Leboyer objected to the prevailing obstetric methods of delivering babies. The baby's umbilical cord was immediately severed. The baby was held upside-down to induce the respiratory system to start breathing, and the baby was given a smack on the bottom causing him to scream. The baby was then washed, subjected to sodium nitrate in his eyes (to prevent syphilis), finger printed, and foot printed before being allowed to rest. Then he was whisked away to the nursery (to give his mother a rest from her labors) at the most crucial time for mother-baby bonding—the first 12 hours after birth.

Leboyer (1975) objected to this treatment of the baby. Why, he demanded, should a baby's first introduction to life outside the womb be such a violent one? He wanted to make a baby's first experience in the world more "loving" and welcoming. So he redesigned the birth experience as follows. Now babies are ushered into a comfortable, warm room and placed on the mother's abdomen (as close as possible to the place he has been growing for the last nine months), where he can feel his mother's familiar heartbeat. The umbilical cord is not severed until it stops pulsating (about six minutes after birth). Leboyer believed that this more gentle and welcoming birth must reduce the birth trauma and have a positive effect on the baby's personality style. He believed that as an adult, the baby would

Figure 6.2 Gentle Birth. Frederick Leboyer took birth trauma very seriously and campaigned against "violent birth."

develop into a more confident, more spontaneous, more authentic, more creative person. Has this proved to be the case? As yet, we do not have any long-term data to substantiate this assumption. We do know the medical professions the world over have taken Leboyer's gentle birth methods to heart by incorporating his methods into their birthing methods.

Environmental Determinants as We Grow

Genetics, however, is only half the story. We develop many of our defending mechanisms as the result of our experiences growing up. Children who have been abused, physically or sexually, carry the scars for the rest of their lives. Perhaps 30 percent (statistics vary) of these adult survivors react by becoming brutal spouses or parents themselves. Some adult survivors of child abuse tend to connect to people who are similar to their abusing parents and continue to live submissive roles as their "lot in life." Still others adopt (or try to adopt) child-rearing methods quite opposite to their parents and "give in" to the child at all costs rather than teach their own children self-discipline. For example, children of alcoholic parents may either use alcohol to bolster themselves when they encounter problems or try to become "perfect" nondrinking personalities (Bohling, 1989). In the latter case, they demand the impossible, not only of themselves but of other people as well, which no one can live up to. If we grew up feeling inferior in any way, we try to compensate (or overcompensate) by becoming physically or academically superior to others. Or we may try to outdo others in monetary affairs or by becoming

---

Box 6.4   A CULTURE DEVELOPS PERSONALITY TRAITS IT VALUES

The Stoical Utku Eskimos. The Utku Eskimos of Alaska discourage anger by cultivating calm acceptance of problematic situations and by dissociating themselves from any display of anger. Utku Eskimos avoid other people who respond highly emotionally. Consider what kind of personality structure it takes to deal with an unexpected and life-threatening blizzard. Utkus do not display fright or desperation. When they perceive such an environmental threat, they mildly and unhurriedly build an igloo to survive the snowstorm. Panic reactions that some of us might express in such a situation would only worsen the situation. It is, therefore, to their advantage to cultivate a non-emotional response to environmental threat (Briggs, 1970).

The Peaceable !Kung and the Fierce Yanomamo. These two tribes from southern Africa and South America, respectively, provide an interesting contrast in values and personality structure. The !Kung have been called the "harmless people" because of their peaceful way of life. They discourage any kind of aggression in their children and resolve disputes calmly. The Yanomamo Indians, on the other hand, are called the "fierce people." Their sons are taught that manhood is attained through such behaviors as fighting each other, pummeling a help-

less victim, and even through killing. That is not to say that the !Kung have developed a perfectly peaceful society. Recent research has revealed that occasional homicides do take place, but this behavior is seen as very deviant, whereas the Yanomamo actually promote physical aggression and homicide (Lore & Schultz, 1993).

The Competitive Americans. According to almost any psychological and sociological cross-cultural studies devised, Americans are the most competitive people in the world in business, sports, education, science—even family relationships. Competition always involves a reference to others: If we win, someone else is losing. The problem is that our jobs often depend on successful competition. Popular slogans and mottoes highlight our attitude toward winning. Vince Lombardi: "Winning isn't everything, it's the only thing." Leo Durocher: "Show me a good loser, and I'll show you a loser." Is this competition harmful? The answer is yes, according to some social scientists. It is making us work harder and longer. We live with the perpetual uncertainty of whether what we are doing is acceptable. The result is that Americans are, more and more, complaining about exhaustion, burnout, and "not a little bit of bitterness" (Halberstam, 1995).

more sexually attractive to others, etc. (Adler, 1954). Finally, you've already learned that your gender and sibling rank influenced your personality.

What we have been stressing here is that the defense system we have developed over the course of a lifetime is the result of many factors. Let's not go in for the blaming game, since that doesn't do us any good. Rather, let's simply proceed in our process of self-discovery and determine how well we are handling our anxieties. If we think our defense mechanisms are working for us (and there are some defense mechanisms that are more beneficial), all well and good. If, however, we are finding ourselves often anxious or depressed or feeling angry then perhaps we can discover what is obstructing our psychological and physical health. The next step is to develop better coping strategies. Let's begin our self-exploration by familiarizing ourselves with the DSM's category of defense mechanisms that are considered to be fairly common in our society.

The *DSM-IV* Seven-Level Hierarchy of Defense Mechanisms

The mental health professions under the direction of the American Psychiatric Association have been working together to devise guidelines to assess the seriousness or adaptiveness of the defense mechanisms people employ. These guidelines can be found in the ***DSM-IV,*** the common name for the ***Diagnostic and Statistical Manual of Mental Disorders,*** **4th Edition** (APA, 1994). We discuss the DSM-IV in more detail in Chapter 9 on abnormal and dysfunctional psychology. In this chapter we focus on the hierarchy of defending mechanisms so that the reader can recognize them, can assess their level of significance (how serious or adaptive), and explore ways to develop a higher-level behavior pattern (see Table 6.2).

Level of Defensive Dysregulation: Breaking with Reality

This most serious level is the point at which the person's defenses are failing to "hold the person together," leading to a complete break with reality. Lay people may describe a person functioning at this level as "really crazy" or "gone bonkers" or "out of his tree." Professionals usually use the words "psychotic behavior." Three typical symptoms of psychosis are delusions, hallucinations, and psychotic denial. We include this level here because even so-called "normal" people can manifest these symptoms as a transient episode, such as during a "bad drug trip," a traumatizing emotional shock, an alcoholic binge, overdosing on medication, or a high-fever delirium. Fortunately, most of these transitory episodes can be alleviated with minimal treatment or simple rest, after which the afflicted person recovers and restabilizes.

Hallucinations are sensory experiences that are not shared by the rest of us and seem to have no basis in reality. Example: A college student may try out an hallucinogenic drug and experience a "bad trip" of nightmarish apparitions for eight or more hours until the **hallucinogen** wears off. An alcoholic may go on such a severe alcoholic binge that she will truly describe "pink elephants" or "giant cockroaches" crawling on the walls. All of these people are experiencing hallucinations. **Delusions** refer to irrational beliefs. The alcoholic woman may believe that the person on TV is talking right to her and may even answer back. **Psychotic denial** is the complete blocking out of a traumatic and painful event. A woman whose child has just been killed by a hit-and-run driver may be in such a state of shock as to insist the child is still alive. She may appeal to others to call an ambulance. At this moment, she cannot

Table 6.2 The DSM-IV Hierarchy of Defense Mechanisms

Level of High Adaptive (*most optimal defense response to stressors*)

Anticipation:	Considering realistic alternative plans of action in advance of possible threat.
Affiliation:	Turning to others for support, help, and advice.
Altruism:	Processing trauma by helping others who (usually) are in like circumstances.
Humor:	Processing trauma by understanding the amusing aspects of a stressful event.
Self-Assertion:	Expressing feelings and thoughts in a nonmanipulative and direct fashion.
Self-Observation:	Reflecting upon and analyzing thoughts, feelings, and events.
Sublimation:	Channeling maladaptive feelings, thoughts, and actions into socially acceptable ones.
Suppression:	Intentional and conscious avoiding of thoughts, feelings, actions.

Level of Mental Inhibitions (*keeping threatening ideas or feelings out of awareness*)

Displacement:	Transferring negative feelings onto those who (usually) cannot retaliate.
Dissociation:	Breakdown of memory, total or in part, of self, others, or situation.
Intellectualization:	Excessive use of abstract thinking to avoid dealing with emotions or reality.
Isolation of Affect:	Remembering the traumatic event but losing touch with associated feelings.
Reaction Formation:	Substituting diametrically opposed behaviors and feelings for the real ones.
Repression:	Expelling disturbing thoughts or experiences from conscious awareness.
Undoing:	Words or behavior designed to reverse unacceptable thoughts or behaviors.

Level of Minor Image-distorting (*distorting image of self or others to regulate self-esteem*)

Devaluation:	Attributing negative qualities to others to protect self-esteem.
Idealization:	Attributing exaggerated positive qualities to others to protect self-esteem.
Omnipotence:	Attributing superior powers to self and behaving in superior manner to others.

Level of Disavowal (*disclaiming responsibility for events; may shift blame onto others*)

Denial:	Refusal to admit reality, sometimes only temporarily until shock wears off.
Projection:	Attributing own unacceptable feelings and thoughts as coming from others.
Rationalization:	Concealing real motivations and behaviors by offering self-serving reasons.

Level of Major Image-distorting (*gross distortion of reality, self, and others*)

Autistic Fantasy:	Excessive daydreaming instead of dealing with people and reality.
Projective Identification:	Justifies own unacceptable thoughts and behaviors by blaming others.
Splitting:	Sees others and self as all good or all bad; sometimes both.

Level of Action (*responding to stress by aggressing or withdrawing*)

Acting out:	Aggressing against others, running away, suicide, hurting self.
Apathetic Withdrawal:	Flight from world of interpersonal relationships.
Help-Rejecting Complaining:	Disguising resentments with pleas for help and then rejecting it.
Passive Aggression:	Seeming to be compliant, but actually sabotaging others.

Level of Defensive Dysregulation (*pronounced break with reality*)

Delusional Projection:	Gross reality impairment through many types of delusions.
Psychotic Denial:	Gross reality impairment by reinterpreting events or reasons for them.
Psychotic Distortion:	Hallucinations of actual events or only certain aspects of them.

conceive of a reality so terrible. She may continue this denial for hours or days, until she can accept the reality of the child's death.

Level of Action: Aggressing toward Others or Self (Commonly Quite Dangerously) or Withdrawing from Society

The person who "acts out" responds to emotional conflict through actions rather than through reason and reflection. They behave impulsively without any apparent regard for consequences at the time. Later, they may rue their actions—when they realize the consequences of their behavior.

Physical Aggression. One of the most primitive forms of defense is physical aggression, in which the person tries to inflict pain on another person. It can be seen in young, upset children who hit each other or their parents. In high school, the formation of gangs actually legitimizes the physical aggression of "gang wars" and vandalism. In some people, alcohol seems to unleash a tendency toward physical aggression whether in a barroom brawl or domestic violence. We are just now beginning to recognize the frequency of aggression that is going on within the family—spouse abuse, sibling abuse, and elderly abuse. Acting out behaviors are reported in the media quite frequently. Example: The Olympic ice skater who hired two accomplices to injure her chief competitor. Example: The adolescent girl who shot the wife of her alleged lover. Example: The "wilding" gang of teenagers who beat and raped a Central Park jogger so viciously that she is crippled for life. Physical violence has become so frequent in our schools that many school children carry knives or guns for self-protection. The high school shootings of the last few years are causing Americans to reevaluate the roots of our violent society and determine what can be done to instigate more peaceful interaction among our young people. Also getting attention in recent years is the form of aggression called **road rage.** Frustrated by more traffic controls (red lights, stop signs, school zones), expressway tie-ups, and bumper-to-bumper driving, aggressive drivers react by forcing other drivers off the road, shouting obscenities at passing cars, and even shooting at other drivers. Aggressive drivers are accident prone and when queried admit to "wanting to kill the guy." So rampant has this form of aggression become, "our roadways are viewed as a lethal mixture of insolence, impatience, and hostility" (Sleek, 1999, p. 1). We seem to be becoming a society of road warriors. Americans sometimes say they are more afraid of road rage than drunk drivers.

Verbal Aggression. Verbal aggression can be heard whenever children call each other names, but it reaches its apex in high school where it becomes the adolescent way of relating to each other. They either make biting remarks to each other, or they tear themselves apart before others do it for them. One of the most damaging of all verbal aggression is what an abusive parent screams at a child. The pain caused by a physical beating can fade over time, but the brutal things a parent screams at a child may be indelibly imprinted on the child's memory forever.

"I wish you had never been born!"
"How can you be so stupid?"
"You're a whore just like your mother!"

Figure 6.3 Verbal aggression is a frequent defense mechanism.

"You're to blame for my headache. Go away! I can't stand the sight of you!"

Passive Aggression. If the child has been severely disciplined for acting out in overt ways (as in physical aggression), the child may turn to an acting out style called *passive aggression.* Overtly, the child may seem to be obeying, but (covertly) the child is actually doing everything possible to sabotage the request or demand. The child may not hear what was asked or reply with that familiar "Huh?" Or they do the job so slowly and so badly that the adult says, "Oh, never mind, I'll do it myself." If that occurs too often, the child has learned very successfully how to manipulate others and feels superior to others by defeating them. Their acts of passive aggression are camouflaged under the guise of being slow or confused. At an adult level, the passive aggressive person can be infuriating to work with. No matter what we ask them to do, it doesn't get done. They may quote a by-the-book rule that is insignificant or obsolete. Or they may respond to repeated requests for urgent action by telling you that there are many other requests or orders which have priority over yours. Secretly, they delight in obstructing their co-workers in the performance of their jobs.

Help-Rejecting Complaining. People who use this form of defense are carrying a lifetime of resentments. When we first get involved with these people, we may feel very sorry for the very real plights of their lives and do our best to help them. But as soon as we begin to get involved, we discover that no matter how we try to help them, they outwit our attempts. They are only seeming to ask for help. What they are actually doing is sabotaging all suggestions, advice, or solutions we offer. "Yes, but . . ." "Yes, but . . ." "Yes, but . . ." is one of their standard responses. They are very much like the whining child who won't stop whimpering even when others are trying to comfort them. They are actually getting satisfaction from their whining and complaining and blaming of others for their misfortunes. After all, if others are responsible for their problems, then they don't have to do anything about their lives. They don't have to change.

Apathetic Withdrawal. A curious and sad thing happens to children who have been left alone too long in hospitals or orphanages. Without a dedicated caregiver to look after their psychological and physical needs, they seem to withdraw from the world. They stop responding to others and sit passively in a crib or corner in a dazed and lonely fashion. When picked up, they seem to have lost their ability or desire to cuddle or be hugged. They remain limp and unresponding as a rag doll (Bowlby, 1977; Provance & Lipton, 1977). We can observe this kind of listless apathetic withdrawal in older adults who have been relegated to "convalescent" or "retirement" homes. We can observe many "homeless people" who do not want to be approached and scurry away as we go toward them. Try to help them, and they tell you "just go away and leave me alone."

Box 6.5

WHY PEOPLE ACT OUT WITH AGGRESSION
Nathan Azrin's Pain-Attack Response

Nathan Azrin describes physical aggression as an instinctive reflex in animals up and down the phylogenetic hierarchy. What Azrin observed was that when animals are shocked by an electric current, they will immediately attack another animal (even though the other animal had nothing to do with hurting the shocked animal). If no other animal is present, the shocked animal will bite and attack an inanimate object, such as a ball. If there is no other object in the cage, the shocked animal may even bite itself. Furthermore, there was no lessening of the attack response over time. The animal attacked every time it was shocked. Azrin concluded that this *pain-attack response* is a kind of "push button" sequence of shock-pain-attack, following each other in rapid order. Moreover, the pain-attack response was consistent through all the species Azrin investigated, including that traditional symbol for peace and gentleness—the dove. Some readers will recognize this response if they have ever had an injured dog or cat. When the owner bent down to help, the dog bit the owner. The pain-attack response may also explain the tendency of angry people to inflict physical or verbal pain on each other. When asked later why they hit the other person or made such vicious and untrue accusations, the person will respond, "I wanted to hurt you," or "I was just blowing off steam."

Source: Nathan Azrin, "Pain and Aggression" in *Readings in Psychology Today* (Del Mar, CA: CRM Books, 1967), pp. 114–121.

Level of Major Image Distorting

In everyday language: People who use this level of defense protect their self-esteem by changing the facts. Listen to the captain or coach of a national athletic team that just lost a game. What you will hear will be a very mature admission of the poor performance. No excuses: *We just fell apart. Our defense was full of holes and our offensive team just did not operate as a team. We're just going to have to tighten up, that's all.* Now listen to two teams of fifth grade boys after they come in from recess. The winning team members will brag about how well they played. Will the losing team members admit they played badly like the captain we just quoted? Not on your life. Loudly, they accuse the others of "cheating." They are not just lying. To salvage their self-esteem, they have actually altered the facts in their own minds. It will take a long time for these youngsters to avoid this kind of distortion of the facts and mature into the kind of mature captain or coach described earlier. Some of the ways in which image distortion works is through the defenses of splitting, autistic fantasy, and projective identification.

Projective Identification. Projective identification provides the person with an excuse to aggress against others. Listen to a spouse abuser explain the reasons that he beat his wife. "She drove me to it!" (In actuality, the woman did everything she could to prevent his abuse.) "All she does is nag, nag, nag. I couldn't help myself." (In actuality, the woman has become a very submissive and silent individual.) Notice how the abusing husband is distorting what happened by placing the blame for his actions onto his wife. Men who molest or rape the young girls in a family grouping sometimes say something like, "She asked for it. She was all the time cozying up to me." Delinquent teenagers use projective identification as a way of excusing their actions. When confronted with their behaviors of truancy, drinking, vandalism, dope addiction, or shoplifting, they defend themselves by blaming their parents, or their teachers, or the shop owners, or "the system." Their conflicts with society are never their fault—not in the least. Somebody else is always to blame.

Scapegoating is a particularly vicious example of this type of defensive mechanism. Hitler projected the economic disaster of Germany onto the Jews and used that distortion to carry out the horrors of the Holocaust. In the United States, scapegoating resulted in the near genocide of our Native American population and the horrors of discrimination (including lynching) of our African-Americans. We now are facing an upsurge in *hate crimes*—the brutal violence of one group against innocent victims. These crimes are receiving harsher penalties from the courts. Sadly, scapegoating can sometimes be observed in the dynamics of a family or classroom. If a child in a family has tended to "act up" and got caught at it a few times, the other siblings soon catch on that they can blame the miscreant and escape the "heat" themselves.

Splitting. Splitting is the tendency to divide the world into "good guys" and "bad guys." The world is mostly "bad guys," while the individual may feel himself to be the "good guy," of course. Sometimes people with this defense system will describe a person as a "good guy" one day and the next day as a "real creep." Splitting is a normal defense in very young children. Consider, for example, the little boy of three years whose parents came home with a new baby sister. When asked why he is sulking, he says. "I don't like the baby's mother. I like my mother!" Of course they are the same mother, but the little boy has conveniently split his mother into two people, one whom he does not like and the other (the one who gives him attention) whom he still likes. In adults, major distortion by splitting was identified by Carl Rogers as one of the personality characteristics of many clients upon entering into the therapeutic situation. They had a tendency to view their mothers or spouses or employers as "bitches," "jackasses," or "bastards." Over the course of the therapeutic situation, the client gradually lets go of this kind of thinking; thinking that other people are good or bad, right or wrong, great or lousy. He begins to accept people for what they are and understands that most of us are doing the best we can (Rogers, 1970).

Autistic Fantasy. Sometimes the person simply withdraws into a world of fantasy. Instead of dealing with the everyday world in which they feel inadequate and unable to cope, they use fantasy to fill the emptiness and loneliness of their lives. Unlike the homeless or runaways, people who use autistic fantasy as their major defense may go to their school or job each day and carry out their tasks as best they can. But they will hurry home to watch TV, which is the only reality they can relate to without fear. Or they may bury themselves in a romantic novel in which the hero and heroine get married at the end and live (presumably) "happily ever after." Children who are failing in school are no longer psychologically present in the classroom. Instead of listening to the teacher, they are tuning in to a better world where they are being successful and admired.

Level of Disavowal: Preventing Self-Awareness of Painful Events

We can observe disavowal quite easily in children. Ask three children, "Who ate the cookies?" and all three children will probably answer, "Not me!" And they are not lying! Disavowal is quite "normal" in children. If it continues into adulthood, then we are dealing with *disavowal*, which is how the individual deals with unpleasant facts.

Denial. Denial is often our first reaction to painful news. Kubler-Ross (1975) lists the shock and denial response as the first stage of a person's response to being told he or she has a terminal illness. Upon being told of the prognosis, the patient often disclaims it with such remarks as, "No, it can't be true. There must be some mistake." Another example: When told that their son has been sexually abusing their grandchild, parents can steadfastly refuse to believe it is true—their son would not do such terrible things!

Rationalization. Rationalization is the concealment of the real reason for thoughts, feelings, actions, and events by proffering an elaborate or self-serving explanation. Some examples of rationalization can be quite amusing because it is so easy to see through them. The sour grapes rationalization was taken from the fable by Aesop. In that story, a hot and weary fox spies a bunch of cool and delicious grapes hanging from a tree—just the thing to quench his thirst. But despite many jumping attempts, he is unable to reach them. Frustrated and weary, he stalks off saying to himself, "They were probably sour anyhow." Rationalization is a frequent defense for all of us when we experience what we perceive as "failure." Here is a real-life example observed by the authors on the beach one day. Several young men were gazing at a lovely young lady in the distance. They all acknowledged her attractiveness in a bathing suit and were fantasizing about how they might approach her without her taking offense. One young man finally approached her and "made a pass." We could not hear her answer at that distance, but whatever she said resulted in his backing off rather quickly. By the time he returned to the group of boys who were now laughing and making sarcastic comments, he had his rationalization ready: "Yeah, she turned me down and was I glad. She looks good from here, but when you get up close, she's really 'a dog.'"

Simple Projection. In simple projection, the person attributes his or her feelings and thoughts to someone else. Unlike projective identification, which is a far more serious defense, the person does not excuse an abominable behavior by blaming the other person for his actions. In simple projection the person assumes that the motivations and behaviors of others are the same as his own. A philandering husband may accuse his wife of having an affair because she comes home late one night from the office (see Tip 6.1). Since he lives by lies, he assumes she does, too. A mother who had a promiscuous life as a teenager may accuse her daughter of having premarital sex whenever she is on a date.

Level of Minor Image-Distortion: Salvaging Self-Esteem by Assigning Unrealistic Attributes to Self and Others

At this level, people bolster their self-esteem by devaluating others, idealizing others, or making themselves seem more superior or even omnipotent.

Omnipotence. People using this defense are protecting themselves against feelings of inferiority by ascribing to themselves superior attributes or powers that set them above others. Omnipotent thinking and behavior can be very easily observed in small children who pretend they are Superman flying through the air. Adolescents who have a negative self-esteem will try to bolster their self-confidence by displaying a know-it-all exterior: flashy clothes, souped-up cars, the adoption of an aggressive posture, and a "tough" personality style. Anyone recog-

Tip 6.1 Simple Projection versus Projective Identification. If the reader is confused between these two defenses, here is an example that may clarify. In simple projection discussed here, a philandering husband or wife may accuse the other of being unfaithful. In projective identification, described earlier, the philandering spouse blames the other person by alleging the other is "driving me to it."

nize these adolescents? Generally speaking, they are not doing well academically. Nor have they found much recognition in sports or other high-school activities.

Devaluation. Some people deal with their sense of inferiority by devaluating the talent, attractiveness, or abilities of others. Most readers will remember how academically bright students in high school were devaluated as "nerds." The athletically talented student was devaluated as a "stupid jock." Students who develop a good relationship with a teacher or who contribute to class discussions were devaluated as "brown-noses" or as "trying to earn brownie points." Listen to workers talk about a person who got a significant raise or promotion. Only the most mature individuals will admit the person deserved it. Less mature workers will attribute the raise or promotion to "favoritism," "sucking up," or "she probably got her promotion in bed."

Idealization. If devaluation is attributing negative qualities to another person, then idealization is attributing positive (and generally unrealistic) attributes to that person. Of a wife who squanders money, the husband may say, "She's a bit extravagant, but she's made our home a showplace I am proud of. And she always looks like a 'million dollars.'" Of a philandering husband, the wife may say, "He is such a physically attractive man, I can't really blame him for being so attractive to other women." The problem of idealizing other people is that it not only blinds us to what is really going on, it also condones their bad behavior. The extravagant wife will continue to run up their credit cards. The philandering husband will continue to be unfaithful.

Level of Mental Inhibition: Repressing Unwanted Thoughts and Feelings

We all forget things from time to time. What distinguishes this kind of forgetting is that the repressed material cannot be recalled easily—sometimes never—except under certain circumstances, such as deep reflective thought, meditation, hypnosis, therapy, a so-called "truth serum" and so on.

Displacement. If someone is threatening us and we are unable to "strike back" at that person, we may transfer our wishes and actions onto a substitute person or object. Generally, the substitute person or object has less power and cannot retaliate and so is "safe" to aggress against. The classic example in most textbooks goes something like this: The boss shouts his anger at his employee. When the employee goes home, he snaps at his wife. His wife doesn't want to further upset him so she "keeps the peace" by not retorting. But at home, she becomes "fault-finding" toward her children. One of the children displaces his hurt feelings by kicking the dog.

Intellectualization. Another way adults can avoid dealing with conflicting emotions is to intellectualize them to such an abstract level that they seem more a philosophical issue than a here-and-now problem. Alcoholics, for example, will refuse to acknowledge they are alcoholic by quibbling over the definition of "alcoholism." Whatever others say to them, alcoholics manage to outmaneuver their arguments. "You're absolutely right. And when my drinking interferes with my work, I'll take the pledge!" To prevent self-awareness, the person has managed to intellectualize his drinking problem as if it were simply an interesting subject that does not have much to do with him personally.

Isolation of Affect. Affect is the professional term for *feelings* or *emotions*. What the person does in this defense is to filter out the emotions from events. Most of the readers may remember a time when someone they knew experienced a traumatic event (death of a loved one, rape, plane crash) and, in the aftershock of the event, discuss what happened in a seemingly calm and rational manner, devoid of emotion. We may even be amazed by their calm account of the event. Later, however, they may "come apart" when the loss of their loved one comes home to them or the horror of the near-fatal plane crash begins to surface. In these situations, isolation of affect is a fairly "normal" shock reaction. However, when this reaction becomes a part of our standard defense system, we are living only a "half-life," since the isolation of affect also robs us of the feelings of love, tenderness, joy, elation, etc. The person lives in a kind of gray area where nothing "gets through" to them at the emotional level. Perhaps the reader knows someone like this. Try as you may to discuss an emotional conflict, it is like "talking to air."

Dissociation. When people have been involved in a traumatic situation that is overwhelming, they may repress the memory of it through a process called **dissociation.** Sometimes these repressed memories come into conscious awareness when the person is able to handle the memory. We have proof now that repressed memories can be very valid, since the revelations of a woman who, only as an adult, began to remember some of the traumatic events associated with her father—such as the rape and murder of her best friend and playmate. The proof came when she could describe the topography of the event so well that the police were able to unearth the body of the child. (Not all repressed memories can be so validated, and health professionals are now involved in determining how to distinguish between actual repressed memories and the phenomenon of false memories.)

Reaction Formation. In the **reaction formation** defense, the person's thoughts and feelings seem to go in reverse. The little girl who is jealous of her baby brother gets punished when she shows any overt dislike of him. Eventually, she becomes so guilty whenever she experiences any negative feelings toward her little brother that she represses these feelings and begins to behave in positive ways toward him. In fact, she becomes a little "second mother" by asking to wheel him in the baby carriage or give him his bottle. However, the negative feelings that have been repressed may surface in ways that are dangerous to the baby. The baby carriage tips over "by accident" or the baby's milk bottle begins to choke him. The readers may remember the motion picture *Throw Mama From the Train* in which Danny DeVito hires someone to kill his mother. At the end of the film, he has become so guilty about his murderous thoughts that he plies her with flowers and candy and tells her how much he loves her—this to surely one of the most repulsive creatures ever depicted in film history.

Undoing. The classic example of **undoing** in adults often used in textbooks is taken from the famous sleepwalking scene in *Macbeth* by Shakespeare. Lady Macbeth, guilty over the murderous events that she and her husband have committed, is observed sleepwalking through the castle rubbing her hands together as if she is washing blood-stained hands, moaning all the while, "Out, out damned spot!" A real-life example: A woman burdened by a houseful of screaming children says to herself suddenly, "I wish they were all gone." In horror at what she has muttered, she proceeds to undo the aftermath of guilt by buying each child a gift. This may sound like *reaction formation,* but there is an essential difference. In reaction formation, the person is unaware of the negative feelings they are reacting against. In *undoing,* the person remains conscious of the negative thoughts and feelings, at least until he or she is convinced the

Box 6.6

STUDENTS VERBATIM
on Defense Mechanisms

Male (19 years): My parents were divorced when I was little and my mother got custody of my sister and me. When I got to be 14 years, I wanted to go live with my father but my mom said no. So to get back at her, I refused to do anything she asked me to do quickly. I used to dawdle about doing my chores, like taking out the garbage. She'd say, "Never mind, I'll do it myself!" I guess that was being passive aggressive.

Female (22 years): When my father died of a heart attack right in front of my eyes, I was in shock and feeling numb for days. After the funeral, I was still not feeling my grief and sorrow. I went through the funeral and all, and I was accepting his death but I had walled my emotions off. I think I was using the defense of isolation of affect.

Male (24 years): When I was in high school I used to make fun of the guys who were making good grades. I used to call them "nerds" and (excuse the expression) "brown nosers." Now that I'm in college and getting pretty good grades, I can see how childish I was being by devaluating them.

Female (28 years): I was so depressed in high school because I was fat, I just stayed in the house and wouldn't go anywhere. I just kept reading gothic novels and eating and getting fatter. Would you call that apathetic withdrawal? Or an autistic fantasy?

Female (26 years): Here's a good example of idealization. When I was in high school, I was terribly flattered by being the girlfriend of the football captain. He was "the catch." So when all my friends kept telling me they saw him with other girls, I'd just say that he was so attractive, other girls just threw themselves at him. I'm not sure whether that was rationalization or idealization. Maybe I was just being a stupid fool.

Female (37 years): When I was a teenager, I lived with my father sometimes and sometimes my mother. I don't know how I did this in my head, but I blamed my mother for the divorce and I hated her. My father I saw as "an angel" because he let me do whatever I wanted. Well, I have two teenagers myself and I understand my mother a lot better. I was splitting all the adults in my world as "good guys" and "bad guys." Needless to say, most of my teachers were "bad guys."

Female (20 years): When I was a freshman, I had a science test that I hadn't really studied for and I was scared stiff. On the way to school, I did a really strange thing. I never got to school. I just kept driving around and around until I ran out of time for the test. I couldn't understand what I had done. Now I understand that I was so scared, I was dissociated!

---

harmful impulse has been reversed through ritualistic behaviors. Most of us engage in some sort of "undoing" behavior, such as knocking on wood (after making a statement).

Level of High Adaptation: The Most Adaptive (Constructive) Types of Defensive Responding

By this time, the reader may be wondering if there are any *healthy* defense mechanisms. That's a touchy question because as long as we are reacting to pain, we are on the defensive, and it is difficult to respond to situations in creative ways if we are on the defensive. What makes them more constructive is that a) they do not do injury to others; b) they are not destructive to ourselves; and c) they may even promote our psychological growth.

Self-Observation. Basic to all higher-level defenses is the ability to examine our own feelings and thoughts through the process variously called self-examination, introspection, meditation, meditative prayer, and so forth. It is not easy to penetrate our defenses since they were erected in order to prevent us from insight. To be truly self-observing takes honesty, stamina, and courage. We have to be willing to see our faults and our own culpability in any situation. We must strive to determine how we participated, no matter how innocently, in the event. What did we do to hurt someone's feelings so that they have gotten angry with us or refuse to talk to us? How did we phrase a sentence so that we hurt someone else unintentionally? How did we actually invite a behavior that was injurious to us?

Suppression. Suppression is confused with repression, so let's make the distinction clear. Repression inhibits the *conscious* knowledge of the wish, thought, or event, while suppression inhibits only the *behavior.* **Suppression** means we remain *conscious* of the impulse, but we do not act it out. The classic textbook example goes like this: Our spouse yells at us for no apparent reason. We may want to hit our spouse in return. If we repress our feelings, we no longer remain aware of that urge to hit. If we remain aware that we would really like to sock our spouse, but refrain from doing it, then we are using the defense of suppression. We are in control of our behaviors.

Affiliation. Affiliation means turning for help to people who can help us sort out our feelings and suggest alternative actions. We do not drop our problems into their laps. What we do is to share our concerns and problems and get their feedback. Obviously, the therapeutic situation is a very appropriate environment for this kind of sharing and feedback, but it is not the only one. We may have close friends who hold what we say in absolute confidence. If our concerns or problems are work-oriented, we may be able to find a *mentor,* an older person who can counsel us. If we are affiliated with a church, we may be able to discuss the situation with our minister, rabbi, priest, or even with a church group of adults who come together for that purpose.

Altruism. One way to cope with our conflicts is through altruistic service to others. Do not confuse *altruism* with the self-sacrificing behavior of the *martyrdom syndrome.* The family and friends of a martyr may eventually realize that the person's self-sacrificing is a type of control. She has succeeded in making others feel guilty in order to get them "to do" for her. By contrast, altruism is not self-sacrificing. Truly altruistic persons experience joy when they are able to help others become more self-supporting or help them over a crisis in their lives. Good examples of altruistic behaviors can be observed when persons who have suffered trauma help others who are in a similar situation. The father of Adam Walsh, a little boy who was kidnapped and murdered, formed an organization to help other parents search for their missing children.

Humor. What humor does is to drain some of the negative charge out of a painful situation. When we are able to see the sheer idiocy of an offensive person's behavior, we can smile (to ourselves) instead of getting angry. Or if we can reply to an angry criticism by a humorous retort, we not only save face, but enable the other person to see the irony of the situation. Abraham Lincoln was a master of this kind of humor. Lincoln was a very tall man with long, gangly legs. His appearance was often ridiculed by the opposition party. To a critic who asked him how long should a man's legs be, he replied, "Just long enough to reach the ground." Such humorous retorts can defuse even the most self-righteous criticism.

Sublimation. We can also channel socially unacceptable motivations into behaviors that are socially acceptable and that may even gain the approval of our society. Sports may be a way for channeling aggressive behavior into behaviors that provide public entertainment and in which no one (it is hoped) gets seriously hurt. Voyeurs (peeping Toms) may sublimate their desire to look at naked bodies by becoming artists who paint nudes. A pyromaniac may sublimate his desire to play with fire by becoming . . . (what else?) a fireman. Incidentally, psychologists have been called voyeurs as well, since we seem to like to peek inside peoples' private worlds.

Anticipation. A highly adaptive coping style to perceived threats is to consider possible consequences or emotional reactions in advance of the event. Professionals refer to this type of anticipation as "worst case scenarios." To be forewarned is to be forearmed! But it is not enough to simply imagine serious consequences. That is only the first step. The second step is to plan alternate courses of action. Let's take a very real-life example close to the hearts of most students. Let us suppose the readers are going to have to enroll in a course in which they believe themselves to be at "high risk" for failure. If they use anticipation to contend with their anxiety, they first acknowledge their anxieties: they won't do well or may even receive a failing grade. They then devise alternative educational plans for themselves. They may take a pre–college-level course to bolster their academic skills. They can participate in a tutorial lab situation to get extra practice in the assignments. They could get themselves an individual tutor to help them get through the course. But supposing their worst fears are being realized and they are in danger of failing, another alternate plan would be to withdraw from the course before the drop deadline. These are all constructive ways to use anticipatory coping strategies.

Self-Assertion. Self-assertion is dealing with an emotional conflict by expressing our feelings to another, not in anger or by trying to "cast blame." True self-assertion is not easily acquired for a number of reasons. Many of us have become afraid of hurting other people's feelings and prefer to "suffer in silence." Others of us are so used to being verbally aggressive that it is difficult to learn more respectful communication methods. Self-assertiveness is a fine line between verbal aggression and submissiveness. It is such a subtle skill that courses in self-assertiveness abound in colleges and universities and professional workshops.

Suppose a person asks us to do something we don't want to do. It may not be illegal, but there is something "unsavory" about the request. If we don't have positive self-esteem, we may comply with their request—even though it goes against our moral/ethical grain. On the other hand, if we respond with verbal aggression, we may shout derisive comments, such as, "Are you crazy? How dare you!" A self-assertive response might be, "Doing that would make me uncomfortable so I think I have to say no this time."

IMPORTANT TERMS AND CONCEPTS TO KNOW

aggression	delusions	penetrance	rebirthing
anticipation	displacement	projection	self-assertive
birth trauma	*DSM*	racial	sibling
coping	gentle birth	rationalization	suppression
defense	nature/nurture	reaction formation	twin

Box 6.7
SCENARIO REVISITED
And the Good News Is . . .

Professor Weitzman: We've discussed the many foibles of humanity. Comments, anyone?

Alec: It's easy to see all these defense mechanisms operating in other people—like in my father. But I guess it's a lot harder to see them operating in ourselves, right?

Professor Weitzman: Absolutely right.

Shannon: It's like in the Bible that we tend to see the mote in our brother's eye before we see the mote in our own eye.

Ernesto: So how do you get to use the . . . highest level of defense mechanism? I know I get defensive sometimes but I really do try to stay reasonable and I think I do . . . well, most of the time anyway.

Dan: But it's hard to stay cool and undefensive when some SOB is getting under my skin with one of his jokes. I'd like to sock it to some of these guys who think they're being funny when they're making wise cracks.

Professor Weitzman: Well, there's some good news to all this. According to a psychologist called George Vaillant, we develop higher and more constructive defending mechanisms throughout our life span. I know that's been very true for me. When I was a young instructor, I used to get irritated when a student challenged something I said. I recall several times snapping back at the student with some sarcastic remark. I'm rather ashamed of that now.

Alec: You don't get angry at a smart-aleck student anymore? How come?

Professor Weitzman: He's not hurting me, is he? I don't take his hostility personally. Somewhere along his journey, he has developed some kind of hostility toward authority. I'm just the nearest available target. I can usually answer with some humor now. And there is something else I've noticed. When I don't take such a verbally aggresssive student so seriously, after a while the student begins to relax and becomes less hostile.

Jonnimae: I guess not taking it personally comes with maturity.

Professor Weitzman: Exactly. Vaillant's data revealed that as his subjects got older, the defense mechanisms they used were higher on his scale. The value of Vaillant's study is that it was longitudinal and not retroactive. He literally followed his subjects up the agescale. (His scale was not exactly like the DSM scale in this chapter but very close.) What he discovered was this: When the subjects were younger and in their late adolescence, the defense mechanisms they used were projection, hypochondria, and acting out behaviors. Later adults used what the DSM calls "high adaptive"—humor, suppression, and altruism.

Jonnimae: Because we have more self-esteem as we get older. I know I do because I know that the people I work with know I do a good job. So when there is some kind of mistake in the accounting, I don't have to get defensive. I just say something like, "Well, let me take a look at the figures and I'll see if I can find out where they don't add up."

Professor Weitzman: Good example: As we get more experience of life and have managed to survive a lot of problems and crises through the years, we gain confidence that we'll be able to cope with future problems. We adopt higher and higher coping strategies.

Alec: Is that true of everyone? Will my father ever get over his prejudices and hatreds (which I see now are his defense mechanisms to cover a lack of self-esteem)?

Professor Weitzman: That's the one caveat! Vaillant discovered that more maturely behaving college students developed higher level defense mechanisms as older adults than students who were behaving at a lower level in college.

Alec: It's like the higher the rung you start on, the higher rung you reach in adulthood?

Professor Weitzman: So it would seem. The higher up we are on the defense scale to begin with, the better our chances for reaching a higher self-actualizing level as we mature.

MAKE YOUR OWN CHAPTER SUMMARY BY FILLING IN THE BLANKS BELOW

Use the "Important Terms and Concepts to Know" to fill in the blanks below.

Symptoms of anxiety. Anxiety comes in many shapes and forms. Anxiety is mental or emotional pain. To avoid the overwhelming pain of anxiety, we develop _____ mechanisms.

The etiology of anxiety. The origin of anxiety begins early, perhaps even before our birth. _____ studies here and abroad indicate a strong genetic component. But because the concordance rate is not perfect, there must also be a _____ factor in the intrauterine environment, such as prenatal infectious disease. The genetic/environmental issue is a basic and ongoing issue of psychology, popularly known as the _____ controversy.

Otto Rank believed that the _____ was the basis of all adult anxiety. While American psychology did not take Rank's theory very seriously, European professionals did. Two examples are Frederick Leboyer with his _____ and Ronald Laing with his radical _____ therapy. Daniel Freedman and his Chinese-American wife discovered genetically temperamental differences in different _____ and ethnic babies. Sociocultural factors determine how we express our anxiety and what defense measures we develop. Another factor that determines our personality relates to our _____ rank.

Defense mechanisms. The mental heath professions have been working together to establish a "common language." This collaboration has resulted in the *Diagnostic and Statistical Manual of Mental Disorders,* also called the _____ which contains guidelines for assessing the seriousness or adaptiveness of common defense mechanisms.

The level of defensive dysregulation. This level is the complete breakdown of reality and includes the psychotic defenses of hallucinations, _____ , and psychotic denial. This level is included in this chapter only because these phenomena can even occur in "normal people" as the result of alcohol, drugs, severe illness, etc.

Analyzing defense mechanisms. In the opening scenario of this chapter, some of the students revealed some of their anxieties and behaviors. Dan is struggling to control his defense mechanism of _____ . Eduardo uses the defense of _____ . Martha admits to using the defense mechanism of _____ .

Maturational effect. There is some good news: Finally, in his life span studies, George Vaillaint noted (fortunately) that as we mature in age and experience, we develop higher and higher _____ strategies.

7 THE PSYCHOLOGY OF HEALTH
The Holistic Approach to MindBodySpirit Well-Being

We are beginning to understand health—not merely as an absence of disease symptoms—but as a joyful experience of creative energy and harmony of the mindbodyspirit.

Box 7.1

SCENARIO
From the Focus on Illness to a Focus on Health

Dr. Weitzman: We are about to study one of the most exciting areas of research into human personality at the present time. And that area is your health.

Alec: Our health! I thought this was a class in psychology!

Dr. Weitzman: And so it is. But what we have learned in the past hundred years is that our "minds" and our "emotions" and our physical bodies do not function separately but are clearly connected and interconnected.

Li Ho: I bet we're going to talk about stress.

Dr. Weitzman: Indeed, we are. And, as a matter fact, Alec, research in the area of stress doesn't belong to any one scientific discipline. How stress affects our physical health is a hub discipline that involves medicine along with the disciplines of psychology, psychiatry, genetics, pharmacology, neurology, and a fascinating new discipline called psychoneuro-immunology.

Dan: That's a mouthful of syllables!

Dr. Weitzman: Yes, so the initials PNI are sometimes used in the literature instead. What that term means simply is the study of how our emotions directly affect the body's nervous system and ultimately the immune system.

Dr. Weitzman: I haven't heard from any of the ladies. I wonder why that is.

Martha: Probably because we know how connected our emotions and health are from our own experience. When I have a good cry, I feel better physically. When I'm upset about one of my kids, I begin to break out with acne. And just let me have a fight with my husband and my asthma acts up. I think women are more in touch with their bodies.

Eduardo: Are you being a feminist again?

Dr. Weitzman: Whoa, Eduardo, there is some research to back up her opinion . . . But let's go back to our discussion of stress. We need to clarify some terms. The general public uses the term *stress* to stand for many things. Researchers use more discrete terms. *Stress* is a general term encompassing the whole subject. The emotional or environmental stimulus that is contributing to the physiological illness is called a *stressor*. How our bodies (and minds) respond to the stressor has been termed our *stress reactivity*. Given the same stressor, our individual stress reactivity varies considerably. Some of us are hot reactors—which is to say that the stressor has a much more intense effect on us.

Martha: I guess I'm a "hot reactor." I am always coming down with colds and aches and pains of all sorts.

Dr. Weitzman: Nothing as yet is as clear-cut as that. Martha, it can also be that you have so many stressors in your life right now that the next small stressor can act like the straw that broke the camel's back.

Li Ho: Now that you mention it, I realize that I get headaches every time my wife wants us to entertain people. I'm not really the entertaining sort, but I go along for her sake. Can that be right?

Box 7.1

SCENARIO
From the Focus on Illness to a Focus on Health (continued)

Dr. Weitzman: It can. You might want to keep a journal when you get headaches and see when you get headaches. And what the pattern seems to be. We've really only begun to understand how the "mind" and the "body" interact. What is remarkable, however, is how our focus has changed in the past 70 years.

Alec: In what way?

Dr. Weitzman: Well, take the title of this chapter, for example. Before World War II, the title could have been something like "Psychosomatic Medicine." In the two or three decades after the war, these chapters were entitled "The Effects of Stress." In the '80s, the chapters were entitled "The Psychology of Health and Illness." Now this chapter is simply called "The Psychology of Health." Then in the last two decades, this new discipline, called psychoneuroimmunology has been developing. We are learning what an extraordinary biological complex the bodymindspirit really is.

Alec: So we'll start off talking about sickness and symptoms but we'll end talking about health.

Dr. Weitzman: Right! And this change in focus has all happened in the last 40 years—since I was your age and in my first psychology class.

A Brief History of Disease Theory

Primitive societies have always had an animistic view of disease. This worldview held that when people get sick, it was because they had offended some malevolent demon or god. Or that some human enemy had a voodoo curse on them. In the twelfth to fourteenth centuries, the Church laid the blame for the bubonic plagues that devastated Europe on the sins of humanity. Priests urged their parishioners to repent of their sins, and many church members even flagellated (whipped) themselves in the hope of forestalling the spread of the contagion (see Box 7.2). Even today there is a belief among certain groups that AIDS is the punishment for evildoing.

Box 7.2   **Primitive Beliefs about Disease**

If thou wilt not observe to do all the words of this law that are written in this book, that thou mayest fear this glorious and fearful name, THE LORD THY GOD;

Then the LORD will make thy plagues wonderful, and the plagues of thy seed, even great plagues, and sore sicknesses, and of long continuance.

Moreover He will bring upon thee all the diseases of Egypt which thou wast afraid of; and they shall cleave unto thee.

Also every sickness, and every plague, which is not written in the book of this law, then will the LORD bring upon thee, until thou be destroyed.

—Deuteronomy 28:58–61

Let a Maori chief lose some valued article, or suffer from an attack of illness, and he immediately concludes that he has been bewitched. Who has bewitched him? He fixes, as a matter of course, on the individual whom he conceives to be his enemy, and orders him to be put to death. Or he resorts to some potent witch, and bribes her to exercise her influence to remove the maleficent spell under which he is laboring.

Source: W. D. Adams. *Curiosities of Superstition;* London: J. Masters and Co., 1882, p. 244.

The Germ Theory and Its Limitations

Then, in the nineteenth century, the discoveries of the great medical researchers—Louis Pasteur, Robert Koch, and Charles Bernard—made us aware of the role of germs in the etiology of disease and how imperative it was to maintain conditions of cleanliness. It is hard for us today to imagine how desperately Robert Lister, an English physician, had to plead with his fellow surgeons not to operate on people until they had first washed their hands. Eventually, however, the role of germs became the accepted theory of contagious diseases. In fact, the germ theory took such hold on the medical professions that, as a theory, very few people saw anything wrong with it. The germ theory went like this: If a person contracted an infectious disease, it was because some germ had taken hold within the person's body and had multiplied in terrible numbers.

Limitations of the Germ Theory.   Make no mistake, the germ theory contributed much to the health professions. But the problem with the germ theory of disease is that it accounts for some of the facts but not all the facts. Why is it, for example, that when a flu runs throughout the country only some people get it and others don't? The usual response to this question was that some persons are "immune." But such oversimplified answers do not really explain this phenomenon so much as to explain it away. Just because we give a "name" to something, doesn't mean we understand it. It simply begs the next question: *What exactly is immunity?* Furthermore, the germ theory of disease doesn't account for the noncontagious diseases such as the heart diseases, cancer, rheumatoid arthritis, and the diseases of respiration. It doesn't account for such burning questions as why do some diseases "run in families" and not others. It doesn't account for why people are more susceptible to disease when they have more problems in their lives.

"Mind Over Matter."   Over the centuries, there have been some hints about other explanations about why we get diseases. For example, an American woman by the name of Mary Baker Eddy (1821–1915) founded a religious sect, Christian Science, based on positive mental attitudes. Perfect faith and love, she declared, produces perfect physical health. In the area of medicine, Franz Anton Mesmer (1734–1850), a French physician, seems to have "cured" many persons by his methods of "mesmerism," now known as *hypnosis*. Unfortunately, he began to get more and more theatrical in his methods and a couple of his patients died in convulsions. He was condemned by the European medical profession and "mesmerism" fell into disrepute. For many years, no honorable physician would have anything to do with the "black art" of hypnosis. Nevertheless, a French pharmacist by the name of Emile Coué (1857–1926) began to practice a kind of autohypnosis in free clinics all over Europe. A major part of his therapeutic approach was to have the patients repeat to themselves over and over again, "Every day in every way, I am growing better and better."

Charcot's Demonstration of Hypnotism: Physical Symptoms Can Have Psychological Etiology

About the same time as Coué, a renowned French physician, Jean-Martin Charcot (1825–1923), began demonstrating what hypnotism could do in front of audiences of European physicians. To a male patient with a severe stutter, Charcot gave the hypnotic command to talk without his usual stammering and (lo!), the man could speak. Charcot gave a hypnotic suggestion to a person who could not walk that she could walk—and she did. It seemed miraculous, a fulfillment of the promise that the mute would speak and the lame would walk. Alas! The two patients were "cured" only so long as they were in hypnotic trance. As soon as they were out of their trance states, their physical symptoms reoccurred. What was significant, however, was that Charcot demonstrated that physical illness can have psychological **etiology** (causation).

One of the persons sitting in the audiences of Charcot was a fledgling physician, Sigmund Freud by name. Freud was deeply impressed by what he observed, but was hesitant to use hypnosis until he met another physician who would become his mentor, Joseph Breuer. To use hypnosis was a courageous step since "mesmerism" was still classified as one of the "dark arts"—and in some quarters, a practitioner was even considered as "being in league with the devil." Breuer had been using hypnosis to treat a young woman with many physical and emotional problems. In his writings, Freud called her by a pseudonym—"Anna O." Among her physical symptoms were semiblindness, the inability to swallow, and the inability to walk. She also suffered from bad dreams at night and frightening fantasies during the day. Breuer would put her into a hypnotic trance and have her recall repressed memories. Over time, some of her symptoms seemed to be alleviated. When the young Anna O. began to express romantic feelings toward Dr. Breuer, he turned her over to Freud. Freud continued with hypnotic treatment for some months until he developed his psychoanalytic method instead. It was through his work with Anna O. that Freud evolved his theory of *conversion hysteria.*

Sigmund Freud: Conversion Hysteria

Freud came to believe that one of the ways people deal with overwhelming anxiety is through what he called conversion hysteria (Freud, 1900). In **conversion hysteria,** the person transforms anxiety into physical symptoms (see Box 7.3). People with conversion hysteria behave quite differently from those the lay public calls hysterical. Hysterical people display a wide range of emotions: crying, laughing, screaming, etc. By contrast, the people who have an hysterical conversion have a calm, even tranquil exterior—even when they are victims of a fatal disease. The French psychiatrists, who were awed by the peacefulness of these patients, called this phenomenon *la belle indifference* ("beautiful indifference"). What gives rise to this surface tranquillity is that the patients no longer feel anxiety; they have successfully converted all their anxiety into physical symptoms (see Box 7.3).

The Era of Psychosomatic Medicine

Eventually, Freud's theory of conversion hysteria began to attract attention both in Europe and America. In the 1920s, a new field of medicine evolved, called **psychosomatic** (meaning mind-body) research. Psychosomatic research revealed a strong correlation between psychological problems and diseases of respiration: hay fever, asthma, and many allergies (Alexander, 1950). Clinicians began to notice that after a family "blow-up" or an on-the-job slight, for example, their patients' respiratory illness would also "blow-up."

Even the "Common Cold"? Even the common cold came under scrutiny. Clinicians reported that their patients would verbally dismiss the family blow-up or slight as unimpor-

Box 7.3

Mr. Smith, as we shall call him, was a man of "moral" fiber, and his conduct in business was ethical to an extreme. Mr. Smith treated his employees with unusual diplomacy and dignity, and they in turn were loyal to the firm. Being a friendly and genial person, he had many friends. His home life seemed to him to be satisfying. His wife was intelligent and his college-age children were doing well in school. But one morning he woke up with a paralyzed right arm. He had made the rounds of physicians and neurologists who could find nothing physically wrong. One neurologist suggested that his difficulty might be psychological. He said there was nothing in his life that could account for "psychological paralysis." The idea that the paralysis of his arm might be psychological seemed to amuse Mr. Smith as he sat in our office. But he was willing "to try anything—even psychotherapy!"

After a few therapeutic sessions, however, some deeply repressed emotions began to surface. He became aware that all was not as "ideal" as he had believed. His wife—whom he deeply respected—tended to be demanding, and sometimes her nagging "got" to him. In the fourth session, he reported remembering a morning when his wife's nagging had been so disagreeable to him that he felt like punching her in the jaw. Raised as a "Southern gentleman" who does not hit women, Mr. Smith was horrified by his own impulse. The next time he came to the office, he showed off his right arm which he could now move. After forgiving himself for his "ungentlemanly thoughts," his paralysis disappeared. He himself was utterly amazed.

"The strange thing," he said with a smile, "was that I had forgotten both the disagreement with my wife and my impulsive urge to hit her."

tant, but two or three days later, the patients found themselves in the grip of a miserable cold. Their patients had resisted the temptation to cry at the time of the negatively charged event, but their eyes were now watering with tears. They were not crying, but the cold was causing them to sniffle. They were not crying, but they were now breathing with gulping sobs. Their eyes became red and puffy, and they had a general feeling of self-pity. Psychosomatic clinicians became convinced that when people do not allow themselves the release of crying that the "common cold" allows them that release (Dunbar, 1955). Now there is some experimental evidence that crying may decrease our vulnerability to contagion (Cohen & Williamson, 1991). Moreover, it appears that strong social ties may reduce the risk of catching a cold. People who have fewer social relationships may be more susceptible to colds (Gilbert, 1999).

Heart Disease and the Type A Personality

The psychosomatic research of the 1920s and 1930s described above relied on clinical studies. There is nothing wrong with clinical studies, per se, but scientists always feel more comfortable if they can find statistical evidence. This kind of statistical evidence began to pour in after World War II. By the 1970s, a number of statistical studies related stress to cardiovascular diseases. A book entitled *Type A Behavior and Your Heart* (Friedman & Rosenman, 1974) called attention to a personality type that is at "high risk" for a coronary attack. In addition to being overweight from lack of exercise and having a poor eating regimen, Type A personalities are also fiercely competitive, have a continual sense of pressure, and the feeling that there is never enough time to accomplish their job tasks. They are aggressive, impatient, highly competitive, and the master of the "hard sell." They hate to wait in line at checkout counters, talk far too fast, and often interrupt others in the middle of a sentence. As managers they "get things done," often at the cost of those under their supervision.

For a while, other researchers who were trying to replicate the Friedman and Rosenman research did not come up with the same conclusive evidence. The literature in this area began to reflect some doubt about the original study—until some researchers began to factor out a Type B personality. The **Type B personality** may also eat and drink and smoke too much, but they are less vulnerable to heart disease. What is the difference between them? They are described as more "laid back," less angry, and less isolated from others. Type As feel themselves essentially alone and without support from others. Their speech reflects this isolation, since

---

Box 7.4

SCENARIO
Dan Westwind Visits the Infirmary

The physician has finished reading the file and turns to Dan Westwind.

Dr. Ling: Good news and bad news. The bad news first. Your blood pressure is sky-high.

Dan: I have high blood pressure? Is that the cause of my headaches?

Dr. Ling: Well, yes and no. "Cause" is a not a very definitive word in health science. While your blood pressure may be responsible for triggering your headaches, there are many possible causative factors, such as diet. Westerners eat far too much fat, too much red meat—in fact, too much protein entirely. Another factor is stress. Pressure in your environment.

Dan: That fits. I'm taking a lot of courses. I have a part-time job at the garage in town. I don't have much time to study, and every time I turn around, there's another test I have to study for! I'm up at dawn, and I don't get to bed till after midnight. This school business is too much for a man of my age.

Dr. Ling: Do you drink?

Dan: I used to drink. I was an alcoholic. I guess I'm still an alcoholic who just happens not to be drinking. At least that's what they say at my AA meetings.

Dr. Ling: So how do you handle your anger?

Dan: What?

Dr. Ling: Well, you used to cover your anger with alcohol. You aren't using that to handle your stress. So the anger may be coming out in other ways—like migraines.

Dan: Thank you Dr. Freud! I didn't come here to get my head shrunk!

Dr. Ling: *(calmly)* We also know that anger and hostility are factors. I detect a lot of anger and hostility in you. What you need is an "attitude adjustment."

Dan: O.K. So I don't like the white man's school. I'm a second-class citizen here.

Dr. Ling: So am I.

Dan: You! You've got it made. You're a physician. You've got a secure job.

Dr. Ling: I am also a Chinese-American. And a woman physician in a male-dominated profession.

Dan: But your people weren't victims of genocide by the whites.

Dr. Ling: Oh, weren't they, though! Have you ever read about the building of the railroads? Or the history of mining? Chinese coolies were imported by the thousands and died by the thousands. Hatred only hurts yourself.

Dan: You're giving me all the bad news. What's the good news?

Dr. Ling: Hypertension is treatable with medication and with some alternative health measures—a change in your diet, a program of daily exercise. Also, do you pray or meditate?

Dan: I thought science was opposed to religion.

Dr. Ling: I think you'll be a little surprised by recent research in health science. How about getting some counseling? It might help defuse some of your anger and hostility.

Dan: You mean counseling would help my headaches and blood pressure?

Dr. Ling: Isn't it worth a try, just as exercise and a change in diet is worth a try? We can set you up to meet with one of our health counselors. Are you willing?

Dan: At this point, I am willing to try anything. Lay it on me!

Dr. Ling: I'm also recommending a psychophysical program to help you develop some coping strategies for your anger. It's called stress inoculation training.

Dan: Is that some kind of sissy therapy stuff?

Dr. Ling: Not exactly "sissy stuff." SIT has been developed to help deal with maladaptive anger—in law enforcement officers, prison guards, and athletes—to name just a few of the populations. You're in good company.

Type A personalities almost always use the singular personal pronouns: "I," "me," "my," "mine." Type B personalities, on the other hand, use the first person pronoun in the plural: "we," "us," "ours" (Fischman, 1987).

The medical profession has put the final imprimatur on the detrimental effects of anger on heart disease and also the risk of having a cerebral vascular accident—what the lay person calls "stroke." (The *Johns Hopkins Medical Letter,* 1999). Part of the susceptibility may be what is called being a "hot reactor." Given the same stimulus as the rest of us, **hot reactors** respond with racing hearts, fast breathing, and tense muscles—all of which may be precursors of heart disease (Siegman, 1989).

Heart Disease and Loneliness. Physicians have long been fascinated by the phenomenon called death by **conjugal bereavement;** that is, the death of a widow or widower soon after the death of the spouse. Mortality rates suggest that there is a high incidence of just such deaths, particularly in the first six months of bereavement (Kaprio, Koskenvuo, & Heli, 1987). Is it too great a leap to suggest that the death is caused by grief? A noted cardiologist, Robert Lynch (Lynch, 1977), wrote a book entitled *The Broken Heart: The Medical Consequences of Loneliness.* Lynch frankly asserted that what is happening to many heart disease patients is that they are really dying from . . . (well, let's just say it!) loneliness! He noted the high rate of heart fatalities among the single and divorced population of Nevada. But Lynch warned us that it is not simply a matter of being unattached. Many people are married in name only. They are really strangers or hostile antagonists living under the same roof. Not only do they experience loneliness, they are also undergoing the pain of never feeling they can come home to a "safe haven" and to a place where they can feel love and a sense of belonging—so necessary to our feeling of well-being (Maslow, 1954).

Warning for Women! The public still seems to make the assumption that heart disease is primarily a man's disease. That may have been true once but the facts are otherwise now. At the present time, heart disease kills six times more women annually (500,000 every year) than breast cancer. Moreover, heart disease is a much stealthier killer in women than in men. Instead of announcing itself with crushing chest pain, says Christina Northrup (1997), a specialist in women's diseases, there are few warning signs in women. Furthermore, she continues, women are much more likely than men to fall victim to depression. The significance of that statistic is that depressed patients are four times more likely to die of heart attack than non-depressed women.

Cancer: Genetic and Environmental Factors

Cancer is the second leading cause of death in the United States but in terms of psychological trauma, it is the most feared of all the diseases. Only a few decades ago, a diagnosis of cancer was equivalent to a death sentence. The picture has changed considerably since that time for several reasons. Early diagnosis, newly developed treatments, and psychotherapeutic support have increased the survival rate dramatically. In the early 1980s, chances for recovery (remission equals five years with no further outbreak) was about one out of every two. As of this writing, the chances for recovery are three out of five (McGuire, 1999). Genetics plays an important part in cancer. But what is intriguing is that environmental stress also plays a part.

Pinning down what environmental factors are cancer-inducing in humans has been hard. But the experimental evidence from "rat studies" has been clearly demonstrated. The question is no longer *Is there a link between environmental stress and cancer?* The question has become

What kinds of stress are cancer-inducing? Factors which promote tumor growth in rats include handling, overcrowding, and being bullied by other dominant animals (Azar, 1999b). These factors become extremely interesting when we extrapolate to other environmental situations. For example, all of these environmental stressors can be (by extension) identified as part of the environmental conditions of poverty and slum-like overcrowding, where heart disease and cancer have a higher frequency. In point-of-fact, all minority populations are in special jeopardy for cancer, says Richard Suinn, the 1999 president of the American Psychological Association (1999). Can we identify the factors here as being manhandled by abusive family members, overcrowding in slum conditions, and bullying by ghetto gangsters? An interesting speculation.

Reacting to the Stress of Life: Investigating the Physiology of the Mindbody Connection

So far in this chapter, we have focused on the correlational evidence of the stress factors in a person's life and obvious ill health. But health scientists have always endeavored to discover the actual physiology of the mindbody complex. What they want to know can be phrased as: *What are the actual physiological processes involved? How can our emotions affect our bodies in such a direct way?* While the discipline of psychoneuroimmunology is a development of the last two decades, the first inroads were made by pioneers in many fields. One of the first of these pioneers was Walter B. Cannon in the 1920s with his model of the flight-or-fight syndrome.

The Fight-Flight-Freeze Response: Emergency Reactions to Perceived Threat

What Cannon discovered was that human life must stay within certain tolerance limits of chemical and fluid balance in order to stay healthy. He called perfect bodily balance **homeostasis** (meaning "stable state") but, of course, no such perfect state really exists in any of us. In reality, the body is continually going through many internal physiological changes to meet the constantly changing external environment. For example, when the body gets too cold, we shiver. Shivering actually raises the body's temperature. When the body gets too hot we perspire, which lowers the body's temperature. If we lose too much fluid (as the result of perspiring), our bodies have a need to replenish the fluid loss—we experience the drive state of thirst, and we drink. If we lack air, we yawn, which allows us to take in more oxygen in one huge gulp (and so on and so forth). These changes are what Cannon called the body's *inner wisdom* by which it adapts to everyday situations (Cannon, 1929). We have come to call this "inner wisdom" of the body by the term **need-drive state.** The body experiences a *need* (lack of water and consequent thirst) and goes in search of water, which is a *drive*. When the person quenches the thirst, the need is satisfied and *homeostasis* (optimum fluid content) is restored.

But every so often, said Cannon, we are faced with more than the usual everyday situations. We are faced with emergencies that require more than the normal amount of energy. When walking down a dark street at night, we may hear footsteps in the dark that seem to be following us. Or we may have to jump out of a window three stories up because of fire. Our physical energies become immediately mobilized in what Cannon called the **fight-or-flight syndrome;** that is, an emergency bodily response to either take flight or to stand and fight (see Figure 7.1).

Figure 7.1 The Fight-Flight-Freeze Response Cannon has said that when we sense an emergency, our bodies respond with an increased energy to meet the threat to run away. Health professionals have extended this theory to include the "freeze" response. It has also been suggested that this theory should be extended even more to include other responses. Perhaps we should call the emergency behavior the "fight-flight-freeze-faint-and-fumble" response.

Adrenalin races through our blood stream arousing nerve and hormonal reactions in every part of our body. The pupils of the eyes dilate which improves our vision. The nostrils expand to let in more air and therefore more oxygen. Respiration and heart rate increase in rate with a corresponding increase in metabolism. The blood withdraws from the surface of the body so that we do not bruise and bleed as much if we are hurt. Blood salts and sugars rise to higher levels. The higher salt level increases the blood's clotting ability. The higher sugar level increases the metabolic rate. We have mentioned only a few of the bodily changes. In fact, our whole physiological system is fired up and racing with literally hundreds of neural, hormonal, muscular, and other bodily changes! This speeded-up energy system is referred to as the **adrenalergic state.**

When we are in this adrenalergic state, we are capable of so-called superhuman feats. Newspapers report stories of people who have reacted with just this kind of strength in times of crisis. A woman lifts up the front end of her minivan to pull out her child pinned beneath it. The football player grabs the ball, dodges eleven other men, and runs the whole length of the football field before he realizes that he has been severely injured. All of us are capable of this kind of adrenalergic energy—for a short while. We cannot sustain this kind of energy for very long since eventually our fluids and bodily chemicals are used up and we simply burn out and get ill. At some point, we have to stop so that our bodily reserves can get replenished and the tissue damage repaired. As we rest or sleep, our bodies change over to the **cholinergic state** in which the toxins are drained out of the body, the chemical and fluid balance restored to normal levels, and damaged tissue is healed (see Figure 7.2).

To Cannon's Original Fight-or-Flight Response Has Been Added the Freeze Response.
The two responses of either fighting or taking flight need the opportunity and the ability to do one or the other. But what if we cannot do either? Suppose the circumstances prevent our escape or the threat is too overwhelming for us to fight it. What then? Health scientists have added a third dimension: the **freeze response.** The freeze response in animals is often a very strong protective device from predators. If the predator uses his visual sense more than his sense of smell, what alerts the predator to prey is movement. If the predator's quarry makes no motion but freezes on the spot, it may escape detection. In humans, the freeze response can result in several different behaviors. For example, the person can literally freeze into an immobile state. The person may be aware of what is going on around but seems almost paralyzed. Because his body has gone into a freeze response, he may have difficulty breathing. He may not hear what you are saying to him. His heart rate may slow down. Or the individual may go into shock by actually losing consciousness (fainting, passing out, etc.). Or the person may dissociate the event from conscience remembrance of it (as we discussed in the last chapter). Although the person has managed to avoid the traumatic consciousness of the event along with the emotions involved, he may eventually have to pay a price for this dissociation. The shocking event may return to the person's consciousness along with the fearful emotions as flashbacks. Or even worse, the person may not remember the event but be experiencing the emotions of fear, anger, guilt, and horror without knowing where it is coming from. The individual may remain unable to deal with his ongoing

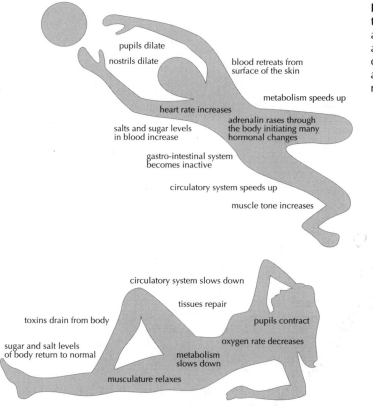

pupils dilate
nostrils dilate
blood retreats from surface of the skin
metabolism speeds up
heart rate increases
adrenalin rases through the body initiating many hormonal changes
salts and sugar levels in blood increase
gastro-intestinal system becomes inactive
circulatory system speeds up
muscle tone increases

circulatory system slows down
tissues repair
toxins drain from body
pupils contract
oxygen rate decreases
sugar and salt levels of body return to normal
metabolism slows down
musculature relaxes

Figure 7.2 The Adrenalergic State vs the Cholingeric State. The adrenalergic state is engaged when we are active and expending energy. The cholinergic state is engaged when we are relaxed and resting and the body is repairing tissues and draining toxins.

feelings of anxiety and terror. (It has been suggested, incidentally, that the syndrome should be expanded even further as the *fight-flight-freeze-faint-and-fumble response*.)

The General Adaptation Syndrome (G.A.S.): The Effects of Ongoing Stress

The fight-flight-freeze response is the bodily reaction to perceived threat. It is a state of emergency. But what happens when we do have not an emergency situation but are subjected to one or more stressors over a prolonged period of time? The term stress is on everyone's lips now, but when it was introduced by Hans Selye some decades ago, it made scientific headlines. What Selye did was to subject healthy laboratory rats to a stressor that would not kill the rats but was definitely traumatic. The stressors he used were varied: electric shock (which Selye used to induce emotional trauma), sublethal doses of poison, extreme cold, and semistarvation diets. Whatever the stressor, the results were the same. The animals went through three predictable stages:

1. **The alarm reaction.** After the healthy animals had been subjected to stress for a period of time, they began to look and act sick. When animals are ill, they stop eating, drinking, and copulating, huddling by themselves in a corner. An autopsy on a few of these rats revealed the ravages of disease: bleeding ulcers, diseased adrenal glands, a withered thymus, abnormally high levels of blood salts and sugars, and a high white blood cell count.

2. **Stage of resistance.** If the stressor was not too severe, many animals seemed to recover. They began to eat, drink, run around, and copulate. Were they really better? Autopsies revealed all the diseased tissues had healed and the bodily fluids returned to normal—but only for a while.

3. **Stage of exhaustion.** If the stressor was not removed, the animals again became sick and died. Autopsies revealed the same bodily ravages as in the stage of alarm. Selye also noted that the animals could resist one stressor for a time, but when another was added, and yet another, death could come instantly.

How Does the General Adaptation Syndrome Apply to Our Health? Selye postulated that if we live and work in an environment where the pressure is constant or the environment is hostile, our bodies deteriorate with what he called the "diseases of civilization"—arthritis, the heart diseases, the cancers, etc. In further work, he differentiated stress from *eustress, hypostress,* and *distress.* There is no way to avoid **stress** since it is normal "wear and tear" on the body that comes from everyday living. Nor would we want to avoid stress for if we did nothing all day long, the boredom of doing nothing would be stressful, which Selye termed **hypostress.** On the other hand, if the stress becomes overwhelming, we are then in a state of **distress,** which has serious consequences on the body (see Figure 7.3). He then defined **eustress** as the excitement and joy that comes of happily challenging situations. His recipe for maximizing eustress is to develop optimistic and altruistic attitudes toward others and toward life in general (Selye, 1991).

Voodoo Death: Can Fear Itself Be a Factor in Disease and Death?

Voodoo death has been reported by anthropologists for several centuries. The unfortunate victim of the curse goes home and, in fear and trembling, waits for death to arrive—and arrive it does—in a very brief time (Richter, 1985). Is it possible? Can people just give up and die simply out of fear (see Box 7.5)? Or, as did the pathetic heroines of Victorian literature, die by "turning their face to the wall"? Or as did the legendary Elaine, the Lily Maid of Astolat, who pined away for her unrequited love of Lancelot? Some light has been shed on "voodoo death" from laboratory studies, as for example, the classic Sawrey and Telford study (1971).

What Sawrey and Telford did was this: They injected laboratory rats with an overdose of insulin. Overdoses of insulin have the same consequence as a lack of insulin; namely, it produces insulin coma. The insulin overdosing was injected with a hypodermic needle under the conditions of bright light. Some of the rats died, but most survived. When the surviving rats had recovered completely from the insulin shock, they were given another injection, but this time the hypodermic needles contained only a

Figure 7.3 Air Traffic Controllers: Always Under Pressure. One of the most stressful jobs in industry is that of the air traffic controller who coordinates the input of radar, weather, panel instruments, and communications to guide airplane landings and takeoffs. Both air traffic controllers and pilots work under life-and-death circumstances, but air traffic controllers are under greater psychological stress, since they must make the final decisions. In a study of health records for 8,435 pilots and 5,199 air traffic controllers, the air traffic controllers were found to have a far greater frequency of high blood pressure, diabetes, peptic ulcers, and so on (Cobb & Rose, 1973).

Box 7.5   **FROM THE SUFI LITERATURE OF THE MIDDLE EAST**
The Relationship of Emotions and Death

How we process (cope with) trauma is often more significant than the trauma itself—a fact that has long been recognized in the literature of civilization. The Sufis of the Middle East relate the following anecdote, which goes back to the times of the Great Plagues of the thirteenth and fourteenth centuries.

A certain Bedouin chieftain, while riding in the desert, met Pestilence. Reigning in his horse, the chieftain cried, "Pestilence, where are you going?"

Pestilence answered, "To Baghdad, where it is ordained that I am to take 500 souls."

The chieftain replied, "Well, see that you don't take one soul more. I am going there to raise an army."

Pestilence agreed and both went on their way.

A few weeks later, the Bedouin chief met Pestilence, once more, riding in the desert and cried out to him, "Pestilence, you lied! You promised you would take no more than 500 souls from Baghdad, but when I got there to look for brave young men for my army, they told me you had taken over 5,000."

"Nay, not so," said Pestilence. "I took only 500 as I promised. Fear took all the rest."

simple saline solution—not harmful at all. Despite the nontoxic solution in the hypodermic needles, most of the rats again fell into insulin shock coma, and if the injection was carried out under conditions of bright light, all the rats fell into coma and many died. These results established a powerful confidence among scientists for the interrelationship of emotions, disease, and death.

Too Many Life Changes—Even "Happy" Changes—Can Affect Our Health

Another advance in health psychology was the recognition that too many changes in our lives, even happy changes, can have the cumulative effect of "excessive stress." A team of researchers developed a measurement for change that they called **life crisis units (LCUs).** After the development of a scale, called the **Social Readjustment Rating Scale,** they followed the health records of their subjects for several years. Some life events are obviously hurtful: death of a family member, illness, or being fired from a job. But, too many *positive* changes—marriage, birth of a baby, advancement, buying a house—could have as detrimental an effect on health as the negative changes. Death of a spouse, of course, has the highest emotional consequence, with a score of 100. Death of a spouse not only causes grief, but also many changes in sleeping, eating, recreation, get-togethers with friends and relatives, etc.

Whether sad events or happy events, the research data indicated a very high **correlation** between a high LCU score and what they called "a psychological or physical depression." In short, too much change within 18 months results in a severe physical or emotional problem. If the LCUs measured 300 in that time frame, 50 percent of the subjects came down with physical or emotional illness. If the LCUs measured 400 in that time frame, 80 percent came down with physical or emotional illness. With this in mind, consider your present circumstances. Becoming a college student brought about significant changes in your life. It probably included most of the following changes: your residence, your eating habits, your study habits, your social habits, your relationships with your family and friends, your church, and your financial status (see Table 7.1). You may be trying to support a family, earn extra money by one or even two part-time jobs, etc. Is it any wonder that you feel tired a lot of the time? Or come down with frequent colds, or worse—the flu? Or have you had a lot of back pain lately? Or how about that popular college disease, mononucleosis? Or how about that "new" illness called

Table 7.1   Self-Exploration: How Is Your College Stress Rating Today?

Rate yourself on your stress factor by checking off the event which has occurred, multiplied by the number of times the event occurred in the last eighteen months. For example, if you broke up with your intimate friend three times, your score would be 150 (see asterisked item).

Changes in educational situation	Your Score
Began college	(60)____
Changed major field of study	(45)____
Transferred from another college	(55)____
Failure in course	(45)____
Hassles with school administration	(20)____

Moved residence

From one country to another	(75)____
From one state to another	(63)____
From one city to another within state	(45)____
Within city	(35)____
Vacation away from home residence	(13)____

Changes in family situation

Got married	(50)____
Got engaged	(45)____
Got divorced	(73)____
Planned pregnancy	(40)____
Unwanted pregnancy	(85)____
Gained a new family member	(39)____
Extramarital affair	(56)____
Increase in arguments with partner	(52)____
Broke up with intimate friend*	(50)____
Reconciliation with spouse/friend	(35)____
Concern for children cared for by others	(42)____
Sexual difficulties	(40)____
Serious problems with parents	(39)____
Trouble with in-laws	(29)____

Changes in work

Held a job while attending school	(38)____
Had a problem with employer	(39)____
Fired or laid off from full-time job	(47)____
Fired or laid off from part-time job	(35)____
Changed to a different line of work	(50)____
Promoted with new responsibilities	(29)____
Changed hours or location of job	(29)____

Change in personal habits

Major change in eating habits (New diet/switch to vegetarian)	(15)____
Changes in sleeping habits	(24)____
Changed church or church activities	(19)____
Changes in family get-togethers (number and type)	(19)____

Changes in recreational activities (dating, hobbies, sports)	(19)____

Personal achievement

Hard studying brought high G.P.A	(22)____
Earned award in some activity (athletics, speech contest, etc.)	(45)____

Change in financial status

Lost significant income	(40)____
Assumed mortgage over $10,000	(31)____
Retired from life work (Ex: army career)	(45)____
Spouse began or ended job	(26)____

Personal trauma

Death of spouse	(100)____
Death of a close relative or friend	(70)____
Close family friend commits suicide	(66)____
Serious drug addiction	(60)____
Personal injury	(60)____
Abortion	(63)____
Recovery from drug addiction	(55)____
Major illness of close relative or friend	(55)____
Infidelity of spouse	(49)____
Major problems with child	(49)____
Jail term (over a year)	(65)____
Prison term of close family member	(56)____
License suspended or revoked	(45)____
Trouble with neighbors	(23)____
Found guilty of minor violations of law	(15)____
Foreclosure of property	(30)____

Total Score   _____

SCORING

0–299	Mild	500–799	Substantial
300–499	Moderate	Over 800	Excessive

Reflective writing: What is your reaction to your stress level?

How does your stress level relate to your physical health over the last 18 months?

If your stress level is high, think of three ways you could reduce your stress overload.

Source: Adapted from M. B. Mark et al., "The influence of recent life experiences on the health of college freshmen," *Journal of Psychosomatic Research 11* (1975), 341–345; A. O'Connell & V. O'Connell, "How much change in your life?" in *Choosing and Changing.* (Englewood Cliffs, NJ: Prentice Hall, 1974), pp. 26–35.

chronic fatigue syndrome (CFS)? In this generally nonfatal but utterly debilitating disease, the victims demonstrate all those factors that make for career success: high achievement motivation, successful accomplishment of career objectives, upwardly mobile aspirations, and, finally, the tendency toward **workaholism**.

The Placebo Effect and Its Applications

The placebo effect is a phenomenon long known to the medical community. The term **placebo** (Latin for "I please") was originally applied to sugar pills, given to patients, that could not, in themselves, have any effect on the symptoms or the illness. Yet patients who get placebo pills seem to get better than patients who do not receive any pills at all. What can be the explanation? Even if pills will not have any effect on flu, we would probably be disappointed if the physician did not give us a prescription and say, "Take two of these and call me in the morning." We feel powerfully reassured by taking medication, and it is that reassurance that seems to be the real healer. So powerful are the effects of placebo that when testing for a new drug, it is necessary to have a placebo control group, a group of subjects who do not take the real drug but take a placebo pill instead. There have even been cases of placebo surgeries, where the patient was wheeled into the operating room, given an anesthetic, a simple scalpel incision, and then sewn up. These patients actually did as well as those who received antibiotics or actual surgeries (Beecher, 1961; Frank, 1964). (This kind of research, like the Baby Albert research, may not be done again since it violates more recent standards of ethics for research.)

Until a few decades ago, the placebo effect was regarded simply as an intervening variable, something that interfered with the "real" treatment of the disease or experimental data. Now the health professions have come to recognize that the placebo effect is not something to be eliminated from the treatment program. Instead, medical teams are incorporating the "placebo effect" into the patient's ongoing treatment plan. The placebo treatment can come in the form of a pill or a hypodermic needle. But it may come also in the form of "laying on of hands" or prayer or the incantation of a shaman or medicine man. The effect of these "placebo treatments" may even seem miraculous at times, such as the powerful healings that happen sometimes at Lourdes in France or St. Anne de Beauprés in Quebec. Such healings may be a demonstration of the power of the patient's "expectant faith" (Frank, 1964). One explanation for the placebo effect is that it encourages the patient to energize the body's ability toward self-healing. Or it may be that the patient is receiving visible affirmation of love and caring and concern—all of which have proved to be efficacious in the healing process.

The Personality Style of Psychophysically Hardy People

We have already learned that the more changes in our lives—and the more stress—the more liable we are to come down with a serious physical or psychological depression. Even day-by-day changes in our moods can contribute to relatively minor ailments such as colds and other respiratory problems. But not everybody! There seem to be a number of people who do not seem as vulnerable to illness as the rest of us, so health professionals began to study these *psychophysically hardy people*. The questions they were asking were as follows:

What keeps these people physically and emotionally healthy?
What regimen of health do they follow that enables them to survive too much change?

Box 7.6

STUDENTS VERBATIM
The Stressors in My Life

My roommates. Female (18 years): My friends all tell me this is an old, old story. I came to the university with three of my high school friends. Being such good friends, we thought it would be wonderful to become roommates. Wow! Did that prove to be wrong. First of all, one of my roommates turns out to be a slob. I don't think she has ever washed a dish in her life. Another roommate has her boyfriend over all the time so we really have five people in the apartment instead of four. The other roommate and I suffer in silence until we can't stand it anymore. Then one of us explodes. Then all hell breaks loose! Everybody is fighting. We have four months till the lease is up. In the meantime, I must be at the next-to-lowest level of Maslow's hierarchy of existence—safety.

Credit card debt. Male (20 Years): I grew up last year when I got into debt over my ears. I got a credit card in the mail with my name on it, and I thought "Wow! What a neat thing," when I was getting an apartment for the first time. So I outfitted my apartment with a computer and a computer desk and a few pieces of furniture. I just figured somehow I would be able to make the payments when the time came. (Talk about a denial system!—that was me!) Anyway, you can guess what happened next. When my first credit card bill came, I couldn't believe it. Whew! Had I really run up that much? I made the first payment OK, but I couldn't make the second one, so I took another credit card out and started in on that one! Of course I was only making matters worse. I began to lie in bed at night trying to figure out how to get out of the hole I had dug for myself. I was scared to tell my parents . . . I got a part-time job. Then I got two part-time jobs. Then my grades began to slip . . . I got put on academic suspension. Then wham! I got the flu. I mean, I got really sick. When my parents came, they were so sympathetic about how ill I was that I confessed what I had done. They just brought me home. My father said I could work off the debt at his place of business (he's a landscape gardener), and so I did. I worked for "nothing" except for board and room and twenty dollars a week. . . . I was really grateful to my Dad for letting me do that. Anyway, I'm back in school and I'm not going to get myself into financial debt any more! The stress is too great.

Too much moving from place-to-place. Female (26 Years): My whole life has been stressful. My father was a career army officer. We moved around the world—Germany, the Philippines, Canada, and a lot of places in the United States. I've heard "army brats" like myself say they loved going from place to place, and my parents are always saying it was a wonderful education. I suppose it was, but all I can remember was the anxiety I always felt when I had to leave all my friends in one place and I was scared I wouldn't make any friends in the next place. Plus moving and moving and moving. It's awful. One year my father got transferred three times (don't ask me why!). Talk about changes in eating and dressing and local customs. Change! Change! Change! No wonder I began to have "acid indigestion" and stomach aches and diarrhea all the time. My whole gastro-intestinal system had gone wacky. I thought that I just couldn't get used to the new food all the time. Now I bet all these changes would be way over 2000! I'm not kidding. I'm better now, even with all the pressure of school. At least I am staying in one place.

My manhood is being threatened. Male (44 Years): My greatest stress level was just after I was released from the Air Force. I had always loved flying and got myself a job as pilot with a commercial airline. I had all the confidence in the world as a pilot for the Air Force, but I began to lose it with the commercial airline. They had stringent exams every six months. Also the FAA official could get aboard our flights at any time (generally three times a year) and give the entire crew a check while en route on our duty trips. The pressure for success was overwhelming. I was older now, and I was getting nervous about whether I would be able to pass the physical tests or the instrument check rides. The stress level is extreme. If you don't pass these tests, you may be looking for a new job. I had a wife and two sons in college, and I was scared of losing my job. I had serious "check-itis." I was anxious all the time. I had insomnia. I had bouts of "acid stomach." I finally had to resign when my blood pressure got so high they didn't dare let me fly. So here I am back in school. There's a lot of stress of course with exams and working and all that, but nothing like the constant fear I had at the commercial airline.

Reflective writing: *Describe a particularly stressful situation in your life, past or present, and how it affected your physical health.*

Box 7.7

RESEARCH METHODOLOGY
The Placebo Control Experiment

Ordinarily, experimental research uses two groups or two treatments. The *experimental group* is the group that receives the new and different treatment. The results of the experimental treatment are then compared to the *control group,* which does not receive the experimental treatment. If the experimental treatment proves to be superior, then the results of the two groups are compared to determine if there is a statistically significant difference. The experimental model is fairly simple as follows:

Control Group	**Experimental Group**
No difference in treatment	Given experimental treatment

However, when human subjects know they are being given experimental treatment (whether it be a different diet or exercise regimen or a new medication), they react differently just because of that awareness (an intervening variable). In terms of medication, the placebo effect is so powerful that the experimental subjects who are given a placebo sugar pill will (on the average) get better faster than a control group who did not receive a similar pill.

Consequently, when pharmaceutical companies develop a new drug, they must use a third group, called a *placebo group* in which the subjects are given a placebo medication (pill, topical ointment, hypodermic injection) so that they can determine whether the alleviation of symptoms is the result of their new drug or simply the placebo effect. When the subjects do not know whether they are being given experimental treatment, it is called the *single blind technique.*

Sometimes even the experimenters also keep themselves "blind" as to which subjects got the placebo, and that method is called the *double blind technique* (subjects and researchers both "blind"). Why would the researchers want to keep themselves blind? Because sometimes the treatment involves the researchers themselves. For example, if the researcher is the physician prescribing the new drug to his patients with ulcers, he does not want to bias his later examinations of them by knowing which patient had the new drug, no change in treatment, or the placebo.

So he tells his assistants to administer all the medications, including the drug he was previously using, the new drug, and a placebo drug—without his knowledge, but they are to keep records as to which patient received which treatment. Since he doesn't know which patients are in which group, his later determination of the results is free of bias. Such an experimental model is more complex, with at least three groups as follows:

Control Group	**Experimental Group**	**Placebo Group**
No difference in treatment	Given experimental treatment	Placebo treatment

The data from the three groups are statistically compared. If the results show that there is no statistical difference between the placebo and control groups, then we can be more confident about the significant differences that appear in the experimental group.

Does this account for the power of faith healers? We simply do not know as yet, but some physicians believe that all the medications before the twentieth century were useless, by and large. They believe that what healed the patients was the powerful effect of the physician's comforting and reassuring bedside manner or the nurse's loving kindness—"the power of expectant faith." It may even be the knowledge that someone cares enough for them to nurse them through illness (Jaffe, 1974). Consider, for example, what some gerontologists (scientists who specialize in the psychology and health of older people) have been observing for a long time. When we place our older relatives in a nursing home (because we believe we can no longer care for them adequately) without their consent or input, we are literally "consigning them to death" (Butler, 1980). Like the tribal member that has a voodoo curse placed on him and is then shunned by the whole tribe, it is likely that the old person feels cast out and unwanted by their families. Conversely, when older people are given some decision-making power in what should happen to them and take part in choosing the nursing home, the mortality rate is much lower.

Figure 7.4 Alternative Holistic Health Approaches. Today, physicians and other health professionals are incorporating many alternate health approaches into their treatment of patients. Reading from bottom left to right, counter clockwise are a few of these approaches: Deep relaxation methods; meditation; self-discipline regimens of yoga, karate, aerobic exercise, weight control, nutrition and exercise; meditational prayer and visualization methods.

Do they have distinct personality characteristics that foster health?

Can we foster these personality traits in other people?

If these traits can be developed, what methods are most efficacious for doing so?

What was discovered should not surprise the reader by now for, in one way or another, most of the characteristics of psychophysically hardy people have already been discussed in previous chapters. Nevertheless, a complete listing of them now is not only a good summation of what we have learned thus far but also focuses our attention to their importance in our lives.

1. **Positive self-esteem.** When people have low self-esteem, they tend to think that they deserve ill health and that it is their punishment for their sins or their inadequacies as a person. In contrast, psychophysically hardy people have high self-esteem and do not blame themselves for their illness but take it in their stride as happening to everyone on occasion.

2. **Internal locus of control.** Psychophysically hardy persons are characterized by a strong internal locus of control. They believe they can monitor their own health. To understand their disease, they engage in deep self-observation of their symptoms in terms of their possible meaning.

3. **Aggressive pursuit of health.** Psychophysically healthy persons are highly motivated to engage in effective preventative health measures. They exercise daily, eat nutritiously, do not smoke, and drink only on occasion.

4. **Believe they engage in useful and creative work.** They do not "work to live" but "live to work," which is to say they enjoy what they do. They may even have a tendency toward workaholism just because they get so much satisfaction from what they work at.

5. **Have a strong emotional/social support system.** Many have strong family ties and take pleasure from family gatherings. Others may not have personal ties, but they are engaged in activities that bring them into contact with persons of similar interests and ideas.

6. **Regard problematic situations as a challenge.** They may have stresses in their lives (as do we all), but they work at solving problems in a logical and motivated effort.

7. **They investigate alternative health approaches.** Among the many approaches are deep relaxation measures, biofeedback training, meditation and meditational prayer, visualization methods, and any of the therapeutic approaches discussed in Chapter 8.

8. **Able to discuss their life problems with openness.** Since they do not feel guilty about problematic situations in their lives, they are able to use their friends as a sounding board for actively seeking opinions and advice. They are willing to consult counselors for aid and assistance for specific problems or in crisis situations.

9. **Have a purpose and meaning to their lives.** They believe that life is worthwhile. They may have a strong religious belief and attend church. Or they may simply have a spiritual

Box 7.8   SHIFTING ASSUMPTIONS OF THE HEALTH/DISEASE PARADIGM

Assumptions of the Traditional Medical Approach	*Assumptions of the Holistic Health Approach*
1. Disease is the focus.	1. Health is the focus.
2. Emphasis on specific organ or area.	2. Emphasis on the whole person: physical, emotional, cognitive, and spiritual—a unity.
3. Origin of illness viewed as an external invasive force.	3. Origin of illness viewed as a complex of forces: expectations, genetics, present stressors, and worldview.
4. Disease viewed as an entity (germs, virus).	4. Disease viewed as changes the body goes through in the process of reestablishing health.
5. Physician diagnoses, prescribes, and treats.	5. Physician, patient, and adjunct health professionals are a team, working together toward patient's well-being.
6. Placebo effect is evidence of power of suggestion and superstition.	6. Placebo effect is evidence of mindbody's ability to employ powerful symbols of self-healing.
7. Primary therapy is chemical or surgical.	7. Alternative methods investigated, used appropriately, in cooperation with the medical team.
8. Physician makes final decision for treatment.	8. Patients make final decisions for treatment based on their values and belief systems.

sense that life is purposeful and that they are contributing, in some measure, to that purpose. They are often oriented to supra-personal goals.

10. **Proactive participation in their own self-healing.** They are not "pill poppers." When they occasionally do experience pain, they do not "pop" pills for instant relief of symptoms. They understand pain to be symptoms that need to be understood by themselves and to be reported to their health team professionals. At the same time, they know themselves to be the most important person in their own "health team." As well, they understand that we have different reactions to different medications and they record side effects of their prescriptions. If they do need surgery, they take care to get as much information as they can concerning the operation, possible aftereffects, and what they can do to aid their own process of recovery. They work with their physician and other health team staff to determine how to prepare themselves for the surgery and to decide what needs to be done afterward, concerning the immediate effects of the operation and long-term recuperative and rehabilitation needs. As well, they discuss these matters with their support system and community resource agents (see Box 7.8).

11. **Investigate and employ alternative holistic healing methods.** They consult with their physicians but realize that they are their own best caretaker. They assess their areas of stress and take proactive methods to reduce stress, employing holistic methods of health such as nutrition, adequate rest, relaxation, and meditation methods to reduce their levels of stress (see Figure 7.4).

Psychoneuroimmunology: An Interdisciplinary Science of Health and Disease

The foregoing discussion brings us finally to the topic introduced at the beginning of this chapter and which is one of the exciting frontiers of health psychology; namely, psychoneuroimmunology—the research and theory about how people get ill or stay healthy. Psychoneuroimmunologists are not as much interested in whether or not our emotional states affect our physical states. That connection has already been established. What psychoneuroimmunologists are more concerned with, at the present time, is how it happens—the physiological processes whereby our immune system is either enhanced or inhibited by our response to environmental stress. What these researchers have discovered has significantly altered our understanding of what we have considered as belonging to "the mind" and what we have considered as "the body." In fact, their discoveries are leading to a surprising implication; namely, that we are not made up of a "body" and a "mind." We are a unity of physiological processes of bodymindspirit striving to harmonize ourselves with the environment.

Psychoneuroimmunology: Antigens versus Antibodies

The body is vulnerable to many and varied invading microorganisms called **antigens,** such as bacteria, virus, fungi, and parasites. Other antigens include dust, pollen, bee stings, poisons, free radicals (unattached oxygen molecules), and cancerous growths. Fortunately, the body has many built-in protective devices to combat these antigens. If it did not, our life spans might be very short indeed. One such protective device is the immune system. The **immune system** is composed of many organs throughout the body and includes the thymus, the tonsils, the thalamus, the lymph system, the spleen, and the white blood cells. Of particular interest to us here are the antibodies produced by the lymph system. These **antibodies,** known as T-cells, B-cells, and NK cells (for "natural killer" cells) hunt down the toxic antigens, destroy them, and get rid of the waste. These antibodies wait in the spleen and elsewhere until they are alerted that there are invading microorganisms or other antigens somewhere in the body. They then race to the infected area and surround and attack the antigens. If the invading antigens are bacteria or virus, they literally kill them. Other antibodies, called *phagocytes,* engulf and gobble up foreign substances, such as dust or pollen, and act like the garbage disposals of the immune system. The immune system is a wonderfully intelligent complex of many kinds of antibodies that do many different kinds of things to protect us. The immune system, as a whole organ system, is a floating, roving body of cells that "seek out and destroy" dangerous invading antigens.

To repeat: All of the information above describing the immune system had been known for some time to *immunologists* (scientists who study the immune system). But the immunologists wanted to get down deeper into the actual physiology of the body-to-mind connection. What are the precise mechanisms by which our thoughts and moods can raise or lower the immune cells? What they dicovered is this: When we are elated and joyful, the brain's neurotransmitters stimulate the immune system to produce more of the antibodies that protect us from the invasive antigens. When we are depressed or anxious or have other negative emotions, fewer antibodies are produced. It is almost as simple as that. While these connections may seem obvious to us now, these discoveries completely upset the medical assumption that we have a "mind" and a "body" which may influence each other but which are basically separate systems. Psychoneuroimmunologists are now suggesting that we do not have a "body" and a "mind" but rather a seamless integrity of bodymind. This integrity of bodymind has been a position advocated by the "holistic" health professions for a number of years now. Indeed, they have gone even farther and speak of a bodymindspirit integrity. For that perspective, we turn now to the area of holistic health.

Box 7.9

**PSYCHONEUROIMMUNOLOGY
Summing up the Factors that Affect Our Immune System**

1. **Toxins in the environment.** Contaminated water supply (caused by the runoff of fertilizers, garbage, and other poisons), poisoned food; and air pollution; including smog.
2. **Poor health practices.** Smoking; not getting enough rest; inadequate nutrition; overuse of alcohol; and drug abuse. Even prescribed medications can inhibit the immune system.
3. **Overwhelming life events and change.** Traumatic events can overwhelm the immune system's ability to cope; even too many positive changes may be stressful.
4. **Naturalistic stressors.** Even expected stress events (such as taking exams, or working extra shifts) can substantially reduce the body's ability to sustain its usual immune defense.
5. **Chronic stress.** Stressful events that last for a longer term, say months or even years (such as caring for a patient with cancer or Alzheimer's disease) have the potential of weakening the immune system. Even more interesting is the fact that the depressed immune state can last for years after the stressful event has ceased. For example, the residents of Three Mile Island suffered depressed immune systems for more than ten years after the nuclear accident that happened there in 1979.
6. **Seriously depressed emotional disorders.** A meta-analysis of over 40 studies suggests that there is relatively strong correlation between severely depressed patients and a lowered immune system.
7. **Day-by-day mood states.** Even transient negative mood states lasting only a few hours in a day reveal that the antibodies which fight disease and foreign substances are at higher levels during good days than during depressed mood days in the same person.
8. **Day-by-day family stress events.** Even small negative upsets in the family system can increase the vulnerability to colds and other respiratory distress.
9. **Lack of good interpersonal relationships and/or support systems.** People who report feeling isolated and lonely have lower levels of immune antibodies than people who report less loneliness. There is substantial evidence also that poor marital relations or marital interruptions (separation, divorce, widowhood, etc.) also affect the immune system negatively, making the person more likely to succumb to flu and other contagious diseases.
10. **Personality.** While the findings have not been consistent, there is some indication that repression and denial (refusal to acknowledge the existence of a disease such as AIDS or cancer) and a pessimistic personality style contributed to a lowered cellular immune function. Particularly important is the role of depression as a contributing factor to earlier mortality in cancer.

(*Source:* From a review of the literature by Cohen & Herbert, 1996).

The Holistic Approach to Psychophysical Health

All of the these converging lines of research—from the clinical studies of ill patients to psychosomatic research to the discoveries of the "placebo effect" and psychophysically hardy people, and finally to the research of psychoneuroimmunology—have led to a new direction in the study of health and disease. This new direction is called the **holistic health movement.** The holistic health movement is not a discipline in itself but an approach that not only views the person as a bodymind or mindbody but as a unity of bodymindspirit. Moreover, say these holistic health professionals, we must understand the person within his/her total complexity of environments of home, school, neighborhood, work, church, and recreational leisure. That last term, *recreational leisure,* is interpreted as the time to re-create (renew) our physical, emotional, mental, and spiritual energies. One of the first well-known examples of this approach is the famous case of Norman Cousins who, with the aid and support of his physicians and medical team, recovered from a particularly fast-raging and venomous form of cancer (see Box 7.10).

Box 7.10   The Famous Case of Norman Cousins

The use of humor in the treatment plan of illness was given a jump-start by the publication of a noteworthy autobiographical account by Norman Cousins about his bout with cancer (1979). Cousins was an internationally famous correspondent for several magazines and newspapers. While on assignment in Russia, he collapsed with pain and had to return to the United States, where he was diagnosed with collagen disease, a progressive and deadly form of cancer.

Cousins refused to accept the prognosis of "terminal" and took a hand in his own treatment. First, he decided that "a hospital is no place for a person who is seriously ill." He was particularly angry about the food, convinced that the hospital's most serious failure was in the area of nutrition. He also concluded that he was being toxified by the painkillers, and he decided to redefine his role as patient. He set himself up in an apartment near the hospital where he could cook his own food. He reasoned that if stress has negative effects upon the body, then perhaps positive emotions, such as love and hope and faith and laughter and the will to live, would have a therapeutic effect. He rented films that were funny and would make him laugh, such as the "Candid Camera" series and films of the Marx Brothers. He found that joyous laughter enabled him to have at least two hours of pain-free sleep. He initiated a vitamin program and after months of slow recuperation was able to resume his work.

Upon his recovery, he emphasized the three most important healing factors for him were (1) the will to live;

(2) his medical team's holistic approach and support; and (3) refusal to participate in the gloom, fear, depression, and panic that so often accompanies a verdict of cancer.

Cousins was eventually invited to join a California hospital (at UCLA) as adjunct professor so that he might introduce the medical staff and students to the healing value of laughter, good nutrition, and the holistic approach to health and recovery from disease. He died ten years after his ordeal with illness, not from cancer, but from heart disease.

Hospitals everywhere are introducing holistic health concepts. Hospitals were once solemn places where noise (including conversation) and visitors were kept to a minimum. That scenario is changing rapidly. Whatever raises the patient's morale is not only permitted but encouraged. Where the number of visitors to hospital patients were once strictly limited (only two at a time and only for 20 minutes), hospital staffs now encourage visiting, phone calls, spiritual healers and "laying on of hands," or whatever might raise the patients' "expectant faith." Walking through a hospital corridor these days is an enlightening experience. Some hospital rooms may seem like a small party with colorful balloons and wonderful laughter. The medical professions are shifting their assumptions about the health/disease paradigms (see Box 7.8) and are endeavoring to enhance the patient's self-healing by whatever physical, emotional, social, or spiritual avenues are significant and meaningful to the patient.

The Therapeutic Value of Humor

In Chapter 6 we learned that humor is considered one of the highest level defense mechanisms. But in fact, the ability to laugh may be more than a defense mechanism. It may be one of the most transcending of all the gifts of nature, as valuable perhaps as what has been called "the miracle of language." Including laughter in the treatment plan of patients has proved beneficial in a number of studies (Dean, 1997). The famous Mayo Health Institute has already legitimized the use of humor not so much as a cure in itself but as a complement to the body's natural ability to heal itself. They explain the use of humor as having a beneficial influence on the respiration system by increasing the amount of oxygen in the blood, by providing an increase in blood circulation which sends nutrients to your tissues faster; and by increasing the concentration of immunoglobulin A in saliva. Immunoglobulin A is known to fight off colds, flu, and sinus infections. Studies have already demonstrated that humor helps patients cope with pain. Because of the efficacious healing effects of laughter, the Mayo Clinic encourages their physicians to expose patients to humorous experiences (Mayo Clinic Health Letter, 1993).

The famous Gesundheit! Institute of Patch Adams, M.D.   Perhaps no one exempliflies this approach better than Dr. Patch Adams, whose work at his famous Gesundheit! Institute was even made into a movie, starring Robin Williams. The German *gesundheit!* means "Good health!" And that is what this now almost-legendary physician named his first clinic/hospital in an economically depressed area in rural West Virginia. He wants to move our society away from needing Xanax and Prozac. With a firm belief in the healing power of laughter and joy, he has created an institute that celebrates laughter rather than sadness, good spirits rather than depression, and life rather than death. He walks around in a clown's uniform and encourages his staff to try out whatever funny faces, comic clothes, and masks may appeal to them. He employs all the healing arts available, which include comic theatrical presentations, art therapy, dance therapy, peer support groups, and all the alternative therapies presently shown. More alternative therapies will be discussed in the next chapter (Adams, 1999).

Carl Simonton: The First Step Toward Self-Healing May Be to Discover the Meaning of Our Ill-Health

Carl Simonton is an **oncologist** (a physician who specializes in the treatment of cancer.) Simonton believes that the first step in recovery from illness is to discover the meaning of it. It is his belief that cancer and many other illnesses afford the person with some secondary gain (Simonton, 1995). The secondary gain can be the need to resign from a work that has become toxic to the patient. Instead of experiencing "burn out," which may seem a sign of "weakness," the patient develops an illness that provides him with the "right" to leave work. Or it may be that the cancer provides a way out from a family situation that is overdemanding to the point of exhaustion. Or it may be the person's only way to be the recipient of more attention from loved ones. It is not easy to recognize the secondary gain we get from our illness, said Simonton. It takes absolute honesty with oneself and a willingness to discover other ways to deal with the underlying difficulty. A lady of our acquaintance analyzed her incapacitating chronic fatigue syndrome (CFS) in this manner:

> I was a chronic workaholic. When I was growing up, nothing I ever did pleased my parents. Nothing! I was always at fault, always wrong, always lacking in some way. I struggled harder and harder and harder "to do right" and to get approval from my parents—to no avail. Since I was never sure that what I was doing was enough, I overdid everything. I had a work style of doing more than I was asked to do. I didn't go the whole nine yards. I went the whole ten yards, and eleven yards—and not for my own gain!—but for the gain of my bosses or the company I worked for. I exhausted myself at home and at work, until finally I came down with CFS. After the worst of the CFS symptoms diminished, I was able to return to work. I did not tell my bosses the nature of my illness—only that I had a chronic muscle disease and had to regulate my life with a little more attention to my physical health. My bosses did not want to lose such a good worker (which I had never realized before) and were only too happy to accommodate my need to "throttle back" just a little. I could have throttled back years ago if I had just understood I was working far harder than anyone else in my department. I could have taken more time for rest and recreation—just to enjoy myself. I have come to regard the CFS as my body's way of slowing me down and letting me have some leisure time in my life.

Simonton and other holistic health professionals suggest that we need to learn to read our own bodily symptoms. If we have a headache, we can ask ourselves who or what is giving us the headache. Is it that office party we dread going to? Is it our boss who is always nagging us to get things done faster? Or the income tax form that doesn't seem to make sense to us. If we have a backache, we can ask ourselves "what burdens are we carrying that are becoming too heavy for us?" Or the pile of work that is getting larger and larger by the day? No one can tell you what the symptom might mean. You and you alone have the clue to your body's state of being ill-at-ease; i.e., diseased. Or does a sudden cold suggest that you need to have "a good cry"? (Some of the other body signals that have been suggested are listed in Box 7.11). This may seem outrageous at first, but many health professionals take it very seriously. As Robert Lynch says, body language is embedded deeply within our language: Does common sense recognize something that scientists and physicians cannot see? Why do we continue to use phrases such as broken heart, heartless, sweetheart? Why do we persist in the notion that people die of broken hearts when no such diagnoses ever appear on twentieth-century death certificates? (Lynch, 1977)

Toward a Definition of Health: Harmony of BodyMindSpirit

Health professionals are working on deriving a definition of health. Strange as this may seem, it is a lot harder to create a definition of health than a definition of disease. Traditionally, health has been defined as an "absence of disease or disease symptoms," but that definition is no longer acceptable to holistic health professionals. Health is not the mere absence of disease or other pathologies, it is something more. But before we can begin to evolve that "something more," we need to make some quantum leaps in our understanding of what disease actually is and what our disease symptoms mean.

The first quantum leap is to understand the difference between the disease and the symptoms of disease. The symptoms of the disease are not necessarily the disease itself but the

---

Box 7.11

CARL SIMONTON
Learning to Read Our Bodily Symptoms

The following are only a few examples of body metaphors. Each person needs to analyze what the meaning of his or her symptoms might be.

Headache? Who or what is giving you a headache?
The common cold? What situation would you like to cry about? What happened within the last forty-eight hours that hurt your feelings or wounded your pride—only you refused to admit it. After all, you figured, you're above such petty feelings.
Stomach problems? Knot in your stomach? Queasy stomach? Nausea? What has you so tensed up, your stomach can't relax? What is it that you can't "stomach"? Nausea? What is making you "sick to your stomach"?
Lump in your throat? What piece of news can you "not swallow"?
Insomnia? What worries are keeping you awake?

Abdominal cramps? Is there something going on in your life that is "cramping your style?" Are you feeling squeezed into doing something you don't want to do? Do you feel like you are caught in the middle of an argument not of your choosing and being squeezed dry by both parties?
Sensitive shoulders? Have you taken on too much responsibility and, like Atlas, feel you are carrying too many burdens on your shoulders?
Constipation? Are you holding on "for dear life" in your job or at home? It could be you are just so busy you are not taking time out for much needed relaxation.
Arthritic fingers? Are you trying to control people or events beyond your control? Does your reach exceed your grasp?

Reflective Writing. Describe one of your chronic bodily ills. What might be the significance of the symptoms?

Box 7.12

SCENARIO REVISITED
Beginning Stress Inoculation Training

Jill Smith, the graduate assistant, has just begun a small group session with three students.

Jill Smith: Let's begin by explaining why we are here. As the leader-participant, I'm adding to my professional "tools," but I'm also working on my own anger and stress.

Martha: You! You always seem so cool.

Jill: I may seem cool, calm, and collected, but I sometimes say things in anger that I'm sorry for later. And words can't be as easily deleted like a mistake on a computer screen. People say this to me a lot: "You're a psychologist—you shouldn't have any problems." I assure you we have our fair share of problems. And we don't always act maturely.

Alec: Jill, I thought stress inoculation had to do with plants and animals.

Jill: Yes, that's where the term comes from. For example, biologists have been inoculating young plants to withstand future severe drought by subjecting them to minimal drought conditions. Psychology has borrowed the term because it is an approach that prepares us to deal with stressful situations that may occur in the future. Of course we can't anticipate every stressful situation you may meet but at least we can develop some coping strategies that have generic application. Stress inoculation training usually begins with becoming aware of our fight-flight-freeze "triggers." So why are you here, Dan?

Dan: It's part of a program Dr. Ling put together to get my blood pressure down and to prevent my migraine headaches. I get so angry when I sense prejudice from whites; I get boiling angry. I've been in a couple of barroom brawls. That was when I was drinking. I don't drink now.

Alec: I'm here for almost the same reason as Dan only kind of turned around. I don't show it like Dan does, but I seethe inside when I hear prejudicial remarks toward nonwhites. I'm completely alienated from my family because they are so prejudiced. I can't even stand to be around them over the holidays.

Martha: My son can irritate me to distraction and I end up screaming at him. I don't want to be the kind of mother always screaming at her kids.

Jill: Now let's identify just what happens to us when we get angry. Martha, what does your son do or say that sets you off?

Martha: He comes home with bad grades and when I get on him, he says (just as cool as you please) "I don't care. I'm going to drop out of school when I'm six-teen." And then I go "ape." "Drop out of school. How can you be so stupid? After all your father and I have done for you. We've been working night and day so you can get a college education." Then he says, "Then you can stop working because I ain't going. I'm going to bum around and have a good time for a while." And there I am being a screaming maniac and that only makes matters worse.

Jill: And how do you experience that anger in your body?

Martha: Experience it? You mean like what do I feel in my body? (*Jill nods*) Sometimes I get tears in my eyes, I feel so frustrated. (*Jill nods*) And my heart begins to pound. And my voice gets so loud I could wake the dead!

Jill: When I get angry, I feel self-righteous indignation. I think, "How dare he say that to me!" (or whatever).

Martha: Me too. How dare this kid turn his nose up at all we're trying to do for him!

Jill: So one of my signals that I'm getting irrationally angry is when I hear that phrase in my head—"How dare he . . . "

Dan: I've got a lot of signals. I think, "That SOB—he's a no good" . . . well, I think a lot of words I can't say here.

Jill: How about body signals?

Dan: Let's see, I clench my fists and I grit my teeth so hard, my jaw hurts later. I get hot—like I'm on fire.

Alec: That's interesting. I go the other way. I get cold, ice-cold. And a strange thing happens to my eyes. Suddenly, the person that has gotten me angry suddenly seems small and far away.

Jill: So let's see. I get indignant. Martha screams. Dan would like to go for the jugular. Alec distances himself from the other person. This is a good beginning to our group. We've described some stimuli that trigger our fight-flight-freeze responses. For homework this week, you're to write in your notebook every day what got you angry or even just irritated that day, what triggered it, and how you reacted. Think about what thoughts went through your head. Get in touch with your bodily responses. And what you actually did in your moment of fear or anger. Finally, think about how you felt when your fight-flight-freeze response subsided. We'll spend a few sessions doing that and we are also going to be learning a few body-calming techniques like deep relaxation, desensitization training, and biofeedback—some of the techniques you have been reading about in the last three chapters.

Source: Donald Meichenbaum. (1993). "Changing conceptions of cognitive behavior modification." *Journal of Consulting and Clinical Psychology,* 61, 202–204.

body's response in getting us well again. Let us take, for example, a cold or viral flu. The cold or flu is running rampant through your system. You feel sick with all the usual symptoms of headache, fever, muscular aches and pains, drowsiness, and the desire to just go to bed and stay there. These symptoms are the result of your body's reaction to the invading bacteria or flu. The fever will burn off the bacteria or flu. The headache and muscular aches and pains are the result of the fever—not the bacteria or virus. All of these symptoms, along with the drowsiness and desire to nod off, are the way your body is urging you to go to bed and sleep. When you go to sleep, your body shifts out of the *adrenalergic state* to the *cholinergic state*. Now you will remember that it is when we are in the cholinergic state that our bodies can drain built up toxins, heal damaged tissue, conserve the body's energy, and speed up the process of healing. You probably should have gone to bed earlier but you told yourself you had too much work to do. So eventually, the fever and the aches and pains and the drowsiness have gotten so great that you now have no choice but to go to bed. You call whomever you need to call and tell them that you won't be able to work or go to class or do those other things on our "to do" list. What we need to understand then is that the discomfort and the pain of the symptoms are not the way Fate in the form of the disease is punishing us, but the body working hard to heal us. Once more: The symptoms we feel (the fever, the aches and pains, the headache, and the drowsiness) are the changes the body is undergoing to combat the disease and restore health.

Now let's proceed toward deriving another definition—that of health. Health professionals are working toward a holistic definition. We have said that health is not merely the absence of disease. It is a matter of our entire psychophysical well-being. Any valid definition of health must include more than the freedom from disease and disease symptoms. It must include the concepts of energy, vitality, enjoyment, zest, and exuberance for life, a sense of fulfillment in living a creative life, and a sense we are living up to our highest potential at the moment. It must include the ecological freedom to grow, adapt, and change—and the willingness to allow others to grow, adapt, and change. Psychophysical health must include such terms as peace, joy, and—yes—the concepts of love and loving relationships. We must consider health as a harmonious ecological unity of bodymind—and even bodymindspirit. Think about a time in your life when you felt your very best, when you were bursting with energy, and brimming over with happiness. That approaches the definition of health. Health must be considered as a total experience of living peacefully, joyfully, creatively, and with purpose and meaning.

IMPORTANT TERMS AND CONCEPTS TO KNOW

adrenalergic	disease	hot reactors	psychosomatic
alternative	etiology	hypnosis	responses
animistic	esteem	hypochondria	stress
antibodies	eustress	inoculation	symptoms
antigens	fight	life-crisis units	sympathetic
change	freeze	loneliness	Type-A
cholinergic	germ theory	placebo	Type-B
conversion	holistic	psychophysically	

MAKE YOUR OWN SUMMARY BY FILLING IN THE BLANKS BELOW

Use the "Important Terms and Concepts" on the facing page to fill in the blanks below.

The history of disease theory has undergone many transformations from _____ theories (in which disease is caused by malevolent entities or voodoo) to the _____ developed by such men as Louis Pasteur and Robert Lister. The contribution of our mental states to our physical health began with the work of Franz Mesmer, who demonstrated cures for physical disease through the power of suggestion, known today as _____ . Jean-Marc Charcot demonstrated that physical symptoms could have psychological _____ .

Sigmund Freud described _____ hysteria, in which the patient's symptoms of anxiety are converted to physical ailments. All of these clinical observations led to the _____ era of disease, which means that the physical symptoms have at least some correlation with social/emotional problems. The term psychosomatic must not be confused with the concept of _____ , a state of mind in which the patient is constantly concerned about health.

W. B. Cannon described the body's reaction to emergency situations which he called the _____ or-flight syndrome. When we sense a threat, our bodies energize the _____ nervous system, which causes many physical changes and increases our energy levels. We are then in a/an _____ state but we cannot remain in this state for too long or we would "burn out." We need time for relaxation and sleep so we can restore our bodily energies, called the _____ state. We now speak of the fight-flight or _____ response, the latter being what the body does when escape is impossible and the threat too overwhelming.

Hans Selye investigated the effects of less dramatic but chronic _____ on our bodies. He later differentiated _____ , hypostress, and distress. The Holmes and Rahe studies revealed that _____ itself can have serious effects on health. A high score of _____ , including "happy" events, can produce a physical or psychological depression. Some people overreact physiologically to minor stress and are called " _____ ."

Personality "type" and certain diseases have been correlated. For example, _____ personality has been associated with heart diseases. Robert Lynch believes that many people die simply from _____ caused by physical or emotional separation from friends and family. Other evidence of the effects of our emotional state on our health comes from the studies of the _____ effect, that includes not only non-medicinal pills but also the "laying on of hands," prayer, laughter, and other mood-elevating procedures. People who seem to manage excessive stress in their lives are described as _____ hardy persons. They have many personality characteristics in common, including positive self _____ , a strong social/emotional network, challenging work, a strong moral/ethical system, and are proactive in their own psychophysical health.

Psychoneuroimmunology is a relatively new field of science that has discovered a direct relationship between the neurotransmitters of the brain and the _____ of the immune system. What has been discovered is that our emotions and mood states affect the number of T-cells, B-cells, and NK-cells, all of which are needed to protect us from invasive _____ . A program of stress _____ is designed to enable people to deal with crises they have not yet encountered by having them identify their mental states and bodily _____ when they under stress. They are then encouraged to discover different ways to deal with the stress.

Holistic health professionals now view health as a unity of bodymindspirit and encourage the patient to seek _____ health measures including nutrition, exercise, prayer or meditation, biofeedback, etc. In their view, the definition of health can no longer be limited to the absence of _____ . We must also include such elements of the bodymindspirit as joyous energy, creativity, a harmonious life with others, and the reward that comes from commitment and service to others.

8 THE PSYCHOTHERAPIES
Many Types, Many Applications

Since Freud's discovery of the "talking cure," there have been many different kinds of approaches developed for the integration of personality. Only a few of these many approaches are pictured here. They are discussed in this chapter and in later chapters.

Box 8.1

SCENARIO
How Do We Know If We Need Therapy? Or What Kind?

Eduardo: Professor, if all of us live with anxiety most of the time, like you've been telling us, how do you know when our problems are serious enough that we need psychotherapy?

Dr. Weitzman: There are many ways to answer that question but perhaps the most direct is simply to ask ourselves: How are we feeling most of the time? Are we usually optimistic and cheerful despite the problems we are having? Or are we generally depressed and anxious and feeling that life is a misery? A good psychotherapist can help you assess what is going on in your life and provide options for you to think about or help you develop coping strategies for working through problem areas.

Martha: But can't you get the same results by discussing a problem with a good friend?

Jonnimae: I tried that once! I thought I had a friend who would keep a confidence I gave her. Never again! I don't trust her with anything I don't want published in the newspaper.

Dr. Weitzman: If what you told her was very serious and traumatic, she may not have been capable of keeping it to herself. It was too much for her. A therapist is legally and ethically bound to maintain the person's confidentiality. Another problem is that friendship is supposed to be mutual give-and-take. Eventually your friend may get tired of listening to your problems.

Alec: I have this friend who's in therapy with a counselor and she raves how it has helped her so much. I admit I see a real change in her—for the better. But she talks like it's the answer to all of life's problems. But it certainly can't cure all the ills of the world, like poverty or disease. It can't keep a person from dying of AIDS.

Dr. Weitzman: Alec, that's a very good point. There are some things psychotherapy cannot do. Therapy cannot wipe out war or social injustices. And, as you say, Alec, it can't keep a person from dying of AIDS. But there are some things a therapeutic situation can do. For example, a therapist with expertise in AIDS counseling can provide information about alternate courses of action. The counselor can also help the family members deal with their concerns, their anxieties, or their guilt feelings if the afflicted person deteriorates to the point of needing institutional placement. Or perhaps the family members can join a peer support group with other relatives of AIDS victims. We can't keep the person from dying but we can alleviate some of the stress and pain of those closest to the patient. Therapeutic support has proved to be very effective with patients undergoing surgery or some other life-threatening illness.

Alec: Can it help with the hatred in our society? I'm on a personal crusade to work against all these hate groups in our nation—even the world.

Box 8.1

SCENARIO (continued)
How Do We Know If We Need Therapy? Or What Kind?

Dr. Weitzman: That's a wide-open question and one which social scientists all over the world are discussing. We know, for example that people who are angry and hostile and who have low self-esteem are more likely to externalize their unhappiness onto others. If these people can get some insight into their unhappiness, they become more open to new ideas and cultures. They are less likely to go in for the destructive defense mechanisms we have already discussed—such as physical violence, projective identification, scapegoating, and so on. They become more respectful of the rich diversity in our country.

Eduardo: There's a joke that if I am thinking about going to a "shrink," I ought to have my head examined.

Dr. Weitzman: (*smiling*) I've heard that joke, too. Actually, if a person has lost touch with reality and is in the midst of an acute psychotic episode, psychotherapy is not going to help. The person needs medical treatment first. Once the person has been stabilized with medication, psychotherapy can be provided for the person. Therapy is more suitable for people who are not psychotic. We deal with the more serious mental disorders in the next chapter.

Eduardo: So getting back to my original question: What I want to know is how do you know what kind of therapy a person needs?

Dr. Weitzman: So glad you asked! That's what we are about to discuss right now.

The Need to Be Therapy Literate

Therapy means healing, and **psychotherapy** means healing of the mind/spirit/soul. We tend to think that psychotherapy started with Sigmund Freud's technique of psychoanalysis, and in one sense that is true. He helped us to understand that expressing our negative emotions through the "talking cure" can alleviate our anxiety and problems. But historically there have been many kinds of therapies. Consider, for example, the story of King Saul of the Hebrews. His episodes of depression were remediated by the soothing music of the young shepherd boy, David, who played to him on his harp. Today, we would call that music therapy. Long before the Christian Era, India was developing several kinds of yoga designed to bring about inner peace and enlightenment. The early Christian Church instituted the rite of confession and today we still say "confession is good for the soul"—an assumption that is not too dissimilar from the insight therapies of today. One hundred years before Freud, Franz Mesmer introduced his method of **mesmerism,** which today we would call **hypnotherapy.** In 1875, Mary Baker Eddy formulated a Protestant sect she called Christian Science, which advocated basic spiritual principles in order to achieve good mental and physical health. At the present time, many churches encourage spiritual retreats in which both clergy and parishioners can get away from "the madding crowd" and enter into self-contemplation and meditative prayers. In fact, all the major religions have advocated prayer and meditation as paths to the healing of the mind/spirit/soul. (We must mention, however, that some practices were not very healing, such as the "snake pit" of the medieval era, or the torturous practices of the Inquisition and the New England Puritans.) Furthermore, it has long been known that people who write about the negative events of their lives experience a cathartic emotional release. Today, we have several types of therapies which would fall under the heading of writing therapy. In fact, the reflective writing activities in this text can be categorized as writing therapy. Psychotherapy, then, has a long history, but the scientific approach began just a little over one hundred years ago with Sigmund Freud.

A good place to start becoming therapy literate is to recognize the three basic categories of psychotherapy. Most psychologists group the various approaches to psychotherapy into three general categories:

Insight therapies.
Behavior therapies.
Cognitive therapies.

The Insight Therapies

Each of the three categories listed above can be further broken down into individual therapies, which are one-on-one interactions (therapist and person), and group therapies, which can involve many other persons. The assumption underlying the **insight therapies** is that when we gain insight into ourselves and our problem, we will experience relief of our symptoms and change our behavior. It was Sigmund Freud who opened up the field of insight therapy with his development of **psychoanalysis.**

Freud and the Psychoanalytic Approach

Freud began his therapeutic work with patients by using hypnosis. In the hypnotic state, the patient would recall unconscious traumatic events and bring them into conscious awareness. Over the course of time, however, Freud discovered that hypnosis was not necessary to bring back repressed memories. He discovered that simply encouraging the person to talk, a technique he called **free association,** would bring up the repressed material as easily as hypnosis (Freud, 1926). The patient was told simply to lie back on the couch and say anything that came to mind, any thoughts or feelings, or whatever. Nor did these associations have "to make sense." The patient could ramble on disjointedly about past events, present guilts, or future fears, etc. He also encouraged his patients to discuss their dreams, which Freud called "the royal road" to the unconscious—by which he meant the swiftest way to uncover unconscious conflicts.

The Aim of Psychoanalysis: To Bring Unconscious Material into Consciousness and Catharsize Traumatic Events. Psychoanalysis was based on the assumption that most of our behavior is motivated by unconscious conflict, generally as the result of repressed childhood memories. Freud explained that repressed memories require much psychic energy to stay in the unconscious. If people have too many repressed memories, explained Freud, so much psychic energy is being drained away from their everyday functioning that they become emotional and/or physical cripples for the rest of their lives. Freud called this emotional and physical crippling by the term **neurosis.** Freud also said that traumatic memories do not have to be "real." They can also be a child's misinterpretation of events. For example, a child may witness his parents having sexual intercourse and misinterpret that as an act of violence of his father against his mother. By recalling this event and understanding its real significance, the adult no longer has to hate his father because of his childhood misinterpretation—that his father was hurting his mother.

As Freud formulated psychoanalysis, it was a long and involved process, consisting of one hour a day, three to five times a week. It often required three to five years to alleviate the person's symptoms. Clearly, the only people who could take advantage of psychoanalysis were those who could afford the time and money involved. "Classical psychoanalysis" was introduced to this side of the Atlantic after World War I and is still practiced today in large urban centers. But as a therapeutic approach, it was out of the reach of most North Americans with modest incomes. What was needed was a more practical and less expensive approach, an approach which was called *counseling.*

Carl Rogers and the Client-Centered Counseling Approach

The counseling approach began in the 1930s as a task-oriented situation—such as vocational counseling, marital counseling, academic counseling, etc. This type of counseling was usually a one hour, once-a-week situation for a limited period of time. Sometimes, as in the case of academic counseling, the task might even be accomplished in one session. Over the course of time, however, counseling also became involved with the individual's entire life-career. Finally in the early 1950s, the counseling approach was molded into a psychotherapeutic model that was significantly different from Freud's psychoanalytic model. The person responsible for this evolutionary development was a therapist by the name of Carl Rogers (1905–1987).

Since Freud had been a physician and a neurologist, it was natural for him to develop a psychotherapy that reflected his medical worldview. Psychoanalysis was a doctor/patient relationship. When Freud's patients entered his office, they listed their symptoms, which Freud then diagnosed and treated. Eventually he pronounced his patients "cured" or "incurable." In other words, psychoanalysis was a **medical model.** Carl Rogers, almost singlehandedly, introduced a **nonmedical model** with the publication of his now classic book *Client-Centered Therapy* (1950). These two models, medical and nonmedical, are built on entirely different assumptions (see Table 8.1).

A Humanistic Self-Fulfillment Model. Carl Rogers had been a minister befor becoming a counselor. His previous ministerial career provided him with a different worldview, which had different assumptions. As Rogers put it, he was not a physician; therefore, he did not have patients. He had clients. Rogers' clients, then, could not have "symptoms." They simply had "problems." In fact, said Rogers, we all have problems. As the French philosopher Herbert Marcuse once wrote, "Life is problematic" (Marcuse, 1974). Since Rogers was not a physician, his job was not to diagnose or treat. Rogers did not view himself as a physician whose job it was to heal patients. His job was to facilitate his clients' self-healing. Clients were people who needed improvement in communicating with themselves and with others. As far as Rogers was concerned, he was simply an expert in interpersonal relationships.

Table 8.1   Assumptions of the Medical Model versus Rogers' Nonmedical (Counseling) Model

Assumption	*Medical Model*	*Nonmedical (Rogerian) Model*
Person seeking help	Is a "patient"	Is a "client"
Therapist	Is a "physician"	Is a "counselor"
Person describes	"Symptoms"	"Problems"
Therapist's role	To make diagnosis and prescribe treatment	To listen empathetically and to reflect empathetically. To enable the "client" to get in touch with center-of-growth
Worldview	Some people are healthy and some people are sick	We all have problems since "life is problematic"
Therapist/person relationship	The doctor is the authority. "Tell me, Doctor."	Therapist is a consultant Therapist is a facilitator of client's self-discovery

Rogers' nonmedical personality model also differed significantly from Freud's model of human personality. Freud's medical model portrays human consciousness (the ego) as a beleaguered battleground on which the id and the superego wage war. It is a conflict model. Rogers' theory, on the other hand, is a **self-fulfillment theory;** namely, that our conscious and unconscious processes are not antagonistic. What is going on, said Rogers, is the attempt of our entire personality complex to harmonize and evolve to higher levels of consciousness. Rogers' theory is that we have a Self and that this Self is seeking to grow into more creative levels of expression. Rogers' model is called a **humanistic model** of personality.

Aim of Therapy: To Harmonize and Expand the Self. Rogers' self-fulfillment model of personality has a direct bearing on his model of therapy. All our early lives are spent trying to live up to what *others* (parents, teachers, adolescent peers) think we should do. If we have tried to conform too much to the expectations of other people, we lose touch with our own center-of-growth. Said Rogers, we all have a center-of-growth—even the most depressed patients on the psychiatric ward of a state hospital. If they did not, said Rogers, they would be dead. The task of the Rogerian therapist is to enable the client to get in touch with that center-of-growth. That means that the Rogerian therapist does not lecture to the clients, or tell them what to do, or offer advice, or in any way try to direct the person's life. Well, if the therapist doesn't do any of these things, what does the therapist do? The therapist listens with empathy (without judgment) and reflects back to the clients what they seem to be expressing. In this way, the client hears his/her own thoughts reflected back. Little by little, the clients begin to listen to themselves, and to trust their own feelings and intuitions. They become self-directing.

Empathy versus Sympathy. Rogers distinguished empathy from sympathy. When we are engaging in **sympathy,** we are feeling superior to that person. One clue that we are being sympathetic is a remark such as "Oh you poor thing, I feel so sorry for you," which really means "How much better off I am than you." **Empathy** has more equality to it. We are looking at the world through the eyes of the client and we can identify some of the same emotions in ourselves. We are not feeling sorry for the person. Nor are we judging the person. We are understanding the person's **phenomenology.** We say something like, "I've been in a similar situation myself." Or "I think I understand a little of what you are going through." At that moment we truly understand the Native American saying mentioned in an earlier chapter: *Never judge a person until you have walked a mile in their moccasins.*

In order for the clients to reveal their "true Self," Rogerian therapists must create a special environment in which the clients feel safe enough to communicate all those emotions they have bottled up for so long. The clients must believe that the therapist likes them, and accepts them for what they are. Rogers called this acceptance of the client in totality as **unconditional positive regard.** The task of the client-centered therapist, therefore, is to create a **warm environmental climate** of mutual respect and liking where clients can feel safe enough to be self-revealing. When the therapist accepts clients in this manner, they can begin to accept themselves. (See Box 8.2 for a transcript of a Rogerian-type therapeutic session.) In later chapters, the reader will discover how Rogers' theories have found their way into marriage counseling, education, child-raising, interacting with adolescents, and business.

Frederick Perls' Gestalt Therapy

Freud's psychoanalysis and Rogers' client-centered counseling are both time-consuming. There are other approaches, however, that are much more direct and economical in time and money. One approach was developed by Frederick Perls, who left his native Germany during the Nazi

Box 8.2   A TRANSCRIPT OF CLIENT-CENTERED (ROGERIAN) THERAPY

Before reading this transcript, reread Box 7.3 (p. 148) in which Mr. Smith's conversion hysteria is discussed. The following is an actual transcript of the therapeutic situation. Notice how the therapist mainly reflects Mr. Smith's feelings and thoughts to him (with only an occasional personal note) and, in so doing, Mr. Smith's mood changes from depression and guilt to one of amusement.

Mr. Smith: I feel depressed . . . I can't get over being ashamed of myself.

Therapist: You feel really badly about yourself.

Mr. Smith: Sure I do. I must really hate my wife if I wanted to smash her face in! If I feel that violently about her, I can't really feel very loving toward her.

Therapist: You believe that you can't have feelings of love and hate toward the same person.

Mr. Smith: Can I?

Therapist: Can't you?

Mr. Smith: (*after some silence*) Well, maybe we can. I can remember times when I hated my father when he disciplined me, but I also loved him. But I was a child then.

Therapist: You think only children can have ambivalent feelings toward someone?

Mr. Smith: I like to think of myself as a rational adult.

Therapist: And rational adults never have irrational feelings.

Mr. Smith: (*smiling at this*) I guess none of us are rational all the time.

Therapist: I'm certainly not rational all the time. In fact I don't know anyone who is rational every single moment. Do you?

Mr. Smith: No one's perfect! . . . (*after a few more moments of silence*) . . . What's irrational is to think I can be perfect. Good Heavens! What an absurdity! I'm only human just like everybody else.

regime and eventually arrived in the United States, where he developed an insight therapy that was quite different from both Freud and Rogers. Like Freud, it was Perls' contention that we do not function as a complete person. But whereas Freud divided human personality into the three component parts of id, superego, and ego, Perls divided human personality into two component parts. He called these two component parts Top Dog and Underdog (Perls, 1967, 1969).

Top Dog and **Underdog** represent our two parents, who vied with each other for control and dominance in the family unit. As we grow up, we introjected the personality characteristics of each of our parents, including their struggle for dominance. When we interact with others, especially in personal and intimate relationships, we sometimes take the Top Dog role and sometimes take the Underdog Role. Make no mistake, however, Top Dog is not always the victor. While Top Dog is the louder, more aggressive part of our personality, Underdog has powerful manipulative devices to get its own way—devices such as martyrdom, weakness, and coyness—which frequently topple Top Dog. For example, if boyfriend or husband is acting in his Top Dog role, he may yell at his girlfriend or wife who (in this situation) is poor little Underdog. He stamps away feeling victorious in this interaction. *Man, did he tell her off!* Later the same day, he approaches the lady in question only to find her cool and quiet and not very responsive in her Underdog role. She may even be tearful. He does not want her in this nonresponsive state. He wants to resume his happy relationship with her so he ends up apologizing for his previous behavior until she smiles and warms up to him. According to Perls, Underdog has won again! Although we have depicted Top Dog as the male in this case and Underdog as the female, the relationship can be just the opposite—the man as Underdog and the woman in Top Dog position.

Aim of Therapy: To Resolve Unfinished Situations from the Past and Learn to Live in the Here-and-Now.   The aim of gestalt therapy is to live in the here-and-now. We do this by resolving the Top Dog/Underdog conflicts of our past. To do so, Perls developed some dramatic and lightning-swift techniques to dramatize our conflicts by imaging the person in a chair and having a dialog with that person, later called the "hot seat" technique. (It might be added that Perls' direct technique is not for the timid or shy person who could be easily daunted by being put on the "hot seat.") But by dramatizing our interpersonal conflicts and exaggerating them, we do gain insight into our unconscious resentments. It does not matter whether our resentments are "real" or exaggerated or distorted or complete fabrications. It was Perls' contention that all our perceptions of the world are products of our own imagination. His worldview was this: How we perceive others is simply a reflection of ourselves. We are looking into a mirror. If we perceive the world as hostile, we are perceiving our own prevailing hostility—products of past unresolved situations. All that mattered is that we resolve the unfinished situations in our own minds, which could be done very quickly in the course of a therapeutic hour.

What Perls often wrote and talked about was that most of us are living out resentments from the past or haunted by specters of the future which usually never come about. In either case we are not really living in the present. We are living as deadened bodies unable to feel alive to the present moment. Perls urged us to live in the **here-and-now.** Looking at Figure 8.1, we see a familiar illusion. If we focus on the black, we see a vase, but if we focus on the white, we see two faces. The black is the figure and the white is the ground (background). The significance of the **figure-ground** relationship for Perls was that we often confuse the past (the ground or background) with the present figure (the figure). The transcript in Box 8.3 provides an example of just such distortion. As you read the transcript, note how Mr. X confuses the present situation (the figure) with events of his personal background (the ground).

Group Insight Therapies: Transactional Analysis and Peer-Support Groups

We have been discussing the individual insight therapies of Freud (psychoanalysis), Rogers (client-centered therapy), and Perls (gestalt therapy). The reader may well have noticed that the gestalt session in Box 8.3 was done in a group, but careful reading of that transcript will reveal that the therapeutic interaction was strictly between Perls and Mr. X. We turn our attention now to the insight therapies that actually do require the active participation of the group members.

Figure 8.1 The Figure-Ground Relationship. Perls used this illusion as a metaphor for our inability to distinguish past conflicts and present events in the here-and-now. The vase represents the figure or present focus. The two faces represent the ground (or background or previous history). People sometimes confuse the ground with the figure. Now read Box 8.3 and identify the ground and the figure.

Advantages of Group Therapies. Group psychotherapy became popular for several reasons. First, the cost is much less, the fee being shared among the group members. Second, the therapeutic session does not have the rarefied atmosphere of a patient/client relationship but more of a realistic everyday atmosphere of adults discussing mutual problems in an atmosphere of trust. Third, the group members develop close emotional/social relationships, similar in some ways to those of a family. Unlike family members, however, the group members do not have a long knotty history of parent/child conflicts, sibling rivalries, and smoldering resentments that lie just under the surface of many family relationships. The value of the group is that the individual members can work out many of their family difficulties in the safe climate of the therapeutic group. Finally, group therapies often take the form of professional training, such as human potential seminars, leadership training, and management

Box 8.3

A GESTALT THERAPY SESSION WITH FREDERICH ("FRITZ") PERLS (continued)

In this group was a pert and attractive young woman (Miss Y), who came into the group with a smile and a hello for each of the other members, all of whom were men. The therapeutic session had not officially started. Mr. X, one of the group members, made a seemingly joking remark to Miss Y, that went something like: "I see you are being your usual flirtatious self." The attention of most of us was immediately riveted on Miss Y, but Perls turned his attention to Mr. X.

Perls: Mr. X, what do you "see" when you look at Miss Y?

Mr. X: (*startled by Perls's question*) I was just making a joke.

Perls: Let us examine your "joke." What do you "see" when you look at Miss Y?

Mr. X: I didn't really mean anything by the remark—it was just a remark.

Perls: Would you direct your attention to Miss Y now?

Mr. X: Sure.

Perls: What do you see?

Mr. X: I see a pretty, kind of flirtatious girl, that's all.

Perls: Would you direct your remarks to her? (*Perls always asked the group members to talk to a person, not talk about the person, which he called gossiping.*)

Mr. X: She heard me.

Perls: We don't allow "gossip." Please direct your remarks to Miss Y.

Mr. X: All right, if you say so. Miss Y, I see you as being a very flirtatious person.

Perls: What are you experiencing now?

Mr. X: I'm looking at Miss Y, that's all.

Perls: By experiencing, we mean what is going on in your body.

Mr. X: You mean inside me?

Perls: Ja!

Mr. X: Well, my heart is pounding. You've made me nervous.

Perls: (*after some silence*) Go on . . . what else do you experience?

Mr. X: I'm feeling angry.

Perls: Could you act out your anger? Could you say what is making you angry at Miss Y?

Mr. X: I don't know.

Perls: Would you be willing to try?

Mr. X: I don't know . . . maybe.

Perls: Let us "see" your "maybe."

Mr. X: Maybe I will; maybe I won't . . . Yeah, I guess I will. (*to Miss Y*) You make me mad!

Perls: Could you tell her more how mad she makes you?

Mr. X: I don't know. (*to Miss Y*) I get mad at women who flirt around with men.

Perls: Could you tell Miss Y that you would like her to flirt with you?

Mr. X: (*suddenly very loud and obviously angry*) Why should I? I resent her flirtatiousness. It's manipulative.

Perls: Would you play Miss Y being manipulative?

Mr. X: You mean act like Miss Y? (*Perls nods.*) I don't know if I can . . . All right, I will. (*He imitates a "female" voice and smiles to various persons in the room, saying "Good morning, dear" to each person. His voice is strangely authentically female.*)

Perls: Could you tell us who says "Good morning, dear" like that?

Mr. X: Miss Y, whenever she comes in the room.

Perls: You didn't hear me. Who says, "Good morning, dear" to you?

Mr. X: I don't know what you mean. (*The rest of us realize that Miss Y has never used the word "dear."*)

Perls: Could you exaggerate "Good morning, dear"?

Mr. X: Good morning, dear. Good morning, DEAR! GOOD MORNING, DEAR! (*He is talking very loudly now, almost screaming. His face has become very red. The room has become very quiet now.*)

Perls: What is going on now?

Mr. X: (*Visibly shaken, it takes a few moments for him to respond.*) That was my mother talking. She always talked like that when she came into the room.

Perls: Go on.

Mr. X: I can see her now, the bitch! (*There follows here a rather involved session in which Perls requests Mr. X to act out each member of the family on one of these occasions: his mother, his father, his brother, and himself. Mr. X describes how his mother played each of them against the other. He seems to have two unresolved situations, an Oedipal conflict with his father, and an unresolved sibling rivalry with his brother. After almost twenty minutes of this role-playing, Perls has Mr. X return his attention to Miss Y.*)

Perls: Can you look at Miss Y now?

Mr. X: Sure.

Perls: What are you seeing?

Mr. X: I see Miss Y . . . (*then after a few moments*). I also still see my mother. It's like a double image.

Box 8.3   A GESTALT THERAPY SESSIONS WITH FREDERICH ("FRITZ") PERLS

Perls: Ah! Can you put your mother into the chair in the corner of the room?

Mr. X: You mean in my imagination? (*Perls nods.*) . . . OK. She's over there in the brown chair.

Perls: Now regard, if you please, your mother in the brown chair. Can you see her clearly?

Mr. X: Yeah.

Perls: Now look at Miss Y, and see if you can see her clearly.

Mr. X: Not very. She looks a little fuzzy.

Perls: Ah! Now, try to shuttle between your mother in the brown chair and Miss Y until you can see them both very clearly.

Mr. X: OK. (*He spends a few minutes "shuttling" his gaze from the chair to Miss Y and back again.*) She's gone now.

Perls: Who?

Mr. X: My mother. She's faded out.

Perls: Now look at Miss Y, please.

Mr. X: Yeah, I can see her pretty good, now. She's sitting there. (*Correcting himself by talking to Miss Y.*) You're just sitting there.

Perls: What is your experience?

Mr. X: (*to Miss Y*): I guess you're not as flirtatious as I thought. You're not my mother.

workshops so this type of group membership is something the participants can be proud of and add to their education/vocational resume.

Transactional Analysis (TA)

This therapeutic approach was formulated by psychiatrist Eric Berne, and psychologist Thomas Harris (Berne, 1978; Harris, 1969). Transactional analysis (TA) is based on this assumption: That personality is composed of three ego states: the **child-ego state,** the **parent-ego state,** and the **adult-ego state.** Sometimes we are acting from our calm, logical **adult-ego state,** but at other times we are acting out our **child-ego state** (our inner child), or our **parent-ego state** (our introjected father, mother, or other significant figures). Thus when any two people are speaking to each other, six ego states can be operating. **Transactional analysis (TA)** got its name from its therapeutic approach; namely, to analyze any transaction between two people to determine which ego state is operating, as in the following hypothetical dialogue between a husband and wife:

Husband: (*in his accusing parent-ego state*) What happened to my cuff links!

Wife: (*in her defensive child-ego state*) How would I know where they are?

Husband: (*still in his accusing parent-ego state*) Because you used them last.

Wife: (*switching to her accusing parent-ego state*) Just like all men, you always blame things on women!

Husband: (*switching to his emotional child-ego state*) I hate it when you get on your woman's lib kick!

Wife: (*switching to her logical adult-ego state*) Quarreling isn't going to help us find your cuff links.

Husband: (*switching to his logical adult-ego state*) You're right. Maybe they're in the shirt I wore yesterday. Yes, here they are.

The Ego States. The child-ego state represents all the drives, needs, and impulses of the internal biological organism. It is the emotional aspect of the personality. It contains all our positive and negative feelings from our conception to the present time. This **child-ego state** within us has both its constructive and destructive elements. Its constructive element is our spontaneity (nobody is as spontaneous as a child) and our adventurous spirit (a child is naturally adventurous) and our creativity (a child delights in discovering what the world has to offer). Our child-ego state laughs, experiences joy and delight, is enthusiastic, and is bursting with energy. The negative aspect of our child-ego state occurs when our feelings dominate our personality (a child can pout or cry at any slight or rage with a temper tantrum), which interferes with our ability to keep a cool head on our shoulders.

The **parent-ego state** begins to develop, said Berne, at the moment of birth and consists of all the conscious and unconscious "recordings" of what our parents (or other caretakers) communicated to us and to each other. And what do these recordings consist of? All those commandments, rules and regulations of our parents, all the "shoulds" and "should nots" of our school teachers, etc. In short, our parent-ego state consists all those admonitions of what we are "supposed to do," and are frequently couched as proverbs, sayings, epithets, and maxims. In addition, the parent-ego state has many nonverbal recordings: Frowns, finger wagging, angry tone-of-voice, hands-on-hips, etc. Parental recordings include the imperatives of "never" or "no" or "It can't be done," or the everlasting "Let me show you how to do it right!" These prohibitions become part of us as we grow up, expressed through our hands-on-the-hip postures, our finger-pointing gestures, and our disapproving frowns (see Tip 8.1).

The **adult-ego state** is the rational, logical part of the personality that can view a problem objectively and solve it with cool scientific reasoning. The alert reader may have already equated the child-ego state with Freud's id or the more modern metaphor of the "child within" us all, even the most sophisticated and mature personalities. The parent-ego state, then, can be equated with the superego. The adult-ego state, however, is quite different from Freud's ego state. Freud's ego is a beleaguered battleground, whereas TA's adult-ego state acts with logic and cool rationality.

Aim of Therapy: To Learn to Use Our Ego States Appropriately. We can never erase the recordings of our child-ego state or our parent-ego state. They are permanent recordings. Nor would we want to erase them, even if we could. The child-ego state represents our joyous, adventurous feelings and creativity ("Isn't it fun!"). Our parent-ego state consists of the admonitions of 5,000 years of civilization that enable us to survive ("Don't run out in the street") and to get along in society ("Mind your manners when you visit them"). Nor would we want to remain forever in our adult-ego state. While our adult-ego state is a rational thinking state, it is devoid of our feelings of joy and exuberance and love.

In the group situation, the group members will call attention to each other's ego states. If we are at the mercy of our emotions and are always getting our feelings hurt, or if we get angry easily, a group member will say something like, "You sound hurt/angry. What's hooked your child-ego?" If we suddenly get a frown on our face or wag our finger while we are talking, a group member will say, "You're lecturing now. Will you get off of your parent-ego state and stop lecturing her!" Verbal and nonverbal clues of the ego states are listed in Table 8.2.

Tip 8.1 Comedians Act Out Our Ego States! One of the reasons we enjoy comedies is because the comedians are acting out our ego states. Some of the great child-ego state comedians have included Jerry Lewis, Lucille Ball, and Gilda Radner. Comedy teams who acted out the parent-ego and child-ego state include Bud Abbott and Lou Costello and Jackie Gleason and Art Carney. The adult-ego state is satirized by Kelsey Grammar. We laugh because these comedians are holding "the mirror up to nature." In short, we are laughing at our own human frailties and foibles.

Table 8.2 Transactional Analysis: Clues to Our Three Ego States

	Child-Ego State	*Parent-Ego State*	*Adult-Ego State*
Permanent Data and Recordings	**Internal Events:** Bodily needs and feelings, sensations, emotions, curiosity, exploratory and experimental drives.	**External Events:** Do's and don'ts, shoulds, admonitions, rules and laws, all the *how to's* and gestures, facial expressions of adults.	**Evaluation of Internal and External Events:** Information and data gathering, thinking, open-ended judgments, and planning.
When Overdominant	**Always in the grip of our feelings:** We remain childlike in our emotional repertoire, easily hurt or always angry and desiring to strike back.	**Generally repressed and over-anxious:** Lack of spontaneity, inhibited, rigid, overly conforming, irrational fears, narrow-minded, and opinionated.	**Too controlled and sober:** Too studied and sober, lack of spontaneity and human responsiveness.
When Used Constructively	High motivation and energy, spontaneity, creativity, ability to enjoy life.	Productive habits, life-saving caution, time-saving knowledge, "common sense."	Able to reinterpret child "injustices" and able to forgive parents for their mistakes, able to deal with family conflicts non-defensively.
Physical Clues	Quivering lip, tears, temper, high-pitched voice, shrugging, rolling or downcast eyes, nose thumbing, teasing, squirming, giggling, feelings of delight, raising hand for permission.	Furrowed brow, pursed lips, pointing index finger, foot tapping, hands on hips, arms folded across chest, wringing hands, tongue clucking, clearing throat.	Listening attitude, thoughtful, interested in what person is saying, unperterbed, calm, focused on task, patient.
Verbal Clues	"I wish . . . " "I guess . . . " "I dunno . . . " "I hate . . . " "I don't care . . . " "You make me mad . . . "	"Always . . . " "Never . . . " "How many times . . . " "That's wrong!" "Let me show you how to do it right!"	"Let me see if I understand this." "Who? What? Where? When?" "What are our options?" "How can we solve this?"

Source: Adapted from Thomas Harris, *I'm O.K.–You're O.K.* (New York: Harper & Row, 1969).

Peer-Support Groups: No One Understands Like Someone Who's Been Through It!

The first peer-support group was Alcoholics Anonymous, organized in 1935 by two recovering alcoholics. The AA concept goes something as follows: No one can appreciate the problems of an alcoholic or how difficult it is to stay "on the wagon" as much as other alcoholics. The members come together for one or more meetings through the week to share their problems, to provide emotional support for each other, to be inspired by religious and other readings, and to formulate goals. The AA members become a kind of family that is willing to help the alcoholic when he "slips" and has "gone under" again.

There has been a lot of criticism of Alcoholics Anonymous for several reasons: because of its quasi-religious 12-step method, because it demands total abstinence (as compared to the method of controlled drinking), and because of its basic assumption that alcoholism is a disease. Evaluation of AA has been difficult because only about 25 percent of people who join AA remain with the organization after 12 months. Of those who do remain, praise for AA is very positive. Often the reclaimed alcoholics give testimony at the group meetings of the long list of psychiatrists, psychologists, pastors, and other counselors who were of little help—nothing was helpful, until they went to AA.

Multifaceted Peer-Support Group Spin-Offs. Negative criticism not withstanding, AA has been the inspiration for (literally) hundreds of spin-off peer-support groups. Peer-support groups were originally organized for women (or men) who have been raped, for adult survivors of incest, for victims of disaster, for parents of murdered children, for abused spouses . . . and the list keeps getting longer and longer. Now there are peer-support groups not only for the victims, but also for the perpetrators—the rapists, the molesters, those convicted of murder, spouse abusers, etc. These kinds of groups, however, generally are led by one or more professionals in these areas. The peer-support group approach is the fastest growing therapeutic milieu at the present time (see Box 8.4).

The basic assumption of all these peer-support groups is that while professional intervention is helpful, no one can be as helpful to a survivor-victim, or to a perpetrator, as those who have had similar experiences. Group members gain insight and inspiration by listening and learning from each other. They help each other struggle with their sense of shame, guilt, their nightmares, and (sometimes) the overwhelming terror that the experience might be repeated. Generally the peer-support groups follow certain guidelines established by a national office, which also provides materials, movies, cassettes, and other types of audiovisual aides. Sometimes, the peer supports function in a hospital setting, in a clinic, in a church, but sometimes, the

Box 8.4   SOME PEER SUPPORT GROUPS

Al-Anon (for families of alcoholics)	Parents Anonymous
Co-Dependents Anonymous	Partners of Survivors of Incest Anonymous
Codependents of Sex Addicts	Partners of Survivors of Sexual Abuse
DD-Anon Group One (Dissociative disorders)	Sex Addicts Anonymous
Incest Anonymous	Sex-Mutilators Anonymous
Men Overcoming Violence	Sexual Abuse Survivors Anonymous
Men in Recovery	Synanon (for drug addiction)
Mothers of Sexually Abused Infants and Children	Transcendental Mediation Ex-Members Support Group
Narcotics Anonymous	Victims Anonymous

meetings can take place in someone's home. (See Box 8.5 for a partial transcript of a peer-support group).

Peer-Support Operates in Many Situations on an Informal Basis. Peer-support has been found so efficacious in enabling people to cope with very real situations that hospitals now group their patients according to the disease or problem. For example, in one study, researchers found that bypass-surgery patients who share the same room do far better, by-and-large, than a control group of patients who had different health problems. The patients with the by-pass surgery who shared rooms with other by-pass patients were less anxious and more ambulatory immediately after surgery and their length of stay in the hospital was 25 percent shorter than the control group. Why would this be so? Well, let's try these possible explanations "for size." While professionals listen to their patients, they do not have that same empathetic listening that does another person with the same symptoms. Second, it simply helps to know that we're not alone in dealing with a life-threatening disease. Finally, another patient can provide supportive information that busy professionals might forget to say or not even know to say.

Feeling queasy? So did I when the anesthetic wore off but it won't last long.

Don't get worried about not remembering what happened before you were operated on. My doctor told me that often occurs. Happened to me too.

You may feel weak now, Buddy, but they'll have you up and walking in 24 hours, like me.

Box 8.5 | **TRANSCRIPT OF AN ADULT INCEST SURVIVOR PEER-SUPPORT GROUP**

The meeting has been in progress for about forty minutes.

Josie: I feel like I'm going crazy lately.

Marion: What about?

Josie: I have this kind of feeling . . . I know it's stupid . . . but I can't get it out of my head. I think about it all the time . . . I can't say it.

Marion: Sure you can. Try.

Josie: What keeps going around in my head is that the same thing that happened to me will happen to Missy (*her three-year-old daughter*). That she'll be raped or seduced by somebody.

Ellen: By whom?

Josie: Anybody. Everybody. Anybody.

Marion: That doesn't make any sense, Josie. The world isn't filled with men who all set out to seduce young girls. We just had hard luck.

Josie: I know that with one part of my mind. But the other part says you can't trust any man with a girl-child.

Marion: Josie, are you afraid of all men you know?

Josie: No, just . . . (*she stops suddenly*).

Ellen: Just who?

Josie: Nobody. It's just stupid.

Marion: Are you afraid of leaving her with your father? (*Josie's father was the perpetrator of Josie's incest experience.*)

Josie: Oh, no. He's too old now and crippled. I'm not even afraid of him anymore.

Marion: Well, who are you afraid of?

Ellen: You're afraid of your husband, aren't you? You're afraid of leaving Missy with your husband.

Josie: Yes, I know it's stupid . . . but every time he picks her up, I shudder.

Marion: Have you talked about this with him?

Josie: No, I'm scared to.

Ellen: Honey, there ain't a gal in this group has a baby daughter hasn't felt the same way.

Josie: Then I'm not going crazy.

Ellen: Lawd, no. It's natural. Just natural.

The Behavior Therapies: Insight Isn't Necessary—Just Change the Behavior

A basic assumption that underlies the insight approach is that insight leads to behavioral change. This assumption has not always proved to be correct. Therapists sometimes complain that despite gaining insight into their problems, insight did not necessarily motivate their clients to make productive changes in their lives. Case in point: Surely by now all smokers must know that smoking is hazardous to their health. Yet they continue to smoke. All their insight has not led them to change their smoking behavior. Now we are about to discuss another approach to therapy, called **behavior therapy,** which aims directly for change in behavior with or without insight. Verbal interchange is minimal and insight into past behaviors is deemed unnecessary. We shall discuss three of them: behavior modification therapy, systematic desensitization training, and biofeedback training.

Skinner's Behavior Modification (Therapy)

Behavior modification is based on B. F. Skinner's operant conditioning (1938). The basic assumption of this approach is that a destructive life style or pattern of "neurotic" symptoms is simply an inappropriate complex of *conditioned (learned) responses*. If that is so, it follows that what has been conditioned can be *deconditioned*. What has been learned can be unlearned. Behavioral therapy, say its advocates, is much more economical in terms of time, money, and professional staff simply because—when it works—it accomplishes its goals in a remarkably short period of time. There is no need for extensive case studies, months of searching for "causal factors" (which may never be discovered), or endless discussion of problems, which may only reinforce and magnify the symptoms. The behavior modification technique described below is called shaping of behavior.

Shaping of behavior is a step-by-step method of teaching a behavior you want a child to learn. The shaping of a child's behavior is done through a series of small, successive, successful steps (memory jog = think of 4 S's). The reader has already encountered Skinner's *environmental engineering* in Chapter 5, but we cannot resist including the following classic example of behavior therapy that was carried out in a nursery school (Harris, Johnston, & Wolf, 1964). It demonstrates many of Skinner's principles of operant conditioning.

In this nursery school, teachers were devoting considerable time and attention to an apparently immature and withdrawn child who spent most of her time on the floor, playing by herself with her back to the other children. When the nursery school teachers failed to get the child adapted to the school routine, they called in a behavioral therapist as consultant for advice and help. The behavioral consultant observed the child in the nursery school for an entire day. Then he called the staff together and explained that what the teachers were doing was actually reinforcing the very behaviors they didn't want. By coaxing her and calling her name and trying to get her to play with the other children, they were giving her more time and attention than all the other children put together. Why should she change her behavior?

When the nursery school teachers got over their astonishment, they asked him what it was they should do. The behavioral consultant outlined a behavior modification plan for them. The first step was to extinguish her isolated behavior by nonreinforcement: Don't wave, talk, call her by name when her back is turned. Only reinforce her behavior when she is turned around toward the other children or when she is standing. In a few days, she was standing much of the time and watching the children play. The next step was to smile and call her by name only when she approached the other children. Within two weeks, she was playing with the other children so that an outside observer could not distinguish her from other children.

The nursery school staff wondered if perhaps she had just gotten over her shyness. To answer that objection, the consultant told them simply to reverse the procedure and reinforce her behavior only when she was turned away from the group and in only a few hours she was right back on the floor again. Quickly, they reversed again and—in only a few hours—she was playing with the other children.

So successful are some kinds of behavioral therapies that these techniques have been adopted in many institutional milieus: classrooms, mental hospitals, physical therapy situations, juvenile delinquency programs, and special education. Despite its therapeutic advantages, however, behavior therapy is not a solution by which to create a perfectly Utopian world. Behavior modification can modify existing behavior. It does not develop new and creative behaviors. Behavior therapy is simply a method by which to solve single concrete situations. Nevertheless, when it works, it works very well indeed (Abramson, Seligman, & Teasdale, 1978).

Joseph Wolpe's Systematic Desensitization

One of the first persons to appreciate the behavioral approach was a physician, Joseph Wolpe, who developed a **counterconditioning** method for dealing with overt fears and phobias (Wolpe, 1958). This method is based on a powerful **assumption:** *The two emotional states of fear and relaxation cannot exist within us at the same time.* When we are anxious, our body is tense, our muscles are contracted, and we are in an **adrenalergic state.** When we are calm and relaxed, our muscles are not contracted, we are not fearful, and we are in the **cholinergic state.** Wolpe's approach is remarkable in its simplicity. All we have to do is to help the person stay calm in the presence of whatever is making the person fearful or phobic. It doesn't matter what the anxiety-provoking stimulus is. It can be the common phobia of snakes, claustrophobia, or a fear of heights. Wolpe's method enables the client to remain relaxed in the presence of the anxiety-provoking stimulus (snakes, cars, heights). He outlined the following three-step process by which to achieve this goal of relaxation.

1. **The client constructs a hierarchy of fears.** The therapist has the person identify as many anxiety-provoking stimuli as possible (at least 15 such associated stimuli). If the phobia is driving, the client may list all of the stimuli noted in the insert (Hierarchy of Fears) along with an assessment of the level of fear associated with each stimulus.
2. **The client becomes very relaxed.** The therapist trains the client in deep muscle relaxation, as developed by Edmund Jacobson, until the client can keep his body in a state of relaxation at will.
3. **The therapist introduces the anxiety-provoking stimulus while the client remains relaxed.** The client puts himself into a state of deep relaxation.

A Hierarchy of Fears
with the level of anxiety associated with each fear stimulus

Anxiety	Stimulus
5	Picture of a car
8	The word "car"
10	Planned honking
20	Unexpected honk
30	Imagining a car
40	Talking about driving
50	Hearing a siren
55	Screech of brake
60	Imaging being in a car
70	Seeing adult drive
75	Imagining self drive
80	Photo of car crash
85	Seeing TV car crash
90	Riding in a car
95	Sitting in driver's seat
100	Actually driving

The therapist then presents the least-anxiety provoking stimulus, for example, a picture of a car for those with driving phobias. If the client remains relaxed in the presence of the picture of the car, the therapist goes on to the next stimulus on the hierarchy, the word *car*. If the client gets fearful and tense, the therapist signals the client to put himself in a state of deep relaxation again. When the client is relaxed again, the therapist again says the word *car* again. If the client can stay relaxed in the presence of this anxiety-provoking word, the behavioral therapist goes on to the next stimulus on the hierarchy (*honking*) and so on up the hierarchy list of anxiety-provoking stimuli.

Using this method, therapists can sometimes dispel a fear or phobia in a few sessions. Obviously, this method would only be an exercise in futility unless the person can actually drive again. And they do! With this method, thousands of people with a driving phobia have been enabled to drive again. We know this because, for many years, driving on the California Freeway was the single most frequent phobia to be treated at Wolpian clinics. (That fact will not surprise anyone who has driven on that freeway.)

Biofeedback Training

It was once thought that basic bodily processes were *autonomic;* i.e., not under our own conscious control. Then a certain Yogi Swami Rama once astonished psychologists by proving that he could voluntarily slow down or speed up his pulse rate, stop his heart from pumping blood for 17 seconds, raise or lower the temperature in his hand, and alter his brain wave patterns (Kassin, 1995). What Swami Rama had demonstrated was that those bodily processes we had previously believed to be autonomic functions (beyond our conscious control) can be altered through our own conscious control. The power of will! Here's how the biofeedback procedure works. Suppose you suffer from simple tension headaches. Tension headaches are most often caused by muscular tension in the forehead, neck, and shoulders that constricts the arteries to the brain and which results in "headaches." Under supervision, you would make yourself comfortable in a sitting or reclining position. The biofeedback trainer would attach an EMG (electromyograph) to your head or finger. The EMG translates muscular tension or brain waves into an auditory or visual signal. The purpose of the auditory or visual signal is to enable you to become sensitive to your body functioning. During the first part of the training, you learn to associate, for example, a higher-pitched tone to increased muscle tension in your head and a lower-pitched tone to decreased muscle tension.

In addition to recognizing the tension in your body, the trainer may accompany the biofeedback with verbal autosuggestions in a calm monotone to lower the temperature in your head as follows:

I feel very quiet. I am beginning to feel relaxed . . . My head feels heavy and relaxed . . . My ankles, my knees, my hips, my shoulders are all feeling relaxed. My neck, my jaw, my forehead are all feeling relaxed. My eyes are closed and relaxed. My whole head is feeling relaxed. My entire body is feeling relaxed . . . Relaxed as I am, the tension is flowing out of my head. My head is already getting cooler. The warmth of my head is flowing into my arms and hands. I can feel my hands becoming warmer . . . I can feel my head getting cooler and cooler.

Within a few sessions, you are able to decrease your muscular tension and reduce your headache strain under your own volition. Eventually, the trainer commits those relaxation phrases which seem to "work" for you on to a cassette tape which you take home and use by yourself when you feel a headache "coming on."

Probably the most revolutionary aspect of biofeedback, say its advocates, is that it shifts the **locus of control (LOC)** from external to internal control. No longer does the client look dependently on drugs to alleviate insomnia, migraine, cramps, hypertension. The client's world-view now includes the understanding that we are not just the victims of external forces. We are, in fact, the perpetrator of our bodily ills. That is good news! If we do indeed perpetrate our "dis-eased" bodies, it follows that we can do something about it. Research studies indicate that 50 percent of the patients who have tried biofeedback for their tension headaches have benefited permanently (Blanchard, 1994).

The Cognitive Therapies: Combining Insight and Behavior Therapy and Changing Our Whole Belief System

A third approach, called cognitive therapy, rests on another assumption; namely that many of our conflicts are based on misperceptions and "errors" of thinking. The aim of cognitive therapy is to gain insight into these misperceptions and "errors" of thinking and to change the way clients process information. Knowing that our perceptual belief system motivates our actions and our interactions, the therapist is attempting to foster a whole new worldview in the client. In fact, he or she will use any method to help us change our ideas and self-image, by playing the many roles of therapist, teacher, coach, friend, and partner. Whatever it takes! To illustrate the cognitive approach, we begin with rational-emotive therapy.

Albert Ellis' Rational-Emotive Therapy (RET): "Get Rid of Your Irrational Beliefs; They're Driving You Crazy!"

Albert Ellis was originally trained in psychoanalysis (an insight therapy) but like other behavioral therapists, he became convinced that insight is not enough. If people want a better life, they must do something on their own behalf. The responsibility for our lives rests squarely on our own shoulders. Also, he had become very impressed with one significant aspect of human discomfort: Our anxiety and depression (and general misery) are not necessarily caused by actual events but by how we respond to them. What drives us "crazy" are our irrational beliefs, which keep us in constant emotional turmoil. What are these irrational beliefs? Some examples can be found in Table 8.3.

Table 8.3 RET: Examples of Irrational Beliefs

I have to be the kind of person everybody likes.	I have to be a perfect wife/husband.
It's my job to "keep peace" in the family.	I have to be a perfect parent.
What happened to me has ruined me for any kind of normal life.	I have to be a perfect adult child to my parents.
	I won't be able to go on if she/he leaves me.
I should not be selfish. I must keep everyone's needs ahead of my own.	Maybe it's just my lot in life to suffer.
	It's too late for me to change my life.
Nothing ever goes right for me.	Bad things aren't supposed to happen to good people.
I've made a failure of my life.	If I don't get approved of by everybody, I must be
I should live my life so that I don't make enemies.	dislikable.

The A-B-Cs (and D-E-F-Gs) of RET. Ellis' underlying assumption is that it is not what actually happens to us that is so catastrophic but how we react to it. Case in point! In the opening scenario of Chapter 1, six people received the same letter but how they reacted to it was dramatically different. One person was jubilant, one was anxious and depressed, and one committed suicide. Ellis could easily cite this example as illustrative that the activating event (A) is not what hurts us but the beliefs (B) we have about what happened. If our beliefs are irrational, it will lead to self-defeating consequences (C). Ellis explains that all people are born with self-defeating tendencies. When something goes against their goals or values or desires (failures or rejections or whatever), they have a choice of responding fairly healthily with appropriate emotions (feeling sorry or disappointed) or making themselves miserable, terrified, panicked, self-pitying, or even suicidally depressed (Ellis & Dryden, 1987). As Ellis continued his work, he enlarged on his A-B-C model to make an A-B-C-D-E-F-G model (see Box 8.6). The person learns to dispute (D); that is, to challenge the irrational belief system that is causing him so much anxiety. Behavioral techniques to dispute the belief system and its consequences may involve any one of a host of activities: public speaking, going for the job interview they are afraid of; approaching members of the opposite gender, etc. If the disputation (D) is successful, the person experiences a new effect (E) of no longer feeling anxious and depressed. So he stops procrastinating, drinking, etc. The person now has a new feeling (F): confidence about getting along in the world.

Aim of Therapy: Substitute Rational Cognitions and Take Risks. The demands we acquire as we grow up set us up for a life of continual misery. Furthermore, we can never succeed in living up to all these "shoulds." We are setting ourselves up for failure. When we experience failure, we get anxious, depressed, and suffer from low self-esteem. So how does the RET therapist shake these kinds of irrational beliefs out of us? By pointing them out to us—very bluntly if need be—using "sandpaper" questions and sarcasm:

Why must you always "should" on yourself?
You'd rather suffer than leave this abusive relationship? Do you like to suffer?
What's ruining your life is not what happened to you. It's your attitude.
There you go again making a mountain out of a molehill! Does it make you happy to worry?
Whatever gave you the idea that life is fair?
You believe that life is always a happy situation? You must still believe in Santa Claus.

Sometimes the therapeutic treatment may seem cruel to an observer and Ellis has been criticized that his unconventional approach is extreme and could be humiliating and damaging. Ellis responds to these criticisms in this way: Our assumptions, attitudes, and irrational beliefs are some of the most difficult personality traits to "shake loose." We have generally lived with these cognitions so long that they have become part of our personality patterning.

Beck's Cognitive Therapy

Like Ellis, Aaron Beck was trained in psychoanalysis. Like Ellis, he was impressed by the self-defeating worldview of depressed patients. They look at the world, he said, not through rose-colored glasses, but through dark-colored glasses. They magnify small events into catastrophic ones. When they have "butterflies in the stomach," they imagine they are having heart palpitations. The smallest social gaffe causes them to imagine they "can never show my face again to those people" (Beck 1991).

Box 8.6   DIAGRAM AND TRANSCRIPT OF RATIONAL-EMOTIVE BEHAVIOR THERAPY

The client came into therapy with the goal (G) of becoming "dateable." When a classmate began to show an interest in her, which was the Activating event (A), her Behavior (B) reflected her anxiety with the Consequence (C) of wanting to drop the class. At this point, the RET therapist disputed (D) her belief she is "damaged goods." If the disputation is successful, the effect (E) will be a new feeling (F) about herself, which should help her attain her goal (G) of being dateable.

Dana was subjected to incest as a child from ages ten to fifteen. She has been dealing with this experience for several sessions.

Dana: I feel like it [the incest] ruined me for life.

Therapist: If it ruined your life, why come to therapy? Why don't you just grovel in your misery?

Dana: You could be more sympathetic.

Therapist: What would you like me to say. . . "Oh, you poor thing, you. I'm so sorry for you"?

Dana: Now you're being sarcastic. I just want to know that you know what I went through.

Therapist: I know what you went through. You've talked a lot about it. It's an obsession with you. Maybe you don't want to get over it. You seem to hang on to it, like a teddy bear. You need an attitude change.

Dana: That's not true.

Therapist: You aren't the only woman it has happened to. It has happened to maybe 30 percent of American women, maybe more.

Dana: Thirty percent? That many?

Therapist: The only thing ruining your life is your irrational idea that it has ruined you. Or has it?

Dana: It hasn't ruined everything. It hasn't ruined my ability to work. I'm a good worker.

Therapist: Well, congratulations, you have finally uttered a rational statement. So it hasn't ruined your whole life. What has it ruined?

Dana: Well, it's ruined how I react with men, emotionally.

Therapist: In what way?

Dana: I feel so ashamed. I feel like damaged goods.

Therapist: We are all damaged goods. That's part of growing up. No one has had a completely "happy childhood." That's one of our absurd modern fallacies.

Dana: No man really wants a woman who had sex with her father.

Therapist: How do you know, have you asked them?

Dana: No, only he made me feel like it was my fault. That I came on to him.

Therapist: All right, let's straighten this out before we go on. He was the adult and you were a child. He was the perpetrator. You were the victim. Say it!

Dana: He was the perpetrator. I was the victim.

Therapist: Again!

Dana: He was the perpetrator. I was the victim.

Therapist: AGAIN! LOUDER!

Dana: HE WAS THE PERPETRATOR. I WAS THE VICTIM! ALL RIGHT. IT WASN'T MY FAULT!

Therapist: You got that straight in your head?

Dana: *(quietly)* I think so.

Therapist: Furthermore, you survived. You are now an adult survivor. Congratulations!

All cognitive therapists share the same objectives (to change behavior, to eliminate self-defeating beliefs, to adopt more rational attitudes, etc.). How they do this is a reflection of their own therapy style. In contrast to the sometimes harsh sounding RET therapists, Beck has a much more folksy, country-style approach. Therapists who use this approach ask Socratic-like questions.

How did you come to that idea?
What's your evidence for that idea?
Are these the facts or your interpretation of them?
Let's take a look at that situation from another angle.
What's the worst that can happen?
Where is it written that we have to put everybody else's needs in front of our own?

Beck particularly stresses learning to replace negative self-talk with more efficacious statements (see Table 8.4).

Albert Bandura's Social Learning Theory and Guided Mastery Technique

One significant way we learn is through what is sometimes called **social learning** and sometimes **observational learning.** The psychologist who has done the most to conceptualize this type of learning is Albert Bandura. He has demonstrated, irrefutably, that we learn simply by watching what others do. Having established that we learn simply by observing, Bandura has sought ways to use it in working with people's emotional and physical problems (Bandura, 1986).

Aim of Therapy: Learning New Cognitions and Behaviors from a Model. Bandura points out that much of what we fear is not just the situation itself, but our presumed inability to cope with it. In that respect, Bandura is like other cognitive therapists. When people come to believe that they do not have the skill to handle a situation, that the situation is overwhelming for them, they begin to break down morally and physically. What is important to Bandura is to help them handle the overwhelming situation. What Bandura suggests is to introduce the person to experts in the area who can handle the feared object or situation. Suppose, for example, a person has a snake phobia and runs screaming from the presence of even the gentlest garter snake. Bandura has the client watch the snake expert handle the snake in a gentle manner. Step-by-step, the client approaches the snake and under the tutelage of the snake expert, is encouraged to pet the snake or even hold it. The client is learning how the snake expert handles the snake and,

Table 8.4 Beck's Cognitive Therapy: Improving Self-Talk

Negative Statements	Positive Statements
"I can't do it. There's no use trying."	"If I get some help, I can master this situation."
"I'm not getting anywhere."	"My progress is slow, but I see definite progress."
"It's too much for me."	"This is going to take some concerted effort but I'll do it."
"I've never been able to do math."	"I'll approach math in a more adult fashion."
"He'll never give me the job."	"I may not get the job but the interview will be good experience."
"I'll make a fool of myself."	"I'll practice until I feel confident and secure of myself."

at the same time, is learning a different emotional response. Eventually, the person walks with the snake expert in the woods, while the snake expert teaches the client how to walk and look for snakes, how to dress for snake protection, and to enjoy the beauty and usefulness of snakes. Eventually, the client ventures out on his own to see if he can take a walk in the woods by himself. He rates himself on his fear reaction (say from 1 to 10) in all the steps we have outlined above, until his snake phobia is no more than his natural fear of any uncertain situation.

Three New Thrusts in Cognitive Therapy: The Use of Rites and Rituals, Humor, and Stress Inoculation

As in all scientific areas, professionals in the field of psychotherapy continue to try out new approaches to the therapeutic situation. In the last two decades, some interesting thrusts have been initiated. The first thrust is the purposeful use of *rites and ritual*. The second is use of *humor,* the third is called *stress inoculation*.

Ritual in Therapeutic Healing

The reader will probably remember this basic concept—that all cultures—whether traditional or modern, rural or industrial, tribal or mass society—develop rituals to mark significant events in a person's life. Some of the rites VanGennop discussed included baptisms, celebrations of circumcision, weddings, funerals, and initiation into the sacred orders. But some therapists bemoaned the fact that we have rites for marriage but not for divorce. We have baptism rites and showers for newborn babies and their biological mothers. We have no such rites for the adoption of children who are older than newborn. And while we have funeral services for the death of a baby, we do not provide a way for a woman to mourn, grieve, and "bury" an aborted or miscarried child.

Furthermore, say these therapists, we ignore some of the most profound transitions of many people. We do not have rites for people who have rid themselves of an addiction (alcohol, cigarettes, narcotics). We do not celebrate with a person who has recovered from a mental disorder after several weeks or months in a mental hospital. In fact we avoid any mention of the hospitalization. We ignore the fact that a person who has always been on some kind of welfare program has become gainfully employed. We will congratulate a young person for acquiring a new car, but we somehow don't congratulate him for a safe driving record over ten years—which surely must be a more remarkable achievement. The following examples illustrate how rituals have been utilized to make up these deficits. An example of a therapeutic ritual follows.

Rocks and Pebbles Ritual. When clients enter the therapeutic milieu, they are generally in such pain of anxiety, depression, and feelings of hopelessness, that they do not see anyway out of their life situation. Their general attitude is one of futility and despair of ever improving their life situations, which have become overwhelming for them. Moreover, because of their anxious and depressed emotional state, they do not know how to "get a handle" on the various elements that are weighing on them. In fact, what frequently happens is that all their concerns and anxieties have become entangled into one great "Gordian knot." Or perhaps a more graphic metaphor is that the client views himself or herself as imprisoned in an environment out of which there is no escape. The following ritual was designed by the therapist to help clients "get a handle" on their problems.

The therapist places an empty box in front of the client along with a pile of rocks and pebbles of different sizes. The client is asked to pick a rock or a pebble that symbolically will represent one of the concerns or anxieties the client is depressed about. A large problem is generally represented by a large rock and a smaller problem is represented by a smaller rock or pebble. The client then is asked to label the rock or pebble with a writing instrument and to place it in the box. The box represents the client's psychological emotional state. The client is then asked to focus on other concerns and to choose rocks or pebbles according to the emotional weight of the concern. Again, the client generally chooses large rocks, although from time to time he may choose smaller ones. This first step is repeated until the client has exhausted all his/her concerns.

Over the course of the therapy, the client begins to perceive that a large issue (symbolized by a large rock) can be broken down into smaller issues. Accordingly, the client exchanges the large rock for smaller ones—or even pebbles. As the client begins to deal successfully with each of the smaller pebbles or rocks, the client discards the pebble or rock that represents that particular issue. This ritual is repeated until the box is empty. The rocks and pebbles that are eliminated from the box are not thrown back into the rock pile but are put in a special container marked "Solved problems."

What makes this ritual so remarkable are the number of underlying metaphoric meanings it can have for the client. For example, labeling the stones and putting them into the box provides a way of externalizing the client's anxieties and worries. Similarly, by externalizing our errands and not having to keep them "in our heads," we become more relaxed and able to accomplish them one by one. In therapy, the client is more able to cope with the smaller-pebble issues than when they were as one big rock. As the client deals successfully with each concern, removing that particular stone from the box, the client gains feelings of self-efficacy—he or she can cope with what is going on. Finally, the container of rocks and pebbles labeled "Solved Problems" is a marker device for the client to appreciate his or her progress as that container is filled up. The clients feel they have become more empowered to solve their problems (Barton & Bischoff, 1998).

The Use of Humor

In Chapter 2, we noted that humor is one of the characteristics of highly creative and self-actualizing persons. In Chapter 6, we discussed the use of humor as one of the most adaptive and constructive of the defense mechanisms. In Chapter 4, we discussed the newest thrusts in medical treatment; namely, the use of humor. Humor is also one of the newest thrusts of psychotherapy today and is gaining much respect as a therapeutic tool. In the last few years, the *APA Monitor* (an official monthly publication of the American Psychological Association) has devoted considerable space to the therapeutic effects of humor in both physical and psychological healing. Taking their cue from the medical uses of humor, researchers are exploring ways to harness this very powerful psychophysiological source of healing and energy (*APA Monitor,* 1997, 1999). One such psychologist is Herbert Lefcourt at the University of Waterloo in Canada. Lefcourt had read Norman Cousins' book, *Anatomy of an Illness* (1979), and has been validating Cousins' remarkable recovery ever since (see Box 7.10). What Lefcourt did was to show a humorous video to a group of graduate students. Then he tested their saliva and compared it to a control group of students who had not watched the humorous tape. What he discovered was that many of the immune antibodies had risen substantially higher than the control group. Like Patch Adams (whom we read about in the last chapter), these researchers tell us that laughter is injurious to our illnesses!

Here is how these psychologists explain their use of humor. Psychotherapists from Freud all the way to the present time focus, generally, on very weighty problems, problems which

Box 8.7 A FEW OF THE MANY OTHER THERAPEUTIC APPROACHES

Art Therapy. Art therapy was originally designed for children as an adjunct to play therapy (see below). As its efficacy became better known, it was adapted and used successfully for many other types of therapeutic situations, such as working with retarded citizens, elderly people, and emotionally disturbed adults.

Crisis Management. This approach is a short-term therapy to help a person recover from the serious events we all experience (death of a loved one, rape, or depression as the result of the loss of job). It has also proved to be effective for persons who have functioned well throughout out their lives.

Family Therapy Systems Approach. It used to be that when a family member was in serious trouble, the person was sent to a therapist to be "straightened out" as if the person functioned in a vacuum devoid of other people. Virginia Satir recognized that every family has a "personality," i.e., there are basic dynamics within a family. The problem may be not in any one individual, but in the way the whole family interacts. Thus the whole family is encouraged to come into the therapeutic situation and to make changes in the family dynamics. The aim of therapy then is to change the way family members communicate and interact with each other. Various forms of family therapy include parent/child therapy, couples therapy, and marriage counseling.

Fight Therapy. George Bach and other therapists have developed a technique of enabling people to fight with each other in nondestructive ways. Their thesis is that in any intimate situation, conflict is unavoidable. We can't always be happily involved with others all the time. If couples don't fight at all, someone is "giving in for the sake of peace." The therapy involves learning to stick up for oneself and fight "constructively." A modified form of this therapy is assertiveness training. (See Chapter 11 for our suggestions for having a marital quarrel.)

Logotherapy. Viktor Frankl, who went through the horrors of Nazi concentration camps and survived, believed that one of the main problems of modern humanity is that we have placed too much importance on material goods and other "pleasures of the flesh." We suffer, he said, from **noogenic neurosis,** a state of apathy, aimlessness, and boredom. A life lived without purpose must ultimately leave us with the taste of "bitter ashes." The aim of **logotherapy** is to develop a philosophy of life that has more transpersonal values, and to engage in suprapersonal activities (service to others and/or working for world peace, world brotherhood, and world ecology).

Play Therapy. First devised by Melanie Klein and Anna Freud, play therapy was legitimized by Carl Rogers' student, Virginia Axline. Play therapy was devised for children who are too young to verbalize their fears and anxieties. The child is taken to a playroom in which there are many toys and dolls representing the family. The child is allowed to color, play with water, make mud pies, or throw the dolls, but the child may not hurt himself or the therapist. In this way, the child can act out conflicts and catharsize unconscious material. The therapist's job is only to reflect upon what the child is doing. (See Chapter 12 for a description of play therapy, pp. 298–299.)

Writing Therapy. Ira Progoff is the therapist most associated with the therapeutic aspects of keeping a journal, but any literature teacher can relate the cathartic effect of autobiographical writing or fictionalized autobiographical writing. In fact, keeping a journal of one's hopes, wishes, fantasies, dreams, disappointments, etc. has become the "homework" aspect of many types of therapies. In fact, the reflective writing assignments in this text are designed for that purpose.

depress the patient and cause him a great of anxiety. Session after session is devoted to the negative events and negative emotions. Introducing a bit of humor lightens the mood and gives the client a sense of distance from his personal hurts. Therapeutic sessions do not have to be deadly serious. In fact, emphasizing the negative side of living all the time may engender an assumption in the client that therapy sessions have to be somber. A humorous quote or anecdote often contains a fundamental wisdom. Comedy is truth—only faster. Humor—along with tragedy, suffering, and perplexity—is woven into the whole fabric of our living experience. The use of humor, in appropriate places, allows the client to realize that they also have the

Box 8.8

STRESS INOCULATION, SESSION TWO
Devising New Self-Talk Messages

Jill Smith is sitting with the small group of students she has been working with.

Jill Smith: Our task for this meeting is to develop some strategies for when we begin to feel the symptoms of anxiety we were talking about last week. I am dealing with saying things in anger that I regret later. The emotion I feel is *righteous indignation.* And the self-talk I engage in is this: *How dare he say that! How dare she treat me this way!* What I have to do now is to derive a new self-talk. I probably can't stop my initial feelings of self-righteousness. But the moment I do feel that emotion coming in strong, I must add another thought to it. Let's see, I could add the thought *I'm feeling self-righteous now. I better not say anything until I'm cool and dispassionate.* Then when I have let go of the strong anger, I can change my thoughts and feelings: *There may be good reasons for his actions. I'll ask him about it later. I'll suspend judgment until then.*

Martha: Yeah, but that's easier said than done. I try not to yell at my son, I really do, but my anger shoots out like molten larva. I can't stop myself.

Jill Smith: Well, I think I can stop myself. I want to replace my external locus-of-control in these situations with an internal locus-of-control.

Martha: Wow! I see what you're saying. If I say I can't stop myself from yelling when my son aggravates me, he's controlling my behavior! Whew! That's something to think about!

Alec: (*laughing*) He's jerking your collar again!

Martha: He sure is! And I'm letting him do it! Well, I don't have to play that game any more. I've just made up my mind! I'm NOT going to scream when he is trying to aggravate me. Oh, I see it all now! He's shaping my screaming behavior and I didn't even realize it. And I'm reinforcing his behavior by screaming! Omygosh! I am so embarrassed!

Jill Smith: We can get embarrassed when we realize how we contribute to our own problems.

Jonnimae: OK, how do I contribute to my problem of getting so anxious in a test situation that I freeze up?

Jill Smith: You weren't here for our first meeting so let me tell you what we did. What each member of the group did was to focus on the feelings or emotions or bodily experiences that trigger their anxiety. Imagine you are going into a test situation. What are your feelings?

Jonnimae: Whew! My throat is dry and I think, *I'm never going to pass this test.*

Alec: With that kind of self-talk, it's a wonder you pass any of your exams. You're actually programming failure.

Jonnimae: I know that's right. So what do I do?

Jill Smith: As soon as you hear your negative self-talk, what can you add to at least modify it?

Jonnimae: Well . . . I can tell myself that my self-talk is nonsense and that I have studied the material and just to stay calm.

Dan: Maybe this will help, Jonnimae. When I get angry now, I just focus on my breathing and concentrate on breathing slower and deeper and slower and deeper, and that distracts me from the angry feelings and slows me down.

Alec: That's sort of like Jacobsen's deep relaxation. You're letting your body relax.

Jonnimae: So when I get into the classroom, I can just sit at my desk and close my eyes and keep breathing. Is that what you all are saying?

Jill Smith: Think you can try it?

Jonnimae: I don't know.

Jill Smith: Try practicing that every so often between now and your next exam. Practice it several times a day at odd times. If you find yourself getting uptight about something, try the breathing exercise again. Make it a habit. Make it such a strong habit that whenever something triggers your anxiety, you will almost automatically start your breathing exercise.

Jonnimae: I'm sort of religious. Is it OK to pray while I'm doing the breathing exercise?

Jill Smith: If that helps you—of course.

freedom to laugh (Castleman, 1997; Goodheart, 1994). So helpful has humor proved to be that there are now professional journals and organizations that study humor and promote its beneficial uses.

Stress Inoculation: Focus on Prevention

Stress inoculation has partly to do with preparing us for stressful situations that might occur in the future. One of the factors that renders us less capable to handle stress and emergency situations is not knowing how to cope with feared or unexpected events. Instead of remaining calm and thinking rationally about what has happened, we may feel ourselves "going out of control." We may react with shock, frozen to the spot, unable to move or speak. Or we may react with hysteria or with screaming rage, lashing out on all sides. We may even react with behaviors that seem bizarre and shocking to others. Underlying this wide range of emotional reactions are feelings of helplessness. Now it is certainly true that we may encounter situations so unexpected and traumatic that no one can prepare us for them. But there are many situations for which we can be somewhat prepared in advance through stress inoculation strategies (Meichenbaum, 1993).

By now, the reader will have noticed how frequently a negative worldview and a negative self-esteem affects our ability to cope with situations. This negativism is one of the prime targets of the cognitive stress inoculation techniques. It follows that the negative self-talk that is going on inside our heads must be replaced with statements of self-efficacy, the belief that we can master a situation and produce positive outcomes. Stress inoculation is designed to prepare the person for unanticipated anxiety-provoking events. This focus has led to a variety of techniques. For example, the therapist encourages the clients to become aware of the physiological changes in their bodies that indicate that their anxiety or panic symptoms are being triggered. The clients may then undergo symptom reduction through formalized biofeedback training, autohypnosis, deep relaxation training, or desensitization training, etc. At the same time, the clients are undergoing self-observation, recording and analyzing their self-talk. If their self-talk is negative, they practice replacing it with self-efficacy statements. Other techniques include modeling, learning self-assertion, anticipation, the use of humor, and so on. All of these techniques enable the person to take control of his anxiety and to prepare for new situations. The final step is to enable the person to develop strategies to face the feared event as in Box 8.8.

IMPORTANT TERMS AND CONCEPTS TO KNOW

adult-ego	deconditioning	hypnosis	perpetrators
Alcoholics Anonymous	desensitization	inoculation	positive
behavior	ego states	insight	psychoanalysis
biofeedback	empathy	irrational beliefs	rituals
catharsize	Freud	learned	self-fulfillment
center-of-growth	free association	modification	transactional
child-ego state	healing	parent-ego	unconditional
client-centered	hierarchy of fears	peer-support	unconscious

MAKE YOUR OWN SUMMARY BY FILLING IN THE BLANKS BELOW

Use the list of Important Terms and Concepts to Know to fill in the blanks below.

The History of Psychotherapy. Therapy means _____ . Psychotherapy has had a long history all the way back to the Ancients. In the eighteenth century, Franz Mesmer developed mesmerism which today we would call _____ , but scientifically, psychotherapy as we know it today was started by _____ .

The medical approach. Sigmund Freud, a physician and neurologist, began to treat people with hypnosis but eventually he developed a "talking cure," which he called _____ . Freud posited the theory that most of our motivation and behavior is the result of opposing forces deep within the _____ . It followed that the therapy consisted of bringing this repressed material to consciousness in order to _____ it. The patient was instructed to say anything that came to mind without feeling that such thoughts or emotions were bad, a technique called _____ .

The Non-Medical Counseling Approach. Carl Rogers introduced a nonmedical approach to therapy, which he called _____ counseling. Where Freud's theory of personality is based on conflict, Rogers' theory is based on a _____ model of human personality. Rogers' believed that we all have a _____ , even the most depressed and catatonic patient in a mental ward—if we did not, we would be dead. Rogers stressed the need for a warm climate of safety and for the therapist to accord the client " _____ positive

regard." Rogers distinguished sympathy, as a feeling of superiority over the client, from _____ in which the therapist understands the client's worldview.

Therapy In Group Situations. This approach considers group participation as an essential aspect of therapeutic treatment. The group members represent society-as-a-whole, and becomes a family unit. TA, which stands for _____ analysis, describes human nature as follows: Each individual is composed of three _____ . The _____ state represents our innate biological drives, energy, and emotion. The _____ state contains all the rules, regulations, warnings, and prohibitions of 5,000 years of civilization. The job of the adult-ego state is to reinterpret the misunderstandings of our childhood. Another approach to group therapy are the burgeoning _____ groups, based on the assumption that nobody understands like someone who has been through a similar situation. The first such group was AA or _____ , started in 1935. Now there are similar groups for victims and survivors of rape, incest, and other traumatic events, as well as for the _____ themselves.

The Behavior Therapies. A third approach to therapy involves the behavior therapies. Their basic assumption is that _____ , in and of itself, does not necessarily lead to more adaptive living. These therapies go directly for change in _____ , through such techniques as Skinner's behavior _____ . The underlying assumption about dysfunctional behavior is that it is simply a complex of _____ responses. It follows that the treatment is simply to eliminate these responses through _____ processes. One such therapy is Wolpe's _____ training. It has been proven especially effective with anxiety disorders and phobias. Wolpe's technique is to have the client list a _____ and then to introduce these anxiety provoking stimuli while the client is in a state of deep relaxation. Another behavior therapy is _____ , which allows clients to monitor and modify physiological changes and thereby reduce their hypertension, headaches, and other physical ailments.

The Cognitive Therapies. Cognitive therapies combine insight and behavioral change to effect a change in the person's belief system. Beck and Ellis developed therapies that seek to substitute _____ statements for self-defeating self-talk. Three recent thrusts of cognitive therapy include stress _____ , humor, and the use of rites and _____ .

9 ABNORMAL PSYCHOLOGY
Trying to Function in Dysfunctional Ways

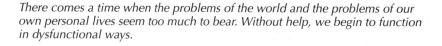

There comes a time when the problems of the world and the problems of our own personal lives seem too much to bear. Without help, we begin to function in dysfunctional ways.

Box 9.1

SCENARIO
Shannon Consults Her Abnormal Psychology Professor

Dr. Weitzman is waiting quietly for the young person in his office to gather the courage to speak.

Shannon: I'm sorry it's taking me so long to talk. I asked for an appointment, and here I sit. When I do this at home, my mother says, "Cat got your tongue?"

Professor Weitzman: Take your time. It must be difficult to talk about it.

Shannon: But I know you're a busy man. OK, here goes. How do you know if someone is just moody or is really crazy or not? I mean really insane.

Professor Weitzman: Terms like "crazy" and "insane" are only used by the legal system. They don't have much meaning for mental health professionals. We prefer other terms, such as disorder or dysfunctional. And the answer to your question is that it isn't always easy to know whether someone has a serious emotional disorder or whether it's a temporary and normal reaction to something that is happening in his or her life.

Shannon: I'm not sure I know what you mean by "normal" reaction.

Professor Weitzman: Let's suppose a person has just suffered the loss of a child after a long and terrible illness, and suppose that the cost of the battle to save the child's life has resulted in an enormous number of bills not covered by health insurance, so that the family is staggering under increasing debt and on top of all that, the man of the family loses his job . . . wouldn't it be normal for him or his wife to suffer a king-size depression? We can all be dysfunctional at times.

Shannon: Sure.

Professor Weitzman: In fact I would be much more concerned if he didn't experience a hefty depression.

Shannon: But I'm not talking about getting depressed once in a while. I know how that is. I used to get depressed sometimes when I had to go to school. I'm talking about really . . . I don't know how to put it—doing really strange things.

Professor Weitzman: Even then we would have to have a lot more information than a description of some of the person's behaviors. Let me give you an example. Delusions and hallucinations are symptoms of schizophrenia. Yet, all those same symptoms can be observed in a person with a very high fever or who has a brain tumor or who is suffering from a bad drug "trip." Before we can say that a person has a serious emotional disorder, we need to know many things; such as the person's health history; the circumstances of the person's life from infancy; and the person's present situation. Whom are you concerned about?

Shannon: Well, actually, it's two people. My mother and . . . and a friend of mine.

Professor Weitzman: Why don't you tell me about them? I'm not a psychotherapist but if I know a little more about what you are concerned about, I would be in a better position to make some suggestions.

Shannon: I'll start with my mother. Until your lecture on bipolar mood disorder, I never thought anything about my mother's behavior. We just always considered her as being "moody" or "high-strung." At least, that's what my dad always says when she has one of her "spells." Sometimes she will cry for hours. It's even worse when she doesn't cry, just sits on the bed all hunched up and saying it would be better for everybody if she would just die. We all tell her that it isn't true. And it isn't true! When she's feeling good, she's just the cheeriest person and takes us all out shopping and gets us clothes. And she'll sew new curtains for the house and make dresses for Gram (that's my grandmother) and me. Wow! We can hardly keep up with her. Dad says she's got more energy than a barrel full of monkeys. Then Dad thinks everything is OK again.

Box 9.1

SCENARIO (continued)
Shannon Consults Her Abnormal Psychology Professor

Professor Weitzman: And isn't it?

Shannon: He says he just has to watch how she spends money. But that isn't the half of it. When she gets into one of these happy moods, she does strange things, like writing checks that bounce. And sometimes she comes home with things I'm sure she didn't pay for. Once they caught her shoplifting. Later, she told me she doesn't even remember doing it. Then suddenly she turns quiet . . . just like that! For days. And for no reason that we can see. Has she got a bipolar mood disorder?

Professor Weitzman: How long have these mood cycles been going on? One of the determining factors is the length of time the behavior manifests.

Shannon: It's hard to say. I've mostly lived with my grandmother. But I think a long time. Ever since I can remember and realized that other people weren't like that. Do you think it's bipolar mood depression?

Professor Weitzman: From how you have described her, it might just be the case. You might suggest to your father that he take your mother for a psychiatric examination. If it is confirmed that she has a serious mood disorder, she could benefit by some medication. In the last 20 years, mental disorders have been much alleviated by drug therapy.

Shannon: (*sighing*) We're just country folk, and my parents are real suspicious about "shrinks." My dad and I are close though. I guess I could at least talk to him anyway when I go home.

Professor Weitzman: Who's the other person you are concerned about?

Shannon: This friend of mine . . . we help each other. He helps me a lot carrying books and stuff. I guess you noticed my club foot. And I help him in his writing. Actually, you know him. It's Dan Westwind. Anyway, even though he's a Navajo, we've gotten friendly, and we confide in each other. Sometimes, though, he talks about things that seem strange to me.

Professor Weitzman: Such as?

Shannon: Such as . . . well, I told him about my family, especially my mother. And he's talked to me about his family, too . . . and particularly about his wife who died. Only . . . he says he talks to her a lot . . . as if she's alive . . . and sometimes he sees her . . . not when he's dreaming . . . but right in daylight . . . and that sounds like a hallucination, doesn't it?

Professor Weitzman: Shannon, we'd have to know a lot more about Dan's culture before we can make a judgment. What would be considered "abnormal" in one culture may be quite "normal" in another.

Why Study Dysfunctional (Abnormal) Psychology?

Sometime, in each of our lives, we will share the same concerns as Shannon in the opening scenario. When is a problem serious enough to warrant professional help? In fact, the readers may have already asked themselves such questions as:

Is my spouse just a social drinker or does she have a serious alcohol problem?
Is my daughter losing weight because she's on a diet or does she have bulimia?
Has my son become addicted to drugs? Should I hospitalize him?
My brother has been so depressed lately; is he "at risk" for suicide?
One of my employees is acting strangely lately; is he having a "nervous breakdown"?
My son's teacher says he is seriously hyperactive. How can I tell?
I get so anxious I feel like I'm going to burst out of my skin. Am I losing my mind?

A few years ago, a survey resulted in an astonishing conclusion by the investigators. Almost half (48 percent) of the American population could qualify for a mental disorder diagnosis at sometime in their lives, and 27 percent could qualify for two or more different mental

Table 9.1 Sources of Our Personal, Social, and Global Anxieties

Personal Anxieties

Pressures to be successful and to climb the social and vocational "success" ladder.
The rising cost of living, and difficulties understanding taxes and paying bills on time, including credit cards.
The obligation to raise happy children and to prepare them for responsible citizenship.
The fear that social security and retirement funds will collapse after a lifetime of working to fund them.
The need to stay healthy, slim, young, and beautiful, as portrayed by advertising.
Fear we cannot keep up our present frantic pace of life.

Social and Vocational Anxieties

Disillusionment with the American Dream of financial success and happiness for all.
The plight of our cities with their increasing problems of ghettos, riots, and crime.
The need to be well informed and to stay abreast of social and financial developments.
Our sense of "rootlessness," as 20 percent of our population move away from home every year.
The need to support equal civil rights for all and to support multicultural diversity.
Our hopes to help the poor, the homeless, the aged, and the infirm.
Fear of being laid off as the result of downsizing.
Pressures to keep abreast of computer technology.

Global Anxieties

Recognition of our "rape of the planet" and the fear that we have poisoned it irreversibly.
Increasing concern for national and international terrorism.
A desperate search to find new energy sources as the world's fossil fuels run out.
The shadow of World War III always hovering on the horizon as the result of tribal disputes and wars.

disorders at some time in their lives (Kessler, 1994). That doesn't mean that all of these people have ever spent time on a mental ward, not at all. Many people who have suffered serious problems may have gone to work every day throughout their emotional crisis and may never have seen a mental health professional (see Box 9.2b). But it does mean that occasional dysfunctionality is a part of "the human condition." And if that isn't enough—our worries today are not just personal and social but global—we wonder each day if some small tribal warfare halfway across the world will be the beginning of World War III (see Table 9.1). Small wonder that so many of us will experience some kind of emotional depression during the course of our lives.

So when are symptoms and behaviors serious enough to warrant consulting a mental health professional? For many reasons, it is not at all an easy task to diagnose a "mental disorder." First, unlike most physical diseases, a "psychological illness" cannot be determined by a single test (such as a blood test or an X-ray). It is more a matter of **differential diagnosis** (a process of eliminating what the condition is *not*). Many factors must be taken into consideration.

> *Are the symptoms or behavior seriously out of the statistical "Average range"?*
> *How long have the symptoms or behavior existed?*
> *What is going on presently that might account for such an intense dysfunctional reaction?*
> *Is the person experiencing such overwhelming anxiety that he or she reports feeling "out of control"?*
> *Are the symptoms so bizarre that they are causing discomfort in the onlookers?*

Is the person unable to function in the everyday world of work and interpersonal events?
Does the person's verbal or physical behavior suggest he/she might do harm to self or others?
Could the dysfunctional behavior be caused by a physical problem—such as a severe reaction to a drug or a brain tumor or the leftover ravages of drug addiction?

DSM-IV: A "Common Language" for All the Mental Health Professions

Another problem of diagnosis concerns the difficulty of communicating across mental health professional boundaries. Because each mental health profession developed more or less independently, it also developed different objectives and training, different definitions for the same disorder, and different perspectives and different vocabularies. While each of these professions made valuable contributions to our understanding of emotional or mental disorders, communication within and across professional disciplines had become extremely difficult. Professional communication had become a "Tower of Babel."

In an effort to improve communication, the American Psychiatric Association decided to standardize professional terminology and improve descriptive classifications. In 1952, the first ***Diagnostic and Statistical Manual of Mental Disorders (DSM)*** was published. The *DSM* (as it is called by most professionals) is similar to the medical doctor's *Physician's Desk Reference (PDR)*. It lists the major symptoms and defense mechanisms most often associated with the disorder. It provides statistics on the prevalence of the disorder, generally worldwide, and within any given subculture, according to gender, age, ethnicity, socioeconomic status, etc. It also lists other variables of the disorder such as medication, psychotherapies, and prognosis.

But since there are so many problems connected with diagnosis of mental/emotional disorders, the *DSM* has always been the subject of intense debate and controversy (see Box 9.3). As well, advances in technology, the development of new drugs, and new psychotherapeutic methods make updating of the *DSM* an ongoing process. And so it should be. Scientific advances are not accomplished by agreement and unanimity of opinion but by disagreement and constant debate. Consequently, there have been several revisions of the *DSM,* the most recent of which is the *DSM-IV,* published in 1994. What is important for the reader to understand is that, despite the ongoing professional debate and argument, all the mental health professions have agreed to use the *DSM* as a classification system so as to speak "a common language." As scientists and practitioners, we will continue to disagree with each other, but at least we will know what it is we are disagreeing about (Frances, First & Pincus, 1995).

The *DSM-IV* lists more than 300 "mental disorders." Sometimes called "the psychiatric Bible," it is an encyclopedia. Obviously, you cannot be expected to become acquainted with all these disorders in the course of one short term. Indeed, mental health professionals out in the field will be studying and working with the *DSM-IV* for several years before they feel proficient in it—and by that time there may be a *DSM-V.* But the reader needs to become familiar with the most frequent of these disorders, familiar enough at least to recognize that you or someone you know may need help. We are fortunate today to have derived some effective treatments for many of these disorders. Unlike previous times, an afflicted person can be helped to live again in society and to find a compatible work.

A Word of Warning: The "Intern's Disease." Medical students sometimes come down with what is called the "intern's disease"; namely, the tendency to believe they have contracted whatever disease is being presently studied. A headache may arouse a concern of having a tumor of the brain. A blister on the foot may arouse the thought: *Ohmygod! I've got leprosy!* Occasionally, interns are known to slip down to the lab in the wee hours of the morning to take a look at their own blood sample under a microscope. This tendency to become somewhat **hypochondriacal** (imagining we have symptoms and diseases we don't have) is also noticeable in beginning psychology students. It is quite a normal reaction when studying abnormal psychology. What the readers need to keep in mind always is that we all have experienced symptoms associated with the various emotional disorders. Experiencing a few of the symptoms does not mean that the reader actually has the disorder being discussed. What makes for a serious disorder is whether the symptoms have existed for a long time, are intense in quality, and are interfering in the individual's personal, educational, or vocational arenas. If the reader believes that these criteria are being fulfilled, the next step is to consult a mental health professional. But before you rush off, remember that all of us experience all kinds of symptoms from time to time, but they are generally transient in nature.

The Anxiety Disorders

We begin with the anxiety disorders because they are the most statistically frequent disorders. Estimates vary, but, in any given year, between 15 and 30 percent of the adult population is afflicted with a severe anxiety disorder. All of us probably have experienced depression of some sort at some time in our lives. While there is some genetic component to the anxiety disorders, as it seems "to run in families," we also know environmental stress plays a major part in its etiology. We know because the **World Health Organization (WHO)** reports that the frequency of anxiety disorders (as a group) have been increasing steadily in the past 50 years (World Health Organization, 1997). Anxiety disorders are the most expensive in terms of economic cost to the nation. Fortunately, they are also the most treatable.

Generalized Anxiety Disorder

Sometimes people have such pervasive fear that it is described as **free-floating anxiety.** These people complain that they "worry about everything under the sun," that they are tired and excessively fatigued all the time, and that they can't seem to do their work because they can't concentrate. They may suffer from insomnia night after night, and this lack of sleep intensifies their problem. They may be afraid they are "losing their minds" or "going crazy." Friends and relatives will accuse the person of "wanting to worry," of "looking for things to worry about," of "being happy only when they are worried about something." Now most of us have probably experienced these symptoms from time to time in our lives, particularly if we are doing too much or if we are having trouble coping with all our responsibilities. That doesn't mean we have an anxiety disorder. In order to qualify as an **anxiety disorder,** the symptoms must be ongoing and of at least six months in duration.

Etiology and Treatment. Life-in-society has become stressful. We are more fearful now about terrorism, about child abuse and kidnapping, about more nuclear accidents, and about safety in our schools. Older workers are awed by the new technologies. Educationally disadvantaged people are feeling overwhelmed by the computer age. Fortunately, advances in medication have been extremely helpful, particularly the tranquilizers and mood elevators.

Specific Phobic Disorders: Often Age-Related

Phobia comes from the Greek word for "fear." A *phobia* is a persistent, exaggerated, and unreasonable fear about a person, an object, or situation. (See Tip 9.1 for some common specific phobias). Most of us (even if we don't want to admit it) are phobic about something. Very few of us (including your authors) feel comfortable around snakes; in fact, the fear of snakes is common at around 20 years of age. In fact, many phobias are related to our age or our circumstances in life. Small children can develop phobic reactions to doctors and particularly to hypodermic needles. School phobias are surprisingly frequent in kindergarten and the early grades. Young adults can be quite phobic about heights. As we get older, we become more frightened of being in crowds (where we may get mugged), of falling (and breaking a bone or hip), of an incapacitating illness, and of death. All of these phobias may even be "the norm" for their age-groups (Agras, 1985).

We all have minor fears of one sort or another. So when does a phobia become so serious as to warrant psychotherapeutic attention? An example should clarify. People with agoraphobia are so fearful that they will exhibit fear, dizziness, palpitations, diarrhea, or nausea in public that they will avoid restaurants, movie houses, museums, college classrooms, or any other space where escape might be difficult. Sometimes their anxiety is less about their physical symptoms than about the fact that they will exhibit embarrassing behaviors. An extreme form of agoraphobia is exemplified by those recluses who will not even venture out of the house but remain, day after day, prisoners in their own homes—people whom the newspapers describe as reclusive. Agoraphobia is experienced in about 4 percent of the population and is twice as frequent among women as men. Fortunately, the behavior therapies and cognitive therapies have proved useful in alleviating specific phobias—particularly Wolpe's desensitization training.

Panic Attack Disorder

One day a friend of yours keels over, his face grimacing with pain. As you go to help your friend, he describes pain in his chest and down his left arm and all the classic symptoms of a heart attack. You rush him to the hospital and (lo! and behold!) his EKG(electrocardiogram) reveals normal heart rhythms. What your friend has suffered is not a heart attack but a panic disorder. Panic attack is characterized by such overwhelming anxiety it can produce all the symptoms of a major disease, including heart disease, an acute diabetic episode, or even a severe occurrence of asthma. The person will describe themselves as "being out of control," of wanting to "scream for help," or sure they are "about to die with nobody around for help." One of the side effects of panic attack is the tendency for the victim to avoid any situation which might trigger another episode—leading eventually to the *comorbid* (two or more diseases or disorders) condition of panic disorder with agoraphobia (described above).

Tip 9.1 Some Specific Phobias

Acrophobia	Heights	Mysophobia	Dirt, germs
Agoraphobia	Open spaces	Nyctophobia	The dark
Astaphobia	Thunderstorms	Ophidiophobia	Snakes
Claustrophobia	Closed spaces	Pyrophobia	Fire
Hematophobia	Blood	Zoophobia	Animals
Melanophobia	Bees		

Etiology and treatment. Many explanations have been offered to account for why certain people are "at risk" for panic attacks. The present estimate of the frequency of panic attack is about one in every 75 Americans. It affects twice as many women as men and typically begins in the late teens or twenties. It also appears to have a genetic component, but while it may have biological underpinnings, it is often triggered by traumatic stress—death of a loved one, divorce, or by a serious physical illness. Sometimes, however, it seems to appear for "no reason at all." A physical explanation has to do with an imbalance of a brain **neurotransmitter,** norepinephrine (Papp & Gorman, 1993). A psychological explanation has to do with the person's over-sensitivity to and misinterpretation of bodily sensations and pain. For example: Suppose a person's anxiety is manifesting as "butterflies in the stomach" or even heart-pounding. Most of us will recognize these symptoms as anxiety. The person with panic disorder, however, is convinced that he has ulcers or is undergoing a heart attack. They have become so anxiety-sensitive that any insignificant event may trigger exactly what they are trying to stave off.

Fortunately, **antidepressant drugs** and **tranquilizers** (particularly the benzodiazepines) seem to be highly effective for panic disorder, particular those which restore neurotransmitter balance. But many victims are also helped immensely just by being informed of the diagnosis. Most people seeking help for their symptoms resist the idea that some or much of their distress is "psychological." Their concept of the psychological aspect of a disease is that it indicates some weakness in their character. Not so with most panic attack victims. Says David Barlow of Boston University's Anxiety and Related Disorders Clinic, "It's usually a big relief" when panic sufferers find out they aren't gravely ill, aren't "crazy," and are treatable. Some are downright happy about it. (Barlow, in Seppa, 1996). The good news is that alleviation of symptoms is about 80 percent at the present and getting higher all the time. The bad news is that 50 percent of the patients experience a recurrence. What is also needed then is the inclusion of cognitive/behavioral therapy in the treatment plan. The cognitive aspect involves helping the patient identify the anxiety-provoking symptoms, and then helping the patient reprogram his cognitive schema so that he knows a serious heart attack (or whatever) is not coming on. They then realize they are in control. They can stop their panic attack. The behavioral component is to teach the person how to handle the anxiety-provoking symptoms: relaxation and breathing techniques, desensitization training, stress inoculation, and the use of cue words such as "stop" or "cancel," and other coping strategies (Meichanbaum, 1993).

Acute Stress Disorders, Including Posttraumatic Stress Disorder (PTSD)

Attention was first drawn to acute stress disorders when social scientists were doing their best to help Holocaust survivors get reestablished physically and psychologically. But sometimes nothing seemed to help the survivors recover from the nightmare of the concentration camps. In one comprehensive study, it was discovered that 97 percent of the Holocaust survivors were still suffering from severe anxiety symptoms many years after their release. Even worse, the suicide rate was considerably higher than in the general population even though they were now "in safe hands." The Holocaust survivors worried their family might be in danger if they were out of the house. Many had nightmares recalling their captivity and dreamed that their children (who had been born after liberation) were imprisoned with them. Eighty percent of the survivors felt guilty that they had survived when so many of their relatives and friends had died (Katzman, Kuch, & Cox, 1992). So acute are the symptoms that mark the Holocaust survivors,

Figure 9.1 PTSD PTSD is the latest in a series of terms for the symptoms that occur as an aftermath of war and other trauma. In World War II, it was called "battle fatigue" and in World War I it was called "shell shock." We know now that it also occurs in victims of abuse, earthquake, devastating floods, tornadoes, and hurricanes.

that the anxiety and despair is known now to affect not only the children but the grandchildren of the survivors (Fox, 1999).

Then the mental health professions began to focus their attention on a similar **syndrome** (symptoms that occur together) appearing in returning Vietnam veterans. Americans are very familiar now with **post-traumatic stress disorder (PTSD),** but it took some time to be defined. The medical services had been used to "shell shock" and "battle trauma" that occurred during or right after the battle. But the Vietnam veterans were showing symptoms long after coming back stateside. After more than 25 percent of the returning Vietnam veterans began to have serious and long-lasting symptoms of anxiety similar to the Holocaust victims, PTSD became a new mental health disorder. Appetite or sleep may be disturbed and frightening dreams may be frequent, and these symptoms may last anywhere from six months to, unfortunately, a lifetime (APA, 1994). In Hawaii, for example, the Veterans Administration has reported a surprising number of PTSD veterans are survivors of the Japanese surprise attack on Pearl Harbor. Also needing treatment are many of the Nisei 442nd Regiment, the Japanese-American soldiers who became the most decorated combat unit in American history. They were returned home to find their homes gone, the family business dismantled, and sometimes their family members interned. While these World War II survivors claim they never had these symptoms before, it is likely they were simply overlooked as just "being grumpy" or "needing to be alone for a while." Today, we might use other terms for their emotional states, such as having *high anxiety* or *social isolation*. But since they kept working and seemed mostly all right, nobody took notice (Sutker, 1998);

Etiology and Treatment. We are becoming aware also that PTSD has occurred as the result of many other situations. Women who have been raped may develop an aversion to sex and display other symptoms such as pounding heart, shortness of breath, or dizziness. Posttraumatic stress disorders may also follow natural or accidental disasters such as earthquakes, floods, tornadoes, fires, airplane crashes, and serious car accidents. There seem to be some factors that make for "high risk" for PTSD. So far, three factors have been identified in those persons who suffer the most severe anxiety disorders. First, they have had a history of traumatic events, such as divorce and death of parents in childhood, or a history of physical abuse. Second, they do not have a sense of control of their own lives. They tend to feel they have always been at the mercy of a cruel Fate. Third, they do not have a strong social/emotional support system whereby they can share their anxieties or experiences (Kobasa, 1990). But it is also true that many "high-risk" victims of PTSD have been functioning very well in society and have been contributing members of their society. What is immediately necessary is the alleviation of the symptoms, which generally means the use of tranquilizers and other medications. Once the anxiety has been somewhat diminished, other treatments are highly recommended, such as behavior modification and cognitive modeling. In addition, all the anxiety disorders are amenable to insight therapies such as counseling or a peer-support group. For example, women who have been brutally raped recover from their trauma much more quickly if they have a strong support system and can share their experiences to a receptive audience (Kushner, Riggs, Foa, & Miller, 1992).

The Mood Disorders

Depression has become a household word. Even children in middle school are able to describe themselves as "being depressed." Fortunately, major and minor depressions are very amenable to medication. Antidepressant drugs are remarkable for their swift mood elevating effects. Major and minor depression are also vastly alleviated through psychotherapy. If a person can talk about what is causing the underlying anxiety and depression and can discover ways to cope with these problems, the person is well on the way to permanent recovery. Sometimes, the mood disorders recover without any specific treatment whatsoever, called *spontaneous remission*. In fact, as many as one-third of all cases of major and minor depression report spontaneous remission. What is the reason for spontaneous remission? At this point, it is anybody's guess. It might just be that in the safe haven of a hospital, they are relieved from the ongoing and overwhelming stresses of their everyday lives. As one woman remarked:

> When the family knew I was having a depression, they laid off me for a while. I was always the one everybody came to with their problems. I was always the "strong one." It just got too much for me. And I sank into a depression. Suddenly, no one was bothering me with the problems. I didn't have to answer the telephone. Other people did the jobs they all thought I should do. I stayed in bed and slept and rested. It was such a relief to have a little rest from everybody's demands and some peace in my life. I began to feel better.

Major Depressive Disorder

A deep and profound depression or *dysphoric* (unpleasant) mood state is the single most obvious characteristic of major depressive disorder. The most remarkable fact of this disorder is how common it is in our society—perhaps 10 to 15 percent of Americans experience a major depressive episode each year (APA, 1994). So common is depression in our society that it has been called the "common cold" of mental disorders. When college students have been asked to describe what it feels like to be depressed, the following answers have been given:

> It's hard to get up in the morning and drag one foot in front of the other just to get to class.
> I just want to get into a hole in the earth and cover it up above me and stay there.
> Being depressed is like hopeless. The world is a maggot hill, and I'm one of the maggots.
> Utter Dejection. Gloom. Despair. Hopeless. Those are the words that come to mind.

If depression is so common and we all have bouts of it occasionally, when is it serious enough to warrant professional help? The answer to that question has to do with several factors. The first factor is the length of time the depression lasts—at least two months, according to the *DSM-IV*. Other factors include whether the depression is interfering with the person's ability to function as a student or as a worker and if the person withdraws from any kind of family or social life. Of course, that does not mean that the person who is depressed has to wait for two

Figure 9.2 Depression. It has been on the rise for the last 50 years and it is still increasing. One estimate is that one out of every four Americans has had a serious depression at some time over the life span.

months before getting help—only that the label of "major depressive mood disorder" is applied after that amount of time. If a person is experiencing an intense depression for more than a week or two, there is no reason to continue to suffer when there are so many drugs available to relieve the misery. In severely depressed people who do not respond to antidepressants, and have either attempted suicide or expressed strong wishes to commit suicide, **electro-convulsive therapy (ECT)** (formerly known as **shock therapy**)—as barbaric as it may seem to some—does lift the depression for some patients for whom no other approach has proven beneficial (Fink, 1992).

Dysthymic (Minor) Mood Disorder

Dysthymia has been gaining recognition as a mood disorder only in the last two decades. The reason for such a long delay is that the symptoms are not as dramatic as they are in major mood depression or schizophrenia. People so afflicted were simply characterized as an underachiever, as lazy, as chronically irritable, or just as always feeling "plain miserable." Because of the nonspecific aspects of the symptoms, statistics are still tentative, perhaps around 5 percent of the population are afflicted. We expect to see a gain in reported cases as the general population becomes more aware of the disturbance.

Dysthymic victims, unlike victims of major mood depression, can often continue to go to work each day, support themselves, and appear to be doing a satisfactory job. But their unruffled external appearance is a camouflage for their internal unhappiness and despair. They manage to get through the workday, but at home they may just seem to "fall apart." They may drink or use drugs to cover their misery. Their families sometimes say they "just aren't there" most of the time—they isolate themselves from family involvement and often ask to just be "let alone." They often describe themselves as "a phony" or "an empty shell." A professional friend of the authors is a good example. She is a speech therapist in a local hospital and is highly regarded by the members of the medical team. She has even been called "a wonder worker." Yet in a conversation about the ability of some people with dysthymia to keep functioning in a limited capacity, she responded that she herself had been such a person—for more than ten years (see Box 9.2b).

Etiology and Treatment. Worldwide studies indicate that the major and minor mood disorders are on the rise in the technological societies and have been increasing since 1915 (APA, 1994). Are the mood disorders, then, a disease of our pressure-cooker society with its emphasis on personal achievement, "getting ahead," and dog-eat-dog competition? Is the rise of the mood disorders a fallout consequence of having to acquire more and more knowledge and skills to compete in the job market? Surely, the increasingly fierce competition for college grades, the pressure to achieve academic and athletic honors, the increasing academic standards being demanded by all the professions and paraprofessions are intensifying the problems of adolescence and adulthood. We may literally be working ourselves into major and minor depressions (at least in part) in our desire to achieve the American Dream of material wealth and of climbing the "success" ladder.

Box 9.2

STUDENTS VERBATIM
The Mood Disorders

a. On Major Mood Disorder: Male Caucasian, (47 years). When my wife died, I thought I couldn't go on living. Everything that mattered to me seemed gone. Sometimes I felt like there was a ton of weight on my chest holding me down. I had trouble breathing. My arms ached. I felt like I couldn't get up on my feet, that they wouldn't hold me. It's hard to go to sleep. It was even harder to wake up to face another dreaded day. Eventually breathing became easier and the terrible weight on my chest got lighter. Then one day it was gone, the whole sad melancholia I had been feeling was gone. I knew it was over and I could live again. Thank God for antidepressants.

b. On Dysthymia (Minor Mood Disorder): Older Professional Woman. I have worked hard all my professional life. I thought I was all right, at least as all right as most people. Then I woke up one day and realized that I had been depressed for ten years. Ten years! I had a feeling of happiness! Actual happiness! When people used to talk about "feeling happy," I really didn't know what they were talking about. I thought I did. But what I assumed was "happiness" were those occasional times when I felt "less bad." At my best, I was living a kind of dull gray existence. I was at my best in my job because I knew how to do my job, but I didn't like social relationships. People expected things I couldn't give them. Then I woke up one morning, and the whole world had become brighter overnight. What caused me to have a ten-year depression, I have no idea. I didn't even know I was having one. I thought everyone felt like me. It was

like a "numbness." In comparison, now I actually wake up most mornings glad to see the sun shining and hear the birds singing.

c. On Bipolar Mood Disorder: Male College Student. My mother was diagnosed with bipolar mood disorder. I don't know which was worse, her bad moods or her good moods. When she was in her bad mood state, she would cry a lot and say that she didn't deserve to live, that nobody loved her, and . . . threaten to commit suicide . . . Then all of a sudden, she would switch for no apparent reason and be full of life and happy, but I can't really say happy exactly . . . it was more like racing, racing, racing, and giggling like she was a little tipsy. One time, she got us redecorating the house and ran up thousands of dollars just to do it. Another time, she said we all needed a vacation. The next thing we knew we were all in the car going out West. It was no use saying that we couldn't leave school, she'd just say we were too conventional. We didn't even have time to pack the things we needed, so when we got to the mountains, it was cold and we had to buy clothes to keep warm . . . Finally, our father couldn't take it anymore and he left, leaving the rest of us with her. I don't think we ever had a real childhood . . . we were always struggling to keep our mother's condition from getting out of hand . . . When she was in her bad mood state, she would cry and say she was no good and go to church and get very religious. I'm very bitter at my father for having left us with her. That was no kind of childhood for us kids.

Bipolar Mood Disorder (Formerly Called Manic-Depressive Psychosis)

People afflicted with **bipolar mood disorder** also suffer periods of depressions, but their depressions alternate with periods of *mania*. In the **manic state,** the person experiences an energetic and optimistic **euphoria,** which is to say that they feel elated and energetic. They become exuberant, full of ideas to improve their situation at work or at home. Their physical energy can astonish other people who may even complain they cannot keep up. They may decide to remodel their homes, to add a swimming pool, to build a racing car, to start a new business, etc. (see Box 9.2c). If they are gifted and creative artists and writers, they may produce remarkable works of art in an extraordinarily short time. In fact, there seems to be a relationship between some types of creativity and bipolar mood disorder. George Frederick Handel, who has been described as having a bipolar mood disorder, may have written *The Messiah* during one of his manic states. As soon as he conceived the idea for this celebrated oratorio, he locked himself in his room for three weeks, saw no one, ate little, and emerged with most of it in finished form. It should be noted, however, that the creative juices flow only when the person is in the euphoric manic stage and not in the depressed stage. One suggestion as to why the creativity seems to flow during the manic phase is that the speeded up cognitive processes heighten the person's natural flexibility and fluidity of thinking: quick associations, energy, confidence, and a general sense of well-being (Goodwin & Jamison, 1990).

Unfortunately, not all is auspicious in the manic phase of bipolar mood disorder. For one thing, the mania also includes a grandiose self-esteem—even a sense of omnipotence. Persons in the manic phase may believe they are capable of anything even when they have little skill in an area. Their self-confidence often borders on recklessness. Once they conceive an idea, they refuse to "listen to reason" no matter how many people tell them they are being "foolhardy" and taking dangerous and stupid risks. They may go on shopping sprees, buy things for which they have no need, run up their credit card debt, write checks that bounce, and give large sums of money away to strangers. If someone tries to restrict their activities, they may become irritable, angry, and turn on anyone who pleads with them to "listen to reason." Their incessant talking will now become a tirade of complaints and angry criticism of the people around them who are "stupid idiots who can't see opportunities being handed to them." Their attempts at wisecracking humor turns to fury. Their remarkable physical energy may become destructive to themselves or to others.

Then, just as suddenly as it began, the manic episode will come to a dead stop. But, generally, these people do not just return to "normal." The sudden end of the manic phase marks the beginning of the depressive phase. All that creative flow drains away, and the person feels life has no meaning any more, and he or she may even become suicidal.

Etiology and Treatment. While the unipolar mood disorders (major and minor depression) have some genetic component to them, the evidence of a genetic component for the bipolar mood disorder is undeniable. The World Health Organization (1997) has reported a consistent 1 percent of the population as having bipolar mood disorder over the last 50 years. Twin studies also support the genetic etiology of this disorder. A twin study in Denmark, for example, revealed a concordance rate for bipolar mood disorder of almost 70 percent for identical twins as compared to fraternal twins who show a concordance rate of only 20 percent. But the fact that the twin studies do not show a 100 percent concordance means that environmental factors must also play a part. Serious emotional trauma, the person's early life history, living at a distance from family and friends, drug abuse, and a lack of a social/emotional support system all effect the chances of bipolar mood disorder (Kendler & Diehl, 1993).

The actual "cause" of bipolar mood disorder seems to be an imbalance of certain neurotransmitters in the brain. Research has revealed that people suffering from mood disorders have abnormal levels of norepinephrine and serotonin. That sounds like bad news, but actually it is also good news. When diabetes was discovered to be a deficiency of insulin, it followed that injections of synthetic insulin would counteract the symptoms of diabetes. In like manner, if the mood disorders are the result of chemical imbalance, it follows that appropriate chemicals will restore the normal chemical balance. And so they do: antidepressants and mood elevators such as lithium, Prozac (which has stirred much controversy), Elavil, Zanax, and other drugs that contain the necessary counterbalancing brain chemicals.

Seasonal Affective Disorder (SAD)

In the 1980s, there came to light (both metaphorically and literally) a disorder that had to do with the fact that some people can experience major depression in the winter months. Now all of us can get a little "high-strung" or "nervous" or complain we have "cabin fever" if we can't get out for days on end because of inclement weather. The moment blue skies break out and we can feel the warmth of the sun, we find ourselves cheered up. That kind of reaction is normal. But some persons are so sensitive to the low levels of light during the long winter months that they get seriously depressed. The person's whole physiology seems to slow down. The research suggests that the person's circadian rhythms have been seriously disturbed. **Circadian rhythms** have to do with those seasonal cycles of the universe that affect all animate life on earth. Examples of the effects of circadian rhythms include the migration of birds, animal mating seasons, and a woman's menstrual cycles. Persons afflicted with SAD have melatonin levels that are "out of sync" or desynchronized. In terms of duration, the depressed phases show a repetitive cycle that can vary as much as months on end to several in a day. That's the bad news, but good news follows.

Etiology and Treatment. If lack of sunlight is the cause of this depressive state, the researchers decided to see if flooding the depressed person with light, called phototherapy, would lift the depression. And it did—in the majority of patients. Perhaps this is why citizens of the northern latitudes (Canada, Great Britain, and Scandinavia) take winter holidays to Greece, Italy, Mexico, Bermuda, and other places south. The researchers even have advice for people who work indoors all day: Instead of the common variety fluorescent light, get what is called full-spectrum lighting which most closely resembles natural daylight (Grinspoon & Bakalar, June, 1999).

The Schizophrenias

Schizophrenia is the professional term for what lay people think of as "crazy" and "insane" because of the seemingly strange behaviors these people display. The term schizophrenia comes from two Greek words meaning a "split mind." But the split is not the same as a person who has split into several "personalities." The patient's **affective** functioning (emotional reactions) seem to be split off from the **cognitive** (intellectual understanding) aspect. This "split" appears as inappropriate responses to what is going on in the environment. For example, the schizophrenic patient may giggle inanely during a funeral. Christmas and other festive occasions may trigger tears, anger, depression, and other bizarre or embarrassing behaviors.

Positive Symptoms

There are two types of schizophrenic symptoms: positive symptoms and negative symptoms. The positive symptoms are fairly easy to identify. A normally clean and well-dressed person may become slovenly and stop taking baths or wear a strange and outlandish costume (perhaps wearing several overcoats, one on top of the other). He may sink into a deep stuporlike state in which he can be motionless for hours, even days—a psychomotor behavior called *catatonia*. She may leave the safety and security of her home and become a "bag lady." Delusions, hallucinations, and disorganized speech are also examples of **positive symptoms. Delusions** are grossly erroneous beliefs that have little to do with reality. Patients who exhibit persecutory delusions may be convinced that people are spying on them; that they are being followed; that their telephones have been tapped; that people are lying to them; or that they are being subjected to ridicule. These **persecutory delusions** may indicate a very serious and very dangerous personality pattern—the **paranoid personality disorder.** Patients who exhibit referential delusions may believe that comments on television or certain gestures people make or articles in a newspaper have to do with them personally (see Box 9.4). Bizarre delusions could be scenes out of our worst nightmares. A person may believe someone has destroyed all his internal organs. Or that "somebody" has control of her mind and body. Patients with grandiose delusions may believe they are superior beings and have superior powers; for example, they may believe they are the President of the United States or God or Jesus Christ. **Hallucinations** refer to sensory perceptions that are not shared by anyone else in the vicinity and can occur in any of the five classic senses: Seeing, hearing, tasting, smelling, and feeling. The most common hallucinations take the form of voices in the head, which makes it difficult to communicate with the afflicted person. As any mental health professional can testify, it is very difficult to interview a patient whose voices are screaming in the patient's head that the mental health professional is a satanic demon. Tactile sensations can manifest as insects crawling over the skin or electric shocks or tingling or burning. Visual hallucinations will distort colors or shapes or the size of objects. Hallucinations of taste can convince the person his food is being poisoned. Hallucinations of smell may lead him to the conviction that the sulfuric fumes of hell are present. (See Box 9.4 for examples of positive symptoms of schizophrenia.)

Negative Symptoms

Negative symptoms are not so easy to pinpoint because they are nonspecific and are recognized only as a diminution of certain faculties and behaviors. They involve such characteristics as affective flattening. **Affective flattening** means a low level of emotional response or interpersonal interaction. The person avoids eye contact, responds to questions in brief and laconic and noninformative answers. They may smile occasionally and even seem to have moments of cheerfulness but they vanish almost as soon as they appear. Their energy level remains at a very low level. They do not have an organized life plan or the ability to sustain a job unless it is very undemanding and repetitive. Many of our "homeless" population or "street people" exhibit this kind of affective flattening.

Etiology and Treatment

The prevailing theory about schizophrenia at the present time is that several factors may be involved: genetic and biological; environmental; and interactive. For some cases of schizophrenia, genetic factors seem to be the primary etiology, which means that these people will develop schizophrenia no matter what kind of environment they grow up in. The evidence for genetic etiology is mounting from the many twin and adoption studies both in the United States and Europe. In a second group of cases, a traumatic childhood may result in a lifelong schizophrenic disorder. Finally, many persons may be born with a genetic predisposition toward schizophrenia, but whether this genetic disposition actually develops depends on environmental factors. For example, studies show that schizophrenic patients also have had a higher incidence of birth complications, such as prolonged labor resulting in oxygen deprivation. And from Holland comes another statistic. During the winter of 1944–1945, the Germans tried to starve the Dutch into compliance. Babies conceived during that time of famine have been studied ever since. One of the findings: As adults, they have had double the risk of hospitalization for schizophrenia as a comparison group in nearby countries that did not suffer the same starvation.

Box 9.3

Evaluating *The Diagnostic and Statistical Manual of Mental Disorders (DSM-IV)*

PRO

1. **Establishes a "common" language among the many disciplines involved with mental health.** There are more than two dozen disciplines (at the last count) presently involved in one way or another in the diagnosis and treatment of mental disorders and more coming into existence all the time. These various disciplines had developed their own unique perspectives and professional vocabularies. The establishment of a "common language" makes possible clear communication among professionals and across disciplines.

2. **More valid research methods and diagnostic techniques.** The first effort to standardize mental health terms and diagnoses was published as the first *Diagnostic and Statistical Manual of Mental Disorders* in 1952 and was modeled after the medical profession's *Physician's Desk Reference (PDR)*. This first edition was based on "inferred causation," which is more appropriate to physical ailments than to mental and emotional disorders. For example: If a man is found to be infertile (cannot produce viable male sperm), and the physician discovers through the case history that the man contracted mumps early in his youth, the physician may well pinpoint the earlier case of mumps as the cause. The physician is likely to be correct in his inferred causation since the correlation of mumps with later infertility is so high. But when it comes to "mental disorders," inferred causation is extremely risky. As we now know, many mental and emotional disorders that were once blamed on poor parenting now turn out to be genetically determined. Retroactive investigation and inferred causation are always at risk for errors of misattribution. To correct this type of diagnosis, the *DSM-III* and *DSM-III-R* developed a classification that did not rely on inference, but on more scientific empirical data. The *DSM-IV* (1994) is the result of the independent observations of "more than a thousand" practitioners and "over sixty professional organizations."

3. **The *DSM* classifications have become the standard for worldwide study.** The *DSM* has not only become the "psychiatric Bible" in this country, it has won worldwide recognition. We now have a "common language" that cuts across national boundaries and diverse cultures.

4. **Having a common language will aid both treatment and research.** Since definitions, diagnoses, and criteria for mental disorders have been standardized throughout the mental health professions, research on mental disorders will be greatly enhanced.

Source: American Psychiatric Association. (1994). *Diagnostic and Statistical Manual of Mental Disorders-IV.* Washington, DC: APA.

CON

1. **By *DSM* standards, we are all of us a little crazy.** With more than 300 disorders listed and the symptoms accorded to these disorders, all of us have to be counted as falling into one or more of these disorders. After the appearance of the *DSM-IV, Harper's* magazine published a wonderfully satiric article, entitled "The Encyclopedia of Insanity: A Psychiatric Handbook Lists a Madness for Everyone" and described it as "a book of dogma in which human "life is a form of mental illness." Critics say that while the *Harper's* article may be exaggerated, the *DSM-IV* is creating psychopathologies by diagnosing the usual normal reactions to stressful situations as symptoms of severe mental disorders.

2. **The *DSM* reflects cultural biases.** Sometimes the *DSM-IV* is more a reflection of social values, political compromise, and a manual for insurance claims than a collection of empirical scientific observations. It is biased toward gender and toward certain ethnic groups. For example, in the process of putting together the *DSM-IV*, the editors proposed a disorder called "victimization disorder." The proposed disorder would categorize women who were having emotional reactions as the result of rape or other types of sexual abuse as having "victimization disorder." When word leaked out about this proposal, the National Organization of Women (NOW) and other groups protested this as a gender bias of men who were making perfectly normal emotional responses a psychiatric disorder. "Victimization disorder" was removed as an official category.

3. **Many disorders are simply "waste basket" diagnoses.** Three of these waste basket diagnoses are oppositional defiant disorder, defiant disorder, and attention-deficit/hyperactive disorder. Children with these

Box 9.3   Evaluating *The Diagnostic and Statistical Manual
                          of Mental Disorders* (*DSM-IV*) (continued)

diagnoses can then be put into special classes, or dismissed from school. The *DSM* is shaping how we think about children in grades K–12, prisoners, welfare recipients, and anyone who has "hit hard times."

4. **Psychiatric diagnoses carry a life-long stigma.** Perhaps the most serious criticism is that by labeling children who are having academic problems in school or reacting against an environmentally stress-

ful situation as this or that disorder, we are giving them a label that will last all their lives. If the behavioral symptoms are transient, there may be no way to delete the diagnosis off the computer monitor or the paper report.

Source: Herb Kutchins & Stuart A. Kirk. (1997). *Making Us Crazy: DSM: The Psychiatric Bible and the Creation of Mental Disorders.* New York: Free Press.

Finally, there is the effect the child has on its parent, which may alter the parent's **interaction** with the child. (*The Harvard Mental Health Letter,* June 1999). An example of this kind of interaction comes from the authors' own close family. In a letter written in her eighties, the mother of a schizophrenic daughter (now in her fifties) made a humble confession. We have changed the name of the daughter (of course), otherwise, the following is the mother's verbatim written words.

> People have always asked me why I treated my two children so differently. For a long time, I denied it. But it has come to me lately that they were right. There was always something different about Louise that made me nervous. I didn't like having her near me. I don't know what it was that made me feel this way. I just had this uncomfortable feeling. When Tommy came along, I felt so much closer to him.

This may be a very good example of an interaction effect. Let us suppose that there was "something different" about Louise from the day she was born. Let us suppose also that this "something different" caused her mother to avoid holding her and caressing her and playing with her. We can then further surmise that this lack of physical contact between Louise and her mother affected Louise still further, manifesting as **shallow affect** (diminished emotional response). Thus the cycle continued to escalate.

How do these several possibilities affect the treatment of the schizophrenic patient? To be frank, many practitioners admit they use "whatever seems to work," but most practitioners also agree that at least three types of treatments are necessary. The first is to alleviate the positive symptoms with medication. The second is to develop a support plan with the patient's family and friends. The third is to develop a long-term psychotherapeutic treatment plan with the patient.

The Dissociative Disorders

Dissociative disorders, which include *amnesia,* the *fugue state,* and *dissociative identity disorder* (formerly called *multiple personality*) have gained a lot of publicity in the media because of their dramatic qualities. The dissociative disorders affect the person's memory to such an extent that whole aspects of the person's personality or history can be lost to the patient's awareness. Now many factors can affect our memories including disease (such as Alzheimer's disease) or chemical addiction (drug and alcohol abuse) or physical trauma (such as an accident

Box 9.4   EXAMPLES OF THE POSITIVE SYMPTOMS OF SCHIZOPHRENIA

a. Delusion. A colleague of ours was sinking deeper and deeper into a delusional state. He was convinced that his salary check contained a message that said he had only so many more days before he was going to be fired and then die. What he was referring to was a notation that appeared monthly on that portion of the paycheck we tear off and keep for our records. The notation was simply an update on the number of sick leave hours that the employee had left in the fiscal year and it appeared monthly on all our checks. His update read: You have 192 hours of sick leave time still available. He had figured out that 192 hours was approximately four working weeks and that at the end of that time he was going to be fired and die. Although a few of us tried to break through this delusion by showing him that we had similar messages on our paychecks, it availed us nothing. When he got back into contact with reality, he told us that what triggered his delusion was the word *sick*. He knew he was sick, and so he believed the notation was meant for him personally.

b. Auditory hallucination. I'm 24 years old now. Ever since I was seventeen years old, I have always heard voices. I may have heard them before that, I'm not sure. They used to be very loud, and I could never get away from them. No matter where I was, they were always in my head and drowning out what other people were saying to me. I tried all kinds of things to keep from hearing them, like playing the piano or turning the TV up loud or humming to myself, but they always managed to be heard anyway. Sometimes they became quite obscene, or they would curse me and tell me how terrible I was. Sometimes they told me about other people and how evil they were. Sometimes they told me how evil I was. I began to think they were the angels that live in Hell and I was their sole victim. Finally, my parents began to believe me about the voices. They took me to a psychiatrist, and he diagnosed me as a paranoid schizophrenic. Thank God for that. Since I've been taking his medication, the voices have become much quieter and there are even times I don't hear them at all. But I know they are always there, waiting around the corner for a chance to take control.

c. Disorganized Thinking and Speech. A psychiatrist reported this unexpected phone call:

Hello, I'm a paranoid schizophrenic from Tampa. Are you the Dr. Maxim [sic] who wrote the book *The New Psychiatry?* [Yes.] Well, I'm 75 years old, but I grew up in the home of the very famous Dr. Zuckerman . . . the Dr. Obsessive-Compulsive Neurosis psychiatrist, who was a brilliant cardiologist, and I was his only psychiatric patient, and he never said he was my father, but my mother was a borderline butch-lesbian personality, and Dr. Zuckerman was the first to take me to the Metropolitan Museum of Art because I have a tooth on the right side that's too big just as in that Picasso painting, and I have a malformed skull and a right leg also longer than my left, and my daughter Infanta Marguarita Pequina lives in Chicago, but Dr. Zuckerman didn't rescue me from a terrible marriage from 1948 to 1966 in which a man beat me and raped me in the Jewish community . . . My brain waves flash too fast, just as you said in the book, which I'm taking to my clinical psychologist, where I go three times a week, although Dr. Zuckerman studied with A. A. Brill and Dr. Freud . . . but that can't help my skull which was genetically deformed and made worse by my sadist husband in the Jewish community. Do you see patients?

Source: J. S. Maxmen, & N. G. Ward, *Essential Psychopathology and Its Treatment,* 2nd ed., Revised for permission *DSM-IV* (New York: Norton, 1995), p. 178.

d. Visual Hallucinations. The following was written by a French woman who described her first acute episode of schizophrenia at the age of six during the school recess period. (Notice that the constancies of size and shape are disappearing.):

I remember the day it happened . . . a strange feeling came over me . . . I no longer recognized the school, it had become as large as a barracks; the singing children were prisoners, compelled to sing . . . My friend approached me . . . the nearer she approached, the taller she grew, the more she swelled in size . . . I cried out, "Stop, Alice you look like a lion. You're frightening me!" . . . The other pupils looked to me like ants under bright light. The school buildings became immense, smooth, unreal . . . I fancied that the people watching us from the street thought all of us were prisoners, just as I was a prisoner . . . when one of my schoolmates came toward me I saw her grow larger and larger, like the haystacks . . . all the children had a tiny crow's head on their heads."

Source: Renee (pseudonym). (1951). *The Autobiography of a Schizophrenic Girl.* New York: Grune & Stratton.

or brain disease). To qualify as a dissociative disorder, the memory loss must be profound and psychogenic (the result of psychological stress and not as a secondary symptom of a physical disease).

Dissociative Amnesia and Fugue

The media tends to exaggerate the intensity and duration of most amnesia. Most cases of **dissociative amnesia** are of short duration lasting for a few hours or a few days at the most. **Global amnesia** involves the person's entire identity. In some cases, the afflicted person may age regress to (say) five years old and be unable to add two plus two. Dissociative amnesia generally follows extreme anxiety resulting from environmental stress at home, in the military, or as the result of earthquakes, or personal victimization, such as rape.

In the **dissociative fugue state,** the afflicted person not only runs from the memory of who they are, but they also run from their physical home place—where they live and work. They just disappear one day. Sometimes they assume another identity in another location and find a job similar to the one they had before. Most fugue states last only a few hours, but some cases of fugue state have lasted for many years. Strangely, if the person's original memory returns, the memory of what they were doing while they were in the fugue state may be lost.

Dissociative Identity Disorder (DID)
(Formerly Multiple Personality Disorder)

No other subject electrifies a college class more than a discussion of this disorder, which used to be called multiple personality disorder. It first came to the attention of the public in 1957 when two health professionals wrote *The Three Faces of Eve* (Thigpen & Cleckley, 1957). At the end of the book, the authors believed that the three personalities had coalesced into a single overall identity. That did not prove to be true. The woman in question later wrote her own account and revealed that after the original therapy had been terminated with the authors of the book, she developed many more personalities—in fact, 21 different alter identities (Sizemore, 1973). A more recent book, *Sybil,* narrated the sad story of a woman who had been horribly abused—psychologically and sexually—by her own demented mother. Over the course of her early life, she developed sixteen personalities, each quite different from all the others. The remarkable stories of Eve and Sibyl made headlines because at that time it was thought that dissociative identity was so rare as to be "one in a million." However, in the past three decades reported cases of DID have been increasing. It is difficult to make an estimate of the number of DID cases in the general population because diagnosis is so difficult. One estimate puts it at perhaps as high as 1 percent of the population.

Etiology and Treatment

Generally, the victims are unaware of their altered identities. They come into therapy because they know they have lapses of memory. They may have headaches—sometimes severe migraines. They do not understand why they find clothes in their closet they don't remember buying. Or why they find canned goods in their kitchen that they would not ordinarily buy. Or why they have the burns or scratches and cuts they find on their bodies. They come because they are scared. It generally takes many months, generally years, for the *alters* (short for "alter identity") to appear. Why so? The alter identities have been in hiding for so much of the person's life, it generally takes a long time for alters to develop trust in the therapist and to feel "safe" enough to come out of hiding. Are these altered identities really different from each other? Yes, that much we know. They may differ in their memories, in their likes and dislikes, in their attitudes, in their learning ability and knowledge, and in their gender, sexual orientation, age, and rate of speech. Moreover, they may even differ in their autonomic nervous responses (blood pressure, brain rhythms, visual acuity, etc.).

Any explanation of etiology at the present time is strictly hypothetical, but one explanation goes like this. We know that most people afflicted with DID were, like Sybil, victims of terrible physical and sexual abuse. And if that was not terrible enough, the child's response to the brutality brought on more mistreatment. However the child behaved (defying the abuse, screaming, crying, hiding) only increased the abuse. The child thereby learned to exhibit as little emotional reaction as possible. The consequence was that the surface identity develops a very

---

Box 9.5

SCENARIO REVISITED
Shannon and Professor Weitzman

Shannon has knocked on Professor Weitzman's door and opens it when she hears "Come in."

Shannon: I'd like to thank you for helping me. I was able to talk to my Dad. I was kind of nervous to bring it up with him, but Dad felt kind of relieved to know she may have bipolar mood disorder. He said he used to wonder if he had done something to bring on her "crying spells." He says he won't feel so bad now, as he knows he's not to blame. Anyway, he's going to take her to the hospital next time she gets into one of her bad spells.

Professor Weitzman: I suggest that he take her when she gets into one of her depressed states and not when she is in a manic phase. She will be more amenable to going when she is depressed. People who are manic don't believe there is anything wrong. Life is wonderful at those times.

Shannon: That's exactly what Dad is going to do. I've been a little worried about me and the boys. If bipolar mood disorder is genetic, what are the chances of us kids getting it—me and my twin brothers?

Professor Weitzman: I won't say there isn't a chance. But I will say this: The drugs that have been developed go a long way toward ameliorating the symptoms. Today, a person who is afflicted with bipolar mood disorder can live as normally as anyone else, if they continue to take the medication prescribed. The problem is that when they are feeling good, they don't feel a need for the medication and stop taking it . . . and the whole cyclic aspect of the disorder begins again. How old are you now?

Shannon: I'll be nineteen next month. And the boys are sixteen.

Professor Weitzman: Have you ever experienced some kind of serious depression for apparently "no reason" or are you inclined toward hyperactivity?

Shannon: No, never. My dad says I'm the most calm and cheerful person he's ever known—at least when I'm home.

Professor Weitzman: How about hyperactivity?

Shannon: Not really, not like my mother.

Professor Weitzman: Do you have any idea when your mother's symptoms began appearing?

Shannon: Dad says ever since they first went together in high school when she was fifteen. He loved her because she was so lively, but sometimes when they were out on a date, she'd just begin to cry. He always figured that he had said something wrong.

Professor Weitzman: Well, if your mother's symptoms began that early, and you are past that age, you may not have inherited it. But at least you have more understanding and can do something about it if it does appear in yourself or your brothers. What about the other friend you were worried about?

Shannon: Dan? Oh, no, that was just me. When I talked to Dan about it, he said that his tribe talks to the Creator when they have problems. He said before we got to talking, he didn't have anyone to talk to so he talked to his wife. You see, he loved her a lot and he said she had the most wonderful spirit he ever knew. He says our friendship (his and mine) means a lot to him because we talk about what we learn in psychology. He doesn't need to talk to his wife any more. I'm not worried about him any more. So thanks a lot. I think I've got it altogether now.

constricted range of emotions and behaviors to deal with the horror and pain of the abuse. The child escapes conscious awareness of the torture by dissociating from it—she is simply not present through the repeated ordeals.

But we already know that repressed emotions seek to be expressed. The child's repressed emotions coalesce as altered identities. So, for example, denied anger may become an alter that is masculine, aggressive, and maybe even sadistic to others. Or the child who has never been allowed to have toys or to play with other children develops an altered identity that is as spontaneous and playful as a toddler and just as irresponsible. A child who was punished severely for masturbating developed only one alter who could enjoy sex. The alter identities may have full-blown personality characteristics, but they may also simply be "fragments" of behavior. For example, one alter first appeared to the therapist when the patient and therapist were walking across a busy street. When the surprised therapist asked the "alter" for a name, the patient could only reply, "I'm the one who crosses the street." Sure enough, that was the only time this alter ever appeared.

Once the therapist and patient become aware of the alter identities, the presently pre-scribed treatment for DID is hypnosis and/or free association to uncover the repressed memo-ries and thus to catharsize them within the safe climate of the psychotherapeutic situation. Besides hypnotherapy, the psychotherapies that have been found successful are psychodynamic therapy and cognitive therapy. But it is a slow process. The average time of therapeutic involve-ment has been set at about four years, with some cases lasting up to a decade. In terms of med-ication, antidepressants and tranquilizers have been found helpful, not in terms of "curing" the person, but in terms of enabling the person to cope with the confusing situations (Putnam, 1989).

Is a "cure" possible for persons with multiple personalities? It depends on what is meant by "cure." If by "cure" we mean the ultimate consolidation of all the fragmented parts of the per-sonality into one unifying "presentation of self," then we may have to respond with the medical prognosis of "guarded." However, if by "cure" we mean the ability for the afflicted person to be able to function in society and to be financially self-supportive, the answer is—many times—yes.

A Controversial Issue: Recovery of Repressed Material or False Memories? At the present time, there is no more heated psychological debate going on than that dealing with whether some recovered memories are actually fabricated, either intentionally or unintention-ally. So heated has been this issue for the last two decades, sometimes with bitterness on both sides of the controversy, that the American Psychological Association (APA) finally called for a "voice of reason" and a cool-headed investigation, rather than the contentious dialogue often dominated by the televised polemics of accusers and accused and their attorneys. A working com-mittee was created to find some common ground and some suggestions for validating actual recovered memories and for the protection of those falsely accused.

Although it has been acknowledged that repressed memories can emerge in the course of simply getting older or during the therapeutic situation, we need to mention that some recov-ered memories have been empirically substantiated. Others may indeed be false. The abuse may not actually take place but was, perhaps, the consequence of hypnotic or therapeutic sug-gestion. For example, in 1993, Steven Cook, a young man of age 34, filed a lawsuit claiming he had been sexually abused by Cardinal Joseph Bernardin. Later, however, he stated that the memory had been "assisted" under hypnosis, and the case was dismissed. On the other hand, one woman's repressed memory was so clearly described that the police were able to find the body of the woman's childhood playmate, who had been murdered by the woman's own father. This issue has been the source of lawsuits, and the whole issue of false memories has become not just a very "touchy" subject, it has become the grist of legal battles played out in the public media as well as in the courts of law.

The Personality Disorders: Let the Reader Take Warning!

Personality disorders differ from all the other disorders discussed so far in several very significant ways. First of all, people with personality disorders generally do not often recognize there is anything wrong with them. They attribute the discomfort or problems they are suffering to other people or to society-in-general. Second, because they have very little insight into how they are contributing to their own problems, they do not often enter the therapeutic situation voluntarily. Third, they are probably the most problematic personality to work with. Although people with personality disorders may never land in a hospital, they often have a long police record that can include prostitution, drug addiction or drug dealing, eccentric and histrionic and even bizarre behavior, and violent or "white-collar" crime. That leads to the fourth difference—they are the people most likely to cause discomfort, pain, and suffering to others—even more than to themselves.

The incidence of these disorders is quite high. Depending on which disorder we are talking about, the statistics range from between 4 and 15 percent of the adult population (APA, 1994). This means that it is highly probable that the reader will discover that a painful relationship with a relative, a "friend," or a co-worker is because that person has one of the personality disorders described in this section. The *DSM-IV* groups the personality disorders under the three categories called Cluster A, Cluster B, and Cluster C. Cluster A involves disorders characterized as having odd or eccentric behaviors. Cluster B involves disorders characterized as potentially dangerous. Cluster C involves disorders characterized by anxious and fearful bahavior.

Paranoid Personality Disorder (Cluster A)

People with this disorder are characterized by distrust of other people. They have a basic belief that no matter how loyal or friendly or kindly people may appear, they are not to be trusted. This suspiciousness leads to perceiving slights where none were intended; responding with anger at innocent remarks; and holding grudges, sometimes for a lifetime. They are hostile, stubborn, preoccupied with "not being made fools of," and need to be in control of every situation. They may carry the proverbial "chip on their shoulders." If they belong to a church, they may point accusing fingers at other parishioners, and they may even instigate a "split" in the membership by insisting on certain beliefs or actions. If they are jealous of another person, they may engage in anonymous accusatory or obscene phone calls or send poison-pen letters. If they feel threatened by others at work, they may spread vicious lies about them to co-workers and superiors. Generally, other people suspect who is behind these acts, but it may be hard to prove. They can also exhibit dangerous "acting out" behavior, physical aggression and violence, lying, and malicious gossip. We should not overlook the fact that the behaviors exhibited by the paranoid personality arouse anger and retaliation in others, which of course confirms the person's belief that "people are no damn good."

Etiology and Treatment. If the readers think they detect a similarity of these behaviors to paranoid schizophrenia as described on previously, they are right. So what is the difference? Simply this: People who suffer from paranoid personality disorder do not have obvious delusions, hallucinations, and disorders of speech that characterize paranoid schizophrenia. Paranoid personalities are still somewhat in contact with reality although they exhibit major distortions in attributing negative motivations to others. Treatment is extremely difficult with these people. If medication does not avail, then electro-convulsive shock treatment may be required to bring them out of their acute paranoid episodes.

Histrionic Personality Disorder (Cluster B)

These people are characterized by their flamboyant personality styles and attention-seeking behaviors. They often don outlandish clothes and assume theatrical postures or gestures. If female, they may wear sexually enticing costumes. If male, they may don exaggerated "macho" attire and wear dark glasses as if they don't want to be seen, but, of course, the dark glasses succeed in drawing more attention to them. They often give the impression of being larger-than-life in their appearance and emotional expressiveness. They may be movie stars or opera stars who storm off the stage in a temper. They can be athletes who consider themselves the "star" of their particular teams and insist on special treatment. They can be overtly smiling, enthusiastic, and friendly and (sometimes) wonderful to have at a party since they will get things going—and how! Even on short acquaintance, they will call you by terms that indicate intimacy, such as Cutie, Lover, Sweet Thing, etc. But don't be fooled by these terms. They are like movie stars who call everyone "Darling"—even strangers on the street.

Borderline Personality Disorder (Cluster B)

The "border" indicated here is the border line between what can be considered as psychotic or nonpsychotic. The personality structure is so unstable as to be marked by violent moodiness, sudden reversals of emotions, regression to very primitive defense mechanisms, and extreme impulsiveness. Because of their erratic acting-out behaviors, they can be very dangerous at times, pulling knives on people, reaching for broken bottles to bring down on someone's head, or throwing dangerous objects at people. They can be extremely dangerous individuals. The serial killer who murdered five college students in Gainesville, Florida, was diagnosed as a "borderline personality." The woman who picked up men by hitchhiking and then murdered them was also diagnosed the same way. So why are they not considered psychotic? Same answer as before: While their understanding of reality suffers from major distortion, they do not have the obvious psychotic symptoms of hallucinations, delusions, and thought disturbance. Other examples may include the woman who plotted the attack on Nancy Kerrigan, the American medal-winning Olympic ice-skater, and the society woman who killed her husband and his new wife. But their violence can also be directed toward themselves, and they may try to hang themselves when locked up, engage in reckless driving, and attempt to show themselves fearless by reckless acts of self-mutilation. In fact, a high percentage of patients that arrive at the hospital emergency room (particularly after midnight) are either borderline personalities or are the victims of this type of personality disorder (Gibson, 1990).

Etiology and Treatment. Clinical case studies of borderline personalities reveal a marked fear of being abandoned. So striking is this fear that it has led to the hypothesis that disturbed child/parental relationships may be a root cause of many borderline histories. This disturbed relationship may have been an abusive one, but research indicates a high percentage of the physical

Box 9.6 ANTISOCIAL PERSONALITY DISORDERS: ONLY THE "MASK" OF SANITY

Harvey Cleckley (1976), who made it his life work to study antisocial personality disorders, described them as having only the "mask of sanity." While they do not have overt hallucinations, delusions, etc., their mask of sanity covers an extremely aberrant personality patterning. He listed 16 traits that are characteristic of their personality patterning. While Cleckley's work precedes the *DSM-IV*, students are able to identify these personality traits in people they have known.

1. Superficial charm and intelligence
2. Irrational thinking
3. Absence of symptoms of anxiety; smooth and calm exterior, although may be fast-talking
4. Unreliable, does not live up to promises
5. Untruthful, insincere, lives by fabrications, the proverbial "pathological liars"
6. Lack of remorse or shame
7. Antisocial behavior, treats others as "marks"
8. Egocentric, incapable of real caring for others
9. Sex life impersonal, trivial, and casual
10. Poverty of affect/shallowness of emotions
11. Little if any insight into self, blames others for problems
12. Unresponsiveness and lack of responsibility to others in social situations, out to get what they can
13. Alcohol stimulates obscene and other undesirable behaviors
14. Suicide threatened but rarely carried out
15. Poor judgment and failure to learn by experience
16. Failure to follow any organized life plan

On reading the sixteen characteristics of personality disorders listed above, a college student, aged 22 years wrote the following about her ex-boyfriend.

He showed almost all of the characteristics described in Cleckley's list. He abused me verbally. He lied. He cheated on me. He accused me of all the things *he* was doing. He used drugs and got me on them. Then he disappeared for several weeks and left me on my own. Oh, but before he left, he took all the cash he could find in the house, emptied our joint bank account (Boy! What a fool I was not to have my own bank account!). Sex? He was a great woman chaser but Cleckley is right—sex was trivial and shallow. He really didn't make love—just "quick fixes." I tried to leave several times before I finally did but he would, get this, threaten suicide if I left. He'd worm money out of his mother by sweet-talking her. But if he got mad at her for some reason—like when she would say she didn't have any money right then—he'd turn around and tell her how stupid she was and what a slob. I think back about him and wonder how I could have been taken in by him. Grrrrrrrr!

loss of parents. This loss can involve being orphaned, being placed in a foster home, or simply suffering the neglect of noncaring parents (Ludolph et al, 1990). There are also discernible biological differences such as disturbance of sleep patterns, a genetic involvement, and abnormal levels of certain neurotransmitters in the brain.

Therapeutic treatment is difficult with these people because of their ongoing underlying anger and resentment of any kind of authority and because they continue to blame others for their difficulties. If the therapist can manage to walk a very careful line between being a caring person and avoiding the parent role, there is a moderate chance for improvement. Group therapy composed of "like people" has proved to have some beneficial results since the other group members can spot the "blaming game" very quickly and call attention to each others' irrational thinking and behaviors. In contrast to other emotional disorders, therapy with personality disorders may have to involve eliciting an element of guilt and anxiety since they seem to have very little of either. Rapists may be faced with a video of people expressing their hate for the rapist and what it did to them. Child molesters may have to come face-to-face with the victim-survivors who tell them what the molestation did to them. Sometimes, these confrontations develop a minimal "superego" in these people where they had none before. The destructive acts and impulses of borderline personalities peak in their early adult years. If they can survive until their thirties and forties, there is some evidence that they can reach a more stable integration and gain confidence in what they can do—particularly with some therapeutic help.

Narcissistic Personality Disorder (Cluster B)

The most apparent character trait of these personality types is their utter self-absorption, like the Greek character they are named for, Narcissus. In the Greek legend, Narcissus was a beautiful young man who fell in love with his own image in the water and pined away for love of his own reflection. The outstanding characteristics of narcissistic personalities are the (seeming) grandiose opinion they have of themselves, their need for admiration, and their lack of empathy for others. They fantasize about having all the social rewards due gifted people (like themselves), vocational and financial awards, and a privileged status wherever they are. They exaggerate their achievements and talents, and have an arrogant attitude when dealing with friends and acquaintances. Their manipulative skills in getting people to work for them are remarkable. As a consequence, they may actually get a promotion on the backs of other people. For an up-close view of the narcissistic personality, we quote directly now from the *DSM-IV*, (pp. 658–659), while pointing out to the reader that few *DSM-IV* disorders are as graphically described, probably because therapists have found personality disorders so infuriating to work with.

> Individuals with this disorder generally require excessive admiration. This often takes the form of a need for constant attention and admiration. They may expect their arrival to be greeted with great fanfare. They may consciously fish for compliments. They expect to be catered to and are puzzled or furious when this does not happen. For example, they may assume that they do not have to wait in line and that their priorities are so important that others should defer to them. They expect to be given whatever they want no matter what it might mean to others and may overwork [their employees] without regard for the impact on their lives. They tend to form friendships or romantic relationships only if the other person seems likely to advance their purposes or otherwise enhance their self-esteem. They often display snobbish, disdainful, or patronizing attitudes. For example, [they] may complain about a clumsy waiter's "rudeness" or "stupidity" or conclude a medical evaluation with a condescending evaluation of the physician.

Etiology and Treatment.   What causes narcissistic personality disorder? Theories range from loss of parental care to being treated too positively in childhood. Some theorists believe that the super-macho exterior is a cover-up for an extremely low self-esteem underneath, similar to Adler's overcompensation theory. The "too positive" theory receives support from the higher incidence of this disorder among firstborns and only children, whose parents often do treat them as having special talents or intelligence. Unfortunately, when these children go to school, they discover they are not accorded the same reverential treatment they receive at home. Their self-esteem crumbles. They bolster their lagging self-esteem by developing a grandiose exterior "Persona." Another theory is that they are afraid they cannot live up to other people's expectations. They may come from a brilliant family with many outstanding relatives but they feel unable to "follow in their footsteps." So they invent a personality that seems (at least to them) to be also outstanding (Curtis & Cowell, 1993).

Generally, narcissistic personalities do not go voluntarily into the therapeutic situation. Many therapeutic approaches have been used, from confronting their grandiose opinion with a mirror of themselves from family members to a more gentle approach such as Rogerian therapy, where the person can feel safe enough to take off the mask of superiority and reveal the frightened and vulnerable child underneath (Masterson, 1990).

Antisocial Personality Disorder (Cluster B)

Of all the disorders we have discussed, the antisocial personality disorder is the one for which you need to be most on your guard. What characterizes these people is their disregard of the rights of others or for societal norms. Their antisocial behaviors may range from vandalism, to harassing others, to employing tactics to cheat people out of their money, to actual illegal acts such as stealing, physical aggression against others (spouse or child abuse is common), stalking, rape, and even homicide. Their have little if any kind of feeling, respect, or empathy for others. They are sexually exploitive, are often irresponsible as parents, and may do illegal things just to see if they "can get away with it," as if outwitting the forces of law and justice is a game. Other behaviors include impulsivity, irresponsible work behavior, risk-taking "for the fun of it," and drinking-and-driving. They take little if any responsibility for their victims and express no remorse for having hurt them; in fact, they often blame their victims and describe them as "stupid" and that "they had it coming to them."

Etiology and Treatment. Although by definition antisocial personality cannot be labeled as such until the person is 18 years or older, the antisocial characteristics are often evident in childhood. The three main diagnostic behaviors that show up in case studies again and again include 1) a tendency toward physical aggression and bullying; 2) pyromania (a fascination with fire), and 3) cruelty to animals. It is estimated that about 3 percent of men are so diagnosed and 1 percent of women. Again, Reader, this is the person to watch out for in terms of your wallet, your spouse, your daughter, and your entire household. Prognosis is guarded, which means in plain English that it is very difficult to treat these people since they have little insight into themselves and they externalize their problems (blame others). There are some medications which reduce their impulsivity and lower their risk-taking tendencies. Group psychotherapy composed of other antisocial personalities has been used and these groups prove helpful because "you can't con a con" and an individual's glib alibis, lies, and excuses are detected and exposed by the other group members.

Dependent Personality Disorder (Cluster C)

Freud called this the passive-dependent personality because of the seeming inability to make the slightest decision. They have such low self-esteem that they feel helpless without a dominant life mate, friends who protect them, or relatives who act as protective guardians. Like avoidant personalities, they are overly sensitive to criticism and go to great lengths to make themselves likable. But whereas avoidant personalities are afraid of initiating relationships with others, dependent personalities are fearful of being abandoned by others. They seldom disagree with others and look to their mates for decisions about where they will live and other important life decisions. They will do anything, even make "slaves" of themselves, to ensure their protectors or lovers or mates will stay with them. They frequently marry people who become a substitute "mommie" or "daddy" and who controls family life.

Etiology and Treatment. Their case histories reveal common themes. They were either "babied" and "pampered" by an overprotective mother who did not encourage the skills that Erik

Erikson called autonomy and initiative. Or they had authoritarian parents who punished independence. This punishment came by way of actual physical spankings, verbal criticisms, or emotional rejection (Bornstein, 1992). In therapy, these persons will try to transfer their dependency needs onto their therapist. Getting them to acknowledge that their lives are their responsibility is one of the chief aims of the therapeutic situation. The biggest problem, however, is that if passive-dependent people become more independent, their family and their friends may not like to have "the worm turn." This person who was so nice and agreeable and so willing to do things for them may not be so obliging any more. The dependent personality may be accused of becoming an unlikable person—just exactly what the dependent personality is afraid of being. Group therapy helps prevent overdependency on one therapist. Also, the other group members will support the person's attempts to make independent decisions despite the sabotage of the person's family and friends (Gabbard, 1990).

Obsessive-Compulsive Disorder (Cluster C)

Obsessions are thoughts, feelings, ideas, or impulses that repeat and repeat and repeat (get the idea?) in a person's consciousness. If the reader has never had such an experience, just remember when a song ran through your mind over and over and over again and you couldn't get rid of it. **Compulsions** are actions that the person feels driven to repeat and repeat and repeat (got it?). All of us have ritualistic compulsions that allay our anxiety: finger-tapping, foot-wagging, tie-stroking, mustache-twirling, and hair-twirling. Minor obsessions, such as most of us have experienced, are sometimes life-saving, as when we check a second or third time to see if we have turned off the stove or locked all the doors. But when the ritual is repeated many times over to the point of incapacitating the person, it is categorized as an obsessive-compulsive disorder. Freud was the first to describe and diagnose this condition. Frightened of any kind of disorder or the slightest suggestion of dirt or dust, obsessive-compulsive personalities have a nagging drive to dust, vacuum, and clean their homes, offices, cars, etc. One student told us that she may spend up to 20 minutes turning a light switch off and on because she is not sure the switch will remain in the "off" position when she leaves the room. Once she did it so long that her finger got bruised. They have a constant, nagging anxiety that whatever they are doing is not good enough. Nothing must be left to chance. Everything must be arranged carefully to preclude mistakes and inadequacies, even holidays and vacations down to the last minute. This utter lack of spontaneity and nagging doubts deprive them from the everyday joys of living. But nothing they ever do will meet their perfectionist standards. Nor can anyone else live up to their standards. They are often inflexible about what constitutes morality or ethics or values. Their rigidity can also be reflected in their limited ability to express affection. Members of their families describe them as "unloving" or "mean" or "picayune" or "always criticizing."

Etiology and Treatment.   Since obsessive-compulsive personalities believe they are simply doing the best possible job they can, they find it difficult to see what's wrong with their need for cleanliness, orderliness, and incessant attention to detail. What is wrong is that they are driving their family, co-workers, and subordinates "crazy." What is wrong is that their need to go over and over the same material is making them inefficient at work. What is wrong is that there is not much joy, freedom, or creativity in their lives. Drug therapy may help them alleviate their anxieties. Psychotherapy will help them get in touch with their basic feelings of insecurity. Behavior therapy will enable them to take risks. The cognitive therapies are sometimes useful in breaking through their worldview that they must supervise and control everything

---

Box 9.7

SCENARIO
Nothing Is Perfect–Certainly not the *DSM-IV* or Our
Understanding of What Is Normal or Abnormal

Professor Weitzman: It should be understood that this chapter only covered a few of the most common mental disorders of the over 300 disorders described in the *DSM-IV.*

Li Ho: What about all those other disorders we have not covered?

Professor Weitzman: We've covered the most statistically frequent. And remember that many of the disorders listed in the *DSM* are not disorders in themselves. Many are the side effects of physical disease. Let's take substance-related disorders as an example. The side effects of substance abuse can produce symptoms much like the mental disorders we have been studying.

Dan: You mean like alcoholism? When I was drinking heavily, the people who took me to the emergency room said they thought I was crazy. I was hallucinating like mad. I wasn't seeing pink elephants, but I kept telling people to get the insects off me.

Professor Weitzman: Alcohol is a good example. It may be the most serious legal drug. It is implicated in 70 percent of fatal auto accidents, 65 percent of murders, 88 percent of knifings, 65 percent of spouse batteries, 55 percent of violent child abuses, and 60 percent of burglaries, according to a 1970 report by the National Commission on the Causes and Prevention of Violence). And, yes, alcoholism can result in hallucinations, paranoia, and many other mental symptoms. But there are many substances that can have toxic effects, such as nicotine, marijuana and cocaine, and even the medications your physician prescribes.

Martha: Medications!

Professor Weitzman: Why is that so surprising? You all must know somebody who has had an allergic reaction to an antibiotic.

Shannon: Oh, I know what you mean! My brothers and I all came down with flu and the doctor prescribed an antibiotic for all of us. The boys did fine but I had a terrible reaction to it. The doctor had to change my prescription.

Jill Smith: Shannon, I hope you carry a card with that notation. Should you ever be taken to the hospital unconscious, the emergency medical team would need to know that!

Shannon: You mean like diabetic people carry? (*Jill nods.*) I haven't but I will from now on.

Jill Smith: Some people even have a negative reaction to caffeine which means they have to limit their coffee, tea, and cola. Cheese and chocolate and coffee can bring on migraines in some people. And those of you who take over-the-counter diet pills had better check the list of ingredients. Many of these pills contain amphetamines—"uppers." And you can have allergic reactions to one or more of them.

Martha: Gosh! I'm always trying one new diet pill after another.

Professor Weitzman: Back to Eduardo's original question, which had to do with all those "other mental disorders." We have said some of them have their etiology in disease. Other disorders will be discussed in later chapters. Bulimia, for example, will be discussed in the chapter on adolescence. Children with special problems are discussed in the chapter on parenting. Are there any other questions or comments?

Natasha: (*raising her hand timidly*) Professor, this chapter frightened me a little.

Professor Weitzman: How is that?

Natasha: My parents have often told me . . . that there was a time . . . people were often . . . put into mental hospitals . . . if they spoke out against the political leaders . . . Does that ever happen here?

Professor Weitzman: You are talking about what they called "dissident thinking." We have to be on guard against that always. Critics of the *DSM* have pointed out that labeling a person as having a "mental disorder" may actually be the same thing in the end. And that can lead to other abuses. Living in a democracy means that all of us participate by being "watch dogs" of societal institutions.

Martha: I heard that a long time ago if a woman was disagreeable to her husband he could have her put away in a mental institution. Is this true?

Professor Weitzman: It is true, even in our democracy, these types of atrocities occurred at a time when women did not have rights equal to men. Furthermore, individuals with a physical handicap, such as blindness, deafness, or muteness were also sometimes institutionalized under the category of mental retardation. We've come a long way in our classifications, therapies, and theories about what is abnormal and what is normal. And we still need to try to alleviate the stigma associated with mental illness.

and everybody in their environment or things will break down. The "letting go" of control will allow their families more freedom to be spontaneous and expressive with each other and their subordinates to make more independent decisions and escape continual and nagging supervision.

IMPORTANT TERMS AND CONCEPTS TO KNOW

affect	common language	fugue	panic attacks
age-related	delusions	hallucinations	paranoid
alter	depression	histrionic	phobias
amnesia	differential	manic	posttraumatic
anxiety disorders	dissociative identity	mental disorder	*SAD*
bipolar mood	*DSM*	mood elevator	spontaneous
borderline	dysfunctional	narcissistic	therapy
circadian	free-floating	older	tranquilizers

MAKE YOUR OWN CHAPTER SUMMARY BY FILLING IN THE BLANKS BELOW

Use the "Important Terms and Concepts to Know" to fill in the blanks below. Use each term only once.

Frequency of mental disorders. All of us, at one time or another in our lives, will have to deal with abnormal (or _____) behavior, either in ourselves or in someone else. In a 1994 survey, almost half of the American population described symptoms serious enough to qualify as a mental disorder at some time in their lives.

The Diagnostic and Statistical Manual of Mental Disorders, known as the _____ , and now in its fourth edition, has been established as a "_____" for the mental health professions, but categorizing a "mental disorder" is not at all simple and generally depends on _____ diagnosis (diagnosing it through a process of elimination).

Anxiety disorders are differentiated from the anxiety we all feel from time to time in that anxiety disorders incapacitate the person in everyday life. _____ are unreasonable and persistent fears about an object, person, or situation. They are often _____ , since fear of school is common in young children and fear of being mugged on the streets is common in _____ adults. Anxiety that is pervasive and spreads to whatever the person is thinking about is described as _____ anxiety. _____ often imitate physical diseases such as heart attack and asthma. _____ stress disorder is the aftermath of an emotionally shocking experience (such as war, earthquake, rape, etc.) in which the person experiences flashbacks and the accompanying anxiety. Anxiety disorders can often be treated with _____ to reduce anxiety and with psychotherapy to develop coping strategies.

Mood disorders are one of the easiest disorders to treat. In fact, 15 to 30 percent of all cases are alleviated without any specific treatment, which is called _____ remission. _____ disorder was formerly called manic-depressive psychosis. In the _____ phase, the person feels euphoric and has high energy, but unfortunately may engage in such behaviors as running up credit card debt, shoplifting, and bouncing checks. _____ refers to the disorder that results from lack of daylight for too long a period of time, which seems to interrupt our natural _____ rhythms.

The schizophrenias involve positive symptoms which include _____ , which are irrational beliefs and _____ , which are sensory experiences not shared by others in the environment. Negative symptoms include a flattened _____ and lack of an organized life plan.

Dissociative disorders include _____ (repression of all or partial memory) and the _____ state, in which the person not only represses self-identity, but literally runs away from the home environment. What used to be called multiple personality is now called _____ disorder.

Personality disorders do not often enter into _____ voluntarily, since they blame others for their problems. People who have an overall suspiciousness and distrust of others are categorized as _____ personality disorders. The _____ personality is theatrical, seductive, and attention-getting. They use whatever means they have to involve others in the dramatic and ongoing sagas of their lives. _____ personalities can be extremely dangerous because of their acting-out behaviors. The _____ personality is characterized by total self-absorption and grandiose self-esteem.

10 INTERPERSONAL COMMUNICATION
Creating Harmonious and Enduring Relationships at Home, at Work, and at Leisure

T. E. Hall's Proxemics

Over and above what we say to each other in words, there is another dimension of our communication with each other— the dimension called paralanguage. *Paralanguage is composed of our body language: our gestures, our facial expressions, and also the distance at which we talk with other people, called* proxemics, *as illustrated here. If we approach a stranger too closely, they feel offended or even threatened. In this chapter, the reader will discover the many subtleties of this paralanguage and also how to use this nonverbal language to create harmonious communication with others.*

Box 10.1
SCENARIO
Our Multicultural Differences in Communication

As the students file into the classroom, Professor Weitzman is writing the following question on the blackboard.

Who do you have difficulty communicating with?

Professor Weitzman: For starters on today's topic, inter-personal communication, I'm asking for volunteers to respond to the question I've written on the board.

Jill Smith: I'll start. I find it very hard to have a friendly discussion with my mother. Every time I visit her, she starts in criticizing everything I am wearing and immediately I'm in my child-ego state. I get back to my own apartment and I'm utterly ashamed of myself. It only takes 10 minutes and we're bickering!

Alec: Ten minutes! What's your secret! I can't talk to my father for two minutes without us getting into the same old arguments. I know what's coming! He wants to know what crazy new-fangled idea I've learned at school! "Filling your head with all that liberal trash?" I can't stand that man!

Eduardo: Gosh, Professor, I don't find it hard to talk with my family at all. They are always eager to listen to me and find out what I'm learning in school.

Li Ho: I feel a little like Eduardo except for one thing. My Japanese family is holding on to a lot of their tra-

ditions. They think I've become too "Americanized." Don't get me wrong. I love some of their traditions. But when I bring home an American girl who's used to speaking up, they're too polite to say anything but I know they think she's too forward. They want me to bring home nice Japanese girls who are respectful toward their elders and keep quiet.

Jill Smith: They should only speak when spoken to?

Li Ho: Something like that. Not quite as bad though. My family has been living in Hawaii for three generations. Once, though, my family went back to Japan to visit the relatives. I was just a teenager and was used to talking up in school. My father gave me a stern dressing-down once when I talked up without being addressed. That was kind of a shocker. I loved Japan but I was glad to get back to Hawaii.

Martha: Tell me how to communicate with my mother-in-law. We have to go to dinner there every other Sunday, kids and all. (The in-between Sundays we go to my parents.) Everything is so polite and stilted and, of course, that's just when the kids start acting up. Dinners at my parents' house are much different. Rod says it's so chaotic and noisy he can't hear himself think. And it's true. There are usually ten or twelve people for dinner and we argue about everything

227

Box 10.1

under the sun. Wow! Talk about not understanding another culture right here in this country (*class laughter*).

Professor Weitzman: How about you, Dan? We haven't heard from you for quite some time now.

Dan: Native Americans don't do as much talking as the rest of you. It's not like what Li Ho was describing—a matter of respect. I mean we do respect the Elders and all that but it really has more to do with not speaking unless you have something important to say. It's just part of us.

Shannon: I talk with my dad and brothers OK and we get along fine, but outside of my family, I'm so shy I can hardly talk sometimes. Sometimes people think I'm just dumb.

Natasha: I would like to say that at home we get along OK. Sometimes Georgi gets a little . . . I think the word is maybe irri . . . irri . . . ?

Professor Weitzman: Irritable?

Natasha: Yes, irritable, but I understand that. We have no family here but ourselves. He was very much important in the old country because he was automechanic—very good. People have much respect for him. Here he is only custodian at the school. He hurts inside.

Professor Weitzman: Very understandable.

Jonnimae: I used to have wonderful communication with my kids. Now they are teenagers and we are always at each others' throats. Can you help poor single mothers like me learn how to communicate with teenagers who think they know it all? (*class laughter*)

Professor Weitzman: We may have to put that off until the chapter on adolescents. That's a topic all by itself. The chapter you are about to read discusses general principles of communication. But we will be coming back to interpersonal communication in the chapters immediately following on marriage, raising children, and dealing with adolescents. Can you survive till then? (*Class laughter and Jonnimae nods.*)

The "Gift of Language"

Many eons ago, at the very dawn of human consciousness, an event took place. Although there have been a multitude of theories suggested, we simply do not know how this event came about. But however it came about, it changed the course and development of our existence on this planet. This development has been called the "miracle of language." It was a quantum leap of evolution. It enabled our life form to put a name to things, to describe what we see, to remember past events, and to imagine a future better than our present. Without language, we could not pose questions, seek answers, and derive hypotheses. Language enables us to share our fears and our hopes, our joy and our pain, our sadness and happiness. Language made it possible for musicians to compose their love songs, for wise men to write their sacred scriptures, and for leaders to create constitutions. But language is also a two-edged sword. While language allows us to work together for our common good, it can also be used to divide and separate us. It can be used to damn as well as to praise, to curse as well as to heal, to declare war as well as to make peace. In our personal lives, as well, how we use the "gift of language" can help us or hurt us.

People Skills: Essential for Success in Our Life-Careers

Used well, language enables us to get along with others. Used badly, we alienate others and create enemies even when we don't mean to. The skillful use of language is the vital key to making friends, maintaining loving relationships, skillful parenting, and success in our vocational pursuits. So important are people skills that it is considered the number one skill for becoming successful managers—ahead of technical skills and conceptual skills. And what that means in everyday language is that it more important to know how to communicate than having high intelligence or having a long list of academic qualifications (Katz, 1974). In fact, when the top executives of six megacorporations were asked why some managers don't get ahead, the response was overwhelmingly unanimous—poor interpersonal skills (Hymowitz, 1988). The axiom that "most problems are the result of a breakdown in communication" may not be completely true but it does contain a large measure of truth. Estimates vary but perhaps as much as 70 percent of our communications are probably misinterpreted, misunderstood, rejected, or distorted (Harley, 1996).

The secret of long-lasting marriages depends largely on how good the interpersonal communication is within the family grouping. Aside from the issues of violence and abuse, the chief reasons for divorce can be traced—not to sexual and psychological incompatibility—but to deteriorating interpersonal communication (Gottman, Coan, Carrere, & Swanson, 1998; Matthews, Wickrama, & Conger, 1996). Finally, raising children to have high self-esteem and intelligent behavior has largely to do with how we interact with them. How we listen to them, speak to them, and convey nonverbal messages.

People Skills and Your Personality "Type"

Much of our communication style has to do with our personality "type." Type psychology is based on the work of Carl Jung, the Swiss psychiatrist, and two Americans, Isabel Myers and Katharine Briggs (Jung, 1968; Pearman & Fleenor, 1996). Type psychology is based on the assumption that we come into the world with different "types" of personality. It is not our environment that has determined our personality patterning but something innate, inborn. In other words, it is our *nature,* not our *nurture.* College students enjoy assessing themselves through this test because it does not stick you into an "abnormal" category. On the contrary, it provides you with some appreciation of your strengths and natural gifts. What it does also is to provide us with insight into people we have difficulty understanding because their personality "type" is so different from our own. Discovering the way others function naturally will enable us to communicate in ways that will have meaning for them. According to type psychology, there are 16 basic personality types consisting of four dimensions:

Extraversion-Introversion (E-I)
Sensing-Intuition (S-N) (Since the letter "I" is already used for Introversion, "N" is used Intuition.)
Thinking-Feeling (T-F)
Judging-Perceiving (J-P)

It is important to remember that we all have some measure of these eight functions or we couldn't survive. But generally speaking, we favor one function or the other. You may already know on which side of these four dimensions you come down on. If not, check out the descriptions in Box 10.2 to get an idea of your personality "type." Even though we usually are dominant on one side or the other on the four dimensions, it may be that you find yourself a little bit of both. In that case, accept whatever seems to be true of you. In fact, in any case, accept only what you think is true of you.

The Extraversion-Introversion Dimension. Most Americans are familiar now with this first dimension—our orientation in the world and where we get our energy from. **Extraverts** are turned toward society. They get their energy from other people. They find delight in social

Box 10.2

WHICH PERSONALITY "TYPE" ARE YOU?

Read over each of these dimensions and choose which function is the more dominant function. If you can't make a decision on one or the other ends of the dimensions, then consider both function "types" when you are reading through the chapter.

EXTRAVERSION-INTROVERSION DIMENSION

Extraverts

Like variety and action.

Tend to like group tasks and have a good time while doing them.

Good at making people feel at home; good hosts.

Enjoy interruptions by phone or people.

At a social, the more people, the merrier.

Like to have people around; a "party animal."

Communicate freely with others.

Like to work with others on a team project.

Like lots of friends, casual or otherwise.

It's 5:00 PM on Friday. What they like to do is meet some friends for THIF meal or drink.

Introverts

Like peace and quiet.

Prefer work they can work on alone if not all the time, at least some of the time.

Have trouble with names and faces.

Like to work without interruptions on long, complicated jobs.

Must get some private time each day "to think my own thoughts."

Can get "peopled out" easily; prefer home base.

Prefer working independently from others.

Prefer one or two intimate friends to many casual acquaintances.

It's 5:00 PM on Friday. They prefer to go home, kick off their shoes, have a drink while they watch the TV.

THINKING-FEELING DIMENSION

Thinking Types

Prefer logic to emotional reactions.

May unknowingly hurt other people's feelings.

Like organization and logical order.

Like to treat people fairly but firmly.

Tend to be firm-minded and objective about others.

Prefer to discuss issues rather than people.

Able to reprimand or fire people.

Dislike emotional scenes; think people often "over-react."

On trips and vacations, like to plan out ahead of time where they are going, where they will stay, and what they will be doing.

Prefer to think and act in terms of theory and principles.

Feeling Types

Very aware of other people's emotions.

Get enjoyment from pleasing people.

Like harmony; office feuds are very upsetting.

Like to treat people kindly.

Tend to be empathetic with others.

Prefer to discuss people rather than issues.

Dislike telling people unpleasant things.

People often consult them with their problems.

"Facts" don't account for everything; they trust their "gut" reaction.

May have a general idea of where they would like to vacation, but prefer to be able to do something spontaneous from time to time.

SENSING–FEELING DIMENSION

Sensing Types

Dislike thinking up new solutions if old ones "work."

Prefer to stay rooted to reality and known facts.

Intuitive Types

Propose what "could be" rather than "what is."

Like to propose new possibilities.

Box 10.2   WHICH PERSONALITY "TYPE ARE YOU?" (continued)

Sensing Types

Patient with details; aim for "zero mistakes."

Good with tools and constructing physical objects.

Distrust "inspiration" and "hunches"; prefer practical solutions to new ones.

"If it is working, don't change it."

Like to finish a job; value job well-done.

Enjoy learning technical skills.

Think most people do not pay enough attention to the nitty-gritty details.

Like to look their best when they step out of the house, even if just going to the store.

Intuitive Types

Work in bursts of energy and slack times.

Enjoy unsolved, mysterious problems.

Rely on inspiration, hunches, sudden insights.

Ideas come so fast, unable to say where they come from.

"It may work OK, but let's figure out a better way to work it."

Prefer to rough in ideas, let others finish job.

Often make new brilliant discoveries.

Dislike working on nitty-gritty details and prefer working on the "big picture" than on details.

Care more about what they are doing than how they look when they are doing it.

JUDGING-PERCEIVING DIMENSION

Judging

Interested in results of jobs and getting it done.

Sometimes told they need "to look before you leap."

Like action and plenty of it.

In a test, they like to answer as best they can and leave without dawdling over each item.

Dislike people who take "too much" on things.

Like to make decisions quickly and act on them rather than have decisions made by indecision.

Like to do something rather than do nothing.

Good at schedules, timetables, and deadlines. Like to get right on the job and finish ahead of time.

Like making a "to do list" and wasting no time getting items accomplished.

Like closure; enjoy checking things off the "to do list."

Perceiving

Like to take time to mull over a project.

Sometimes told "to hurry and make up your mind."

Prefer a calm atmosphere to too many things at one time.

In test situations, don't like to rush through the test but rather think carefully about each answer. Also like to go back over it even if they are last to leave.

Sometimes feel like people are always trying to rush them.

Tend to procrastinate on finalizing a project and turning it in because new facts may come to light.

Like to keep options open rather than make up mind too soon.

Often finish a project at the very last minute by staying up all night.

Will spend the whole day, if need be, to find the "just right thing" for what they need.

Reflective Writing: What is your personal response to Jung's typology? Does it accord with your understanding of yourself? Where does it seem to fit your personality style? Where does it not seem to fit your personality style? Ask someone who knows you well, if it accords with your personality style?

situations and enjoy people-related tasks. Because they are interested in others, they make delightful hosts, friendly companions, and good committee chairs. Generally speaking, they are adaptable and affable and can get people to work together on projects and tasks with comparative ease. That is why they make such good managers. They can make good counselors and grade school teachers because they like people. However, they have a desire to be liked, so they may pursue popularity and adopt whatever fads are going around. They may vote for

Figure 10.1 Extraversion versus introversion. It's the end of the workweek. Given the opportunity to rest and relax, extraverts would relish the chance to socialize with others. Introverts would probably prefer to read the day's mail, watch TV, or curl up with a good book.

government officials, not because they have truly examined the issues, but because they want to join "the band wagon."

In contrast, **introverts** are turned inward, toward their own thoughts and feelings. They dislike crowds and prefer activities that involve introspective concentration. They are less interested in public opinion than in their own opinions. They are independent in judgment and, when necessary, can be a "minority of one" when everyone else is caving in to popular opinion. They are, therefore, less impressed by status or the material wealth of a person, and they do not judge a book by its cover. Introverts are capable of working on projects that require long, isolated stretches of time. People may sometimes get the impression that they don't have feelings for other people. They do, but they keep their feelings, for the most part, to themselves. However, persons who are *extremely* introverted may be so out-of-touch with other people as to be difficult to get to know and hard to work with. But once they make a friend, they will keep that friendship for life (see Figure 10.1)

The Sensing-Intuition Dimension.   There are two ways of "making sense" of the many events that are taking place from moment to moment—through our senses or by intuition. **Sensing** is using our physical senses to derive information and conclusions about the world we live in. When we walk into a room we observe its size and shape. We make a map "in our heads" when we drive around a city. People with a strong sensing function can remember a route even though they haven't traveled it for years. *Sensors* like to make order out of chaos and enjoy figures and tools that take measurements. They are eminently practical in their approach

Figure 10.2 Sensing versus intuition. The woman is a good sensor. A mistake in a pharmaceutical could be deadly. The composer is playing out the melodic structures within his psyche. He is strong in intuition.

to living-in-the-world. They perform well as engineers, construction foremen, carpenters, bookkeepers, and managers in any area that requires accurate perception of environmental details. They may be good also at remembering names and faces and be able to describe what a person was wearing a day later. They also like to keep order in the world. Their houses tend to be neat, their cars washed, and the lawns manicured nicely. Their clothes are well matched in color and accessories, and somehow they generally manage to keep spotless no matter the temperature or terrain.

The second way to derive understanding about the world is through what is called intuition. **Intuition** is much harder to pin down and define. It is the function that is operating when we do not know how we arrived at the answer or conclusion we came up with. It has been called "a hunch" or a "lucky guess" or even quantum leaps of cognition. Whatever intuition may be (and there are lots of theories), intuitive persons are sometimes capable of such new and creative perception as to astonish others. But strong intuitives are not as sure-footed in the physical world as strong sensors. They can get lost while driving, forget where they've parked their cars, and lose their wallets. The reason for their "absent-mindedness" is that they are often so absorbed in what they are working on "in their heads," they forget to pay attention to what is going on "outside." Sometimes they can come up with ideas that prove impractical or even wildly inaccurate. Nevertheless, when a group of people have a hard time solving a problem, the intuitive person can cut through the "Gordion Knot" with an incisive shortcut or a brand-new concept no one has thought of. Since intuitives cannot detail how they came up with their conclusion or idea, they can drive sensors to distraction. Sensors may accuse intuitives of "not sticking to the facts." Intuitives, on the other hand, may think that sensors "can't see the forest for the trees" and lack imagination (see Figure 10.2).

The Thinking-Feeling Dimension. All of us think, and all of us feel. But most people lean in one direction or another. Strong **thinking types** like facts and figures before coming to a conclusion. They distrust emotion and prefer "logic." They want to evaluate the pros and cons, the plus and minus factors of any situation, and to weigh them all with a cool, level head. They try to account for all the pertinent data and to present it in as clear and objective way as possible. For that reason, they often make excellent executives and administrators. They enjoy research and knowledge for its own sake. If they go into education, they prefer to teach higher grades—high school or college. If they go into medicine, they prefer research to patient care. The limitation in their style is that they do not recognize the nonintellectual aspects of working with people. Unintentionally, they may seem uncaring, if not downright cruel, in their executive style.

By contrast, people who are strong **feeling types** have a genuine regard for the feelings of other people. Furthermore, they can sense a person's feelings even when the person is unable to express concerns and anxieties. For that reason, feeling types make good therapists, counselors, nurses, and physical therapists. They also make good grade school teachers because their hearts go out to the children who are having problems of one sort or another. They are particularly good at reading body language and other nonverbal clues. They are "heart people" and rush to the aid of others in distress. Their limitation is that their feelings can become so overdominant that their feelings can overwhelm them. Parents will say of children that they "don't use their heads" and, as adults, may get so overinvolved with other people's problems that they wear themselves out. Strong Thinkers will say people with a strong feeling function are overly

Figure 10.3 Thinking versus feeling. Strong thinkers are interested in principles and theories. Grade school teachers need to be strong feelers to enhance the child's self-esteem along with academic skills.

sensitive and get their feelings hurt too easily. Strong Feelers will say that strong Thinkers don't consider a person's feelings (see Figure 10.3).

The Judging-Perceiving Dimension. This dimension has to do with how we act upon the conclusion we have drawn from our sensing-intuitive and thinking-feeling processes. Having drawn some conclusions and making decisions, what action do we now take? And how quickly? A popular misconception is that judging means judging others as in stereotyping but that is wrong. Judging refers to the quality and swiftness of the decision-making. Strong **Judgers** will keep their eyes firmly fixed on the target and the target date. If there is a paper due, the strong judger will prepare it well in advance and get it in on time. Strong Judgers are capable of sizing up a situation quickly and accurately, seeming to be able to take in enough details of a situation for swift action. Consequently, they are the type of people that are valued in occupations that need that kind of instant decision making and fast action, such as S.W.A.T. team members, fire-fighters, emergency room attendants, and courtroom attorneys—anywhere immediate action is needed. On the downside, they may jump to conclusions without knowing all the facts, make too-hasty decisions, and leap before they look.

Perceivers like to take their time making decisions and taking action. They want to get all the facts possible. They want to keep their options open and to be very thoughtful before coming to conclusions. They are not as time-conscious as strong Judgers and they dislike being hurried. They are the kind of people you want on a committee when an issue needs to be looked at from many angles before deciding what to do. If they are given one perspective, they will immediately consider the situation from another one, which can be infuriating; but this makes people stop and think about what they are doing. If they are too far extended on the perceiving side, they may postpone making decisions until it is too late to make a conscious choice at all,

Figure 10.4 Judging versus perceiving.
For occupations such as piloting airlines, the person should be strong in the judging (action) function. For an occupation such as building large buildings, the architect needs a strong perceiving function so as to consider the many various factors and possible problems.

and so decisions are made by indecision—by default. Judgers accuse perceivers of never being able to make up their mind. Perceivers say of Judgers that they don't give enough thought before taking action (see Figure 10.4).

As you continue on in this chapter, you will discover how your personality "Type" affects how you interact with other people—what you do well and what you need to become aware of and practice as you develop your "people skills."

The Most Important of the People Skills: The Art of Listening

People who are unsophisticated in the area of interpersonal communication tend to think that improving our "people skills" is a matter of improving our ability to speak. Good oral communication is certainly one of the important "people skills," but it is not the only one. In fact, in studies of effective communication at home or at the office, the most important of all the people skills turns out not to be how good we are at *speaking* but how good we are in *listening* (McKay, Fanning, & Paleg, 1994). Surprised? Most people are. So we shall start our discussion of people skills with listening.

Hearing versus Listening

Would you be surprised to learn that we listen very poorly? *Listening* is not the same as *hearing*. Hearing refers to our sensory ability—how well our hearing mechanisms are working, including the eighth auditory nerve that goes from the inner ear to the brain. Listening is a psychological process (perception): how much actual information we are taking in and how accurately (Whitney, 1998). Our actual hearing can be very good, even very acute, but our ability to understand what people are trying to tell us (our listening skills) can be very poor. Do any of the following complaints sound at all familiar?

Wife:	He listens to everybody at the office and then doesn't hear a thing I'm saying to him.
Father:	My son can hear what I don't want him to hear, but he gets deaf if I give him a chore to do.
Mother:	As soon as my teenager rolls her eyes, I know she's tuning out everything I'm saying to her.
Worker:	We keep telling the "higher-ups" what's wrong down here, but they don't pay any attention to us.
High schooler:	I told my father my math teacher wouldn't accept his method of calculating, but he wouldn't listen to me.
Manager:	I hated firing the guy, but he kept ignoring what the customers were complaining about.

Barriers to Listening. Considering how important it is to listen and to listen well, we need to discover what blocks our ability to listen. Even when two people talking together have no auditory or brain dysfunction, speak the same language, and come from the same general cultural background, chances are they still are not understanding each other completely. You have already come across some barriers to listening in previous chapters, such as poor self-esteem, a bitter worldview, negative self-talk, prejudice, stereotyping, either/or thinking, irrational cognitions, and so on. But when we examine all of these specific **cognitive shortcuts** (the way we group people, events, and objects, so we don't have to take too long to make a decision), we discover that they could all be grouped under the heading of making quick judgments (see Box 10.3). These cognitive shortcuts help us get through the day with its hundreds of events and people. If we had to think about every object and event and every person we encounter in the course of a day, we would hardly be able to function at all. So the ability to make quick judgments enables us to respond to situations in an efficient manner. The other side of the coin, however, is that when we make judgments about people we meet or interact with, we may be erecting a major barrier to good listening. We are judging the person instead of understanding the person.

Carl Rogers: Reflective Listening

When Carl Rogers (1961) taught his counselors, he instructed them like this over and over in many, many ways: Listening is not just sitting back and saying nothing. It is a process by which you give your entire attention to the person. You don't think about something else. You don't let your mind wander. You don't make judgments about what the person is saying. You don't act impatient. You don't fidget. You don't swing your foot or tap your pencil. You don't wait till the person has stopped talking so you can say something. And, most important of all, you don't make judgments about what the person is saying. If you are making a judgment about what a person is saying, you are not listening to the person. You are listening to the thoughts in your head. And most important of all, you don't tell the person what you think is the answer to the problem with statements like the following:

> *I know what you should do. It's as plain as the nose on your face.*
> *I've got the solution to your problem. Here it is . . .*
> *If you'll just listen to me for a minute, I know exactly what your problem is.*

The counselor's job is not to be a parent or a boss but simply someone that will listen empathetically and make it possible for the person to discover his or her own solutions.

Empathy versus Sympathy.   Carl Rogers distinguished *empathy* from *sympathy*. Sympathy is feeling sorry for someone. Empathy is understanding what the person is feeling. To truly understand a person, said Carl Rogers (Rogers, 1970), the counselor must see the world through the person's eyes—just as if you were that person. Once you have gained that perspective, all judgment ceases. You are experiencing the speaker's problem as he or she is experiencing it. You understand the person's dilemma. Rogers spent many years training counselors to listen empathetically. It is not easy to do. In fact, it takes a long time to learn to be the type of counselor who listens well. Listening in this way involves an attitude of listening without judgment. The reason it is so important to listen without judgment is to create a **warm climate of trust** so the person can feel free to say anything without being condemned by you as bad or stupid or crazy or whatever. Rogers called that attitude **unconditional positive regard** and that attitude on your part will be conveyed to the listener. You will maintain eye contact (but not give the person a hard stare). Your expression will be friendly and your body will be relaxed and receptive (you won't have your arms crossed with a scowl on your face). You will nod occasionally to let the person know you understand his or her message (but you won't nod so often it becomes distracting). You may smile if appropriate.

Aren't you allowed to respond at all? Of course you are. In our focus of making sure that you listen well, we have probably given you the impression that you must keep your lips

Box 10.3   TEN BARRIERS TO ACCURATE LISTENING

Given that there is nothing wrong with your hearing itself, the following conditions and cognitions block our ability to listen well.

1. **Poor health or pain.** How much we are able to take in depends often on our health. When we have a headache, for example, our ability to listen is greatly decreased.
2. **Multicultural diversity.** If we have grown up in different cultures or subcultures, another person's accent or gestures may confuse or even irritate us, making it difficult to understand them.
3. **Poor self-esteem.** Poor self-esteem makes us hypersensitive to criticism and blocks our ability to accept compliments.
4. **A bitter worldview.** If we think that people are "no damn good" or that "everybody has his price," we will be unable to believe good things about a person when we hear them.
5. **Negative self-talk.** If we are constantly listening to the "voices in our head" that tell us we are dumb, stupid, clumsy, selfish, etc., we are not going to be able to listen to the voices outside our head that tell us we did a good job or thanks us for being so generous.
6. **Prejudice.** If we have grown up hearing adults speak ill of certain groups, we are not going to be able to listen to members of this group with any degree of open-mindedness.
7. **Stereotyping.** If we take the cognitive shortcut of stereotyping people according to their obvious group membership, we will listen to what they have to say through the filter of the stereotyping shortcut.
8. **Either/or thinking.** If we are in the habit of using either/or thinking, we will fall into the cognitive trap of thinking people are all good guys or bad guys, with a tendency to believe most people are bad and to tune out what they say to us.
9. **Irrational cognitions.** If we believe that we have "to love everybody" and be self-sacrificing, we will be too ready to introject every negative criticism that people level at us—whether it is true of us or not.
10. **Defense mechanisms.** Any of the many defense mechanisms listed in Chapter 6 will prevent us from hearing anything that might bring us anxiety, guilt, shame, etc.

---

zipped tightly shut. Nothing can be further from the truth. You will be responding to the speakers while they are talking to you. Your body language will tell them that you are interested in what they are saying. You may smile and nod your head occasionally. You may intone an utterance, such as "Hhmmmm" or "Unh-hunh" spoken in your most understanding way.

Reflecting, Confirming, Paraphrasing, and Validating. The speaker needs more than your ears. The speaker needs your empathetic support. You can provide that empathetic support in several ways. You can let the person know you understand his or her feelings by **reflecting** what the person has been saying. You may want to **confirm** that you are getting the right picture by asking gentle (not probing) questions or by checking your understanding. Every so often, you may want to summarize what the person has been saying by **paraphrasing.** You may even want to take the final step of **validating** the person's phenomenology; i.e., that how the person is feeling and reasoning sounds appropriate and authentic (see Box 10.4).

Listening for Feelings. One very important aspect of reflective listening is not to pay attention to just the person's verbal utterances. First all, many people find it difficult to talk about what is really bothering them. They may talk all around a subject and avoid what is really bothering them. Even when we communicate well, words are very inadequate for expressing our deepest emotions. Finally, many people try to hide their sad or anxious feelings with a "brave front" even as they are describing a traumatic situation. So we need to listen for more than words. If people find it difficult to express their sad, frightened, angry feelings, these emotions

Box 10.4

FACILITATIVE COMMUNICATION
Reflecting, Confirming, Paraphrasing, and Validating

Reflecting *means repeating back what the person has been saying.* Confirming *means checking out our understanding of what the speaker is saying through gentle (not probing) questions.* Paraphrasing *means summing up the person's dilemma, feelings and thoughts.* Validating *means affirming the person's thoughts and feelings and actions as appropriate and authentic.*

Reflecting
"You're feeling betrayed/forgotten/left out."
"You're saying you're not sure what to do next."
"You're feel the situation is getting desperate."
"What I'm hearing is . . ."

Confirming
"Are you saying that . . . ?"
"Am I understanding you right–you feel . . ."
"I'm not sure what you mean by that."
"Can you give me an example?"

"I think I understand. See if I have it right . . ."
"I'm a little lost. Can you explain that a little more?"

Paraphrasing
"You feel damned if you do, damned if you don't."
"You feel you have to make a decision one way or the other."
"Sounds like everything you've tried hasn't worked."
"Sounds like you want to give it your best shot."
"If I'm understanding you right, ..."

Validating
"Of course I haven't heard it from his (or her) side but it seems to me you've been straightforward and honest about it."
"I don't blame you. I'd feel that way too."
"After all you've been through, I don't blame you for feeling emotionally drained."

may come through the voice quality, which is tense or seems to sound like sobbing. Another way people speak is through their body language. This kind of listening demands observing the person. Are his hands gripping the arms of the chair? Is the person drumming all of her ten fingers nervously? Is she biting her lips?

Your Personality Type and Ability to Listen and Reflect Feelings

Some personality types will have a hard time learning to listen actively. Strong Judgers who are in the fast lane of communication will have a hard time slowing down long enough to listen, and the good active listener needs to be willing to take time to listen. Perceivers have a better chance at being good active listeners since they are not at all in a hurry, but their natural tendency to conjure up alternative perspectives may prevent them from reflecting the person's feelings. Thinkers and Sensors may pay so much attention to the words the person is saying that they miss the feelings underneath the words. Extreme Introverts may be too engrossed in their own thoughts and feelings to pay attention to another person's thoughts and feelings. Who then has a head start in reflective listening? Well, Extraverts enjoy other people and since they gain energy from being with other people, they may well be a good listener. Feelers will pick up other people's feelings easily of course, not just from what they say but from what they don't say. Intuitives may have a head start in perceiving what the real problem actually is—even before the persons themselves. What the Intuitive has to learn to do is not to take the discovery of the problem away from the person. The intuitive person needs to learn patience and not blurt out his/her insights into the person's dilemma.

Gordon Thomas: Active Listening

Rogers' reflective listening was a therapeutic method designed for a one-on-one counseling situation. Nevertheless, psychologists began to adapt Rogers' reflective listening to the world of family life and the business world. Thomas Gordon was one of the first to do so. In order to distinguish his adaptation of Rogers' reflective listening, Gordon called his adaptation **active listening.** Whether dealing with children, students, or employees, Thomas urged those in charge to speak less and listen more. Thomas' three books, *P. E. T.: Parent Effectiveness Training* (1970), *T. E. T.: Teacher Effectiveness Training* (1974), and *L. E. T.: Leadership Effectiveness Training* (1977), became, one after the other, best sellers among the general population. The principles of active listening have been used to train teachers, business leaders, policemen and policewomen, medical teams, athletes, labor-management negotiators, and church leaders to name but a few arenas of society. As well, his books have been translated in every major world language including Chinese and Japanese. Considering how popular this technique has become, it is a vital people skill to become familiar with and to learn to use. Since Gordon began his active listening principles with children, that's where we will begin as well (see Box 10.5). Then we'll see how Gordon adapted it for other situations, such as the business world.

Active Listening with Children: Parent Effectiveness Training (PET). The basic purpose of P. E. T. is to foster facilitative communication between parent and child through the process of "active listening" on the part of the parent. Gordon has two major purposes for what he called "facilitative communication" between parent and child. The first purpose is to foster the child's communication with us. The second purpose may be even more important: He wants adults not to try to solve a child's anxieties and problems. To fully understand these two purposes, Gordon wants us to incorporate the following four principles of facilitative communication.

1. Make the assumption that the child is struggling to discover how to relate to others. The first requirement of Thomas' facilitative communication is to hold onto one basic assumption about a child's behavior, no matter how destructive it seems to be. All children, according to Thomas, are always trying to understand the world around them and to discover a place for themselves. It is difficult enough for an adult to do. It is a Herculean task for a young child. No matter what she does, it sometimes seems to her that she is wrong! If an adult believes that a child is just being "bad" or that he is "just trying to aggravate," he needs to remember the one basic premise of P.E.T.: The child is always trying to adapt to his environment—even if his behaviors seem confusing and destructive to the rest of us.

2. Develop active listening skills. It is not an easy skill to learn and takes the therapist-in-training many years before he is good at it. As parents, it is even more difficult. Instead of listening to children, parents tend to put them off: *I can't pay attention to you now. Can't you see I'm busy?* Instead of making the child wait, give the child your attention NOW if at all possible. He generally needs only a few minutes. In addition to giving the child our full attention, Gordon wants parents to avoid the most common nonfacilitative ways of communicating with children: judging, ordering, directing, reassuring, moralizing, lecturing, advising, distracting, preaching, explaining, scolding, nagging, threatening, shaming, blaming, persuading, disagreeing, criticizing (see Box 10.6). People who look over this list for the first time frequently

Box 10.5

PET
Thomas Gordon's Facilitative Communication

The following are examples of how parents turn off the child's communication.

Megan: I'm never going to play with Chrissie ever again!
Mother: That's silly. Chrissie's your best friend.
Megan: She is not! I hate her!

Since her mother doesn't believe her, Chrissie picks up her marbles and leaves. By denying Chrissie's feelings, her mother has effectively stopped the communication between them.

Father: Hurry up and get in the car, Michael, or you'll be late for school.
Michael: I'm not going! I hate school! I'm not going.
Father: You have to go whether you like it or not! I don't want to hear any more of that nonsense. If you don't get in that car right now, you're asking for it!.

Michael is now in tears. His father has not only been unsympathetic to his feelings, he has told Michael that he has to go back to the place where something has happened to make him feel miserable. Again, the child's ability to express his true feelings has been effectively cut off.

The following are examples of how parents can facilitate communication and foster self-efficacy.

Megan: I'm never going to play with Chrissie ever again.
Mother: You must be pretty angry with Chrissie!
Megan: Yes, I am! She doesn't play fair!
Mother: Oh, she doesn't play fair!
Megan: She cheats.
Mother: And that's not fair.
Megan: And then she always wins.
Mother: It hurts to always lose.
Megan: I don't always lose. Sometimes I win too.
Mother: You both lose and you both win.
Megan: Yeah, she doesn't always win. Sometimes we both win.

Michael: I hate school!
Father: Something must have happened at school to upset you.
Michael: My teacher yelled at the class. And I wasn't doing anything.
Parent: You don't like it when she yells.
Michael: No! I hate it.
Parent: It's hard to be yelled at.
Michael: It's awful. Course, she doesn't always yell. Mostly she's nice.

ask: If parents eliminate all the items in the list, what is left? The reader has probably guessed the answer: *We listen. We listen actively.*

3. Reflect the child's emotional message. When a child expresses some kind of emotion, parents tend to deny them their feelings: *Oh, don't be silly, there's nothing to be afraid of.* Or we scold them: *That's a terrible thing to say.* Or we threaten them: *That's fresh. Say that again and you'll get a spanking.* Or we lecture at them: *You musn't say—it isn't nice.* Or: *It's wrong to feel like that.* These kinds of responses from us inhibit the child from confiding in us. In fact, we just turn him off. *No use trying to tell Mom or Dad. They won't listen to me anyway.* Moreover, we are delivering a very strange message to the child. What we are saying, in effect is: *What you say you are feeling isn't really what you are feeling.* If this message is repeated often enough, the child begins to mistrust what he is feeling which leads the child away from what Rogers called his or her **center-of-growth,** that deep well-spring of feelings, intuitions, and creativity that guides us throughout our lives. (See Box 10.5.)

People become alienated, said Rogers, because as children, they were denied their feelings in the ways we have just described. Rogers wanted us to accept this psychological truth: *Our feelings are our feelings.* We may have mistaken ideas. Or prejudicial thoughts. Or confused perceptions. But *our feelings are not right or wrong*—they just belong to us like our eyesight

Box 10.6

EXAMPLES OF THOMAS GORDON'S NONFACILITATIVE METHODS OF COMMUNICATION

The sentences marked Adult to adult could be Husband to wife; Wife to husband; Roommate to roommate; Friend to friend; or Sibling to sibling, etc.

Ordering, Directing, Commanding:
Parent to child: You'll do what I tell you and not another word.
Supervisor to worker: Don't give me any ifs, ands or buts. Just do what I tell you.
Adult to adult: Get up here when I ask it, damn it!

Warning, Admonishing, Threatening:
Parent to child: You're asking for it! And I'll give it to you!
Supervisor to worker: Well if you don't like it here, you know what you can do.
Adult to adult: One more crying fit like that and you can start looking for another place to live.

Moralizing, Preaching, Imploring:
Parent to child: If I've told you once, I've told you a thousand times . . .
Supervisor to worker: Well, you went off half-cocked so it was bound to happen!
Adult to adult: You want my advice now? I told you what I thought before you got into this!

Advising, Suggesting, Problem-Solving:
Parent to child: I'll tell you what you can do.
Supervisor to worker: My suggestion is . . .
Adult to adult: If you want my advice . . .

Persuading, Lecturing, Arguing:
Parent to child: You don't like Marsha anymore. Why, she's your best friend!
Supervisor to worker: Just cool off and think about it objectively.
Adult to adult: Why don't you think about it from his perspective.

Judging, Criticizing, Disagreeing, Blaming:
Parent to Child: I see you've decided to be naughty today.
Supervisor to Worker: All right! Let's find out who did this!
Adult to adult: Yeah, I know you got taken for a ride, but you went into this with your eyes wide open.

Praising, Agreeing, "Buttering-up":
Parent to child: You didn't win. So what! We think you did the best anyway!
Supervisor to worker: I wouldn't worry about the customer who complained. We all know you.
Adult to adult: Hey, cheer up and smile. You may feel depressed, but you look great!

Name-calling, Ridiculing, Shaming:
Parent to child: You big baby! That's no way to act at your age.
Supervisor to worker: Can't you do anything right today? Do I have to tell you every little thing to do?
Adult to adult: I can't believe you did anything as stupid as that, you nudnik!

Interpreting, Analyzing, Diagnosing:
Parent to child: You're just scared. Everybody is scared the first day.
Supervisor to worker: This is what you've been doing wrong.
Adult to adult: You're oversensitive. You're too thin-skinned is what's wrong with you.

Reassuring, Consoling, Sympathizing:
Parent to child: So you didn't make the team. You will next time.
Supervisor to worker: You're worrying too much. It'll work out just fine.
Adult to adult: You're always nervous when we start out. You'll enjoy yourself once we're there.

Probing, Questioning, Interrogating:
Parent to child: What possessed you to say that?
Supervisor to worker: Where did you ever get the idea this was the way to do it?
Adult to adult: You realize now it was a dumb thing to do but why didn't you realize it then?

Distracting, Diverting, Kidding:
Parent to child: You feel bad now but wait till you see the surprise I brought.
Supervisor to worker: Ah, let it go. Today's Friday and we've got the weekend off.
Adult to adult: Cheer up, Sad Sack! It's too beautiful a day to stay gloomy. Just look at that blue sky.

and our sense of touch. To tell a child that he does not have the feelings he is having is akin to telling him that what he is seeing or tasting is not what he is seeing or tasting. The child begins to become alienated from his center-of-growth (Rogers, 1961). Small wonder the child loses his or her sense of Self. What Gordon wants us to do is not deny the child his or her feelings but to affirm them by making statements that reflect the child's feelings. When the parent does that, the child knows that his parents are listening to him, understanding him, and affirming him. He gains confidence in himself and learns to trust his feelings.

4. Encourage the child's self-efficacy. We want to foster the child's **self-efficacy;** i.e., the child's confidence and ability to solve his or her own problems. Self-efficacy leads to the development of an internal locus-of-control. Admittedly, it is very tempting to try to solve a child's problem. If we try to solve all the child's problems, however, we are not giving the child an opportunity to learn to solve problems. So we do not advise, counsel, explain what to do, or falsely reassure that "it will all work out." If the child learns to solve one problem and then another, the child will develop self-efficacy; i.e., confidence in solving problematic situations. This is the best gift we can give to our children. There will be times, however, when a little assist from an adult is necessary and proper, but whenever possible let's encourage the child "to talk it out" first. When we talk things out with a friendly and empathetic listener, we often find the solution to our problems—adults and children alike.

Making Friends: The Paralanguage of Timing, Rhythm, and Space

All the previous discussion of active listening with children and adults applies also, of course, to making friends and maintaining our relationship with them. In that discussion, we mentioned that active listening requires an attitude of attention that is reflected in our attitude, our nods and gestures, and our entire body language, which is sometimes called *nonverbal communication*. But making and maintaining friendships also involves additional dimensions, which are subsumed under the term **paralanguage.** Paralanguage includes the nonverbal communicators (mentioned previously) such as facial expression and body language, but includes other dimensions as well. These dimensions include such factors as distance between people; territoriality and boundaries; touching, kissing, and embracing; the all-important dimension of timing and rhythm; clothing and other matters of appearance. All of these dimensions are culturally determined and what is thought to be good manners in one ethnic or cultural group may be considered bad manners in another group. The people skill of understanding and using appropriate paralanguage is part of the step-by-step procedure for making friends with others.

Personality "Type" and Friendship Needs

When it comes to the subject of making and keeping friends, we must keep the following fact in mind: Depending on our personality type, we all have different kinds of friendship needs. If we are strong Extraverts, we will like having a lot of friends and make friends easily. We may phone a dozen people a day, party with them, study with them, and interact with them in a number of different projects. Introverts need some time to themselves each day to maintain their emotional health. To be involved with that number of people would wear out a strong Introvert.

Box 10.7 REAL-LIFE EXAMPLES OF SOME PSYCHOLOGICAL "TYPES"

Extravert versus Introvert. Peter Fonda tells a wonderful anecdote about his father, Henry Fonda, and his father's friend, James Stewart—two of Hollywood's superstars. The two men were hobbyists and built miniature trains and planes, etc. Peter Fonda says he remembers the two of them spending whole evenings working on them hardly saying a word to each other. All he could hear were long silences punctuated only by such phrases as "Do you have the screw for this part?" and "I need that piece over there." They were both Introverted types.

Sigmund Freud had hoped that one of his student-colleagues, Carl Jung, would eventually take over the leadership of the International Psychoanalytic Congress as president, but that was not to be for several reasons. One of the chief reasons, explained Jung in his autobiography (1963), was because of the differences in their personality "types." Jung described himself as an Introvert who did not want or seek students and colleagues, whereas Freud was an Extravert who was perfectly capable of leading a group of highly intellectual and educated men and women.

Sensors versus Intuitives. Thomas Edison is a very good example of a strong sensor. He had a remarkable genius for utilizing the elements of our world to create hundreds of inventions, including the electric light and the phonograph. Albert Einstein, on the other hand, left us nothing of a practical nature. As an introvert, he simply gave us a whole new way of looking at the physical universe.

Thinkers versus Feelers. Woodrow Wilson, the twenty-eighth president of the United States, typifies a strong Thinker. He had studied at Princeton and Johns Hopkins University, became first a lawyer, then a university professor, and then president of Princeton University. He was responsible for three amendments to the Constitution, and in true thinking fashion, proposed "fourteen points" for peace, including a League of Nations as part of the Treaty of Versaille after World War I. However, he was not in touch with the American feelings of traditional isolationism, and the Senate rejected this most ardent of his peace policies.

There may have been no more feeling-type president than Abraham Lincoln. Although he was able to reply humorously to any criticism or insult, his biographers always note his great sadness concerning the Civil War. His strong feeling nature led him to propose nonretaliative peaceful policies toward the defeated South. His speeches and writings, such as the Gettysburg Address, reflect his deep feelings for all humankind—a true Feeler.

Strong Extraverts like a lot of friends and are forever involved with arranging group activities: watching a televised football game at someone's house; organizing a festive occasion at work; arranging a block party in the neighborhood. Strong Introverts might even scoff and say that all those people Extraverts call "friends" are really "acquaintances" or "buddies." Introverts prefer to have a few "real friends" with whom one can discuss a wide range of subjects from philosophy to "cabbages and kings" in the peace and quiet of their homes or on a walk in the woods.

Furthermore, we will be more attracted to persons who are more like us than very different from us. Strong Thinkers may be ill-at-ease with people they consider "too emotional" (Feeling types) or "spooky" (Intuitive types), and they will prefer the company of other Thinkers and even Sensors. Thinkers and Sensors share a "problem solving" approach to interpersonal communication. We simply gravitate toward those whom we understand and who are similar to ourselves.

Proxemics: Interpersonal Distance

A well-known dimension of interpersonal communication is the distance at which we communicate. The seminal research of Edward T. Hall (1966) is still the classification we use today for categorizing how close or how far apart we sit and stand when interacting with others:

> **Intimate space, from 0 to 1½ feet.** This is the zone of intimacy, reserved for our most dearly loved persons, generally our families, our sexual partners, and closest friends,

but only at times of intimate situations, many times involving touching, embracing, and kissing.

Personal space, from 1½ to 4 feet. This is the zone of most of our conversations with families and close friends. Interactions here are informal and friendly.

Social space, from 4 to 12 feet. This zone involves most group and working relationships. These interactions can be quite friendly, but leans in the direction of formality.

Public space, from 12 feet and beyond. Interpersonal communication is formal. Some communication can occur toward the 12 foot end but as the distance increases, the amount of interpersonal communication diminishes and becomes a matter of public speaking before an audience. (See the frontispiece to this chapter, p. 227.)

Cultural differences. These spaces vary according to gender, age, size, and cultural affiliation—and yes, personality type again. Children under ten years of age can invade the personal space of strangers without offending them, but if an adult stranger moves into our personal space, our instinct is to back away. Larger people like to have more space around them than smaller people. Women tend to cluster closer together than men. Mediterraneans (Greeks, Arabs, Italians, Hispanics) cluster closer than Nordic types. Japanese and Chinese adults tend to keep respectful distances from even their closest family members (Harris & Moran, 1991). Learn about the cultural context of other ethnic groups. You don't want to startle them with a cultural *faux pas*. To the male gender reading this text: Consider how you would feel if you were embraced by another man. Yet this is part of the friendly paralanguage of the Italians, the French, and the Russians. French officers, by the way, not only shake the hands of soldiers receiving the *croix de guerre* (a very high medal of honor), they also embrace and kiss them on both cheeks. (Ivy & Backlund, 1994).

While Westerners regard eye contact as a sign of friendship and honesty, the Japanese regard it as rude staring. Northern Europeans avoid personal questions until they have gotten to know each other fairly well. Greeks, on the other hand, will ask personal questions upon meeting you as a way of indicating their interest in you. Conventional wisdom in the United States is to avoid discussing politics and religion if we want to establish a friendly relationship. The French will avoid personal questions on first getting to know you, but they find argument over the political situation as a delightful way of establishing a relationship right from the get-go.

It can be seen that how we approach someone we would like to get to know has a lot to do with their cultural background and our ability to time our overtures in accordance to the person's cultural rhythm. Americans generally move in fairly quickly in making friendships. Perhaps we do this because we are living our lives in the fast lane, particularly in the cities where the pace is simply faster. We do everything fast including establishing friendships. Or perhaps it is because we move so often—about 20 perccent of Americans move yearly, many times hundreds or even thousands of miles across this vast country. But other cultures are not so quick to make friendships. Family members are considered the primary source of friendships, and it is not easy to be admitted into their circle of family-and-friendship. A British family may invite the reader to tea but that invitation may not include an invitation for friendship. As they are wont to say: *We open our houses but not our homes to other people.* To be invited to their house for tea is not unusual; to be admitted to their home (their circle of friends) may take months and years. On the other hand, Mediterraneans and Hispanics on this side of the Atlantic tend to be inclusive rather than exclusive. They open both their houses and their homes to strangers and treat them as "family": *Mi casa es su casa* (Alba, 1990).

In terms of personality types, Extraverts and Feelers can both be approached very quickly. But we may offend the sensibilities of introverted types or perceiving types. Introverts only admit a few people into their circle of close friendships, so give them plenty of time as well as space. And never rush Perceivers! They take their time in deciding if they want to make a commitment to another friend. They are well aware that friendships take time and energy, and they weigh the cost-benefits carefully.

Examples of Conversation Openers. Conversation openers then are the slow and gentle way of initiating friendships. Conversation openers may not mean much in terms of information exchange but they serve as subtle but powerful indicators of interest or friendships. They are also an invitation to respond. The following are some examples of conversation openers.

Hi! Were you here yesterday? I'm missing some notes.
Gosh! It's raining again! Is it ever going to stop?
This lecture is so boring, I'm going to sleep.
Is it just me or are you finding it hot in here? I'm stifling.
Do you have the date of the next exam? I left my notebook in the car.
What's happened to all the students in this course? Have a lot dropped out?

It really doesn't much matter what kind of a conversation opener you use, as long as you remember to let it be neutral in tone until the person signals they are ready for the next step. If the person indicates a willingness to respond, then you can take the next steps. In a classroom setting, you can indicate that you are having a hard time settling on a major. If the person responds with any degree of interest, you might want to ask the person what his or her choice of major is. If the person responds to that question, you may want to follow it up with: *How did you decide on that as a major?* Or *You must be pretty good at that. I hear it's a really hard major.* Or, *What do you intend to do after graduation?* Notice that you are showing interest in the person but notice also you are keeping to fairly neutral territory. At this stage of the relationship, you are proceeding slow and easily, testing the water at all times. After two or three such conversation openers, you might just introduce yourself: *By the way, I'm Tony Smith.* Or, *My name is Sally Jefferson.* Don't ask for the other person's name. One of the clues that a relationship is developing is that the person will state his or her name as well. From now on, each small conversational remark is establishing a bond between you. You and the other person are becoming familiar with each other and at ease with each other. In a classroom full of strangers, he or she will look forward to each new exchange with you. Again! Don't rush things. Take your time.

Self-Disclose S-l-o-w-l-y

In 1971, a psychologist by the name of Sydney Jourard wrote a book entitled *The Transparent Self* (1971). In this book, Jourard explained that deep friendships are the result of self-disclosure, and that the more we self-reveal, the more transparent we become. The more transparent we become, the more authentic we are. What Jourard meant by **transparent** was that we should not hide parts of our personality from others. What he was saying went something like this: When we are "an open book" and reveal intimate parts of our life, we engender trust in others and they in turn engage in self-disclosure. Jourard's book caused a sensation and readers by the thousands began to self-reveal. Many times, the self-disclosure did make for openness and trust in others and encouraged their own self-disclosure. But not always. Sometimes the self-disclosure backfired in negative ways. Some people were put off by the information they received so suddenly and so early in the relationship.

Later studies of self-disclosure confirmed that *timing* and *rhythm* is all important. When appropriately used, self-disclosure does engender trust in another person and a willingness to reciprocate. When we are at the initial stages of a relationship, we can disclose low-risk information. When the other person reciprocates, we can then move to disclosing more high-risk information. Finally, as we reach more and more openness and trust with each other, we can disclose our most intimate life-events. But at every level of self-disclosure, it is wise to wait until the other person reciprocates with self-disclosure on his or her part. Men do not find it as easy as women to self-disclose so it will take longer for two men to reach a high level of intimacy Berger & Bradac, 1982).

The Paralanguage of Building and Maintaining Relationships

The sensitive and skillful use of paralanguage is also involved in maintaining relationships. Keeping friendships requires as much attention as establishing them. While some friendships come to a nightmarish end because one or the other feels betrayed, lied to, and "used," most friendships that end have simply faded away from lack of frequent contact (Duck, 1994). One or the other friends may get a change of job so that frequent contact is no longer available. One or the other of the friends may move away or go back to school, which limits the time available for social events. Or the intense pace of our lives has left little room for intimate dialog. In any of these situations, a major facet of maintaining a friendship has to do with how we use the paralanguage of communication. In this very common situation, we utilize a paralanguage technique that has been described as "stroking."

Mutual Stroking.   Some years ago, Eric Berne described what he called "strokes" (1978). "Strokes" are the little verbal or nonverbal interactions between two people which do not seem to contain much cognitive information but which are powerful emotional transmissions. These strokes include smiles, hand greetings, a "Hello" or "Hi," remarks about the weather, and non-questions such as "How are you?" which should be answered with a conventional, "Fine, thanks and you?" These seemingly insignificant remarks are actually sending powerful affirming messages. Berne called them "strokes" and are conversational exchanges that tell each person that the other still acknowledges him as worthy of a greeting. After a few strokes, each person continues on their way. No real news has been exchanged, but the stroking has validated that they are still friends.

Staying in Touch.   Friendships can quite literally simply wear away from disuse when they are not renewed occasionally. If the circumstances of your lives prevents you from frequent contact occasionally, then you need to be very creative in finding ways to keep the relationship alive and nourished. It will take effort to maintain that kind of friendship but friendships which have been growthful for both parties are well worth the effort and creativity it takes to maintain them. As people get older, they often discover that the friends they value the most are those they have known the longest.

One way to maintain a long distance friendship is by phone or writing. At the suggestion of maintaining a correspondence with friends who move away, some readers may groan and say something like: *But I'm no good at writing letters. I hate writing.* At which point, we retort that, in this day-and-age, e-mail technology has changed the way people communicate with each other. For almost the entire twentieth century, literary commentators had been decrying the lost art of letter writing—an endangered people skill on its way to extinction. But correspondence between people has had a resurgence thanks to electronic correspondence. Literally, millions of people worldwide are e-mailing messages to each other. They have discovered they don't have to go in for lengthy letters. Short e-mail notes do just fine. In fact, e-mail is replacing "snail-mail" all over the world. Since the single most important consideration for maintaining relationships is frequent contact, e-mail provides us with the opportunity for doing so. But, since electronic mail is much shorter than letters, it is more difficult to express emotion. Furthermore, e-mail lacks the warm expressiveness of body language and voice quality so that jokes and kidding can be misunderstood. In order to place the words within a context, there has been developed a whole lexicon of **emoticons,** keyboard symbols used to convey emotional subtext (Duck, 1944). (See Box 10.8.) There are also some conventions that need to be adhered to when we use electronic mail. Unless it is an emergency or a real plea for help, SHOUTING, by using capital letters, is considered impolite. Do we need say that off-color language and jokes are prohibited and the person that uses them may find themselves off-line?

When Problems Arise: Setting the Environmental Stage for Conflict Resolution

In all relationships, there are bound to be some occasional squalls. If you believe that there is something amiss in the friendship, ask the other person if the two of you can straighten it out. What we would like you to understand here is how important is the setting you choose in which to iron out your difficulty. Most people choose their home or their office to discuss a problem. We suggest not doing this. The person's home or office is the person's turf and the other person is in the diminished status of being a guest. Choose a neutral environment, where both of you are on an equal footing. And (if possible) choose a friendly environment. You want to keep the discussion of what is wrong in as friendly a manner as you can. If the difficulty seems to be something fairly minor, suggest the friendly atmosphere of a pub or restaurant. This suggestion already communicates a friendly overture. Furthermore, when two people are having drinks or sharing their mealtime in a pleasant environment, such at a public restaurant, they have already made a headstart in conflict resolution. The paracommunication taking place is that you are still good enough friends to eat together.

Box 10.8   ELECTRONIC EMOTICONS

Electronic mail has adopted a short-hand system for indicating the emotional subtext of the written message. Below are some of the more frequent symbols presently in use:

:-)	Smile face	:-&	Tongue-tied	((((0))))	Lots of hugs
:- |)	Smiley with a mustache	:- J	Joking	| -)	Giggle ("hee-hee")
D	Big smile	: P	Sticking out tongue or raspberry	: /	Not funny
;-	Wink	: *	Kiss	> : - <	Angry
:- @	Scream	: ** :	Returning kiss	: - (	Sad
: X	Keeping mouth shut	( )	Hug	:' (	Really sad; crying

Source: Charles Bowen. (January, 1995) *Home PC.* p. 109.

If the problem seems not to be the sort that can be discussed easily during a meal, there are several other settings that are conducive to conflict resolution. Try taking a walk together while talking. Walking involves movement and movement allows us to deal with hurt or angry emotions. Walking also provides the opportunity to be occasionally silent. Sitting together face-to-face while discussing a problem often increases the intensity of an emotional discussion. Silences are embarrassing for many people and they tend to want to fill it with words—and unless we are careful, these words may be negative in content, which only increases the problem. Walking allows the two people the opportunity of talking, and it also allows them to be sometimes silent without embarrassment while they reflect on what has been said and how they would like to respond. Discussing a problem can then be done with much more ease and comfort.

Another idea for a setting is working on a task together. There is nothing like helping a person wash and wax his or her car to "wash and wax" the relationship. Washing and waxing takes considerable effort and the physical exercise involved is another way of draining the negative emotions. Further, the other person cannot help but be appreciative of your willingness to help. The same applies for other jobs such as window washing, grocery shopping, and leaf raking—any job that allows for verbal interchange (mowing the lawn is out). So how do you offer to help? Listen to the person's answer when you suggest discussing the problem. The person may provide you with the very lead you need as in the following interchanges:

You:	I'd really like it if we could take some time to straighten this out.
Friend:	I'd like to but I've got to wash and wax the car this afternoon.
You:	Great! I'll come over and help you, and we can talk while we're washing and waxing your car.

You:	What do you say to discussing the problem?
Friend:	I don't know. I'm so busy right now. I've got to go to the mall to return something.
You:	I've got an errand I'd like to do at the mall myself. How about we meet there? What time do you want to meet?

Finally, one of the friendliest things a person can say when dealing with a problem is "I'm sorry." Those two words, perhaps followed by an explanation has a tremendous healing effect for both parties concerned.

Speaking: A People Skill for Career Success

It was not surprising that educators and teachers and parents began to take seriously to Gordon's facilitative communication. But it came as something of a surprise when megacorporations began to organize leadership effective training (L.E.T.) workshops not only for their front-office managers and line supervisors but also for their top executives. At the beginning of this chapter we noted that, over and over again, top business leaders have named "people skills" as more important than technical skills or academic background. In fact, interpersonal communication has become a nationwide requirement of a degree in business. Call it part of public relations if you want to, but organizations want people who can communicate successfully with customers, with co-workers, with clients, and with executives of other organizations nationally and globally.

To understand the emphasis that business and other organizations (charitable, governmental, political, and religious) are placing on people skills we need to know a little bit about the transformation of organizational philosophy in the twentieth century. Until just after World War II, theories of management had to do with issues of bureaucratic structure: how to get the most out of the workers and how to prevent sitdowns, strikes, and sabotage, etc. For the most part, workers were perceived as people who had to be directed (told what to do) and controlled (by signing in and out on time clocks, by pay-docking for tardiness or excessive absence, and by negative notations in their employee records. Managers issued orders and workers followed them—at least in principle.

Douglas Macgregor: Theory X and Theory Y (and Now Theory Z)

Then in 1960, a man by the name of Douglas Macgregor wrote a book that substantively changed the managerial theories of business organization. Macgregor had once been the president of Antioch College but he was not just a professional educator. He had been associated with the corporate world for many years and was disturbed by the lack of insight that management at every level had into the psychology of their workers. It was his philosophy that workers were a lot more responsible and creative than management gave them credit for. In fact, Macgregor was convinced that the business world was mismanaging most of their workers. He did not believe that the way to get things done was to shout orders, treat workers like mindless robots, and watch them so they didn't stop working—a management style he called the Theory X. It was his belief that the way to achieve the goals and objectives of management was by treating the workers as intelligent human beings who want to work and who are responsible and creative if given the chance. He called his approach to management Theory Y. The title of Macgregor's book was *The Human Side of Enterprise,* and it swept Corporate America like wildfire. Workshops on the new organizational philosophy were organized and literally thousands of business leaders all over the nation were trained in the Macgregor's approach to management (see Box 10.9).

To carry out the new management style of Theory Y, Macgregor knew that organizations had to change the atmosphere of the work place. Carl Rogers (1950) had written about the need to develop a warm climate of trust in the counseling situation. Macgregor now wrote about the need to develop a warm **climate of work.** The manager was no longer to stay locked up in an office

---

Box 10.9

DOUGLAS MACGREGOR
Assumptions of Theory X and Theory Y

Theory X Assumptions
1. Workers are inherently lazy and shun work whenever possible.
2. Workers must be directed, controlled, and motivated by fear of punishment or deprivation to impel them to work as the company requires.
3. Workers have little ambition and work solely for money.
4. Workers cannot be trusted because they avoid responsibility.
5. Workers have little imagination and creativity.

Theory Y Assumptions
1. Work is as natural to human nature as play and rest.
2. Workers do not always need to be directed and control by management; workers can be self-directing and are happy to be given responsibility.
3. Workers want to work in order to fulfill their highest potential.
4. Workers don't avoid responsibility; they seek responsibility.
5. Workers are capable of creativity when given the opportunity.

but to adopt an "open door" policy and make it a friendly place to enter. Punitive managerial policies, such as pay-docking for lateness and the ever-present threat of being fired were replaced with invitations to suggest innovative problem-solving and with some control by the workers over their work situation, encouraging them to participate in the decision-making process.

Macgegor then applied Maslow's **hierarchy of needs** (see Table 1.1) to the work situation. A paycheck provides the basic needs of safety and security. Having co-workers provides people with a sense of belonging. Being able to contribute something valuable to the organization provides for the need of self-esteem. And there is probably no more direct route to self-actualizing, said Macgregor, than through the world of work. Macgregor urged managers not to think of workers as irresponsible employees always looking for ways to avoid working. Think of employees, he wrote, as workers wanting to be useful and productive. Macgregor concluded that people do not always work to live, they also live to work—if we can help them find a work that makes them feel good about themselves.

Eventually, **Theory Z** would be added to Macgregor's theories X and Y (Ouchi, 1981). Theory Z acknowledges that we must continue to have a participative management style for workers. But there will always be some workers (let's call them goldbrickers) that call for a more direct and authoritative approach. So Theory Z is also called a contingency approach to management, meaning the management style we use should be appropriate to the situation. Let it be clearly understood, however, that Theory Z still calls for giving every worker the benefit of every doubt, and wherever and whenever possible treating them with every courtesy and all due respect. And what that means is that not only do we apply all the listening skills we have been discussing but also that we adopt a speaking style that is different from directing, ordering, threatening, etc. We don't treat people as naughty children who have to be scolded. We treat them with dignity and give them every due courtesy. And what that means is that we have to learn a facilitative speaking style.

Adopting a Facilitative Management Speaking Style

Every textbook in organization management opens up with the classic definition of management that goes something as follows: *Management is the process of working with and through others to achieve organizational objectives in an effective manner.* Now what this definition is saying is that your job as manager is to motivate and coordinate the people you work with (notice, please, we didn't say "the people who work *under* you."). In other words, you can't carry out the goals and objectives of your organization by yourself. Your job is to provide the kind of work environment that encourages people to be their most fully functioning and creative. What encourages workers to become fully functioning and creative? Answer: Knowing that they can ask questions, relate problems, make suggestions, and trust you to relate to them more as friend-to-friend than as employer-to-employee, as in the seven guidelines that follow.

1. Be friendly and supportive when you talk with employees. Treat your workers as you would your friends and neighbors. That means you talk with your workers in a comfortable tone of voice even when discussing a problem. You don't get angry or irritated as that will simply close off communication and what you want to do is to facilitate communication. Only in that way, can we discover what has caused problems. You are the model for the rest of the staff. If you speak kindly with them, they will speak kindly to each other. If you are understanding, they will be more understanding with each other. If they understand that you are not "out to get them," they will be less fearful to tell you what you need to know. There is an axiom in organizations that goes like this: *Good news travels up; bad news travels down.* What that means is that workers avoid reporting problems to superiors and are more apt to send up good news to management. That is not what you want to happen. The way to keep small problems from snowballing into big ones is by discovering the small problems as soon as they happen. Employees will come to you faster when problems begin if you establish and maintain a good rapport with them.

2. When problems arise, look first for environmental factors, not people to blame. If there is a problem, don't look immediately for someone to blame. Finding someone to blame may make us feel better but we are probably not getting to the crux of the matter. In Chapter 2, we discussed **attribution bias,** the tendency to attribute problems to people rather than to the situation, generally assigning blame to some negative characteristic of the people involved—their inherent laziness or irresponsibility or whatever. While fundamental attribution bias operates everywhere, nowhere is it so obvious as in the work situation. Managers and supervisors have a tendency to assign the cause of problems to people rather than to external factors (Miller & Lawson, 1989). The truth is that, more often than not, problems are caused by external factors and there are a multitude of them. Inclement weather can delay the delivery of parts. When the reason for the late delivery is investigated, it turns out that the truck overturned on a super-highway (and that happens more frequently than is generally known). An overheated or cold workplace or poor quality air can cause such discomfort among the employees that production suffers. Too much noise in the workplace can interfere with good communication. A machine part may wear out and produce faulty parts. Or a worker is out sick and "the temp" is doing his or her best to do the job, but it is tough sledding and it is no one's fault that the work is slower than usual. And here is an external factor that everyone can appreciate: Computer breakdown! And things just seem to come to a halt until the "tech" arrives.

3. When discussing problems with others, use the pronoun "we" or "us" instead of "you." Whatever we are doing in our position, we are doing it together. When interacting at any level (manager, supervisor, or simply as worker), there is one swift and effective thing you can do to change your speaking style and engender confidence in those who work with you and for you. That one thing is to change your pronouns. Wherever appropriate, stop using the word "you" and replace it with "we" and "us." Adopting the first person, plural pronoun style of speaking immediately conveys to others that you regard problems and successes alike as the result of team work. When a problem arises, instead of saying, "OK, what did you do wrong?" try something like "OK, let's see if we can discover what went wrong." That way the people involved don't have to feel they are going to get blamed for something. They will be much more able to talk freely and undefensively. You are concentrating on the issue, not on someone to blame. (See Box 10.10 for more suggestions for changing pronouns.)

4. Look for win-win solutions to problems. When working out problems with people, avoid win-lose situations. When people come out on the "losing" side, damaged feelings may never get repaired. Start with the assumption that there is no one in the wrong and find solutions in which everyone "wins" at least to some degree. If two people are having a problem working out a difficult situation, help them find a common solution that will satisfy both of them. If department heads are at loggerheads, form an *ad hoc* committee (a temporary committee that exists only until an assigned task is completed) to find a solution that will be beneficial to all concerned.

5. Speak only the truth (as you know it) in the most straightforward way possible. Establish your reputation as a trustworthy person who deals square and fair with everyone to the best of your ability. Nothing will engender more confidence in others than knowing you are not "two-faced." No one wants to deal with somone who says different things to different groups. Duplicity is a sad characteristic of many types of leaders, including governmental leaders. So often did the U.S. government break treaty with Native American nations that one of the sayings of Native Americans became *White men speak with forked tongues*. Don't be known as that type of person. No one will ever trust you again.

Answer people's questions truthfully, in so far as you know what that truth is. Don't be afraid to say something like, "I'm sorry. I don't know the answer to that" or "Your guess is as good as mine" or "That's what the people in the front office told me and that's all I know." That kind of candid and truthful response may surprise people, but they will have trust in what you say when you do have answers. But suppose, for example, that you do have information they would like to have but it is still confidential in nature. Don't lie and say you don't know. Far better would be a reply like this: "I have some information on that but I'm under a pledge of confidentiality. When I am able to tell you, I will do so straightaway."

6. Ask for feedback to make sure your communications are being heard correctly. We have made this point before (in many different ways) but it deserves repeating. No matter how we good we are at communicating, what we say is never completely understood by anyone in exactly the way we intended. Whatever we say (the message we think we are sending) is transmitted through a series of filters that have to do with our gender, our age, our health, our socioeconomic status, our profession, and cultural background, and many other variables as well. These filters will eliminate some of the information we are trying to send, distort other information, and magnify still other parts of the information. Ultimately, we may discover that what the person heard was far different from the message we were trying to convey.

7. And pay attention to your paralanguage. Most people are aware of body language—messages we are communicating with our gestures, postures, and facial expressions. If we sit with our arms crossed with a frown on our face and our jaws clamped tight, we are probably sending a message that we are angry, irritated, disbelieving, insulted, or whatever. On the other hand, if we are facing the person in an open position, with an interested and receptive expression and nodding our head occasionally, we are sending a message that we are pleased to be with

---

Box 10.10   CHANGING THE PRONOUN "YOU" TO "WE" AND "US"

Have someone read the first sentence of each pair of sentences below. Then after a slight pause, have the person read the second sentence. Decide which of the sentences would most likely encourage you to be open and candid in your response.

a. What's your problem?
b. What's our problem?

a. What can you do about it?
b. What can we do about it?

a. How could you have made such a blunder?
b. How could we have made such a blunder?

a. You need to clear up this mess pronto.
b. We need to clear up this mess pronto.

a. How did you discover the mistake?
b. How did we discover the mistake?

a. You'll have to tell the front office fast.
b. We'll have to tell the front office fast.

a. You must have overlooked that part of it.
b. We must have overlooked that part of it.

a. Where did you go wrong?
b. Where did we go wrong?

Box 10.11

SCENARIO
Improving Our Communication

Jill Smith: So that brings us back to our original question: What can we do to improve our communication? Since I am the group facilitator, I'll go first. Before we read the chapter, I talked about my inability to have an adult conversation with my mother. I act like a child—always on the defensive. So what I have to learn to do is to shift out of my child-ego state and get into my adult-ego state.

Alec: That goes for me too, I guess. The minute my father starts talking, I can feel myself getting cold as ice. I know he's going to say something nasty about my so-called "liberal" ways and, sure enough he does and, sure enough, I make some snide remark of my own, and we're off and running. I storm out in my child-ego state.

Martha: Alec, are you aware of your body language? Your fists are clenched and your jaw is jutting out.

Alec: I know! My jaw is so tight it hurts! What is it they call that? TMJ?

Jill Smith: It stands for temporomandibular joint problem. It's a common symptom of tension.

Shannon: (*turning to Dan*) I've seen you clench your fists like Alec just did. That's when I get scared you're going to start fighting.

Jill Smith: Notice how we all get hooked into our child-ego state. It just takes different forms. I feel like a little girl in front of my mother and want to run out of the room so I don't start crying. Alec expects his father to say something he doesn't like and he gets ice-cold with anger. Dan gets hot-angry on the slightest suspicion someone is uttering a prejudicial remark. The symptoms may be different but tearful or angry or ice-cold, we are caught up in child-ego emotions.

Alec: How do you get yourself out of your child-ego anger state anyway?

Jill Smith: Anybody got any ideas?

Li Ho: How about never getting into your child-ego state in the first place?

Alec: That's easy to say but how do you do that?

Shannon: I used to get very nervous around my mother because I knew she didn't like me as much as the twins. She's always been very touchy and I thought it was because of me all these years because of my club foot. Then, after we read the chapter on abnormal psychology, I had a talk with Professor Weitzman and I realized that my mother has bipolar moods. It wasn't always me that made her nervous at all. That helped a lot. So now when I see my Mom looking at me with that awful look on her face, I don't clench up so bad.

I just say, "Hi, Mom, I'm doing the dishes. Is there anything you need?" Sometimes she answers me; sometimes she doesn't. But that doesn't matter. I don't take her sad moods or angry moods so personal anymore.

Jill Smith: Shannon, that's wonderful! You've jumped way ahead of the rest of us.

Martha: We've never heard you speak so much at one time.

Jill Smith: So what is there in what Shannon just said that the rest of us can apply to ourselves? I expect my mother to start criticizing what I wear or what I'm doing—even before I see her. So what happens? My mother sees me acting like a child and immediately she's in her parent-ego state. So I need an attitude change—big time!

Alec: But how do you change your attitude?

Jill Smith: Next time I see my mother, I'm going to say something complimentary before I say anything else. She's a spotless housekeeper. I can tell her how nice the house looks. That should put her in a good mood.

Dan: I know my attitude isn't good. I know I have a tendency to hear prejudice where there isn't any. Shannon is right when she says it's mostly in good fun. (*Looking around the room*) You people have helped me, by the way. You've all been open about yourselves and that's helped me look into myself as well. If someone makes a joke about my being "an Indian" or says "How!" I can go along with the gag, "How, White Man!"

Alec: Yeah, but how do you fight *real* prejudice—like the kind my father has. That's not me just thinking it. He really is!

Dan: I've been thinking about your problem, Alec. You know you're probably never going to change your father. He's what . . . 50 years of age? He grew up in a more prejudiced society than we have now. I'm half in and half out, being younger than him. But you're part of the new generation that is freer of all these prejudices.

Alec: Not exactly. Look at all the hate groups in our country! We still have neo-Nazis parading around big as you please.

Dan: That's a fact all right! But the amount of prejudice is so far less that it was when I was young and when your father was young. Society doesn't change overnight. Just be glad you're part of the new generation.

Alec: What do you want me to do, kiss him?!

Box 10.11	**SCENARIO (continued)** **Improving Our Communication**

Dan: Of course not! Just say something quiet like, "Let's not get into it again, Dad" or "Let's not fight, Dad, let's wash your car instead." He might just go for that.

Alec: It sounds great when you read it in a textbook but how do you know if it works in real life.

Dan: Well, we won't know unless we try, that's for sure.

Jill Smith: And keep trying. And keep trying. If it doesn't work the first time, Alec. If he is still sarcastic, don't feed his prejudice by reacting as you usually do. Just go out and wash his car by yourself. That is sure to reach his heart even if he isn't going to show it. That's all we can do—keep trying.

---

that person and that we are pleased to be engaged in a mutually beneficial dialog. But there is much more to paralanguage than that.

Our paralanguage has to do also with how close we allow people to get to us. Do we keep them at a distance with a desk between us? That puts us in the formal managerial role and the person talking to us in the position of being an employee, perhaps even a suppliant. Or do we come around from behind our desk and sit comfortably with them within what is called the personal distance, between 18 inches to 4 feet? Now we are on more equal footing and conversation will also become more personally equal. Many higher echelon college administrators and chairpersons arrange seating where they and other personnel can sit comfortably side by side or in an L-shaped seating arrangement. King Arthur's Round Table was symbolic of the equal standing of his knights—no one had superior status. Another consideration is whether we make people wait in an outer office before seeing them even when they've made an appointment with us. One of the most demeaning acts we can do to another person is to make them wait for more than 5 to 10 minutes. And it isn't enough to say, "I'm sorry I had to make you wait. I have a deadline on this report." Making someone wait sends a demeaning message that the person does not have enough standing to warrant time courtesy.

Test yourself! We think by now you know the answer to the following situation. If the door to your office is closed and the person who has the scheduled interview knocks on it, will you shout "Come in!" Or will you get up and open the door yourself, welcome the person with a friendly smile and handshake, and issue an invitation to sit down? After reading this chapter, we think you know the answer.

IMPORTANT TERMS AND CONCEPTS TO KNOW

active	hearing	personal	team captain
attribution	introverts	prejudice	thinking
contact	judgment	public	timing
e-mail	language	resolution	win
emoticons	listening	revealment	we
environment	openers	social	X
esteem	paralanguage	self-efficacy	Y
extraverts	people	stereotyping	Z
disclosure			

MAKE YOUR OWN CHAPTER SUMMARY BY FILLING IN THE BLANKS BELOW

Need for people skills. The most frequent reason for the derailment of the careers of managers and executives comes under the heading of _____ skills, which are essential for harmonious relations at home, with friends, and in our place of work. The most important of these skills is _____ , which is different from the sensory process of _____ .

Barriers to good listening include our defending mechanisms, poor health or pain, low self-esteem, and negative self-_____ .

Reflective listening means listening to a person without _____ and repeating the message back to the speaker. Reflective listening also includes body _____ and focused attention. Rogers' reflective listening was translated by Thomas Gordon into what he called _____ listening, to indicate that nonprofessionals were capable of adopting this skill. Parent effectiveness training is learning to use active listening with children and fostering the child's _____ ; i.e., the child's self-confidence in solving problems.

Our needs for friendship varies with our personality style. For example, _____ like many friends whereas _____ prefer a few intimate friends. _____ types prefer people who are not "emotional."

Making friends depends in large measure how we approach the person including being aware of the person's ethnic background, paying attention to the timing and rhythm of our interactions, called _____ . Self-_____ encourages trust in the other person, but we should do so S-L-O-W-L-Y. Different cultures have different comfort levels for interaction, which includes intimate, _____ , and _____ distance. Public distance is reserved for _____ speaking. A gentle approach is achieved with the use of neutral sentences, called conversation _____ .

Conflict _____ can also be aided by the _____ in which we discuss problematic situations. Most friendships that end are caused by simple lack of _____ because of external circumstances such as moving or lack of opportunity for contact. Fortunately, _____ can be used to maintain frequent communication and can go a long way toward maintaining friendships.

Career success depends a lot of how we interact verbally with those we work for. The old-fashioned "boss" has been replaced with the _____ . We need to replace the Theory _____ assumptions of workers with the Theory _____ (and Theory _____ , which is also called a contingency theory). When resolving conflicts, we look for win-_____ solutions. One of the simplest and quickest ways to become a modern manager is by replacing the pronouns "I" and "you" with the pronouns _____ and us.

11 MARRIAGE AND FAMILIES
Learning to Live with Other People

Surviving the winds of social change
Surviving the winds of social change
Surviving the winds of social change
Surviving the winds of social change
Surviving the winds of social change

The S.S. Marriage

Social change has been avalanching upon us. Social upheaval seems to be happening everywhere. In the last hundred years, the structure of family life has altered dramatically. Can modern marriage sustain these winds of change? In this chapter, we take a quick look back at some of the traditional marriage-and-family styles of the past. We then examine some of the trends of family life of the last several decades, and the challenges men and women face today. Finally, we discuss the forging of community-based families and family grouping, living and growing and exploring together new ways of relating to each other in the twenty-first century.

Box 11.1
SCENARIO
A Heated Discussion Over Marriage-and-Family!

Professor Weitzman: How many of you are married or intend to get married? (*Many hands are raised.*) OK, that's almost all of you. Now let me ask you this question: How many think your marriage will end in divorce? (*No hands are raised.*) But we know that at least one out of every two marriages will end in divorce. What makes you think yours will be different?

Eduardo: My parents had a good marriage. I never heard them quarrel. That would mean they were good role models, yes? Now my sister, she has not such a good marriage. Her husband beats her sometimes. I would never do that. I would be like my father.

Professor Weitzman: But your father went to work and your mother stayed at home. Is that what you are expecting from your marriage—you'll work and your wife will stay at home? Yes? Do you plan to have children?

Eduardo: Of course. Lots. I love kids. I want a housefull.

Professor Weitzman: Do you want them to go to college?

Eduardo: Yes, even the girls. I want the best for all of them.

Professor Weitzman: If you want this house full of children to go to college, how will you finance it? At the present time, it costs $500,000 to raise a child and finance him or her through four years of college. Think of it! A half million dollars for each child. Are you going to be able to do all that on your single salary with a house full of kids?

Eduardo: I didn't think of that.

Jonnimae: I'll never get remarried. My father beat my mother and the kids. And then I married young just to get out of the house, I think, and I discovered I had married a man as abusive as my father. I got out and I'm glad I'm not married anymore. Single parenting is hard, let me tell you, but it's better than an abusive husband.

Alec: I don't blame Jonnimae. I never want a marriage like my parents. That wasn't a home I lived in. It was a battleground! I used to ask my mother why she stayed with him. Why didn't they just get a divorce! And you know what she said? She said they were staying together for the sake of us kids!

Natasha: I've been listening to you all and I am . . . surprised! Aren't there any happy marriages in America? When I see American movies, Americans seem to all have happy lives, mostly.

Alec: You mean like the TV sitcoms, where there is this happy little family with perfect parents and almost perfect children. And whatever problems they have get solved in 30 minutes and they live happily ever after. What a joke!

Shannon: I think our family was pretty happy . . . except for Mom. I mean my grandmother and Dad and the twins, we all got along. We just learned to watch out for Mom's moods.

Professor Weitzman: This discussion points up what we are going to be talking about throughout the next few days. Marriage is not a "crib" course. It's probably the most difficult relationship we will ever form.

Box 11.1

SCENARIO (continued)
A Heated Discussion Over Marriage-and-Family!

Jonnimae: But is it really worse now than in times past? With the divorce rate so high, is it really true that our society is in "moral decay?"

Professor Weitzman: That's a good question, Jonnimae. There are two schools of thought on this. Traditionalists call attention to all the problems of modern family life—the high divorce rate, the difficult task of single-parenting, "latch-key" kids, and children being raised with several sets of parents and stepparents. Stepfamilies, which will soon be more common than otherwise, are fraught with problems. On the other hand, nontraditionalists argue that what is really going on today is not moral decay but a renunciation of all the abuses that "traditional marriage" covered up. Several of you right in this class have described physical abuse, and we are discovering just how widespread it is—not just in this country, Natasha, but worldwide. Other types of domestic violence have been unearthed in the last several decades—child abuse, incest, and screaming conflict-ridden homes where the weapon of choice is verbal abuse or worse.

Eduardo: Are you saying we can't go back to the old traditional marriage like my parents had?

Professor Weitzman: We can never turn back the clock. We are living in a different society from that of our grandparents and even from our parents. We can only forge ahead. What is needed is to forge a new type of family, a family that retains traditional values of love and respect and commitment but without the hypocrisies and abuses of previous generations.

Eduardo: But some of these strange new family combinations coming about these days make me sick!

Professor Weitzman: Eduardo, I hope that in a couple of days, you will grasp this one significant fact, that some of these "strange new family" arrangements that repulse you are not new at all, but simply updates of centuries-old love-and-family arrangements in modern dress. An analogy would be some of the movies you young people think are new, but we "oldsters" recognize as "remakes" and "updating" of old movies. But let's see if we can put together some guidelines for creating and maintaining successful family interactions.

Introduction: Despite the High Rate of Divorce, We Still Believe in Love and Marriage

As a society, we give a lot of attention to the "politics" of marriage. The publishing business abounds with books on how to make a success of marriage. Other books offer advice on how to get out of a marriage that isn't working or which may even be abusive. Monthly magazines offer articles in every issue on how to stay young, slim, and attractive to our spouses; how to get into the dating social scene and get married; how to make a stepfamily work, and how to be a working wife-and-parent. Yet, despite all of this expert advice, the divorce rate does not seem to be lessening. When the no-fault divorce laws swept through the state legislatures, the divorce rate took a phenomenal upturn although it seems now to have leveled off to about 50 percent of American marriages—statistics vary according to the sample and the way it is collected. That does not mean that 50 percent of the American adult population has or will be divorced. Keep in mind that some people get married and divorced a number of times, which skews the "head count."

To add to our confusion, during the last several decades we have witnessed extraordinary changes of the social scene with experimental ways of bonding, child-bearing, and living together. We have learned about conception *in vitro* (test-tube babies), open marriage, gay marriage, and single parenting, the increasing numbers of single working mothers, the double income family as a norm, open adoption, adoption by single persons, surrogate mothering for childless couples, and children divorcing their parents. And as if that is not enough, scientists have cloned animals—where will it all end? We are feeling lost and alienated by the onslaught of "the new and novel."

Amid this onslaught of "the new and novel," we are searching desperately to hold onto what was good in "the old and traditional." Traditional marriage is not going out of style, not at all! We may be divorcing in huge numbers but we are marrying and remarrying in even higher numbers (Coleman & Ganon, 1990). We still believe in romantic love, and we still believe in marriage. As of 1998 figures, the Census Bureau reports that 56 percent of all American adults are married and living with their spouses, while only 10 percent are "currently" divorced. So what happened to the other 44 percent of those who got divorced? Well, if they didn't die of some dread disease, they got remarried.

So What Is Going Wrong? Great Expectations, Great Disappointments

What is going wrong may well be that modern men and women have greater expectations from our long-term relationships than ever before in history. We want a life-partner who is not only an ardent lover and faithful spouse and devoted parent, but who is also an astute financial manager, a homework supervisor and athletic coach for our children, an able house and car maintenance engineer, a lively recreational partner, a competent host or hostess, an outstanding cook and . . . (whew!) need we go on? Not only do we want all this from our single life-partner, but we also want that person to be someone with whom we can always be in harmony, with whom we can grow, and with whom we can develop a more creative life style. How can one person live up to so many expectations? Romantic love is too fragile a bark to carry all those expectations and demands. When the realities of living overwhelm two young people just setting out on their voyage of marriage, romantic love capsizes very easily.

Romantic Love versus the Realities of Living. Before we discuss the failure of romantic love, we need some insight as to the nature of romantic love. Romantic love has to do with sexual attraction. It has to do with the arousal of the physical senses. It has to do with the euphoria two people experience when they discover each other. It has to do with the sheer wonder of finding intimate companionship in a world of strangers. Romantic love is so compelling an experience that poets have spent their lives trying to express it in words and song.

But romantic love does not have much to do with the realities of everyday living together. The realities of everyday living have to do with cooking meals and washing clothes day after day. The realities of life have to do with cleaning the house and changing diapers. They have to do with paying bills, fixing plumbing leaks and mowing the lawn, taking care of a sick spouse and ailing children, and conferences with the school when a child is having problems. Reality has to do with the shock of being laid off from a job and not knowing where the next dollar will come from. Reality has to do with those times when an adolescent runs into trouble with the law. Reality has to do with debilitating diseases that occasionally strike down the hardiest family member or an accident that derails a carefully planned future.

Young people do not anticipate these realities when they set sail so optimistically into marriage. The two persons begin to feel inadequate to the problems they are facing, disappointed in each other, and disillusioned by the destruction of their romantic dream. *If love is blind, marriage is an eye-opener*. Damaged self-esteem arouses hostile and destructive defense mechanisms. They blame each other for the problems they are encountering. They may take solace in extramarital affairs or one-night infidelities. If alcohol enters the picture, abuse is also highly likely to enter the picture. The couple may become so alienated from each other that divorce follows quickly. If they do not divorce, the relationship that was once so joyful devitalizes into tiresome routine, or becomes conflict-habituated, or is reduced to a cold atmosphere of strangers living under the same roof (Cholst, 1991).

From Marriage Past: Left-Over Obsolete Traditions and Beliefs about Marriage and the Family

Part of the failure of modern romantic love-and-marriage is that most of us are carrying obsolete and destructive attitudes, behaviors, and expectations left over from the last two centuries—even those of us who think we are most liberated. We begin our present discussion on these outmoded traditions and beliefs with the Victorian Era because we can trace many of our present confusions about what a "man" is (or should be) and what a "woman" is (or should be) from that era. (See Box 11.2 for earlier historical marriage-and-family traditions along with their updates to "modern times").

Victorian Sexual Repression. "Good women" of the Victorian era were often told that sex was a "necessary evil" in order to have children, and they were told to "lie back and do it for England." It was a scandalous announcement for Benjamin Disraeli, prime minister of England, to say (publicly) that his wife was an "angel in church," a "lady on the street," and a "courtesan in bed." Proper British society was hiding some "bare facts"; namely, that the city of London had 100,000 prostitutes and streetwalkers. Why so many? Should a family have "too many mouths to feed," a daughter would be told they could no longer support her. If she did not have a marriage proposal, her only recourse was to become a "working girl." There was no other kind of work available to women without education—except to go into service and those jobs were hard to get. Or suppose a girl did succumb to the attentions of a young man and became pregnant out-of-wedlock, she might be told to "leave this house and never darken these doors again." This **double standard** of sexual behavior for men and women was, not infrequently, demonstrated in another way. There were often illicit relationships of aristocratic men and the female servants of the house. Nor was it unusual for a father to introduce his son to his first sexual experiences by taking him down to a house of prostitution or to an obliging servant in the house (with a generous tip for her courtesies).

Intellectual Debasement of the Victorian Woman. But perhaps even more hurtful than the sexual debasement of the woman was the psychological debasement of the woman. She was frequently treated as if she were a child who must be taken care of, or as a pretty creature incapable of serious thought. While aristocratic men were encouraged to fulfill themselves intellectually, socially, and vocationally, women were not supposed to be too "intellectual" or to engage in too much serious endeavor. They were encouraged to develop any small talent they might have, such as the piano or singing—but never, never to make a career of it. Working outside the home was considered demeaning. In short, the "lady of the house" was a prisoner of her own home and hearth.

If she yearned for some deeper meaning to her life than always making herself attractive, spending endless hours at afternoon teas, and cutting a dazzling figure in her society, there were certain activities she could engage in. She could volunteer a few hours of her time in charitable activities (helping "the poor and needy") (Wiesner, 1993). (See Tip 11.1.)

Updating. This intellectual debasement of the woman has a correlate in today's market place—the sexual harassment that women are still subjected to in the workplace. Not only is such harassment an assault on her sexuality, it is a debasement of her intellectual capability to perform the job she has been hired for. Career women may be subjected to rude sexual jokes and innuendoes when they are in an male-dominated environment. Or there may be scuttlebutt that she was advanced to her position of authority because she "slept her way to it."

The Evolution of a New Breed of People: The American Family

In our early history, first as colonies and then as an independent nation, we developed a different kind of family from what was traditional in Europe. America was settled by many groups seeking religious and political freedom to worship and live according to the dictates of their conscience. They found the freedom they wanted, but they had to wrest their survival out of a wild and forested land. They had come from countries that had been cultivated and farmed for centuries. In the new land they had to ax down trees, to shape logs for cabins to live in, to drag tree roots from the earth and fish the dangerous rock-bound seas. It was backbreaking work. Fierce winters brought illness and death. When spring came late and plantings were delayed, vegetables and fruit were scarce. To prevent starvation, the men had to take to the woods for days and weeks at a time to hunt for rabbit, turkey, venison, and anything else that could be eaten. Sometimes they had to chase Native American War parties for miles in order to save their homes and families from massacres. At these times, their wives and daughters had to become head-of-household, managing the financial affairs of the homestead and business and educating the children. Fortunately, their women folk were equal to these tasks for they were not the women of the Old World. They were not the illiterate peasant women who walked humbly behind their husbands. They were a different breed of woman largely unknown in the history of Western civilization. They had been raised to be literate, intelligent, independent, and assertive.

The Evolution of a New World Personality Style for Women. It may have been the duty of New World fathers to read the Scriptures at family devotions, but it was the duty of New World mothers to teach their children to read the Scriptures. Colonial women had to be literate themselves. This "brave new world" required women who were firm in their convictions,

---

Tip 11.1 On Women in Previous Eras. We must not think that the value system of the Victorian eras was necessarily the mainstream of sex-and-gender throughout the history of Western European civilization. While the peasants of the feudal era were illiterate, many noble ladies were highly educated and owned a library of books. A woman who did not want to be married to a man twice her age (and without most of the teeth in his head) could escape to a religious order where anything was better than being married and reduced to servitude. Other women chose convent life to continue their education for to be in the holy orders often necessitated being educated. The imprisoned Victorian "lady of the house" certainly does not represent women throughout history who worked not only inside the home cooking and washing and cleaning but also out with their men at planting time and harvest time stomping the grapes for wine and the hops for beer. Painters like Pieter Brueghal (c. 1520–1569) have immortalized them in his scenes of the peasantry of France, Italy, Germany, and Holland.

Box 11.2

MANY "NEW" MODERN FAMILY BONDINGS ARE SIMPLY REMAKES OF PREVIOUS HISTORICAL ERAS

Read the following descriptions of previous eras and then note the "updating," which states how these bonding traditions are still with us—although sometimes appearing in modern garb.

Hebrew and Muslim Polygamy. Although the Judeo-Christian tradition holds that a husband and wife should "cleave together" forsaking all others, that tradition was not always followed through the centuries. The Hebrew patriarchs (Abraham, Isaac, and Jacob) might have had one principal wife, but they were also allowed to have *concubines* or even other wives. Even after the Ten Commandments were written down, the Hebrew Kings (Saul, David, and Solomon) continued to have more than one wife and many concubines, sometimes out of ardor but many times as a way of cementing international relations and keeping Israel out of war.

Updating: Harems and concubines still exist today in certain Arab cultures of the Middle East. The *Koran* specifies that a man may have as many as four legal wives provided he can afford them and he treats them all equally (and as any Muslim will testify—that is not an easy thing to do). In our country, polygamy (one man, more than one wife) existed in the Mormon tradition until outlawed by the United States. The existence of concubines occurs most often in those countries whose religious or national laws do not allow for divorce. In Mediterranean countries, a man may hold his marriage as a sacred institution, but he feels free to support one or more mistresses, escort them to night clubs, and have children by them. On Sunday, however, he goes to Mass with his wife and legal children. In our own country, this tradition was prominent among the Mafioso. A Mafia saying goes, *Saturday night for the wife; Friday night for the mistress.*

Greek Bisexuality. At the time of its greatest flowering, Athens was a bisexual society. We admire the remarkable fifth-century B.C. Greeks for their achievements in philosophy, science, math, and the arts, and for their experiments in democracy. But when we take a closer look at the lives of famous Greek philosophers and writers, we discover that their idea of a fully developed, loving relationship was not with women, but with other men. Ideally, the most perfect relationship was between an older, wiser, and more experienced man-of-the-world and a younger man, still physically beautiful but inexperienced in the culture and politics of Athenian society (Kitto, 1950). The relationship between these two was also that of mentor and student. Later, when the relationship dissolved and the younger man became more mature, he in turn took a younger male lover whom he

instructed in the politics and aesthetics of Athenian society. In modern times, homosexuality has come out of the closet only in the last few decades. Before World War II, homosexuals and bisexuals may have stayed hidden but the annals of science, art, literature, the military and the government record these illustrious homosexual personages of history: Alexander the Great, Julius Caesar, Richard the Lion-Hearted, Michelangelo, Walt Whitman, Frederick of Prussia, Peter Tchaikovsky, Virginia Wolfe.

The question has often been raised why Athens became an essentially bisexual society. A plausible answer has been suggested as follows. While Greek men lifted the arts and sciences to extraordinary heights, women (even aristocratic women) were still being kept illiterate and performing menial household tasks. Their essential duties included maintaining the house; surveillance of servants and slaves; overseeing the cooking, baking, and storing of food grown on the land; keeping watch over their herds of sheep and the weaving of wool into fabric; and producing at least one male heir. In fact, Athenian men were living off the labors of their wives and slaves. Historians tell us that Athenian wives must have been rather pathetic creatures, illiterate, treated like chattel, not the kind of person with whom the great Greek philosophers could share ideas about "the good, the true, and the beautiful." If they wanted companionship, these gifted men could only turn to those like themselves, men with whom they could not only share the pleasure of bed but also the pleasures of philosophic and artistic discourse.

Updating: The Greek treatment of their wives is not too different from rural America's adage that the best way to treat women was to keep them "barefoot, pregnant, and in the kitchen." In some Muslim countries today, women are forced to remain within the confines of the house unless accompanied by a man. When they do leave, they must be entirely covered up, including their hair and faces. Reports out of Afghanistan (as of this writing) describe terrible stories of women being stoned to death for any violation of this law. Professional women may no longer work outside the home and some are committing suicide rather than return to a prisoner-like existence.

Roman Marriage and Divorce. If women had a debased status in Greece, it was quite otherwise in Rome. Aristocratic Roman women had an elevated status almost unparalleled in ancient civilizations. Although Roman women could not hold political office or vote, they could inherit land and wealth and were often as highly educated as Roman men. Lavish dinner parties were not just orgies (as Hollywood would have us believe) but occasions by which to share influence and power, and where persons of both sexes could discuss politics, aesthetics, and philosophy. Early Roman society was family-based. Even in the later centuries of the decadent Roman empire when both partners in the marriage engaged in semi-public extramarital affairs, the family was still the basis of Roman society. Although a woman could be divorced by her husband, he could not simply abandon her. Not only did he have to continue to support the legitimate children from this marriage, he had also to provide for his divorced wife's security, household maintenance, and even luxurious life style (Rawson, 1991).

Updating: Divorce laws today still hold that the major income producer (whether it be husband or wife) must support the other partner and provide for the children (as in Roman times). In some circles, extramarital affairs are acceptable as long as they are not too frequent and remain discrete, another value of the Roman times.

Medieval Courtly Love.   During the Middle Ages a rather interesting romantic tradition arose. The young princess, duchess, or countess had little to say about whom she would like to marry. She was first the property of her father and then the property of her husband. In fact, since part of the marriage arrangement was a dowry (a gift of money or territory from the bride's family to the groom's family), the marriage might not be anything more than a financial transaction. Women of noble blood were valued as political assets to be married off to foreign royalty and nobility in order to establish and cement diplomatic relationships. Sometimes a woman was raised from early childhood in the court of her husband-to-be in order to learn the language and etiquette of that country. Other times she might not even see her bridegroom until just before the wedding ceremony. That brief premarital encounter accorded the couple little opportunity for romance. The lord demanded fidelity from her (sometimes with chastity belts) but his *droit de Seigneur* (right of the liege-lord) allowed him the privilege of deflowering the peasant virgins of his lands or raping the wives and daughters of his enemies. Although these marriages occasionally did produce warm attachments, being the "lady of the manor" could not have been a pleasant situation. Medieval castles were cold and damp, unsanitary, and smelly. Nor was the medieval lord a glamorous person. Beneath his elegant robes and glistening knight's armor was a rather unsavory being who seldom bathed, lost his teeth early on, and was illiterate. Even the great Charlemagne, who established one of the first schools

for higher education (c. A.D. 800) could himself neither read nor write. But Charlemagne himself admitted that he had even hung the alphabet over his bed but he could "never get the hang of it" (Bronowski, 1976).

When the lord of the manor was off on hunting trips or making war, his lady led an even harder and more exhausting existence for it was up to her to oversee his huge estates. Her lonely position in life sometimes led to a romantic and lengthy affair of the heart, called *courtly love*. The man involved might be a member of her lord's retinue, a courtier, or a noble of a neighboring estate—someone worthy of her love. The rules of courtly love were intricate. He wooed her with poetry, music, and pleas of despair if she did not favor him with her heart, mind, and body. She, in turn, was supposed to resist him—at least for a time. When she finally gave way to his despair and pleas of love, it had to remain secret at all costs. The real sin of courtly love was not the affair itself but discovery (Hunt, 1959). But keeping an affair secret must have been extremely difficult since the castle had many eyes and ears and few places to hide. When found out, both persons were punished. The story of King Arthur, Queen Guinevere, and Sir Lancelot is an excellent literary example of courtly love. How much of the tradition of courtly love was fact and how much is simply literary myth we cannot say, but it certainly produced some of the loveliest poetry, song, and stories the world has ever known.

Updating: Courtly love as a romantic phenomenon has some obvious modern correlates. Since the medieval man could only view his love and sexual ideal from a distance, his passion for her was of the same nature as that of soldiers in World War II who developed a "love" for their favorite "movie star." The medieval man valued a dropped handkerchief or glove. The World War II soldier valued a "pin-up" of his particular screen idol.

Colonial "Bundling."   For those who believe that premarital exploration is "sinful," we cannot resist describing the Colonial tradition of "bundling," even among the Puritans of New England. Having no heat in the lofts or on the second floor, bedrooms were extremely cold, especially in the harsh winter months. If a man came courting a young maid, the two were allowed "to bundle" together in her bedroom. Generally, a board was laid down in between the two young people with the idea that anything they were able to do together without climbing over the board was permissible. It was a practical way of keeping warm and a delightful way for the young couple to get to know each other, and (presumably) have them happily anticipating the bridal bed. (Stiles, 1992).

Box 11.3 CONTRASTING ATTITUDES AND VALUES OF MEN AND WOMEN

What some men have said of women.

Aristotle (Greece, 384–322 b.c.): Woman may be said to be an inferior man.

New Testament (I Timothy 2:11): Let the women learn in silence with all subjection.

Medieval Proverb: A woman, an ass, and a walnut tree, the more they're beaten, the better they be.

Lord Chesterfield (England, eighteenth century): Women are only children of a larger growth . . . They are to be talked to as below men, and above children.

William Thackeray (England, nineteenth century): There are some meannesses which are too mean even for man. Woman, lovely woman alone, can venture to commit them.

John Knox (Scottish church reformer, sixteenth century): Nature doth paint them further to be weak, frail, impatient, feeble and foolish; and experience hath declared them to be unconstant, variable, cruel, and lacking the spirit of counsel.

Grover Cleveland (U.S. president, 1837–1908): Sensible and responsible women do not want to vote. The relative positions to be assumed by man and woman in the working out of our civilization were assigned long ago by a higher intelligence than ours.

What two women have answered.

Abigail Adams (wife of John Adams, U.S. president, 1744–1818): Highly literate, she wrote to her husband, then drafting the Declaration of Independence:

That your Sex are Naturally Tyrannical is a Truth so thoroughly established as to admit of no dispute, but such of you as wish to be happy willingly give up the harsh title of Master for the more tender and endearing one of Friend. Why then, not put it out of the power of the vicious and the Lawless to use us with cruelty and indignity with impunity. Men of Sense in all Ages abhor those customs which treat us only as the vassals of your Sex. Regard us then as Beings placed by Providence under your protection and in imitation of the Supreme Being make use of that power only for our happiness. *Source:* (http://longman.awl.com/history/primarysource_6_1.html.)

Sojourner Truth: *This emancipated slave gave her famous speech at the 1851 Women's Rights Convention in Akron, Ohio. Several ministers were attending and they were voicing their opinion of the natural superiority of men. One spoke of "superior intellect." Another of the "manhood of Christ." A third spoke of the original sin of "our first mother." Suddenly a woman stood up, Sojourner Truth, who was then at the end of a long and hard life. Several women whispered loudly not to let her speak, but Sojourner Truth marched doggedly to the podium, took off her bonnet with great dignity and gave her famous speech and when she was finished, the women at the convention cheered wildly: From* And Ain't I a Woman: That man over there says that women need to be helped into carriages, and lifted over ditches, and to have the best place everywhere. Nobody helps me to any best place. And ain't I a woman? Look at me! Look at my arm. I have plowed, I have planted, and I have gathered into barns. And no man could head me. And ain't I a woman? I could work as much, and eat as much as a man—when I could get it—and bear the lash as well. And ain't I a woman? I have borne children and seen most of them sold into slavery, and when I cried out with a mother's grief, none but Jesus heard me. And ain't I a woman? (*pointing to another minister*) He talks about this thing in the head . . . intellect . . . What's intellect got to do with women's rights or black folks' rights. If my cup won't hold but a pint and yours holds a quart, wouldn't you be mean not to let me have my little half-measure full?" (*pointing to a third minister*) That little man in black there! He says women can't have as much rights as men 'Cause Christ wasn't a woman . . . Where did your Christ come from? Where did your Christ come from? From God and a Woman! Man had nothing to do with him! . . . If the first woman God ever made was strong enough to turn the world upside down all alone, these women together ought to be able to turn it back and get it right-side up again. And now that they are asking to do it, the men better let them. *Source:* Carleton Mabee, *Sojourner Truth: Slave, Prophet, Legend.* (New York: NYU Press, 1993.)

courageous in trying times, and who had strength of character. The frontier needed women who could do more than tend the hearth. Frontier women had to help clear the wilderness, sometimes with shovel, ax, and plough. When the men were called upon to leave for weeks at a time on scouting parties or on hunting-and-trading trips, they needed women who could manage the homestead intelligently, who could buy and sell products with financial acumen, and who could defend the homestead from raiding parties or the unscrupulous. The New World man needed a New World woman—a true helpmeet. So strong and assertive was the New World woman that Abigail Adams (wife of President John Adams) could entreat him to make laws to free women from the tyranny of men:

> Remember the Ladies and be more generous and favourable to them than your ancestors. Do not put such unlimited power into the hands of the Husbands. Remember all men would be tyrants if they could. If particular care and attention is not paid to the Ladies, we are determined to foment a Rebellion, and will not hold ourselves bound by any Laws in which we have no voice, or Representation.

While Abigail was protesting the tyranny of men, she could not have done so had women of that period not gained a certain amount of stature and equality. So sure is she of herself, she even threatens a woman's revolution.

The Evolution of a New World Personality Style for Men. The men of the New World were also developing a different personality style. The Old World with its class society had bred obsequiousness among working-class men and an intricate formality among upper-class men. Old World youngsters were taught to bow to their elders and "to be seen and not heard." But the New World settlers did not have time (or desire) for either obsequious manners or ritualized formality. New World men addressed each other by first names or as "Brother." They addressed neighbor women by their first names preceded by a respectful "Sister" or "Mistress." "Good day, Sister Prudence." Or, "You're up bright and early, Mistress Rachel." When a Frenchman by the name of Alexis deTocqueville (1830) came over here to see what kind of people the New World was producing, he was amazed by the informality and friendliness of everybody (see Box 11.4). In fact, the American family was based, not on class distinction and power, but on a community of equality and cooperation. It was a family style in which every adult—even the hired hands—had a say in the management of the homestead. While we are extolling the early American settlers, however, we must be careful not to over-romanticize them. There were deep pockets of prejudice, intolerance, and superstition even in the New World. The Salem witch hunts testify all too well to that. But the ideals of "town hall democracy" were reflected in community-based family life.

Marriage Present: The Exhausted Nuclear Family

How then did we lose this sense of community within the family? Why are so many modern marriages ending in alienation, conflict, and divorce? Why can't we end the "war of the sexes"? These questions have been the earnest study of many social scientists, and they have identified a myriad of causal factors. They point out that we are still trailing obsolete and destructive traditions of interpersonal relating based on power and dominance. They point to our increasing anxiety to survive and to achieve in our complex and competitive society. They point to the pressure of continually needing to update our technical skills. And, in particular, they point to the pressures

Box 11. 4   ALEXIS deTOCQUEVILLE DESCRIBES THE NEW WORLD FAMILY

Alexis deTocqueville was a remarkable Frenchman who came over here in the early part of the nineteenth century to observe what kind of people the "American experiment" in democracy was producing. He was doing what anthropologists do today—travel the globe to study other cultures. DeTocqueville was studying the people of the New World. His travels led him from Canada to Florida and from the Eastern Seaboard to the frontiers of the Mississippi, after which he returned to France and wrote his amazing treatise on the American character, entitled *Democracy in America.* He had lots to say about Americans, and it was not all complimentary. Some of what he had to say, however, was quite glowing.

He described North Americans as the friendliest peoples he had ever come across. He noted how everyone called each other by their first names: husbands and wives; parents and children, employers and employees,

even village acquaintances to each other. He found that remarkable. He commented on the warm-hearted hospitality that he (a stranger from overseas) received from everyone he met. He was also deeply impressed by how educated everyone seemed to be, even humble hired hands could read the Bible or the works of such poets as Bobby Burns. And he was particularly impressed by the women he met.

When asked to what the prosperity and growing strength of the American people ought mainly to be attributed, he replied without hesitation, "The superiority of their women." In contrast to the women of his country, he described them as literate, educated, and assertive. His description of the New World woman was a radical departure from the European tradition that a woman is to be from her house three times: When she is christened, married, and buried.

of the modern nuclear family. In order to understand the problems of the modern nuclear family, we need a bird's-eye view of what came before our modern urban family; namely, the extended rural family (see Figure 11.1).

The Rural Extended Family. The community-based rural family, with its extended family, was a physically supportive environment. In addition to Mom and Pop and the children, the extended rural family might also include one or both grandparents, widowed Uncle Will, young orphaned Cousin Hester, and maybe a "hired hand." There was a sense of community to these family groupings. The housekeeping tasks, the farm tasks, and the tasks of child raising were shared among the several adult members of the extended family. We hope that no one believes the extended rural family lived in idyllic harmony as portrayed in a Norman Rockwell magazine cover. There will always be some dissension among a group of people living in close proximity over a long period of time. And the more people that live together, the more issues there will be to argue over. But at least there were people to share the tasks and responsibilities. If Mom fell ill, Grandmother could take over the cooking and Cousin Hester, though young, was a built-in baby sitter. If Father hurt his back, Uncle Will or Grandfather could take over farm chores, and even the women could help out.

Role Overload of Today's Exhausted Parents

In moving away from the rural homestead and into the city and then into the suburbs, the extended rural family became a **nuclear family** (two generations composed of parents and children). While the urban nuclear family was advantageous in terms of privacy, more income opportunities, and better schooling for the children, the nuclear family also contained some inherent problems. One of the most difficult problems of the nuclear family is the sheer number

Figure 11.1 The multiroles of the modern nuclear family.

of roles each partner has to play—which is exhausting them. By contrast, the rural extended family (more than two generations living under one roof) provided both physical, emotional, and social support for all members of the family.

Consider now the nuclear family composed only of one generation of adults. They are having to play a multitude of roles, some of which were shared by others in the extended family. So when Mother falls ill with the flu, she can expect very little help with the children or household tasks. Her husband can't afford to take off more than a day or two from his job to help out. Too often the grandparents live too far away to come and help her or are themselves working at full-time jobs. Even when she is well and working at top efficiency, she finds herself a combination housekeeper, cook, chauffeur, nurse, bookkeeper, homework supervisor, and coordinator between home and school (Steinberg & Silverberg, 1987). If she is a full-time working mother or a single working mother, her problems are increased many times over.

The Plight of the Modern Husband-and-Father. Consider also the plight of the modern husband/father. He finds himself working a full-time job and maybe "moonlighting" as well. When he is not working, he may have to take more courses or attend conferences on the weekends, coach his son for his Little League participation, become the house maintenance engineer, and "pick up" a few things on the way home from work. He has to acquire the skills of plumber, carpenter, electrician, garage mechanic, mason, gardener, and roofing expert. Modern life has not allowed us to have more leisure. What modern life has done is to raise our desire for a higher and higher standard of living which in turn demands that we work as much at home as we do at our jobs. We are overwhelmed by the number of roles we have to play and the number of skills we have to learn. In working conferences of the 1980s and 1990s, the one overwhelming problem employers and employees alike talk about is being overworked to the point of continual fatigue (Davidson, 1995).

While women are now working in greater and greater numbers to supplement our desire for a higher standard of living, men have lost that sense of belonging to the home place. As we have divided up the gender roles of our modern society, it seems to the man that his work place is his domain and the home place is her domain. She buys the things for the house. She is in charge of the food. Even if father and children have a good relationship, they run to Mom when they are hurt or scared or need help with something. She tells him what they need in the way of house needs or children needs or the needs of family and friends. She has become the social chairperson and has control of their visiting schedules. She pays the bills and controls the cash flow. His sense of powerlessness makes him feel like "a wimp." At work he feels competent. At home, he is not sure of himself and what his role is. In short, the "man of the house" has been replaced by a "lost soul" (Bly, 1992).

The Plight of the Modern "Super Mom." From her point-of-view, he has turned over the responsibility of the house to her completely, and she is overwhelmed by the number of things she has to do: the shopping, the cooking, the meal planning, seeing to it that the kids take baths and are clean when they go to school, supervising their home work, trying to keep the house clean, worrying about who needs what in the way of clothes or other supplies and how to balance the budget. It isn't so much that any one job is too much but put them all together and there is not enough time in the day or energy to do everything she is "supposed to do." She too is exhausted. She feels that she gives and gives and gives and gets less and less in return. Even when she asks him to do something simple, such as take the garbage out or fix the living room lamp, he gets resentful of it.

The Stresses and Strains of Modern Parenting

There is a centuries-old tradition that the more children that are produced, the more advantages to the family—and the more marital satisfaction. This may have been true of previous traditional societies when children were an economic advantage. Children were free labor. They were also deemed to be the staffs who would care for an aging parent. In an agrarian economy, children can help with the planting, weeding, and harvesting, etc. The situation today is quite reversed. Studies of marital satisfaction actually show a reduction in happiness with every child that comes along. Why so? The reasons include the additional financial responsibilities each additional child requires, the draining of energy with every child that comes along, and the longer period of time required to take care of them.

Huge Demands on Our Time and Energy. We want our children to have "every advantage," and we devote our time, our energies, and our financial resources to that end. We urge our children to go on for further education after high school and further education means additional financial support of them. Moreover, all those music, dance, and swimming lessons cost money. So do athletic uniforms and band uniforms and cheerleading uniforms. The more we want for our children, the more it costs. If a child with a debilitating disease needs extended medical help, only a portion of it will be paid by insurance benefits. We can afford this kind of physical and emotional energy with one or two children. By the time the third and fourth child come along, our energies (both financial and emotional) are exhausted. As children come, one by one, and grow into their teens, the sad truth is that marital satisfaction declines—shown in study after study over the last 50 years (see Figure 11.2).

Financial Stress. The research data in this area are unequivocal. Financial security and adequate income are basic indicators of marital success. It is more truth than poetry that when bills fly in the window, loves flies out. When credit card balances climb and debts pile up, the normal stresses and strains of married life are compounded by anxiety and despair. Small tensions become large ones. Quarrels about how to spend the available money and accusations about each other's wastefulness become hot and explosive. She may vent her anger and despair on her husband with unjustified accusations that he is an inadequate breadwinner. His feelings of inadequacy and failure may lead to drinking or a night out to "have a little fun." That "fun" may involve other women who seem to restore in him his sense of adequacy and masculinity. The drinking may result in abuse of wife and children (Gelles & Straus, 1989).

Lack of Privacy and Quality Time. Because we want to give our children "every possible advantage," American parents have become chauffeurs to band practice, play

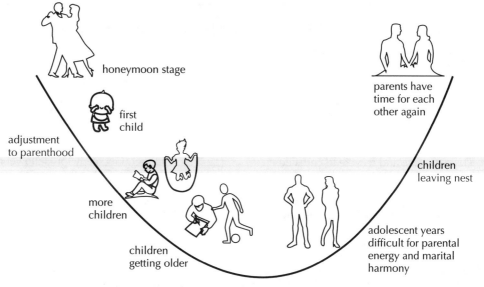

Figure 11.2 The Life Cycle of Marital Satisfaction

practice, athletic games, boy and girl clubs. We attend teacher conferences and PTA meetings. We squire them to their doctor appointments, dentist appointments, to their music lessons or gymnastic lessons. We are on the run to do whatever we can for them. But all that running, all those errands, all that quality time we make for our children means less time we have to spend with our life-partner. If the catch phrase for parenting in the 1970s and 1980s was quality time with our children, the catch phrase for the present decade might need to be quality time with every member of our family, and that includes our Significant Other. Moments of intimacy between two persons cannot be expressed when other people are in the immediate vicinity. Maintaining the glow of intimacy requires privacy—without friends, without relatives, without business associates, and without children present. (There is nothing like two parents wanting some intimate time and privacy to themselves in their bedroom only to have children bang on the door: "What are you doing in there? Can we come in?") Privacy and quality time was what the two people who fell in love valued most dearly. The problem is that the older we grow and the more responsibilities we take on, the harder it is to find that kind of time and intimacy (see Box 11.6). Maintaining intimacy is vital for long-term, enduring love and marriage. Guidelines for maintaining intimacy are discussed later in this chapter.

Domestic Violence

The statistics on reported domestic violence is shocking. Statistics indicate that the spouse murder rate in this country is the fifth highest in the world, ten times higher than in England and 25 times higher than in Spain (Wallach, 1995). Our most recent information indicates that one out of eight husbands is physically aggressive at least once toward his wife each year. Think of it! In 12 percent of marriages, a woman has been physically assaulted by the very man who once declared his love for her and promised to cherish her (see Table 11.1). People frequently

Box 11.6   LITANY OF MODERN FAMILY RESPONSIBILITIES

Daily:
Pick up newspaper
Pick up mail
Meal preparation
Supervise children's homework

Weekly or Semiweekly:
Take garbage and recycle to curbside
Grocery shopping
Laundry
Chauffeur children to and from after-school events
    (sports, band, Scouts, 4H, Sunday school)

Monthly or Bimonthly:
Pay bills within "grace time"
Parent-teacher meetings and conferences
Take children to doctor if needed
Sign and send back report cards
Car maintenance or repair
Dental appointments for someone in family

Yearly:
Birthday Month: Driver's license renewal
February 14: Remember Valentine cards

April 15: Personal income tax deadline
May: Remember mother and mother-in-law
June: Remember father and father-in-law
June: Graduations at every grade level from kindergarten to grade school to college
July 4: Plan festivities
September: Get children ready for school
October: Get ready for Halloween
November: Get to the voting headquarters
November: Thanksgiving preparations
December: Cards, cards; gifts, gifts

Variable:
August/September: Preschool physical exams
August/September: School clothes for everyone
Variable: Renewal of car insurance
Variable: Renewal of house insurance
Variable: Pay state taxes
Variable: Pay local taxes
Variable: Yearly health checkups for everyone
Variable: Clothes for religious holidays: Easter, First Communion, Confirmation
Variable: Birthdays for all family members

ask, "Why doesn't the battered woman just walk away from the marriage?" Her friends and family usually cannot understand why she just does not walk out the door. They get her to escape to a shelter for abused women, only to discover she has returned to the abuser's domicile. Angry and frustrated, they assume she must want to be abused. But those who have done case studies of battered women explain it this way. She has been brainwashed. Her image of herself has been virtually destroyed. She has been taught that she is ugly, incapable, and incompetent. Her self-esteem and self-confidence have been eroded. Her will has been paralyzed. Her perceptions of reality are seriously skewed. If she has been a "homemaker," the battered woman may have no vocational skills. She may have two or more preschool children and no one to leave them with so she can find some kind of job, no matter how menial. Family members who do not believe in divorce may even tell her that she "made her bed so she has to lie in it."

Some abusers apologize for their abuse and promise never to do it again. Some abusers live up to their promise, but, unfortunately, most abusers simply repeat the cycle of (1) romantic involvement, (2) irritation, jealousy, etc., (3) violent abuse, and (4) apologies and promises to do better in the future. And then back to (1) romantic involvement. But when the abuse is repeated over and over and trips to the emergency room are repeated, eventually the abused spouse will be forced to leave or the "next time she'll be dead" (Jones, 1988).

Table 11.1   Signs of an Abusive Relationship

Separation: The batterer isolates his victim from her support system of friends and family. He insists that they are making her unhappy or interfering in their marital relationship. He may move her to an isolated area so that she has little opportunity to see other people.

Surveillance: He wants to know where she is at all times. He convinces her that he needs her presence constantly. If he cannot force her to quit her job, he may drive her to work, meet her for lunch, and pick her up at closing time to drive her home.

Verbal abuse: He may accuse her of infidelity with others when that is what he is involved in. He may tell her she is sexually incompetent in one way or another. He will criticize her constantly. He complains continually that she is a "lousy" cook and a "lazy" housekeeper.

Exhaustion and hunger: He may deprive her of sleep by keeping her up late and making her wake up early in the morning while he sleeps late. He makes her work on projects that are overwhelming for her, like helping to build a new home or starting a new business in addition to her other responsibilities.

Hostility and paranoia: He may throw food, break furniture, burn or tear her clothing, threaten her life, or the life of the children. She often describes him as a Dr. Jekyll and Mr. Hyde, charming in public but brutal in private.

Chemical dependence: Batterers will often encourage a woman to become dependent on drugs or alcohol as a way to control her and make her totally dependent on him.

Financial dependence: He will try to make her financially dependent on him. If she works, he will make her give him her paycheck and spend it on things he wants. Or he will convince her not to work so that she will be dependent on him for money.

Financial deprivation: When she is totally financially dependent on him, he will mete out money to her penny by penny. Then he will accuse her of not managing the budget competently, even though he does not give her enough money to pay the bills. He may prevent her from having transportation to get around, so that she becomes a prisoner in her own home. She then stops buying clothes, begins to look bedraggled, and may even cut her own hair rather than go to the beauty shop.

Battering: Once she is isolated from her emotional support system and becomes convinced that she is an incompetent adult who cannot survive without him emotionally and financially, the battering increases. It starts with irrational arguments followed by mild threats, and then escalates to shoving, pushing, hitting, and slapping, and ultimately to the use of objects and dangerous weapons.

Cycle of violence: After the violence, he convinces her that he just couldn't control himself and that it will never happen again. After the battering, he may apologize, shower her with gifts, love, and swear he'll never do it again. Or he may convince her that she was responsible for the beating. In either case, she is expected to conceal her bruises and cuts and lie about what really happened. She is then the one who feels guilty. He has convinced her that she "drove him to it." The perpetrator has transformed himself into the victim.

Sources: Lenore Walker. *Terrifying Love: Why Battered Women Kill and How Society Responds* (New York: Harper & Row, 1989).

Let's Not Go In for Man-Bashing: Women Have Also Been Violent. Even though the majority of victims are women, too many books have presented a one-sided picture. Men, too, have been insulted, humiliated, and assaulted by women. While discussing this subject one day in one of our classes, we said something like this: *No physical violence is allowed by either party. Just as men should not sock their women, women should not think it permissible to slap their men.* A few of the female students expressed surprise. Evidently, they were assuming that somehow a "slap in the face" by a woman was acceptable even though they railed against being slapped in the face by a man. Counting acts by both men and women, more than 10 million Americans experience physical violence every year. Violence is a hangover from previous power-dominated relationships and is not limited to our nation. It is pandemic worldwide.

Children and Elderly Abuse. Children are frequent targets of parental violence, sometimes to the point of death. We are also learning about abuse of the elderly by the very children they gave birth to and whom they supported for the first two or three decades of their lives. Finally, there is another type of violence: The abuse of brothers and sisters to each other. For years, we have not paid attention to the amount of abuse that has been going on among sisters and brothers. Sibling abuse is finally coming out of the closet. Siblings have committed numerable acts of atrocity on each other, including torture, mutilation, and murder.

It Isn't Really a "War Between the Sexes"—It's Regressing to Primitive Defense Mechanisms. We have been listing, one after the other, the problems of the nuclear family. At this point we are beginning to understand that when problems strike at the heart of the family, the nuclear couple turn on each other with impossible demands and power tactics, hostile accusations, and vengeful retaliations, leading—ultimately—to either a house of hostile silence or screaming arguments or domestic violence. We call it the "war between the sexes," but that is a misnomer. What is happening is the collapse of love and trust and faith in each other followed by the pain-attack response (see Box 6.5, p. 134). The "war between the sexes" is really a regression to more primitive defense mechanisms.

Marriage Now and for the Future: Rebuilding the American Family Based on Community Once Again

But enough of discussing the problems of modern marriage. What the readers want and need are ways to counteract the stresses and strains on the nuclear family. Alas! It is always easier to list problems than to suggest solutions in any area of life. But let us try. Based on the observations of professionals in the field, it is obvious that we need to restructure the modern family, based not on power and dominance, not on hostility and violence, but with that spirit of community that marked the early colonial families. While we cannot turn back the clock—at least, not for very long—we can at least take inspiration from those early settlers. We may not be struggling to survive in a wilderness, but we are certainly struggling to survive the complexities of modern life. The early colonial families used the tools of ax, pick, shovel, and rifle to forge a homestead for themselves. The tools that we shall use to forge a home place for ourselves will be psychological insight, supportive interpersonal communication, and a focus on establishing and maintaining intimacy among family members. We need our home place to be a sanctuary of harmony and strength. We need a community-based family.

What Is a Community-Based Family? Supportive Relationships Built on Faith, Hope, and Love

A community-based family is composed of a group of people, related by blood or by commitment, who receive and give physical and emotional support and strength to each other. A community-based family develops in a prevailing atmosphere of freedom that allows each and every family member to grow, mature, and evolve according to each person's individual differences and needs. But let's be very clear what this freedom means. It is not hedonistic "license" to do whatever we want. It means not striving for dominance and power over other family members. And it certainly does not mean promiscuousness and infidelity (especially now, with the shadow of AIDS always hovering over casual sexual relationships). A community-based family is a responsive and emotionally supportive family, one in which there is a "warm climate of trust" (Rogers, 1961). A warm home climate of trust means that the conflicts that arise can be resolved because the inter-actions among family members rest on the principles of faith and hope and love.

Early Warning Signs of Nonsupportive Relationships: Taking Others "For Granted." Generally we provide a warm climate of love and caring for our young children but, as the pressures of working and raising children increase, we begin to neglect that kind of love and car-ing for our Significant Other. The longer the relationship, the more tendency there is for hus-band and wife to take each other "for granted," a very common expression of dismay of both men and women. The thinking that underlies the following statements are one of the indicators that this kind of neglect is beginning to happen:

> That means I'll have to tell Jane I won't be able to fix the washer tonight, but she'll understand.
> I told John I'd pick up the suit at the cleaners, but he'll understand I had too many errands to do.
> I told Eleanor I'd take them to the game, but I'll just have to tell them I have too much work to do.
> Kevin asked me to call her this morning, but he'll know that something more important came up.

Breaking these kinds of promises (and saying that we will do something is a promise)—as insignificant as they may seem—is one of the first indications that we have made someone or something else more important. We're not talking here of sudden emergencies that preempt all other activities. Nor are we talking about a business trip out-of-town. We are talking about those small requests that may not seem important to us but are very important to the person who made the request: husband, wife, roommate. We may make a sincere apology and that person may say, "Oh, it's all right" but that does not repair the person's feeling that somehow we don't value him or her enough to keep our word.

Young couples "in love" start out with this sense of community. How does it disinte-grate? A large part of it is due to the fact that men and women have different communication styles. In fact, some writers on marriage and family, believe that men and women grow up in two distinct cultures, two cultures that have different orientations, different values, and differ-ent expectations (Gilligan, 1982; Philpot, Brooks, Lusterman, & Nutt, 1997).

Coming from Two Different Cultures, Men and Women Develop Different Communication Styles

Men are goal-oriented. Men value power, competency, efficiency, and achievements. Their sense of self is defined through their ability to get results. They are fulfilled through achieve-ment, such as building skyscrapers and super highways. Women, on the other hand, are relationship-oriented. Women value tenderness, communication, beauty, and intimate inter-personal relationships. They spend a lot of time supporting, helping, and nurturing one another. Their sense of self is defined by their feelings and the quality of their relationships. They express fulfillment through sharing and caring. Rather than building structures and highways, women are concerned with building relationships.

Boys-becoming-men are taught to be tough, to be self-reliant, to not show weakness, to do what has to be done, and to bite-the-bullet when they are hurt. Girls-becoming-women are taught to be gentle, to comfort and care for others, to be of service whenever possible (Gilligan,1982). He is taught to "stand up for himself." If he can't fight the other guy, he can at least yell at him. So while she is learning to be polite and soft-voiced, he is learning to argue and shout. Let's not blame our parents for this. These values are everywhere sanctioned in our society and have been for thousands of years. Men can argue and shout one minute and in the very next go off and have a drink together. This is true on the athletic field, on the job site, or in the office. A man does not understand that when he shouts at a women, she gets hurt. He thinks: *Doesn't she realize he was just blowing off steam?* No, she doesn't. Brought up to be soft-spoken, those words and names he has shouted at her are daggers in her heart. (Kipnis & Heron, 1995). The problem with verbal abuse is that it can never be truly erased, no matter how sincere an apology is offered, It remains in the person's verbal memory.

Men Are from Mars, Women Are from Venus

In this best-selling book by psychologist John Gray (1992) points out that men and women speak in different languages. Men and women may use the same words, says Gray, but the words don't mean the same thing. So different is the communication between men and women that they misinterpret each other. When she shares her probems with him, he supposes that she needs him to provide her with solutions. When he has nothing to say, she concludes he doesn't want to have a conversation with her. Her interpretation of his silence is probably wrong. He may be cogitating her problem and wondering what he can do to "fix it" for her. Mistakenly, he offers her advice—a quick fix to her problem and an end to the discussion. She becomes offended by his simplistic quick-fix when the problem has so many long-range ramifications. She didn't ask for a quick-fix solution; she only wanted him to be aware of all the things she is contending with every day of her life that do not have quick-fix solutions but just go on day-after-day.

There are no "quick fixes" to what she has to contend with, such as Jimmie's school problems or Jenny's trips to the doctor for her allergies or his mother's agoraphobia. All she wants to do is update him on what is going on in the family or in the neighborhood or with some distant relative or friend. All she wants is for him to listen. Listening, however, is not the communication style of most men. Most men, when they get together, do so for a purpose: to discuss a project, to work out a contract, to meet with the representative of another company, etc. Men go to lunch to discuss business or a project. Women go to lunch to nurture a relationship, giving and receiving emotional support. Women study psychology, are involved in personal growth, nurturing life, healing, and beauty. A sign of great love is to offer help and assistance to another woman without being asked. Offering help is not offensive, and needing help is not a sign of weakness among women. Offering help to a man implies he is incompetent, weak, and even unloved. When women try to improve men or offer help, the men receive the message that they are broken and need to be fixed. They feel humiliated. Thus women unknowingly and unintentionally hurt and offend the person they want most to please.

When his simplistic "fix-it" advice meets with disgusted reactions, he becomes either infuriated or depressed. His infuriation or depression leads to his withdrawal from her. John Gray says they need an interpreter. With this we disagree. What men and women need to do is to learn to speak "a common language." Building community means learning a mutually supportive communication style.

Building Community with a Mutually Supportive Communication Style

As unacceptable as it is, a major reason that people resort to verbal abuse is that it is a direct expression of their feelings. There is a maxim in international politics: War is the last stage of diplomacy. So too is verbal abuse often the last stage of trying to get a message across, messages such as:

> You were so hurtful that I hate you for it!
> You take back what you just said to me.
> Stop nagging me!
> Stop belittling me!
> That's a lie!
> What a brutal thing to say.
> You are being so hateful, I want to hurt you in return.
> I'm so hurt by what you did, I am brokenhearted.

Developing a common language may sound ultrasimple but maintaining supportive communication in a long-term relationship is a discipline no less exacting than developing team work among a group of athletes. He needs to learn to admit mistakes honestly and rationally without "blowing up." He has to learn that the admission of mistakes is not a sign of weakness, but a sign of strength. She needs to back off from moralizing, lecturing, using I-told-you-so statements, and making him feel as if he is a moral idiot. She needs to remember that he is new at this way of interpersonal communicating, allowing him the time and space to learn it without humiliating him (see Table 11.2).

Developing a "Common Language" by Changing Our Pronouns. It makes us feel good to blame others for problems. We tell ourselves: *It was his fault—not mine*. Or how about: *She started the argument, but I'm going to finish it.* Finding other people to blame absolves us from guilt and the responsibility to make amends. We use many defense mechanisms to protect our awareness: Projection, rationalization, displacement, etc. The blaming game comes out in accusations and the use of the pronoun *you. You did this!* or *you did that!* What we need to do is exchange the pronoun *You* for the pronoun *I,* and the pronouns *I, me, mine* for the pronouns *we, us, ours*. When we use first person plural pronouns, we do not send accusing statements. We send the message that no one person is to blame for problems. We send the message that all problems are to be shared. We send the message that solutions must be arrived at jointly. Avoiding the "blaming game" is easy to learn but hard to remember to do in the heat of raging emotions. Like skill on the athletic field or in the concert hall, it takes determination and practice, practice, practice to develop a supportive communication style.

If a Quarrel Does Break Out, We Can Quarrel Intelligently and Constructively

A few psychologists have suggested that if we follow certain guidelines for domestic harmony and peace, the couple may never again have another argument. With that premise we disagree. Wherever people live together in close contact over a period of time, friction happens. It happens in the office. It happens on the athletic field. It happens even at social functions. Arguments will break out despite all our attempts to stay cool and rational. That is the nature of things—human

Table 11.2   Developing a Supportive "Common Language" for Men and Women

Non-Supportive Communication	*Supportive Communication*
Both partners need to avoid "you" statements, accusations, and the blaming game. "You were flirting with every girl at that party. I saw you, you s. o. b.!!" "You're jealous, that's what you are, just jealous!" "You're always sticking up for the kids against me. You always make me the 'meany.'"	**Both partners need to learn how to own their own feelings and actions.** "I felt left out at the party last night. You were being sociable but I didn't have any one to talk to." "Hey, if you don't like them, that's good enough for me. We don't have to have them in the house." "Let's decide together a play/chore/homework schedule for the kids so we don't get into a good cop/bad cop routine."
He needs to avoid replying sarcastically to what she is saying. "I was late, so what!" "OK, so it was a mistake. Big deal!" "All right. I heard you. Can we forget it now?" "Well, spit it out!"	**He needs "to own" his mistakes and respond authentically to what she is saying.** "Sorry. The time got away from me. I'll call from now on when I'm late." "I didn't realize it meant so much to you. I'll check with you hereafter." "O.K. O.K. I hear you. It won't happen again." "I can tell something is bothering you. What is it?"
She needs to avoid saying "always" and "never." "We never go out any more." "I'm always working like a drudge in this house." "Nothing in this house is working right." "I'm never appreciated around here."	**She needs to be specific about her feelings.** "I've got cabin fever. Let's go out tonight." "This was one of those days. Dinner is ruined! I burned the sauce. Johnny dropped a dozen eggs on the floor. Let's eat out." "I know you'll love this. The washer is stuck and I can't wring the clothes out." "I'm feeling overwhelmed today. The twins have been fighting. Suzy told me she wishes she had been born in another family. My sister was on the phone for an hour this morning with her problems. I need some TLC."
When she is making an earnest request . . . "I'm feeling like a drudge. What do you say we go out without the kids—just us." "I'm so tired. I'd love us to relax a while." "Everything seems to break down at once. Now the dryer just quit." "I did all of the jobs on this list, Captain. I deserve a salary raise, a medal, a gold star or a happy face. But I'll settle for a pat on the back and a hug."	**he needs to respond supportively.** "Sounds like a great idea. Got any ideas when and where?" "I know what you mean. It's been a hectic day." "How does that principle go?—Things break down. Just when you need them the most." "You got it. I sure appreciate it. You've done a lot this week. Thanks." "I'll do better than that! How about I make dinner tonight?"
When he owns up to a mistake . . . "I should have called when it was getting late." "I made a mistake. I'll try not to let that happen again." "Sorry. I didn't realize how important that was to you." "I've been so busy that I really haven't been listening. Try me again."	**she needs to be supportive of him in return.** "I'd really appreciate that a lot. I'll do the same." "You're really a neat guy! Thanks." "Thanks for realizing it now." "That's what I like about you—your willingness when you're so busy."

nature. But quarreling does not have to be a knife to the jugular if both parties understand that even a quarrel can have several legitimate purposes: namely, to give vent to unexpressed feelings and needs, to get problems out in the open, and to work through to solutions.

We can quarrel constructively if we follow a few simple rules. If this comes as a surprise, remember that wrestling matches, Olympic competitions, and football games all have rules. Even warring nations are supposed to abide by the Geneva Convention. If we have never tried to argue within a framework of guidelines, it will not be an easy habit to learn, but it *can* be learned. It is also a skill that couples develop in successful long-standing relationships. We suggest our set of guidelines in Table 11.3, but each couple may want to work out adaptations of their own.

Intimacy: The Keystone of a Community-Based Family Once Again

If we are going to rebuild modern marriage into a community-based family once again, just how do we go about it? Answer: We build and protect our moments of intimacy with each other. It is intimacy through which we develop a warm climate of trust within the family. It is through maintaining intimacy by which we keep our romantic love for each other. And it is this intimacy that is the keystone of loving relationships. In today's society of external pressure and multitude of strangers, we need moments of intimacy with each other, now more than ever.

Ten Guidelines for Creating and Maintaining Intimacy Among Members of a Family

Each family grouping is different today, so some of the seven guidelines below may work better for one family than another. But in general, they are adaptable to most families, whether single- or double-parenting, stepparenting, or grandparenting.

1. Intimacy is maintained through verbal communication. When we are in love, we can't seem "to get enough" of the other person. We talk constantly. We call each other on the phone. We write letters to each other. We may even write poems. We want to know what the Other is thinking and feeling. We ask questions. We debate issues until we come to a mutual resolution. There doesn't seem to be enough time to say all that we want to say to each other. All that is before marriage. And all that talking is one way we achieve that precious quality of loving intimacy. Alas, after marriage all that verbal interaction begins gradually to lessen. As couples learn to know each other seven days a week, they feel less need to talk. Unfortunately, that is when we begin to take the Other for granted. We stop checking with the other person about his or her needs and desires. We forget to listen. And that is where the ship of marriage begins to founder. Studies have revealed that as the years go by, married couples begin to talk less and less to each other—on the average, only 11 minutes a day. What is even more confounding is that as couples begin to grow a family and put down roots in a community, they should be talking more to each other, not less. They need to talk about how to cooperate with each other's parenting style and philosophy. They need to talk about what they need or would like for their home and their vacations and how to budget for it. They need to talk, not argue, about events in general, before they become problems and conflicts.

2. Intimacy is achieved mainly through one-on-one moments with each other. Genuine intimacy is not possible in group situations (except in special psychotherapeutic situations).

Table 11.3   When Arguments Break Out, Guidelines for Constructive Quarreling

Guideline 1. Quarrel about only one thing at a time. Perhaps you have known couples who, when they argue, drag out every conflict they have had since Day One. When this happens, there are so many tangled threads to the argument, the result is one huge Gordian Knot that can never be untangled. Problems can only be resolved when a single issue is under discussion. This is a basic tenet of Robert's Rules of Order. It is a basic tenet of most guidelines for intelligent argument.

Guideline 2: "Hit-and-run" drivers not allowed under any circumstance. You probably know what we are talking about even before we explain it. It's saying or doing something that really hurts the other person and then storming out, getting into the car, and leaving. That's not just a cheap shot—leaving the scene of a crime is a criminal act. If you find yourself running off, turn around and come back. Apologize for the terrible thing you said and for leaving. (It's OK to still be angry—just not OK to be a reckless driver.)

Guideline 3: Keep your voice as calm as possible. Don't start shouting. Keep your voice down and as normal as possible. When we shout at people, we are deafening them. They cannot hear the words because they are defending themselves against the noise of shouts and screaming. Furthermore, if one person shouts, the other has to shout louder in self-defense. Neither person is listening anymore. They are simply screaming. It has become a madhouse.

Guideline 4: Keep to the truth. People who are quarreling tend to exaggerate their complaints or to throw a red-herring lie into the argument. Not allowed! Lies are neither intelligent nor constructive. It's tempting to exaggerate, but it only confuses the issue. What is needed is clarity about where things are going wrong.

Guideline 5: Don't go in for the blaming game. Just remember that in a problematic situation, everybody is involved. All problems are shared. Use "we" instead of "you."

Guideline 6: Don't play the silent game. Say openly and honestly what is upsetting you. Here's the scenario: The husband comes home and knows right away something is wrong. His wife does not have her usual smile on. In fact, she goes on with what she has been doing and hardly seems to notice his presence. "OK," he says, preparing for an all-out encounter, "What's wrong?" Does she tell him? Not on your life! "Nothing," she says in a tone that says "There's plenty wrong, but I'll be damned if I'll tell you." This script could be entitled "Guess What I'm Annoyed About." There will be times when you don't feel able to talk about it rationally. Simply say so. "Yes, there's something I'm disturbed about, but I just can't discuss it now. I need to wait until I'm calmer."

Guideline 7: When the argument is reaching "critical mass," call for "time out." Sometimes even the calmest persons can begin to feel that the argument is getting out of hand. If so, call for "time out" so that both of you can collect your thoughts and feelings and return to a calmer place. Simply say, "Look, this argument is getting too much for me, and I can't handle it rationally any more. Let's talk later when we are both cooled down."

Guideline 8. Look for win-win solutions. We can win a battle, but no one really wins in a war. The defeated party may acquiesce or surrender but the hurt, the anger, the bitterness will come out in covert ways. Instead of looking for who's to blame, look for solutions. Instead of concentrating on win/lose solutions, seek win/win solutions.

Guideline 9. Avoid acts of terrorism. Don't bomb the other with catastrophic statements. When some couples argue, they begin to threaten each other. "If you do that again, I'll leave you." "If you walk out that door, don't bother to come back." "I'll never forgive you for that! Never!" "I guess you want a divorce. Call the lawyer in the morning." Whatever you were quarreling about has now been blasted out of memory by the bomb you have just tossed into the argument. If the other person calls the lawyer, remember that you asked for it.

Guideline 10. No violence. Not any! Not of any sort! No pushing, shoving, hitting, beating, slapping. No throwing things even if you know you aren't going to hit the person. A person we know once threw all the food the other had just finished preparing on the floor. That is violence. Throwing a cup or a glass is violence. Slamming cabinet doors or bedroom doors is violence.

To keep our communication going, we need private time with each other. While families often do things together, it is through one-on-one situations that we become close to one another. Build in quality time for any two members of the family to be with each other without the others. We can say some things only in the company of one other person. Quality time can mean shopping for clothes with one child, not the whole family. The task of shopping with that one child provides you both with time and space to do something quite enjoyable together and in an intimate situation your child can say things to you that might be embarrassing in front of siblings. Having your mother over for Sunday dinner is fine, but having lunch with your mother once or twice a month, without anyone else around, is what will build and maintain intimacy. Try having a one-on-one lunch with your mother-in-law. As long as you don't criticize her son, she will be flattered by your willingness to develop a relationship with her—and her alone.

3. Intimacy with your Significant Other is only achieved through private times with each other. Children simply interfere with our connectedness with a Significant Other because they need so much of our attention and energy. Some of our attention and energy needs to be directed toward each other. So, again, unless we wedge out some private, personal time for each other, these terms of endearment can fall by the wayside and the only time to yourselves that remains is when you both fall into bed, too tired to talk—or do anything else. The popular magazines are replete with ways-and-means for bringing this kind of romantic intimacy back into a couple's life with each other—all the way from special terms of endearment to extended cruises away from home and children. Whatever the circumstances of your time and budget, the essential thing to remember is that you two have as much right to privacy as your teenage children. When you were romantically "in love," you sought every opportunity to be together. Now you must fight for that opportunity to be with each other and no one else. Don't wait for the children to grow up and leave the nest before you connect to each other again (look at Figure 11.1 again). Get involved together in at least one activity you are both interested in, whether it is a bird-watching society, joining them on their "Christmas bird watch," or working together a few hours a week in the garden. Or if you both love sailing, motorcycling, bowling, fishing—make this a sacred activity for yourselves and no one else. Doing something together provides you with time to talk, to share what's been happening, and to develop exciting plans together.

4. Promote intimacy among the other members of the family. Do you want your grandchildren to have the benefit of a grandparent relationship? Then provide time for a child to spend time with that grandparent without other siblings. If two or more siblings share grandparent time, they will either gang up on that grandparent or vie for attention in sibling rivalry. Children do not need to be treated equally. They need to be treated fairly. If little Donnie likes to visit Grandpa, let Donnie do so without big brother, Eddie. Eddie can have another treat, perhaps going with Dad on his next fishing trip. Is there a childless aunt, uncle, or cousin who misses having children? Don't just invite that relative to the house to share the Holidays, encourage their interaction by themselves at other times.

5. Promote family intimacy through family rituals. In saying that intimacy is best achieved through one-on-one situations, we did not mean to give the impression that we discredit the value of family rites and rituals. We believe in rituals. Repeating family rituals creates bonds of memory which tie us together and which affirm every person, no matter how young or how old, as valid members of the family grouping. We have already mentioned Thanksgiving as a rite that celebrates family membership. Other rituals have to do with the sacred: Sunday dinner after church is one such ritual. Some families pray together, say grace together, and bless each other upon leave-taking. Rituals can also be secular: We celebrate festive occasions such as weddings, graduation days, and other school events. Even funeral rites, with all their mourning and sense of loss, are rituals whereby we rebond with each other.

6. Providing intimacy through sharing of household tasks. Building family intimacy is also achieved through task sharing in the home place. In the early days of colonial settlement, the homestead was the home of everybody in the family. Everyone helped out; everyone worked. When it was haying time, everyone turned to—men, women, and children—to get the crop in before rain spoiled it. Whether mending fences on the farm or away on trapping and hunting trips, the husband-and-father had a feeling of pride and ownership in the homestead that he and other family members were building. If Super Mom is doing everything in the homeplace, Dad doesn't have much ownership of it. If only the parents are involved in household tasks, then only the parents are going to have a sense of accomplishment. While there are often clear division of duties, there are many tasks than can be shared with others. Task sharing replenishes our energies. Task sharing fosters family intimacy. Task sharing builds family community.

7. Intimacy is fostered by not appearing "perfect," but by being willing to reveal our vulnerabilities. No one is more difficult to achieve intimacy with than someone who appears to be perfect. If we attempt to appear perfect with our children, they will feel themselves inadequate in comparison. If we allow them to witness our "humanness" occasionally, we make it possible for them to be a little more equal to us. We let them know when we have made a big mistake. We apologize when we accuse them of something they didn't do. We let them in on our moments of pain and confusion. When they see that we too have moments of doubt and anxiety and then see us recover from them, they have more hope that they too will recover from their moments of doubt and anxiety. Too, we allow them to reach out and touch us—and that is true intimacy.

8. Remember, also, to allow each other some time to be "on our own." With everything we have said about the need for private time to be with each other, remember to allow each other "get-away" time. Give the other person room to breathe, to grow, to follow his/her own interests and recreation. People who are jealous are jealous about every relationship the other person has. They are jealous of the other's relationship to their children. They are jealous of the other person's friends. They are jealous of the time their spouse spends with the in-laws. They are even jealous of the other person's time at work or recreational hobbies. What this amounts to is virtual slavery of the other's time, interest, and energy. Instead, encourage the other to engage in what is creative and growthful for him/her unless it is seriously detrimental to your relationship and family grouping. As we develop our talents and skills, we become more enamored of each other because we have become more interesting to know—provided that we continue to talk and share what we are doing with each other.

When Divorce Is Inevitable

This chapter has been devoted to the building of a marriage-and-family partnership, based on commitment to community values. But we would be remiss if we did not discuss divorce as an ever present possibility and to provide some guidelines for living through the divorce procedure and subsequent "singlehood" status. With divorce as frequent as it is today, divorce is no longer considered scandalous or shameful as it was once. In fact, divorce has become almost as much of an institution as marriage. The factors that used to hold marriages together no longer do so today.

Women were once shackled to abusive marriages because of economic necessity. With women entering the work force in larger and larger numbers, the economic factor no longer holds. Men who used to be willing to remain in a loveless marriage "for the sake of the children" are no longer willing to do so. They do not believe that it is better for children to be subjected to years of verbal bickering, insults, and screaming arguments. With the shadow of AIDS ever present, neither men nor women are as forgiving of adultery. To reiterate the opening theme of this chapter, modern persons expect much more from the marriage contract than in previous eras. They want fidelity. They want responsible life-partners. They want to come home to a safe harbor of loving companionship and an expectation of continued growthful interaction. When that is no longer possible, they want out (Jones, 1990).

Divorce is never easy. Divorce may be a quick end to the most painful aspects of a conflict-habituated marriage that may include verbal and physical abuse, philandering and incessant lies to cover up, gross neglect of the family unit, etc.—but divorce brings other problems for which the man and woman are usually quite unprepared. No matter how brutal has been the marriage, or how deep the feelings of betrayal, divorce is also experienced as a kind of "dying." The divorce may come as a relief to years of agony, but nevertheless both partners will experience the loss. The loss may not be that of losing someone we love, but it is the loss of the someone and something that was once the central focus of our lives. Not only are we divorced from our spouse, we may also go through divorce from our children, from our neighbors, and from friends that we shared in common. When a person dies, we process the loss of the person we have loved through the rites of passage we call funerals. We grieve, we mourn, and then we let go of the person so we can begin to heal (vanGennep, 1908/1960). Death is final. The person is no longer on this plane of existence. Consumatum est.

Moreover, there are no cultural rites of passage by which to process our change in status from married to single/divorced. We suffer the pain of divorce mostly by ourselves. After all, who wants to listen to the woes of a person in a failed marriage? If the divorce proceedings are dragged out, the suffering can be extended over months and years. Just as we are beginning to heal, wounds are unintentionally reopened when old friends, unaware of the divorce, ask, "How are Annie and the kids?" or "What is Charlie doing now?" It is then the divorced person has to reiterate the painful disclosure that they are "no longer together" before leaving hurriedly to escape from detailed explanations of "what went wrong." Even when the heaviest responsibility for the splitting up of the family falls on the "other," even the most "innocent" of the partners will still feel a sense of guilt and shame for the "failure of the marriage."

When Custody Is Shared, a Divorce Is Never Final

The courts once generally gave custodial custody of the children to the mother—unless there were very extenuating circumstances, such as a charge of "unfit mother." Today in most states, the custody of the child and child support is now awarded to both parents—although how much time the child spends with each parent depends on the state laws and the particular family situation. As long as the parents share the custody of the children, the divorce has put an end to the marriage only on paper. The necessity of talking to each other on the phone to arrange visits or to keep the other informed about illness or school problems, and so on, continue to connect the divorced couple to each other. To make matters worse, the divorced spouses and their children are not the only characters in this drama. There are generally a lot of people off-stage who are coaching the main characters and stirring the plot:

> He has some nerve not calling you if he was going to be late picking up the kids.
> You tell that no good ex-wife of yours to teach your children better manners.
> Don't you let him/her dictate the rules of the visitation. You insist on your rights.

Sometimes these off-stage coaches involve the children by asking them questions about what goes on in their other house.

The Effects of Divorce on Children

The effects of divorce on children is a highly controversial subject. On one side are those who believe that children without a two-parent home are part of the "moral decay" of society. On the other side are those who believe that the real issue is not whether children can survive divorce but whether they can survive an atmosphere of screaming arguments and abuse. There are a few fairly consistent findings, but they do not enlighten us as to whether or not it is better for a hostile or abusing couple to stay together "for the sake of the children" or to divorce. They only enlighten us about what to expect in terms of the children's consequent responses and behaviors.

There is no doubt that the children miss and mourn the loss of one parent or the other—even ten years later (Wallerstein & Kelly, 1980), Boys in particular were not only "unhappy and lonely" and felt they had "missed a lot" by not having a father, they found it difficult to relate to girls. A British study found that girls from divorced homes were more apt to leave home immediately upon their eighteenth birthday, more apt to have babies out of wedlock, and much less apt to go on for post-secondary education. Obviously, the splitting of their own families by divorce did not instill in them much confidence or respect for the institution of marriage (Jones, 1990; Furr, 1998).

Children Do Feel Guilty and They Resent Stepparents. Unless divorcing couples are very quick-witted, children can very easily work one parent against the other to get what they want. When parents are divorced, children can become even more skillful in manipulative tactics. But, probably the single most overwhelming effect on children is guilt. While they may not voice their anxiety, children of divorcing parents tend to believe it is their fault that their parents are splitting up. Perhaps they have heard the parents screaming how the other one coddles or brutalizes the child. Because children believe they have been the cause of the split, they also believe it is up to them to bring the parents back together, and so they will resent any other person in the life of their parents. They will try to undermine the divorced parent's new relationship. What can you do when children feel "to blame"? Listen attentively to what they are saying and what they are not saying. Make sure you tell them they are not to blame. And tell them that over and over again. Gently, without probing, ask them why they think they are to blame. When the reason comes out (such as a misdeed or something someone said), let them know otherwise. And tell them that over and over again. Long-held guilt is not easy to overcome. Divorce counselors often advise open communication with the children, and, if possible, with the other parent (Krantzler, 1999). But it may be better to wait to reestablish communication at a heart-felt level. When the divorce has been bitter, it is perhaps better to avoid communication until some of the negative feelings have diminished. If the divorce has been heartbreaking, opening up communication may be tantamount to opening up the wounds (Dowling, 1999).

Problems of the Custodial Parent

Even when the divorcing spouses have made an attempt "to be civil" and have promised "not to involve the children"—a promise born of good intentions but unrealistic in actuality—they will have problems they did not anticipate. For example, the children of shared custody often have to spend weekends and holidays such as Thanksgiving or Christmas or the summer vacation with the non-custodial parent. The custodial parent, bereft of losing the child over the Holidays (say, Christmas), may react by having a second "Christmas morning" complete with gifts. The non-custodial parent may try to woo the child's affection and loyalty with costly gift-giving, or by treating the child to "Disneyworld" or other theme parks, and by generally having fun with them. The custodial parent, while happy to hear of the wonderful places the child was taken, may feel somewhat wistful that the child seems to have "lots of fun" with the divorced spouse. The custodial parent is the one who has to take care of the everyday raising of the child, which includes supervision of homework and consultations with the school, nagging to brush teeth and take baths, disciplining the children in instances of misbehavior, and so on. (Compston, 1998).

In addition to the problems of having the responsibility of custodial care, single parents (particularly mothers) have additional problems. No matter how prepared they thought they were for the single life, most mothers now find themselves facing financial hardship they never expected. Some even lose any financial support for the children because of fathers who abnegate all responsibility for their children. Happily, the court systems throughout the United States have instituted measures to track down these "deadbeat Dads," and to extricate support money from them. Still, that is not the only problem of the single mother. She discovers that while a new man may be interested in her, his feelings for her children are not nearly so fond. Diapers and dating do not make a good match. And what does one do about baby-sitters? Reputable baby-sitters are often signed up long in advance and most mothers have watched, with horror, TV movies about abusive baby-sitters. In addition, she may not even have the money to afford one. And so it goes. The woman may feel safely away from an abusing husband but she now bears the duties of child raising and child care that were once shared by two people on top of the problem of working full time.

Problems of the Noncustodial Parent

But noncustodial parents also have their fair share of problems. In the beginning it was fun to take the child to the zoo or the park or the movies. Eventually, however, noncustodial parents may begin to wonder if the child really has a genuine affection for them. Or are the child's shows of affection the result of "buying the child's love"? Furthermore, the visiting child is also divorced—divorced from playmates and friends, divorced from familiar toys and objects of interest, divorced from the child's own room (which is the child's "home place" of safety and trust). No matter how well the noncustodial parent and child get on, the child is a "guest" in someone else's house (Kendal, 1999).

Parenting Education Programs. Effective on January 1, 1994, Public Act 93-319 went into action. This act requires that all court systems establish parenting education programs for people involved in issues concerning divorce and children. The primary goal of this legislation is to make sure that parents are aware of the effects of divorce on children, when the divorce is final and the family structure is changed. The programs are designed to prepare the divorcing couple (and any interested relatives) for the way the divorce may affect the children and also to help the children adjust to the situation. The programs specifically focus on how to provide cooperative planning, parental dispute resolution and conflict management, and guidelines for visitation. An interesting part of the program provides for educating the divorcing parents about how to reduce the stress in their relationship and also how to reduce the stress on the children. The parents are also instructed on how the issues change according to the age of the children. The charge for the program is minimal and can be accomplished in about six hours. Finally, the judge has the option to excuse the parents from the program if he or she deems it unnecessary based upon parental attitudes and behaviors (McKnight, 1999). Whether these programs are proving effective is even now being studied.

Alternatives to Divorce Court Battles: Mediation, Prenuptial, and Living Together Contracts

One of the disheartening aspects of the divorce procedure is the bitterness that arises during divorce litigation—bitterness over character assault, unfair property settlements, and custody of the children. Such bitterness cannot help but affect the children, even if both parties agree never to talk badly about the other. The bitterness and the heartache inevitably leaks out in nonverbal ways when the other parent is referred to—a stiffening of the body, a tone of voice that is unmistakable, or a grim set to the jaw. Moreover, if the divorce proceedings are dragged out month after month, the only winners become the divorce lawyers who are charging by-the-hour. In an effort to avoid the negative fallout of divorce proceedings, an alternative method of ending marriage has emerged in a process called **mediation.**

The assumptions and process of mediation differ from traditional divorce in several significant ways. The assumption that underlies divorce is that the marital partners are in an irreconcilable battle that requires representation by attorneys and refereeing by the court. The assumption underlying mediation is that the marital partners are committed to cooperative resolution of the failed marriage. Instead of two warring attorneys presided over by a judge, mediation involves the two marital partners and a single mediator who has training in counseling and other types of "people skills." Third, the marital partners do not leave the decisions up to a third party judge but make all the divorce settlements and custodial decisions themselves. The mediator's job is solely one of facilitating communication between the spouses (Emery & Wyer, 1987; Folberg & Taylor, 1984). The chief advantage of mediated divorce is that the control is in the hands of the two persons and not in the hands of attorneys, court judges, and biased witnesses in the courtroom procedure.

Mediation would seem to be a superior route to the dissolution of marriage, but has mediation worked out in practice? Well, yes and no. Follow-up studies of mediated proceedings reveal more satisfaction generally by the women than the men. Children seem to make better adjustments. Women report more satisfactory financial settlements. But fathers often feel that they have been given the bad end of the financial stick (Emery & Wyer, 1987). Nor should mediation be considered for everyone. If the couple are already engaged in revengeful warfare, no amount of mediation seems to cool their feelings of hatred and resentment. If there has been any physical or sexual abuse of one of the partners or of the children, legal action must be taken to prevent further damage. Finally, if one of the partners is submissive and the other dominant, then the submissive partner may indeed need the protection of a strong attorney (Schulman & Woods, 1983).

Another approach has been gaining some popularity, particularly among the more affluent classes—the **prenuptial agreement.** Before the marriage ceremony, each partner lists his and her financial contributions to the marriage along with the personal possessions each of them brings. After that, the partners agree on what each divorcing spouse should get if divorce becomes inevitable. For example, suppose one partner brings very few financial assets to the marriage but agrees to work in order to put the other one through graduate school. The working partner would expect to get some compensation for his or her contributions to the increased financial potential of the educated spouse. This list becomes a legal contract so that there is no question about the material division should the marriage need to be dissolved. Although many young people tend to view prenuptial agreements as demonstrating a lack of faith in their forthcoming marital career, it has more to do with the kind of memory loss that happens over the course of months and years and when divorce emotions are running high. What belongs to whom can be a cause of furious resentment. A small vase of little financial worth but of significant emotional value can lead to furious battling. Who gets the family pet—while it might seem trifling to others—has not infrequently become a court issue.

More popular than prenuptial agreements is the contract that has become increasingly more popular since the 1960s; namely, living together agreements. **Cohabitation** may sound like a realistic way of discovering how compatible two people are, but recent studies on living together before marriage does not guarantee "marital satisfaction." In fact, some studies show more divorce after living together than those who did not live together until marriage. But there are also unexpected results from this kind of arrangement—even more legal trouble for separating after cohabitation than there is from the dissolution of a marriage.

Since the laws affecting cohabitation are different from state to state and are swiftly changing, we can discuss the personal and legal issues of cohabitation only in very general terms. First, let it be clearly understood that separating unmarried couples have the same loss of memory as do divorcing couples—what belongs to whom? What if (as has happened in more than one case) one partner takes off with all the money in the joint account or all the furniture the couple possess? Obviously, the other partner cannot resort to the courts if cohabitation is illegal. Or try this: In some states, there may be an underlying assumption that all possessions belong equally to both even if one party came into the living together situation with nothing. Despite the recent *palimony* rulings, in many states, unmarried partners still do not have the same rights as spouses to share property or to receive alimony or child support. Of course, if one partner wishes to pursue their "rights" or their possessions in those states that do officially recognize cohabitation, the litigation may end up in civil court with a jury trial that may entail weeks and months. Unless there is some kind of written agreement, courts generally do not give much credence to "verbal agreements" between a couple, since that kind of testimony comes down to "your word against your partner's word." If you are thinking about living with another person or are already doing so fairly comfortably, it is wise to draw up a **living-together agreement** (LTA). There are books and inexpensive "kits" on the market that can be used to detail property division. Roughly, however, the procedure is as follows:

1. To decide if either partner has rights to the property or income of the other.
2. To decide which assets belong to which partner.
3. To make a list of debts and to decide whose debts belong to whom.
4. To decide how your assets will be divided if you make an investment in both your names.
5. To declare yourselves a common-law marriage if you so choose (where legal).
6. To decide on possession of the home and custody of children in the event of separation.
7. To decide the circumstances under which one or the other would be justified in ending the relationship (infidelity, spouse or child abuse, etc.)

Investment counselors also advise making up a will if you want the other to inherit. Otherwise, the inheritance may go to the deceased's family—even if you have been living together for many years.

Reintegrating Oneself into Society

Unless the person has another partner to go to, life after marriage or cohabitation may be freer, but it is not necessarily easier. Unlike marriage, there are no rites of passage to reintegrate the person back into society—although it is somewhat easier for the man than for the woman in this case. In our society, divorced and widowed women have an ambiguous social status, even today, as we acknowledge the legitimacy of single career women. Formerly married women complain that while they are interested in real companionship, the men who make an approach are more interested in a casual sex relationship. If the woman moves too quickly toward a more committed relationship, she may discover that the man has made a fast getaway. A divorced woman's complaint: "I'm good enough to go to bed with, but I'm not good enough to marry."

But lest it be thought that the formerly married man is having an idyllic bachelor's existence, let it be understood that he too has his problems—of a somewhat different kind. Divorced men are besieged with invitations to "fill in" at a party and pressured by friends to be introduced to another woman. Furthermore, the newly single man gets the impression he should be an aggressive "Lothario" at all times. The formerly-married man may enjoy his new sexual freedom in the beginning and may even "play the field" as he never did when he was younger. But as men get older, the excitement "of the chase" becomes very old very quickly, particularly after the midlife transition—when more transcendent values (such as the companionship of another mature adult and children) come to the fore.

Second Marriages and Stepfamilies. As difficult as divorce or separating may be, most divorced persons do remarry despite the feeling that they will never let anyone get that close to them or hurt them again. After the first five years, however, second marriages seem to work out fairly satisfactorily. The reasons are fairly logical. Both persons are older now and (in most cases) more mature. They are also marrying for different reasons. Ask teenage females what they value in a boyfriend and they very frequently answer that they want him to be good-looking and a good dancer, to make a good impression on her friends, and to be generous when taking her out or giving her gifts. Ask that same question of her at age thirty-five and the answers will probably revolve around being "a good father and provider." Making an impression on her friends does not concern her now, and she would rather he be frugal with the family finances. Male teenagers who also are looking for a pretty face and figure will appreciate other aspects of personality as they get older. In their thirties and forties, they appreciate thoughtfulness, genuineness, cheerfulness, and all those qualities that make up a kindly and generous nature.

Stepfamilies (sometimes called *blended families* or *reconstituted families*) have unique problems of their own. It is always difficult to get used to the ways of people you haven't grown up with (any person unhappy with a roommate can tell you that!). Children who have been allowed to do something may suddenly discover the stepparent doesn't think it should be allowed. Or a stepparent may suddenly be shocked to discover behaviors in stepchildren that they wouldn't permit in their own. If it isn't easy for biological siblings to get along with each other, it becomes even more difficult for foster siblings to relate to each other. Furthermore, there is in the very concept of stepfamilies, an ingrained prejudice that stepchildren fall prey to—the wicked stepmother of fairy tale and folklore.

In fact, the whole stepfamily is fraught with fairy tale archetypes. In addition to the wicked stepmother, there is the stern and unbending stepfather, the badly treated stepchildren, and the favored stepsiblings. Children are natural fairy tale creators and will rationalize their behaviors and dislike of imposed discipline by dramatizing the stepfamily roles: "My own mother wouldn't do this to me," or "You aren't my father. You can't boss me around!" No matter how fair the stepparents try to be, the first minute they must side with their own children in any squabble, they will hear the inevitable accusations that they always "stick up" for their own children. It salves the stepchild's bruised feelings to cast them in the "wicked stepparent" role.

So What Is a Poor Stepparent to Do? Tips for the Novice Stepparent. Read everything you can about stepfamilies. Libraries have many books with advice and suggestions about relating to stepchildren. We have provided many guideline and tips for adult-child interaction in previous chapters, and we have more to say in the next one devoted to parenting. But since stepfamilies are such a special situation, we are inserting here just a few of our favorite tips for the novice stepparent or stepparent-soon-to-be.

1. Be friendly, but don't try to "make friends" too soon. Stepchildren or children of "your friend" are suspicious of anyone "usurping" the place of the biological parent. If you try to smother the child with affection before the child wants it, you will only raise the child's resentment even more.

2. Allow the child to make the first real bonding approach. Eventually, the child will become used to your presence and your general friendly demeanor and will begin to accept you. Let the child make the first approach. Be on the alert for this approach as it may come in very disguised form. For example, the child will ask you what to call you. If that happens, ask the child what he or she would like to call you. Or the child may ask you some personal (and sometimes embarrassing) questions about yourself. It's not just curiosity but a way of getting to know you.

3. Don't be the disciplinarian—just be the friend. Remember that the child will always be more resentful of any discipline you administer than if the biological parent administers it. If the child engages in an undesirable behavior, let the biological parent take care of it. Your job is to be the child's friend. If the child asks permission to go someplace (where you feel he or she should not go), refer it always to the child's biological parent: "Oh, that's something you better ask your father (or mother) about. I'm unsure of that." If the child is "acting up" inappropriately, you can say, "Hey, I don't think your mother/father would want you to do that." If that does not suffice, you can say in a friendly (and confidential way), "You don't want me to have to tell your mother/father, do you? I sure don't want to tell her/him, but I'll have to if you keep it up. Why not . . ." (and then suggest another behavior or activity he can do.)

4. Make sure you carve out some quality time for your stepchild alone. When the time is right and the child is exhibiting more acceptance, take the child (by yourself) for special things to do, such as buying clothes, having a lunch out together—without your own children or without the other biological parent. Those kinds of experiences will produce a sharing/bonding/cementing of your relationship because it doesn't include other people.

5. Discuss all these questions with your intended even before the wedding. Before you enter into a committed relationship with the biological parent, have many discussions about your relationship to the child beforehand, including some of the tips we have just mentioned.

Where Is Marriage Going? Trends and Possibilities Suggested by Demographic Statistics

It is very clear that the institution of marriage—and indeed that of the whole family—is undergoing a transformation. Divorce almost doubled between the 1940s and the 1980s, particularly after the "no-fault divorce" laws. Single parenting due to divorce and out-of-wedlock births is at an all time high. There is an epidemic of teenage pregnancy, particularly among the lower socioeconomic levels. One way to look at these trends is to bemoan the breakdown of traditional family values and to worry that the moral fiber of our society is disintegrating. Another way to look at these trends, however, is to view them as the rejection of marriage as it has been—with its brutalities, conspiracy of silence about incest, and acceptance of infidelity. What may really be happening is the reformulation of what marriage should be, based not on ownership, power, and violence, as it has been so often, but based on true commitment and fidelity to each other.

There are some interesting statistics that may foreshadow what is ahead (Furstenberg, 1996). Men and women are marrying later. The mean age for women has risen from 20 years of age in 1960 to 25 years in 1994 and the mean age for men has risen from 23 years to 27 years—and that bodes well. Later marriage may mean more maturity in the two people getting married. Later marriages and more maturity seem to be leading to fewer children. Many couples are having two or even one child and in that respect, we are approaching the birth rate of Europe since the last century. Fewer children allows for more care and quality time with each child and more financial support toward their education and successful life-career. Moreover, the divorce rate that sky rocketed in the 1960s to the 1980s has leveled off. The fact that women are not nearly as dependent on men for their economic security may indicate that married couples are staying together because they want to and not because they have to.

Marriage is no longer simply a way of having children and securing financial stability or even community respect. Psychological surveys in the last decade indicate that both men and women want more from marriage than they used to. What women want from a committed marriage these days is warmth and caring, increased communication, and more sharing of household tasks. What men want from a committed marriage these days is more leisurely time off. With the majority of couples now out working, we may be witnessing the reemergence of a community-based family with men and women sharing income, household tasks, and the care of the children. At present, women are still bearing most of the household tasks, and men are still leery of being seen with a carriage or baby-tender. Nevertheless, there is definitely more symmetry in the relationship of the working couple and that is the basis of a community-based family.

No one of course can predict what the future holds, but it will certainly be interesting to watch the transformation of marriage-and-family in the twenty-first century. Despite all our scholarly and statistical research studies, love transcends anything we can say or predict about it.

Box 11.7

SCENARIO
So Where Is Marriage Going in the New Millennium?

Jonnimae: This chapter doesn't encourage anyone to get married. What good did it do us to read it? I'm not speaking for myself because I know I'm not going to get married again but the younger students in this class must feel a little discouraged after reading it.

Professor Weitzman: Let's find out. I'm going to ask only the students who have never been married to respond to an informal survey. How many of you think you will find and marry Miss or Mr. Right. (*Most of the class members raise their hands.*) Well, Jonnimae, it seems as if we haven't discouraged too many students from their marriage intentions.

Natasha: American marriage is scary for me . . . I know that my Georgi is . . . how you would say something . . . "authoritarian"? But it makes for . . . security. He is the head of my family. My children and I . . . we do what he says. it is easier than . . . what you call democratic marriage. . . . Do I have that right?

Professor Weitzman: Absolutely. And I have to agree with you that attempting to make marriage more equitable, we are facing huge problems—divorce and children growing up without two biological parents close at hand; single mothers trying to raise their children while holding a job and often without enough financial security; and divorced men and women trying to find another life for themselves often in their forties, fifties, and even older.

Martha: The chapter should have said some positive things about long-term marriages. I really believe that Rod and I have a good marriage—even though we fight and quarrel and feel like outlaws with our in-laws. At least we laugh a lot. And we talk and talk and talk.

Professor Weitzman: A lot of talking and laughing are two of the significant indicators of a good and long-lasting marriage.

Alec: I showed the box on "constructive quarreling" to a . . . friend, well, girlfriend of mine but she said that when she is having a fight, she doesn't want to have any rules.

Professor Weitzman: Tell her that only barbarians do not fight by rules. As the chapter noted, there are even rules of warfare which we call the Geneva Convention. She needs to understand that the rules you agree upon are not to hurt each other but to clarify the problems that have arisen and to find win-win solutions. Let her think it over and approach her again. Remember what you agree upon (or don't agree on) now will determine your future relationship.

Alec: What you're saying is that if she fights with me all-out now with screaming and vicious accusations, I should expect that's how she would fight with me after we were married. That's a sobering thought.

Jill Smith: The way we are with each other in the first year of a relationship establishes the pattern of the relationship more-or-less forever.

Ernesto: But what I want to know, Professor, is where is marriage going? Is monogamous marriage doomed? That would make me very sad, having been raised very traditionally.

Professor Weitzman: No one can predict with any certainty but there are some interesting trends which suggest interesting possibilities. The mean age for both women and men marrying has increased in the last two decades. Men are marrying (on the average) around 27 years of age and women about 25 years of age. Being more mature, more marriages will become more stable. As well, older parents may be more responsible and judicious parents. If the birth rate continues to drop as it has been, we may well be raising a more intelligent generation because we know that parents can put more energy and time into one or two children than on a raft of children. And that leads us to the chapter on parenting young children.

IMPORTANT TERMS AND CONCEPTS TO KNOW

aggressive	financial	love	prenuptial
bisexual	friendly	mediation	rites
community	gentle	moral values	rituals
cooperation	guilt	multiroles	romantic
courtly love	intellectual	nuclear	stepparent
cultures	intimacy	polite	task-sharing
divorce	language	polygamy	violence
extended	literate	power	win-win

MAKE YOUR OWN SUMMARY BY FILLING IN THE BLANKS BELOW

Use the "Important Terms and Concepts to Know" to fill in the blanks below.

The present family scene. Despite the high rate of _____ , we still believe in love and marriage. So what is going wrong? One of the chief problems is that _____ love has little to do with the everyday realities of living, such as bills, illness, house and car maintenance, etc. There is widespread anxiety that the modern bonding styles of the last several decades represent the breakdown of _____ . Actually, many of these "new" styles are simply reinterpretations of the bonding arrangements of former cultural eras.

Historical bonding styles. Although the Bible exhorts the cleaving together of one man and one woman, the Hebrews themselves often engaged in _____ , with multiple wives, concubines, and harems. Ancient Greek society was essentially _____ . While Roman life was essentially family-based, Roman men could divorce their wives, but they had to provide _____ support for their children and divorced wives. The Medieval Ages developed a romantic adulterous tradition called _____ . The educated elite of the Victorian Age repressed female sexuality, but perhaps even worse was the _____ debasement of women.

The New World family produced a different style of family relationships. The pioneer woman was a true helpmeet to her husband, being strong of character and highly _____ . Alexis deTocqueville described the people of the New World as being the most _____ he had ever come across. The New World was producing a new breed of people who were building a _____ -based family style.

The urban family. As people migrated away from rural areas to urban centers, the _____ family became a _____ family. While urban life offers more privacy and financial opportunities, modern parents are exhausted by their _____ , leading to short-tempered retorts and a poor communication style.

Gender differences. Another problem is that men and women grow up with different personality styles and do not speak a common _____ . As well, men are taught to be _____ and competitive, while women are raised to be nurturing and _____ and _____ . Men and women come from different _____ .

To achieve a satisfactory long-term relationship, we need to replace relationships based on _____ and domination with relationships based on cooperation and _____ . The first requirement is to disallow _____ of any sort by any family member to any other. Other aspects include _____ of family responsibilities. Finally, if a quarrel cannot be avoided, we can quarrel intelligently and constructively but not by accusing or blaming but by finding _____ solutions. To achieve a community-based family, we need to provide quality time and one-on-one moments of _____ with every member of the family with every other member. We also need time for family _____ .

Divorce is always painful no matter how terrible the marriage has been. Children often experience _____ since they believe the divorce was their fault. They hold out a fantasy for a reconciliation for their parents and have a natural dislike of the new _____ . An alternative to the divorce court with its assumption of antagonistic positions is _____ with its assumption of cooperation. Another way to avoid the divorce court is through _____ contracts, treating the assets of both parties as a merger.

Post-script. Despite all the statistics and scholarly writings about marriage, sex, and bonding styles, in the long run, _____ still transcends everything we know about it.

12 PARENTING
Families Growing Together

Play was once considered something children did because they did not have anything more serious to do. Now we know that play is an important factor in a child's physical, emotional, social, cognitive, and moral/ethical growth. We know now that children's play is very serious business, indeed!

Box 12.1
SCENARIO
What's the Right Way to Raise Children

The instructor has been discussing the many problems that parents face in raising children.

Martha: So what the right way to raise children?

Professor Weitzman: (laughing) You have just asked the traditional American question.

Jonnimae: A baby doesn't come with a manual of instructions.

Professor Weitzman: That aphorism sums it up rather neatly. We know a lot of things that are not good to do but there are few hard and fast rules about what is right to do. It depends on so many other variables: The child's genetic structure, the child's personality "type," sibling rank order, gender, and even the traditions the parents have come from.

Li Ho: I'm going to pick up on what you just mentioned—traditions. My families on both sides are very tradition-oriented—like filial piety, meaning they want us to respect them and use their wisdom in guiding our lives. Their traditions differ somewhat and I respect both of their traditions—a lot. But their traditions don't always fit into what's going on today. Here I am living in the computer age and still trying to please my parents who don't even understand what is meant by the "information society." They still believe that children should listen and I have had to contend with that. But what will happen when I present them with grandchildren who are loud and rowdy and haven't been taught to be so respectful?

Professor Weitzman: What Li has just said applies to our society in general in another way. In previous eras, young parents could rely on centuries-old tra-

ditions to guide them—a kind of tribal parenting. Today we are being influenced by a mix of cultural models, subcultural models—even TV–family-sitcom models. We are living in a time when each new set of parents has to make parenting decisions on their own. That's not easy. We're all beginning at Square One again.

Martha: In other words, there is no right way to raise kinds . . . only "wrong" ways.

Professor Weitzman: Well, I wouldn't put it quite that way. But I do say modern parenting is a paradoxical situation. Most young people genuinely assume that the job of parenting "comes naturally." The trouble is that what comes naturally is that we generally imitate how our parents raised us. They are role models that have been "hard wired" in us—without our even being aware of it.

Alec: If that's true, I sure don't want to have children. My father beat the hell out of us when we didn't jump at his commands.

Professor Weitzman: In that case, Alec, your parents may be role models of a different sort—negative role models.

Li Ho: Negative role models? What's that?

Professor Weitzman: It's trying to do things in reverse from the role models we have inherited. Alec, for example, shudders when he thinks how his father raised him—which may lead him to try to do everything quite oppositely from the way he was raised.

Alec: You bet I will!

Box 12.1

SCENARIO (continued)
What's the Right Way to Raise Children

Eduardo: But, Alec, that may just lead you into doing things that may not really be good either. You would be just reacting and not thinking about what you are doing—if you can understand what I'm saying—like playing defensively instead of offensively. I'm not sure how to express it.

Martha: I know what Eduardo means. A lot of things my parents did with us I wouldn't want to do with my kids. Yelling was part of our family environment. But, gosh, the love that was all around. It poured out like the spaghetti sauce on the pasta—that was something marvelous. That feeling of being loved is something I do want to hang on to.

Professor Weitzman: Parenting is probably more difficult today in our society than it has ever been before. Yet when things go wrong, others in our society are too willing to point a blaming finger at the parents who have done everything as well as they have known how to do. In fact, so difficult is it to raise children that it is high on the list of reasons for divorce. Parents fight continually over each other's treatment of the child and what the children are expected or not expected to do. We all want to raise our children to be loving, intelligent, authentic, assertive, morally responsible adults. How to do that . . . is the question.

Shannon: I have a relative that keeps quoting the Bible, "He who chastiseth not his child, hateth him."

Professor Weitzman: But how shall we interpret that? Chastising a child with gentle words will make a more permanent impression on him than beating him. If we beat children, we are only teaching them that we believe in violence.

Eduardo: I suppose you're going to say modern marriage partners need modern types of parenting. Right?

Professor Weitzman: We can only cover general principles of parenting in this course. Unfortunately, even the healthiest children have many more specific problems than we can cover. Some children are hyperactive. Some children are born with serious birth defects. Twins and triplets are a special problem of child raising. The publishing market is flooded with books on how to raise a loving child, an intelligent child, an authentic child, an assertive child, a morally responsible child, etc. If you're serious about parenting, peruse your library for books on parenting and raising children. Use your parents, grandparents, and friends as another resource. But most of all, have fun with them. Let them know you love them as Martha said. Then they'll forgive you your "mistakes."

The Child's Personality Style: A Mix of Many Factors

We are raising the tallest, healthiest generation in history. We have learned a lot about nutrition, for example, and it shows up in the fact that the children of immigrants are generally taller (on the average) than their parents. The second generation will be even taller (on the average) than the first and so on. We know from historical data, that the first *menarche* (first menstrual period) of girls in the last century did not take place until the ages of 15 to 18 years of age, simply as a matter of enough weight. Girls need a certain amount of fat on their bodies to have regular menstrual cycles and girls today on average experience menarche much earlier. Since 1930, there has been a steady increase in IQ scores worldwide (see Box 12.2) (Flynn, 1987). Through the medium of television, children know more about life-in-society and its problems than any generation in history. In comparison to previous generations of children who were taught to "be seen and not heard," our present generation of children are highly verbal and have advanced learning skills (such as knowing computer technology) that even some older adults cannot handle. But even with our highly intelligent, highly verbal, strong and healthy generation of children, there will probably never be such a thing as "perfect parenting" and "perfect children."

Many Influences on the Child's Development Are Not Under Parental Control

A child's personality is a mix of many variables not always under parental control. For example, the child may be conceived with a genetic weakness. The difficulties of pregnancy, labor, and birth may cause problems that will only show up later. Size of family, gender, and rank order will affect the child's self-concept. Marital stability and divorce, moving from place to place in the country, unemployment, and financial stress will all add to the environmental "mix" that will be part of the child's background. Where children grow up (city, suburb, ghetto, barrio, or rural countryside) will influence their moral/ethical values. Finally, our society is in such flux that what was right for other generations of parents is no longer considered "right" for the present generations. Nevertheless, we have learned something about what makes for psychophysically hardy children.

Parenting Begins Before Birth! Even Before Conception

Parenting begins long before birth—it begins in the nine months while the growing child is developing in the womb. Young people who want to raise healthy children need to understand that the nine months before birth are perhaps the most important nine months in a child's life, followed by the first two years of infancy. In fact, parenting begins even before conception. We are speaking not only of the genetics of physical health but also of mental, emotional, and moral/ethical health, discussed in previous chapters.

Ensuring a Healthy Environment for the Unborn Child

We used to think that the placenta was a wall that protected the infant from antigens in the mother's blood stream. We know quite differently now. It has long been known, for example, that rubella (German measles) transmitted through the placenta can not only cause deafness, blindness, and other incapacitating problems, it can even kill the embryo. Another factor is drug addiction that can severely damage the growing embryo. By now, most people know about

---

Box 12.2   THE FLYNN EFFECT: A RISE IN IQ SCORES WORLDWIDE

The "Flynn effect" is the name of the phenomenon that IQ (however we measure it) has increased over successive generations around the world since 1930. When psychologists examined the data, they were amazed to discover that each generation is about 15 points higher than the previous generation—a very powerful jump. And this amazing jump has occurred in technological societies all over the world. The effect must be environmental because it is obvious that there has not been enough time to produce that kind of genetic mutation. To what, then, can it be attributed? Well, obviously better nutrition, fewer incapacitating childhood diseases, greater educational attainments of the parents and so more information about how to care for children. More educational attainment of parents usually results in fewer children—which in itself leads to higher verbal ability, because each child typically enjoys more attention and financial resource.

"crack babies" (babies born of mothers who were cocaine-addicted) and who manifest physical and emotional difficulties of addiction. Obvious symptoms include irregular sleep patterns, feeding problems, and a high-pitched crying. Most people know by now about the effects of alcohol on the child, including the disease called **fetal alcohol syndrome (FAS).** And of course there is the example of the **thalidomide babies** who developed "flippers" instead of proper arms and legs because their mothers had taken this drug to prevent morning sickness during pregnancy. But many people are still unaware of the possible harmful effects of other drugs, including the prescriptions your physician may subscribe and even popular over-the-counter medications. In fact, many health organizations now urge prospective parents to guard against all the items listed in Box 12.3. It should be noted, however, that many women have ingested one or more of the toxins noted while pregnant with no apparent harm to the child. For example, it is estimated that only 10 percent of pregnant women who drink alcohol have children with congenital birth defects. Nevertheless, a 10 percent risk estimate is reason enough to play it safe now rather than be sorry later.

Health organizations also urge pregnant women to take other measures in order to ensure the health of the child they are carrying. For example, they suggest that to avoid chance encounters with people who are sick, pregnant women should avoid crowds of people. This measure is particularly urged in December when the Christmas shopping season takes place. Another health measure is to make sure the expectant mother consumes a nutritious food regimen. Too often, pregnant women have been so fearful of gaining weight and not being able to lose it again that they tend to diet. What has been discovered is that poor nutrition can lead to low birth weight and low birth weight can lead to problems apparent at birth or which show up years later. For example, it has been statistically demonstrated that premature babies or simply **low birth weight babies** (5.5 pounds or less) have a lower-than-average life span. They are 40 times more likely to die in their first month than normal weight babies. Those who survive are at risk for life-long disabilities including mental retardation, cerebral palsy, and visual and hearing impairment (Abel, 1997). One of the most recent discoveries is that low birth weight has a correlation with breast cancer—a particularly dangerous cancer for women. Most particularly of all, even before the pregnancy, get under the care of an obstetrician. He or she will be happy to get to know you, get your vital statistics before pregnancy so as to have a base line for comparison later, and finally to detect any problems that might occur before they happen.

Box 12.3   POSSIBLE TOXINS TO BE AVOIDED BY MOTHERS-TO-BE

Alcohol	Mercury (used in teeth fillings)
Amphetamines (pep pills)—often found in diet pills	Nicotine
Aspirin	PCP
Caffeine	Prescription drugs
Cocaine	Rubella
Folic Acid	Tranquilizers
Heroin	Vitamin A (in excess)
Marijuana	X-rays

The Unwanted Child and Later Lack of Self-Esteem

Social scientists have been wanting to investigate empirically (and therefore unequivocally) the importance of warm personal mothering for the psychophysical health of the child. That kind of study needs to be a well-researched ongoing longitudinal study of the growing infant and the caregiver. Such a study has been going on by teams of researchers which has confirmed the work of the personality theorists, such as Freud, Erikson, Leboyer, etc. (Axinn, Barber, & Thornton, 1998). The purpose of this ongoing research study was to determine if unwanted or unexpected pregnancy correlated with later lack of self-esteem in the child. The researchers were careful to note the limitations of the study (and there are some) but what is significant in this research is that the study was not retroactive but has been carried on for a period of 23 years. Previous research had strongly indicated that unwanted pregnancies increased the incidence of child neglect and child abuse. One of the purposes of this ongoing research is to discover if "unintended" pregnancies have an effect on the child's later mental health (Axinn, Barber, & Thornton, 1998).

In the first year of the child's life, the mothers were asked whether or not they wanted another child before the child was conceived. There were two types of "unintended" pregnancies: those that the mother did not want and those that came earlier than the mother intended. The researchers reasoned that if the pregnancies were unintended or unwanted, the quality of parenting might include lack of parental support, low parental involvement, and substantial parental rejection—all of which would affect the child's self-esteem. The mothers (matched for race and socioeconomic variables) were interviewed several times over the course of the study and their children (all born in 1961) were interviewed twice, around their eighteenth and twenty-third birthdays. The children, now in their late adolescence and early adulthood were given a standard self-inventory of self-esteem. The findings of this research reveal the following:

1. The more number of children in the family, the less the pregnancy was desired.
2. Children who were unwanted by their mothers scored significantly lower on the self-esteem scale than the children who were *not* unwanted.
3. The lower self-esteem continued into early adulthood.
4. The unwanted pregnancy seems to have more effect on lowered self-esteem than even the divorce of the parents.

Several factors have been suggested for this unwanted child effect. First, the mere fact of being (say) a fourth child (or more) in the family tends to lessen the amount of time the parents can spend with that child as compared to the first child. The first child usually gets lavish attention and each child thereafter gets less as parental time and energy diminish. Just looking at the photographs of the first child, we note that there are generally more of them and they are of a more costly type than the photographs of later-born children. Second, the lack of wantedness may lead to less active support of the child's scholastic studies or special interests such as hobbies, sports, and talents. Third, since many unwanted pregnancies occur to young unmarried adolescents, they do not have the kind of skills or motivation that older and/or married mothers enjoy with the children. Fourth, unwanted pregancies may be so abhorrent to the mother (and father, if there is a visible one) that she (or they) totally neglects or abuses the child. Finally, if the child came earlier than expected with disabilities that sometimes accompany premature and low-birth weight babies, one or both parents may be unequipped emotionally or physically to deal with the added physical and emotional care required.

Parenting Infants

After the nine months of intrauterine growth, the next most important time in our lives consists of the years of infancy. Even though the child is no longer developing in the womb, the whole nervous system, the skeletal, muscle, and organ systems, are undergoing tremendous growth. What children experience at this time will shape their perceptions about themselves and about other people. If they are screamed at often, they will learn to avoid adults. If they are neglected or abused, they will not be able to form healthy attachments to other people and that can lead to any of the disorders discussed in the chapter on abnormal behavior. If little girls are made to feel ashamed of themselves, this may set the pattern for accepting an abusive husband. If little boys are abused, this may set the stage for being the husband that abuses. But perhaps the most insidious of parental deficiencies is *neglect.*

Neglect can result from the inability of the care-takers to relate to a child that is not as healthy as others and who may exhibit a difficult personality style from birth. For example, if a baby is born far ahead of time or is frail for others reasons, the baby may not react to the mother's love with the coos and smiles of the healthy child. Disappointed that their infant is not what they expected or wanted, the parents may withdraw emotionally from the child. Instead of holding the infant and soothing its crying (which may seem endless), the parents may tend to ignore the child's cries and leave the child in the crib "to cry itself out." If there is suspicion of neglect, then others in the family circle need to help out. They can relieve the mother from all the caretaking of the infant and other children so she can get some rest and "playtime" for herself. They can help with the cleaning and household chores. They can volunteer to do some of the shopping and cooking. With this kind of support, the rested and supported mother can begin to find some joy in the caretaking of her "difficult child" which we describe next.

Thomas, Chess, and Birch: The Easy Child, the Slow-to-Warm Child, and the Difficult Child

We must not oversubscribe to the idea that all problems with infants and children is due to inadequate mothering. Mothers have too long been blamed for anything that "goes wrong" with their children. There is evidence now that problematic children are "just born that way." All parents will tell you this: *Children are different!* From the time they are born, any two siblings show vast differences in temperament; in sleeping and eating habits; in the way they relate to others; and in their interests, talents, and gifts. These differences in personality traits have been observed in children from earliest infancy, and for the majority of children they are long-lasting, persisting right up to adulthood for the majority of children (Thomas & Chess, 1980).

Impatient with the assumption that parents are entirely reponsible for "problem children," Thomas & Chess compared families of "children with problems" with families of "children growing well." As far as the team of researchers were concerned, the differences in personality style had little, if anything, to do with the family environment. They did discern that there were distinctly four different kinds of baby temperaments, which they described as the easy child, the slow-to-warm child, the difficult child, and the changeable child (see Table 3.3)

The **easy child,** which made up 40 percent of the sample, has a generally moderate activity level, is generally positive and cheerful in mood, has a low or moderate intensity of reaction, is adaptable, and quickly establishes regular sleeping and feeding schedules. Later this child participates easily in school routines. The **slow-to-warm child,** 15 percent of the sample, has a moderate activity level, but, unlike the easy child, tends to withdraw from new situations and is slow to adapt. These children are somewhat negative in mood and need some time to get used to new routines. Once they do become familiar with the routine, they do what is asked of them. They just need a little time to adapt. The **difficult child,** 10 percent of the sample, is difficult from birth. This child has difficulty eating and sleeping and many exhibit colic. These children find it hard to adapt to new situations and cry a great deal in their later childhood. Their crying has a characteristic quality that their parents find unnerving. Finally, there is the **changeable child,** 35 percent of the sample, who doesn't seem to fit very neatly into any category and who seems to go through a lot of "phases."

There are many other personality differences among children. In the chapter on communication, we described four different personality dimensions of "type psychology." Other dimensions include whether a child is impulsive or reflective, analytic (seeing details and problems) or superordinate (appreciating the "whole picture" and similarities) (Kagan, Reznick, Snoidman, Gibbons, et al., 1988). Every child is uniquely different. The issue is not to treat each child equally but to treat each child in accordance to what is appropriate and growthful for that child.

Play as Preparation for Life

In previous centuries, a child's playing was viewed as something children did when they didn't have anything better to do. Amusing to watch, yes, but before the twentieth century most philosopher-psychologists thought of play as not much more than the drain of excessive energy. Twentieth-century psychologists have taken children's play a lot more seriously. Freud's theory of play was that a child catharsizes his anxieties, his resentments, and his confusions through play (Freud, 1926). Watch a child play with her dolls after she has been disciplined. She may scold them, make them stand in a corner, or even spank them. She is displacing her hurt onto her dolls. Erik Erikson viewed play as part of the child's whole psychosocial development. If children are allowed "free play," they learn the tasks of autonomy and initiative. The pretend games of childhood are ways children learn their gender roles: "I'll be Daddy and you be Mommie and Jimmy can be the baby!"

Piaget placed even more importance on the activity of play. For him, play was essential to cognitive development (Piaget, 1973). While playing, children are developing perceptual skills, improving their physical hand/eye coordination, and validating the perceptual **constancies.** Finally, through cooperative play with other children, they are making advances in their moral/ethical development. Playing is the serious business of early childhood.

Play as Therapy

In addition to the "free play" we have been discussing, there are some specialized play techniques employed by those who work professionally with children. It was Freud's daughter, Anna, and another German psychoanalyst, Melanie Klein, who began to investigate the possibilities of using play as a therapeutic device for nervous or "high-strung" children or children who were having emotional problems (Klein, 1960). In this country, play therapy for children was popularized by Virginia Axline, a student of Carl Rogers. The account that she wrote regarding a frightened and mute little boy electrified the psychological and educational worlds. The book was entitled *Dibs in Search of Self* (Axline, 1964). The story of Dibs is well worth telling.

Dibs was the only child of two very brilliant parents who gave him physical care but who were emotionally cold and regarded the birth of Dibs as an interference in their careers. Dibs was referred to Axline because of his mute and bizarre behavior. He kept to himself, crawled under the chairs and tables, and acted more "like a wounded animal" than a little boy. The nursery school teachers wondered if he were autistic or mentally retarded. Axline undertook play therapy with Dibs for an hour a week in a play therapy room. A play therapy room has many toys and paints and even sand and running water. The child is allowed to do anything he wants, including marking on the walls with crayons and splashing water all over the floor. There are only two rules in this magical play therapy room: He cannot hurt the therapist, and he cannot hurt himself. The therapist sits quietly and reflects to the child what he is doing and expressing: "Oh, you are stamping on the father doll. You must be very angry at the father doll!"

In the hours that Dibs spent with Axline, the child used the small dolls to act out the confusion, the meaninglessness, and coldness of his life at home. A particularly absorbing chapter of the book describes a scene in which Dibs creates a play fire, after which he picks up the mother and father dolls and throws them into the fire. In psychoanalytic language, fire is equated with emotional rage. But fire can also be symbolic of inner cleansing and purifying—a transformation toward recreation. It is through the fires of self-examination that we learn to become more self-aware. It is in the fire of purification that heroes, like Siegfried in Wagner's opera, are transfigured. It was through the fire drama that Dibs began to purge his inner torments. Following the fire scene, Dibs began to make his way back to the world of people. The hitherto unexpressed fears and guilts and hatreds were dissolved in calmer and quieter hours of play therapy—until at last his usual woebegone expression began to brighten. He began to smile, to talk, to laugh, and to develop interactions with others in the world. Dibs eventually revealed himself as brilliant as his parents, and he went on to college and professional school.

Art Play as Diagnosis

After World War II, children's art also became a diagnostic tool in cases of alleged or suspected physical or sexual abuse. Unfortunately, many times people who are not qualified to make diagnoses can see what they want to see in children's art. Nevertheless, children's art can sometimes reveal what is going on in the house. For example, Drawing A in Figure 12.1 was a shock to the teacher who collected the papers. The little boy who drew the picture (whom we shall call Tommy) was six years old, the youngest sibling of three children. The immediate family consisted of mother, older brother (11 years), and older sister (8 years). The mother had divorced the father, a physician, two years prior to the drawing. Although very neat and clean in appearance and physically healthy, the boy was not doing well in school.

Tommy described this Drawing A in the following way: "This man is kissing her and they are laying on the bed with the pillow over their heads, and clothes off. But their shoes are still on." He described the boy as "Danny," who is 7 years old, and the girl as "Ginny," who is 6 years old. Alarmed, the teacher wisely refrained from saying anything more to the child. She took the child's drawing to the principal and school counselor who referred the matter to the proper authority. From the drawing itself we cannot infer whom Tommy may have seen. Is it the mother and a "friend?" Is it his older brother and sister? The latter seems the more likely, but we cannot make any valid judgment. We can say, with a good deal of certainty, that this bright six-year-old witnessed something that he could not comprehend and that was causing him considerable anxiety.

Drawing A

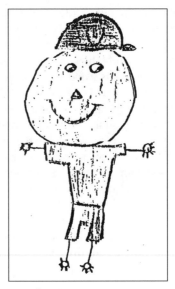

Drawing B

Drawing C

Drawing D

Figure 12.1 Children's Art. Drawing A. The six-year-old boy who drew this said, "This man is kissing her and they are laying on the bed with the pillow over their heads, and clothes off. But their shoes are still on." **Drawing B.** This first-grader complained of headaches, but no one took them seriously until an alert art therapist noticed that she had drawn huge heads on all her figures. The mother consulted the family physician and the diagnosis was "migraines." **Drawing C.** Drawn by a 10-year-old boy. A generally happy household including grandparents, mother, and himself. But who is the stick figure on the right? Said the boy, "That's my father. He's divorced from us. But I don't know how to draw him." But notice how well drawn all the other figures are. **Drawing D.** Another 10-year-old boy. What struck the art teacher was the strange elbows and knees. He drew all the other figures in the same way. The art teacher said, "This would seem to me to be a pretty good description of how the boy feels about his body. He is very awkward and uncoordinated. Very immature physically."

Sensitive art therapists can pick up on other kinds of physical or psychological problems. No one realized the severity of a little girl's headaches until she drew figures with huge heads on top of tiny figures (Figure 12.2, Drawing B). Ordinarily, a huge head is typical of a child emerging from the "tadpole people" stage, around five or six years of age. But this child was quite intellectually advanced for her age and her figures show sophisticated details. Why then these huge heads so out of proportion to the rest of the drawing? The mother took the child to the family physician, who diagnosed the child as having, not occasional headaches, but severe and lasting migraines. It is a wonder that the child was doing as well as she was.

But a child's art can also be representations of happy scenes. When we see a sun shining and a rainbow in the sky and smiles on the faces of the people, we may infer that—no matter how serious a child's present problems may be—the child still has an optimistic worldview.

Figure 12.2 Rhoda Kellogg: Stages in Children's Art As Kellogg analyzes children's art, it has clearly recognizable stages as follows:

Stage 1 (before 2 years of age). Simple marks or scribbles on the paper. Although the scribbles on the page may seem to be stray hit-and-miss marks, those marks represent a magnificent achievement on the part of the infant. The child is learning to focus on a small area (the paper) and make a mark on it. In other words, he is learning eye/hand coordination and direction: up/down, center, and around and around.

Stage 2 (between 2 and 3 years). Geometric shapes. The child is developing shape awareness, making crosses, circles, even squares and triangles, which someday will be reflected as part of a reading readiness program in the early grades.

Stage 3 (after 3 years). Combining shapes. For example, a circle and some straight lines make a person. Kellogg was also fascinated by the child's obsession at this stage with creating circles and then the tadpole people that emerge at this stage. It was Kellogg's theory that this circle can be equated with Jung's concept of the **mandala,** the Eastern symbol which represents wholeness, health, and harmony. Jung had noticed that his patients began to dream and draw these symbols when they were reaching new levels of personality integration. Kellogg believes the circles of this stage denote a new level of cognitive and personality achievement. Eventually, the circle-head clones a circle-torso, and the body becomes more and more refined with hands and fingers, feet, and so on. As children become better able to integrate their physical coordination and to orient themselves in space, their figures become more complex, complete, and "human." In other words, their drawings reflect their own cognitive and emotional self-concept.

Stage 4 (beginning at 4 to 5 years). Pictorial objects. Children are attempting to make representations of their world, those familiar pictures they draw of houses, people, trees, and animals. She cautions parents and teachers *not* to tell them how to draw but to allow them to develop their understanding of "reality" through free art play.

A typical "tadpole" person.

When the child depicts flowering plants and tall trees growing straight, we can presume that the child feels that she too is blooming and growing tall and straight and being productive—at least to some degree.

Helping Children Cope with Their Fears

Except for falling, loud noises, or of the sudden introduction of unfamiliar objects within their visual field, infants have few real fears. Babies have an "experimental" approach to exploring their environment (Piaget, 1970). Given a reasonably healthy infancy, babies are relatively unafraid of the dark or new territory. In the words of a first-grade child, "Babies are just too dumb to know any better." As children grow older, around two to three years of age, they develop a distinctly human cognitive ability, which we can call imagination. Imagination allows children to make up pretend games and to invent a world of their own. But this very same ability leads also to imagining frightening possibilities. What are they afraid of? Lots of things. For example, they are afraid of getting hurt.

Fear of Bodily Injury. Sometime in their third year of life, children become aware that they are vulnerable to injury. The little girl who has scratched herself yells, "Mommie, my blood is running out!" The little boy becomes panic-stricken when he watches his sun-burned skin begin to peel off. The best thing a caretaker can do is to apply a band-aid to the child's scratch, no matter how small it is, and top it off with a kiss "to get better." The band-aid's curative effect owes as much to its magical powers as to its healing properties. For the little boy whose sunburned skin is beginning to peel off, other magical remedies can be used (such as calamine lotion), even if the medication is only a psychological placebo.

Fear of Castration: Yes, It's Real! Yes, Freud was right in this respect. Little boys do develop a fear that their penis may wither away, die, and fall off! Freud assumed this anxiety occurred only in children who are threatened in this manner when they masturbate, causing castration anxiety. But more recent research indicates that this is a normal anxiety for most or all male children, even in the most permissive of homes (Conn & Kanner, 1947). When little boys observe that little girls don't have such a magnificent organ, they develop secret fears that they might lose theirs as well.

Fear of Monsters that Lurk in the Dark. Somewhere between age two and three, children begin to develop fears about the dark, about kidnappers that might steal them, or about monsters lurking under the bed or in the closet. They may even wet the bed out of fear of going to the bathroom by themselves at night. As for the monsters under the bed, several college students have volunteered that they still get nervous when they step off their beds and onto the floor in the middle of the night. A night light is a wonderful protection against "things that go bump in the night."

Fear of the Monsters in Their Night Dreams. Children may also start having bad dreams from which they wake up screaming. The frightening dream symbols may actually be monsters or "bad men" who will kidnap them or big animals. When a child has such a frightening dream, the important thing is not to say something like "there are no such things as monsters." The child knows there are! He has just dreamed them! A child has very little ability, as yet, to distinguish between what we adults call "reality" and the dream state (Piaget, 1962).

So what can we do to help the child get over a frightening dream? We can let the child talk and talk about "the monster" or "bad men" until the child quiets down (see Box 12.4). Talking is just as cathartic to children as it is to adults. Furthermore, you are building the child's trust in you. You are someone who believes him. He feels safer. Don't start impressing on the child that "it was only a dream." Save that until the next day. Then in front of the child, say to anyone in hearing, "Lucy had a bad dream last night." A discussion about scary dreams that other members in the family have had will not only be therapeutic, it will be the first step in Lucy's understanding that dreams are not the same as "real life."

Children's Literature: Understanding the Children's Phenomenology

By the late 1800s, there had grown up in Europe and Great Britain a field of study that investigated legends as a way to study the psychology of ancient peoples and tribal societies. Certain of these nineteenth-century scholars became especially interested in myth and fairy tales as keys to the phenomenology of children—a Rosetta Stone by which we could discover how children think and what they believe. Freud drew from these studies in his formulation of a child's psychosexual development. The Oedipus legend, for example, formed the basis for his Oedipal complex theory. But fairy tales also fascinated him.

Box 12.4 HELPING A CHILD COPE WITH A NIGHTMARE

A colleague of ours reported a conversation with his four-year-old daughter following a nightmare that had awakened her. The remarkable aspect of this conversation was that her father refrained from denying her reality and enabled her to catharsize her fear of the monster. Although he had come to us to ask what he should have done, there was nothing we could suggest to improve how he handled the situation. All we could do was to congratulate him for his parental intuition.

Child: It was a monster. A big monster. He was after me. Big! Big!

Father: A very big monster?

Child: Yes! Big! Big!

Father: As big as me?

Child: Bigger!

Father: As big as a horse?

Child: Yes!

Father: As big as this house? (*The child has become a little quieter. The question-and-answers have become gamelike.*)

Child: Yes!

Father: Where is the monster now?

Child: Under the bed!

Father: Under the bed?

Child: Yes. Under the bed.

Father: How can a monster as big as a house get under the bed?

Child: I don't know. But he's there just the same!

Father: Can I look and see if he's there?

Child: (*after a moment*) Yes.

(*Her father pretended to look under the bed. He remained "looking" for several moments not saying anything. At last the child's curiosity got the better of her and she broke the silence.*)

Child: Do you see him?

Father: Nope.

Child: Are you sure, Daddy?

Father: I'm sure. Just your old teddy bear.

Child: Let me see! (*The little girl maneuvers herself so that she can hang her head down and peer under the bed.*) I want my teddy bear!

Judging that the child was calmed down now, he helped her settle back into bed.

The Fairy Tale as Metaphor of the Child's Worldview. Why do fairy tales have such appeal for young children? Because the characters in the typical fairy tale represent the child's phenomenological world. As fairy tales evolved over the centuries, handed down from generation to generation in oral tradition, they developed stock characters. A typical fairy tale involves a Good King and a Beautiful Queen and either a Princess or a Prince, and one more very important character—the Wicked Witch or the Wicked Stepmother. The King and the Queen obviously represent our parents who, after all, were the King and Queen of our young world. The little boy identifies, of course, with the Prince and the little girl identifies with the Princess. But who can the Wicked Witch or Wicked Stepmother be? Ah! Therein lies the value of the fairy tale!

As young children, we adored our mothers. She was the giver of all good and all pleasure. She comforted us when we were hurt or scared. She provided us with all kinds of goodies to eat. She was indeed the Beautiful Queen of our small world. But she was not always a Good Queen. Sometimes she did not give in to our demands for more candy—"Not until after supper." Sometimes she frustrated our desires—"No, you can't stay up. It's bedtime!" Sometimes she could be outright mean—"You threw your food on the floor? You clean that up right now!" When our Mommies acted like that, they weren't good at all. We didn't love them then. In fact, we may have even hated them then. We may have even fantasized a terrible revenge on them like Hansel and Gretel who threw the Wicked Old Lady into her own oven. We knew we weren't supposed to hate our Mommies—we are supposed to love them. Besides, Mommies are only mean sometimes. A serious dilemma of our child psychology! Fairy tales solve this dilemma very nicely. Fairy tales devised two mothers: A Beautiful Queen, who died when the baby was born, and the Wicked Stepmother the Good King married after the Beautiful Queen died. Oh, she is so nice to us when the Good King is around. When he is gone, she becomes her old mean self!

Or take, for example, the problems of the youngest child in the family who generally feels shoved around by his or her older siblings and can be actually heard to complain of having nobody "to boss around." Such resentments and desires are wonderfully portrayed in fairy tales in which the youngest child is the hero or the heroine. A typical tale begins: "There once was a miller who had three sons, and the youngest of them went out to seek his fortune . . ." Now the youngest son is frequently referred to as a "simpleton" or "dolt." But who winds up with the fortune? Who slays the dragon? Who is it that marries the princess? The older, more intelligent and capable brothers? Not at all! It is the "dolt and simpleton," of course. Which just goes to show that younger siblings will some day outdo their scornful and more powerful older brothers, so there!

The Value of Fairy Tales: Cartharsizing Childhood Fears and Anxieties. Fairy tales are not sweet "Dick and Jane" type of stories. They may start off with an innocent "Once upon a time long, long ago . . ." and they may end with an optimistic ". . . and they all lived happily ever after," but in between that innocent beginning and optimistic ending, fairy tale plots involve all the evils of the world. In fairy tales, the hero or heroine suffer from a variety of injustices: insults, calumny, kidnapping, child abuse, rape, or—like Hansel and Gretel—the threat of cannibalism. The child experiences all these kinds of anxieties and fears. In fact, children have already suffered many frightening experiences. Her older brother has said he will flush her down the toilet! Her parents tell her that is being silly, but she still believes he will do it. The little boy has been beaten by the bully he calls "Daddy!" And he threatened to do it again! But the worst fear and the worst anxiety the child must confront each day is, wrote Bruno Bettelheim, a noted child psychiatrist, the child's own inner self, the baby **id,** that urges him to do things he shouldn't. A child's worst anxiety is himself (Bettelheim, 1987).

Box 12.5

The following are the responses of college students regarding a significant fairy tale, folklore, or story of their own childhood.

Female: The story of "The Three Billy Goats Gruff" was a very important story to me. I guess because the three goats gruff all were aspects of me. I am usually very shy and quiet and can only make a little noise like the littlest goat gruff, and I am kind of defenseless. The middle-size goat is like me when I have enough courage to assert myself a little more. And the large billy goat gruff is me when I'm angry and can make a really loud noise. But I can't do that very often.

Female: I think the story of "Snow White and Rose Red" meant a lot to me. Although my sister and I were very close, I always felt like Rose Red. For some reason, Snow White is the main person in the story, and she gets the prince, and Rose Red only gets to marry the prince's friend. My sister was fair and I was dark, just like Snow White and Rose Red, and I always thought she was much prettier than me and had more boyfriends than me somehow.

Male: I was the youngest of four children and came late in my parents' life. I had three sisters who were all in their teens when I was born, which made it seem like I was living with five big grownups, all of whom were always telling me what to do. My favorite story was "Jack and the Beanstalk." I used to get a charge out of the fact that he outwitted the giant and brought him down. I can see that I identified with Jack, and the giant was all the grownups in my family. And I also have a sneaking suspicion that I get a charge still out of outwitting my boss, or my father, or anyone in authority. I'll have to look into this.

Conquering the "Beast Within." Freud and other psychologists have noted the fierceness of children's sibling jealousy when they have been displaced by a baby brother or sister. Their sibling rivalry stems from their desire to be the only object of their parents' love and devotion—particularly from their mother. Children would like to do away with the father and siblings who grab mother's attention. Although we may think children are innocent of such thoughts and feelings, Bettelheim (1987) called our attention to a child's violent thoughts and urges. As Freud explained it, the socialization process takes many years and the desires and urges of the ferocious "id" will make itself felt from time to time. Despite the violence and brutality of fairy tale plots, Bettelheim says fairy tales actually provide children with hope that they will someday be able to conquer the Monster inside them. The Prince who slays the Dragon provides that hope—for the Dragon is a wonderful representation of the "beast within." Bettelheim's thesis is that we should not deny fairy tales to our children because they are violent. Their very violence helps children catharsize their inner torments and frights.

Fairy Tales as Moral/Ethical Instruction. Erich Fromm, another noted psychologist, explained it this way. Just as we read adult fiction to catharsize the woes of our lives, so too do children love to listen to fairy tales for precisely the same reasons. Furthermore, fairy tales deal with morality at a level the child can understand. The real themes of fairy tales are good versus evil, the poor versus the rich, the weak and the helpless versus the strong and the mighty. Ultimately, fairy tales are teaching about crime and punishment and the existential problems of death, injustice, and despair. Fairy tales hold out the promise of ultimate justice and ultimate success. Evil is eventually punished, the good are eventually rewarded, and all who deserve it live "happily ever after."

They also teach lessons in parable form. In the words of one writer of children's fiction, "Beauty and the Beast" should be read by every pretty girl who places too high a value on masculine good looks, and also by every unfortunate boy [with acne] who knows that he's a prince down deep" (Hornyansky, 1969). We add the note that a little introspection into the favorite fairy tales and stories of our own childhood may give us an insight into our struggle for personality integration as we were growing up (see Box12.5).

Parenting the Child for School Readiness

Parenting Styles: Authoritarian, Permissive, and Authoritative

One of the tasks that children encounter when going to school for the first time is discovering they are not the center of the adult's world. They have to learn to share their toys. They have to learn that they must stay seated sometimes and "do seat work." They have to learn how to raise their hands to talk. They need permission to go to the bathroom. They can't run in the halls. They have to learn to write the letters and numbers between two lines at a time when their fine motor coordination is not yet developed. They have to learn to read despite the fact that the English language, being as unphonetic and huge as it is, may be *the* most difficult language to learn to read. At this early age, children have to learn endless rules and, at the same time, to acquire many language and computing skills. What can parents do to foster the child's adaptation to the school environment is suggested by the classic Baumrand studies (1973) on styles of parenting.

Our ethnic background will naturally influence our parenting style. We may have come from a patriarchal family where the father's word is law. Or we may have come from a family in which the mother played the dominant role. Our ethnic background also influences the child's personality. Children from Mediterranean backgrounds will tend to be more expressive. If our background was more Nordic, we probably grew up in a more reserved and less emotionally expressive family. But whatever our family background, our parenting styles will fall into one of the following three categories: authoritarian, permissive, or authoritative.

Authoritarian Parenting. This is the traditional and historical parenting style and is based on the use of power. The parents assume the responsibility for their children's welfare and upbringing. The assumption underlying this style is that "parents know best" what is good for the child. Since parents are the adults and have more experience of the world, they feel they must take charge of the child's education and experiences. The parents make the rules, and the children are expected to obey them without question. If they disobey, physical force or punishment may be used. When the children are little and question why they should do something, the answer goes, "Because I say so." These families are adult-centered and adults make the rules of the house. When the children reach their adolescence and want to kick over the traces, the answer goes, "As long as you're under my roof and I am paying the bills, you follow my rules." This style of parenting is still the predominant style of the working class. It is also consistent with the type of jobs working-class people have where there is a boss who says what should be done and when. No excuses! No alibis! Just do it! Period! Some of these parents have never experienced any other way of relating to authority, and this is the way they relate to their children.

Permissive Parenting. This style emerged in the 1960s as the result of our changing views about personality development. It was based on Rogers' model of self-discovery and nondirective counseling style. Rogers (1960) had posited that each of us has a center-of-growth that is uniquely our own. When we are in touch with our center, we act appropriately. When we are always being told how we should be and how we should think, we grow up confused and alienated from this center-of-growth. Rogers' therapy was to listen reflectively to clients but not to interpret for them or tell them what to do. Permissive parents applied Rogers' theories to raising their children. These parents believed that in a democratic society, it is more appropriate to raise children, not in an authoritarian style, but in a more "democratic" style. Their homes were "children-centered" and freer in atmosphere. In child-centered homes, children were given as few rules as possible. Permissive parents wanted their children to discover the world for themselves without adult "interference." They would then grow up more in touch with their center-of-growth, and therefore more spontaneous, more authentic, and more creative.

Authoritative Parenting. This style evolved out of the criticism leveled at permissive parenting. Critics were particularly concerned about allowing children to have complete freedom of choice, such as what time they wanted to go to bed. Children, they said, are simply not yet capable of making mature judgments. Another criticism: Permissive parenting sometimes led to such loud and unrestrained attention-getting behavior on the part of the children that visiting these homes was often a nightmare. The most serious criticism was that children had so much "center stage," they were growing up to be attention-demanding adults with little respect for the needs of others.

Authoritative parenting is based on Skinner's **operant conditioning,** which stresses positive reinforcement for constructive behavior. Environmental engineering is used instead of ordering or physical force. Instead of rules there are guidelines. Parents use themselves as role models. If a child leaves a tricycle in the driveway, parents may remind the child several times to put it away. If the child continues to leave the tricycle on the driveway, the parent simply puts it away until the child demonstrates the required behavior. Punishment is used but only rarely since parents are aware that punishment only raises hostility in the child and the behavior doesn't cease—it merely goes underground. Authoritative homes are not adult-centered but neither are they child-centered. They are family-centered.

Adaptation to School. Baumrind's objective was to discover how these three parenting styles affected the child's adaptation to school. The results clearly revealed the children's parental upbringing. As we might have guessed, children from authoritarian homes were belligerent and aggressive with other children. They tended to regard teachers and other adults somewhat suspiciously and to keep their distance from them. Adults mean "trouble" so stay away from them! They fought with other children more often on the playground and more often were verbally abusive toward other children in the classroom. While a minority of these children remained antisocial, however, the majority eventually adapted quite well to the classroom situation. After all, they were used to rules in their home; they simply had to learn new rules. The negative side, however, was that they had a hard time doing "independent seat work" or working creatively with others in joint projects.

Children from the authoritative home were clearly the most at ease in the new classroom situation. They conformed easily to the school rules and responded well to praise and direction, particularly if the teachers used the same kinds of positive reinforcements as the parents. But these children also demonstrated socially responsible and self-controlled exploratory behavior. All in all, the child from the authoritative family was the best adapted to the new school environment.

Box 12.6   PARENTING STYLES AND ADJUSTMENT TO SCHOOL

Parenting Style	Assumptions	Values	Behavioral Consequences
Authoritarian Adult-centered *Based on authority and power.*	Parents have responsibility for child's welfare.	Obedience to rules. Respect for authority. Parents supervise and punish transgressions.	Initially belligerent but makes quick adaptation to school. Avoids adults. Some remain belligerant but most settle down. Not motivated to do "seat work" or creative projects.
Permissive Child-centered *Based on Rogers' client-centered counseling.*	Freedom from rules or parental interference enables child to actualize center-of-growth.	Children encouraged to discover the world and to express themselves.	Lost in new environment. Lacked self-reliance and unable to adapt to not being center of attention. Good at creative projects, but difficulty in sharing.
Authoritative Family-centered *Based on Skinner's operant conditioning.*	Children acquire responsible behavior through observational learning and adult role-modeling.	Parents set guidelines. Child's autonomy is respected.	Adapted quickly to school routine. Able to play cooperatively with other children Good "inner resources."

Reflective Writing: What Kind of Parenting Did You Have? Respond to the following Items.

1. What kind of ethnic or cultural background do you come from?
2. If your ethnic background is not "mainstream America," how did it affect your ability to cope in school?
3. In your family, who had the supreme authority or was it democratically equal?
4. Were your parents authoritarian, permissive, or authoritative?
5. Describe your family environment in terms of health and harmony.
6. Were you raised androgynously? Whatever your answer, describe how it affected your personality?
7. Reflecting on your own upbringing, describe:
   a) one thing you would keep the same
   b) one thing you might change as you bring up your children.

Surprisingly, the poorest adaptation was displayed by the children from the permissive home. They seemed at a total loss in the new environment. They lacked the very self-reliance that permissive parents were trying to foster. From an environment in which they were the center of attention, they were now only one child in a classroom full of thirty other children. It took these children a lot longer to get their "sea legs" and learn what was expected of them.

Using the Three Parenting Styles Appropriately. So how should we parent? Perhaps there is a place for all 3 parenting styles. If a child runs into a street full of cars, this is not the time to be permissive. That kind of situation calls for a loud *Get out of the street!* In times of danger or crisis, we may need to be very authoritarian indeed! When the situation is dangerous, as in playing near water, there are certain restrictions and rules the child must learn to obey. If the children are playing safely on the beach making sand castles, parents can afford to be very permissive indeed (while keeping one eye out). At other times, we can do our best to be authoritative which means that while we keep an eye on their safety, we foster their own exploration of the world.

As children approach kindergarten age, they need to have learned to obey certain house rules.

- No playing in the street.
- No crossing the street unless accompanied by an adult.
- Washing hands before each meal.
- Washing hands after a trip to the bathroom.
- After dinner, putting their dishes on the kitchen counter.
- Putting their toys away before going out to play.
- Coming in when called for meals or bedtime.

These rules may seem obvious and absurdly simple but the point is that the child does not have a choice in these matters—the child is simply learning to mind a few simple do's and don'ts. If the child learns to follow the house rules, learning to follow school rules will come easier and problems of discipline will be less liable to rise. Learning to pick up their toys before going out to play will enable them to follow the teacher's instructions to put away their paste and coloring tools before they line up for recess.

Psychological Androgyny: A Larger Worldview and Expanded Capabilities

Originally, the term **androgyny** meant a person who had both male and female sexual characteristics. The social sciences borrowed the term and applied it to psychological characteristics. As a medical term, it indicates a sad condition, but as a psychological term, it connotes something quite beneficial. **Psychological androgyny** refers to children who have developed skills, interests, and abilities of both genders. The androgynous girl-child has not been severely punished for being a "tomboy" or for showing interest in competitive sports, mechanics, math, science, or business. The androgynous boy-child has not been severely punished for his interests in art, music, reading, nurturing, and other pursuits that our culture has labeled "feminine." Androgynous children show a wider range of intellectual pursuits and a more sophisticated palette of emotional responses. They can be both competitive and cooperative, and they have a larger worldview. By contrast, all-girl families tend to foster "lady-like" behaviors such as politeness, courtesy, and an

Figure 12.3 The androgynous child. This type of child will have a broader range of interests and abilities and therefore will have higher intellectual and emotional intelligence.

interest limited mainly to domestic affairs. All-boy families tend to encourage sports, aggressiveness, and competition. In mixed-gender families, however, boys grow up interested not only in athletics and cars but also in their sisters' games and puzzles and reading material. Likewise, girls who grow up in mixed-gender families show an interest not only in dolls and games, but also in their brothers' sports, science projects, and mechanical pursuits. Sandra Bem (1975) pioneered studies of androgyny. Studies indicate that psychologically androgynous children have higher IQ scores, get better academic grades, and have higher educational/vocational goals. Furthermore, the boys have healthier interpersonal relationships since they are able to express tenderness and are more comfortable with intimate relationships. Their psychological androgyny does not make them confused about their sexual identity. In fact, they are more sure of their gender roles and secure in who they are as male or female. Most important of all, they have better coping mechanisms to survive the stresses and strains of adult life (Bem, 1985).

Raising Emotionally Intelligent Children

In 1916, Lewis Terman of Stanford Univerity published the first American IQ test, which was supposed to measure some global ability of intelligence (see Tip 12.1). Terman's test, called the *Stanford-Binet Test of Intelligence* became the measurement by which children were admitted into advanced scholastic courses or put into institutions for mental retardation. As the test became used over time, it was noticed that many children were being rated as below "Average" in intelligence: Native American children on reservations, black children living in ghettos and rural areas, Southern Appalachian White children, children of coal miners, and so on. It began to dawn on psychologists that there was something seriously wrong with using the Stanford-Binet as the sole criterion of a child's level of intelligence. What was wrong was that Terman had standardized his test on middle-class children in and around San Francisco. That means that any child who came from locales other than urban/suburban San Francisco was severely disadvantaged.

Many other tests of intelligence were also devised over the next 75 years, including the famous **Wechsler Intelligence Scale for Children,** the so-called **WISC.** And of course both of these tests for children have been revised from time-to-time to keep abreast of sociocultural changes. But the WISC was also discovered to disadvantage certain populations such as the Hispanic child who is not highly verbal in the English language, the hard-of-hearing child, or a child who stutters. As a consequence, many psychologists called into question the whole concept of intelligence, as defined by American tests of intelligence, which are highly verbal in nature. As a matter-of-fact, today some psychologists resist using the word "intelligence" at all, since they believe the term as we use it has become as useless as a corrupted disk. Other terms that are used to replace it include *human abilities, academic skills, cognitive processes,* etc. These psychologists point out that while the IQ score has some predictive ability about how much education a person can achieve, other factors are equally, if not more, important. Success in school and even career success has even more to do with factors such as motivation,

---

Tip 12.1 The Origins of the Stanford-Binet. This test did not originate in the United States. It was actually developed in France and it was not considered an intelligence test at all. It was simply a way to "weed out" children who were so slow to learn, they were disrupting the teacher's attempts to teach. When Terman brought the test and adapted it to English-speaking children, it evolvd into what people thought was an "intelligence test."

Box 12.7 HOUSE RULES

If you dirty it, wash it.	If you borrow it, return it.
If you open it, close it.	If you break it, get it fixed.
If you drop it, pick it up.	If you play with it, put it back.
If you use it, put it away.	If you wear it, put it in the hamper.
If you spill it, clean it up.	If you empty it, fill it up.

personality stability or pathology, sensitivity to social situations, ability to communicate with others, and the continual striving to learn more. Furthermore, the concept of intelligence differs in different cultures. In addition to high verbal ability, Western nations value problem-solving and what has been called "technological intelligence." African and Asian cultures value (among other qualities) **social intelligence (SQ)**—defined as the ability to live harmoniously and thoughtfully with others (Sternberg & Kaufman, 1998).

In the early 1980s, it was suggested (Gardner, 1993) that human beings have **multiple intelligences (MI theory)**. **MI theory** includes *linguistic* intelligence (writing a poem or reading a book), *spatial* intelligence (fitting a box into a trunk), *musical* intelligence, *bodily-kinesthetic* (athletic) intelligence, *interpersonal* intelligence (the ability to get along with others), and *intrapersonal* intelligence (insight and understanding of oneself) and so on. Other intelligences have since been added, such as *natural* intelligence (ability to discern patterns in nature), *spiritual* intelligence (concern for cosmic understanding) and *existential* intelligence (what we understand to be the meaning of life) (Gardner,1998). But of all of the multiple inteligences suggested, however, the one kind of intelligence that took strong hold of the psychological community in the 1990s is *emotional* intelligence.

"What Is Emotional Intelligence (EQ)?" The two psychologists who first used the term **emotional intelligence (EQ)** defined it as a set of skills involving the ability *to understand our own feelings and the feelings of others and to use this information to guide one's thinking and actions* (Salovey & Mayer, 1989). If the reader is beginning to suspect that emotional intelligence is another term for good "people skills," that may not be too far off the mark. Social intelligence is what enables us to deal with difficult situations without panic. However it is defined, emotional intelligence or EQ has become recognized as far more important than "IQ" scores for academic achievement, vocational success, and family relationships (Goleman, 1995). The definition of emotional intelligence has not yet stablized. But most psychologists agree that the following traits and abilities are included:

- Empathy
- Understanding one's feelings
- Expressing feelings
- Controlling one's temper
- Independence of thought
- Independence of action
- Persistence
- Friendliness
- Respect for others
- Adaptability
- Ability to get along with others
- Sensitivity to the feelings of others
- Optimistic and smiling demeanor
- Kindness
- Self-awareness and desire to improve
- Ability to understand other people's feelings

Box 12.8

RAISING EMOTIONALLY INTELLIGENT CHILDREN
Some Guidelines

Establishing Firm Disipline. *Don't be afraid to state your expectations of behavior. Sometimes the child simply does not know. Establish a firm but gentle need for appropriate behaviors as follows:*

1. Praise the child for appropriate behaviors but do not overpraise and be accurate. Appropriate praise needs to be specific rather than gushing. "Nice job on the car!"

2. Demonstrate your interest in what your child is doing by participating in the activity. Or simply describe what you see is going on. *"Hey! That's a great tower you two have constructed. May I take a look at it?"*

3. Make clear rules and stick to them. EQ professionals suggest writing these rules down and posting them where they can be seen—in the kitchen, in the children's bedroom, in the bathroom, and all over (See Box 12.7).

4. Give the child a warning if he is pushing the rules too hard. Everybody deserves a second chance. Maybe even a third. Warnings can be verbal but eventually you will want to be able to warn him with a look or an upraised finger rather than words. Reason: Verbal warnings repeated often enough begin to sound like nagging. Body language signals are more effective. Long before we had language, we were able to read the body language of other human beings in our world. That still holds true as we grow up.

5. If the child deliberately breaks a rule, follow up immediately with an appropriate response. Sometimes a simple remonstrance will do—especially if the child is generally obedient and sensitive. Get the child to state what it was that he did that he should not do. It is much more effective if the child tells you than if you tell him (which is simply nagging). If the child repeats the offense deliberately, follow it with kindly but appropriate consequences. The consequence of misbehavior should fit the misbehavior. If the child made a mess on the floor, he cleans it up.

6. Utilize the technique of overcorrection if the child keeps forgetting. For example, if the child "forgets" to bring in his bike to the garage, have him walk the bike back and forth to the garage (say) six times. He won't willingly "forget" again. If the child still "forgets," perhaps the best thing now is to take the bike away until the child understands that leaving a bike outside is the same as inviting someone to steal it.

7. Limit the amount of TV watching in the house. The time that has been eliminated can be used for homework, family discussions, creative home projects, etc. TV has been found to have a depressing effect on young children, especially when they are in the habit of watching violence of overstimulating programs. When children are young, you need to monitor their TV viewing.

8. Use the shaming technique if the child shows no remorse for an action. One of the distinquishing characteristics of juvenile delinquents and career criminals is their lack of remorse for what they have done. What they are sorry for is that they got caught. Instead of trying to spare the child's feeling, it may not be a bad strategy to shame the child if the wrongness of the behavior has not penetrated. A common example used by parents is to take a child back to the store she has stolen something from and make her apologize. A one-time consequence of this nature early enough in the child's life may be a cure for all time.

Fostering Emotional Intelligence. *The suggestions above are fairly easy to institute. They are clear and easy to follow. The second set of suggestions have to do with developing the positive attributes mentioned earlier (empathy, kindness, cheerfulness, self-efficacy, etc.)—which are not easily spelled out and require thoughtful planning by the parent.*

1. Act as role models. If we want to have honest children, we need to be honest with them. If we want polite children, we need to be polite to them. If we want optimistic children, we need to be cheerful around them. Our children are watching us and they are imitating us. If we don't want our children to smoke, we had better not smoke. We know now that saying "Do as I say, not as I do" is only teaching them that adults can be hypocrites.

2. Apologize to the child when we make a mistake. Being good role models does not mean being perfect. It is OK to make mistakes—just admit them. It's OK to scream occasionally—just apologize later. It's OK to cry in front of children once in a while—just let them know you are feeling better and that even adults need to cry once in a while just like children. In fact, to know that even adults give way to irrational behavior (as they do) or have sad feelings (as they do) helps children understand that parents are people—like themselves.

3. Encourage random acts of kindness and senseless acts of beauty. Allow the child to witness your own acts of kindness and beauty. While walking, pick up litter. Encourage the child to do so as well. If the child has a friend who is hurt and home from school, find something the child can take to his friend while he is home. If a playmate has a contagious illness, you can both pick out a get "well card" for the child.

Box 12.8   RAISING EMOTIONALLY INTELLIGENT CHILDREN
Some Guidelines (continued)

4. Teach the child how to apologize by way of words or action. If the child has hurt someone accidently or deliberately, discuss it with the child. Together, decide on something that the child can do to make up for the hurt. The ability to apologize is one of the great people skills organizations appreciate in a manager or executive. If you can teach this to a child, you are doing that child a great service.

5. Read stories of courageous men, women, and children to the youngster. Choose fairy tales and stories that embody a virtue in the hero or heroine. Don't just read the story, however; encourage the child to tell you what was noble in the main character. As the child gets older, you can substitute biographies of real men and women who were outstanding for some virtue or other.

6. Encourage the child to draw, paint, or color how he's feeling. When the child is feeling depressed (and children do get depressed), encourage the child to talk, following Thomas Gordon's guidelines for facilitative communication. If the child is unable to verbalize it, encourage the child to draw his feelings. He doesn't have to draw anything special—angry black strokes will be just as efficacious as a well-delineated scene. What the child is doing is externalizing his black feelings. Don't throw the drawing away! Hang it up on the refrigerator along with all the other pretty pictures as a way of

legitimizing the child's expression. Later, the two of you may want to laugh over it (and laughter is a wonderful healer) and even entitle the picture as "Robbie's black mood day."

7. Teach optimism. One of the "big five" personality traits validated in one research study after another is the quality of optimism. There is a strong genetic aspect to optimism but it can be developed. When Robbie has a black mood day, encourage the child to find something that would be "fun to do" and cheer him up. Don't you do this! What you want to do is enable the child to discover these activities, so the child will be able to use this technique later.

8. Teach the child efficacious self-talk and efficacious behavior. If Robbie says, "I'll never be any good at arithmetic" or "football" (or anything else in which he is suffering low self-esteem), find a quiet place to discuss the problem. Ask Robbie what would he need to be good at it. If he says he needs to practice more, then you and he can find a way for helping him get more practice. A talk with the coach or the teacher or someone you know that can help Robbie may be the next step. If Robbie says that the "other guys go to soccer camp" perhaps you and Robbie can discuss how to get him to soccer camp. However your discussions turn out, the final decision must be Robbie's.

There is presently much discussion about the possible neurological underpinnings of emotional intelligence. When something happens that arouses concern, persons with a high EQ have the ability to temper their fight-flight-freeze response and act in a cool and constructive manner. People who have low EQ fall victim to the fight-flight-freeze response, which may then trigger runaway emotions and explosive behaviors, as for example:

- We are invited to join a risky adventure and leap before we take a good look at what is involved.
- Or we find ourselves trapped in an awkward situation from which it will be embarrassing to extricate ourselves.
- A chance remark insults us (when no insult was intended) and we fly off the handle at the speaker.
- Scared that we are not prepared for a test, we panic at the first item we are not sure of and run out of the room.

Most of us have experienced one or more of these kinds of runaway emotions and behaviors. More extreme examples have made the headlines. Probably the most tragic of such loss of emotional control are the high school shootings and suicides that occurred at Littleton, Colorado, and Conyers, Georgia and elsewhere. But each of the incidents listed below has also made newspaper headlines. Psychologists who support the concept of emotional intelligence believe that the perpetrators had a low emotional intelligence (Goleman, 1995).

- A child cries off and on all night until one or the other of the parents beats the child into insensibility.
- An abused woman, frightened for her life, sets on fire the bed her husband is sleeping on.
- A student on the way to class gets so frustrated by the bumper-to-bumper traffic, that road rage takes over and she causes a serious accident.
- A teenager, enthralled by his passionate feelings for a teacher, is talked into killing her husband.
- Two adolescent brothers have an argument outside their home. The younger brother gets his rifle and shoots his older brother in the head.

Although the definition of emotional intelligence is still being hotly argued, psychologists and educators are already involved in teaching children (and adults) how to raise their EQ. Some of these teaching concepts (see Box 12.8) have not been validated by rigorous research but they are certainly worth considering. These teaching concepts are already being introduced to grade school children.

Finally, What Can We Do About Child Abuse?

As unfortunate and distasteful a topic as child abuse is, we cannot leave it out of a chapter on children and what can be done to protect them. The amount of child abuse is difficult to determine since each state has its own definition of what constitutes child abuse. The incidence of child abuse, including incest, is appalling. In the United States, reported cases hit the 3,140,000 mark in 1994 and the figures are still rising (Wiese & Darrow, 1995). Of course, it is highly probable that the increasing statistics is not so much a matter of more actual child abuse than it is a measure of more public awareness and willingness to report it. Professionals in the area of child abuse distinguish several kinds of child abuse (Baumrind, 1995) as follow:

- **Physical abuse,** which is easily determined by medical examinations and X-rays. Physicians are able to detect broken arms, legs, and ribs that could not be the result of simple falls. Other signs of physical abuse that are not uncommon are burns in the shape of a cigarette or iron, lacerations, missing teeth, and abrasions. (21 percent).
- **Mental/emotional and miscellaneous abuse,** usually involving screaming, name-calling, and blaming the child for the problems of the family. (19 percent).
- **Neglect,** which is the hardest to determine. This kind of abuse can take the form of inadequate nutrition, rest, and sleep; inadequate parental involvement with the child's school achievement, and inadequate medical treatment (not taking the child to the doctor when needed). Medical examinations may also reveal deficiencies of nutrition and even the ingestion of poisonous substances. When this is occurring during infancy, the child may even suffer **failure to thrive** and die. (49 percent).
- **Sexual abuse.** (11 percent).

We know, too, that certain variables contribute to child abuse, such as substance-abusing parents, single parenting, large families, poorly educated parents, and teenage mothers who are too young to cope with babies. When bills pile up and there are too many mouths to feed, and there is no one to turn to for help, the parents may see the children as the source of their problems. A young mother with several children and either isolated from supporting relatives or crowded into slum conditions is very likely to be at risk for any one or several of the types of child abuse described above. There are other variables that may contribute. Mothers who themselves were abused physically, emotionally, or sexually are significantly more likely to continue the pattern of abuse with their own children. Altogether, the research supports the view that styles of parenting are carried on from one generation to another (Spieker, Bensley, McMahon, Fung, & Osslander, 1996).

The consequences of child abuse can be short- or long-term. Short-term consequences may appear as being frightened of and avoiding adults (particularly in school), poor social skills (including being "picked on" by other children, since the child has not learned to defend herself), learning problems, and fear of exposing parts of the body (such as when they are supposed to "dress out" for gym). Long-range consequences include all the symptoms of post-traumatic stress disorder discussed in the chapter on abnormal behavior. Many cases of extreme pathology, such as personality disorder and dissociative identity disorder, have been traced to a brutal childhood (Baumrind, 1995).

At the present time, many mental health professionals are looking for solutions and preventions for child abuse. The tragic aspect is that the abusing parents may actually love the child, but under the influence of alcohol or drugs may suddenly pound a crying child into silence. Whether they have been inadequate parents, neglectful parents, or even abusing parents, taking the children away from them is not necessarily the best answer and may actually have worse consequences on the children. To the astonishment of many professionals, abused children (particularly when young) cling to their abusing parents. They don't want to be put into a place of shelter and safety. Until they are older, most abused children genuinely believe that they have deserved the abuse and just want to be "good" so their parents will love them. Taking them away from their parents seems to the child's mind to be punishment for having been "bad." As a consequence, agencies involved with child abuse have taken a different direction. They are trying out educational support programs for abusing parents, teaching them about how to care for their children, how to discipline them without violence, and how to connect to support persons to overcome their physical isolation and emotional despair. Thus far, however, the programs are few and far between and the results somewhat disappointing—probably because the programs have been underfunded and therefore not long enough or adequate enough to produce a change in parental behavior. Of course, the most effective approach to the whole problem is prevention and for that we need to educate teenagers about what it takes to be parents, and to make a nationwide effort to stem the epidemic of teenage pregnancy and to educate them as to the consequences of alcoholic and drug-abusing parents.

Single Parenting and Child Abuse. The problems of single parenting were discussed in the chapter on marriage and the family. We need, however, to add a note here concerning the increased incidence of child abuse in a single parent household where there is an unrelated male also in the house. There is a reported eight times higher incidence of child abuse when there is a man living in the household of a single woman parent. Sometimes the woman is not aware of the abuse (physical or sexual), but sometimes the woman is aware but remains, hoping against hope, that the situation will improve. She does not want to separate from the man because she is attached to him or doesn't believe she can find another male partner. Even sadder is the fact that fatalities on children under five in 1994 was reported as 88% under five years of age. The largest proportion of these fatalities occur when there is an unattached male in the house.

What can single mothers do then? One answer has been to encourage foster parenting by welfare mothers who also have children to care for and cannot work. That obvious answer

---

Box 12.9
SCENARIO REVISITED
A Small Group of Students Discuss Their Childhoods

Six students are seated in a circle with Jill Smith, the graduate assistant.

Jill Smith: You all volunteered for this small group session. But, in keeping with my practice of role modeling, I will self-reveal first. I was the fifth of six children. When I was born, both my parents were very disappointed because they were told they were going to have a boy after four girls. Instead, I was born, making the fifth girl and no boys.

Shannon: Didn't they have sonograms when you were young? My mother knew she was going to have twin boys.

Jill Smith: Oh, yes. But somehow they made a mistake. What they thought was a boy's penis was an unusual looping of the umbilical cord. Hospitals do make mistakes—even to the point of mixing up children as all of you know from the news media. I was a mistake.

Eric: So how did your parents abuse you?

Jill Smith: I'm not saying my parents abused me—only that because of circumstances of being an unwanted child in a large family of only girls, I was neglected. No matter how good my grades in school, they never praised me—all the praise went to my little brother. Nor did they encourage me to go to college. All their pride and praise was centered on Billy. So I grew up feeling as if I was never good enough to warrent any attention from them. I think the result of all this is that I'm a workaholic, never really believing that what I do is good enough. (*After a period of silence, Shannon raises her hand.*)

Shannon: I haven't wanted to admit it but I guess I can face up to it now. My mother never wanted me around her. When she was in one of her depressed bipolar moods, she used to say things to me that really hurt—like I was the cause of all her unhappiness. My father told me that was not true, and I think I knew it was not true but it hurt just the same.

Jonnimae: None of you had the kind of physical abuse I had growing up. First there was my father who beat all of us. I used to hide, but I think it was just as hard hearing my sisters and brothers scream—like it was happening to me. Later, my husband beat me, and I was just a teenager. I ran away after I had two children so it wouldn't happen to them. And you know something! Neither my father or my husband was a bad person—it was only after they got some alcohol into them that they got so mean.

Dan: You've made me think about my two sons. I really haven't given them much fatherly attention. After their mother died, I became alcoholic and I guess I've treated them mean sometimes. Their grandmother has taken care of them mostly.

Jill Smith: Alec, do you want to add anything to this discussion?

Alec: Yeah. But I'm not sure what to say. I think it is that the whole atmosphere in the house was like a mausoleum. Nobody was ever really happy. I don't remember people ever telling a joke or laughing—only shouts and fighting and those awful days when nobody would talk to anybody else. It was like living in an ice world. I've made a connection, lately. You know when we were discussing how we react to negative interpersonal communication? I talked about how I just get cold and very distant. I think it has to do with that icy feeling in the house. I just revert to it. I've started calling that part of myself "the Iceman." You know, like Eugene O'Neil's play *The Iceman Cometh*. (*To Jill*) Do you think I'll ever get over it? I can't tell you what it's like when it happens—it's like I'll never be warm again. I don't even want to be around people, I feel so cold.

Jill Smith: There are no absolutes, Alec. But you've made a good beginning. How are you feeling about the people in this room after telling us about "the Iceman"?

Alec: (*after looking around at everyone in the group*). It was hard to do and I'm still a little embarrassed. But I'm glad I did. It's like we're a family, only a good kind of family that I never had. Thanks. This may sound strange but I'm actually feeling warm sitting here right now.

has not worked out in reality, because many of these mothers have inadequate parenting skills themselves and the children are even more at risk for abuse or neglect. Are daycare centers the answer? Well, better than the welfare foster mother. But daycare centers need to be adequately investigated since child protective agencies have had to investigate reported abuse there too (although some accusations have been demonstrated to have been false). What then is the best answer at present? Well, to develop willingness of family members to care for the children. If the child's grandparents are willing and able, they sometimes provide the best foster care. If the divorce has been at all civil, the ex-husband's parents may also be delighted to have some young ones in the house again and grateful to the mother for encouraging a grandparenting relationship. In the meantime, educational institutions all over the country are instituting child care programs to train people to be more adequate foster mothers or daycare workers.

IMPORTANT TERMS AND CONCEPTS TO KNOW

adult	emotionally	moral/ethical	power
art	environmental	mother	psychological
authoritative	fairy tales	multiple	role models
castration	family	Native American	self-esteem
center-of-growth	Flynn	neglect	therapy
child abuse	gender	operant conditioning	toxins
cognitive	genetic	permissive	verbal
culture	intelligence		

MAKE YOUR OWN CHAPTER SUMMARY BY FILLING IN THE BLANKS BELOW

Use the words from "Important Terms and Concepts to Know" to fill in the blanks below.

Personality development. A child's personality is a mix of many factors. Children today are exposed to a richer, but more complex environment. The _____ effect is the evident increase in IQ scores over the last 50 years.

Parenting begins before birth. We have become aware of the many _____ factors that deterimine physical defects and emotional problems. But _____ factors also play a big part, even at the embryo-fetal stage. Prospec-

tive parents are cautioned against many _____ that could affect the child. Unwanted pregnancies can also affect the child-to-be in later life in regard to _____ .

Parenting the young child. Theories of the purpose of play are numerous. Piaget considered play to be necessary for the child's _____ development. It is generally accepted now that play is preparation for life. Play _____ can be used to help children alleviate their fears and anxieties, as in the case of the frightened young boy, Dibs. Children's _____ can be used as a diagnostic tool to discover the child's worldview or specific problems.

Children's Fears. Children are afraid of many things, including injury such as _____ , and of "things that go bump in the night." Psychologists believe that _____ represent the child's phenomenology. The child is the Prince or Princess while the Beautiful Queen and the Wicked Witch represent different aspects of their _____ . These stories represent the child's _____ development (good versus evil) at a level the child can understand.

Parenting the child who is soon to go to first grade. First-graders have many things to learn. Baumrind studied the adaptation of children to school as based on the parenting styles of their families. Authoritarian parenting is traditional and is based on _____ . A more _____ parenting style was evolved from Rogers' client-centered therapy and its objective is to foster the children's own exploration of the world and to help the child stay in touch with their _____ . Authoritative parenting is based on _____ . One of the strategies for enabling a wider spectrum of talents, interests, and abilities is to encourage _____ androgyny.

Stepparenting. This is a special type of parenting. The very nature of the stepfamily is fraught with the myths of the mean stepmother and the uncaring stepsiblings. Then there is the very problem that the child is being introduced into a different family _____ , which is hard enough for adults but overwhelming for children. Guidelines for stepparenting are quite distinctive.

Raising emotionally intelligent children. Intelligence as defined by _____ tests has been shown as disadvantaging special populations of children, such as African-Americans, _____ children on reservations, ghetto children of the cities, and white Southern Appalachian children. As well, children who are less _____ , such as hard-of-hearing or use English as a second language will also test lower than average. Some personality theorists even question the use of the term *intelligence,* preferring other terms such as *human abilities* or *academic skills*, etc. Others have suggested we have _____ intelligences (*MI theory*). Raising _____ intelligent children became a hot topic in the 1990s. This approach to child raising advocates teaching children to be mindful of the rules of the house, and also becoming _____ for them by including them in acts of generosity, kindness, and beauty.

Child abuse. Child abuse takes many forms including physical abuse, mental/emotional abuse, _____ abuse which is a lot harder for the courts and professional agencies to define and deal with. _____ is eight times more prevalent in houses with unrelated male living in the house.

13 THE AGONIZING JOURNEY THROUGH ADOLESCENCE
The Need for More Understanding of the Adolescent Changes

Puberty and Adolescence: In a short space of time, the former enemy suddenly has become very attractive.

Box 13.1
SCENARIO
Shannon Confides in Her Friend, Jonnimae

Shannon and Jonnimae are having lunch together in the cafeteria.

Shannon: There's somebody I like a lot and I think he likes me. How can you tell if a person is interested in you, I mean really interested?

Jonnimae: Bless your heart, Honey, I think I know who it is! Eduardo, right?

Shannon: *(blushing)* How did you guess?

Jonnimae: I got eyes. You got a king-size crush.

Shannon: Is it that obvious? *(Jonnimae nods).* Oh, dear, I hope everybody hasn't noticed. I hope Eduardo hasn't noticed.

Jonnimae: Why don't you want him to know, for heavens' sake!

Shannon: Because maybe he doesn't feel that way about me.

Jonnimae: Of course he does! How come you don't know he's got a crush on you too?

Shannon: Does he really? How come he hasn't said anything to me?

Jonnimae: Honey, he's probably just as scared as you to make the first move. You gotta let him know.

Shannon: How do I do that?

Jonnimae: Well, the first thing you can do is when he looks at you, don't look away like I see you do. Smile at him. Let him know you like him.

Shannon: What will he think of me if I smile like that. My mother would call that being "brazen."

Jonnimae: These are things girls learn how to do naturally when they reach about thirteen.

Shannon: Gosh, I'm so ignorant about guys. You see, I've never been on a date—not a real one. We used to go on church picnics and we got paired, sort of, by the organizers. Girls brought the picnic and guys brought things to sit on and games to play. I hated those picnics because I never really knew if the guy liked me or just felt sorry for me because . . . well, you know . . . because of my club foot.

Jonnimae: A pretty girl like you afraid of boys? You just got to let them know you like them. Boys aren't nearly as tough as they put on. They can brave eleven other men out on the football field, but make a speech in front of a class or approach a girl they like, and their knees turn to sand and they get tongue-tied. I guess I 'm going to have to tell you about how girls and boys go about getting to know each other and dating. I've been talking to my teenagers about sex and dating and all that. I might as well talk to you, too—if you wouldn't mind, that is.

Box 13.1   SCENARIO (continued)
                    Shannon Confides in Her Friend, Jonnimae

Shannon: Mind! I've been dying to have someone talk to me. I'm just plain ignorant. Compared to all the boy-girl movies I see on TV, I'm so backwards about sex, I could cry. I never had any girlfriends in high school. Please talk to me about dating and sex—if it wouldn't embarrass you. My mother never talks to me about anything except what she wants me to do in the house and for the boys and all. And it's the one subject my daddy and I never talked about. I guess it would have been too embarrassing for him—and me too, I guess.

The Troubled Adolescent: More Frightened and Insecure Than Adults Realize

It was an early American psychologist, by the name of G. Stanley Hall, who called our attention to the turbulence of this time of life by coining the term **adolescence**, from Latin root words meaning "to grow up" (Hall, 1904). He described this age/stage as a period of *sturm-und-drang* (German for storm-and-strife). It will come as no great surprise to the readers that adolescence is an even more difficult age/stage today than a century ago (see Tip 13.1). Parents of this age group freely admit adolescence to be the most trying time of parenting. High school teachers not infrequently get "burned out" by trying to teach classes of students who have intense adolescent problems. Nor do adolescents themselves experience this time of life as a happy one. Studies reveal that the self-esteem of adolescence is lower in high school than at any other time of the life span (Beane & Lipka, 1986). If the readers are still in their late teens and early twenties, they can probably still remember some of the confusions, anxieties, and problems of their own high school years. The pressure to perform, to excel, to be pretty, to be thin, to be an athlete, to be a "jock," to dress, to drive a car, to be just accepted by one's peers—in short, to compete with others in every dimension of high school life—all make the years of junior and senior high school a misery for most young people.

For many years, Hall's metaphor was quite accepted, but as the decades passed and particularly after the "soft" revolution of the 60's and 70's, Hall's metaphor fell into disfavor. American students were no longer living out their lives as naive "flower children" who preferred to "make love, not war." The drug-happy "hippie" was fast disappearing from the street scene. The adolescents who had idolized the frenetic activities of the Beatles or screamed at the frank sexuality of the Rolling Stones seemed to have turned their attention to the more prosaic and homespun country music artists of this country, Jimmy Buffett, Garth Brooks, and the Judds, mother and daughter. Hall's metaphor of the teenage years as being a time

---

Tip 13.1 On the Term, Sturm un Drang. Hall saw a correlation between the emotionally expressive poetry and life styles of the Romantics of the eighteenth century (Byron, Shelly and Keats, for example) and the adolescent's emotional turmoil. He compared the Romantics' struggling for freedom with the adolescent struggle for freedom—with this essential difference: Where the Romantics were struggling for the freedom from Europe's oppressive governments, today's adolescents are struggling for their own personal freedom. In the worldview of today's adolescents, the rest of us are a supporting cast, either helping them to achieve their quest for self-expression or interfering with their freedom to do so. Generally speaking, the people who are hindering them the most are their parents, but others in the supporting cast of their romantic drama are their teachers, principals, officers of the law, etc.

of turmoil was largely discarded as not typical of the "average" teenager. Psychologists and educators began to describe "most adolescents" as quite well adjusted and growing well. And then in the decade of the 90s, the nation was rocked by news of violence among the nation's 10-to-18 population, particularly by the high school shootings of Littleton, Colorado and Conyers, Georgia. Americans are now asking themselves: *What is going wrong?*

Under a Calm Exterior: Anxieties, Fears, Emotional Mood Swings

When we watch teenagers walking across a high school or college campus, the landscape seems to be one of busy but unexciting clusters of students. When we ask them what they have been doing or learning, their verbal replies seem to corroborate the scene we are watching: *Nothing much. You know, school, homework, hanging out with friends—the usual.* But our observations and their answers do not match the roller coaster of moods and emotions of their interior landscape. Studies of teenagers reveal that their moods and emotions swing from ecstatic satisfaction to the depths of depression several times a day, particularly in the first two years of high school (Fischman, 1987). Both their ecstatic elations and their dejections revolve around peer acceptance or rejection and a lack of meaning in their lives. They attempt to fill up the void they feel by socializing with their peers, talking on the telephone with their friends, watching TV, and—when all else fails to alleviate their feelings of emptiness—by sleeping. Their parents, who are nagging them to do their chores or trying to get them involved in family affairs (which they mostly hate) wonder (as do we all): *Just what are teenagers troubled about?* From the point-of-view of their bewildered parents, teenagers today have more money in their pockets, more "advantages," than they had, and more leisure activities to get involved in than any previous generation. So what is ailing them? A lot of things!

The Problems of the Adolescent Girl

The Need to be Attractive and "Sexy." The teenage girl is obsessed with her appearance. Having developed two years (on the average) earlier than boys, she has been waiting for them to show an interest in her. She studies the young movie stars and what they look like. She rips through fashion magazines and spends hours at the shopping malls to find clothes that will make her look slim, smart, and "sexy." Often, there is also a subtle and covert campaign going on with mothers and their daughters. While mothers do not want to see their daughters engage in destructive premarital sex, many mothers apply subtle pressure on their daughters to demonstrate their sexual attractiveness. She outfits her daughter with bras, guides her in selection of clothes, and instructs her in the subtleties of make-up. When the daughter is besieged with requests for dates, both mother and daughter feel validated. The mother can be reassured that she has brought up her daughter to be poised, socially gracefully, and able to handle herself in the "dating game."

The Need To Be Slim and Slimmer: A Warning Concerning Anorexia and Bulimia. While young men are finally adding the much desired muscles to their frame, young women, on the other hand, are gaining fat in the breasts and hips and thighs as a result of puberty. These changes are in direct opposition to what our society (as portrayed in the media) finds attractive. The teenage girl is obsessed about her appearance. Even when she is slim, she misperceives herself as fat when she looks in the mirror. If she is overweight, she goes on a diet. Or she avoids most food at all costs and may become a victim of **anorexia nervosa,** that is, eating so little that she has not the required 85 percent of the required average weight for her height and frame. Since a certain amount of weight is necessary for a normal period, she may even experience **amenorrhea,** the absence of her monthly periods. Other consequences are anemia, dry skin, brittle hair and nails, sensitivity to heat and cold and changes in temperature, and cognitive deficits. Sometimes they even develop growth of downy hair on their legs and cheeks. If she is hungry and cannot resist food and is afraid she is getting fat, she may become bulemic. **Bulemia** is binge eating followed by vomiting and regurgitating the food she has binged on. She may also use diuretics and laxatives and enemas to keep her weight down. Whether anorexic or bulemic, they will develop strategies to avoid treatment and recovery. They will mouth what family and physicians want to hear—that they need to gain a few pounds and are working on it. They will even prepare food for the family as a way of camouflage and then pretend to eat it (Wolf, 1992).

The Ever-Pressing Question for the Girl-in-Love: Shall I or Shan't I? Having proved themselves datable, girls are now troubled about what to do with their boyfriends who are pressing them for sex. Their boyfriends are no longer content with simple necking, and they pressure their girlfriends to "give in"—*if you really loved me, you would!* If the girl chooses to remain virginal, she may find that she has lost her boyfriend to someone who has been willing to comply with his demands. On the other hand, if she continues to date him and wants to restrict their sexual involvement, she may discover one afternoon or evening that she has gotten herself into a situation from which she cannot escape and falls victim to "date rape." It is difficult to obtain statistics on premarital sex, teenage pregnancy, and rape for obvious reasons, and the estimates vary widely.

Problems of the Sexually Active Girl. If the girl has become sexually active, she lives with the fear, not that she will get a sexually transmitted disease (that really doesn't occur to her) but that she may get unexpectedly pregnant. If her period is late, she lives through anxious day after anxious day until her period does arrive. If she discovers she is pregnant, she now has the anxiety of deciding what to do now.

Even yet, a girl's reputation suffers if she is sexually active in high school. If she gets a reputation that she is sexually promiscuous, she may discover that she suddenly has a lot of bids "for a date." This sudden popularity may make her feel good about herself for a while, but she may discover, alas, that her popularity is the result of "locker room bragging." Having gained a reputation for **promiscuity,** she is now the open target for any adolescent male eager to have a sexual experience (see Box 13.2). In certain adolescent crowds, a sexual "conquest" may be one of the "rites of passage" to membership. He may use any manipulative device to win her compliance.

The Problems of the Adolescent Male

They Are Even More Confused and Bewildered Than Adolescent Girls. If the adolescent female is confused, the adolescent male is even more deeply troubled. Puberty is one of the most intensive growth spurts of the entire life span. Between the ages of ten and fifteen (sometimes earlier, sometimes later), there is a general flooding of many hormones through his body, causing wide-spread physical changes. The hormones speeding through his system are also triggering widespread *psychosocial* changes. Of course, these psychosocial changes are going on within the female teenager as well but he is not as able to cope with them as she is (see Tip 13.2).

Teenage Boys Are Frightened of the Physical Changes They Are Experiencing. Their emotional makeup has undergone a remarkable change, and they find themselves having feelings they have never had before. Their sexuality, which has been more-or-less dormant for some years now, is emerging in daytime fantasies and in nighttime dreams. At times, biological urges seem to take over their everyday consciousness. If we do not accept this one basic fact, say the social scientists who research this area, we will simply not understand the young boy-becoming-man (Goedert, 1991; Rice, 1989). If the young man does have **erotic dreams,** they may interrupt his sleeping and he wakes up to discover he has had **nocturnal emissions,** known popularly as "wet dreams." During the day, he may have **spontaneous ejaculations,** which embarrass him. If he has not masturbated since his early childhood, he may now discover he has the urge to do so again. But whereas masturbation came easily as a child, he is older now and the desire to masturbate is masked with shame and fear. He is caught between the twin furies of desire and guilt. He yearns to talk to someone about his awakened sexuality but does not dare. Instead, he joins the boys in locker room bragging, which he knows is mostly "sound and fury signifying nothing."

Boys, Too, Are Worried About Their Appearance. Like girls, boys are tremendously worried about their appearance. If he is a late developer and sees himself in the mirror as a gangly, thin, and undersized or as the fat boy everyone calls names, he is stricken with low self-esteem. He wants the girls to find him attractive but they obviously prefer the jocks. He must endure the insulting names he is called by the other boys: Skinny, Fatso, String Bean, Shortie, Half-Pint, Peanuts, Jumbo, Noodle-Head, etc. He dresses in a far corner of the locker room so his lack of sexual maturity is not obvious. To compensate for his lack of "manliness," he watches for signs of beard growing. He works out in the gym to develop muscles in order to look more virile. Nothing seems to work. Life seems mean, and he hasn't found many activities he can do which will bolster his self-esteem. If he's good at his school subjects, the "jocks" will call him a "nerd"—so getting good grades doesn't give him any pleasure. In fact, if he's smart, he'll make sure no one finds out the high grades he has been getting (Hall, 1999).

They Are Afraid of Being Bullied. Bullying is rampant. Investigations into the possible causes of the Littleton shooting (and there have been many), reveal that one variable appeared, time and time again: the bullying that was going on by the larger, macho boys against the smaller and more vulnerable boys. Teachers, say high schoolers, turn a blind eye on anything that doesn't occur in their classrooms. Yet the bullying is going on all the time in the halls, in the boys' bathrooms, in the locker rooms, on the playground, and on the school bus (Fitzpatrick,

---

Tip 13.2 Why Girls Become "Boy Chasers." Girls mature, on the average, about two years earlier than boys. For example, it is not unusual for their skeletal growth to begin as early as the fourth grade and their breasts may bud out by the sixth grade, while boys can be as late as high school before their bodies begin the pubertal process. Nature has made her eager to pair up with a boy she likes. He, on the other hand, remains disinterested. Result: She pursues him and he runs the other way. She is labeled a "boy chaser" and her behavior is thought of as aberrant. Actually, she is simply responding to Nature's prodding. What she has not yet learned to do is to be subtle about her attraction to the young man. Over time, she will develop these subtle sexual cues so as not to appear "on the make."

1999). In any school can be found an intricate and locked-in hierarchy. One writer (Fischman, 1987) describes the hierarchy of a relatively progressive high school in New Hampshire.

> . . . the popular kids tend to be wealthier and the boys among them tend to be jocks. The Gap Girls—Tommy Girls—Polo girls compose the pool of desirable girlfriends, many of whom are athletes as well. Below the popular kids, in a shifting order of relative importance, are the druggies (stoners, deadheads, burnouts, hippies or neo-hippies), trendies or Valley Girls, preppies or neo-hippies, skateboarders and skateboarder chicks, nerds and techies, wiggers, rednecks and Goths, better known as freaks . . . There are troublemakers, losers and floaters—kids who move from group to group.

On Moving to a New School, They Are Afraid of Not Being Able to Make Friends. As traumatic as it is to move for the entire family, it is probably hardest on teenagers. Moreover, since the cliques and groups of the high school hierarchy have been firmly established by the sophomore year, both adolescent girls and boys are daunted by the prospect that they may not be able to find a group with whom to relate. Teenage boys, in particular, need the support and strength of friends in order to fend off the bullying that goes on. Or else they have to learn to endure insults or develop protective devices by which to fend off the insults and the bullying—in short, to accept being an outcast. To be an outcast boy is to be a "nonboy" to be feminine, to be weak. Apparently, the bullying that was going on in the halls, in the cafeteria, in the restrooms, and on the school grounds seems to have been part of the terrible high school shootings at Littleton and Conyers. The outcasts are accustomed to the daily onslaught of bullying. Outcasts survive by their stamina, sometimes by their fists, but mainly, if they're lucky, with the help of the family they've created among their outcast friends (LeBlanc, 1999).

The Former Enemy Have Become Objects of Desire and He Has No Idea How to Make an Approach to Them

The young man's awakened sexuality not only astonishes him, it puts him into an embarrassing position. Since the first grade, young boys have regarded the opposite sex as "the enemy." While girls between six and puberty have been willing to share confidences about which boys in class they like, boys of the same age have been only sharing their mutual dislike and disgust of the female gender. They smirked at the romantic affairs of their older brothers, and while they may have poured over a magazine of female nudes, their interest in breasts and buttocks was mostly academic. In their worldview, they considered girls to be inferior in every way. They can't play football or baseball! They like to play stupid games! And all they talk about is movie stars and clothes. *What do older guys see in girls anyway?* Now, almost overnight, their feelings about the opposite sex have undergone a "sea change." The very personages they have been disparaging for so long are now the focus of their eager interest. They are bewildered by their realization that their former enemies have turned into objects of desire.

The young teenage boy has no idea how to institute diplomatic relations with the former enemy. Girls are different! They talk differently. They act differently. They seem to giggle over things that boys can't fathom. And they seem so . . . soft, ah that's not right. *So delicate, yeah, delicate, that's the word.* How do you get to talk to one of them? He doesn't know how to make an approach and he is too embarrassed to ask someone who could advise him. Unable to solve this dilemma, he does nothing. Well, not exactly nothing. He engages in a lot of covert girl-watching. He listens to the guys brag in the locker room. He peruses those magazines filled with girls in bathing suits (or less), and hides them where he thinks his mother or sister won't find them.

Homosexual Adolescents: "High Risk" for Suicide

Another problem that some adolescents will have to deal with is homosexuality. No one can imagine the utter bewilderment and loneliness, or the guilt and despair of adolescents who wonder, as they are growing up, if there is "something wrong" with them. They know they are not experiencing the same reactions as other guys in their peer group. They may even have inklings that they might be homosexual but are not quite sure (and many desperately hope they are not). Their growing self-awareness is accompanied by anxiety and guilt since it is so overtly condemned by so many in society. In the meantime, they have to withstand the onslaught of jokes and slurs about "gays," "fags," and "fruits," all through the day. It has been estimated that the high school male hears about 25 anti-gay remarks in the course of a day. Not only does the adolescent fear his own difference and being "found out" by his peers, he also does not want to hurt his parents if their beliefs and feelings toward homosexuality are **homophobic** (an exaggerated fear and dislike of homosexuality).

The DSM: Homosexuality Is No Longer Listed as a "Disorder." In the 1980s, the *DSM-III* removed homosexuality from the list of abnormal disorders "to be cured." Mental health professionals have also rejected many other fallacies concerning homosexuality. For example, we know that homosexuality does not come about generally as the result of seduction by an older person. As well, the evidence of a genetic and biological basis is mounting. In the "soft revolution" of the 1960s and 1970s, homosexual men and women organized themselves into activist communities and called themselves gay. They came out of the closet not only in America but all over the world. They revealed themselves not as the stereotypic "drag queen" but as responsible men and women in many endeavors: as scientists, as military officers, and as some of our most notable writers, artists, entertainers, and athletes. Furthermore, the Supreme Court upheld the right of American homosexuals to have the same civil rights as other minorities in our society; i.e., they may not be fired from a job solely on the basis of being gay. Our society was becoming more realistic in its understanding of homosexuality, and we began to acknowledge their creative contributions to our culture and civilization (see Tip 13.3). Gradually, more enlightened attitudes were taking over the prevailing homophobia in the United States.

Then something happened which resulted in a sudden whiplash of intolerance: The discovery of AIDS in the early 1980s. Because it was first detected among the homosexual population, the disease itself was blamed on homosexuals. (In Africa where it originated, however, AIDS is a heterosexual disease.) Then a number of terrible abuses of adults on children came to light. Ministers, priests, Sunday school teachers, and boy scout leaders were brought to trial as child molesters. Once again, homosexuality was indicted as being an aberration and in terms of children (pederasty)—it certainly is! (What we were ignoring was that a much higher percentage of heterosexual adults have been child molesters than homosexual adults). But the courts have ruled that what occurs between two consenting adults is a private situation. Nevertheless, homophobia began to increase again.

Self-Awareness of Sexual Orientation Comes About in Adolescence. If that is so, then what these youngsters-becoming-adults need is education, including sex education, just as all our young people do. They need the kind of education that will enable them to become responsible and moral individuals, as all our adolescent youngsters need. They need to understand the stresses and strains that go along with a "gay" life style that must still be covert in many areas. They need to be even more aware of the danger of STDs in general and AIDS in particular. They need not just education but counseling about what it means to be a minority, and in some places, even yet, a rejected minority. They need effective education to build their self-esteem. They need vocational counseling to enable them to find a work that leads to responsible citizenship. If they do not get this kind of intervention, they are at high risk for suicide. In a health survey carried out on 35,000 students in Minnesota public schools, homosexuals have a much higher rate of suicide than the general population. Fully 28 percent of the bisexual and homosexual boys reported a suicide attempt compared with 4 percent of the heterosexual boys (Remafedi, French, & Story, 1998). Clearly, they need adult understanding, adult acceptance, and adult support.

What Parents Are Concerned About

Personality Changes of the Adolescent: Have We Created a "Monster"?

We noted in the chapter on marriage and the family, that the most difficult time of the life span of marriage is during the adolescent years. After congratulating themselves for having raised decent human beings at about age eight through ten, they suddenly find that their "decent human beings" have become over-emotional, unreasonable, hyper-critical, victims of wild mood swings, and selfish to the extreme. If that is not enough, parents discover that their teenagers are convinced they "can handle" anything—including skipping school, drugs, alcohol, dating, sexual exploration, and seem to take deadly risks. *What has happened to their "decent human beings?"*

In addition to their fears and concerns, adolescents have developed several personality traits their parents haven't seen before. David Elkind (1984), our most notable adolescent psychologist, has described them in the following ways. On the surface they can strike us as amusing or simply irritating. But these characteristics can also prove to be dangerous—even lethal!

An Exaggerated Belief in Their Abilities. First, they begin to have an exaggerated idea about what they can do and accomplish. They consider themselves now as adults who do not need or want parental guidance. Question teenagers who have run off (and perhaps gotten into drugs, prostitution, and other destructive life styles) as to how they thought they were going

---

Tip 13.3 Famous Homosexuals and Bisexuals in History

Alexander "the Great," world conqueror	Erasmus, medieval Cleric and philosopher
Julius Caesar, emperor and world conqueror	Michaelangelo, Renaissance sculptor and painter
E.M. Forster, writer	Sappho, Ancient Greek Poet
John Maynard Keynes, economist	Richard Turin, scientist and British Intelligence
Leonardo da Vinci, Renaissance painter and inventor	Peter Tchaikovsky, musician and composer
Frederick "the Great," Prussian king	Tennessee Williams, playwright
Richard Lionheart, King of England and crusader	Virginia Woolf, writer

to survive without money, without a high school diploma, or a way to make a decent income, and the typical answers are: *I thought I could handle it. I thought I could make it on my own.* They do not yet know what they don't know—that kind of understanding comes with more experience of the world and is the benchmark of creative philosophers, writers, and scientists—and generally all mature adults.

Adolescent Egocentrism. When children transit to the stage of concrete operations, they can begin to appreciate the feelings of other people. Ten-year-old Tommy may say, "There are only three cookies left for me and Tammy. I'll cut one in half and then we'll both have the same. That's fair, isn't it?" When Tammy is ten, she volunteers to watch her younger sibling so her Mom can take a quick nap. Parents beam and congratulate themselves on having raised such good family members and responsible citizens.

But as Tommy and Tammy transit into adolescence, the social conscience they have been developing for people in far-off corners of the world does not seem to apply at home and the people closest to them. Tammy "hogs" the bathroom despite the fact that other family members have been pounding on the bathroom door for some time. She also monopolizes the telephone until Dad yells, "Get off the phone—I'm expecting a business call"—or until he finally gives in to a "children's phone." When Tommy gets permission to use the car, he returns it with so little gasoline in the tank that Mom can't get it started the next morning. Tammy "borrows" her mother's best blouse without asking, although she would be outraged if mother invaded her closet. Tommy "forgets" to return his father's tools after using them and they are now rusted out. When confronted with their behaviors, they storm upstairs and slam their bedroom doors. But even behind closed doors, they can be heard all over the house.

"No matter what I say or do, I'm always wrong."
"Why must EVERYONE keep treating me like a child. I know what I'm doing."
"Nobody in this house cares about my feelings."

They have "retrograded" into what Elkind has termed **adolescent egocentrism,** unable to appreciate the situation from any point-of-view but their own. In their search for their own identity separate from their parents, they draw away from them emotionally (Erikson, 1950). They probably regard their parents as "old fogies" or "really dumb" and "behind the times." They are already making plans to avoid all their parents' "mistakes." They are going to be "perfect" parents and have "perfect" children. Of course as they get older (and especially when they do become parents themselves), they will be much less disdainful of their parents. In the words of Mark Twain, "When I was fourteen, my father was so ignorant I could hardly stand to be around him. When I reached my twenty-first year, I was amazed at how much the old man had learned in seven years."

The Personal Fable. As the hero and heroines of their life stories, they are prepared to set forth on crusades to help feed the poor, to aid the victims of hurricanes and earthquakes, and to set forth on missions of peace. They are John Glenn, Joan of Arc, Robin Hood, Florence Nightingale, young Tom Edison, Madonna, their favorite rock musician, and James Bond. They see themselves as special and what applies to other people should not apply to them. For example, when they don't get a paper in on time, they imagine that their circumstances are unique and they should be given special consideration. Their failure to get a term paper or term project in on time should not result in points being taken off for lateness because . . . because their little sister had to go to the hospital last night. Because the family car broke down two days ago. Because they had to help clean the house this past weekend. The term paper deadline was set six weeks ago but, be that as it may, the ordinary consequences of forfeit or discipline that apply to other students should not apply to them: Their situation is different.

But the personal fable refers not just to the hero and heroine role they are acting out; it refers to their belief that they are invincible. The accidents and tragedies that touch the lives of other people will never happen to them. Waking up in the hospital, their parents ask them what on earth induced them to drink and drive. Didn't they know they could have an accident that way? The usual answer: "I didn't think it would happen to me." When they become pregnant, and are asked why they didn't take precautions: "I didn't think it would happen to me." And tragically, when they practice unsafe sex and contract AIDS, the answer is still "I didn't think it would happen to me."

The Imaginary Audience. The adolescents' heightened self-importance gives rise to a phenomenon Elkind calls the **imaginary audience;** namely, that they are being watched by everyone in their social environment. Preoccupied with themselves as the "star" of their personal fable, they are constantly concerned how they appear to others. They are afraid that the slightest deviation from the accepted dress, the accepted speech, the accepted way to react will result in their expulsion from their clique or crowd or gang. And they are desperate for acceptance. Pulling away from their families emotionally, they cannot as yet stand by themselves so they cling to their peer group. In fact, the lower the self-esteem they feel, the more they will engage in **social conformity:** they adopt the same dress, the same slang, the same taste in music and entertainment, etc. But no matter how much they ape their peers, they are never sure of their acceptance by others. They alternate between bouts of self-aggrandizement and self-abasement and from elation to depression during the course of the day. The agony of being unaccepted may even end tragically in high school violence.

The Dating Game: From the High School Crowd to "Pairing Off" and the Dangers of Intimacy

Convinced that they know what they're doing, adolescents begin the dating game, which is another anxiety-provoking situation for their parents. The beginning of the dating game starts out as all-girl or all-boy cliques. Slowly, the cliques begin to merge into the girl-boy crowd. The crowd has several socializing advantages. It provides a framework for the first social interaction between the sexes. The "crowd" goes places together: to the movies, to the football game, to the shopping mall. It is an impersonal arena where the boys and girls can joke and josh with each other without it getting too personal. Since no one is pairing off yet, no one has the uncomfortable pressure of having to keep up a conversation with any one individual for too long a period of time. The crowd provides teenagers a sense of "belongingness" and "esteem" at a time in their lives when they need it most. Having pulled away from parental support, they are still not ready to stand on their own—they are deindividuated persons (Jung, 1968). As well, crowd life allows the adolescent some experience by which he and she can acquire the social graces in casual settings. Clique and crowd standards also serve another function. If parents do not oblige the adolescent's requests or demands for expensive "designer jeans" or permission to go to a rock-and-roll concert, the adolescent can apply pressure: *All my friends have them, Mom. You don't want me to be the only one in the crowd with stupid jeans, do you?* Or

Come on, Pop, all the other guys are getting to go to the concert. I'll be the only one not going. These strategies are usually very effective.

Pairing Off. For a while, the crowd will "hang out" together at football games or at the shopping mall, providing the teenagers with time to get used to just being around the opposite sex. The young boys-becoming-men are learning how to cope with the emotions that are being aroused by the presence of the fair sex. They are rediscovering all those emotions of tenderness and caring that they have been repressing since first grade so as to become "one of the guys." At times, they may feel dominated and overwhelmed by their sexuality, but they are also learning to modify their behaviors when they are around girls. They are learning how to speak quietly with the "gentle sex." They are learning to slow their pace to theirs, to open doors for them, and all the other rules of etiquette that are the standard for their society. They discover that these new feelings and new modes of behavior are not robbing them of their masculinity. It's OK to be tender and caring in the presence of the female sex (never around the guys). The release of these feelings sometimes transports the young man to levels of consciousness and heights of emotion he never imagined possible.

Eventually, however, the crowd will begin to dwindle as couples begin to pair off. If this early pairing begins too early (say around age 12 to 15), the young couple may be negatively sanctioned by their families and even by their peer group. Parents may indicate their disapproval verbally, restrict the number of nightly phone calls, insist on a curfew, and limit their dating so they "don't get into mischief." Younger siblings may tease them and deliberately reveal everything they have observed at family mealtime to the humiliation of the teenager: *Suzie and Jimmy were kissing on the porch last night!* As the youngsters get more and more involved with each other, the couple's connection to the "crowd" will begin to loosen. Their friends will observe that they "just aren't fun to be around anymore." The deep affection the pair are developing for each other cannot be expressed in the presence of others and so they look for ways to be alone. Although adults may laugh at their "puppy love," their feelings for each other may be much more profound than the adults realize. Romeo and Juliet, after all, were just young teenagers. Shakespeare makes it very clear that Juliet had not yet reached her "fourteenth summer." But for most adolescents in the middle class, serious dating generally begins a little later, around age 16 or 17 (Berndt & Perry, 1990).

The Double Standard of Parental Expectations. We come now to the crux of the adolescent dilemma. Just as parents have a *double standard* for girls and boys regarding educational/vocational achievement, so too do most parents have a *double standard* for their sexual behaviors. Fathers joke that when they were young, all the girls were "fair game," but now as fathers of daughters, they joke that what they would really like to do is keep the adolescent boys away by sitting on the porch with a shotgun! Joking? Yes, of course, but underneath, there is some truth to that fantasy. Fathers may harbor some notion (if not always admitted overtly) that it is natural for young lads to sow their "wild seeds"—but not with *their* daughters.

Furthermore, although parents may overtly encourage their daughters to go on for college education, it may only be a facade. What they may really be hoping for is that their daughters should meet an acceptable young man and to get safely married. By doing so, the daughter may avoid children out of wedlock and avoid sexual promiscuity and the risk of sexually transmitted disease (STD). In addition, there is perhaps the hope of grandchildren.

On the other hand, parents generally do not encourage early marriage for their sons. *Son, why do you want to tie yourself down with responsibilities so young? Go out and see the world.*

Have some fun. You can always get a family later. Perhaps parents are intuitively aware that when a son marries, he tends to move away emotionally and socially from his biological family (the family he was born into), and he then devotes his time and energies toward his family of procreation (the family he creates). A daughter becomes even closer to her parents when she is married and becomes a parent herself. There is much truth to the old English maxim:

> My son is my son till he has got him a wife;
> My daughter's my daughter all the days of her life.

This double standard has also diminished somewhat in the last decade and a half with mothers urging their daughters to stay single for a while and have some fun before becoming a mother.

Adolescents: Caught in a Sexual Vise. Parents are also concerned about adolescent sexuality. While they want their teenagers to be "popular," they are nervous about the dating game and the initiation into active sexuality. They are worried about the teenagers going "too far," about possible pregnancy, about teenage parenthood, about the possibility of sexually transmitted diseases—and most dreaded of all their fears—about the possibility of AIDS. They try to warn their adolescents of these possibilities. But teenagers are listening only with their heads. Their bodies are not listening.

While the beginning of "going steady" may involve only walking close together, holding hands, and sharing experiences, as the two young people become more and more involved with each other, they find themselves drawn biologically to each other. Were they being raised in more traditional societies in Asia, in Africa, in the Middle East, they would now be married and having children. This earlier timetable is more in the natural "order of things." But technological societies require longer and longer periods of schooling to prepare young people for adulthood, which prevents the young people from following their biological inclinations to cohabit and to begin a family. They find themselves in a sexual vise: Their psychophysical readiness and urgings are opposed to the prohibitions of society. Added to the prohibitions of society, the ever-present specter of sexually transmitted diseases hovers over the sexual act. If the young couple engage in sexual activity and do not use some method of birth control, they may end up getting married when the girl becomes pregnant. If they do not get married, their passionate attachment may soon wear itself out and one or both of the partners may want OUT. The couple then separates from their commitment to each other. These sexual dilemmas frequently result in some not-so-nice sexual experiences (see Box 13.3).

The Darker Side of Adolescent Sexuality

Parents have every right to be worried about their adolescents. Along with the many other topics that are coming out of the closet, so are the topics of stranger rape, date rape, and sexually transmitted diseases. They are also fearful of their children becoming parents and being married far too young. Adolescents who find themselves as parents-to-be may actually believe it will be fun to "get away from the home" and set up housekeeping for themselves. But their parents know only too well the difficulties inherent in teenage marriage.

Rape: The Reported Figures Are Rising

Although the definition of rape is different from state to state, **rape** is generally defined as *the forcible sexual intercourse with a person who does not give consent.* (In some states, however, rape of a woman by her husband is legal since antiquated laws consider that behavior as part-and-parcel of a man's conjugal rights.) Let there be no misunderstanding. No matter what fallacies and fantasies have been generated about rape, rape is a violent and horrible act that leaves the victims with many physiological and psychological symptoms. Besides the possibility of an unwanted pregnancy or a sexually transmitted disease (STD), the victim is often injured by the brutality of it. Psychologically, the victims can suffer from symptoms of anxiety and panic attack, a sense of shame, feelings of being "spoiled" or "dirtied," insomnia and nightmares, and a sense of distrust and fear of the sexual act, which may affect future sexual activity in adverse ways.

Only a percentage of rape crimes are reported—somewhere in the vicinity of 200,000 annually, but this figure may be only one-fourth of the total rape crimes, which means that more than a million persons (women and men) are raped every year. When surveyed, college students report that in the period between 14 years of age and entry into college, as many as 28 percent have had experiences that can be defined as rape (Caron & Carter, 1997). This figure does not, of course, reflect rape reported by women after college age. Victims are naturally reluctant to report rape for many reasons. First, the victim does not want to go through the humiliation of exposure. Second, there is still, even yet, a popular fallacy that if a person is raped, the victim somehow "asked for it." (That is the equivalent of saying that if a man beats his wife, she somehow must have "deserved it".) Third, it is very difficult to prove the crime of rape (unless there are witnesses) and to get a verdict of guilty in the courts. Fourth, the victim may be scared that the rapist will come back and get revenge by another rape attack. Fifth, the victims may fear family members will abandon them if they make the crime public (and this is sometimes the case!). And at the base of all her fears, she may wonder guiltily if she really was to blame for the crime against her (see Box 13.3). We should note that although most victims are women, men are also raped—particularly in prison—and generally by heterosexual men. In this case, the rape is a means whereby the prisoner establishes his power and domination over others. (see Tip 13.4).

Date and Acquaintance Rape.   One of the disturbing features of rape is the percentage of crimes that occur as the result of "date rape," which is rape by someone with whom the individual is at least casually acquainted. The figures on college date rape keep increasing. A survey of college men revealed that two-thirds of them admitted to fondling women against their will and over one-half of them admitted to forcing women into coitus (Bohmer & Parrot, 1993). College men give the following kinds of rationale to defend their behavior:

If she didn't want sex, why did she come to my room?
When she invited me in for a drink, I took that as an invitation to have sex.

Tip 13.4 Gang Rape as a Rite of Passage of Street Gangs. In contrast to rape by an individual, gang rape is perpetrated on the victim by two or more persons. This brutal act is often a "rite of passage" for admittance to gang membership. Even an unwilling rapist may not be able to oppose the group standards in this situation.

Box 13.2

STUDENTS VERBATIM
On Their Adolescent Experiences

Female (23 years): I was betrayed by my boyfriend. I was one of those who got "used" by my boyfriend. I really was. I believed everything he said to me. He kept saying how much he loved me and how he couldn't wait till we got married—that the other girls were doing it for their guys and if I really, really loved him, I'd let him. I knew it was wrong. My head told me "no" but it got to the point in our necking, I couldn't say "no" anymore. So I did let him. I love him and I love our sex together. People may think young teenagers have puppy love. Well, it may have been puppy love, but it was love. The more sex we had, the more I loved him. Every chance we could, we were at it. I began to notice looks I was getting from girls and boys I knew. My girl friends were suddenly very nontalkative. Boys began calling me up for dates, guys who wouldn't have looked at me twice. I kind of suspected a little, but I wouldn't let myself believe that he was doing a lot of "kiss and tell." He had promised me faithfully, he would keep it a secret. So I kept fooling myself until suddenly he dropped me for one of the "good girls" in the school. I know it sounds like an old story. The funny part is I laughed at my mother when she used to warn me about the guys. I'm not saying every guy is like that. I've met other girls who had sex with their guys and their guys were lots nicer than mine. They kept it a secret. Besides the fact that I had gotten a "bad reputation," what hurt me the most was how he had used me to make himself big.

Male (18 years): I am eighteen years old and I've been involved with Anne for three years. I really love her. We are both freshmen in college and living together. But Anne wants us to get married. She says that if I don't make up my mind soon, she's going home after the term ends. I really don't know what to do. I feel too young to take on the responsibility of marriage. But I don't want to lose Anne either. It's hard for me to express how I feel to Anne since I've never been able to talk about feelings with anyone. The only time I can do so, I guess, is when I am "three sheets to the wind" and then I must say things that hurt her. Also this is the first serious relationship I've ever had, and I don't know if I want to tie myself down with Anne for the rest of my life. I'm just too young to know what I really want.

Female (27 years): There's something about me I guess that just attracts real "losers." I could go on and on but I'll just tell you about my first guy. When I first met him. I was almost fifteen and he was nineteen, just kicked out of the Marines. He had been mixed up with drugs and disowned by his family even. Yet there was a certain magic in his touch that quickly made me fall head over heels in love with him. Now I had been brought up to believe that I wouldn't have sex until I was married for I was taught that my virginity was sacred. My friends were losing theirs, one-by-one, until I was the only virgin left. This was when I changed my mind to give myself to the person I loved that loved me back. One night in a drunken stupor, Randy finally said he loved me (after a year of me saying I loved him). That was maybe the worst night of my life. He made me do seven different positions and told me he didn't love me in the middle of it. When I started to cry he told me to shut up. All I wanted was to be held, but he wouldn't even do that. Instead he told me that I should go out, meet more guys, and practice. Really! That's exactly what he told me. After this, my eyes were opened and I never saw him again. I wouldn't even speak to him when he phoned. It took me a long time to trust any man again.

Male (22 years): I have been secretive about my affairs but I'm going to level with you now. I've been pretending that all the affairs I have had are with girls. Well some of them have been, but I've come to believe I'm gay. Don't get me wrong. I'm still attracted to girls occasionally and I think maybe my attraction to men is just a "phase" I'm going through, although I can remember playing doctor with a boy across the street. I couldn't have been more than four or five at the time. In high school, I was too scared to let anybody know "the real me," so I pretended I had a girl friend in another city. Of course, I didn't but that helped me get out of a lot of embarrassing situations. I had a brief affair when I was seventeen with a friend. I thought we were life mates. Then he dropped me and didn't even tell me why. So for several years I played it "straight." I went with girls even, but none of them were serious episodes. I enjoyed petting with them but I never went "the whole way with them." After high school, I went into the army. I hoped that would "straighten me out," being with a lot of other men. It did keep me busy, too busy to think about sex. But when I came out of the army, I had the same old problem. Being gay doesn't bother me so much. It's all the rest of it that I hate—the gay bars, the one-night stands, the coded dialogue with its innuendos. I want a relationship that has meaning. I sometimes just get depressed because I don't know what to do with my life.

Female (22 years): When I discovered that I was lesbian I was terrified. In Korean families, it is a bad shame. I

Box 13.2

was terrified that my mother would find out. I was only twelve years old when I first knew I loved another person like myself. She was in my school. I tried hard to resist her. She was my first and only girlfriend for many years. She, however, had many other girl friends. And I used to be so jealous of them. But sometimes she would stay over night at my house. My mother and father were proud of the fact that I was not like other girls chasing the boys. They would have been so ashamed of me if they had found out about us. Then my parents received notice that we could come to United States. I was so disheartened. So was my friend. We cried in each other's arms many times together. So now I am here and very alone. I like all

my friends in college but I can never forget my girl friend who lives on the other side of the world. We write but little by little, the letters take longer and longer to be answered. Will I ever find anyone else that I can love? Then there is my mother who is always asking me when will I settle down and get married. She wants to see her grandchildren before she dies. She introduces me to many Korean men and I pretend to be interested. But I tell her I cannot get married until I finished my college and graduate work which will take a long time because I am going into pharmacy. What will I tell her after I am graduated and have a job and still not have a boyfriend? I do not know.

I figured her "no" was really a cover-up for her desire to have sex.

I was getting tired of her playing hard-to-get.

I thought she really wanted it but didn't want to admit it.

I was so worked up, I couldn't control myself.

Rape Is Less Common in Other Countries Than in Ours. There are several reasons for this. In Middle East countries, women are kept in seclusion before and after marriage. Also if a young woman is raped by a relative, she would bear the brunt of the blame and though illegal, it is still tradition that the males of the family kill the young woman to get rid of the shame, hence rape is under-reported. In the predominantly Catholic countries of Europe and Central and South America, females are strictly chaperoned even when in the presence of their fiances. In societies which are made up of small tribes and clans, fear of discovery prevents the pubescent male from forced sexual entry. Discovery would mean the expulsion of both parties from the only community they have ever known, or possibly they may even be put to death. But we cannot lay the blame solely on the freedom of women in our nation. Other nations who have evolved more gender equality do not have nearly as many rape crimes (see Tip 13.4). Countries such as Holland and Sweden have far fewer sex crimes than in our country, less unwanted pregnancies, less teenage pregnancies, and fewer abortions (Wallis, 1985). At the same time, both of these countries have extensive sex education programs and governmental counseling for adolescents. We need more enlightened attitudes about the rights of women to consent to sexual intercourse, and we need more frank and open sex education to keep our adolescents safe from AIDS and other sexually transmitted diseases (see Box 13.3).

Tip 13.5 Prime Minister Golda Meier's Retort. Under the leadership of Israel's first woman prime minister, the Israeli Cabinet was discussing the rise of reported rape in Jerusalem. When one of her cabinet members suggested establishing a 10:00 P.M. curfew for women, Meier responded, "Why should the women have a curfew? It is men who are committing rape."

Box 13.3   FACTS OF ADOLESCENT SEXUALITY

1. **Age of First Average Intercourse.** About 16, regardless of gender, education, social class and other factors.
2. **Proportion of Sexually Active Youngsters, Age 15–17.** The proportion of sexually active youngsters of this age period increased by 18 percent in the 1980s—with increases mostly among white teens in high-income families.
3. **Teenage Pregnancy.** Every year, one out of every ten adolescent girls in the United States becomes pregnant, which amounts to 1 million adolescent females every year. Eighty percent of these pregnancies are unintentional. Our rate of teenage pregnancy is the highest in the world powers, exceeded only by Chile, Hungary, Romania, Cuba, and Bulgaria. About 500,000 of these pregnancies result in birth. Of the other half million, 13 percent end in miscarriage or stillbirth and the rest in abortion.
4. **Rape.** As of the early 1990s, only about 200,000 rapes are being reported each year, but the estimate is that this figure represents only a small percentage of the cases. It is probable that over a million rapes occur every year if we include date rape and marital rape. Reported rape has increased to four times the rate of reported overall crime in the last decade. It is not clear whether that means the actual crime of rape has increased or the willingness of women to report the crime has increased. From the statistics we do have, 36 percent were raped in their own home.
5. **AIDS.** The best estimate at the present time about the number of cases of AIDS in this country is about 1.5 million. Reported deaths from AIDS is about 60,000 per year. Although it is difficult to get a true cross section of a community's adolescents, we know that the two fastest growing rates of AIDS are among teenagers and heterosexual women. Surveys in Washington, DC, of 13–20-year-olds over a three-year period revealed that the infection rate had risen from one in 250 teenagers to one in every 90 teenagers. The prediction is that the rate will soon rise to one in every 30 in the next few years. A 1990 survey done on college students on 19 different campuses found one student in every 500 to be positive. By the end of June 1994, 401,749 cases of AIDS were reported to the CDC (Centers for Disease Control) of which 51,235 were women. The number of AIDS cases is rising at a more rapid rate among women than men, and in certain urban centers has become the leading cause of death among women.
6. **Other Sexually Transmitted Diseases (STD).** These diseases are on the rise and include gonorrhea, syphilis, human papilloma virus, chlamydia, and herpes of the genitals. For example, in 1988, there were 720,000 new cases of gonorrhea reported to the National Center for Health Statistics. After the 20–24-year-old group, the next highest "at-risk" group are the 15–19-year-olds.

Sources: The University of California at Berkeley Wellness Letter, 7(7). School of Public Health; Newsweek 116 (4), 46–53; Newsweek 128 (5); Amaro, H., American Psychologist 50 (6.), 437–441.

Sexually Transmitted Diseases (STD)

Diseases which are contracted primarily through sexual intercourse used to be called *venereal diseases* but that term has been replaced professionally by the term *sexually transmitted diseases.* The most common *STDs* include gonorrhea, syphilis, chlamydia, herpes genitalia, and AIDS. We have to understand that when the term sexual transmission is used, it does not necessarily mean genital-genital contact. These diseases can also be contracted through oral-genital and anal-genital contact. These diseases have become an increasing health problem in the United States, and particularly among adolescents. The highest numbers of STDs are among the 10–14 age group but the next highest is the 15–19 age group. Our adolescents are engaging in the most unsafe-sex possible despite the urges of public health officials and the public media. In fact, in some locales, the Boards of Education still refuse to consider teaching their high schoolers "safe sex" use of condoms in their sex education programs (see 13.4).

Box 13.4   WHAT TO TELL YOUR DAUGHTER/SISTER/COUSIN ABOUT RAPE AND HOW TO PROTECT HERSELF

Facts About Rape:

1. **Rape is the number one crime against women.** In the years between 1973 and 1982, 1.5 million rapes or attempted rapes were reported on telephone hot lines. The actual number far exceeds that, of course, because many victims do not want to go through the humiliating procedures of police and hospital reporting.

2. **Most rapes are perpetrated by people the victim knows.** We teach our children about strangers who want to give us candy or go with them somewhere. We should teach our girls that rape is perpetrated by people they know so they must be on the alert at all times.

3. **The crime of rape is difficult to prove unless there are witnesses.** This fact makes it even more uncomfortable for women to report rape and prosecute.

4. **Rapists seem like respectable men until the rape.** And so they are. They are not the borderline personality who goes on rampages. Tell your daughter that most rapists can be "good citizens" of the community, good fathers, and (seemingly) good husbands—another factor inhibiting reporting of the crime.

5. **Rapists usually blame the victim.** If the young woman tries to escape the rape, the man will say something like,"You're a big girl. You came up here on your own. You must want it."

6. **The average age of victims of reported rapes is 18 years.** But victims have ranged from babies to an 80-year-old woman.

7. **Half of the known perpetrators were dates:** The victims were shocked by the fact that their dates raped them. They did not expect it.

8. **The rape may last for a long time:** Sometimes for hours.

9. **The rape may be accompanied by other brutality.** Knifing, mutilation, and death are not infrequent with stranger rape, but they may also accompany rape by a person the victim knows.

10. **Rape trauma syndrome follows most victims.** Phobias, flashbacks, general distrust of men, sexual dysfunctioning, and a lasting feeling of shame and lowered self-esteem are the consequences.

Sources: Dizon, Dorian, "Hidden Rape: The Shocking Truth Behind the Statistics." *Redbook,* (July, 1988) 92–93. "This Pamphlet is About Rape," Santa Fe Community College, 1990.

How to Protect Herself:

1. **Acquaintance rape occurs most often between 10:00 P.M. and 2:00 A.M.** Be particularly careful about late-night dating after the football game, the dance, the fraternity party.

2. **Rapes often occur on the man's turf.** Be very alert to invitations to his apartment, house, office, fraternity.

3. **Rapes also occur in secluded areas.** Carefully plan dates that are *not* secluded in your first several dates with the man and until you get to know him and can trust him.

4. **Most date rapes occur on the first several dates.** Most rapes occur early in the "dating game"—generally in the first, second, or third dates. Be especially careful when first dating someone new. It is a good idea to double date with another couple several times. Or to arrange the dates in public and not secluded places.

5. **The perpetrator has often been drinking or is on drugs.** Be wary if your date shows up obviously tipsy or drunk or seems to be "high." He may want you to drink. Girls who have been drinking are more vulnerable to rape.

6. **Most rape victims were slow on-the-uptake.** No matter how well you think you know the man, stay alert and be aware to possible signals that the man wants more than you want to give. If he feels he has been "short-changed" or "led on," he may resort to revenge by rape.

7. **Don't be afraid to say No.** You don't owe him anything, no matter what kind of a nice time he has given you or how much money he has spent.

8. **Call a designated other adult for a bailout.** If you feel in anyway unsure of the situation, call someone to come and get you.

9. **If you can't call someone you know, approach someone in the vicinity to help get you to a police station.** Obviously, we recommend approaching a woman, but in an emergency approach a couple or a man. Most people will respond immediately to a distress call.

10. **If the worst should happen, tell someone.** You need to get medical attention and psychological counseling, whatever it takes to get over it.

The most feared of STDs, of course, is AIDS, because of its death-sentence. AIDS stands for acquired immune deficiency syndrome. People do not die of AIDS; they die of AIDS-related diseases. What happens is that the body's natural ability defense system breaks down. The person dies from cancer, pneumonia, heart disease, leukemia, and so on.

From the Harvard Medical School Comes a Warning! There Is No Such Thing as "Safe Sex" Only "Safer Sex."'s When queried, a high percentage of people admit they lied about their state of health or the number of sexual partners they have had to their new partners (Cochran & Mays, 1990). That adolescent phenomenon of the personal fable (discussed earlier in the chapter) hinders them from realizing that AIDS *can* happen to them. A typical attitude: *He can't possibly have AIDS. He comes from a good family and he's a nice guy.* (Some of the nicest people we know have died of AIDS.) Another typical attitude: *I can't have been exposed to AIDS. I've only had sex once.* (But once is all it takes.) Finally: *He's so sweet and kind. He'd have told me if he had AIDS.* (Maybe he doesn't even know it himself.) Despite the advances being made concerning the detection and prevention of AIDS, it should be emphasized to our young people that neither condoms nor the new simplified AIDS test is 100 percent safe. The moral of our discussion of sexually transmitted diseases is that, barring abstinence, there is no "safe sex." There is only "safer sex."

And Now Another Warning to Women!: Promiscuity Is a High-Risk Factor for Cervical Cancer. Studies of women with cervical cancer have led to the discovery of the **human papilloma virus (HPV),** a sexually-transmitted disease. Since this cancer is caused by a virus, the more sexual contacts a woman has, the higher risk the woman has for contracting it—just as the more people we kiss during a flu epidemic increases our chances for catching the flu. Fortunately, the so-called pap test can detect this virus and it can be treated and "nipped in the bud" so to speak. Untreated, HPV not only leads to cervical cancer but also death. In other words, a simple pap smear test every other year could save your life (Mayo Clinic Women's Health Source, 1999).

Early- and Late-Maturing Adolescents: A Surprising Reversal of Self-Esteem

We have been discussing several difficult and unpleasant topics; namely all the problems that our adolescents may encounter in their growing up. We prefer not to end this chapter on such a "down note." So we turn the reader's attention to another adolescent problem, but one that often, very often, has a happier ending. The problem we are discussing has to do with those adolescents who are slower-than-average in their pubertal growth and are called "late maturers."

The Advantages of Early Maturation

It becomes obvious that early pubertal maturation has definite advantages for the adolescent. All of a sudden, the young girl has become a young woman and the young lad has become a young man. Their status within the peer group rises considerably. She has been transformed into the fairy tale princess for whom brave young men compete. His early maturation results in a more muscular body, which results in superior athletic prowess, which leads to heroic achievement on the playing field. He has become the "Alpha Male" that attracts the females of the group. In addition, their maturation brings about higher (Piagetian) cognitive skills and heightened social awareness. In addition to their heightened status within the peer group, the adults in their society begin to treat them with more respect and equity. Mom will ask her daughter which blouse looks better on her—this one or that one? Instead of telling his son to stay out of the way, Dad will ask his help while adjusting the points on the family car or holding the end of a board while he makes a cut on it. Teachers at school will give the obviously more mature students those jobs that require responsibility. Thus, their early physical and psychological maturity will result in heightened self-esteem. So our early-maturing teenagers have the advantage of being treated as more adult which leads them to act more adult, a phenomenon known as the **self-fulfilling prophecy** (we become how others treat us or think of us).

The Disadvantages of Late Maturation

We have discussed some of the problems of late maturing teenagers. But let's just enumerate a few other disadvantages. She does not get those looks of admiration from the boys in the class. He does not get chosen for team sports until the end because he lags behind in physical prowess. They don't have the prestige, generally, to get nominated and elected to school office. They lag behind in the "dating game." All-in-all, their self-esteem gets dented fairly regularly and they yearn earnestly for signs of maturation. He begins to shave before he needs to. She asks her mother for a bra even though it won't make much difference to her silhouette.

So Where Is the Happy Ending?

Well, here it is. Early maturers are given the gift of "popularity" by virtue of their physical attractiveness. Members of their peer group court their favors. They reign supreme without having to make too much effort to "make friends." People (both male and female) gravitate to them as if attracted by a magnet. Late maturers who do not get elected to student government, who are not chosen as cheerleaders, who do not get to play first string on the school teams— all these late maturers have to do something else. What do they do? They join the band or glee club, take part in school theatrics or special interest clubs, write for the school newspaper or work on the school log. In point of fact, they frequently become the "movers and shakers" of the high school, the ones who "get things done." Through these extracurricular activities, they are developing their talents, skills, and interests, which will prove valuable in college and also later in their adult vocational and avocational arenas. It will stand them in good stead to speak in front of a group of people or to work with others to create a publication or to develop their artistic talents. They are, in effect, developing what teachers call their "inner resources."

Furthermore, where the early maturers have not had to work hard to attract friends and dates, late maturers recognize that they must develop personality traits which attract others. What kinds of traits make them attractive? For starters, a cheerful nature, a ready smile, and a willingness to help others. They may be developing into "good listeners," which is an attribute everyone appreciates. They may have a natural "sense of humor" which they discover causes other people to want to add them to a party, to an outing, or as a great addition to a crowd.

How do we know all this? Because longitudinal studies have revealed that early maturers who have higher self-esteem in high school and college did not always hold on to that level of self-esteem throughout the life span. As the years creep on and their initial good looks and attractiveness begin to wane, their self-esteem begins to diminish. So much of their self-value was vested in their attractiveness, that they did not develop their other gifts and talents. In contrast, late-maturers had a better chance of gaining self-esteem throughout the life span just because of those "inner resources" they were forced to develop in high school if they wanted to make friends. As they get older, they are valued precisely for being the interesting persons they are and for their generosity in using their skills and talents for the general good (Cochran, 1990; Goldberg, 1991). In other words, they have a better chance to develop more gemeinschaftsgefühl, which Adler described as being the measure of a truly authentic, creative, and self-actualizing human being.

A Theory of Adolescent Development: Some Discoveries About the Adolescent Brain

There is much excitement being generated today over what may be behind the bewildering and noncompliant behavior of adolescents. The conventional wisdom has been that their adolescent bickering and rebellion is a reflection of their struggle to establish their own identities apart from their family membership (Erikson, 1950). In their efforts to discover their unique identities, adolescents reject the authority of adults, particularly the members of their own family. The conventional theory of the last 50 years is that the sexual hormones racing throughout their bodies are the primary cause of their confusing and often contradictory behaviors. While we know that these sexual hormones do play a big part in the psychosocial changes of the adolescent, some recent neurological discoveries are also pointing to the adolescent brain itself.

The Traditional Theory of Adolescent Brain Development

For almost a century now, it has been assumed that the three-pound organ we call the brain was more-or-less developed long before the time a child reached puberty. Moreover, it has always been assumed that we are born with all the neurons we will ever have—some 100 billion of them. When these billions of neuronal cells are destroyed, we were told, they could never be replaced since neurons do not regenerate as do blood cells or skin cells or any of the other cells in the living body. It has long been known that the high frequency nerves in our ears can be destroyed by being exposed to intense noise and that drugs and alcohol can actually destroy brain cells. We knew of course that the baby's brain is very immature at birth and that the 100 billion neurons already in place continue to form hundreds of thousands of interconnections and pathways throughout the brain over the next several years. But finally the young child would have all the connections it needed so as to learn at the remarkable rate it does. Except for some relatively minor connections being made as life continues, the adult brain was more or less formed by early childhood.

The Teenage Brain: Also Undergoing Sweeping Pubertal Changes

But with the advent of recent neuroscientific technologies, such as magnetic resonance imaging (MRI), it looks as if the brain—along with all the skeletal changes, muscular changes, and sexual changes—is also undergoing changes during puberty. In fact, suggest the neuroscientists, the brain is undergoing a complete transformation—changes that may also be responsible for the adolescent's stormy mood swings and strife with authority. In retrospect, it seems obvious that *if the rest of the body was undergoing sweeping transformation, why not the brain?* The most recent discoveries about the adolescent brain suggest that it is still immature and more like a child's than an adult's brain. We know that the infant's brain (birth to 2 years of age) is undergoing thousands of neural connections. Now it appears that the adolescent brain is exploding with many more thousands of neural connections, starting around 9 or 10 years of age and continuing on into young adulthood.

The Primitive Emotions of the Midbrain Versus the More Intelligent Reactions of the Neocortex

In order to understand what is going on at this time, we need to know just a little about the functioning of the brain. Inside the mammalian brain, there are three major divisions, sometimes called the old brain, the midbrain, and the new brain. The midbrain is the area of our highly primitive emotions—the **fight-flight-freeze response** discussed in the Chapter 7. The midbrain and its fight-flight-freeze response evolved to enable the animal to respond quickly to a perceived threat. When this system is alerted, we can suddenly (and sometimes apparently for no discernible reason) dissolve in tears, go into shock, or became so enraged as "to come out fighting." In human society, these primitive emotional responses can produce behaviors that are not only inappropriate to the situation but also destructive to ourselves and others.

As evolution continued, however, another part of the brain developed, variously called the *new brain* (or forebrain). This **new brain,** with its many more millions of neurons, allowed for more "intelligent" life—particularly in those species with a wrinkled **cortex** (outer covering). The more wrinkled the cortex became, the more intelligent life became—as in the canine species, in the various species of monkeys and apes, and finally the human species. But in the human species, there is developed also another very thin layer (a bare 1/4″) of brain calls which we call the **neocortex** (meaning the newest and outermost layer of cells). *It is this neocortex which forms the basis of our most conscious, aware, and intelligent cognitive processes—in other words, our increased ability to perceive things more accurately and to make more rational decisions.* But it takes years for this neocortex to mature. In small children, the neocortex is very immature, and their emotional responses are under the control of their more primitive midbrains. As small children, when we perceived a threat to our survival or general happiness, we reacted by crying, screaming, running away or fighting—the primitive emotional responses of the midbrain. As adults, the brain comes under the control of the calmer, more clear-thinking processes of the neocortex. A situation that would threaten a child's feeling of safety is perceived by the more rational adult as a situation that can be taken care of very easily.

The Adolescent Brain: Sometimes Still under the Control of the Midbrain. We have assumed for many years now that the neocortex—the area where we make our most intelligent, logical, and quietly calm interpretations of information and decision-making—was more-or-less formed before the adolescent years. With this model of the brain's neuroanatomy, all that remained to do for the adolescent was to provide him with a few educational skills—how to write a decent letter, how to compute numbers and keep a checkbook, and how to assume the responsibilities of being a good citizen—and the adolescent was ready for adult life. That had been the theory until only a few years ago when neurological discoveries began to change this picture (Brownlee, 1999). The adolescent brain is far from mature and the neocortex is not yet fully developed in the adolescent. In fact, the neurological evidence suggests that the most mature part of the brain (the neocortex) will not be fully developed until the person reaches the early twenties. Of course in some people with brain damage or those who have severe personality disorders, the cortex may never be fully developed. Thus it is that the adolescent's emotions are more often under the domination of the highly primitive fight-flight-freeze response than they will be in the mid to later twenties. There will be times when the adolescent is not feeling threatened and rational thinking is possible. What is happening, according to the new theory, is that the adolescent's emotional response swings back and forth between the higher neocortical brain and the primitive midbrain system, accounting perhaps for the fact that the adolescent can seem to be mature one moment and, in the next moment, behave in erratic and irrational ways.

Is the Immature Adolescent Brain Responsible for the Adolescent's Impulsive and Irrational Behavior? The sudden shifts going on in the brain of adolescents may explain why they do those impulsive things that are life-threatening, such as getting high on drugs or alcohol, drinking and driving, or engaging in unprotected sex. Given an atmosphere of peer fellowship and wanting peer acceptance, they respond to emotional pressure of the limbic system. It may explain why a chance remark may touch off tears in a teenage girl or a rage in a teenage boy. They shoplift impulsively, strike out against another teenager, or engage in gang rape under peer pressure while caught up in the excitement of the forbidden act. This may possibly be what is going on when certain high schools students come out shooting. There is much we do not know as yet.

But the adolescent's immature brain development can also result in risky life-death decisions that prove destructive and even fatal. Teenage drivers have an accident and mortality rate so high that insurance for this age group is exorbitant. We get exposé documentaries on the rise of juvenile prostitutes, both male and female. The United States has a reported 1 million missing children, of which teenage runaways constitute one-third to one-half of them. Drug use is on the rise. Premarital sex is beginning as early as the middle grades. And despite the pleas from health agencies, adolescents are not engaging in "safe sex." More and more teenagers are having babies of their own in and out of wedlock at an age when they are not very grown up themselves. Street crime is higher among our adolescent youth than among any other age group. Carrying guns to school has reached all the way down to middle grades and is pandemic in the high school. And in 1999, the tragic high school shootings in Littleton, Colorado, and Conyers, Georgia shocked the entire nation. But aside from these extreme and tragic situations, a recent survey reveals that one out of every four youth are "at risk" for engaging in some type of behavior that will have negative consequences (Fitzpatrick, 1999). And the figures for victimization in the middle and high school grades are still rising. All of these phenomena are symptoms that our society needs to develop a very effective means by which to support the adolescent in the long and difficult transition to adulthood. So serious have the problems of this age level become for our society that the law courts are taking a firmer and firmer stand with them. In some states, juveniles are being tried as adults. Some states have begun holding their parents responsible for the crimes of their adolescent children. Some social scientists, however, point out that laws may stem some of the violence but that what is needed is a united family-school-church-governmental advocacy against violence at every level from grades K through 12. So do we.

What Can We Do to Foster Emotional Intelligence in Our Adolescents?

This question is the "bottom line" issue of any textbook dealing with adolescence. Parents and teachers and all adults who work with teenagers want more than just a list of problems. They want and need suggestions on how to foster all those personality traits that make for a constructive and responsible life style. So we conclude this chapter with just a few basic rules for moral/ethical development.

Lawrence Kohlberg: They Need Experience in Making Moral/Ethical Judgments

Remembering the work of Lawrence Kohlberg (Chapter 4), we may have some clues. Recapping Kohlberg's three levels of morality (we do not need to worry about the stages here), we remember that Kohlberg listed three main levels. **Preconventional morality** is based on fear and later on self-interest (what do I get out of it?). **Conventional morality** has to do with conforming to societal standards. **Postconventional morality** has to do with abstract principles of justice and mercy for each and every individual. It involves becoming lawful and responsible citizens. It involves a compassionate empathy for all persons, young and old; rich or poor; men, women, or children who are not as competent or fortunate as the rest of us. It involves that gentle loving-kindness that has always been the highest expression of our multicultural philosophic and religious traditions.

While Kohlberg agreed essentially with Piaget that cognitive development and moral/ethical development go hand-in-hand, Kohlberg emphasized the fact that just because a youngster is expanding cognitively, moral/ethical development may lag behind. Certainly, the recent discoveries and theories (mentioned just above) seem to confirm that. To develop higher moral/ethical consciousness, said Kohlberg, youngsters need experience. They need experience in evaluating their past behavior. They need experience interacting with others. They need experience in being confronted with ethical/moral dilemmas. They need the experience of participating in free and open discussion with their peers and with adults. They need experience in participative democracy. They need experience in making moral/ethical decisions. These kinds of experience can only happen in an environment that encourages free and frank exchange of opinion. It means a family environment where children are not only seen but heard. It means a school environment where teachers don't just lecture at the students, but listen to them as well. It means a church environment that does not insist on blind obedience to dogma, but encourages personal introspection on spiritual principles (Kohlberg, 1984).

Replacing Rules and Restrictions with Guidelines and Principles

Laws, rules, regulations, policy statements define specific situations and behaviors. To define something is to draw a circle around it, to limit its meaning. "An eye for an eye and a tooth for a tooth" means that no punishment can be no worse than the crime; i.e., it limits the punishment. On the other hand, principles and guidelines expand in meaning over time. A well-known example should suffice. The framers of the Constitution considered the concepts of *equality* and the ability to vote to apply to white males over 21 who owned land. Over the next two hundred years, equality was expanded to mean all white men (not just the wealthier landowners). Lincoln signed a proclamation to include all men (not just white). In 1919, women earned

Box 13.6   **SO WHAT CAN WE DO TO HELP OUR ADOLESCENTS SURVIVE HIGH SCHOOL?**

Eduardo: I didn't have so many problems in high school, Professor. In fact, I hardly saw any problems at all.

Alec: Oh, come on, Eduardo, I saw lots of hazing going on. I saw the drug-dealing. I saw it all. Sometimes I had to fight my way to school and home again. And I saw guns, too.

Professor Weitzman: Alec, I believe you did see that, but I also believe that Eduardo did not. Let me ask you two a few questions. Eduardo, how many students were in your high school?

Eduardo: It was just a small school—about 350 students in all.

Professor Weitzman: How big was your high school, Alec?

Alec: Big, maybe 3000 students.

Professor Weitzman: Well, there's part of the answer. It's the very largeness of schools that make for our inability to know what is going on among our high school students. Did you know most of the students in your high school, Alec?

Alec: Heck, no. The only kids I really knew were the ones that were with me in grade school. We all rode the bus together so we kind of hung out together. All the other kids I only knew from seeing them in classes. But we changed classes every 45 minutes, so how could you get to really know anybody?

Professor Weitzman: And you, Eduardo?

Eduardo: Did I know the all the kids in my high school? Sure, in one way or another. Of course, I knew the kids in my grade more than the ones above or below us.

Li Ho: So are you saying that our schools should be smaller so there will be more camaraderie?

Professor Weitzman: That's an interesting idea but perhaps not financially feasible at the present time. But what I am saying is that in some way we have got to provide a friendlier atmosphere in our schools where there is a climate of trust. We have spent so much time increasing academic standards, and that's fine for cognitive learning. But adolescents are at the most vulnerable time in their lives emotionally. We need to incorporate a lot more *affective* learning in our schools.

Martha: Affective learning?

Professor Weitzman: Learning that has to do with emotions and feelings.

Alec: Like a class in emotional intelligence that we learned about in the last chapter.

Jonnimae: But isn't that exactly what this course is?—Learning how to be emotionally intelligent?

Professor Weitzman: I certainly hope so or Jill and I have failed to meet our course objectives.

Alec: You really think courses like this would help high schools to be less violent?

Professor Weitzman: I can't say definitely yes, but I think we need to do something for our teenagers. We could at least try it out and see what happens.

Shannon: I could have used a class like this just to make some friends.

Natasha: I am so amazed by this class. It is so different from what I am used to in the Old Country. But I think I like it, yes. I would like my children to be in such a class.

Professor Weitzman: We need more male models for our youngsters. In the place of absentee fathers, we need more high school teachers who are men. We need more counselors who are men. We need to involve our high school teenagers in the community through service learning. By becoming involved with our aged persons in convalescent homes; with our hospitalized patients who don't get many visitors; with our mentally retarded citizens in institutions—there is where they will get the experience Kohlberg talked about. Service learning provides them with a meaningful outlet for their energies and a place to develop their higher moral/ethical natures. If they are "jocks" and athletes then they receive a lot of reward from the schools and the other high school students. The scholars and the "movers and shakers" need to get more recognition. In history classes, we need to emphasize not just generals who won wars but the heroes of peace. We need to provide opportunities outside of school, in the many work arenas where students not only can get paid (thereby developing self-esteem) but also where they connect to older adults (and thereby observe how working men and women interact with others responsibly and reliably in our society).

the right to vote as well. The civil rights act of 1954 expanded the meaning of equality even further and still the meaning of equality continues to expand. It can be seen from this that **moral/ethical/spiritual principles** are expressed, not in specific rules and restrictions but in guidelines for human interaction and responsibility for our planet Earth.

Very often these moral/ethical/spiritual principles are put in the form of proverbs or metaphors or biblical parables or Japanese koans that can have multiple interpretations—many undertones and overtones of meaning. These subtleties and nuances are unraveled by "taking thought" via discussion and through personal introspection and/or prayerful meditation. Kohlberg explained that moral/ethical/spiritual principles do not pose right or wrong answers so much as questions: Given a moral/ethical dilemma, what would be the better of two or more alternatives? These kinds of decisions require a bit of head-scratching, pondering, self-reflection, arguing with others, turning the matter over in one's mind, sleeping on them, etc. Ultimately, each person must make his or her own decision. We tell a child what he may or may not do in every situation: *You may not go on the road.* Later, teachers instruct them not to cheat: *Keep your eyes on your own test; do not look at other people's answers.* But adolescents are not children any more. They are stretching their wings and trying to fly by themselves. They are out of our sight (and our control) for long periods of time. They will be confronted with many dilemmas over time and they need principles and guidelines by which they can make judgments when we adults are not looking over their shoulders. Consider the principles and guidelines couched in the following parables, koans, maxims, proverbs, and so forth.

Look before you leap! A stitch in time saves nine!
Don't be a sheep and follow the crowd. Use your own head. Do your own thinking.
When you are thinking about doing something, think about the consequences.
Don't do anything you wouldn't want everyone to know about.
It's not a beautiful face that counts, but a beautiful heart.
Pride goeth before a fall.
Do unto others as you would have them do unto you.

These sayings, proverbs, and maxims may not have much meaning to the youngster on first hearing them. But as they are applied to many situations, the multilevel meanings of these sayings become woven into the youngster's psychology. They will sound and resound in his memory as he contemplates the events of his life or anticipates future ones. As he matures, he will come to understand their deepest, most profound meanings and be guided by them according to his stage of moral/ethical understanding.

IMPORTANT TERMS AND CONCEPTS TO KNOW

AIDS	crowds	homosexual	pubertal
anorexia	date rape	late-maturing	safe sex
appearance	early-maturing	midbrain	safer
audience	egocentrism	personal fable	storm-and-strife
brain	emotional	primary	venereal
bulimia	fight-flight-freeze	puberty	vise
bullied			

MAKE YOUR OWN SUMMARY BY FILLING IN THE BLANKS BELOW

Use the "Important Terms and Concepts to Know" to fill in the blanks below.

Adolescence is part of human development, but it is a modern phenomenon. Young people in more traditional societies do not experience what G. Stanley Hall called the period of _____ . The physical growth spurt is due to _____ maturation.

Personality Changes. Unfortunately, they develop less attractive personality traits, such as adolescent _____ (the inability to consider anyone else's perspective) and the _____ (the idea that they are unique and special). Their constant self-consciousness is the result of their belief in an imaginary _____ .

From Crowds to Pairing Off. The "dating game" begins when adolescent girls and boys get together in _____ . Eventually a couple pair off and start real dating. At this junction, the adolescent is in a sexual _____ between their sexual drives and the prohibitions of society.

Dangers of Dating and Sexual Exploration. Daughters should be warned against acquaintance or _____ . Unfortunately, too many adolescents are at high risk for sexually transmitted diseases (once called _____ disease), and of course the fatal disease of _____ .The Harvard School of Medicine has issued a warning: There is no such thing as _____ , only _____ sex.

Troubled Teenagers. Adolescents are also at high risk for suicide, particularly _____ adolescents who are more than four times as likely to attempt suicide as other adolescents. Their self-esteem is low because they are depressed about their physical _____ . Girls may develop an unreasonable fear of gaining weight and develop _____ , or go in for binge eating and vomiting, called _____ .

Early- and late-maturing boys are often threatened and _____ . But there is an up-side to the story of late-maturer. _____ adolescents are forced to develop their talents, skillXs, and other inner resources and so develop attractive personalities. By the time they are in their thirties, the late-maturers have more self-esteem than the _____ adolescents.

The confusing behaviors of the teenager may be explained by a new theory of the adolescent's _____ , which is apparently still in an immature state. The growth changes of _____ have also produced changes in the brain. But since the brain is still immature, the adolescent's emotional responses are often dominated by the midbrain which is the seat of the _____ response, and which incites impulsive behavior and violent mood swings. We foster _____ intelligence by providing them with experience in making moral/ethical decisions.

14 THE MANY LEVELS OF CONSCIOUSNESS
Dreaming, Daydreaming, Hypnosis, Prayer and Meditation, and Creativity

CHUANG TZU

Last night I dreamed I was a butterfly,
Now I do not know if I am Chaung Tzu
Who dreamed I was a butterfly, or a butterfly
Who dreamed it was Chuang Tzu.

Box 14.1
SCENARIO
"Altered States" May Simply Be Different Levels of Consciousness

Professor Weitzman: Eduardo, when was the last time you experienced an "altered state of consciousness" (ASC)?

Eduardo: Hey, Professor, you got me wrong! I don't do drugs. Oh, when I was a kid I had to try out some grass like kids do, but that was a long time ago.

Professor Weitzman: I didn't say anything about drugs. I said "an alternate state of consciousness." They don't only come by way of drugs, illegal or legal. They are happening to us all the time. Anybody have an ASC in the last 24 hours?

Jonniemae: I had a really vivid dream last night. When I woke up, I wasn't sure if I was awake or still dreaming. How's that for an ASC?

Professor Weitzman: Exactly. Anybody had a daydream today? Maybe of a pretty girl?

Eduardo: I have those all the time. Wow! I have a lot of ASCs! (*class laughter*)

Shannon: When I am in a special deep kind of praying, I sometimes feel carried away. Would that be an ASC?

Professor Weitzman: Sounds like it to me.

Li Ho: What about hypnosis?

Professor Weitzman: There's another one.

Eduardo: Sometimes when I play my guitar, I feel . . . well kind of . . . you know . . . gone. Not here any more. Somewhere else. Like real inspired. I guess that would be an ASC.

Martha Vining: ASCs are beginning to sound pretty common.

Professor Weitzman: Exactly! We used to discuss all ASCs as if they were the result of some esoteric Eastern meditation or illegal drug-induced states. Now we know that in the course of a day, we are continually undergoing changes in our level of consciousness. In fact, psychologists are beginning to let go of the term "altered states of consciousness" altogether. We're beginning to use other kinds of terms like "levels of consciousness." Freud started us off with several levels of awareness, which he called the conscious, preconscious, and unconscious. You all just added many more levels of consciousness. Then there are other experiences we can add to the list of ASCs; for example, when we have just imbibed some alcohol, or when we have taken pain-killers, or when we are watching a movie or reading a book that is so engrossing that it feels like an actual experience we are having. And so on. We are continually flowing from one level of consciousness to the next every day and night of our lives.

Alec: So what you are saying is that ASCs are very common indeed.

Professor Weitzman: Exactly!

Dan: Hold on, Professor. I have to challenge that statement. We have a man in our village—white men would call him a "medicine man"—who goes into a trance state every so often. It's awesome to watch.

Box 14.1	SCENARIO (continued) "Altered States" May Simply Be Different Levels of Consciousness

When he comes out of the trance, he says very wise things. I don't think that's very common.

Professor Weitzman: Granted! And psychology is very interested in what is happening in those uncommon levels. Psychologists the world over are presently pur-

suing studies of yogis, sufi dancing, meditation and prayer, and what many religions call the "mystic experience." But to begin our discussion, let's start with those experiences which are more common—which all of us have had all our lives.

Defining the Many Levels of Consciousness

Let us define **consciousness** as our everyday perception of the world as we go about our usual routines of getting-up in the morning, eating breakfast, going to school or work, interacting with our classmates and co-workers, driving home, having dinner, etc. Unless something grabs our attention, we are operating "on automatic," in which we are hardly aware of what we are doing. Strange to say, much of what we experience as normal consciousness is largely unconscious and conditioned by our previous life events. No wonder some personality theorists consider us as not much more than mindless robots or trained monkeys.

Then every so often, something jolts us out of our conditioned consciousness. It may be an event so startling that from thence forth our whole worldview has been altered, which is why these events have been called **altered states of consciousness (ASCs)**. ASCs have been described as taking us "out of ourselves" or as the sudden widening of "the doors of perception" (Huxley, 1963). We look at the world with "new eyes" and listen with "new ears." Maslow described one type—what he called a "peak experience"—as one in which the person feels "at-one-ment" with the universe.

Altered states of consciousness can also be triggered by dramatic changes in our health and physical well-being, such as fever or a change in diet or loss of hearing or deprivation of sleep. Or they can be initiated by extra-physical exertion, such as marathon running ("runner's high") or overextended stays underwater ("rapture of the deep"). They can come by way of emotionally traumatic experiences such as a car accident or rape or earthquake or the loss of a dearly beloved friend or relative. Anyone who has experienced the dissolution of a love affair or a heart-rending divorce will freely admit that the shattering of their relationships led to a shattering of their basic assumptions about love, sexual fulfillment, and marital happiness (see Tip 14.1).

Creative Breakthrough in All Areas of Endeavor Through Altered Levels of Consciousness. It is unfortunate that what we have called ASCs came to be associated with

---

Tip 14.1 Operating on "Automatic." Consider, for example, how you drove to work. Can you describe exactly how you pulled out of your driveway onto the street this morning? Can you remember stopping at every stop light and stop sign? Can you remember street after street as you drove? Can you actually recall making the turn into your college or place of work? Probably not, and that is just as well. If we had to think about every movement we made every minute, we would be in serious trouble. The fact that we can do much of what we do "automatically" enables us to concentrate on more important events.

hallucinogenic drugs (drugs which target the central nervous system and change our perception of reality, such as LSD, certain mushrooms (like peyote, etc.), and mysterious practices from the East. ASCs also manifest as many common experiences, experiences we have everyday of our lives. Dreaming, day-dreaming, fantasy, meditation and prayer, creativity and scientific thinking are all levels of consciousness that can produce changes in our perceptions of the world. Maslow's self-actualizing subjects paid a great deal of attention to their inner world of dreams. The great breakthroughs in science are often the result of perceiving a totally new *gestalt*—a sudden, new interpretation of events. In fact, all truly innovative thinking and creative achievement, whether in science, art, literature, or business, are the result of altered levels of consciousness; i.e., a new way of looking and understanding the world. Artists paint the world in colors and shapes hitherto unseen. Musicians play sounds so new that they penetrate our jaded sense of hearing. Poets restring the ordinary words of our language so that they produce new meaning. But altered perceptions are not the sole bailiwick of creative artists. The reformers of all ages have broken through to higher levels of human justice and human mercy.

The Altered State of Dreaming

Dreams have fascinated humanity since the beginning of time. In dreams, we do not seem to have to obey the physical laws of time and space as we do during the day. We can go forward and back in time. We can put people together who never knew each other. We can fly through the air. And a nightmare can haunt us for days. It is obvious that the dreaming state is a quite different reality than our waking state.

A Brief History of Dreams and Dreaming

Today it is difficult for us to realize that dreams were considered so much "stuff and nonsense" by the educated elite of the nineteenth century. For them, dreams were simply a bodily response to physical distress. If someone dreamed of being guillotined, it was because the dreamer was being choked by bedclothes. If someone dreamed of drowning in a sinking boat, the explanation was that he needed to urinate. Ebenezer Scrooge, in Charles Dickens' *A Christmas Carol,* was relying on this *physicalist* theory of dreaming when he reacted to his "night visitor" as nothing more than "a bit of undigested food."

The physicalist approach to dreaming came as a relief to the educated elite of the nineteenth century and was a step in the right direction since previously, in medieval times, bad dreams were believed to be caused by night monsters (in Old English, *nicht mares*). During the medieval witch hunts, erotic dreams were seen as the work of devils (*incubi* and *succubi*) that invaded the souls of innocent men and women. Many an unfortunate young woman was burned to death as a witch because a man had had an erotic dream about her (Huxley, 1986). It was comforting for the educated elite of the nineteenth century to dismiss their embarrassing dreams and frightening nightmares as simply physical discomfort.

Dreams in Ancient Times

It was disturbing, then, for Sigmund Freud to announce to the world that our dreams are far from meaningless—that, in fact, they come from a very deep part of our personality which lies hidden below the conscious mind. According to Freud, dreams are the "royal road" to our unconscious wishes, urges, desires, angers, etc, which we cannot consciously admit to ourselves. Dreams, said Freud, reveal the savage, infantile, uncivilized aspects of the self we prefer to ignore. Furthermore, Freud insisted that the lusty, exhibitionistic, violent, childlike dream self is just as valid (if not more so) than the polite, civilized self of the waking state. And most extraordinary of all, Freud said that while this new understanding of dreams might seem revolutionary, he was taking his stand with "the Ancients"—with the prophets of the Bible, with the scribes of Egypt's Pharaohs, and with the seers of other ancient religions who believed that dreams are very significant messages for human beings.

The *Old Testament* is not only a source of ancient dreams, it is also one of the first handbooks on dream interpretation. Joseph (he of the coat of many colors) gained such a good reputation as an interpreter of dreams that eventually it gained him a high position in the Court of Pharaoh. The Hebrews had long believed that dreams were one of the ways men and Jahweh communicated. The famous dialog between Jahweh and Solomon takes place in a dream dialog. The fall of Jericho to Gideon is predicted in a dream of a soldier of Canaan. All the way through the Old Testament and into the New Testament, dreams continued to play a very important role in the Judaic-Christian tradition. The Book of Matthew highlights the birth, childhood, and death of Jesus with dream messages (Box 14.2).

Mohammed, the prophet of Islam, made a practice of relating his dreams each morning to his top lieutenants, and he had them relate theirs as well. Mohammed considered dream interpretation as an important study of philosophic science. Our Native Americans had a practice of isolating themselves in the wilderness and fasting until they had a "big dream." Today, most psychologists would agree with the first century rabbi who said, "A dream uninterpreted is like a letter that is not read" (see Figure 14.1). The fact that so many ancient religions believed that dreams were of special significance was the meaning of Freud's statement, "I stand with the Ancients."

Freud: Dreams as Catharsis and Wish-Fulfillment

To Freud, dreams were neither divine revelation nor prophecy. While he believed dreams were significant, he believed the significance was of a different kind. According to Freud, dreams are unconscious thoughts and feelings that surface at night in our dreams. Freud discussed two kinds of dreams: Repressed impulses that our consciousness finds unacceptable and **wish-fulfillment** of what we would like in the future. While we are asleep these impulses and wishes come to the fore, but in disguised symbolic form. Why in disguised symbolic form? Freud's answer: If these unacceptable wishes were to appear in undisguised form, we would wake up in horror—as we often do with nightmares. For example, suppose a man dreamt that he wanted to kill his father. He would be as horrified as Oedipus was at the Oracle's prophecy. Instead he simply dreams that he throws a wheel at a snowman, and the snowman melts away. It just so happens that the snowman is wearing a hat like his father has, smoking a pipe similar to his father, and is sporting a red plaid scarf such as his father wears. And why a wheel? Because it revolves—and the word suggests the gun we call "a revolver." By camouflaging his desire to kill his father with dream symbols, the dreamer's unacceptable thoughts and feelings are catharsized and he is permitted to continue sleeping. For Freud, dreams were the "guardians of sleep."

According to Freud, we dream whatever we repress in our everyday life. Since the society of his times was so sexually repressive, it follows that his patients had dreams that were highly sexual in nature. Elongated objects such as knives, sticks, spears, rifles, and even bananas

Box 14.2

DREAMS IN THE BIBLE

Solomon's Dream. It must have come as a surprise to Solomon to be anointed as the heir to David's kingdom. He was one of the youngest of David's sons, and the Bible records his true humility in becoming King of all Israel. He retreats to a "high place" and prays to the Lord God for guidance. He then falls asleep and has a dream in which, God speaks to him thus, "Ask what you would like me to give you?" Solomon replies as follows:

My God, you have made your servant king in succession to David, my father. But I am a very young man, unskilled in leadership. Your servant finds himself in the midst of this people of yours that you have chosen, a people so many that its number cannot be counted or reckoned. Give your servant a heart to understand how to discern between good and evil, for who could govern this people of yours that is so great?

Pleased, the Lord God answers:

Since you have asked for this and not asked for long life for yourself or riches or the lives of your enemies, but have asked for a discerning judgment for yourself here and now, I do what you ask. I give you a heart wise and shrewd as none before you has had and none will have after you. What you have not asked I shall give you also; such as riches and glory as no other king ever had. And I will give you a long life, if you follow my laws and commandments as your father David followed them.

To remind us again that this dialogue between the Lord God and Solomon has come by way of dreaming, the scribe writes, "Then Solomon awoke; it was a dream." (Kings 1:3).

Dreams in the Book of Matthew. When Joseph discovers his bride-to-be, Mary, is pregnant, he is very distressed. But being a man of honor, he does not want to expose her publicly. Instead, he decides to divorce her quietly. The Lord's angel, however, Matthew tells us, appears to Joseph in a dream and tells him not to refrain from taking Mary as his wife, for her conception is by "the Holy Spirit." (Matthew 1:20).

After making adoration of the "new king" of Israel, the Magi are instructed "in a dream" not to go back to Herod and inform him of the whereabouts of the Babe, but to return instead to their own country "by another route." (Matthew 2:12).

The Angel of the Lord appears twice again to Joseph in his dreams: first, to tell him to flee with Mary and the Child to Egypt, and the second time, to tell him that it was safe to return to Israel with his family (Matthew 2: 12–13 and Matthew 2: 19–20).

In the last hours of Jesus' life, at the moment in which he is standing before Pontius Pilate and the crowd, Pontius receives a message from his wife. She is not named in the Bible (although tradition has it that she is called Claudia). The message is a plea of mercy.

Now as he was seated in the chair of judgment, his wife sent him a message, "Have nothing to do with that man; I have been upset all day by a dream I had about him" (Matthew 27.6).

were representative symbols for the penis. Hollow containers such as boxes, chests, cupboards, even ovens, could represent the vagina and uterus. A train going through a tunnel could be a symbolic representation of intercourse. But sexual symbols are not the only kind of symbols in dreams, said Freud. Conflicts of all kinds can emerge in disguised symbolic form. Dreams can be the repository for our anger, our hurts, our jealousies, our desire for revenge, etc. Whatever emotions or thoughts that we repress or do not want to deal with are the substance for our dreams.

An important aspect of dreams, said Freud, is their laconic quality. They say what they have to say as briefly as they can. One soldier can represent a whole army. Thus a judge in a dream may stand for authority of any kind. Freud called these collective objects or collective persons. Freud provided this example of a collective person: Suppose the dreamer is a professor who has not been publishing and consequently is not getting raises and promotions. He dreams of A and B and C and D, who are all publishing papers and getting credit for it. The dream is a

Figure 14.1   Rabbo Chisda A dream uninterpreted is like a letter that is not read.

disguised expression of his own jealousy. Conversely, several people can really be indicating one person. Freud wrote that a person in a dream can "look like A perhaps, but be dressed like B, may do something we remember C doing, and at the same time we may know that it is really D." The *dream work* (Freud's term for unraveling the meaning of dream symbols) is to discover what A and B and C and D all have in common. A and B and C and D must have something in common, which Freud called a *condensed object* or *condensed person*.

The Jungian Approach: Dreams as Inspiration, Creativity, and Prediction

Freud's student and colleague, Carl Jung, developed another approach to dreaming, one which differed significantly from Freud's in many ways. While agreeing with Freud that dreams can use nonsexual symbols to disguise sexual phenomena, Jung came to believe that the reverse is also true. A sexual symbol can have nonsexual meaning,—even a spiritual meaning. For Jung, dreams were a source of inspiration and creativity. For example: Suppose a man dreams that he is pregnant and about to have a baby. A strictly sexual interpretation might result in the hypothesis that the man has "female envy." In a Jungian interpretation, the symbols of pregnancy and birth of a baby could be metaphors for something else. What kind of metaphor? Well, suppose the man is a business man or a scientist who has been working for months and months on a project. The dream then could be a metaphor that after many months of "being pregnant with an idea," he may now be on the verge of a breakthrough (finally), symbolized as "giving birth." Another example is provided in Box 14.3.

Dreams as Spiritual Guidance and Intuitions of the Future. Freud believed that dreams had to do with the past, that we dream at night of conflicts we have had in the previous 24 to 48 hours. Jung believed that dreams could predict the future. He provided examples of such dreams from his own clinical practice.

Here's an example of a predictive dream, a man who confessed himself to be a workaholic had the following dream. He is bicycling along a road going uphill all the way and struggling to get to the top. All along the road there are signposts that read: STOP, SLOW DOWN, DON'T EXCEED THE SPEED LIMIT, 180 MPH. The dreamer insisted he could not fathom what the dream might mean since he was a very careful driver and never exceeded the speed limit. Others who were present in the dream workshop were nonplused by the man's inability to penetrate his dream symbols. They proposed that his dream was a warning that if he didn't slow down and take it easier, he was headed for a serious illness. At that, the man admitted that his last blood pressure reading had been 180 over 130!

Synchronicity. The idea of *synchronicity* has struck such a deep chord in the hearts of some artists and writers that it has become an accepted word in our everyday vocabulary. The

Box 14.3

DREAM TRANSCRIPT
I'm Being Kidnaped!

The following are excerpts from an actual dream. Ginny, an 18-year-old freshman has had a dream which has disturbed her greatly. (The ellipses mean that a few sentences have been omitted.)

Ginny: In my dream, I am in my car and I am going to my boyfriend's house. Only I can't see anything around me like houses and cars because it is all gray and dark . . . I come to my boyfriend's house—only it's a garage. I pull up in my car and he puts gas in it. Then suddenly I am not there at all, but sitting in a room in a house, and it seems as if he has kidnapped me, which I can't understand because my boyfriend is very nice.

Therapist: Try playing the grayness and darkness in your dream.

Ginny: Well, I'm the grayness in Ginny's dream. It's foggy and the fog is covering everything up. I make it hard to see . . . Hey, does that mean I feel like . . . I don't know where I'm going? I'm kind of confused?

Therapist: Sound right to you?

Ginny: Yeah . . . So when I get to my boyfriend's house . . . he comes over and pumps gas in my car, I guess that means something sexual. I guess it means I want to sleep with him.

Therapist: Let's find out . . . Become Tim [her boyfriend] in the dream and let's see what he is doing. Talk like you're Tim.

Ginny: . . . I'm Tim putting gas in Ginny's car . . . (smiling) That's really funny. That's what he does. Every time I get moody, he kind of fills me up . . . He's so enthusiastic about everything . . . He kind of straightens out all my problems . . . and he's always cheerful and good humored.

Therapist: OK. Getting back to your dream.

Ginny: Then I'm at my Tim's house, only . . . I'm crying . . . and the strange thing is Tim is sitting there and laughing at me . . . and so are my father and brother. It seems like I've been taken there against my will . . .

Therapist: . . . Play your father laughing at Ginny.

Ginny: I'm Ginny's father and I'm laughing at her . . . Only Ginny's not laughing. That's strange. I guess I'm not taking her crying seriously.

Therapist: So in some way, your father is not taking you seriously. Is that the same for Tim and your brother? What might that be in your waking life?

Ginny: They think I worry about foolish things.

Therapist: Such as?

Ginny: Like getting married or not. I keep trying to tell them that maybe I'm too young to get married. But they all just tell me I''m being silly. I really feel as if I haven't lived yet!

Therapist: . . . Do you feel like a "child bride"?

Ginny: Yeah!

Therapist: . . . Ginny, do you feel a bit as if you're being kidnapped into marriage?

Ginny: Wow! That's just how I feel. Oh, wow!

Later we asked Ginny to translate her dream symbols into everyday language.

Ginny: I guess I feel lost and confused about getting married and I don't know if I should or not. I am pretty young, I guess. Anyway, every time I tell Tim how I feel, he just tells me not to worry about it . . . I 'm not really sure if it's the right thing to do because he makes it sound so exciting. But I guess I'm not really sure. I feel like a kid and I'm being kidnapped. And no one is taking me seriously.

---

reader may even know a song entitled "Synchronicity," written and played by a rock group that called themselves "The Police." Jung had come from a long line of Calvinist ministers. Although rejecting the orthodoxy of formal religion, he came to believe that there are forces beyond human understanding that are sometimes glimpsed through our intuitions, our art and artifacts, and our dreams. He believed that what other people call coincidence is not coincidence at all, but evidence of our psychic connectedness. Have you ever had the experience of thinking of someone when, all of a sudden, the phone rings and it is the person you have been thinking about? Or have you ever received a letter from a person you have just written to? Jung said these are not coincidental events, but evidence of our connectedness to each other, which he called **synchronicity.**

Box 14.4

DREAM TRANSCRIPT
A Jungian Approach

Jung came to believe that the universal symbols developed in all cultures were deeply buried in the person's collective unconscious. The following dream is a good example. The Ancient Greeks had developed the concept of the basic four elements of the universe: earth, air, fire, and water. Notice how this dreamer uses these elements to point to something missing in her life. The dreamer was an older woman who had lived a life of many experiences, including the suicide of her husband two years before. She was raising her two girls by herself on her 120 acre farm, virtually alone, and had become a kind of recluse, fearing to go out into society.

Brooke: In my dream, I am in a plowed field, which seems to be very fertile, but nothing is growing on it. As I am looking at the plowed fields, I am suddenly aware that I am leaving the ground, and rising into the air. I see the blue sky around me like a dome. As I look down, I can see the furrowed fields are no longer earth but water, ocean, only with the same texture and quality of the plowed fields. . . . I think I know the meaning of my dream.

Therapist: Relate what you understand.

Brooke: Well, I'm like the furrowed fields. I have a lot of richness in me, fertile like the land, but I haven't produced anything for a long time . . . since my husband died.

Therapist: Go on.

Brooke: The rising in the air seems to mean that I am beginning to leave off being so rooted to the earth and allowing myself to expand like the air.

Therapist: New ideas, new goals. What about the water?

Brooke: The water represents the nourishment of the earth so things can grow. The only thing is that the water-land is still brown—nothing growing yet. But the potential is there. I am at a place where I want to do something for myself.

Therapist: Brooke, do you notice that your dream contains three of the four universal elements? . . .

Brooke: Earth, air, and water.

Therapist: What's missing?

Brooke: Fire!

Therapist: What does fire represent to you?

Brooke: I have to put a fire under myself.

Therapist: The fire of creation?

Brooke: Yes, that fits very well. I better get "fired up."

In his search for universal spiritual themes, Jung studied many philosophical systems and their symbols: the Chinese Tao; the Tibetan mandala; Kali, the Hindu goddess of destruction; even medieval alchemy. While Freud viewed Jung's interest in mysticism as so much superstition, Jung believed the symbols of these ancient ethical/philosophic systems held great wisdom for modern humanity—if we can but discover their meanings. American psychologists, too, were skeptical about Jung's forays into esoteric symbolism until the post–World War II decades of the 1960s and 1970s. Young people, the world over began using the ancient Egyptian ankh as a universal symbol for peace. American psychologists began to take Jung's explorations into other cultural paradigms more seriously. (See Box 14.4 for a Jungian dream.)

The Key to Jungian Dream Symbols: The Polarities of Human Existence. From his study of other cultural systems, Jung formulated a personality theory based on his study of The Tao—a traditional Chinese philosophic system of knowledge. Jung came to view the yin/yang symbol as revealing a great truth about human nature. Human understanding, Jung believed, is a matter of distinguishing between opposites. We are able to sense cold because we also sense hot. Other polarities include up/down, light/dark, creation/destruction, male/female. In a similar vein, our understanding of our emotions comes about by way of contrast. An example from everyday life: If we have grown up fairly happily with few problems, we tend to take what we have for granted. Then, somewhere over the course of time, our lives are overshadowed by ill health or financial stress. After a bout of illness, we appreciate good health as we never have before. If we have been buried in debt, we will be more sensitive to living within a budget. Having experienced the dark, we now appreciate the light. The polarities of personality are reflected in many other ways; specifically, in what Jung called the **personal** and **collective** or **racial unconscious;** and in what he called the **Archetypes** of human phenomenology (a person's worldview).

Two Levels of Unconscious: Personal and Collective.

Like Freud, Jung (1964) believed that we have an unconscious aspect to human personality. But whereas Freud postulated only a personal unconscious, Jung postulated also a collective or racial unconscious. This deeper level of unconsciousness has to do with the evolution of the human race and connects us to everyone on earth. (If the reader finds that difficult to accept, we can use the analogy of the DNA by which we are related not only to all other human beings but to all life on earth.) This racial unconscious connects us not only to all other living persons (thus explaining the psychic elements of synchronicity) but also to all previous generations of humanity.

The Polarities of Our Personal Unconscious: Persona and Shadow.

Jung distinguished two aspects of our personality, the *Persona* and the *Shadow.* Notice that the word *Persona* is closely related to the word *personality.* Actually, the **Persona** is what we would like to think our personality to be. It is the "public image" we put on when we put our best foot forward. It is what T. S. Eliot meant when he wrote of putting on "a face to meet the faces that you meet." The Persona can also be thought of as the roles we take on in life as "the Doctor," "the Lawyer," "the Drill Sergeant." The Persona also contains those qualities we portray ourselves to be, such as "sexy" or "pure" or "noble" or "macho" or whatever.

If the Persona is everything we like to think that we are, then the **Shadow** is everything we reject about ourselves. The traits we reject coalesce in our unconscious as our Shadow. We can deny the shadow side of ourselves but we cannot get rid of it. Like our physical shadow, our psychic shadow is always with us. When disagreeable aspects threaten to emerge in our consciousness, we protect ourselves by projecting our bad feelings onto others, sometimes making others our scapegoats. Some of the classic scapegoats have been the Jews, African-Americans, Native Americans, the Gypsies, etc. Sadly, even at the present time, ethnic groups all over the world are killing each other in demonic ways. In our dreams, the Shadow is often that fearsome person or something that frightens or chases us. For a man, it may be a person with a knife or a gorilla, all of which are symbolic of the "beast within" that the man fears might be getting out of control. A woman's Shadow may appear as something opposite to her public image. If she is a conservative person, modest in dress and speech, her Shadow may appear as a fun-loving seductress. If she values herself as intelligent and mature, her Shadow may appear as a retarded child.

Our Shadows are not necessarily "evil"—they are simply parts of ourselves we want to deny, some trait perhaps that embarrasses us or we think of as "childish" or "foolish." Example: A businessman who prided himself on being pennywise once threw some dollar bills into the coffers of the traditional Christmas bell-ringers. That night he had a dream in which he was a beggar giving his last dollar away. In his own eyes, his bit of spontaneous charity was a bit of foolishness. He would have done better to write them a check so as to have evidence for a tax credit!

Our Rejected "Male" and "Female" Aspects: Anima and Animus.

Freud had shocked many of his readers when he wrote that we are all biologically double-sexed—a fact that modern readers take for granted. Now Jung extended this thesis. What he said was that every culture develops certain ideas about which personality traits are appropriate for males and which are appropriate for females. Every child growing up learns the appropriate behaviors for his or her gender and rejects all those traits his family or culture deem inappropriate. The denied "female" traits in the young boy coalesce as the **Anima.** The denied "male" traits in the young girl coalesce as the **Animus.** As long as all goes well, the man and the woman can hang on to their culturally accepted Personas and hide their Shadow, Anima, and Animus.

But there come those moments in life, when the man and the woman are jolted by the circumstances of their lives and, suddenly, the man's Anima takes over his personality and the woman's Animus takes over hers. It is a confounding event to the man and the woman involved (and fascinating to watch). Let us consider a young lad who is taught to feel ashamed of crying or tears of any sort. He grows up with a "macho" style personality, always tough, able "to take it on the chin" or "bite the bullet." Aggressive acts come easily to him. Other female traits, such as caring and tenderness, have been repressed and have coalesced as his Anima. For much of his life, he is able to hang on to his macho style until one day something happens that penetrates his toughness. His wife walks out on him or his son is in an accident—and suddenly he cannot "hold it together." His Anima breaks through and takes over his personality. Behaviors he has denied for a lifetime suddenly break through as tears, copious weeping, bewildering sadness, and utter loneliness. These strange emotions may make him feel that he is "losing his mind." Said Jung, he is not losing his mind but actually getting in touch with the part he has denied for so long—which is part of what happens to him in the midlife crisis.

According to Jung, this denied part of the man, the Anima, is a true wellspring of creativity. Those who are more in touch with their Anima, said Jung, become the artists, reformers, visionaries, and creative scientists. Indeed, said Jung, poets and composers and writers, for centuries, have talked about their Muse—the goddess to whom they pay homage as the source of their inspiration. And who is this goddess? She may be called Harpsichord or Diana or Aphrodite but whatever she is called, he is calling forth his own Anima, and reaching deep into that rich source of his creative unconscious (see Figure 14.2). Like the psychologically androgynous child, men who can call on both sides of their psyche have a much wider spectrum of cognitions and emotions available to them. Is that only Jung speaking? Not at all. American psychologists who have been studying truly creative individuals validate Jung's thesis (Barron, 1970; Kubie, 1967; MacKinnon, 1978).

Furthermore, said Jung, when he falls in love with a woman, a man is really falling in love with himself—a way of uniting that other part of himself he has denied for so long. In the presence of his lady-love, he is able to express his repressed emotions of tenderness and caring. (see Tip 14.2). That is why love makes us feel so good—we are feeling and expressing more sides to our personality than we ever have before.

Tip 14.2 Three Aspects of the Anima. Jung was a friend to all of the women in the world when he explained male psychology in this way. There are three aspects to the Anima: the innocent *nymph* (or virgin), the gracious and loving *madonna* (the gracious and loving mother), and the hideous *hag* (or witch). Man falls in love with the young and innocent *nymph* and captures her in marriage. As his wife, when she becomes the mother of his children, she is transformed into the archetypal madonna. As he gets older and disenchanted with married life, he begins to call her "the old lady," the "nag," the "ball-and-chain"— he has come to view her as the *hag*. Now has she changed over the course of time? Of course not. Only his perception of her has changed. Furthermore, his vision of her (whether nymph, madonna, or hag) has never been based on reality. Each aspect of her is really an aspect of his own unconcious Anima, which he has thrust upon her.

Figure 14.2 Three Aspects of the Anima: the Virgin, the Mother, and the Hag!

In cultures such as ours, where the girl-child has been taught to repress her intellectuality and independence, those aspects of her personality will go underground as her **Animus.** If she has been defining herself all her life only as the wife of her husband and the mother of her children, she will have no identity of her own when her husband is taken up with his work and her children are grown away. Or her denied Animus may take another route. Instead of subjugating herself, she may subjugate her husband and children in either martyrdom or subtle sabotage of her husband as a person worthy of respect. Thus she comes to dominate the house. The Animus may appear in a woman's fantasies and dreams as the ideal lover of her romantic hopes or romantic disillusionment. The Animus may appear as a father figure from her child-like desire to remain "Daddy's little girl." Or as the priest or savior of her unfulfilled life. The Animus may also emerge as a nameless, faceless ogre, the ruffian who brutalizes her. This ogre may seem a little far-fetched to the reader. Who would want to be so brutalized? We have only to point to the women who have offered themselves in marriage to convicted murderers—even serial killers—for the psychological truth of this form of the Animus Archetype.

The Polarities of Our Collective (or Racial) Unconscious: The Archetypes. The Persona/Shadow and Animus/Anima polarities reside in our personal unconscious. There are certain aspects of our personality, said Jung, that have their roots in a far deeper part of the unconscious—they are the Archetypes of our racial or collective unconscious. Jung devised the term Archetype to convey something very old, buried in the most archaic aspects of the personality. As the offspring of previous generations of humanity, we still contain "psychic remnants" of our ancestral forebears. As personality traits, these Archetypes are "predispositions" to perceiving the world in certain ways and expressing ourselves. So potent are these Archetypes in our racial unconscious that they have appeared in the legends, the literature, the art and artifacts of previous cultures. They continue to appear today in our dreams, in our fantasies, in our art, and in our literature. They crop up even in the most modern of dress, in movies and television, and in cartoons and comics. Just as our personal unconscious is characterized by the polarities of Persona/Shadow and Anima/Animus, so too are the Archetypes polarized. The adult Archetypes are composed of the **Wise Old Man** and **Wise Old Woman.** The children Archetypes are represented by the **Wise Child** and the **Trickster.**

The Wise Old Man. The **Wise Old Man** is the personification of the tribal wisdom collected in one person. Over the course of centuries the Wise Old Man has appeared as the medicine man, the shaman, the witch doctor, the rabbi, the minister, the priest, and as a tribal elder. The Wise Old Man formulates principles of conduct for the individual, for the tribe, for the clan, or for society-at-large. Moses of the *Old Testament* is a perfect personification of the Wise Old Man since he was the leader who laid down the wisdom of the Commandments. For Catholics, he may be represented by the Pope. Mythology, folklore, and literature have idealized the Wise Old Man as King Arthur, as Father Time, as Shakespeare's Prospero. In whatever form he appears, his wisdom is the wisdom of experience that comes from having lived many years on this earth, learning the cyclical laws of nature, and the psychological motivations of men and women. However he is represented, his society or culture looks to him for help and guidance. On TV today, he may be the Father who "knows best" or the Beverly Hillbilly who looks like a country bumpkin but who knows about what comes naturally to human psychology. He may appear as the genial, popular talk show host or the all-knowing newscast anchorman. In our dreams, the Wise Old Man Archetype may come in the form of a deceased relative such as a father or grandfather, who counseled us in his lifetime, and now comforts us in our dreams. He may even come in the form of the president of a corporation or even the President of the United States.

The Wise Old Woman.   This archetype is the female polarity of the Wise Old Man. Over the course of centuries, she has been personified as the oracle, the gypsy, the fairy godmother and good witch, the Nordic rune-thrower, the vestal virgin, and the high priestess whose symbol is the writhing snake of wisdom. Her wisdom, however, is of a different kind from that of the Wise Old Man. Her wisdom is not of this earth at all. The wisdom of the *Wise Old Woman* is that of intuition, the intuition that can see around corners and into the future. This wisdom vexes the men in her family. They scoff at "woman's intuition" but are awed by it. In the past, women who were deeply in touch with this aspect of themselves learned to listen to it but to keep still about it—or risk being burned at the stake. Despite their suspiciousness, men of other ages consulted the Wise Old Woman in form of the oracle, sibyl, or the gypsy fortune teller. Today, we legitimize the appearance of these Wise Old Women at certain times—at Halloween in the forms of witches and as "psychic readers." On TV, she appears as Samantha of *Bewitched.* In the movie *The Wizard of Oz,* she is the Good Witch of the North, Glinda.

The Wise Old Woman can take the form of a man—but a very special type of man, a man who is innocent of life's carnal pleasures. Merlin is a good example. As long as he remained chaste he retained his mystic powers and lost them only when he allowed himself to be seduced by the witch-woman called Vivian. In the TV series "M*A*S*H," he is that mystical character "Radar" who seems to know what people want before they ask him and can hear the helicopters before they come into listening range. He, too, the series makes plain, is a virgin innocent of the pleasures of the flesh.

The Wise Child.   This Archetype represents the wisdom of goodness and purity, innocence and sweetness, joy and radiance. This is the wisdom we all had as children when we were more trusting and loving and open to the world. It is the wisdom we lost (alas!) as we grew older and became more cynical. With his lack of worldliness, Francis of Assisi was a Wise Child of the Church. In literature, the Wise Child has been portrayed by Antoine de St. Exupery as the Little Prince and by Charles Dickens as Tiny Tim and David Copperfield and Oliver Twist. But the Wise Child can also been portrayed a girl, as Heidi and Pollyana or the Little Mermaid. In more modern form, the Wise Child is represented by Woody, the naive and trusting bartender of "Cheers." Sometimes the Wise Child comes in surprising form. Although outwardly tough and highlighting all his sentences with all the four-letter words of the English language, Holden Caulfield (from the novel by J. D. Salinger) can see through the hypocrisy of society and wants none of it. Huckleberry Finn is another such Wise Child. Both Huck and Holden see through the sham of "The Emperor's New Clothes" and know him to be naked. And who among us will ever forget the Wise Child who befriended "E.T." The supreme example of the Wise

Child is, of course, the Christ Child whose message is "Peace on earth, good will toward men." Perhaps that is why our favorite holiday is the Christmas season for it is at this time that we are able to renew our childhood wisdom of faith and hope, and to express our love to others through the sending of cards and the giving of gifts.

The Trickster. If we believe that children are all sweetness and kindness and loving-ness, we beguile ourselves. There is also in children a mischievious, fun-loving, and unsocial-ized side. Jung called this aspect of personality the **Trickster** and he is the humorous polarity of the Wise Child. The Trickster can be impish at times, like Puck in Shakespeare's *A Mid-summer's Night Dream* or the Irish leprechaun or the Scandinavian troll. Tom Sawyer tricks his friends into whitewashing his fence for him, and Dennis the Menace outwits all of us adults.

Like the other Archetypes, the Trickster has a unique wisdom all his own. It is the wis-dom of comic relief. We cannot always be "good" and "lady-like." There are times when we sim-ply must strip off the conventional standards and prohibitions of society and allow some sheer animal exuberance and wild laughter into our lives. He is Charlie Chaplin's Little Tramp, and the irrepressible Marx Brothers, and Jerry Lewis. Because of his opposition to the conventions of society, the Trickster is often portrayed as an outlaw, like the movie portrayal of the Sun-dance Kid or Loki (of Native American lore) who stole the fire of heavens and gave it to humani-ty. For that, Loki was severely punished and was condemned as a pariah! (Thank you, Loki). The Trickster is frequently portrayed as the "beast within" us in the form of Fox or Beaver in Native American folktales or Br'er Rabbit of the Uncle Remus stories. Or he may be Rousseau's Noble Savage, as in Kipling's Mowgli (the boy raised by wolves) or Tarzan (the boy raised by Apes). The Trickster is a shape-shifter.

The Integration of Personality: Our Search for Soul! If our basic nature consists of these many dualities, it followed logically for Jung, that our basic task in life is to integrate these polarities within us. It was Jung's belief that for most adults, it happens most often at the midlife crisis. It is then that we take stock of our lives and reevaluate where we are and what we want to do with the rest of our lives. Men who have been workaholics until then may suddenly find themselves struggling to express tenderness, caring, and love—all those parts of his Anima he has repressed for so long. Women, who have had the opportunity to express nur-turing and love, may now reach for their repressed Animus, the assertive and intellectual side of themselves. But the process of integrating these aspects of ourselves can begin at any time in our lives.

Joseph Campbell: The Hero Archetype with a Thousand Faces

Like Freud and Jung, another scholar believes that our mythologies, ancient and modern, rep-resent profound truths of the human experience. If folklore and fairy tale have meaning for the child, the great mythic themes have meaning for adults. Each one of us, said Campbell (1988), is not only the Hero (or Heroine) of our life story, each of us is living out a mythic theme. For example, if we are a young man on the threshold of our adult life, we may be living out the tradition of the archetypal hero setting off to accomplish a great deed. We may be Jason pursuing the Golden Fleece or Saint George slaying the Dragon or Galahad in search of the Holy Grail. The Hero has "a thousand faces," said Campbell, but whatever his face, his Quest is always the same. The capture of the Golden Fleece and the slaying of the Dragon and the search for the

Holy Grail are all simply metaphors for the Quest. And what is that Quest? It is the same for all of us: The integration of personality which (for Campbell) is to know ourselves as not simply conditioned rats or mindless robots but to feel ourselves truly whole, truly human, and truly alive.

Sometimes, the Hero may have to become an outlaw to achieve his Quest. A rebellious teenager or a delinquent in and out of jail for shoplifting may be living out a Robin Hood myth since he may envision himself as stealing from the rich (the stores) and giving to the poor (himself and his adolescent friends) and hiding out from the Sheriff of Nottingham's law (the police). In which case, we need to help him reinterpret the Robin Hood legend in a constructive way. Or consider the traditional interpretation of Lucifer's revolt against God. As a sacred myth, it relates the rebellion of a light-giving angel (Lucifer means light) who fell from the heavens in defeat. Mythologically, it has to do with some of our most unconscious motivations to challenge authority and to become an outlaw, if necessary, in order to be heard. Everyone deserves to be heard, said the Medieval Church, even Lucifer. Thus was born the tradition that all persons, even those accused of heresy and witchcraft, have a right to be defended by the "Devil's Advocate." Today, we accord the same privilege to all defendants, even those who have admitted to heinous crimes—representation by an attorney. If the defendant does not have an attorney, we will provide one for him. Everyone has a right to a defense.

Stephen LaBerge: Lucid Dreaming

In 1980's, Stephen LaBerge introduced lucid dreaming. Lucid dreaming is a technique by which dreamers can become aware they are dreaming and can alter the outcome of the dream. As an example, LaBerge related a lucid dreaming experience of his own. He dreamed that he was in the middle of a classroom riot in which a mob of people was raging about, throwing objects here and there and actually fistfighting. At the center of this dream was the dreamer himself, who was being pinned down by a large, pock-mocked "Goliath." At this point, LaBerge recognized he was dreaming and immediately stopped struggling. He realized, he writes, that the struggle was within himself. On awakening, he knew that the "odious barbarian" of his dream was some Shadow-Ogre aspect of himself and the best (and perhaps the only ultimately effective way) to end the conflict was "to love my enemy [his Shadow-Ogre] as myself."

LaBerge goes on to say that lucid dreaming did not originate with him. Tibetan Buddhists have been using this technique since the eighth century. Furthermore, he is sure that most of us have experienced lucid dreaming at least once in our lives, and that it is easy to learn. What advantages does lucid dreaming have? LaBerge believes it fosters our growth and evolution by light years. Furthermore, if we believe that life is all too brief, he suggests that we stop being unconscious of that one-third of our lives which is spent asleep by becoming aware of what is on going during our sleep. Do we want guidance about a problem? Or are we concerned about our relationship with someone? Then all we need to do is to tell ourselves ahead of time to "dream on it" (LaBerge, 1985).

Insomnia and Our Need for Cathartic REM Sleep. For centuries, philosopher/psychologists argued about whether dreams were instantaneous (like stray thoughts) or whether they extend over time as some seemed to do. This age-old question was finally answered when researchers discovered REMs. **REMs** is short for **rapid eye movements** and they occur during a very light stage of sleep that occurs in cycles about every 90 minutes. What the researchers discovered is that by awakening people during REM sleep, they report more dreams than in non-REM sleep. So the question was answered: Dreams extend over time and can range from a few seconds to twenty minutes in length. If a dreamer feels that she was dreaming for a long time, she probably was. In addition to rapid eye movements, both men and women may show movements indicating they may be having erotic dreams. The penis may become erect and a woman's nipples may undergo hardening. But of paramount importance has been the research on our need for REM sleep (Dement, 1978).

For example, some research suggests that Freud may have been right when he said we need to dream for our psychological health, that dreams may be a way we catharsize our emotional conflicts. Persons who are deprived of REM sleep (by being awakened when REMs occur) for more than 100 hours will begin to demonstrate considerable personality disintegration. They become overtly hostile toward others and seem to develop paranoid suspiciousness. Eventually, they may even begin to hallucinate. Clearly, we need to develop good sleeping habits, and specifically we need REM sleep (Johnson, 1982). What happens then if we have a tendency toward insomnia or if we simply are burning the candle at both ends and not giving ourselves more sleep time? Our physical and mental well-being suffers. Our ability to focus on tasks and concentrate is diminished and we feel generally irritable. Becoming drowsy of course leads to more accidents at work, at home, or in traffic. In recent years, a number of major world disasters have been blamed in part on lapses in judgment and attention due to sleep deprivation, such as the nuclear accidents at Three Mile Island and Chernobyl and the running aground of the *Exxon Valdez*. Many sleep researchers believe that, as modern life intensifies, we simply are not getting the sleep we need. We may not even know what being fully awake and alert feels like.

Daydreaming

Another level of consciousness is daydreaming which involves drifting off into fantasy. It used to be thought that daydreams are simply an "escape from reality" or fulfilling an erotic desire. In nineteenth-century books on parenting, authors frequently warned against allowing children to daydream, lest they slide into a life style of idleness and shiftlessness! The psychologist who legitimized daydreams as an important human event was a man by the name of Jerome Singer (1975). By having his subjects keep a diary on what they daydream about, Singer was surprised to discover that very few daydreams are erotic in nature—even the daydreams of healthy, red-blooded college students. Nor are they very often violent. In actuality, our daydreams cover every aspect of our daily lives: Our work, our studies, our family conflicts, our emotional relationships, our plans for the future. Of course, more of our daydreams will occur at moments of boredom or leisure. Lifeguards and truck drivers daydream to ease their boredom. But daydreams can also help "psych us up" toward some threatening event. Soldiers daydream how they will act in battle. Employees going in to ask for a raise may spend considerable time imagining the scene, going over it "in their heads," preparing the dialog. In a very important sense, daydreaming is a kind of "rehearsal of the mind" (Klinger, 1990).

Furthermore, daydreaming is a vital source for our creativity, although we may call it by other terms: Imagination, intuition, drawing on our inner resources, etc. Daydreams enable

Box14.5

TRANSCRIPT
A Hypnosis Session

The subject was to have an operation. She was experiencing severe panic, not because of the operation but because of her extreme fear of anesthesia, so severe it bordered on phobia. Before the hypnotherapeutic session began, she related the following:

Subject: My parents died before I was eight . . . and I was raised by an aunt and uncle . . . who received a weekly sum of money from the insurance money that came from my father's death . . . My aunt and uncle had three children of their own . . . and they did not like me, since I was half Jewish, and they were very anti-Semitic. It was a horrible situation, and I was a scapegoat for their anti-Semitism. When I was eleven, I had a severe attack of appendicitis . . . I lay on the couch for a long time in pain. Finally, I was taken in a taxi to the hospital and put under anesthesia. I remember being very scared and wanting to tell someone, but when I started to say something, they simply clamped the anesthetic mask over my face, and I remember feeling like I was choking to death. When I woke up, people came in and out of my room, but no one ever seemed to talk to me . . . I was in a room by myself and never saw anyone else, except my aunt. For ten days I was visited by my aunt and one or two nurses and the doctor. I never had other visitors. I never even saw the other patients in the hospital . . . the only gift or toy that I received was, one day, a bunch of letters came written by my classmates, I suppose written under the direction of the teacher. Ever since that experience, I have had deathly fears of doctors, hospitals, and particularly any kind of anesthesia. I hated our family physician after that and all doctors ever since. He made such a big gash in my abdomen that I have had a scar ever since.

We have reproduced excerpts from the transcript. The subject has been trance-induced and has had the suggestion of awakening in the hospital room.

Hypnotherapist: How are you feeling?
Subject: All right. No pain. Glad of that . . .
Hypnotherapist: Can you see your hospital room?
Subject: Yes.
Hypnotherapist: Can you describe the room?
Subject: Yes.
Hypnotherapist: What color are the walls?
Subject: Kind of brown. Light brown. More like beige. Curtains. Kind of lacy. Arm chair brown. Dresser

is brown, just brown wood. Everything brown wood . . .
Hypnotherapist: Can you hear [anybody] moving?
Subject: No. I can't hear anything. I'm supposed to call them but I don't know how. They don't seem to hear me.
Hypnotherapist: Can you hear anything at all?
Subject: No, everything is so quiet. I seem to be by myself. I can see trees out the window. The tops of trees.
Hypnotherapist: You said "house."
Subject: This seems like a house.
Hypnotherapist: It doesn't seem like a hospital?
Subject: No, just a house . . . *(The hypnotherapist told us later he proceeded extremely carefully now because of what this might mean and he didn't want to lead the subject or induce false memories.)*
Hypnotherapist: What is happening now?
Subject: Someone came in the room. I am telling them I have to pee. They say they will bring a bedpan.
Hypnotherapist: Male or female?
Subject: Female.
Hypnotherapist: How is she dressed?
Subject: Dress with flowers on it. Yellow flowers. Pink flowers. Different colors.
Hypnotherapist: She is not in a uniform?
Subject: No one in this house wears a uniform.

The hypnotherapist had the subject move forward in time to when she was going home. She is helped to walk by her aunt and someone else, not in uniform.

Hypnotherapist: Where are you?
Subject: Holding onto stairs.
Hypnotherapist: Can you see anything else?
Subject: People . . . old people . . . yes, very old people . . . Wait a minute . . . I think this is not a hospital.
Hypnotherapist: You think it is not a hospital?
Subject: No . . . more like . . . more like . . . just a house with upstairs and downstairs . . .

The hypnotherapist instructed the subject to return to her usual consciousness and to retain the memory. The following is an interview held immediately afterwards.

Hypnotherapist: How are you feeling?

Box 14.5
TRANSCRIPT (continued)
A Hypnosis Session

Subject: Strange. It's like I understand something I never understood before. It wasn't a hospital at all. It was just a house. I don't know how to fathom that. How could I have had an operation in a house? It was more like an old folks' home.

Hypnotherapist: An old folks' home?

Subject: My God! That would explain a lot, . . . wouldn't it? . . Why I never saw anybody or heard anything . . . like other children. It was . . . always quiet. They had me tucked away from the other patients. . . . There really weren't any nurses. More like attendants.

Hypnotherapist: How do you explain all this?

Subject: I think my aunt was trying to save money. They were poor. I think now that explains why I was there. A hospital would have cost too much.

Hypnotherapist: But you said there was insurance money for you being there.

Subject: Yes, but my aunt was so stingy. I guess from being poor. That would account for why there was no ambulance either. I went in a taxi. I remember that. I went home in a taxi. We didn't even have a car. There was no hospital in our town. Oh my! I just remembered. There was an old folks' home there. There really was. That's where I was!

Box 14.6
STUDENTS VERBATIM
On Peak Experiences, Meditation, and Meditational Prayer

Female (19 years): I come from a very religious home. We pray together a lot at the table and sometimes in the evening. We go to church together too. Praying together seems to harmonize us as a family. That is not to say we don't squabble a lot. With five brothers and sisters (six of us), we have a lot of heated arguments. But praying together reminds us that we're not supposed to be enemies, that we're all on the same side.

Male (21 years): I don't pray very often, usually only when I'm in trouble. I relate all the things I've done wrong and ask for help not to repeat them. When I think to pray, I sure feel better later. I just wish I would remember to do it more often.

Female (26 years): I belong to a meditation group, not TM, but one from my church. We also discuss important things in our lives sort of like a peer-support group. But the meditating in a group is a wonderful experience. Sometimes I am so taken out of myself, I feel like I understand the reasons for life.

Male (27 years): I've been practicing TM meditation for many years, maybe more than a dozen. I don't know if I'm just this kind of person naturally or if these years of practicing TM turned me into this. I'm nonviolent. I don't get angry easily. I coexist peacefully with others. In fact, I'm very good at interpersonal communication just because I approach each person as peacefully as possible. People can't help but respond to that.

Male (45 years): I have prayed and meditated most of my life so that it has become second nature. In fact, sometimes I feel as if I'm in a kind of prayerful and meditation state even when I am talking to people where I work. That may sound very strange but I know when I am. I feel as if I am in a constant state of grace. In that state of grace, everything just sails along. Problems get solved easily. I have wonderful interpersonal experiences. Doors that have been closed suddenly open. Don't get me wrong, I'm no saint. I have those days when I'm irritable, and I can't seem to do anything right—just like everyone else. But I credit my good days (which are more frequent the older I get) to prayer and meditation.

Female (30 years): When I pray, I feel as if I'm talking to God and Jesus. I tell them all my troubles. I ask them for help. I really unburden everything on my mind, even what I feel guilty about, that I haven't done right. When I come out of my prayers, I really feel as if I've left it all behind me. I'm ready to meet the day. I feel like God is on my side.

Reflective Writing. Describe an experience when you were either practicing meditation or engaging in deep meditational prayer that illuminated your consciousness. In fact, one investigator (who has been studying transcendental meditation for several decades), believes that meditation is a kind of deep relaxation response. (Benson 1975).

us to know what directions we want to take in our lives. Singer gave an example from his own life. Like other adolescents, he had many daydreams. The most frequent were of Singer, the Great Lover; Singer, the Hall-of-Fame Athlete; Singer, the World-Famous Surgeon; and Singer, the Concert Violinist. But Singer early realized that his athletic career would end with his high school graduation. It took a little longer to realize that he would never be a first-rate violinist. But his surgeon daydream did eventually lead him to his studies in psychology and to his career in a university setting. Singer concluded that, for most of us, daydreams are often the lodestar for the possible directions we may want to travel someday.

But not for everyone! Singer discovered that our daydreams tend to reflect our personality style. Persons who achieve their goals and who have a positive attitude toward life have positive fantasies with happy endings. Persons who are depressed or suffer from severe emotional problems tend to have unhappy daydreams that end with a depressing resolution. Persons who tend to be passive tend to have daydreams that are rather aimless and meandering.

Hypnosis

As a healing art, hypnosis has had a curiously roller-coaster existence. The reader will remember that hypnosis got its start when a physician in the eighteenth century by the name of Anton Mesmer discovered he could cure some of his patients' symptoms by putting them into a trance and altering their "animal magnetism." Unfortunately, after a few mishaps in which his patients had convulsions and a few reported deaths, he was literally run out of town and denounced as a charlatan. "Mesmerism" remained a "black art," until a Scottish physician, by the name of James Braid, gave it the name of hypnotism in 1843 (Hypnos was the Greek god of sleep). Braid tried using it for minor surgeries and apparently it seemed to work, but since trance induction takes a fair amount of time, it was not appropriate for an emergency situation.

Freud began his practice using hypnosis to uncover repressed memories but later dropped its use when he discovered that unconscious material could be brought to consciousness by the simpler method of free association. In the first half of the twentieth century, hypnosis was treated as kind of a "parlor game" and taken no more seriously than as a seance or Ouija Board. Today, however, it is being explored as a valid healing art in many areas. Dentists are using it to allay the anxieties of "apprehensive patients."

Psychologists are using it to catharsize the stressful events of post-traumatic stress disorders. Although inadmissible in court, hypnosis is sometimes used in law enforcement to enable a victim or witness to recall significant details of a crime. Physicians are using it to induce more rapid healing for surgery. As a self-improvement method, autohypnosis is used as way to enable people to become more confident in themselves, more self-directive, and more self-assertive. As a healing art, research is being conducted worldwide on the effectiveness of hypnosis. (Gibson & Heap, 1991).

But What Exactly Is Hypnosis? The irony is that while we are finding many uses for hypnosis, we still don't know what it is. Theories abound! In fact, there are almost as many theories about what it is as there are scientists studying it. It is a state of narrowly focused attention. It is a state of deep relaxation. It is a state of creative fantasy. It is conditioned susceptibility to suggestion. It is split-consciousness. It isn't even an altered level of consciousness, it's simply role-playing. It is a "puzzlement." But some of the pieces of the puzzle are emerging. What we do know is that people who are easily hypnotizable tend to be creative and spontaneous. By and large, people can not be made to do things that are illegal or immoral. (Hilgard, 1986; Meyer, 1992).

Is there anything else that we can say, then, about hypnosis? Perhaps the best summary statement we can make at the present time is to say that hypnosis is a very special and intense kind of communication between the trance inducer and the hypnotized subject. Within this intense communication, people can be enabled to catharsize past trauma, to cope with present problems, and to become more self-directive in the future (see Box 14.5).

Peak Experiences, Meditation, and Meditational Prayer

Meditation tends to be associated with esoteric Eastern philosophies. Actually all major religions, including the Judaic/Christian tradition, have developed specific techniques to attain this level of consciousness. These techniques may utilize visual symbols, such as the **mandala** of Tibetan Buddhism; the cross for all of Christianity, and the Star of David for the Jews. Other techniques use auditory techniques to induce the meditational and prayerful states, such as the Buddhist **mantra,** which can be a long, drawn-out *OHHHhhhmmmm* or the intonation of the Tibetan phrase *OH MANI PADME HUM.* The Catholics intone the familiar Hail Mary, fingering bead after bead of the Rosary. All Christians repeat the Our Father as a preamble to the prayerful state. The Jews intone the ancient Judaic prayer, the **Shema,** the most fundamental and ancient of Hebraic prayers. Auditory symbols can involve the beating of drums, the ringing of bells, and the sound of chanting. Incense and other scents may be used to alter the person's state of consciousness. Nor are the paths to altered mediational and prayerful states limited to the classic five senses. Some traditions utilize physical postures not ordinarily used by people in their everyday routine. Catholics and Protestants kneel. Orthodox Jews bend their heads and torsos repeatedly in front of the famous Wailing Wall of Jerusalem. Hindus and Buddhists use various yoga positions. The Sufis of the Middle East are renowned for the spinning dance technique they use, going round and round, to induce an altered state. But the meditational state can be reached simply by the technique of *deep relaxation* (discussed in Chapter 7).

But what do meditation and meditational prayer accomplish? When well practiced, we remove ourselves from our ordinary mind-sets and conditioned responses, which allows us to perceive larger universal paradigms. We are withdrawing from the everyday hurly-burley to a place of interior calm. Some have described prayer as "interior talking" and meditation as "interior listening." In religious terms, people have described the difference as "talking to God" and "listening to God." However they are described, they are methods by which people are reaching for higher levels of consciousness (see Box 14.6).

Results of Meditation and Meditational Prayer. Advocates of meditation assert that it can enhance learning, creativity, cognitive development, energy level, and happiness while reducing tension and anxiety caused by stress and thereby increasing longevity. Are the claims of meditators borne out by research? Studies which have investigated meditators in the laboratory have reported that long-term meditators do show actual physiological changes. There is a change of brain wave patterns from predominantly beta waves (our usual

Box 14.7

SCENARIO REVISITED
Creating a Life–Plan to Raise Your Level of Consciousness

Alec: OK, so altered states of consciousness are common experiences which we just have not recognized. Have I got that straight, Professor?

Professor Wietzman: More-or-less.

Alec: Earlier we learned that highly self-actualized people consciously pursue these experiences. What if I wanted to become more self-actualized, how could I go about it?

Li Ho: Well, we can get in touch with our dreams. I'm kind of interested in the lucid dreaming that the chapter described.

Martha: I'll tell you something that happened to me. When we decided to go on a health plan, back toward the beginning of this course, I decided it was time for me to learn to eat better and take off some of these pounds I've been complaining about for years. Hasn't anyone noticed how much thinner I am? I'm not so blubbery.

Jonnimae: I have. You look wonderful, years younger. Congratulations!

Martha: Well, not only did I lose weight but when I stopped eating sugar, I became much more sensitive to the natural sweetness in things—I can smell an apple now on the other side of the room. And it tastes wonderful. Isn't that an altered level of consciousness, Professor?

Professor Wietzman: I certainly would say so!

Dan: I know what I need more of—more physical activity but not just physical activity—activity out there in the natural world. With all my studies and working a full-time job, I miss that part of my life a lot. I seem to be more in touch with who I am when I'm not stuck in buildings all the time.

Professor Wietzman: Mother Nature is a source of harmony we lose touch with if we spend all our time in the concrete jungles of the city. Dan, I would say for you, Nature is crucial.

Jill Smith: If we can't garden or take an occasional walk in the woods, we can grow our own small jungle of indoor plants. Industrial psychologists are urging people who work in windowless offices to bring plants into their work place since it has been found that a "touch of Nature" in our environment is therapeutic. I think that's what I'm going to do this very week—buy some plants for my office space.

Professor Wietzman: I've been working late into the wee small hours for several weeks. I'm getting dull from all work and no play. I'm planning to take some afternoons off for a few rounds of golf.

Alec: OK, I get the point. What you're saying is that each of us must find out what is missing or needed in our lives and that would be different from person to person. Dan misses his outdoor life so he should get more of that. Martha needed to lose weight and when she did, she enhanced her self-esteem and I guess brought about an altered level of awareness for her. And I need to get in touch with my center-of-growth (as Carl Rogers would put it . . . and maybe I could quiet down and not be so worried about hate groups.

Shannon: I love my quiet times. I'm sort of an introvert and while I like all the friends I've found in this class, I find I need more quiet time to myself. I can't get it at home with everything that is happening there. The twins are so noisy—they're teenage boys and that's natural for them. I'll have to find more time for myself. Sometimes I sneak into the chapel for—what did the book call it—meditational prayer? I think that's what I do when I want to get back to my center.

Natasha: Yes, more quiet time would be good for me too. Just being a good wife and going to school and being with my small children at night—I think I have no time for me. I don't complain about that because my husband is working so hard too.

Professor Wietzman: Haven't heard from you Eduardo. What's going on? A class discussion without your input seems lacking somehow.

Eduardo: I've been thinking. When everybody started to talk about more quiet time, I thought maybe this is what I need too. I'm such an extrovert, I'm always with people. But then I remembered that I get a lot of happiness being with people. So I discarded that idea. It's like what Alec just said—we all have to discover what's missing in our lives. And then it came to me. What's been missing for me is more time with my guitar. I used to play regularly—every chance I could. That's what I've been needing.

Shannon: That's one of the places you're so creative, Eduardo. You should hear him, Professor.

Professor Wietzman: I would like to—very much. Music is Eduardo's way of centering himself. We all have our own unique ways of getting in touch with our center of growth. They help us to catharsize our anxieties. Only in those quiet moments of reflection, can we inaugurate more centered ways of being-in-the-world.

waking brain-wave activity) to alpha waves and theta waves, which are slower and deeper. Most studies also show changes in heart rate, respiration rate, oxygen consumption, skin resistance and a decrease in blood lactates (which are built-up toxins after physical activity). All of these physiological changes are similar to the changes that occur after deep relaxation. In fact, one investigator (who has been studying transcendental meditation for several decades) believes that meditation is a kind of deep relaxation response (Benson 1975).

While some of the claims for meditation and meditational prayer may be somewhat "hyped up," there seems to be no doubt that faithful practice of prayer and meditation is good for body and soul. Although varied in expression, their answers suggest the attainment of joy, of loving compassion for the whole world, and for what has been called "the peace that passeth all understanding." At its most basic level, meditation is a centering of oneself within oneself, a way of getting in touch with one's center-of-growth (Rogers, 1961; 1970). At its most exalted level, it partakes of what Abraham Maslow called the **peak experience,** a feeling of exultation, peace, and *at-one-ment* with the universe (Maslow, 1954, 1976).

Drug-Induced ASCs

What is not so good for body-and-soul are the altered states of consciousness that come from "drug trips." We are not debating here the legality of the drugs nor even the mind-altering insights that can come from hallucinogenic drugs. What we are concerned about are the negative effects that can decimate even the most successful personality structure. We have enough examples now of famous men and women in the arts and entertainment fields who used drugs to stimulate their creativity, only to fall victim to drug use later. We are saddened by the loss of these wonderfully talented people: John Belushi, Janis Joplin, Jimi Hendrix, Marilyn Monroe. Before their brilliant careers became a trajectory toward death, they endured many physical and psychological difficulties, including loss of memory (difficulty in remembering lines, appointments, time of day), physical depletion, frequent insomnia, loss of self-confidence, the inability to make decisions, heightened sensitivity to painful stimuli, sexual impotence, anxiety to the point of panic attack, catatonic reactions, and so on.

IMPORTANT TERMS AND CONCEPTS TO KNOW

Ancients	creative	instantaneous	synchronicity
Anima	fantasies	lucid	Trickster
Animus	future	mental	unconscious
ASCs	healing	missing	wisdom
big dream	hero	neurotransmitters	Wise Old Woman
catharsis	heroine	peak	Wise Child
collective	hypnosis	REMs	Wise Old Man
consciousness	interpreter	stimulants	

MAKE YOUR OWN SUMMARY BY FILLING IN THE BLANKS BELOW

Use the words in the "Important Terms and Concepts to Know" to fill in the blanks below.

Levels of Consciousness. It used to be thought that _____ were very rare experiences. Now we know that they are common phenomena that occur everyday and psychologists are now defining them simply as different levels of _____ . Other levels of consciousness include daydreams, hypnosis, meditation and meditational prayer. Abraham Maslow described self-actualizing persons as having had many _____ experiences through active involvement of their dream states and other ASCs. In fact, any _____ breakthrough in the arts or sciences must be considered as an ASC.

History of dream interpretation. Freud startled his society by declaring that dreams were meaningful and that, in this respect, he stood firmly with the _____ . In both the Old and New Testaments, dreams were a medium through which the Deity spoke to people. Joseph, for example, became a dream _____ for the Pharaoh and other Egyptians. Other cultures also gave great meaning to dreams. Native Americans, for example, underwent a fast so they could have a " _____ ."

Freud versus Jung. Freud called dream interpretation as the "royal road" to the _____ . He believed that dreams are an avenue for the _____ of emotional trauma and unacceptable thoughts. While Freud believed that dreams represented the past, Jung believed they could also predict the _____ . Jung regarded dreams as a source of _____ and spirituality. Jung's model of human personality involves two levels to the unconscious: the personal unconscious and the racial or _____ unconscious. This deeper level of the unconscious connects us psychically to all other persons who exist now on earth and is responsible for the phenomenon that we call "coincidence," but which Jung called " _____ ." The wisdom of a learned counselor or tribal elder is represented by the Archetype of the _____ . The wisdom represented by intuition and prophecy is represented by the _____ . The wisdom of innocence is represented by the _____ . The wisdom of "comic relief" is represented by the _____ . Within the personal unconscious are elements of our denied opposite gender characteristics: the _____ for the male and the _____ for the female.

Joseph Campbell helped us to understand our fascination with mythic themes. We are all the _____ or _____ of our life drama. Stephen LaBerge has introduced the concept of _____ dreaming or dreaming consciously.

Modern sleep research has demonstrated that our "dreamiest" dreams occur every 90 minutes and can be detected by _____ (rapid eye movements). Sleep research has also answered the age-old question of whether or not dreams are _____ or occur over time since REM states often last for 20 minutes or more. It has also been determined that REM sleep is necessary for our _____ health. Many modern uses for ASCs. Daydreams are not just useless _____ but one of the ways we prepare ourselves for coming events. Furthermore, active use of our creative imagination is being used for _____ arts. _____ , introduced by Anton Mesmer, fell into disrepute as one of the "black arts," is also being used in medicine, dentistry, and therapy.

More healthful ways to induce higher consciousness. Since any change in perception is a change of consciousness, an ASC can be induced in any number of ways. One way is to determine what has been _____ in our lives and to reinstate it such as quiet moments of meditation, meditational prayer, physical exercise or any creative act, etc.

15 BUILDING A LIFE-CAREER
Your Educational, Vocational, and Personal Future

In this information age with its emphasis on team work and the need for good "people skills," the ability to communicate with others is the major key to a successful career.

Box 15.1

SCENARIO
So Where Do We Go From Here?

Professor Weitzman: The final topic of our course has to do with the work environment. You all know by this time that our society has changed radically in the last one hundred years. From being a predominantly rural nation, we have become an urban nation. Two centuries ago, we were an agricultural society. In the last century, we became an industrial society. In this century we became a technological society, and we are fast becoming an informational society. All of this change has affected our understanding of the work environment.

Eduardo: I've heard the term *informational society,* but I don't really know what it means.

Professor Weitzman: It means a lot of things that are beyond the scope of this course. But let's see if I can give you some idea. Information is what most of your professional careers will consist of. Education as the way to gain information is the first obvious example. But there are others. If you go into scientific careers, you will be observing data and analyzing it and sharing it. The same is true in business and government. Local governments have to gather information on traffic control, usage of utilities, and school achievement. State governments need information on industry trends and setting standards of vocational areas like plumbing, heating and air conditioning, and auto mechanics. Our national government has to keep in touch with global markets, population trends, employment and unemployment figures, and how to raise money to finance itself. Shall I go on?

Jonnimae: And we're going to learn all that now?

Professor Weitzman: (Laughing) Not quite. Most of that is beyond the scope of this one course. Your entire college career is involved in getting you ready for the information society whether you are going to be a doctor, lawyer—or (looking at Dan)—or Indian Chief.

Dan: You make it sound as if college is nothing but a vocational school.

Professor Weitzman: Well, in one respect college, even graduate school, prepares you for your professional career. But a college education is supposed to do many things. We hope also to foster good citizenship, which means a sense of responsibility toward your family, your neighbors, and all the citizens of our global society. We presume you are learning how to lead healthier, more creative lives. We hope we are preparing you for the leadership roles not only at your place of work but also in your community. You've already learned a lot about the "people skills" needed to become an effective professional. Now we are going to see how modern management is applying those people skills in the work environment. The day of the isolated scientist and legendary inventor and single entrepreneur businessman is mostly over. The information age requires people working together, sharing knowledge, learning to be a team—even if members of that team are separated by thousands of miles and communicating over the global Internet.

Box 15.1 — SCENARIO (continued)
So Where Do We Go From Here?

Li Ho: Wait a minute, Professor. I understand about scientists having to work together these days. But I'm thinking of becoming a physician, maybe a surgeon.

Martha: And you don't think a surgeon has to interact with his surgical team?

Li Ho: I see what you mean! A surgeon needs all the input he can get from the anesthesiologist and the techs watching the patient's vital signs.

Jill Smith: We even speak of classroom management. It's no longer a matter of teaching a subject. It's a matter of learning about the students in the class, what information they need and how best to convey that information.

Professor Weitzman: The work situation has changed in another way. We used to think of education as something that ended with high school or college or graduate school. Now we know that if we are to stay abreast of the developments in this information age, education has become a life-long process.

Alec: A life-long process!

Professor Weitzman: Exactly. We may not be registered formally at a college student but we will have to be upgrading our knowledge and our skills all the time. For example, sometimes several times a year I attend psychological conferences where I listen to lectures and discussions of new developments.

Jonnimae: I've been told by my accounting professors that CPAs (certified public accountants) have to gain dozens and dozens of CEUs every year just to keep up with the tax changes every year.

Professor Weitzman: That's right. We call them *conferences* or *workshops* or *in-service training,* but they are all basically educational avenues to upgrade our knowledge and skills. Just as education is no longer confined to a college campus, so also is our work schedule no longer confined to a nine to five daytime schedule. People are working many different kinds of hours and many different kinds of work schedules. Finally, we will "come full circle" and discuss the changing family situation with both marriage partners working and raising children. Just as the workplace is changing, so also is our homeplace changing.

Eduardo: That's great, Professor, but first I'd like to know how to get a good job. Do you have some tips on how to get a job?

Professor Weitzman: I sure do. And also how to write a resume that will get you your first interview. And how to make a success of your first job. So let's begin.

Work as Essential for Our National and Personal Well-Being

In all studies of healthy and creative people, one of the essential ingredients has been the inclusion of a satisfying and productive work. When asked what constitutes a healthy personality, Freud's famous answer was, "To work and to love." One of the characteristics of highly integrated, creative, and self-actualizing persons is that they have a work that provides them with both economic and psychological satisfaction. A work we can be proud of is not just a means to an end but an end in itself. In contrast to those who "work to live" (working at any job to get money), they "live to work" (look forward to each new day and getting back to work). Working is a process by which we grow, mature, and evolve. When we are happy at our jobs, we feel good and we are healthier. In contrast, when we have trouble in our jobs or when we are out of work, our personal health suffers. So does our self-esteem and general morale (McGourty, 1988).

Furthermore, a good job can also sustain us through the darker moments of life. We may experience physical suffering through a debilitating disease or an accident. We may feel betrayed by those we love. We may lose those that are nearest and dearest to us. If fact, the longer we live, the more liable are we to experience the problems and crises of living. Those who have come through those kinds of losses successfully have often said that they were grateful to have a work which sustained them and kept them "centered."

A good job also provides us with an avenue for contributing to the growth of others. When we become skilled and knowledgeable in our work, there comes a time when we want to share that skill or knowledge with others. We gain a joy by mentoring another person who is just beginning on his or her life-career or who may be having difficulty in their work. There is a special satisfaction that comes from helping someone else become successful and self-sustaining. *If I give a man a fish to eat, he will not be hungry for a day. If I teach him how to fish, he will not go hungry for the rest of his life.*

Finally, a good job is the "royal road" to self-actualizing. Studies find that "happiness," "goal achievement," or "need attainment" is highly correlated with a job we like doing. Not only does a good job contribute mightily to our well-being, it is often the route of personal evolution.

If You Don't Know What You Want to Do When You "Grow Up," Take Heart!

Some of you reading these pages may know exactly where you are going. You enjoyed math or science in high school, and you decided early on that you would obtain an engineering or mathematics degree. Congratulations, but you are in the minority. Most students who come to college are really not sure what they should major in. Or because they can't make up their minds, they change their majors frequently. Some of you may not be sure that you should even be in college. We have good news for you. That's what you are here in college to do: to discover what it is that you would like to do. That is why educators insist on a "liberal education." By experiencing a wide spectrum of educational disciplines, you may find yourself attracted to an area you didn't know about before. Moreover, you will rub shoulders with other students who will talk about their majors. Listen to what they have to say about their courses and career possibilities. You can take advantage of all the "career days" your college offers. If you become interested in a certain area, ask your college counselors for an opportunity to gain firsthand experience by "shadowing" a person working in that area for a day or two. Shadowing has become a popular method of introducing people to possible career areas.

Furthermore, vocational choice is not a target—it's a direction. Whatever major or minor you choose is not so much a permanent work choice as a direction. In our swiftly changing society, the work place is changing constantly. People who have been employed in one job will discover, five years later, that their job description has very little similarity to what they are actually doing. Job specialties will appear that weren't even on the job market when you entered college as a freshman. Actually, not being sure of what you want to do may even be an advantage in such a swiftly changing job market, because you will be more open to new career possibilities.

What Organizations Are Looking for in Prospective Employees

If you have been reading the paper or just scanning the headlines, you must be aware that corporations are "downsizing" their companies, including the number of employees. During previous recessions, the "unskilled worker" has been hit the hardest. Today layoffs are happening across the employment strata: skilled and unskilled, blue- and white-collar workers, middle and top management. What does that mean in terms of your career hopes? Will you be able to find a job in your vocational interest? Yes, you can—if you know what corporations are looking for. They are looking for managers who can take responsibility, who can work with people and bring out the best in them, and who know how to interact with many levels of their organizations. They need people who have "people skills."

1. They are looking for people who are "team players." In the last several decades, management has been slowly moving from authoritarian leadership to democratic participation. Until the twentieth century, most employers held the traditional authoritarian style of leadership; that is to say, the employer gave orders and the employees followed them, no ifs, ands, or buts! But research in business management reveals that when we treat people as mindless robots, they behave as mindless robots. They are not acting as thinking human beings in the jobs they are given to do. The results of this robotization are employees who care about collecting a pay check but not much else. They shrug their shoulders if there are mistakes occurring on the assembly line. Their attitude is "You can take this job and shove it!" They treat clients, customers, and the general public in cursory fashion. The results of this kind of employee workforce are automobiles and appliances with many defective parts, poor customer relations, and a negative public image for the company—all of which are destructive to an organization's success. Furthermore, as an organization gets larger and larger, these problems increase substantially.

Recognizing the problems of the traditional authoritarian leadership styles, business schools began to teach team leadership, an approach that fosters the maturity and creativity of every employee at every level (Homans, 1950; McGregor, 1960). The employee is no longer to be considered as a cog-in-the-wheel worker carrying out orders from above but as a thinking, rational human being willing and wanting to do the best possible job. This type of organizational leadership needs managers who view the people in their departments not as employees but as members of a team all working together. That means the wise manager and professional does not see themselves as a "boss." A more apt metaphor would be a *coach* or a *captain* inspiring his team to think creatively toward their job tasks, encouraging them to assume responsibility, and providing them with the trust and the authority to act autonomously.

2. They want people who have good people skills. To become a participative and democratic manager or leader requires good "people skills"—all those constructive verbal and nonverbal communications discussed in earlier chapters. For example, they want supervisors and managers who are able to listen actively. They want people who understand the differences in the communication styles of both genders. So important are "people skills" considered that business schools from Harvard to Berkeley have required courses in psychology and interpersonal communication.

3. They want people who have a well-rounded education and a variety of skills and talents. Students sometimes get irritated by having to take courses that do not seem to have direct relevance to their chosen job or vocation or professional specialty. That is a short-sighted viewpoint. The day of the specialist is receding into history. We used to need specialists who had a deep knowledge of specific areas but we have computers now by which to store gigabytes of data. Thus it is that the computer is taking the place of "the specialist." We simply no longer need people who have a depth of knowledge of a topic. We need people who can connect with and exchange information across many departments, many technologies, and many professions.

4. They want people who are computer literate. If you haven't been told this already in most of your classes, it is time you became aware of this: Become computer literate. It will increase your employability tenfold. Don't be afraid of computers. They were once cumbersome and spoke in foreign languages (Basic, Fortran, Cobalt, etc.). Most programs now are "user-friendly"—meaning they are easy to work on—and lots of fun. It is extremely advantageous to answer YES to the item on your job application that asks if you have any computer skills.

5. They want people who view education as a life-long process. We used to think of education as a four-year program (or an eight-year program), after which you went out into the field and worked. That is no longer a realistic picture. Technological advances in every area of business, science, and the media are making it necessary for employees to update their knowledge and skills. We may choose to get more advanced degrees from the college of our choice. We may need to register for workshops or evening courses to gain CEU credits. If we are in the professions of medicine, psychology, engineering, etc., we may have to get back into the classroom to get updated on recent advances. All the professions encourage their members to attend their local or national conferences. Organizations want people who are not going to stagnate on the job but who are eager to continue their life-long learning.

6. They don't want just "A-getting grinds"; they want multidimensional people. Work organizations want people who have a lot of "know how" and are "problem solvers." They are not looking for the "grind" who is an "A"-getter and not much else. They are looking for "doers" as well as "thinkers." In your curriculum vitae or résumé, they want to see what else you've done besides "study." They like to see that you have been active in extracurricular activities. They like to see that you took on an important project and completed it, whether it was designing and constructing the Homecoming float or working for Habitat for Humanity (community-based projects for building or restoring houses for the poverty-stricken of our nation). If you have been an officer of a club, they know you are willing to take on the problems and responsibilities of leadership. If you have been a member of a dance troupe, or choral group, or in the cast or crew of a play, they know you have had experience being a team member. If you have collected funds for a charitable organization or put on a benefit performance, they know you have compassion and a concern for those less fortunate than yourself. These activities and events on your résumé glow like jewels in a crown.

7. They value college students who have held full- or part-time jobs. If you have had previous work experience before coming back to school, that is of interest to future employers since they know then that you are a person willing to continue your life-career education. If you held one or two or three part-time jobs while attending college, so much the better for you. Your willingness to take some financial responsibility for your life looks good on a résumé. Prospective employers know you have gained much knowledge and experience even in the most menial jobs. They know that you have learned the importance of good public relations. They know that you have learned to juggle work and school, and some of you are juggling work, school, marriage, and parenting. These responsibilities have enlarged your worldview and your judgment has become more mature. Prospective employers know that you have experience now in working with other employees and (presumably) have developed "people skills."

Six Strategies for Landing Your First Real Job!

By the time you graduate, over 1 million students will begin the process of "job-hunting." You may find yourself asking the same questions that most other graduates will be asking themselves: *How does a person land a first real job? Will I be able to find a job?* Some vocational and professional departments actually run workshops and mini-courses on how to go about job-hunting, how to write a résumé, how to dress, how to be interviewed. A few pages of a text cannot take the place of these learning opportunities, but we can provide you with a few of their tips and guidelines. Some of these tips and strategies will already be familiar to you. Skip over them. But some of these tips and strategies may surprise you.

1. Take your time finding a job. It pays to be patient. If you are having to take some time to get that first real job, don't panic by grabbing the first job that comes along. It may take you three to nine months to find that special job just made for you. What do you do for money in the meantime? Well, if there isn't someone supporting you while you job hunt, you have two other options. You can get a part-time job to put food on the table and keep your car running while you job hunt on your off-time. You say you also have other hungry mouths to feed and you can't ask your spouse to continue supporting you? In that case, you can get a full-time job in the evening, and during the day do your job-hunting (when you aren't sleeping). What you need to do is to explain to your family that the first job is an important one, and it takes time to find it. Hasten to assure them that you are not avoiding a job; in fact, a few months of patient job hunting will result in a financial pay off eventually. You might even want to let them read these pages so they can see you are getting this information from "a reliable source."

An important note: You do not have to wait for graduation before job-hunting. It can begin while you are still a student. Your college probably has a list of job opportunities. So will the head of your department. If you want to speed up the process of landing your first job, avail yourself of one or more private employment agencies. They not only have a variety of better-paying jobs in your locale, they are often able to interest an organization in a person of your qualifications. If you don't mind moving away from your college area, make sure to go to state and national professional conferences in your field of work. In addition to the latest updates in your professional field, they usually have a room devoted to job market opportunities. Finally, don't be hesitant in asking a professor or instructor to keep you in mind for information on jobs that may pass their desks. Instructors are always happy to help their students locate employment.

2. Create a résumé that is distinctive. Once you have some leads on a job, the next step is to secure an interview. Employers and personnel departments are flooded with job applications. To secure an interview, create a résumé that (1) is distinctive enough to catch their eyes and (2) indicates that of all those applicants, you are definitely a person worth interviewing. Start by putting together a concise but comprehensive résumé form. There are many paperback books on the market that show you how. If you are computer literate, there are several programs that also make it easy to put together a respectable résumé. That is only the first step, however. After you have put together a conventional but comprehensive résumé, spend some time making it distinctive. We are not saying to make it bizarre or so radical that you scare off the prospective employer. But prospective employers get so many résumés that look alike, nothing sets them apart. You want something that gets their attention (see Figure 15.1). What can get their attention that won't look bizarre? Well, a modest photograph in the upper right-hand corner will turn an impersonal résumé into something more personal. After you have put together a fairly conventional résumé, think about how you can make it just a little more distinctive from others in your field (Corewen, 1988). We'll give you a few examples.

- Don wanted a job working with computers. With his résumé, he enclosed three disks containing programs he had devised himself, along with user-friendly instructions for their immediate use.
- Deidre wanted to break into the children's literature field. Publishing houses are besieged by manuscripts. Since Deidre has an artistic talent, she used her talent even on the brown paper she wrapped the manuscript in. When the first editor saw a brightly illustrated package on his desk, he was immediately attracted to it and opened it before he opened anything else in the mail. Her book was published.
- Jason was applying for a high-paying oil job in the Middle East. He was smart enough to realize that knowing even a little Arabic would be a valuable asset. In his last year at the University, he took an independent study course in Arabic. Although he added that skill to his résumé, he wanted to be sure it was noticed. In the place marked "Special Skills and Abilities" he wrote: "I am learning to read and write in Arabic." That grabbed their attention!

3. Prepare ahead of time for your interview.   Until you have been interviewed a few times, the interview situation may be anxiety-arousing: *How should I act? What should I say? What will the interviewer ask me? What should I wear?*

Finding out what to wear is probably the easiest question to answer so we'll start with that one. You probably know that you need to look well-dressed but not garish. If the location of the interview is not too far away, it might be wise to visit the job site or company before your interview day. Take a walk around inside and out and get an idea of what clothing styles are being worn by both management and workers. If you want them to know you are their "kind of person," wear something within the range of their clothing styles. Take your best friend with you if you are going to buy that special "interview" outfit. In this situation, two critical heads are definitely better than one. If you do buy an "interview outfit," wear it before your interview until you feel comfortable and natural in it and until it looks and "feels right." If you are not used to a collar and tie, get used to wearing them long before the interview situation.

The next step is to go through some dry runs of the interview situation. Wear your "interview outfit." Get some of your friends or an instructor to act as an interviewer. You might want to tape record the sessions. Make a note of some of the questions they ask. Prepare answers for the questions they ask you. But always prepare good answers that are not phony but represent who you genuinely are. "To thine own self be true." Ask different people to act as interviewers because each of them will have different ideas and questions. Tell them not to be afraid of being critical. (Tell them you will do the same for them if they so choose.) The more interview situations you enact, the less anxiety you will experience. Familiarity diminishes

Jennifer was looking for a job in drafting. Drafting is a field that has been male-dominated. She knew once she was interviewed, she could show them her portfolio of work. But how to get past their resistance to females? She devised a stationary on which she drafted a border composed of drafting tools. It was not an example of real creativity, but it certainly was different enough to get her an interview.

Figure 15.1 Jennifer's Résumé

the anxiety of the unknown. Then practice again and again until you feel comfortable and can speak fluently and naturally.

4. Prepare some questions that you would like answered by the interviewer. Interviewers also like prospective employers to ask questions. Give some consideration to the following items and choose ones that seem important to you as you plan your life-career:

What are the chances for advancement?
How are salary increases decided?
Are there possibilities for flex-time so you can continue your education?
Does the organization foster education through full or part tuition payment?
How does the organization react to necessary or emergency needs that must be done during company hours, such as taking a child to the hospital or meetings with teachers?
How does the organization see itself in terms of contributing to the community?
Who would you be working directly under?
Which other areas would you be relating to?
Who else besides your immediate superior will you be interviewed by?

5. When you have obtained an actual interview, read up on the history and goals of the organization. Nothing will impress an interviewer more than to realize you have been reading the history of the organization and have become familiar with its short-term objectives and long-term goals. Don't show off about it. As the interview continues, your responses, both verbal and nonverbal, will make apparent your knowledge of the organization. Eventually, the interviewer may say something like, "You seem to be familiar with this" at which point you modestly reply, "Well, I've been familiarizing myself with the organization's history and goals." Spoken without any sense of self-aggrandizement, it will be very impressive!

6. If you really want a job with the organization, don't take a "no" as a permanent answer. Some people get discouraged by getting turned down for a job. They simply walk away and never go back. That's because they don't know human psychology. If you like the organization and the people who interviewed you, don't give up. It pays to be persistent. If you are told that someone else got the job, ask the interviewers what you lacked. Find out what qualifications were deemed important. If it was a special skill, acquire it. If it was experience in a certain area of work, go about getting it. Then, when a position opens up again, get another interview with them. Do you have to be embarrassed? Not at all. They will be impressed by your dedicated and sincere desire to work for them. They will be impressed by your willingness to acquire more qualifications. They will be impressed by your persistence. They will be impressed by your patience and determination. All of these attributes are what employers are looking for.

Ten Principles for Success in Your Job: Applying All the Principles of Psychology You Have Been Learning

Let us suppose now that you have been hired. How do you go about doing your job not just well but in a way that leads to salary raises and promotions? Will you be surprised if we call your attention again to your communication and "people skills"? We hope not because they are the key to success in every area of your life—with your spouse, with your children, with your employment, and with just about every situation that involves people.

1. Effective managers are not expected to act like the "boss" anymore; they act more like team captains. We have already learned that the chief reason for firing someone is not because they didn't do their job. It is because they didn't know how to work with other people. What that definition implies is that the effective manager has to be sensitive to other people's needs. He or she has to be receptive to other people's concerns, always being friendly and approachable. There is an axiom in organizational life that effective managers do not wall themselves up in their offices but maintain an "open door" policy for anyone, including workers, to discuss what they are doing or to ask some advice. But no one is going to walk into the manager's office if the manager finds fault with everyone—no matter how wide open the door to his office. If a manager is known to say, "I am surrounded by fools," that manager needs an attitude change. If a manager gets exasperated by "mistakes" other people make, that manager needs an attitude change. If a manager begins to delegate responsibility and ends by saying, "Oh, never mind, I'll do it myself," that manager needs an attitude change. The attitude they need to adopt is the understanding that things only get done when everybody works together in a cooperative and friendly manner.

2. Effective managers understand themselves as head of the organizational family. The position of a manager is not dissimilar to the position of the head of a family. Whether you are the night manager of a fast-food franchise or the department head of a large university, you may be astonished how often the people who work for you and even your colleagues will behave like a family. Co-workers will behave like sibling rivals. Collaborative colleagues may behave like divorcing couples if their conflicts become too volatile. Perfectly competent workers may revert into their child-ego states. Eventually, you will witness most of the defense mechanisms being enacted where you work. Your job as manager will be to keep your organizational family as functional as possible. How? By using all the psychological techniques you have been reading in previous chapters. Effective managers have been using them for several decades now.

3. Provide positive feedback. The most effective way of bringing out the best in your workers is to find something good they have done and tell them so. Better still, write it on a note that not only goes to them directly but gets put into their file. In Skinnerian language, it is reinforcing the desirable behavior. It is so easy to point out mistakes. Mistakes are glaring. It is less easy to note what people are doing right. An axiom of effective management goes: *Catch them doing something right!* (Blanchard & Johnson, 1982). Good jobs are deserving of words of praise and concrete actions, such as good performance appraisals, and approval of salary raises or promotions. If these actions are not possible during the downsizing of an organization, at least let the person know you have recommended it. Ask her, by way of compliment, if she would like to take on added responsibility. In the place of salary increase or promotion, such a question certainly will meet some of her esteem needs. It will also convey to her that you are appreciative of her talents and efforts. The positive feedback needs to be sincere, concrete, and objective. It is not enough to say, "Mary, you're doing a great job!" or "Joe, your sales are looking good!" or "Eddie, thanks for your help on the project!" Be more specific. "Mary, your accounting report was very helpful to me in the meeting." Or "Joe, you're the high-scorer this month for sales!" Or "Eddie, your assistance on the project was so valuable that I had occasion to tell the president that you were mostly responsible for its success."

4. For workers who are having difficulties meeting their job responsibilities, assume an attitude of helpfulness. If someone is consistently late or frequently absent or not doing the job to satisfaction, don't make the assumptions that the employee is simply being irresponsible or shiftless. Try to discover what is wrong. It may be simply a very concrete problem requiring a simple solution. The worker who is always late may be having transportation problems. See if you can find ways to help that worker by finding a car pool. The employee who is not doing the job well enough may lack a simple skill such as faster typing, or they may need tutoring on the computer. The person who has had considerable absenteeism may have a chronically sick child, and there may be some kind of baby-sitting solution that can be worked out. They may be going through a divorce with all the heartache that entails. Their spouses or children (or even themselves) may have landed in jail, and they may be overwhelmed by the legal aspects of what is going on. Everyone needs a hand now and then. What these workers need is not to be fired or blamed for their predicament. They need a little help. As a manager, it is not your job to be a therapist, but you can encourage them to get therapeutic help. As a manager, it is not your job to loan them money, but perhaps you can get them financial assistance. As a manager, it is not your job to act as social worker, legal counsel, or physician. But you can become a referral source. Experienced employees who are having problems are not people to get rid of. They are people who need help through the occasional hardtimes we all go through.

5. Good news may travel up and bad news may travel down, but the effective manager keeps all lines of communication open. You have heard this axiom many times, and you will probably hear it many times again: *When things go awry, nine times out of ten, there's been a breakdown in communication.* It is not just a truism, it is a truth. As organizations get larger and larger and the number of workers increase, the more there is a chance for communication breakdown. Most of the time, miscommunications are accidental. But when the work climate has become hostile, much miscommunication may be deliberate. Another organizational maxim then goes: *Good news travels up; bad news travels down.* What that maxim means is that in an organization in which workers are treated on the assumptions of old Theory X (see Box 10.8), employees will not want to report problems to the upper echelon. They will tend to cover up mistakes. Or shrug their shoulders when they read instructions that seem incorrect. Things may be going wrong up and down on the production line and no one is informing the management.

On the other side of the ledger, bad news travels down. Management may discover a costly mistake and seek to find blame among the employees, following the centuries old phenomenon of **attributional bias.** Blaming a person (or even a whole group of people such as an entire department) may make us feel better but casting blame impedes the open communication we want.

6. The effective manager knows how to resolve conflict: Assumptions and guidelines of conflict resolution. Conflict and conflict resolution is one of the chief "people skills" of the effective manager. If you become known as a person who can resolve difficulties between people or departments, you will be targeted as a person who can handle greater responsibilities. Before we begin discussing how to handle conflict, we need to make note of the assumptions of conflict resolution: First, conflict is inevitable. We noted in our chapter on marriage that conflict is inevitable in any area where people are living in close proximity for a period of time. It is also true of the work arena. Today, as in every era and culture, we have many legitimate areas of conflict:

labor/management, minorities, conservative/liberal, environmental/nuclear, right-to-life/right-to-choose, and so on. The second assumption of conflict resolution is that if the conflict is not legitimately recognized, it will go underground and emerge in costly and dangerous ways, such as in interdepartmental warfare, worker-management disputes, and organizational sabotage. The third assumption is that conflict is not necessarily destructive. In fact, conflict prevents stagnation and promotes new and creative ideas. The scientific professions actually promote conflict by inviting opposing points of view.

Wherever there are different departments or work sites, there will always be differences in perspective and points-of-view. The effective manager knows how to legitimize these opposing points-of-view and resolve them. The principles of conflict resolution are very similar to those we have discussed in Chapter 10 on Interpersonal Communication and Chapter 11 on Marriage and the Family. Nothing will be more esteemed by the top echelon of your work place as the ability to resolve conflict, and, in Box 15.2, we have listed some of the general principles of conflict resolution formulated by experts in the field.

7. The effective manager must be sensitive to issues of sexual harassment. Legally, sexual harassment has been defined as unwelcome advances or requests for sexual favors or any other verbal or physical behavior of a sexual nature. Although sexual harassment has been discussed in various organizations in both the private and public sectors, it was not until 1991 that sexual harassment in the work place became such a large issue. It was in that year that Supreme Court nominee Clarence Thompson was accused of sexual harassment of law professor Anita Hill. Although Thompson was ultimately appointed to the Supreme Court, the hearings instigated corporate America to investigate their policies of sexual harassment and to institute policies against such practices. While sexual harassment is difficult to define precisely, organizations are making it clear that many behaviors are no longer acceptable in this country. These behaviors include unwanted touching and verbal sexual advances, and veiled threats that a woman can lose her job if she is unwilling to comply with an employer's sexual requests. But what constitutes sexual harassment does not stop with these behaviors. Sexual harassment also includes off-color jokes or comments by co-workers, sexual artifacts placed around the workplace (such as pictures of nudes), and power tactics based on gender (expecting women workers to make coffee, arrange parties, or do other stereotypic female activities, if the woman does not perceive that as being a normal part of her job description).

It also includes unwelcome female behaviors toward men. Sexual harassment is not limited to unwelcome male behaviors toward women. Sexual harassment also includes hostile anti-gay jokes and comments. In the largest possible sense, sexual harassment includes any behavior which makes the work environment a hostile climate for anyone. This a particularly sensitive area for the effective manager to deal with if there are no other witnesses but the two persons involved. As well, there may be accusations of sexual harassment where none exist. Yet the manager must deal with any and all such complaints. To that end, institutions and organizations have inaugurated workshops, forums, in-service training, and computer-based programs to sensitize managers and executives to sexual harassment issues and how to deal with them both here and abroad (Carrie, 1999).

8. The effective manager is sensitive to gender differences in working with others. The workforce has changed radically in the last two decades and it is continuing to change. One major difference is the increasing numbers of women joining the workforce. Although men are still heading most of the higher echelon corporate positions, women are more and more

Box 15.2

PRINCIPLES OF CONFLICT RESOLUTION

Concentrate on the issue, not on personalities. To resolve any conflict, do everything you can to depersonalize the issue. Never allow it to become a matter of this person versus that person. If personality conflict becomes the focus of the problem, the only solution may be to get rid of one or the other of the persons. Getting rid of someone is never a good thing to do because of the fear and distrust it sets up in the rest of the organization. Successful managers, therefore, do everything they can to veer the problem away from being a personality conflict. Your job is to get everyone concerned to focus on the issue or issues, not on each other.

Ask to interview each person in the conflict separately. When people are fighting with each other, especially in front of other people, their disagreements get larger and their arguing gets louder. What is needed is to separate the disputants from each other by asking them to go back to their jobs and you will speak personally with each of them later. In the individual interviews, your first job is to defuse their emotions. When people are angry or hurt or feel an unjust accusation has been made, their emotions cloud reality. When people are steamed up or suffering in other ways, they cannot think logically or from any other viewpoint than their own. There is a professional maxim about people who are brought to a treatment center for alcoholism: *Let them dry out first. There is no use speaking to the alcohol.* The same holds for hot feelings or hurt feelings. So encourage them to speak about how they feel. Use the technique of active listening. Once their negative feelings have been defused, they will be more open to logic and reason and more able to discuss the matter more objectively.

Maintain a calm, smooth, and interested exterior. No matter how emotional the situation has become, your job is to remain calm and collected. Don't allow yourself to feel insulted or shocked or irritated by the person as he or she is throwing accusations all around. It is part of the person's emotional baggage that is draining off. Communicate the feeling that you are not blaming them in any way for the conflict. As a matter-of-fact, you might even add the idea that you are glad that the problem has surfaced so the problem can be brought out into the open and solved.

Look for win-win solutions. Ask all the participants individually for their suggestions on how to solve the problem. When you have heard everyone's suggestions, put them together and formulate several alternative plans of action. Present your plan and alternate courses of action toward win-win solutions (everybody wins in the end). Win-lose solutions mean there will be losers, and losers never feel good about losing. They may actually turn their negative feelings against you instead of the people or departments they are losing to. Encourage every member present to voice opinions or to make additions, deletions, and modifications. Rather than vote on alternative plans, keep the discussion going until everyone (or almost everyone) seems to favor one of the plans. Then concentrate on implementing that one plan.

Negotiate real differences. Although your objective always is to find win-win solutions, sometimes that just doesn't happen. Don't cover that fact up. Admit it openly and honestly to the party or parties concerned, but with a sense of humor, with remarks such as: "Well, Bob, there's nothing I can do for you in this instance. Your people will just have to bite the bullet this time. But we'll owe you a big one! And I won't forget that!" Or "Janet, we can't do what you need done at this time. Let's see how this is going to work. If we still have the same problems, you have the right to convene this committee again."

Give the team plenty of time to work out the bugs. Don't think conflict resolution can always be done immediately or that solutions can be thought through on the spot. Like so many other processes we have discussed, conflict resolution is a process. It requires time. Your conflict resolutions group may have to meet several times before some viable and creative solution is worked out. If finally everyone concludes that the plan is not working, find out why it isn't working and work out another plan.

Make the pronouns of "we," "us," and "ours" a habitual part of your language. There are many books on the market that give you "do's and don'ts" for conflict resolution. Study them. But for a quick overall tip on how to resolve a conflict, exchange the pronouns "I" and "you" for "we" and "us"—for all the reasons discussed in Chapter 10.

reaching managerial and executive ranks. Given the increasing number of women at all levels of professional and business organizations, men are going to have to communicate with women in a different style. Men tend to shout and argue with each other, which women find offensive and rude. Women managers generally use a more cooperative and friendly style of communication with co-workers and those for whom they are responsible. Managers may expect women workers to be more absent than their male counterparts (generally because of illness or problems with children), but this fact notwithstanding, women will be as productive (if not more productive) than men in most organizations (Beebe, Beebe, & Redmond, 1996).

9. The effective manager stays alert to the multicultural diversity in the workplace. Our vastly different ethnic differences will have different communication styles. Workers with a Mediterranean and Arabic background will tend to huddle together while talking loudly in their common language, but what may look like arguing from the outside may in fact be their directness in working out a problem. Asian immigrants or Asian-American citizens will, on the other hand, seem to agree with everything that is being said because to be too direct or argumentative is, in their cultural background, appalling rudeness. Finally, there are many initiatives across the nation to provide jobs for people with many kinds of disabilities, including physical, emotional, and mental disabilities. We have gone a long way in providing both jobs and services for the physically disabled—according to a recent report about 70 percent are now employed. But we still have a long way to go for the emotionally and cognitively disabled (Rabasca, 1999).

Finally, the downsizing (laying off of workers) of the last two decades has resulted in the use of many more temporary workers ("Temps"—workers who are hired only part-time). In order to compensate for their lack of financial benefits, corporations are offering a wide spectrum of employment opportunities. Students who are going to school may be offered evening and night shifts so they can continue to go to college during the day. As our nation's population grows older, we will have many more senior citizens looking for part-time work if their social security and retirement benefits do not meet their bills. Mothers may be offered the flex-time of working while their children are in school. Other professionals are being hired for ten or twelve hours for three or four days, which means they can take the other days off.

10. Finally and above all, use the following words, phrases, and sentences frequently.
I appreciate what you did/contributed/achieved.
What do you think?
Thank you.
Please.

Coming Full Circle: Applying the Principles of Effective Professional Management to Your Home Management

It is more truth than truism that we deal more sensitively and creatively with the people at our work place than we do with the people in our home place. When we disagree with another person at work, we are more tactful and diplomatic than we are at home. When a problem shows up at work with our co-workers, we try not to tear into them or lower their self-esteem; yet, we often say rude things to those at home. At home, we do not always take the extra time and energy needed to establish or reestablish diplomatic relations with the other members of our home place, as we usually do with others in our work place. And why is that? Because we have different assumptions about the two arenas of work and home. We assume that people at home do not need the courtesy and consideration that we give to people in the work place. We assume that "they'll understand" if we break promises or are going to be late for dinner and don't bother to phone and say so. Yet, being respectful for a dinner date is as important to the family team as a committee meeting is to the work team. We assume that others will know what is needed for a situation even though we do not discuss *en famille* as we do with members of our work department.

It behooves us, then, to begin to change our assumptions about our home place and realize that it is just as important to pay attention to our family management style as it is to pay attention to our work management style. For that reason, we are about to apply the principles of effective work management to our home place and personal life.

Treat Your Family Microeconomics as You Would Your Departmental Budget

The saying goes: When bills fly in the window, love flies out. Nothing can be more true. It is not enough to avoid the horrors of mounting credit card bills and eventual bankruptcy. A sound and fair financial operating procedure is just as beneficial for family health as it is for corporate life. Together with your life partner (and your children as soon as they can comprehend money and finance), plan budget strategies for immediate and long-term goals. Rather than keep the bill-paying secretive, provide all family members with knowledge of the large month-by-month expenses that must be met. Then make a list of the special bills that come yearly. Examples: In January, Christmas expenses must be added up and paid for; in February, the house insurance must be paid; in March, the property taxes; in April, income taxes; and so forth. Make sure that everyone understands that their requests come after the mortgage payments, the budget allowed for groceries, their school clothes, etc. Even after these expenses are met, a certain amount has to be put aside for unexpected expenses and emergency situations.

After these "must" expenses are listed, have everyone put in their budget requests over and above their allowance and earned chore monies. When the list has been made up, negotiations can begin. Mom says she would like to take a vacation this summer and maybe visit her parents. Can we do both at the same time? We could find a vacation spot near them. We can visit them for three days and the rest of the time will be "our " vacation. Perhaps Eddie's teenage request for a motorcycle is way out of line financially. *Eddie, if we back you financially for half of it, would you be willing to save for the down payment, the insurance, and pay part of the monthly payments for it from your allowance? Or by doing extra family chores? Or by a part-time job?* Or perhaps ten-year-old Rachel would like to take ballet lessons with her friends, which would cost a sizable chunk of money every week. *Rachel, you are taking music lessons and karate lessons. If you want dancing lessons now, you either have to do some serious baby-sitting and earn the money or give up one of your other lessons. Why don't you think about which you want more.* Each person is allowed so much weekly or monthly toward their special requests, which can then be charted and placed on the refrigerator—surely as important a learning experience and record of achievement as good school papers. The children are learning about family expenses and how to budget. Every person has a chance to make requests. They are participating in negotiations. They are learning the difference between *wants* and *needs*. They are learning about the financial side of life in their own home as they grow up.

So much for the family *microeconomics* (the economics of everyday personal life). Family economics is only half the story for securing a firm financial base. We are living in an age in which the economic operation of family finances requires planning, detailed record keeping, and a thorough understanding of mortgage loans, interest rates, insurance benefits, local, state, and federal taxes. You are being inveigled in the media to subscribe to this or that credit card, to invest in stocks, bonds, and treasury notes. If you are in business for yourself—you need to learn about bookkeeping, accounting, tangible and intangible taxes, I.R.A. and Keough accounts, and what kinds of medical and liability insurance coverage you need. Although your children are still small, you may be thinking about investing in a college education plan. Management of your business and family finances means that you need to learn everything you can about financial management. Become literate in such areas as insurance, estate planning, taxes, and investment. Read everything you can on financial planning in books and monthly magazines. Take a course in financial planning. We are living at a time when most of us will be living longer and healthier lives. Look for ways and means to secure yourself a financially secure future. The last thing you want is to have to depend on the charity of others when you are in your mature years. Finally, stay abreast of the financial news daily in this era of rapidly fluctuating economic cycles. (For tips on how to avoid money conflicts, see Box 15.3.)

When Conflicts Arise: Apply the Principles of Conflict Resolution

Apply the principles of conflict resolution when disputes and arguments arise. You have already learned principles such as don't look for blame, look for solutions. When children are bickering, separate them and listen to each side individually. If you try to straighten out the mess with both of them yelling and screaming, the situation can only get worse. When you are listening to them individually, employ active listening techniques. Help them to articulate what they are feeling and not to continue blaming each other and making accusations. Whether it is husband and wife, roommates, parents and children, look at where the confusion arose and identify the problem. Start with the assumption that it is a communication breakdown. (It may be that the root cause is far deeper than just "communication breakdown," but at least start with that assumption.)

If the problem is not just a "communication breakdown," give the problem time. Generally speaking, very few problems have to have immediate decisions. In fact—unless it is an emergency situation—nothing should be decided immediately when the participants are all "hot under the collar." Let time do some of the processing of fading angry or hurt feelings. In a few hours, or overnight, people's angry feelings will diminish, and they will be more open to solutions. Ask everybody involved to offer solutions and alternative plans of action. Negotiate new social contracts, particularly in parent/adolescent interactions, but this holds true for everyone. Negotiate with each other toward win-win solutions.

Catch Each Other Doing "Something Right." It is so easy to find fault and criticize. Take advantage of the "one-minute manager" concept of taking one minute to compliment other people in the family for something they have done. It can be done verbally at dinner, in a hand-written note, or by phone.

The Crisis Management Approach: When the "Hard Times" Hit. By and large Americans do well in times of high energy. We are a vibrant and energetic people who operate best when we are "on the go." Despite the occasional prophets of doom who tell us we are headed for a major recession or a third (atomic) world war or the end of human life on this planet, we are still the optimistic and hard-working people that de Tocqueville (1830) described 150 years

Box 15.3   TEN GUIDELINES TOWARD AVOIDING MONEY CONFLICTS

The following suggestions are very practical steps for dealing with the complexities of financial management.

1. Prepare your financial budget and financial planning together, item by item. Use principles of negotiation so that no one feels shortchanged and everyone has some discretionary funds. Make sure that your financial planning includes saving for future goals.

2. Make priority lists for your needs and wants. Discuss what each of your financial needs and wants mean to you. If you are harboring a secret desire (a fishing boat, a better and larger appliance, a piano, a pool table) bring it out into the open. Have your children do the same thing. Make two lists of needs and wants and allow each person some discretionary funds to save toward those goals in order of priority. Have fun with it. If a family member has a financial need or want that would cost (say) $175, make a chart similar to those in charitable and business organizations that documents how much of the financial goal has been reached. Let everybody prioritize the financial goals and make it family fun at the dinner table.

3. Make sure each person has some discretionary funds. Discretionary funds mean funds that do not have to be accounted for. They can be used in any way—for fun and recreation, clothes, savings, presents, whatever.

4. Give all children ways and means to earn their financial goals. Ways and means may be through direct allowances or chores that they can earn money for or the time to make money in the neighborhood through baby-sitting, mowing lawns, etc.

5. Prepare for "worst case scenarios." Financial management should prepare for those emergency times when some kind of disaster strikes, such as a loss of job, medical bills, and accidents that place a financial burden on the family. Realistic planning means learning about insurance, having quick access to emergency funds, and a solid savings account to draw from.

6. When making decisions that involve large financial investments, avail yourself of every possible resource to educate yourself. If you are thinking about buying a house or a car, read everything you can about house buying. Consult experts in the area, but don't accept anything anyone tells you without corroborating the advice. Take your time making major decisions. Avail yourself of consumer advocacy magazines and articles. Become literate in every major financial undertaking you are considering.

7. Remember this! No matter how carefully you plan, things always cost more than you planned for. No matter how carefully you have planned your budget, no matter how honest your building contractor, no matter how much you have read on the subject, somehow you almost always end up paying more than you anticipated. And many times a lot more! You mean to spend a few hundred dollars on a refrigerator and you get so attracted to a model that costs twice as much, you end up buying it. Your physician says it will only cost X amount of dollars to do what you need to do for your health and it ends up costing a lot more than you were told. And so it goes. So whatever you are told, you are wise to figure in 50 percent more than is estimated. If the overage is less than you figure, so much the better—you can go on that vacation you have always wanted.

ago. We still believe that hard work coupled with enthusiasm, determination, and a good education are all that is needed to get ahead. That is still true to a large extent.

But there will be times in all our lives when hard times will hit. An unexpected illness may cripple a young child. A tragic accident may end in the death of an adolescent. An aging parent may come down with a "stroke" or other debilitating disease. In these days of "downsizing," the major breadwinner may suddenly be "laid off"—or discover the toxic effects of job burnout. All of these crises can happen to anyone at any level at any time. These situations may exhaust our financial resources. And, most assuredly, they drain our emotional energy. No survey text such as this one can discuss in great detail all these possibilities, particularly since each family is different and each crisis is unique. These are the times when we need to employ the crisis management approach. **Crisis management** involves general guidelines and coping strategies that enable us to process the pain and anxiety and get us through "the hard times." These are the times when families can truly build a sense of community by which family members can become closer and learn to be mutually supportive.

When Crises Arise: Employ the Organizational Tactic of Consulting, Consulting, Consulting. As a manager you would never, never set out to do something without consulting experts, advisors, other department managers, and so on. This also applies to making major financial purchases, dealing with personal problems, and learning how to interact with your adolescent children. We have given you some basics in this text, but crises and problematic situations will arise that will need in-depth study and unique coping strategies. Just as you do in your work place, use all the community resources available to you. Your libraries are filled with books on all kinds of personal problems written by professionals who have expertise in that particular problematic area. As well, there are many valuable books by people who have lived this kind of situation and are sharing the ways and means by which they coped (see Recommended Readings) . Do you have a family member that has AIDS or Alzheimer's Disease? Are your children having physical or emotional problems? Are you suffering profound grief because of the death of a loved one? Books by the carload are available to you.

And, above all, get on-line! There are hundreds, even thousands, of resources on the information highway—and they're available to you. These resources offer a wide spectrum of help on almost any topic you can think of from quick question-and-answer first aid to the latest research data, to where you can get help from agencies in your area, to chat rooms where you can ask specific questions of others who have had the same problem.

If the problems and crises in your life are reaching "critical mass," avail yourself of the therapeutic situation to help you get through it. You may want to get professional help or you may want to join a peer-support group. Your church may run groups for parents with teenagers. Or there may be adult education classes that provide knowledge and skills that will be helpful for your situation. If there isn't one, get some one to help you initiate a community resource similar to those we have been describing. Our society is fraught with problems, many of them discussed in this text. But one of the brightest aspects of our society is that when we need help, there are always resources available and someone willing and able to respond.

Sharing Problems and Anxieties with Other Family Members

There are people who tend to moan or complain over any triviality that arises. But most of us tend to hide our anxieties. It is easier to share our happiness and successes than it is to share our unhappiness and pain. Pain is more private. Unhappiness is hard to admit. Moreover, we hide our pain from others because we don't want to burden them. But when we keep these kinds of feelings to ourselves, we isolate ourselves from others just at the time when we should be connecting to others. It may take some courage to open up discussion of the crisis, but by doing so, we provide the way for others to share their concerns.

I'd like to share a few of my concerns with everyone. Anyone else feel that way?
I think we need to set a time-and-place to talk about what's going on as calmly as we
  can. Anybody got any ideas about how, where, and when?
We're all hurting, and we aren't sharing it. Do you think we can have a family talk ses-
  sion? Maybe we can help each other figure out how to manage what's happening.

Include the children you believe are old enough to understand what's going on. We have a tendency to "keep things from the children" so they won't get scared. But a house full of whispers and sudden silences may simply make children more anxious. Children are very sensitive to the mood of the house. And they may think they have done something wrong to cause whatever-it-is-that-is-going-on. By including them in on what is going on, we give them something to hang on to and encourage them to express their fears and anxieties as well. Of course, what we say when they are present may be quite different from what we would discuss without them. We may want to have a discussion with them present and another discussion with "just the adults," but those adults might very well include the adolescents in the family. When family members can process the crises together, strong family cohesion is forged.

> OK, we have to move out-of-state and that's not easy. Let's each of us volunteer what the worst thing will be for us.
>
> Dad's lost his job through no fault of his own. Before he finds another one, money is going to be a little tight. Each of us needs to think about how we can save money. So let's brainstorm some ideas.
>
> Mom is going to have to go through chemotherapy, which means there will be times she isn't going to feel good at all. She won't be up to cooking or cleaning or even making her own bed. It's going to be up to us to get her through this. So the subject at hand now (and probably for several weeks to come) is how do we take care of things so she doesn't have to worry about us?

If, on the other hand, you believe the family is not able to communicate real feelings without unnecessary hostility and resentment, it may be more appropriate to get a professional person with expertise in this area. What kind of professional will depend upon the situation. A problem of someone's health might need a person in the health professions. A juvenile in trouble at school or the law may need an educational counselor. An adolescent who may be showing signs of bulimia or anorexia nervosa probably needs a psychologist or psychiatrist familiar with this kind of a problem. Make sure you get a professional with expertise in this area. Not all professionals have expertise in all areas. How do you get some information about knowledgeable professionals? Call an agency that works with this area and ask for the names of people skillful in family crisis management. By making it a family process, you will be teaching them valuable skills that they will be able to use when they are adults. We can't save children from ever having problems. We can build the confidence they will be able to manage critical times when they come. They are fostering their self-efficacy.

Reprise: Using Our Business People Skills to Build a Community-Based Family

It is an axiom that it is easier to live with the people we work with than to work with the people we live with. That is because we are often operating on Theory X assumptions (McGregor, 1960) with our children, spouse, and other relatives. We have insisted on "bossing" them, on being authoritarian, directing, and ordering. Because we have not given our attention to their growing and changing, we have not recognized their present hierarchical level of needs. We have tended to treat each other as people to be shouted at or criticized instead of people who deserve our best "people skills." In this chapter, we have discussed how to use the "people skills" you have been learning about in previous chapters in your work environment. Now you can apply the principles of effective management to your home environment, your church work, your work in community agencies, and wherever else you will spend your time as you continue in your life-career. You will understand that as your children grow up into their teenage years, their needs, wants, and motivations will be different. You will understand the need to have "house meetings" about important events and the responsibilities of all members of the family to each other. You will not so much lecture as listen, not so much give orders as encourage family members to participate in rule-making and task-sharing. Accomplishments of each person will be shared with all family members. Aspirations of each person will come up for discussion and consideration of how to enable them to reach those aspirations. Budget requests by each member of the family will be prioritized and remembered. All persons in the house will be treated with the same respect as we treat those we work with. In this way, children will learn some of the responsibilities and realities of adult life. Finally, the peer/friendship couple will be creating a family community where all are working together for the common good.

IMPORTANT TERMS AND CONCEPTS TO KNOW

abuse	esteem	personality	tenacity
authoritarian	extracurricular	positive	unemployment
climate of work	generalists	problem	us
computers	jobs	pronouns	vocational
crime	liberal	resources	wants
depersonalize	national	résumé	we
direction	patient	right	win-win
emotional	people skills	shadowing	

MAKE YOUR OWN SUMMARY BY FILLING IN THE BLANKS BELOW

Use the "Important Terms and Concepts to Know" to fill in the blanks below.

Importance of work. Work is essential to our _____ and personal well-being. When there is high unemployment, there is more spouse and child _____ , more suicide, homicide, and street _____ . A satisfying and creative work contributes greatly to our self-_____ .

Vocational choice. It is wise to take advantage of vocational _____ days offered by your college. A good way to get a realistic view of a career is by _____ someone already in the field throughout the work day. Do not be overly concerned, however, if you are not sure what you want to do. Career choice today is less a target than a _____ .

Career success. The day of the _____ "boss" is over. Organizations want employees with " _____ " and who know how to communicate and motivate their co-workers and employees. They do not want people who are just "A-getting grinds." They are looking for people who have taken part in _____ activities and who have learned how to be _____ - solvers. They value people who have had full or part time _____ . They need people who are _____ and can relate to many departments and areas. The specialist is no longer as necessary because _____ can store gigabytes of specialized information.

Securing your first real job. To land your first real job, create a _____ that is attention-getting without being outlandish. To prepare yourself for the interview, _____ with your friends by going through several dry-runs. Don't necessarily take "no" as an answer. Don't be afraid to return time after time. They will admire your _____ .

Career success. Effective managers build a warm _____ . Effective managers catch their employees doing "something _____ " and provide for _____ feedback. Do not allow arguments to assume a " _____ problem." Instead, focus on issues. Effective managers are skilled in conflict resolution because they seek _____ solutions. The reader is reminded to use the words _____ and _____ instead of "your" when problems arise.

Using Your Management Skills at Home. Coming full circle, the reader can use the principles of management at home. Plan a family budget but allow every "department" to put in for both needs and _____ . When conflicts and problems arise, consult books, your on-line information highway, and professionals in the field. Take advantage of your community _____ just as you would at work when problems arise.

GLOSSARY

Note: This glossary gives brief definitions of important terms and concepts in the text. For a fuller explanation of a term, look it up in the index and refer to the pages indicated.

abnormal behavior: Dysfunctional behavior that deviates markedly from the average range of behavior and which is disturbing or destructive to the person or others.

AIDS: Initials which stand for *acquired immune deficiency syndrome:* A retroviral disease that breaks down the body's natural ability to resist illness.

active listening: A people skill consisting of the willingness to listen to another person with empathy and understanding, thereby encouraging further communication.

adolescent egocentricity: Elkind's term for the adolescent's self-absorption and inability to consider another person's point-of-view.

adrenalergic state: The many physical changes that accompany the flight-or-fight syndrome by which the body expends energy.

adult-ego state: (Eric Berne). That part of the personality that mediates between the child-ego state and the parent-ego state and is the logical thinking part of the personality.

affect: The professional term for emotions or feelings. A person who is emotionally cold and unresponsive to others' feelings is said to have a flat affect.

age/stage theory: The theory that human beings change *qualitatively* throughout the life span in all dimensions: physically, intellectually, emotionally, and spiritually.

aggression: The defense mechanism by which we attack others physically or verbally. See also passive aggression.

alarm stage: (Hans Selye). The first stage of the general adaptation syndrome in which the animal exhibits external and internal symptoms of disease.

altered levels of consciousness (ASCs): Qualitative changes in one's perception of reality.

anal personality: (Freudian theory). Fixation of the personality at the anal stage of psychosexual development.

anal stage: (Freudian theory). The second stage of psychosexual development in which the libido is centered around the anal area.

analgesic: A drug which blocks only pain receptors.

androgeny: A mixture of masculine and feminine traits.

Anima: (Jungian theory). The personification of a man's neglected feminine traits.

Animus: (Jungian theory). The personification of a woman's neglected masculine traits.

animism: The belief that natural events have supernatural causation.

animistic thinking: (Piagetian theory). The belief that inanimate objects have human feelings and thoughts, characteristic of the preoperative stage of cognitive development.

antipsychotic drugs: Medication to alleviate the positive symptoms of psychotic disorders.

anxiety: Mental or emotional pain which can be experienced as apprehension, dread, or uneasiness.

Archetypes: (Jungian theory). Images and symbols that personify and express the deeply imbedded values and experiences of human personality.

assumptions: Unquestioned and, generally, unconscious beliefs.

attribution bias: The tendency for people to ascribe their good fortune to their own positive characteristics but to ascribe another's good fortune to external (situational) factors.

authoritarian parenting: Parenting that assumes that "parents know best," uses power and force, values obedience, and is adult-centered.

authoritarian personality: People who blindly follow authority, demand obedience from subordinates, and whose thinking is dogmatic, prejudicial, rigid, and stereotypic.

authoritative parenting: Parenting which is "family based" and respects individual differences and rights of all family members.

autonomy: (Eriksonian theory). Stage 2, which is the task of learning to take care of the basic functions of eating and controlling bladder and bowels.

aversive conditioning: Conditioning which avoids painful stimuli.

basic trust: (Eriksonian theory). Stage 1, in which the baby develops healthy physical and emotional responses.

battered woman: A woman who is subjected to physical and verbal abuse by her husband or other spouse equivalent.

behavior modification: Therapeutic change through planned shaping of behavior and other techniques of environmental engineering.

behavior therapy: Therapy that focuses on the non-reinforcement of undesirable behavior and the reinforcement of desirable behavior.

biofeedback: Bodymind therapy by which the person learns to gain control of his/her biological functions.

bipolar mood disorder: The *DSM* term for a person who suffers from extreme mood swings, formerly called "manic-depressive psychosis."

birth trauma: (Rankian theory). The concept that human birth is so painful as to be the etiology of all human anxiety.

bystander effect: The tendency for persons to accept or to decline the responsibility of aiding another person.

caritas: Lovingkindness.

case study: A research methodology investigating a single person, a specific group of people, or an event.

castration complex: (Freud). A little boy's belief that something negative will happen to his penis.

center-of-growth: (Rogerian theory). Inner knowledge or intuition by which a person is guided to make constructive choices.

centrated: (Piagetian theory). A child's cognitive focus.

child-centered home: The result of permissive parenting in which there are few rules and children are allowed to explore and discover their environment on their own.

child-ego state: (TA theory). That part of the personality which records and expresses feelings.

cholinergic state: The physiological state (opposite to the adrenalergic state) in which the body is repaired and renourished while the body is at rest.

classical conditioning: (Pavlovian theory). Learning acquired when a neutral stimulus becomes a conditioned stimulus as the result of pairing it with an unconditioned stimulus.

classical management/leadership style: The first theory of management, which relies on a hierarchy of authority and top-down communication and direction.

client-centered therapy: Rogerian therapy in which the therapist does not interpret but only reflects the client's feelings and thoughts.

climate of work: The friendliness (or lack of it) between employees or between management and labor.

cognition: Professional term for thought processes (as distinct from affect or emotions).

cognitive development: 1. How we develop our ability to think. 2. The growth of thinking in a child, first analyzed by Piaget.

cognitive dissonance: (Festinger). A state of internal disharmony. The psychological state in which two or more beliefs, understandings, or perceptions conflict with each other.

cognitive schema: (Piaget). The term used to indicate a thought, idea, or belief.

cognitive therapies: Therapies that combine insight and behavior therapy and aim to change beliefs.

collective unconscious: (Jungian theory). Human memory in which are stored Archetypal symbols of previous generations.

compensation: The defense mechanism in which the person performs well in one area to make up for a limitation in another.

concrete operations: The third stage of Piaget's theory of cognitive development.

concrete thinking: (Piagetian theory). One of the characteristics of the preoperational stage; the inability to comprehend abstractions.

conditioned stimulus: A previously neutral stimulus that when paired with an unconditioned stimulus eventually arouses a conditioned response.

conditioned response: A response aroused by a conditioned stimulus.

conditioning: Learning as the result of the pairing of two stimuli or the reinforcement of certain exploratory behaviors.

conflict resolution: The process by which disputes are settled.

conjugal bereavement: The grief of a widow or widower.

contingency approach: The most recent management theory, which uses a variety of leadership approaches sometimes called Theory Z.

conventional morality: (Kohlbergian theory). The second stage of moral/ethical development, characteristic of the majority of adult Americans.

conversion hysteria: Converting anxiety into physical symptoms such as paralysis, numbness, or other illness.

coping techniques: The manner in which a person deals with problematic or traumatic events.

crisis: 1. Turning point. 2. Life crisis. (Eriksonian theory). The developmental tasks with which we are confronted and need to learn at various life stages in order to continue our psychological growth and evolution. 3. Very troublesome situation.

crisis management center: A community resource for persons with specific problems such as rape, spousal abuse, suicidal thoughts.

decentration: (Piaget). The ability to consider a previous cognition despite the presence of an opposing one; a cognitive schema that develops in the stage of concrete operations.

defense mechanisms: (Freudian theory). Unconscious maneuvers by which we convert the pain of anxiety, shame, guilt, and other overwhelming emotions such as denial, projection, reaction formation. etc.

deindividuation: (Jung). When personal identity and standards of behavior drop away and the person identifies with group standards of behavior.

delusions: Irrational beliefs.

delusions of grandeur: The irrational belief that one is an important person, such as Napoleon, Superman, or Jesus Christ.

demographics: The objective data of human status such as age, gender, socioeconomic status, religion, etc.

denial: (Freudian theory). The defense mechanism by which we block out unacceptable perceptions.

depressants: Drugs that slow down the functioning of the nervous system.

depression: The feeling of being "down," feeling helpless and apathetic, characterized by a lack of energy.

desensitization training: Wolpe's deconditioning therapy in which the person is presented with anxiety-provoking stimuli.

difficult child: The infant and child that manifests problematic behavior as a life pattern.

displacement: (Freudian theory). Agressing against an innocent person, generally a person or group of people who generally cannot retaliate.

dissociative disorders: 1. Feelings of unreality. 2. The splitting off of the personality as in amnesia and DID.

dissociative identity disorder (DID): The dissociative patterning characterized by several alternative identities which may or may not be aware of each other. Formerly called **multiple personality disorder (MPD).**

distress: Selye's term for stress overload.

distributed practice: Spreading study or skill building over more than one session.

dogmatism: Narrow, rigid, and uncritical belief systems.

double standard: The attitude that what is appropriate for one group is not acceptable for another.

double-bind: The condition of being in a "no-win" situation in which any response that is made results in confusion and pain.

DSM: Initials standing for the *Diagnostic and Statistical Manual for Mental Disorders.*

dysfunctional behavior: 1. Abnormal behavior. 2. Behaviors which seriously interfere with one's ability to sustain mind-body well-being.

dysphoria: Chronic mild depression as contrasted with severe depression.

easy child: The infant and child that manifests a flexible, adaptable, and healthy personality style.

eclecticism: A mixture of approaches, as in using various psychotherapeutic techniques.

ego: (Freudian theory). Latin for "I"; the conscious part of the personality.

ego states: (Bernian theory). The three "recordings" of the personality that equate to the child, parent, and adult ego states within each person.

ego strength: The amount of psychic energy a person has in order to cope with and work through the problems and crises of living.

egocentric thinking: (Piagetian theory). Characteristic worldview of the stage of preoperations which prevents children from seeing the world from any other view than their own.

Elektra complex: (Freudian theory). The attachment of the daughter for her father.

empathetic listening: (Rogerian theory). The skill and art of listening without judgment so that we understand the speaker's phenomenology.

empirical: Evidence obtained through the senses and which can be agreed upon by two or more observers.

enculturation: The process by which we are socialized to the prevailing cultural and mores.

endorphins: The endogenous morphines produced by the brain that act as analgesics or mood-elevating hormones.

environmental engineering: Skinner's term for creating ideal learning situations, including "time-out," the shaping of behavior, and learning methods that provide immediate feedback and reinforcement.

ethnocentrism: The tendency to judge another person or culture in terms of our own culture.

etiology: Beginning(s) or cause(s).

eustress: Selye's term for good stress.

experimental extinction: Pavlov's term for the elimination of conditioned behaviors.

extended family: The family constellation of the preurban society in which several generations lived under one roof.

extraneous responses: Behaviors which are not desired.

extraversion: (Jungian theory). The thrust to extend ourselves outwardly into the world and to form relationships with others.

facilitative communication: Gordon's term for parent-child communication based on Rogerian empathetic listening.

fantasy: 1. A defense mechanism. 2. The process by which we create new images and possibilities.

favorable ratio: Erikson's emphasis that no life task is permanently achieved, but rather that our character achievements always remain a delicate balance.

fear of success: The tendency of women to lower their level of aspiration so as not to threaten men with their intellectual, academic, or vocational ability.

feedback: Immediate knowledge of results and the most efficient method of learning.

feeling function: (Jungian theory). The function in which feelings predominate.

figure-ground relationship: 1. The Gestalt school of psychology term for a factor of perception. 2. Perls's term to indicate the influence of past experience on here-and-now perception.

fixation: 1. Neurosis. 2. Being stuck at a primitive level of emotional development.

fight-or-flight syndrome: Cannon's term for the bodily changes that occur as the result of emergency and threat. This phenomenon has been extended to include the *freeze response* so that now we speak of the *fight-flight-freeze syndrome.*

folklore and fairy tale: Stories handed down over generations.

formal operations: (Piagetian theory). The fourth and highest (adult) level of cognitive development. The person is now able to invent truly creative solutions to problems.

free association: Freudian therapy in which the patient relates whatever stray thoughts or emotions come to mind without having to feel guilt, shame, or remorse.

free-floating anxiety: Anxiety that becomes attached to anything the person is thinking about.

Freudian slips: Slips-of-the-tongue and slips-of-the-pen that are presumed to be discharges from the unconscious.

functional thinking: (Piagetian theory). The tendency for preoperative children to believe that everything has a purpose related to them.

fundamental attribution bias: The tendency to attribute better motives to oneself than to others.

games people play: Berne's term for the repetitive life scripts we write for ourselves.

gemeinschaftsgefühl: Adler's term for the love of all humankind.

gender bias: Preconceptions about a person based upon whether the person is male or female.

gender splitting: Levinson's term for the division of roles that limit women's lives and destinies.

General Adaptation Syndrome: Selye's term for the changes that occur as the result of prolonged stress, and which ultimately produce disease and death.

generalized responses: Behaviors that are similar to conditioned responses and aroused by generalized stimuli.

generalized stimuli: Stimuli that are similar to conditioned stimuli.

generativity: The crisis and life task of Erikson's psychosocial development that occurs after age 40 and before old age.

genital stage: (Freudian theory). The final stage of psychosexual growth, or adult stage.

genetic counseling: Counseling that focuses on the probability of having a child with birth defects, and the community resources available to deal with this situation.

genetic factors: Any physical, mental, or emotional trait that is not due to environmental factors.

gentle birth: Leboyer's term for his nonviolent birthing methods.

gestalt: The German word meaning the whole pattern or configuration.

gestalt therapy: The therapeutic approach formulated by Frederich Perls, which emphasizes the here-and-now.

global anxiety: Anxiety that has to do with the destruction of the planet and the very survival of the human race.

growth groups: Groups of individuals who assemble for the purposes of increasing the effectiveness of our everyday life and fostering our creative thinking and behaviors.

growth model: The personality theories that emphasize free will and our human ability to make conscious choice and change.

guided mastery: A therapeutic technique that focuses on replacing negative fantasies and self-talk with positive and constructive ones.

hallucinations: The acceptance of certain phenomena as external reality when, in fact, the phenomena are private and autistic experiences.

hallucinogenic drugs: Drugs which produce hallucinations or altered consciousness.

hedonism: The philosophy of life that emphasizes earthly pleasures.

here-and-now: Perls' therapeutic emphasis to enable people to become focused on their present experience.

Hero Archetype: (Jung and Campbell) Each person's personal fable.

heterogeneous: Mixed; made up of many elements.

hierarchy of needs: Maslow's seven-stage theory of motivation.

high risk: Vulnerable to a particular disease or defect.

holistic health approach: Treatment of the entire person, including the physical, cognitive, social, emotional, and spiritual dimensions.

homeostasis: An ideal state of chemical balance within the body which exists only in theory.

homosexuality: A preference for a same-gender person as a sexual partner.

hormones: Chemicals produced by the body and which influence behavior.

hot reactors: People whose physical responses are extreme.

human becoming: Allport's term to indicate that we are continually growing, maturing, evolving.

human relations approach: Management style that incorporates Theory Y assumptions.

humanistic psychology: Personality theory that fosters personality integration and creative growth, base on the assumption that we are capable of free will, choice and change.

hypnosis: An altered level of consciousness marked by an intense communication process between the transductor (hypnotist) and the subject.

hysterical paralysis: Paralysis whose etiology lies in psychological factors.

id: (Freudian theory). The unconscious, unsocialized aspect of the personality dominated by the libido and the pleasure-pain principle.

individuation: Jung's term for the process by which we know ourselves as uniquely individual beings. At that point of evolution of personality we act from inner convictions and not as the result of group pressure or mob psychology.

industry: (Eriksonian theory). The crisis and life task of the school-age child, which is learning to work.

inferiority-superiority complex: Adler's term for our need to find some ways in which to be superior to others, while all the while feeling ourselves to be inferior.

initiative: (Eriksonian theory). The crisis and life task of the pre–grade school child.

innate: Inborn, genetic, nativist, inherited.

insight therapies: Therapeutic situations which seek self-understanding and look for the etiology of a psychological problem on the assumption that insight will lead to catharsis.

insulation: The defense mechanism by which we ignore problematic situations.

intervening variable: The extraneous factor that interferes with our intended research objectives.

intimacy: (Eriksonian theory). The crisis and life task of the young adult stage to relate to others.

introjected values: Beliefs we adopt through the socialization process and of which we are largely unaware.

introspection: The process of self-examination and self-analysis.

introversion: Jung's term for our need to withdraw from society and center ourselves in our thoughts and feelings.

intuiting function: Jung's term for the way we take in information that we cannot logically explain.

Lamaze method: A drugless birthing method that emphasizes enabling the mother to work with the birthing process through breathing and muscular cooperation.

latency stage: (Freudian theory). The stage of psychosexual development in which the libidinal drive is quiescent, between ages 6 and puberty.

latent dream: (Freudian dream interpretation). The real meaning of the dream symbols.

learned helplessness: Seligman's term for the person who has not developed adequate coping skills.

learning: Behavior that is not attributable to innate and maturational factors and which is relatively permanent.

left-brain/right-brain research: Research that studies left brain and right brain functioning and the differences between the two halfs of the brain.

libido/libidinal drive: (Freudian theory) 1. In its narrowest sense, the sexual drive. 2. The drive toward pleasure.

life crisis units (LCUs): The units of measurement for the amount of change in one's living.

life dream: The romantic goal that an adolescent develops about the future, often unrealistic in terms of the adolescent's abilities and financial means.

life lie: (Adler). Living in a way that is not in harmony with one's own life style.

life scripts: The repetitive and nonproductive dramas that people play out, rather than seeking ways to learn more effective behavior.

life span: The broad length and process of one's life.

life stages: Those personality theories that assume the human life span is characterized by qualitative changes in our needs, wants, satisfactions, values, etc.

life style: Adler's term to describe the direction, flow, and meaning of a person's life.

life tasks: (Eriksonian theory). The competencies that each person must achieve during the various life stages toward personality integration.

locus of control (LOC): A person's worldview of whether one's fate is externally controlled by outside forces or internal and under one's own control.

logotherapy: The therapy devised by Viktor Frankl that focuses on the need for meaning in one's life.

long-term memory: More-or-less permanent memory.

lucid dreaming: Conscious dreaming.

management theory: The scientific study of work motivation, leadership, and organizations.

mandala: An Eastern circular or quadrilateral figure representing wholeness, health, and personality integration.

manifest dream: Freud's term for the surface dream, as contrasted with the latent dream.

massed practice: Studying a given amount of material over long periods as opposed to distributed practice. Example: Crash studying.

maturation: Growth as the result of the unraveling of our genetic program as contrasted with learning.

mediation: 1. Piaget's term for the cognitive process. 2. An alternative to divorce with an assumptive base of cooperation.

metastudy: Research that analyzes and summarizes many other pieces of research in a particular area.

midlife crisis: (Jungian theory). The upheaval that comes around age 40 as the result of spiritual bankruptcy.

mindgames: A therapeutic technique in which groups are directed toward certain fantasies in order to foster inner awareness and the person's creativity.

mnemonic devices: A memory technique.

mood disorders: Dysfunctional personality patterns that include depression and bipolar mood disorder.

mores: Strong ideas of right and wrong a society or culture develops.

motor learning: Learning with use of muscles; this learning is very resistant to extinction.

multisensory approach: Using two or more sense modalities to get material into the long-term memory.

myth: A story, tale, fable, or epic that attempts to explain the natural and social history of the world.

need-drive state: The psychophysical motivation to restore homeostasis.

negative role model: A person we do not want to be like.

neoFreudians: Psychoanalysts trained in Freudian theory and methods but who include other motivational factors of human behavior over and beyond the sexual drive, such as birth order and cultural determinants.

networking: Managerial organization that fosters lateral communication instead of the authoritarian top-down communication.

neurosis: Freud's term for the fixation of emotional development at a primitive level, no longer included in the *DSM*.

neurotransmitters: The chemicals released by a neuron that fire neighboring neurotransmitters (or that prevent them from firing). At present, more than 200 neurotransmitters have been discovered, such as *dopamine, adrenalin, noradrenalin, seratonin,* and so on. Only a few of these transmitters are understood in terms of their function.

neutral stimulus: A stimulus that does not arouse a conditioned response.

nocturnal emissions: Orgasms or emissions of semen while asleep, generally during erotic dreams.

nondirective counseling: Rogers's therapeutic technique that emphasizes reflective listening and avoids interpretations.

noogenic neurosis: Viktor Frankl's theory that the present psychological illness of our times is lack of meaning.

nuclear family: The urban/suburban type of family that consists of parents and children as contrasted with the extended family.

obedience experiments: Milgrim's studies of the tendency of people to obey authority without question.

object permanence: Piaget's term for the infant's ability to comprehend that objects exist in the world even if they are not seen.

obsessive-compulsive personality: Freud's term for persons who are characterized by the need to repeat ritualistic actions, who are excessively tidy, and who value money and cleanliness as goodness.

Oedipus complex: (Freudian theory). The tendency of the boy child to develop a strong emotional attachment to his mother.

open-mindedness: Adorno's description of persons who have a democratic worldview.

operant conditioning: Skinner's approach to conditioning, which emphasizes learning by the reinforcement of emitted behaviors.

opiates: Drugs derived from opium.

oral stage: (Freudian theory). The first stage of psychosexual development in which the libidinal drive is focused in the area of the mouth.

oral personality: (Freudian theory). A person fixated at the oral stage of psychosexual development.

organizations of mind: Piaget's term for the four different cognitive stages.

overcompensation: Adler's term for the human tendency to exaggerate one aspect of their psychophysical development in order to be superior to others.

pain-attack response: Azrin's term for the innate tendency to attack other animals or objects as the result of pain.

panic attack: An attack of anxiety that is so severe that it can mimic heart trouble, asthma, extreme phobia, paralysis, etc.

paradigm: 1. A framework of thought that explains certain aspects of reality as we construe it from one era to another. 2. Material studied intensively over a given period of time.

parasympathetic system: The organ system functioning at times of quiet, relaxation, or sleep wherein the body repairs and renourishes, as contrasted to the sympathetic system.

parenting styles: Three common styles of parenting have been identified: the authoritarian, the authoritative, and the democratic.

passive aggression: The defense mechanism of seeming to cooperate but covertly sabotaging the other person's request or demand.

passive-dependent personality: (Freud). Fixation of the personality at the oral stage of psychosexual development.

peak experiences: Maslow's term for the experience that has been variously labeled as the mystic experience, satori, Zen, enlightenment, at-onement, attunement, cosmic consciousness, and the "peace that passeth all understanding."

peer-support groups: A therapeutic group situation whose members come together for the purpose of processing a common life situation or problem.

people skills: 1. The ability of a leader to foster communication between individuals and groups. 2. The ability to engage in friendly communication with everyone.

perception: The meaning we attach to sensory experience.

perceptual defense: A defense mechanism by which a person screens out disagreeable perceptions.

permissive parenting: The parenting style that is child-centered based on nondirective counseling.

Persona: (Jungian theory). The public face or mask we wear (our outward personality) and which we believe ourselves to be, as contrasted with the Shadow aspects of our personality.

personal fable: Elkind's term for the adolescent's belief in his own special uniqueness, the Hero of his society.

personality: A person's characteristic but dynamic way of responding to people and events, influenced by factors of age, gender, health, heredity, intelligence, socioeconomic and cultural factors, etc.

personality integration: The process or processes by which persons assimilate and harmonize their physical, cognitive, and social/emotional life experiences.

personality theorists: Social scientists who construct models of personality development over the life span.

persons-in-process: Rogers's term for those persons who are aware of their need for self-understanding and continual growth throughout the life span.

phallic stage: (Freudian theory). The third stage of psychosexual development in which the libidinal drive is focused on the genitals.

phenomenology: A person's worldview; the perceived possibilities in life or lack of them.

phobia: An unreasonable and exaggerated fear that renders the person dysfunctional.

placebo control group: An experimental group used for the purpose of measuring the placebo effect.

placebo effect: Healing as the result of a belief in an object, person, or event.

placebo pills: Pills which are not medicinal, but which are given to patients for the placebo effect.

play therapy: A therapy devised for children based on the principles of free play.

pleasure/pain principle: (Freudian theory). The tendency to seek pleasure and avoid pain, the chief psychological attribute of the id.

polarities: Jung's theory of personality based on oppositional forces, as in introversion/extraversion; sensing/feeling; Persona/Shadow, etc.

polygamy: Marriage of one man with two or more women.

positive reinforcement: Any event which increases the probability of a response.

postconventional morality: The third and highest level of Kohlberg's theory of moral/ethical development.

posttraumatic stress disorder (PTSD): A physical or emotional reaction to stressful situations such as war, natural catastrophe, or personal tragedy.

prana: According to Hindu philosophy, the energy of the universe.

pranayama: In Hindu philosophy, breathing patterns which increase the person's prana.

preconventional morality: The first level of Kohlberg's theory of moral/ethical development, typical of young children and delinquents.

prejudice: 1. Prejudgment. 2. Judgmental thinking about a person or group without personal knowledge of the person or group.

preoperational stage: The second stage of Piaget's theory of cognitive development.

primary group: The family we are born into or adopted into.

primary perception: Sensory input independent of symbolic meaning.

primary reinforcers: Reinforcers based on need/drive states such as food, water, etc.

primary sexual characteristics: The reproductive organs.

progressive relaxation: Jacobson's method of inducing an extremely calm state of bodymind.

projection: Assigning our own thoughts and feelings to others.

propriate strivings: Allport's term for those conscious motivations specific to human beings and which vary according to each person's uniqueness.

psychoanalysis: Freud's specific therapeutic approach, which seeks to reveal the person's psychodynamics.

psychodynamics: The unconscious conflicts that are the wellsprings of human motivation.

psychonauts: Persons eager to adventure into their highest possible personality development via self-awareness, growth and evolution.

psychoneuroimmunology: A relatively new interdisciplinary science that studies the connection between our emotions, the nervous system, and the immune system.

psychophysical hardiness: Persons who have an unusually strong and healthy body integration despite the stresses and strain of modern life.

psychoprophylactic method (PPM): The Russian method of birthing that gave rise to the Lamaze method.

psychosexual development: Freud's five-stage theory of human emotional development.

psychosis: The acute stage of mental disorders.

psychosocial development: Erikson's theory of social/emotional maturation and learning, which is composed of eight life stages.

psychosomatic disease: Emotional and/or physical problems as the result of stress.

psychosomatic medicine: Research that investigates the psychological correlates of illness.

psychotherapy: Healing of the mindbody.

puberty: The physical changes that occur between 10 and 15 years of age as the result of maturation.

qualitative changes: Personality changes that are not simply quantitative or additive but are changes in essence.

quantitative changes: Changes of the additive type, as contrasted with qualitative changes.

racial unconscious: Jung's term for inherited memory or dispositions toward certain cognitive schemas and behaviors.

rational-emotive therapy (RET): Albert Ellis's form of therapy, which focuses on behavioral changes, especially those that eliminate irrational and self-destructive beliefs.

rationalization: The defense mechanism by which we deny the real problem by constructing an alibi to protect our self-esteem.

reaction formation: The defense mechanism by which we deny our unacceptable thoughts and feelings by expressing opposite behaviors.

reality therapy: Glasser's form of behavior therapy, which is based on social contracts or agreements between the person and others.

reality principle: (Freudian theory). As a result of the socialization process, the acquisition of principles of behavior that warn us to be careful about our behaviors because of their possible consequences.

rebirthing therapy: A therapeutic technique of having persons reexperience their traumatic birth or infantile rejection so that they can feel welcomed into the world.

reductionist theories: Theories that reduce the achievements of humankind to the reduction of need-drive states.

replication: Repeating a research study or experiment.

repression: Freud's term for the basic defense mechanism by which we "forget" unacceptable or painful material.

rite: A public ceremony that has become traditional and formalized.

rites of passage: VanGennep's term for the rituals and ceremonies that mark a transition in the person's status, such as a christening, a confirmation, a marriage, and a funeral rite.

ritual: A formal or informal ceremony that is repeated and public.

ritualistic behaviors: Repetitive behaviors characteristic of the obsessive-compulsive personality.

role model: A person who seems to us to exemplify the kind of person we would like to emulate.

role expectations: What society believes a person's behavior should be because of sex, age, work, etc.

rote memorization: Memorizing without understanding the meaning. Such memorization is extremely vulnerable to forgetting.

rule making: Piaget's term for the need of 10- to 12-year-olds to establish what is "fair" and "not fair" in their games.

sacred rites: The rites that initiate the person into the sacred orders.

scapegoating: The defense mechanism by which we project our unhappiness or guilt upon other persons who are usually helpless to retaliate or to defend themselves.

schizophrenia: The mental disorder marked by delusions, hallucinations, speech and thought disorders.

scientific skepticism: A basic tenet of science that asserts the need for empirical evidence.

script: The playlets that we write for our life roles.

second half of life: (Jungian theory). Our life span after the age 40 crisis.

secondary group: Peers and friends we develop outside our biological family.

secondary sexual characteristics: Changes of the body structure as the result of puberty that affect other parts of the body besides the reproductive organs.

secondary reinforcers: Reinforcers that are learned, such as smiles, honors, applause.

self-actualizing: Maslow's term for the highest level of human personality development.

self-concept: How we think about ourselves in terms of demographic variables, such as gender, race, age, political affiliation, sibling rank, etc.

self-esteem: How we feel about ourselves, particularly when we compare ourselves to others.

self-talk: The inner dialog that we have with ourselves. The aim of cognitive psychologists is to replace negative self-talk with more positive and constructive self-talk.

sensing function: (Jungian theory). Our grasp of the physical world.

sensory memory: The memory that connects our moment-by-moment neural firing, composed of momentary and fleeting sensations, thoughts, emotions, etc.

sensory-motor stage: (Piagetian theory). The first stage of cognitive growth and organization of mind.

serial monogamy: Two or more marriage mates in sequence, punctuated by divorce.

severe depression: A personality disorder that is characterized by early onset, profound intensity, and long duration.

Shadow: (Jungian theory). The parts of our personality that we disown but which coalesce in our unconscious levels of personality.

shaping of behavior: Reinforcing of desired behaviors through small, successful, successive steps.

short-term memory: The second stage of memory that makes it possible for us to retain small chunks of information for a brief time (such as a telephone number).

sibling: Sister, brother, or litter mate.

sibling rivalry: The competition of children for their parents' attention and affection.

similarity filter: Mate selection influenced by similarities of age, socioeconomic level, education, intelligence, and personality.

simple forgetting: Forgetting as the result of decay of nonmeaningful material.

slips-of-the-pen: (Freudian theory). So-called "accidents" of writing that are actually discharges of unconscious material.

slips-of-the-tongue: (Freudian theory). So-called "accidents" of speech that are actually discharges of unconscious material.

slow-to-warm child: The child who is shy and irritable in new situations but who eventually adapts to the environment.

social anxiety: Anxiety as the result of the real or perceived obligation to live up to certain societal standards.

social learning theory: Bandura's theory for how we learn by observation and imitation.

social loafing: Tendency for persons in a group to let others do the work.

social sanctions: The positive and negative responses of society toward certain behaviors.

socialization: The process by which we are molded in certain ways by our culture, parents, teachers, peer group, colleagues, etc.

sociopathic personality: The personality disfunction of the person who is seemingly without compassion for other persons' welfare; sometimes called a "moral moron."

spiritual bankruptcy: Jung's term for persons who have neglected the spiritual dimension in the first half of their lives.

spiritual dimension: That aspect of personality functioning that is based on a transcending model of human nature.

spontaneous recovery: The reappearance of the conditioned response as a function of time.

spontaneous remission: The disappearance of symptoms without the use of medication or psychotherapy.

stage of alarm: The first stage of the General Adaptation Syndrome, characterized by "sick" behavior and physiology.

stage of exhaustion: The last stage of the General Adaptation Syndrome, which leads to death if the stress or stressors are not removed.

stage of moral realism and restraint: (Piagetian theory). The first stage of a child's moral/ethical development, which has to do with obedience, a rigid "black or white" system of justice, as contrasted to the stage of moral relativity and cooperation.

stage of moral relativity and cooperation: (Piagetian theory). The second stage of a child's moral/ethical development, in which the child can begin to comprehend relative values and the concept of mercy, as contrasted to the stage of moral realism and restraint.

stage of resistance: The second stage of the General Adaptation Syndrome, in which the animal seems to recover from stress.

stereotypes: Value judgments about a person or group of persons by those who have no personal knowledge on which to base their judgments.

stimulants: Drugs that cause the nervous system to act and react faster.

stress: The problems and challenges that produce wear-and-tear on the body.

stress inoculation: Techniques by which people are given experience in solving *possible future* crises and dilemmas.

sublimation: The defense mechanism by which we transform unacceptable behaviors into socially acceptable behaviors.

superego: In Freudian terms, the introjected societal values, which Freud equated with the conscience.

suppression: Consciously controlling an impulse to act.

sympathetic system: The body's state when expending energy, as contrasted to the parasympathetic system.

systematic desensitization: Wolpe's therapy that seeks to eliminate phobic reactions through deep relaxation followed by introducing a hierarchy of anxiety-provoking stimuli.

teleology: An explanation for events that presumes there is a purposeful end. Teleological explanations go against the grain of most researchers as being outside of the realm of scientific investigation and belonging more properly to the realm of philosophy and theology.

Theory X: A term for the authoritarian approach to management.

Theory Y: McGregor's term for the human relations approach to management.

Theory Z: A modification of Theory Y which considers the willingness of the employee to act responsibly or not, sometimes called the "contingency theory."

therapy: Healing methods.

thinking function: Jung's term for the process whereby we come to rational decisions as opposed to decisions made by feelings.

time out: A technique of Skinner's environmental engineering.

tip-of-the-tongue phenomenon: Knowing that we know something but feeling that we are unable at the moment to call it up.

transactional analysis (TA): A therapeutic situation based on analyzing transactions according to ego states.

transcending model of human nature: Personality theories based on assumptions of continual growth, free will, and evolution of the human spirit.

transcending personalities: 1. Persons who rise above the limitations and worldviews of their culture and time-space situation. 2. Those who go beyond material need/value states to higher, more universal values.

transpersonal: Referring to universal themes of human existence (the meaning of life, death, rebirth, and the unfolding of generations, etc.).

trauma: An injurious event, whether physical or psychological.

Trickster: An Archetype that polarizes the mischievous, spontaneous, and creative aspects of human personality.

twice-born: William James's term for those who have undergone depression and have recovered.

twin studies: Studies of identical twins separated at birth and brought up in different environments.

type psychology: Jung's term for his personality theory based on innate characteristics of human functioning.

Type-A behavior: Behavior characterized by a fierce competitive drive and correlated with a tendency toward heart attack.

unconditioned stimulus (UCS): Any event that arouses an unlearned (reflexive) response.

unconditional positive regard: Rogers's term for the therapist's attitude toward his client in creating a warm and safe climate for the client to reveal his inner self and thereby to grow and evolve.

unconditioned response: Any unlearned (reflexive) behavior.

unconscious: Those memories, thoughts, and feelings driven out of our conscious awareness.

unconscious motivation: Behaviors arising from psychodynamic conflicts.

Underdog and Top Dog: Perls's terms for the conflicts of our parents, which we have introjected as part of our unconscious dynamics.

unfinished situations: Perls's term for the unresolved conflicts of our earlier life.

Universal Unconscious: Jung's term to indicate the relatedness and purposefulness of all phenomena.

visualization technique: Simonton's term for his holistic health approach to illness.

voodoo death: The sickness and ultimate demise of a person as the result of having been cursed by natural or supernatural beings.

win-win solutions: Solutions of conflict that to some extent benefit everyone involved.

wisdom of the body: Cannon's term for the physiological changes of the body as it seeks to restore homeostasis.

Wise Child Archetype: The representation of our innocent and trusting love of the universe and all creatures within it.

Wise Old Woman Archetype: The representation of our intuitive knowledge.

Wise Old Man Archetype: The representation of the knowledge that comes of years and experience.

wish-fulfillment: Freud's term for the symbolic meaning of many dream symbols.

work ethic: The philosophy that work is beneficial for the development of human character.

workaholics: Persons who tend to work over and beyond the normal work schedule.

worldview: 1. One's whole outlook on the meaning and possibilities of one's life. 2. The translation of the German word *Weltanschaung,* indicating the unconscious total fabric of one's beliefs and assumptions about what one chooses.

Zeigarnik effect: The tendency for us to remember uncompleted tasks more than completed tasks.

REFERENCES

Abel, M. H. (1997). Low birth weight and interactions between traditional risk factors. *The Journal of Genetic Psychology, 158,* 443–456.

Abramson, L. Y., Seligman, M. E. P., & Teasdale, J. (1978). Learned helplessness in humans: Critique and reformulation. *Journal of Abnormal Psychology, 87,* 32–48.

Adams, P. (1999). *House calls.* Montréal: Coffragants.

Adler, A. (1954). *Understanding human nature.* NY: Fawcett.

Adorno, T. W. (1973). *The jargon of authenticity.* Evanston, IL: Northwestern University Press.

Agras, W. S. (1985). *Panic: Facing fears, phobias, and anxiety.* NY: W.H. Freeman.

Akir, A. & Glick, S.M. (1998). *Medical Education, 32*(2), 133–137.

Alba, R. D. (1990). *Ethnic Identity.* London: Yale University Press.

Alexander, F. (1950). *Psychosomatic medicine.* NY: W.W. Norton.

Allport, G. (1955). *Becoming: Basic considerations for a psychology of personality.* New Haven, CT: Yale University Press.

Amato, P. R. (1981). Urban-rural differences in helping field studies based on a taxonomic organization of helping episodes. *Journal of Personality and Social Psychology, 114,* 289–290.

(A.P.A.) American Psychiatric Association. (1994). *Diagnostic and statistical manual of mental disorders,* 4th ed. *(DSM-IV).* Washington, DC: Author.

Apps, J. (1982). *Returning to school: Study skills for adults.* NY: McGraw-Hill.

Arbel, N., & Stravynski, A. (1991). A retrospective study of separation in the development of adult avoidant personality disorder. *Acta Psychiatrica Scandinavia, 83*(3), 174–178.

Arendt, H. (1970). *The human condition.* Chicago: University of Chicago Press.

Arivizu, D. R. (Spring, 1995). The care voice and American Indian college education. *Journal of American Indian Education, 34*(3), 1–17.

Asch, S. (1951). Effects of group pressure upon the modification and distortion of judgments. In H. Guetzkow (Ed.), *Groups, leadership, and men: Research in human reactions* (pp. 177–190). Pittsburgh, PA: Carnegie Press.

Axinn, W. G., Barber, J. S., & Thornton, A. (November, 1998). The long-term impact of parents' childbearing decisions on children's self-esteem. *Demography, 35*(4), 435–443.

Axline, V. (1964). *Dibs in search of self.* Boston: Houghton-Mifflin.

Azar, B. (June, 1999a). Does group therapy mean longer life? *American Psychological Association Monitor, 30*(6), 13–14.

Azar, B. (June, 1999b). Probing links between stress and cancer. *American Psychological Association Monitor, 30*(6), 15.

Azrin, N. (1967). Pain and aggression. In *Readings in "Psychology Today,"* pp. 114–121. Del Mar, CA: CRM Books.

Bandura, A. (1986). *Social foundations of thought and action: A social-cognitive theory.* Englewood Cliffs, NJ: Prentice Hall.

Barron, F. (1970). *The shaping of behavior: Conflict, choice and growth.* NY: Harper & Row.

Barton, M. A., & Bischoff, R. J. (1998). Rocks and rituals in producing therapeutic change. *Journal of Family Psychotherapy, 9*(3), 31–44.

Baumeister, R. (1991). *Escaping the self.* NY: Basic Books.

Baumrind, D. (1973). Childcare practices anteceding three patterns of preschool behavior. *Genetic Psychological Monographs, 75,* 43–88.

Baumrind, D. (1995). *Child maltreatment and optimal caregiving in social contexts.* NY: Garland.

Beane, J., & Lipka, R. P. (1986). *Self-esteem, self-concept, and the curriculum.* NY: Teacher's College Press.

Beck, A. T. (1991). Cognitive therapy: A 30-year retrospective. *American Psychologist, 46,* 368–375.

Beebe, S. A., Beebe, S. J., Redmond, M. V. (1996). *Interpersonal communication: Relating to others.* Boston: Allyn & Bacon.

Beecher, H. K. (1961). Surgery as a placebo. *Journal of the American Medical Association, 176,* 1102.

Bem, D. J. (1985). Androgyny and gender schema theory: A conceptual and empirical integration. In T. B. Sonderegger (Ed.), Nebraska symposium on motivation, 1984; *Psychology and Gender, 32.* Lincoln, NE: University of Nebraska Press.

Benson, H. (1975). *The relaxation response.* NY: Morrow.

Berger, C. R., & Bradac, J. J. (1982). *Language and social knowledge: Uncertainty in interpersonal relations.* Baltimore, MD: Edward Arnold.

Berndt, T. J., & Perry, T. B. (1990). Distinctive features and effects of early adolescent friendships. In R. Montemayor (Ed.), *Advances in Adolescent Research.* Greenwich, CT: JAI Press.

Berne, E. (1978). *Games people play.* Westminster, MD: Ballantine Books.

Bettelheim, B. (1976). *The uses of enchantment: The meaning and importance of fairy tales.* NY: Knopf.

Blanchard, K., & Johnson, S. (1982). *The one minute manager.* NY: Berkeley.

Bly, R. (1992). *A book about men.* NY: Random House.

Bohling, C. A. (1989). *On the Monday side of the street: A text on alcoholism for professional and lay people.* St. Albans, MO: Bohling, Corey.

Bohmer, C., & Parrot, A. (1993). *Sexual assault on campus.* NY: Lexington Books.

Bornstein, R. F. (1992). The dependent personality: Developmental, social, and clinical perspectives. *Psychological Bulletin, 112*(1), 3–23.

Bouchard, Jr., T. J., Lykken, D. T., McGue, M., Segal, N. L., & Tellegen, A. (1990). Sources of human psychological differences: The Minnesota study of twins reared apart. *Science, 212,* 1055–1059.

Bowlby, J. (1977). The making and breaking of affectional bonds. *British Journal of Psychiatry, 130,* 201–210.

Brodnick, M. B. (1986). Born on borrowed time. *Science, 7,* 68–69.

Brownlee, S. (August 9, 1999). Inside the teen brain. *U.S. News & World Report, 127*(6), 45–50.

Brownstein, R (1995). America's anxiety attack. *Annual editions: Life management,* pp. 220–228. Guilford, CT: Dushkin.

Butler, R. N. (1980). *Why survive? Being old in America.* NY: Harper & Row.

Campbell, J. (1988). *The power of myth.* Garden City, NY: Doubleday.

Cannon, W. B. (1963). *The wisdom of the body,* 2nd ed. NY: Harper & Row.

Cannon, W. B. (1929). *Bodily changes in pain, hunger, fear and rage,* rev. ed. NY: Appleton-Century-Crofts.

Carrie, H. (1999). *Preventing sexual harassment at work.* Geneva: International Labour Office: Conditions of Work Branch.

Capacchione, L. (1991). *Recovery of your inner child.* NY: Simon & Schuster.

Capone, P. (1991). *The little girl within: Overcoming memories of childhood.* Saratoga, CA: R&E.

Caron, S. L, & Carter, D. B. (October, 1997). The relationships among sex role orientation, egalitarianism, attitudes toward sexuality, and attitudes toward violence against women. *The Journal of Social Psychology, 137,* 568–587.

Change, K. A. (1996). Culture, power and the social construction of morality: Moral voices of Chinese students. *Journal of Moral Education, 25*(2), 141–157.

Cherry, M. J. (1994). *Gilligan's "different voice" theory: A just cause for composition inquiry or just another conceptual bandwagon?* Paper presented at the 45th Annual Meeting of the Conference on College Composition and Communication (March 16–19, 1994), Nashville, TN.

Chess, S., Thomas, A., and Birch, H. (1976). *Your child is a person: A psychological approach to parenthood without guilt.* NY: Penguin Books.

Cholst, S. (1991). *Finding love in a cold world.* NY: Beau Rivage.

Chopra, D. (1990). *Quantum healing.* NY: Bantam Books.

Clark, H. H. (1991). Words, the world, and their possibilities. In G. R. Lockhead & J. R. Pomerantz (Eds.), *The perception of structure,* pp. 263–277. Washington, DC: American Psychological Association.

Cobb, S., & Rose, R. (1973). Hypertension, peptic ulcer and diabetes in air-traffic controllers. *Journal of the American Medical Association, 224,* 489–492.

Cochran, S. D., & Mays, V. M. (1990). Sex, lies and HIV. *New England Journal of Medicine, 322,* 774–775.

Cochran, L. (1990). *The sense of vocation: A study of career and life development.* NY: State University of New York Press.

Cohen, S., & Herbert, T. B. (1996). Health psychology: Psychological factors and physical disease from the perspective of human psychoneuroimmunology. *Annual Review of Psychology, 47,* 113–142.

Cohen, S., & Williamson, G. M. (1991). Stress and infectious diseases in humans. *Psychological Bulletin, 109* (1), 5–24.

Coleman, M., & Gannon, I. H. (1985). Love and sex-role stereotypes: Do macho men and feminine women make better lovers? *Journal of Personality and Social Psychology, 49,* 170–176.

Compston, Christopher. (1998). *Breaking up without cracking up: Reducing the pain of separation and divorce.* London: HarperCollins.

Conn, J. H., & Kanner, L. (1947). Children's awareness of sex differences. *Journal of Child Psychiatry, 1,* 3–57.

Corewen, L. (1988). *Your resume: Key to a better job,* 3rd ed. Englewood Cliffs, NJ: Prentice Hall.

Cousins, N. (1979). *Anatomy of an illness as perceived by the patient: Reflections on healing and regeneration.* NY: W.W. Norton.

Csikszentmihalyi, M. (1997). Happiness and creativity. *The Futurist, 31,* 34–38. Bethesda, MD: World Future Society.

Curtis, J. M., & Cowell, D. R. (1993). Relation of birth order and scores on measures of pathological narcissism. *Psychological Report, 72,* 311–315.

Darley, J., & Latane, B. (1986). Thy brother's keeper, Classic experiment 11: Diffusion of responsibility. In S. Schwartz (Ed.). *Classic studies in psychology,* pp. 122–142. Mountainview, CA: Mayfield.

Davidson, J. (1995). Overworked Americans or overwhelmed Americans? *Annual editions: Sociology,* pp. 22–25. Guilford, CT: Dushkin.

Dean, A. R. (Spring, 1997). Humor and laughter in palliative care. *Journal of Palliative Care, 13*(1), 34–39.

Dement, W. C. (1978). *Some must watch while some must sleep.* NY: W.W. Norton.

deTocqueville, A. (1830). *Democracy in America.* NY: Knopf. (Many editions available.)

Dew, R. F. (1994). *The family heart: A memoir of when our son came out.* Reading, MA: Addison-Wesley.

Dollard, J., & Miller, N. E. (1966). What is a neurosis? In R. L. Wren (Ed.), *Basic contributions to psychology readings,* pp. 206–211. Belmont, CA: Wadsworth.

Dorman, M. (1999). *The killing of Kitty Genovese* [WWW document]. URL. http://www.lihistory.com/8/hs818a.htm.

Dowling, E. (1999). *Working with children and parents through separation and divorce: The changing lives of children.* NY: Macmillan.

Duck, S. (1994). Steady as (s)he goes: Relational maintenance as a shared meaning system. In D. J. Canary and L. Stafford (Eds.), *Communication and relational maintenance,* pp. 45–60. San Diego: Academic Press.

Dunbar, F. (1955). *Mind and body: Psychosomatic medicine,* rev. ed. NY: Random House.

Dunn, J. (1988). *The beginnings of social understanding.* Cambridge, MA: Harvard University Press.

Durkheim, E. (1884). *Suicide.* NY: Free Press.

Dym, B., & Glenn, M. (1993). *Couples: Exploring and understanding the cycles of intimate relationships.* NY: Harper-Collins.

Ebbinghouse, H. (1913). *Memory: A contribution to experimental psychology* (H. Ruger & C. Bussenius, Trans.). NY: Teacher's College Press. (Original work published 1885.)

Elkind, D. (1984). *All grown up and no place to go: Teenagers in crisis.* Reading, MA: Addison-Wesley.

Elkind, D. (1988). *Growing up: Too fast, too soon.* Reading, MA: Addison-Wesley.

Elkind, D. (1989). *Miseducation: Preschoolers at risk.* NY: Knopf.

Ellis, A., & Dryden, W. (1987). *The practice of rational emotive therapy.* NY: Springer-Verlag.

Emery, R. E., & Wyer, M. M. (1987). Divorce mediation. *American Psychologist, 42,* 472–480.

Erikson, E. (1950). *Childhood and society.* NY: W. W. Norton.

Fancher, R. (1979). *Pioneers of psychology.* NY: W. W. Norton.

Farber, I. E. (1957). Brainwashing, conditioning, and DDD (debility, dependency, and dread). Iowa City, IA: Sociometry.

Feist, G. J. (1998). *Personality and Social Psychology Review, 2*(4), 290–309.

Festinger, L. A. (1957). *A theory of cognitive dissonance.* Stanford, CA: Stanford University Press.

Fink, M. (1992). Electroconvulsive therapy. In E. S. Paykel (Ed.), *Handbook of affective disorders.* NY: Guilford.

Fischman, J. (May, 1987). The ups and downs of teenage life. *Psychology Today,* 56–57.

Fischman, J. (1987). Type-A on trial. *Psychology Today, 21,* 42–50.

Fitzpatrick, K. M. (1999). Violent victimization among America's school children. *Journal of Interpersonal Violence, 14*(10), 1055–1069.

Flynn, J. R. (1987). Massive IQ gains in 14 nations: What IQ tests really measure. *Psychological Bulletin, 101,* 171–191

Folberg, J., & Taylor, A. (1984). *Mediation: A comprehensive guide to resolve conflicts without litigation.* San Francisco: Jossey-Bass.

Forsyth, D. R. (1983). *An introduction to group dynamics.* Monterey, CA: Brooks-Cole.

Frances, A., First, M. B., and Pincus, H. A. (1995, June). The DSM-IV: Its Value and Limitations. *The Harvard Mental Health Letter, 11,* 4–6.

Frank, J. (1964). The faith that heals. *Johns Hopkins University Medical Journal, 137,* 127–131.

Frankl, V. (1962). *Man's search for meaning: An introduction to logotherapy.* Boston: Beacon Press.

Frazier, S. H. (1994). *Psychotrends: What kind of a people are we becoming?* NY: Simon & Schuster.

Freedman, D. G. (1974). *Human infancy: An evolutionary perspective.* NY: Halstead Press.

Freud, A. (1926). *The psychoanalytic treatment of children.* NY: Halstead Press.

Freud, S. (1900). *The interpretation of dreams.* London: Hogarth Press.

Friedman, H. S., & Rosenman, R. H. (1974). *Type-A behavior and your heart.* NY: Fawcett.

Fromm, E. (1956). *The art of loving.* NY: Bantam Books.

Fromm, E. (1976). *Escape from freedom.* NY: Avon Books.

Furr, L. A. (Fall,1998). Father's characteristics and their children's scores on college entrance exams: A comparison of intact and divorced families. *Adolescence, 33,* 533–542.

Furstenberg, F. F. (Spring,1996). The future of marriage. *American Demographics, 18,* 34–37.

Gabbard, G. O. (1990). *Psychodynamic psychiatry in clinical practice.* Washington, DC: American Psychiatric Press.

Galbraith, K. (1985). *The affluent society,* rev. ed. NY: New American Library.

Gardner, H. (1993). *Multiple Intelligences: The theory in practice.* NY: Basic Books.

Gemignani, J. (November, 1998). Curbing the tobacco craving. *Business & Health, 16*(11), 45–46.

Gilbert, S. (1999). Social ties reduce the risk of a cold. In *Annual Editions 99/00: Social Psychology,* 3rd. ed., (pp. 114–115). Guilford, CT: Dushkin/McGraw-Hill.

Gilligan, C. (1982). *In a different voice.* Cambridge, MA: Harvard University Press.

Glasser, W. (1967). *Reality therapy.* NY: Harper & Row.

Glenn, N. D. (1995). What's happening to American marriage? *Annual Editions: Marriage and Family,* pp. 80–83. Guilford, CT: Dushkin.

Goedert, L. W. (1991). *The troubled teens: Too old for the pediatrician, too young for the gynecologist.* NY: Vantage.

Goleman, D. (1995). *Emotional intelligence.* NY: Bantam Books.

Goodwin, F. K., & Jamison, K. R., (Eds.). (1990). *Manic-depressive illness.* NY: Oxford University Press.

Gordon, Thomas. (1970). *P.E.T.: Parent effectiveness training.* NY: Peter H. Wyden.

Gordon, Thomas. (1974). *T.E.T.: Teacher effectiveness training.* NY: David McKay.

Gordon, Thomas. (1977). *Leader effectiveness training, L. E. T.* NY: Wyden Books.

Gottesman, I.I. (1991) *Schizophrenic genesis.* NY: W. H. Freeman.

Gray, C.S. (1998). A case history based assessment of female genital mutilation in Sudan. *Evaluation & Program Planning. 21*(4), 429–436.

Gray, J. (1992). *Men are from Mars, Women are from Venus.* NY: HarperCollins.

Gurling, H. M., Sherrington, R. P., Brynjolfsson, J., Read, T., Curtis, D., Mankoo, D. J., Potter, M., & Petursson, H. (1989). Recent and future molecular genetic research into schizophrenia. *Schizophrenia Bulletin, 15*(3), 373–382.

Haavio-Mannila, E. (1995). Family, work, and gender equality: A policy comparison of Scandinavia, the United States, and the former Soviet Union. *Annual Editions: Human Sexuality,* pp. 17–21. Guilford, CT: Dushkin.

Halberstam, J. (1995). How competitive are you? *Annual Editions: Personal Growth and Behavior,* pp. 114–116. Guilford, CT: Dushkin.

Hall, E. T. (1959). *The silent language.* Garden City, NY: Doubleday.

Hall, E. T. (1966). *The hidden dimension.* Garden City, NY: Doubleday & Co.

Hall, G. S. (1904). *Adolescence.* NY: Appleton-Century-Crofts.

Hall, S. S. (August 22, 1999). *The bully in the mirror. New York Times Magazine,* 30–35.

Harris, F. R., Johnston, M. K., & Wolfe, M. M. (1964). Effects of positive social reinforcement of child behavior on regressed crawling of a nursery school child. *Journal of Educational Psychology, 55,* 35–41.

Harris, P. R., & Moran, R. T. (1991). *Managing cultural differences,* 3rd ed. Houston, TX: Gulf.

Harris, T. (1969). *I'm O.K. You're O.K.* NY: Harper & Row.

Hartshorne, H., & May, M. A. (1930). *Studies in the nature of character.* NY: Macmillan.

Harvard Mental Health Letter. (August, 1997). Hearts and mind: Part II. *The Harvard Mental Health Letter, 14*(2), 1–4.

Hilgard, E. R. (1986). *Hypnotic susceptibility*. NY: Harcourt, Brace & World.

Hoffler, M. L. (1991). Empathy, social cognition, and moral action. In K. Kurtines and J. Gewirtz (Eds.), *Handbook of moral behavior and development, Vol. 1: Theory*. Hillside, NH: Lawrence Erlbaum.

Holtzworth-Munroe, A. (1995, August). Marital violence. *The Harvard Mental Health Letter, 12*, 4–6.

Homans, G. C. (1950). *The human group*. NY: Harcourt Brace & World.

Horner, M. (1972). Toward an understanding of achievement-related conflicts in women. *Journal of Social Issues, 28*, 157–175.

Hornyansky, M. (1969). The truth of fables. In S. Egoff, G. T. Stubbs, & L. F. Ashley (Eds.), *Only connect: Readings in children's literature*, pp. 121–132. Toronto: Oxford University Press.

Huxley, A. (1932). *Brave new world*. NY: Harper & Row.

Huxley, A. (1963). *The doors of perception*. NY: Harper & Row.

Huxley, A. (1986). *The devils of Loudon*. Washington, DC: Carroll & Graf.

Hymowitz, C. (May 2, 1988). Five main reasons why managers fail. *Wall Street Journal, 6*.

Ivy, D., & Backlund, P. (1994). *Exploring gender speak: Personal effectiveness in gender communication*. NY: McGraw-Hill.

Jacobson, E. (1938). *Progressive relaxation* (2nd ed.). Chicago: University of Chicago Press.

Jaffe, D. (1974). *Healing from within*. NY: Simon & Schuster.

James, W. (1890). *The principles of psychology*. NY: Dover.

Jenkins, C. D. (1992). The mind and the body. *Annual Editions: Personal Growth and Development*, pp. 59–61. Dushkin, CT: Guilford.

Johns Hopkins Medical Letter: Health after fifty. (July, 1999). *Taking anger to heart*, pp. 1–2. Baltimore, MD: Medletter Associates.

Johnson, L. C. (1982). Sleep deprivation and performance. In W. B. Webb (Ed.). *Biological rhythms, sleep and performance*. NY: Wiley.

Jones, A. (1988). *Women who kill*. NY: Fawcett.

Jones, E. E. (1990). *Interpersonal perception*. NY: W. H. Freeman.

Jourard, S. M. (1971). *The transparent self*. NY: Van Nostrand Reinhold.

Jung, C. G. (1955). *Modern man in search of a soul*. NY: Harcourt Brace Jovanovich.

Jung, C. G. (1963). *Memories, dreams, reflections*. NY: Pantheon Books.

Jung, C. G. (1968). *Analytical psychology: Its theory and practice*. NY: Vintage.

Jung, C. G., & Aniela, J. (1964). *Man and his symbols*. Garden City, NY: Doubleday.

Kagen, J., Reznick, J. S., Snoidman, N., Gibbons, J., et al. (1988). Childhood derivatives of inhibition and lack of inhibition to the unfamiliar. *Child Development, 59*, 1580–1589.

Kasser, T., & Ryan, R. M. (1996). Further examining the American dream: Differential correlates of intrinsic and extrinsic goals. *Journal of Personality and Social Psychology, 22*(3), 280–287.

Kassin, S. (1995). *Psychology*. Boston: Houghton Mifflin.

Kellogg, R. (1970). *Analyzing children's art*. Palo Alto, CA: Mayfield.

Kendler, K. S., & Diehl, S. R. (1993). The genetics of schizophrenia: A current, genetic-epidemiologic perspective. *Schizophrenia Bulletin, 19*, 261–285.

Kety, S. S. (1988). Schizophrenic illness in the families of schizophrenic adoptees: Findings from the Danish national sample. *Schizophrenia Bulletin, 14* (2), 217–222.

Kipnis, A. R., & Heron, E. (1995). Ending the battle between the sexes. *Annual Editions: Sexuality*, pp. 229–234. Guilford, CT: Dushkin.

Kleitman, N. (1953). *Sleep and wakefulness*. Chicago: University of Chicago Press.

Klinger, E. (1990). *Daydreaming*. Los Angeles:Tarcher.

Kobasa, S. C. (1979). Stressful life events, personality, and health: An inquiry into hardiness. *Journal of Personality and Social Psychology, 31*, 1–11.

Kohlberg, L. (1984). *The psychology of moral development: Essays on moral development*. NY: Harper & Row.

Kohn, A. (1998). Challenging behaviorist dogma: Myths about money and motivation. *Compensation and Benefits Review, 30*(2), 27.

Krantzler, M. (1999). *The new creative divorce: How to create a happier, more rewarding life during, and after, your divorce*. Holbrook, MA: Adams.

Kubie, L. S. (1967). Blocks to Creativity. In R. L. Mooney & A. T. Raik (Eds.), *Explorations in creativity*, pp. 33–42. NY: Harper & Row.

Kubler-Ross, E. (1970). On death and dying. Riverside, NJ: Prentice Hall.

Kubler-Ross, E. (1975). *Final stage of growth*. Englewood Cliffs, NJ: Prentice Hall.

Kuch, K., & Cox, B. J. (1992). Symptoms of PTSD in 124 survivors of the Holocaust. *American Journal of Psychiatry, 149*, 337–340.

Kushner, M. G., Riggs, D. S., Foa, E. B., & Miller, S. M. (1992). Perceived controllability and the development of posttraumatic stress disorder (PTSD) in crime victims. *Behavioral Research and Therapy, 31* (1), 105–110.

Kutchins, H., & Kirk, A. K. (1997). *Making us crazy: DSM: The Psychiatric Bible and the Creation of Mental Disorders.* NY: Free Press.

Laberge, S. (1985). *Lucid dreaming: The power of being awake and aware in your dreams.* Los Angeles: Tarcher.

Laing, R. D. (1970). *Knots.* NY: Random House.

Lamaze, F. (1956). *Painless childbirth: Psychoprophylactic method.* Chicago: H. Regnery.

Latané, B., & Nida, S. (1981). Ten years of research on group size and helping. *Psychological Bulletin, 89,* 308–324.

Latané, B., Williams, K., & Harkins, S. (1979). Many hands make light the work: The causes and consequences of social loafing. *Journal of Personality and Social Psychology, 37,* 308–324.

LeBlanc, A. N. (August 22, 1999). The outsiders. *New York Times Magazine,* 36–41.

Leboyer, F. (1975). *Birth without violence.* NY: Knopf.

Leman, K. (1987). *The birth order book.* NY: Dell.

Leonard, L. (1996). Female circumcision in southern Chad: Origins, meaning and current practice. *Social Science and Medicine, 43*(2), 255–263.

Leung, K., Lau, S., & Lam, W. (April, 1998). Parenting styles and academic achievement: A cross-cultural study. *Merill-Palmer Quarterly, 44*(2), 157–172.

Levine, B. (1990). *Your body believes every word you say: The language of the body-mind connection.* Lower Lake, CA: Asian.

Levine, D. U., & Havighurst, R. J. (1992). *Society and education,* 2nd ed. Needham Heights, MA: Allyn.

Levinson, D., Darrow, C. N., Klein, E. B., Levinson, M. H., & McKee, B. (1978). *The seasons of a man's life.* NY: Knopf.

Linden, W., Stossel, C., & Maurice, J. (April, 1996). Psychosocial intervention for patients with coronary heart disease: A meta–analysis. *Archives of Internal Medicine, 156,* 745–752.

Little, S. G., Sterling, R. C., & Tingstrom, D. H. (June, 1996). The influence of geographical and racial cues on evaluation of blame. *Journal of Social Psychology, 136,* 373–379.

Ludolph, P. S., Westen, D., Misle, B., Jackson, A. (1990). The borderline diagnosis in adolescents: Symptoms and developmental history. *American Journal of Psychiatry, 147*(4), 470–476.

Luria, A. R. (1982). *Language and cognition.* NY: Wiley.

Lynch, R. (1977). *The broken heart: The medical consequences of loneliness.* NY: Basic Books.

Mahoney, R. (Sept. 16, 1999). *Divorce, nontraditional families and its consequences for children.* http://www.stanford.edu/~mahoney/Divorce.html.

Marcuse, H. (1974). *Eros and civilization: A philosophic inquiry into Freud.* Boston: Beacon Press.

Martin, C. L., & Halverson, C. F., Jr. (1987). The role of cognition in sex role acquisition. In D. B. Carter (Ed.), *Current conceptions of sex roles and sex typing: Theory and research.* NY: Praeger.

Maslow, A. (1954). *Motivation and personality,* 2nd ed. NY: Harper & Row.

Maslow, A. (1976). *The farther reaches of human nature.* NY: Penguin Books.

Masterson, J. F. (1990). Psychotherapy of borderline and narcissistic disorders: Establishing a therapeutic alliance. *Journal of Personality Disorders, 4,* 182–191.

Mathews-Simonton, S., Simonton, O. C., & Creighton, J. (1980). *Getting well again.* NY: Bantam Books.

Maxmen, J. S., & Ward, N. G. (1995). *Essential psychopathology and its treatment,* 2nd ed. NY: W. W. Norton.

Mayo Clinic Health Letter. (March, 1993). Laughter. *MDA Health Digest, 11*(3), 6. Baltimore, MD: Medletter Associates.

McCall, R. B., & Lombardo, M. M. (February, 1983). What makes a top executive? *Psychology Today, 26,* p. 28.

McEarchern, R. W. (1998). Meeting minutes as symbolic action. *Communication Abstracts 21*(5).

McGourty, C. (September 22, 1988). Report cites unemployment as major health risk in Britain. *Nature, 335,* 290.

McGregor, D. (1960). *The human side of enterprise.* NY: McGraw-Hill.

McGuire, P. A. (June, 1999). Psychology and medicine connecting in war on cancer. *American Psychological Association Monitor, 30*(6), 8–9.

McKay, M., Fanning, P., & Paleg, K. (1994). *Couple skills: Making your relationship work.* Oakland, CA: New Harbinger.

McKnight, M. S. (1999). *Mediating divorce: A step-by-step manual.* San Francisco: Jossey-Bass.

Meichenbaum, D. (1993). Changing conceptions of cognitive behavior modification: Retrospect and prospect. *Journal of Consulting and Clinical Psychology, 61,* 202–204.

Mencken, H. (1963). *History of the American language.* NY: Knopf.

Meyer, R. G. (1992). *Practical clinical hypnosis: Techniques and applications.* NY: Lexington.

Milgram, S. (1974). *Obedience to authority: An experimental view.* NY: Harper & Row.

Mischel, W. (1973). Toward a cognitive social learning conceptualization of personality. *Psychological Review, 80,* 252–283.

Mischel, W. (1984). Convergences and challenges in the search for consistency. *American Psychologist, 39*, 351–364.

Morris, D. (1967). *The naked ape*. NY: McGraw-Hill.

Morris, D. (1970). *The human zoo*. NY: Dell.

Myers, I. B. (1980a). *Introduction to type*. Palo Alto, CA: Consulting Psychologists Press.

Myers, I. B. (1980b). *Gifts differing*. Palo Alto, CA: Consulting Psychologists Press.

Neugarten, B. L., & Neugarten, D. A. (1987). The changing meanings of age. *Psychology Today, 21*, 29–33.

Northrup, C. (1997). Your emotions and your heart: Learning to heed their messages could save your life. *Dr. Christiane Northrup's Health Wisdom for Women, 4*(8),1–2.

Novello, J. R. (1992). *What to do until the grown-up arrives: The art and science of raising teenagers*. Kirkland, WA: Hogrefe & Huber.

Ouchi, W. G. (1981). *Theory Z: How American business can meet the Japanese challenge*. Reading, MA: Addison-Wesley.

Papp, L. A., & Gorman, J. M. (1993). Pharmacological approach to the management of stress and anxiety disorders. In P. M. Lehrer & R. L. Woolfolk (Eds.), *Principles and practices of stress management,* 2nd ed. NY: Guilford.

Parker, R. J. (1999). The art of blessing: Teaching parents to create rituals. *Professional school counseling, 21*(4), 429–436.

Parker, J. G., & Gottman, J. M. (1989). Social and emotional development in a relational context: Friendship interaction from early childhood to adolescence. In T. J. Berndt and G. W. Ladd (Eds.), *Peer Relationships in Child Development*. NY: Wiley.

Pavlov, I. P. (1927). *Conditioned reflexes: An investigation of physiological activity of the cerebral cortex*. London: Oxford University Press.

Pearman, R. R., & Fleenor, J. (1996). Differences in observed and self-reported qualities of psychological types. *Journal of Psychological Type, 39,* 3–17.

Perls, F. S. (1967). *In and out of the garbage pail*. Lafayette, CA: Real People Press.

Perls, F. S. (1969). *Gestalt therapy verbatim*, J. O. Stevens (Ed.), Lafayette, CA: Real People Press.

Perry, C. M., & McIntire, W. G. (Fall, 1955). Modes of moral judgment among early adolescents. *Adolescence, 30,* 707–715.

Philpot, C., Brooks, G., Lusterman, D. D., & Nutt, R. (1997). *Bridging separate gender worlds: Why men and women clash and how therapists can bring them together*. Washington, DC: American Psychological Association.

Piaget, J. (1970). *Genetic epistemology*. NY: Columbia University Press.

Piaget, J. (1973). *The child and reality: Problems of genetic psychology*. Brooklyn Heights, NY: Grossman.

Pines, A., & Aronson, E. (1988). *Career burn-out: Causes and cures*. NY: Free Press.

Provence, S., & Lipton, R.C. (1963). *Infants in institutions*. NY: International University Press.

Putnam, F. W. (1989). *Diagnosis and treatment of multiple personality disorder*. NY: Guilford Press.

Quinn, J. B. (1995). The luck of the Xers. *Annual Editions: Life Management,* 218–219. Guilford, CT: Dushkin.

Rabasca, L. (November, 1999). Knocking down societal barriers for people with disabilities. *APA Monitor, 30*(10), 14–29.

Rank, O. (1941). *The birth trauma*. NY: Dover.

Remafedi, G., French, S., & Story, M. *et al.* (1998). The relationship between suicide risk and sexual orientation: Results of a population-based study. *American Journal of Public Health, 88* (1), 57–60. (Cited in *Harvard Mental Health Letter*, December, 1998, p. 6.)

Rest, J. R. (1986). *Moral development: Advances in theory and research*. NY: Praeger.

Rice, F. P. (1989). *Adolescent development: Relationships and culture*. Boston: Allyn.

Richter, C. P. (1985). On the phenomenon of sudden death in animals and man. In C. Peterson, P. Bobko, and W. Schicht (Eds.), *Readings for introductory psychology: Psychology as a social science,* (pp. 37–45). Acton, MA: Copley.

Rogers, C. R. (1950). *Client-centered therapy*. Boston: Houghton Mifflin.

Rogers, C. R. (1961). *On becoming a person*. Boston: Houghton Mifflin.

Rogers, C. R. (1970). Toward a modern approach to values: The valuing process in the mature person. In C. R. Rogers & B. Stevens (Eds.), *Person to person: The problem of being human*, pp. 19–20. NY: Pocket Books.

Rogne, C. (1991). *Understanding and enhancing self-esteem*. Fargo, ND: Discovery Counseling and Educational Center.

Rosenthal, E. (1995). When a pregnant woman drinks. In *Annual Editions: Human Development*, pp. 39–41. Guilford, CT: Dushkin.

Rotter, J. B. (1990). Internal versus external control of reinforcement: A case history of a variable. *American Psychologist, 45*, 489–493.

Ruark, J. (July 31, 1999). *Redefining the good life: A new focus in the social sciences* [WWW document]. URL. http://www.apa.org/ed/goodlife.html.

Rothenbuhler, R. J. (1998). *Ritual communication: From everyday conversation to mediated ceremony*. Thousand Oaks, CA: Sage Publication

Rutter, V. (1995). Lessons from stepfamilies. *Annual Editions: Marriage and the Family,* pp. 196–201. Guilford, CT: Dushkin.

Salovey, P., & Mayer, J. (1989). Emotional intelligence. *Imagination, Cognition and Personality, 9*(3), 185–211.

Sanders, T. (1991). *Healing the wounded child: A 12-step recovery program for adult male survivors of child sexual abuse.* Freedom, CA: Crossing Press.

Sawrey, J. M., & Telford, C. W. (1971). *Psychology of adjustment.* Boston: Allyn and Bacon.

Schreiber, F. R. (1963). *Sybil.* Chicago: Regnery.

Schulman, J., & Woods, L. (1983). Legal advocacy and mediation in family law. *Woman's Advocate, 4,* 3–4.

Schwartz, S. (1986). *Obedience to authority: Classic studies in psychology* (112–121). Mountainview, CA: Mayfield.

Schweitzer, A. (1980). *Reverence for life* (R. H. Foller, trans. 1960 reprint). NY: Irvington.

Seligman, M. E. P. (1990). *Learned optimism.* NY: Pocket Books.

Selye, H. (1956). *The stress of life.* NY: McGraw-Hill.

Selye, H. (1974). *Stress without distress.* NY: Signet.

Selye, H. (1991). History and the present states of the stress concept. In A. Monat and R. S. Lazarus (Eds.), *Handbook on stress and anxiety.* San Francisco, CA: Jossey-Bass.

Shengold, L. (1989). *Soul murder: The effects of childhood abuse and deprivation.* New Haven, CT: Yale University Press.

Siecus Report, 1993. (1993). *Sexuality information and education council of the United States,* 21,6, NY: New York University Press.

Siegler, R. S. (1994). Cognitive variability: A key to understanding cognitive development. *Current Directions in Psychological Science, 3* (1), 1–5.

Siegman, A. W. (1989). The role of hostility, neuroticism, and speech style in coronary-artery disease. In A. W. Siegman & S. A.. Dembrowski (Eds.), *In search of coronary-prone behavior: Beyond Type-A.* Hillsdale, NJ: Erlbaum.

Silver, D., & Rosenbluth, M. (1992). *Handbook of borderline disorders.* Madison, CT: International Universities Press.

Simonton, O. C. (September 15, 1995). Mind-body essentials: How to use the power of the mind to beat diseases. *Bottom Line,* 9–10. Greenwich, CT: Boardroom.

Singer, J. L. (1975). *The inner world of daydreaming.* NY: Harper & Row.

Sizemore, C. (1973). *I'm Eve.* Garden City, NY: Doubleday.

Skinner, B. F. (1938). *The behavior of organisms.* NY: Appleton-Century-Crofts.

Skinner, B. F. (1971). *Beyond freedom and dignity.* NY: Knopf.

Skoe, E. E. (1998). *The ethic of care: Issues in moral development.* NY: Routledge.

Skolnick, A., & Rosencrantz, S. (1995). The new crusade for the old family. *Annual Editions: Marriage and the Family* (pp. 8–13). Guilford, CT: Dushkin.

Slater, P. (1980). *Wealth addiction,* p. 25. NY: Dutton.

Sleek, S. (May, 1998). Older vets just now feeling pain of war. *APA Monitor,* pp. 1, 28–29.

Sleek, S. (1999). Car wars: Taming drivers' aggression. *APA Monitor, 27*(9), 1.

Smith, L. (1994). Landing that first real job. *Annual Editions: Life Management,* pp. 148–150. Guilford, CT: Dushkin.

Snarey, J. A. (June, 1987). A question of morality. *Psychology Today,* 6–8.

Snyder, S. (1991). *Drugs, neurotransmitters, and the brain.* NY: Scientific American Library.

Solzhenitsyn, A. (1971) *We never make mistakes.* NY: W. W. Norton.

Sommers-Flanagan, R. (1998). *Breaking up without cracking up: Reducing the pain of separation and divorce.* London: Harper-Collins.

Speiser, V. M. (1998). Ritual in expressive therapy. In: Robbins, Arthur (Ed); et al; *Therapeutic presence: Bridging expression and form.* London, England UK: Jessica Kingsley Publishers, Ltd., 1998, 280.

Spieker, S. J., Bensley, L., McMahon, R. J., Fung, H., and Osslander, R. (1996). Sexual abuse as a factor in child maltreatment of preschool aged children. *Development and Psychopathology, 8*(3), 497–509.

Spitzer, J. (1990). On treating patients diagnosed with narcissistic personality disorder: The induction phase. *Issues in Ego Psychology, 13*(1), 54–65.

Steinberg, L., & Silverberg, S. B. (1987). Influences on marital satisfaction during the middle stages of the family life cycle. *Journal of Marriage and the Family,* 751–760.

Sternberg, R. J., & Kaufman, J. C. (1998). Human abilities. *Annual Review of Psychology, 49,* 479–502.

Stiles, H. R. (1992). *Bundling: Its Origin, Progress, and Decline in America.* Detroit: Omnigraphics.

Suinn, R. M. (June, 1999). Cancer: A special look. *American Psychological Association Monitor, 30*(6), 2.

Sullivan, H. S. (1953). *The interpersonal theory of psychiatry.* NY: W. W. Norton.

Sulloway, F. J. (1998). *Born to Rebel: Birth order, family dynamics, and creative lives.* London: Abacus.

Sumerlin, J. R., & Bundrick, C. M. (June, 1996). Brief index of self-actualization: A measure of Maslow's Model. *Journal of Social Behavior and Personality, 11*(2), 253–271.

Sutton-Smith, B., & Rosenberg, B. G. (1970). *The sibling.* NY: Holt, Rinehart & Winston.

Taggert, W., & Robey, D. (April, 1981). Minds and managers: On the dual nature of human iformation processing and management. *Academy of Management Review,* 190.

Tellegen, A., Lykken, D. T., Bouchard, T.J., Jr., Wilcox, K. J., Segal, N. L., & Rich, S. (1988). Personality similarity in twins reared apart and together. *Journal of Personality and Social Psychology, 54,* 1031–1039.

Thigpen, C. H., & Cleckley, H. M. (1957). *The three faces of Eve.* NY: McGraw-Hill.

Thomas, A., & Chess, S. (1980). *The psychodynamics of psychological development.* NY: Bruner/Mazel.

Throll, D. A. (1982). Transcendental meditation and progressive relaxation: Their physiological effects. *Journal of Clinical Psychology, 38,* 522–530.

Toffler, A. (1970). *Future shock.* NY: Random House.

Vaillant, G. E., & Vaillant, C. O. (1990). Natural history of male psychological health, XII: A 45-year study of predictors of successful aging at age 65. *American Journal of Psychiatry, 147,* 31–37.

Vakoch, D. A., & Wurm, L. H. (1997). Emotional connotation in speech perception: Semantic associations in the general lexicon. *Cognition and Emotion, 11*(4), 337–340.

VanGennep, A. (1908, 1960). *The rites of passage.* Chicago: University of Chicago Press.

Vigil, J. D. (1996). Street Baptism: Chicano gang initiation. *Human Organization,* 55:2, 149–153.

Walker, A. (1989). *Terrifying love: Why battered women kill and how society responds.* NY: Harper & Row.

Wallach, L. B. (1995). Helping children cope with violence. *Annual Editions: Marriage and the Family,* pp. 150–155. Guilford, CT: Dushkin.

Wallerstein, J. S., & Kelly, J. B. (1980). *Surviving the breakup: How children actually cope with divorce.* NY: Basic Books.

Wallis, C. (December 9, 1985). Children having children. *Time,* 78–88.

Walls, R. A. (1991). *Life plan–Finding your real self: The journey through life.* Mclean, VA: Inner Search Foundation.

Watson, J. B., & Raynor, R. (1920). Conditioned emotional reactions. *Journal of Experimental Psychology, 3,* 1–14.

Whitney, P. (1998). *The psychology of language.* Boston: Houghton Mifflin.

Wiese, D., & Daro, D. (1995). *Current trends in child abuse reporting and fatalities: The results of the 1994 Annual Fifty State Survey.* Chicago: NCPCA (National Committee to Prevent Child Abuse).

Wiesner, M. E. (1993). *Women and gender in early modern Europe.* Cambridge: Cambridge University Press.

Whitney, P. (1998). *The psychology of language.* Boston: Houghton Mifflin.

Wolf-Smith, J. H., & Larosa, R. (1995). After he hits her. *Annual Editions: Marriage and the Family,* (pp. 155–161). Guildford, CT: Dushkin.

Wolf, N. (1992). *The beauty myth: How images of beauty are used against women.* NY: Anchor Books/Doubleday.

Wolpe, J. (1958). *Psychotherapy by reciprocal inhibition.* Stanford, CA: Stanford University Press.

Wood, D. B. (1995). Hispanics: To be or not to be. In *Annual Editions: Race and Ethnic Relations,* pp. 106–107. Guilford, CT: Dushkin.

Woods, P. (1990). *The happiest days? How pupils cope with schools.* Bristol, PA: Falmer Press.

Yeh, S., & Creamer, D. G. (1995). Orientations to moral reasoning among men and women leaders of higher education in Taiwan. *Journal of College Student Development, 36*(2), 112–122.

Zahn-Waxler, C., & Radke-Yarrow, M. (1986). The development of altruism. In N. Eisenberg-Berg (Ed.), *The development of prosocial behaviour.* Corpus Christie, TX: Academic Press.

Zimbardo, P. G. (1976). Pathology of imprisonment (277–279). *Readings in Psychology: Annual Editions 75/76.* Guilford, CT: Duskin.

Zimbardo, P. G. (1990). *Shyness.* Reading, MA: Addison-Wesley.

INDEX